The
Law & Practice
of
DILIGENCE

The
Law & Practice
of
DILIGENCE

G Maher

Advocate,
Senior Lecturer in law
in the University of Glasgow

Douglas J Cusine

Solicitor, Senior Lecturer
in conveyancing and
professional practice of law
in the University of Aberdeen

Butterworths
Law Society of Scotland

Edinburgh   1990

Butterworths

United Kingdom	Butterworth & Co (Publishers) Ltd, 88 Kingsway, LONDON WC2B 6AB and 4 Hill Street, EDINBURGH EH2 3JZ
Australia	Butterworths Pty Ltd, SYDNEY, MELBOURNE, BRISBANE, ADELAIDE, PERTH, CANBERRA and HOBART
Canada	Butterworths Canada Ltd, TORONTO and VANCOUVER
Ireland	Butterworth (Ireland) Ltd, DUBLIN
Malaysia	Malayan Law Journal Sdn Bhd, KUALA LUMPUR
New Zealand	Butterworths of New Zealand Ltd, WELLINGTON and AUCKLAND
Puerto Rico	Equity de Puerto Rico, Inc, HATO REY
Singapore	Butterworth & Co (Asia) Pte Ltd, SINGAPORE
USA	Butterworth Legal Publishers, ST PAUL, Minnesota, SEATTLE, Washington, BOSTON, Massachusetts, AUSTIN, Texas and D & S Publishers, CLEARWATER, Florida

Law Society of Scotland
26 Drumsheugh Gardens, EDINBURGH EH3 7YR

A CIP Catalogue record for this book is available from the British Library.

ISBN 0 406 11121 9

Typeset by Phoenix Photosetting, Chatham
Printed and bound in Scotland by Thomson Litho Ltd, East Kilbride

PREFACE

Our aim in writing this book is to provide a systematic and comprehensive statement of the law and practice of diligence. The practical importance and the complexity of this branch of the law are in themselves sufficient reasons for a book on the subject. Moreover, there have been significant reforms and changes in virtually every topic within the subject of diligence since the last full survey in Graham Stewart's *The Law of Diligence* in 1898. The Debtors (Scotland) Act 1987, the Civil Jurisdiction and Judgments Act 1982, and the many rules of court which implement these statutory provisions, have resulted in significant reforms on poinding and sale, arrestment of earnings, time to pay debts, recovery of taxes, rates and community charges, officers of court, warrants for diligence, and enforcement of foreign decrees. On other topics, such as arrestment on the dependence, arrestment and furthcoming, and inhibition, a steady body of case-law and statutory reform has added to the law. It may also be noted that further statutory reform of areas of diligence not covered by the 1987 Act is likely to follow proposals for reform which will ensue from the continuing consultation process on diligence being carried out by the Scottish Law Commission. Furthermore, there have been some noteworthy writings on certain aspects of diligence, such as G L Gretton's *Inhibition and Adjudication* (Butterworths, 1987), a work we are happy to acknowledge to have relied on considerably in this book.

These features have dictated our approach in this work. We have attempted to discuss every aspect of diligence, including the bases of diligence in court decrees and other documents of debt. We have sought to give particular emphasis of treatment to those areas of diligence which have been subject to recent reform and change, or on which there is no up-to-date detailed guide elsewhere. We have not examined in the same detail some aspects of the subject which have little contemporary significance in practice or on which there can be found reliable discussion in other texts.

In writing this book we have received much assistance and help, and we wish to record our gratitude to Gordon MacPherson, Messenger-at-Arms, to George L Gretton WS, to Messrs Brodies WS, and to Messrs Dickson Minto WS. We also think it right that we should acknowledge the excellent service provided to us by Messrs Butterworths. We must emphasise that we alone are responsible for any errors of commission or omission in relation to all statements in the text of this book.

Although the authors accept full joint and several responsibility for all statements in the text of this book, it may be noted that in terms of collaboration, this work represents a common rather than joint effort. The division of labour is that Maher prepared chapters 1, 3, 4 (paragraphs 4.01–4.62) 5, 6, 7, 8 (paragraphs 8.01–8.22), 11 and 14; and Cusine prepared chapters 2, 4 (paragraphs 4.63–4.85), 8 (paragraphs 8.23–8.71), 9, 10, 12 and 13.

We have sought to state the law as at 14 July 1989 though we have anticipated the provisions of the Finance Act 1989 and have noted certain other subsequent developments.

G Maher
School of Law
University of Glasgow

Douglas J Cusine
Department of Conveyancing
University of Aberdeen.

CONTENTS

Note – the following abbreviations have been used in the text:
SCR   summary cause rules
SMCR   small claim rules

TABLE OF STATUTES

TABLE OF ORDERS, RULES
AND REGULATIONS

TABLE OF CASES

H

CHAPTER 1

BASIS OF DILIGENCE: 1. DECREES

INTRODUCTION

1.01 Diligence is most commonly based on court judgments. In Scots law the term judgment has no technical or precise meaning, and is used to refer to almost every aspect of a court's decision or determination of a cause, including the opinions of the judges or court. The term is used as a heading in the rules for ordinary actions in the sheriff court[1], where the rules themselves refer to 'interlocutor', 'decree', and 'order'. The technical terms normally applied to the operative aspects of judgments are interlocutors and decrees. These two terms are often used as identical in meaning but this usage, though common, is not exact. The clearest distinction between interlocutor and decree, which reflects earlier usage, is that an interlocutor is an incidental order of a court issued in the course of a cause, whereas a decree is the court's order which finally disposes of a cause[2]. In more modern usage the distinction is one of form and substance: a decree is the substance of the court's decision, and an interlocutor is the expression of the decision[3].

Two further types of court order which may be noted are warrants and acts. In the context of diligence the term warrant has two meanings. When a court issues a decree an official copy, or extract, of the decree is authority, ie warrant, for diligence. Warrants are also used to refer directly to a type of court order, usually addressed to court officials such as messengers-at-arms or sheriff officers, which requires or permits some action to be done[4]. Acts are court orders which do not call for execution or diligence and in modern practice are used for regulating court procedure.

1 OCR 32, 89.
2 Maclaren *Court of Session Practice* (1916) p 1089; cf Stair *Institutions* IV, 46, 2: 'The judicial sentences of judges are of two sorts: The one is intermediate between the dependence and termination of processes, which are therefore called interlocutors, and are done by acts of process: The other sentences are definitive, which terminate and end processes, as to the instance, action or plea. These we call decernitures or decreets.'
3 Compare C W G Guest 'Decree' in *Encyclopaedia of the Laws of Scotland* (ed Lord Dunedin and J Wark) vol 5, para 1055: 'The decree is in fact the judgment itself; the interlocutor is the instrument which contains the decree.'
4 J M Lees *Notes on the Structure of Interlocutors in the Sheriff Court* (2nd edn) p 27.

CLASSIFICATION

1.02 There are three main bases for the classification of interlocutors or decrees, namely (1) according to whether the case was contentious; (2)

according to the extent with which the decree deals with the issues of an action; (3) according to the outcome of the decision[1].

> 1 There is no neat relationship between these three types of classification and the different divisions cut across each other. Decrees in absence tend to be in favour of the pursuer and as such are decrees of condemnator, but in certain circumstances a decree in absence may dismiss the action.

Decrees classified according to whether the case was contentious

1.03 One division of decrees depends on whether or not the action was defended. Actions not defended[1] result in decree in absence, whereas those which are defended[1] result in decree *in foro* (*in foro contentioso*). The chief importance of this distinction lies in the difference in remedies available to the party seeking to overturn the decree.

Two categories of decree call for consideration under this heading: (a) decrees in absence and (b) decrees by default.

> 1 The meaning of 'defended' in this context is explained below at para 1.04.

DECREES IN ABSENCE

Definition

1.04 In the Court of Session, where a defender fails to enter appearance in an action, or having duly entered appearance fails to lodge defences as specified in the rules of court, decree in absence may be pronounced by the court[1]. In the sheriff court, decree in absence may be pronounced only if the defender has not lodged a notice of intention to defend the action or does not state a defence at the first calling of a summary cause or small claims action[2].

A decree in absence cannot give rise to a plea of *res judicata*. However, in certain circumstances a decree in absence is to be treated as if it had all the characteristics of a decree *in foro*, including its giving rise to *res judicata*[3]. These consequences attach to a decree in absence where the summons has been served personally on the defender or where the defender has entered appearance. The decree must be one upon which a charge is competent. After the decree has been extracted and upon expiry of sixty days after a charge based on it the decree will be treated as a decree *in foro* unless it has been recalled or the charge has been brought under review by suspension[4].

> 1 RC 89(a).
> 2 OCR 21; SCR 18, 55; SMCR 10. See ID Macphail *Sheriff Court Practice* (1988) p 232.
> 3 RC 89(i).
> 4 The equivalent sheriff court rule is expressly made subject to the Land Tenure Reform (Scotland) Act 1974, s 9(7): OCR 26.

Special actions

1.05 Special procedures exist for obtaining decree in absence in actions of reduction and adjudication for debt[1]. In actions of proving the tenor[2] and consistorial actions, decree can only be pronounced after proof, though in consistorial actions proof may be by way of affidavits[3]. In the sheriff court, decree in undefended actions relating to parental rights may be granted after such inquiry as the sheriff thinks necessary[4].

Where the defender has not made appearance or in the sheriff court lodged or stated a defence, any decree granted is nonetheless a decree in absence, even if there has been a proof[5].

1 *Maclaren* pp 686, 803; D Maxwell *The Practice of the Court of Session* (1980) pp 362–363, 383.
2 RC 188.
3 See RC 168; Court of Session Practice Note, 11 April 1978; OCR 21(3), 23 (which applies to undefended actions of divorce, separation, declarator of parentage, legitimacy, legitimation or illegitimacy).
4 OCR 22.
5 *Paterson v Paterson* 1958 SC 141, SLT 205.

Procedure

1.06 Where decree in absence can be competently granted by the court, the procedural steps are as follows. It should be noted that the court has no power to grant decree in absence *ex proprio motu* and such decree can be granted only where the pursuer takes the appropriate steps to seek one. Accordingly, a pursuer may wish to go for proof even where decree in absence is competent (which may arise if he wants to record and preserve the evidence[1]). However, the expense of such further procedure will fall on the pursuer.

1 See eg *Russel's Trustees* (1865) 3 M 850.

1.07 Procedure in the Court of Session for obtaining decree in absence is regulated by RC 89 which requires the pursuer to enrol for decree in absence by motion. The motion must state the ground of jurisdiction of the court as well as the domicile[1] of the defender as far as this is known to the pursuer. It has been argued in the context of the sheriff court rules that it is necessary to show that the court's jurisdiction has not been excluded either by the parties having prorogated the jurisdiction of another court or by another court of competent jurisdiction having earlier been seised of the action[2]. As the Rule of Court refers to 'the' ground of jurisdiction being specified in the pursuer's motion for decree in absence, it would appear to be necessary to make the appropriate negative averments in that motion and it is the recommended practice. The cause then appears in the roll of undefended causes on the next available day. Provided the motion is in proper form the court must grant decree in absence but has power to grant decree subject to restrictions.

As there is an element of unfairness in decree being granted in the absence of one of the parties to the litigation, provision exists to ensure that the defender has been made fully aware of the proceedings against him before decree in absence is granted[3].

1 This requirement applies only to actions governed by the Civil Jurisdiction and Judgments Act 1982. Domicile here means domicile as determined by ss 41–46 of the 1982 Act.
2 R Black 'Pleading Jurisdiction: Negative Averments' 1987 SLT (News) 189.
3 RC 89(b), 89(c).

1.08 In the sheriff court, the sheriff is empowered to grant decree in absence on the expiry of the time-limit for the defender to lodge notice of intention to defend (or minute of intention to defend on amount of aliment only). The pursuer endorses a minute for decree on the initial writ. The attendance of the pursuer is not required when decree is pronounced[1].

1 OCR 21(1). For summary cause procedure, see SCR 18(6), 55. Small claims procedure is regulated by SMCR 10.

1.09   However, there are three important qualifications to the sheriff's power to grant decree in absence:
(a) where the defender has his domicile, as determined by Schedule 1 to, and sections 41 and 42 of, the Civil Jurisdiction and Judgments Act 1982, in another contracting state or in another part of the United Kingdom, decree in absence will be granted only if the pursuer shows that the defender had been able to receive the initial writ in sufficient time to arrange for his defence and that all necessary steps had been taken to that end[1];
(b) where the initial writ (or summons in a summary cause action) was served in a country to which the 1965 Hague Convention on the Service Abroad of Judicial and Extra-Judicial Documents in Civil or Commercial Matters applies, decree in absence shall not be granted until it is established to the satisfaction of the sheriff that the requirements of article 15 of that Convention have been complied with[2];
(c) a sheriff may not grant decree in absence unless it appears ex facie of the initial writ that 'a ground of jurisdiction' exists under the 1982 Act[3].

1 This rule applies to ordinary cause, summary cause, and small claims actions: OCR 21(1)(b); SCR 18(8); SMCR App 3.
2 OCR 21A; SCR 18A; SMCR, App 3. See *Macphail*, pp 110–112.
3 OCR 21(1)(a); SCR 55(5); SMCR 10(5). For discussion see R Black 'Pleading Jurisdiction: Negative Averments' 1987 SLT (News) 189.

Obtaining extract of decree in absence

1.10   Generally speaking, a pursuer can extract a decree in absence only after the expiry of a period allowed for the defender to seek recall of the decree against him. In Court of Session actions this period is ten days[1]. Where service of the summons on the defender has been made under RC 74B (which deals with citation and service furth of Scotland) *and* the defender has no known solicitor in Scotland, the court must supersede extract when granting decree in absence for a period of at least seven days. The precise period will depend on whatever time is necessary to allow the pursuer to send a letter to the defender and a reply from him to be received in Edinburgh[2].

In the sheriff court ordinary actions, extract of decree in absence can be granted by the sheriff clerk after the expiry of fourteen days following the granting of decree but the sheriff has power to order extract at an earlier date on cause shown[3]. Motion for extract is at times incorporated in the minute which craves decree in absence; in this case the pursuer moves for extract to be issued in due course[4].

1 RC 89(aa).
2 RC 89(b).
3 OCR 25.
4 B Kearney *An Introduction to Ordinary Civil Procedure in the Sheriff Court* (1982) p 45. There are no specialities concerning obtaining extract of decrees in absence in summary cause and small claims actions. On extracts generally, see further below at paras 1.50–1.64.

Recall (reponing) of decree in absence

1.11   As there is a possibility of unfairness in decree in absence, provisions exist for a non-compearing defender to seek recall of the decree within a short period of time after it has been granted. (In the Court of Session and in sheriff court summary cause and small claims proceedings this procedure is known as recalling, and as reponing in the sheriff court ordinary procedure.) In the sheriff court it is accepted practice to allow a defender to enrol a motion to allow a notice of appearance to be received late and this is granted provided the decree in absence has not been signed[1].

In the Court of Session, the procedure is for a non-compearing defender[2] within ten days of the date of the decree in absence to enrol for recall of the decree and for allowing defences to be received[3]. If the last day of the ten-day period is not an enrolling day, the defender's motion may be enrolled on the next immediate enrolling day. The defender must pay to the pursuer the sum of £4.20 and on proof to the clerk of court of payment of this sum, the court must recall the decree in absence and allow the defences to be received. Unlike the position in the sheriff court ordinary action, the court has no discretion to refuse a motion to recall a decree in absence where all the requisite procedural steps for recall have been taken. The case then proceeds in the normal way as if the defences had been lodged timeously[4].

The recall of a decree in absence under RC 89 does not of itself affect the validity of anything, including diligence, done or transacted in terms of the decree[5].

1 *Kearney* p 47; *Reilly Glen & Co v Beaton* 1964 SLT (Sh Ct) 73. Compare OCR 1 (dispensing power of sheriff).
2 In *Ross v Ross and AB* 1909 2 SLT 117, the trustees of a co-defender who did not enter appearance were allowed to have decree in absence recalled.
3 RC 89(f).
4 Special procedure for recall of decree in absence exists where the defender is furth of Scotland: RC 89(d), (e).
5 RC 89(j).

1.12 In ordinary procedure in the sheriff court, a reponing note may be lodged with the sheriff clerk before implement in full of a decree in absence[1]. On lodging a reponing note the defender must also consign in the hands of the sheriff clerk the sum of £10. This sum is uplifted by the pursuer after the sheriff has dealt with the note unless the sheriff directs otherwise. A reponing note, when duly lodged and served on the pursuer, sists any diligence based on the decree in absence.

A reponing note must make clear two matters: (1) the proposed defence to the action, and (2) explanation of the defender's failure to appear. The note must be frank and sufficiently detailed on both aspects[2], and the sheriff has a discretion to accept or refuse the note[3]. However, the detail required in relation to the proposed defence is such as to show that the defence is statable, and does not call for the exactness associated with specification of a closed record[4].

1 OCR 28–32.
2 *Dixon Street Motors v Associated Rentals Ltd* 1980 SLT (Sh Ct) 46; *Kearney* p 46.
3 *McKelvie v Scottish Steel Scaffolding Co Ltd* 1938 SC 278 at 280; *Hoggan v McKeachie* 1960 SC 461, 462; *Guardian Royal Exchange Group v Moffat* 1986 SLT 262 at 266.
4 *Nisbet v MacLeod* (1923) 39 Sh Ct Rep 248 at 250; *McKelvie v Scottish Steel Scaffolding Co Ltd* 1938 SC 278 at 281; *Consultants and Technologists North Sea v Scott* 1986 SLT 685 at 686.

1.13 There are many illustrations in reported cases of the adequacy, and lack of adequacy, of grounds in reponing notes in relation to the defender's proposed defences and explanation for failure to appear[1].

1 See eg *Scotplastics Ltd v A D Hegney (Plumbers)* 1972 SLT (Sh Ct) 47; *Olsen v Keddie* 1976 SLT (Sh Ct) 64; *Wailes Dove Bitumatic Ltd v Plastic Sealant Ltd* 1979 SLT (Sh Ct) 41; *Dixon Street Motors v Associated Rentals Ltd* 1980 SLT (Sh Ct) 46; *Guardian Royal Exchange Group v Moffat*

1986 SLT 262; *Consultants and Technologists North Sea v Scott* 1986 SLT 685. For discussion see *Macphail* pp 240–243.

1.14 An interlocutor recalling a decree in absence is not subject to review[1]. However an interlocutor refusing a reponing note may be appealed to the sheriff principal and the Court of Session[2].

1 OCR 32.
2 Sheriff Courts (Scotland) Act 1907, ss 27, 28.

1.15 The summary cause rules for recall of a decree in absence follow those of the Court of Session rather than the rules for sheriff court ordinary actions[1]. A defender at any time not later than fourteen days after the earlier of (1) execution of a charge or (2) execution of arrestment following a decree in absence, may apply for recall of the decree by lodging with the sheriff clerk a minute in the requisite form. It is not clear whether the term 'execution' here refers to the date of the actual carrying out of the diligence or the official report (the 'execution') of it. At the same time as lodging the motion for recall, the defender must also consign in the hands of the sheriff clerk the sum of £5. The pursuer is entitled to this sum unless the sheriff orders otherwise.

Not less than seven days before the hearing of a minute for recall, the pursuer must be sent a copy of the minute and also intimation of the date of the hearing. The court lacks discretion to refuse recall but can grant it only so far as the decree has not been implemented at the date of intimation to the pursuer. Minute to recall a decree in absence operates as a sist of diligence but in relation to a decree in absence in an action for recovery of heritable property against persons who lack any right or title to the property, such a sist operates only if the sheriff so directs.

1 SCR 19, form M. The procedure in small claims action is broadly the same as that in summary cause proceedings: see SMCR 27.

DECREE BY DEFAULT

Nature of decree by default

1.16 A decree by default is a decree pronounced after both parties have joined contestation, pronounced without consideration of the merits of a case, and usually follows a failure by a party to take the appropriate procedural steps in conducting his litigation. A decree by default may be pronounced against any defaulting party, unlike a decree in absence which is usually pronounced against a defender. However, some of the rules of court use the expression decree by default to refer only to such decrees against a defender, but this usage is not correct[1].

It is generally thought undesirable that a decree should be pronounced in a case without full consideration of the merits merely because of a procedural default. The award of expenses can be used as a more effective and practical weapon to deter non-observance of rules of court. Accordingly, courts are usually given discretion as to awarding decree by default[2]. Rule 59(3) of the ordinary actions in the sheriff court expressly gives the sheriff power to prorogate the time for lodging any production or step of process or for implementing any order. In a summary cause and small claims action after a defence has been stated, where a party fails to appear or be represented at a diet, or fails to implement an order of the court, decree by default cannot be granted in respect of such failure and the cause must be continued to a later diet not earlier than fourteen days from the failure in question. Intimation must be given to the party in default by the sheriff clerk, stating that if failure continues in the later diet or the party fails to appear at that later diet, decree by default may be awarded[3].

A decree by default is a decree *in foro*, and will give rise to a plea of *res judicata*, so long as it subsists[4]. This is so even if the decree is pronounced in the absence of the party in default[5].

1 Cp RC 94(d); SCR 28(3); SMCR 23(3).
2 See the terms of RC 91(5), 94(d), 173; OCR 59; SCR 28; SMCR 23, which state that the court or the sheriff 'may' grant decree by default rather than 'shall' do so.
3 SCR 28; SMCR 23.
4 *Mackenzie v Smith* (1861) 23 D 1201; *Forrest v Dunlop* (1875) 3 R 15.
5 *Bain v Lawson & Son* (1899) 1 F 576; *McKenzie v John R Wyatt (Musical Enterprises) Ltd* 1974 SLT (Sh Ct) 8; *Turner v Edinburgh DC* 1977 SLT (Sh Ct) 38.

Challenge of decree by default

1.17 The appropriate mode of challenging a decree by default granted by a sheriff is not the process of reponing, which is available only in respect of a decree in absence[1], but to appeal to the sheriff principal or to the Inner House as against any other final interlocutor[2]. A decree by default granted in the Outer House may be challenged by reclaiming note. Where the default has been in failing to lodge a paper or document, that paper or document must be lodged on or before the enrolment of the motion for review[3]. A decree by default of the Inner House can only be set aside by appeal to the House of Lords[4].

Appeal against decree by default must be made before decree is extracted[5].

1 *West v Hair* (1926) 43 Sh Ct Rep 118.
2 Sheriff Courts (Scotland) Act 1907, s 27, 28.
3 RC 264(e). Reclaiming a decree by default does not require the leave of the Lord Ordinary (RC 264(c), (e)).
4 *Tough v Smith* (1832) 10 S 619. *Maxwell (p 617)* cites this case as authority for the view that such a decree must be set aside with the consent of the opposite party.
5 RC 264(e); *McKenzie v John R Wyatt (Musical Enterprises) Ltd* 1974 SLT (Sh Ct) 8. *Tennents v Romanes* (1881) 8 R 824; *Weir v Tudhope* (1892) 19 R 858.

Decrees classified according to the extent to which the decree deals with the issues of the action

1.18 Decrees may be classified by the extent to which they deal with all or only part of an action. Here the division is between interlocutory, interim and final decrees.

INTERLOCUTORY DECREES

1.19 The expression interlocutory decree, although a misnomer, refers to a decree pronounced during the course of an action and dealing with a matter of procedure or some incidental part of the case. RC 264 specifies certain Outer House interlocutory decrees which may be reclaimed only with the leave of the Lord Ordinary, as well as certain such decrees reclaimable without leave[1].

Certain interlocutory decrees of the Inner House require the leave of the particular Division before they can be appealed to the House of Lords[2]. The types of interlocutory orders in the sheriff court which can be appealed to the sheriff principal or the Court of Session are set out in sections 27–29 of the 1907 Act[3].

1 RC 264(a)–(c); *Maxwell* p 547.
2 *Maxwell* p 592.
3 See also OCR 91–96 and discussion in *Kearney* pp 132–135; *Macphail* ch 18. See also AS (Sheriff Court Appeals) 1949, SI 1949/2062.

INTERIM DECREES

1.20 Interim decrees are of two types:

First, the court may make an order dealing with the action *ad interim* until the merits of the case are finally disposed of. Examples of such interim decrees are interim interdict[1], interim aliment[2], and interim appointments[3]. A frequently-used power of the court is that of making interim awards of damages in actions of personal injuries[4]. In interim damages cases, the court in making final judgment is empowered to make the appropriate adjustment to the terms of the decree to reflect the interim award. In particular, the court can order repayment by the pursuer to the defender of any excess by which the final award falls short of the interim award[5].

An interim decree, granted during the dependence of an action, is extractible *ad interim*[6].

1 Court of Session Act 1988, s 47(1), (2); RC 79, 236.
2 Family Law (Scotland) Act 1985, s 6.
3 *Macphail* pp 348–349.
4 RC 89A(1); OCR 147–148. For discussion see *Macphail* pp 690–694.
5 RC 89A(2); OCR 148. The court has power to award interest in respect of money repaid by the pursuer to the defender: *Walker v Infabco Diving Services Ltd* 1983 SLT 633.
6 Cp Court of Session Act 1988, s 47(3).

1.21 A second type of interim decree relates to the merits of a case but is pronounced in respect of only part of them. For example, where it appears from the defences that part of the sum claimed is admittedly and plainly due, the pursuer may obtain interim decree for that part. Similarly an interim decree can be pronounced in respect of one of several craves or conclusions. An interim decree can be pronounced for a balance admittedly due both before[1] and after[2] the record has been closed but interim decree is competent only where the sum is presently exigible[3]. Maclaren[4] notes the situation where one part of a case is decided upon in the pursuer's favour at the procedure roll, resulting in interim decree, and proof ordered in respect of the rest of the case.

Interim decree should not be pronounced in respect of part of an action in respect of which the parties are genuinely in dispute[5], or where the defender defaults in complying with a rule of court or court order[6]. Interim decree, rather than summary decree, should be pronounced where the court disposes of part only of a conclusion or of an action[7].

1 *Crawfurd v Ballantyne's Trs* (1833) 12 S 112; *McKinlay v McKinlay* (1849) 11 D 1022; *Conacher v Conacher* (1857) 20 D 252.
2 *Cameron v McNeill* (1822) 1 S 389 (364); *Lauder v Fraser* (1822) 1 S 439 (407).
3 *Banks v Lang* (1845) 17 Sc J 536.
4 *Maclaren* p 1091.

5 *Scottish Flavour Ltd v Watson* 1982 SLT 78.
6 *Nivison v Howat* (1883) 11 R 182.
7 *Stanley Miller Ltd v Ladhope Developments Ltd* 1987 GWD 22–826.

1.22   An interim decree dealing with only part of the merits of a case can be reclaimed without leave within fourteen days of its date[1]. Where an interim decree has been implemented and is subsequently altered or recalled on a reclaiming motion by the Inner House, the Inner House may order repayment of the money paid or pronounce an order to give effect to the alteration or recall. This power of the Inner House is available even after the interim decree has been extracted and diligence executed on it.

1 RC 264(b). The period is twenty-one days where the decree is pronounced during vacation.

FINAL DECREE

1.23   The notion of a court decree being final has two quite distinct meanings. In the first place, a decree may be final in the sense that it is not open to review or appeal by a superior court, as with judgments within the privative jurisdiction of the sheriff court[1].

A second sense of final decree is that the decree determines the whole cause before the court issuing it. This sense of final decree finds expression in section 3(h) of the 1907 Act[2]; ' "Final judgment" means an interlocutor which, by itself, or taken along with previous interlocutors, disposes of the subject-matter of the cause, notwithstanding that judgment may not have been pronounced on every question raised, and that expenses found due may not have been modified, taxed or decerned for.'

A similar definition has been used in respect of final decrees of a Lord Ordinary[3], but it is not clear that the same approach would be adopted as to final decrees of the Inner House, where final decrees includes a decree on the whole merits of a cause, including expenses. However it is not clear that an Inner House decree is a final decree where it deals with the whole subject matter of the cause but does not deal with every issue of fact or law raised[4].

In the sheriff court, the sheriff must append to all interlocutors, except those of a formal nature, a note setting out the grounds on which he has proceeded. In respect of final decrees the sheriff also sets out separate findings in fact and in law[5].

1 Sheriff Courts (Scotland) Act 1907, s 7 (as amended by the Sheriff Courts (Scotland) Act 1971, Sch 2, the Law Reform (Miscellaneous Provisions) (Scotland) Act 1980, Sch 3 and SI 1988/ 1993), which provides that 'all causes not exceeding £1,500 in value exclusive of interest and expenses competent in the sheriff court shall be brought and followed forth in the sheriff court, and shall not be subject to review by the Court of Session: Provided that nothing herein contained shall affect any right of appeal competent under any Act of Parliament in force for the time being.'
2 This definition applies also to summary cause actions: Sheriff Courts (Scotland) Act 1971, s 45(3). Compare SCR 87, 88.
3 Court of Session Act 1868 Act, s 53, repealed by the Court of Session Act 1988, s 52, Sch 2.
4 See AJG Mackay *Manual of Practice* p 309; *Maclaren* pp 1091–2.
5 OCR 89(1), not applicable to summary cause or small claims actions.

1.24   The importance of a decree being a final decree is twofold: (1) generally speaking no motion can be made in a cause before a judge who has pronounced final decree and, (2) in general the party against whom final decree has been pronounced has the right to appeal against the decree without leave[1].

Much of the case law on appeal without leave concerns the meaning of final decree[2]. In the normal case a final decree is one which disposes of the question of liability for expenses[3]. Thus an interlocutor dealing with the merits but reserving the question of liability for expenses is not a final interlocutor[4].

1 RC 264(a); Sheriff Courts (Scotland) Act 1907, ss 27, 28; Act 1971, s 38. These sections also set out non-final decrees which are appealable without leave.
2 See discussion in *Maclaren* pp 975–976; *Maxwell* pp 567–568; *Macphail* pp 603–606.
3 *Baird v Barton* (1882) 9 R 970; *Burns v Waddell & Son* (1897) 24 R 325; *Caledonian Rly Co v Glasgow Corporation* (1900) 2 F 871.
4 *Parochial Board of Greenock v Miller and Brown* (1877) 4 R 737; *Russell v Allan* (1877) 5 R 22; *Tennents v Romanes* (1881) 8 R 824; *Thompson & Co v King* (1883) 10 R 469; *Stirling Maxwell's Trs v Kirkintilloch Police Commissioners* (1883) 11 R 1; *McKinstery v Plean Colliery Co* (1910) 27 Sh Ct Rep 62. See further below at paras 1.38–1.43.

1.25 There may be more than one final decree in a cause. Where the merits have been dealt with and expenses granted, a decree will still be final even if it contains a reservation as to modification of expenses. The subsequent decree which deals with the modification of expenses is also a final decree[1]. A decree awarding provisional damages under section 12 of the Administration of Justice Act 1982 is a final decree[2].

1 *Taylor's Trs v McGairgan* (1896) 23 R 738; *Inglis v National Bank of Scotland* 1911 SC 6; *Sanderson v Sanderson* 1921 SC 686, 692: 'If "final decree" is pronounced *without reservation* – and there are many cases in which a reservation is inappropriate or not desired by the parties – then, if extract is asked for, the extract is a *final* one, and the process is, so to speak, "killed" and cannot be further moved in.'
2 RC 134D.

Decrees classified according to the outcome of the decision

1.26 Decrees may also be classified in terms of the disposal of the action in favour of one or other of the litigants. The classification is of decrees of dismissal, absolvitor and condemnator. A decree may also embody more than one of these outcomes, in which case it is known as a mixed decree.

DISMISSAL

1.27 A decree of dismissal is a decree in favour of the defender which does not deal with the merits of the case but is to the effect that the action in its present particular form is put out of court. It does not found *res judicata* and allows the pursuer to raise another action on the same matter[1]. In *Stewart v Greenock Harbour Trustees*[2], Lord Deas said: 'if there be a distinction established in our practice, it is that the word "dismiss" is used when it is open to the party to bring another action, and the word "assoilzie" when it is not open.'

However an interlocutor may be taken as one of dismissal, although that particular word is not used. Where an interlocutor was to the effect that the court 'assoilzied the defenders from the action as laid', this was held to be a decree of dismissal[3].

1 *Stewart v Greenock Harbour Trs* (1868) 6 M 954; *Waterson v Murray & Co* (1884) 11 R 1036;

Wallace v Baird (1900) 2 F 754; *Cunningham v Skinner* (1902) 4 F 1124; *Govan Old Victualling Society Ltd v Wagstaff* (1907) 14 SLT 716.
2 (1868) 6 M 954, 958. Compare Lord Watson in *Menzies v Menzies* (1893) 20 R (HL) 108, 110–111: 'The dismissal of an action upon relevancy, without any inquiry into the merits, can never be *res judicata*.'
3 *Gillespie v Russel* (1859) 3 Macq 757; *Waterson v Murray & Co* (1884) 11 R 1036. See also *Shirreff v Brodie* (1836) 14 S 825.

ABSOLVITOR

1.28   A decree of absolvitor is a decree by which the merits of an action are finally determined in favour of the defender. It may also be pronounced against a pursuer for failure to conform to a peremptory statutory requirement or order of the court, but otherwise should be pronounced only after consideration of the merits of the case[1].

A decree of absolvitor is *res judicata* against the pursuer in respect of all matters covered by it. However decree of absolvitor does not prevent a pursuer raising a further action on grounds omitted from the earlier action, the plea of competent and omitted applying only to defenders, not to pursuers[2].

1 *Reid v Russell* 1971 SLT (Sh Ct) 15; *East Coast Finance (Scotland) Ltd v Smith* 1977 SLT (Sh Ct) 7.
2 *Dawson and Hill v Murray* (1706) Mor 12149; *McDonald v McDonald* (1840) 2 D 889, affd 1 Bell's App 819; *Phosphate Sewage Co Ltd v Molleson* (1879) 4 App Cas 801 at 820, per Lord Blackburn.

CONDEMNATOR

1.29   A decree of condemnator is a decree on the merits in favour of the pursuer. It operates as *res judicata* and will bar the defender from raising a later action based on any defence pleaded in the original action or on a matter which might have been pleaded in that action but was omitted from it[1].

1 *Barbour v Grierson* (1828) 6 S 860; *Campbell v Brown* (1831) 9 S 258; *Hamilton v Wright* (1839) 2 D 86; *Glasgow Shipowners' Association v Clyde Navigation Trs* (1885) 12 R 695; *Crawford & Co v Scottish Savings Investment and Building Society* (1885) 12 R 1033; *Edinburgh and District Water Trustees v Clippens Oil Co Ltd* (1899) 1 F 899. See also *Ewing v Wallace* (1832) 6 W & S 222; *Phosphate Sewage Co Ltd v Molleson* (1879) 6 R (HL) 113; *Rennie v James* (1907) 15 SLT 56.

MIXED DECREES

1.30   A decree which contains more than one of the outcomes of the dismissal, absolvitor and condemnator is a mixed decree. Examples are a decree dismissing or absolving the defender in respect of some of the conclusions of the action but finding him liable to the pursuer in respect of the rest[1]; and a decree of condemnator against one or more defenders and absolvitor (or dismissal) in favour of the rest[2]. A further example of what is truly a mixed decree is where some defenders are assoilzied and the rest are granted dismissal: here the effect of the different parts of the decree can be seen from the point of view of the defenders in terms of *res judicata* against the pursuer and the possibility of further action by the pursuer.

1 *Stair*, IV, 46, 3: 'Decreets are absolvitor, whereby the defender is freed or assoilzied from the conclusion of the libel or process; or they are condemnator, whereby the conclusion of the process is found just and true, against the defender, in whole or in part; or they are mixed,

whereby the defender is absolved from some part of the conclusion of the process, and is
condemned in other parts thereof.'
2 *E Ancaster v Sandeman* (1893) 1 SLT 291.

INTEREST ON DECREES

Necessity for crave or conclusion

1.31 A decree requiring the payment of a sum of money will normally state
that interest at a certain rate will run on the sum decerned for from a specified
date until payment. It is probably the case that award of interest on a principal
sum and expenses runs *ex lege* from the date of decree[1], and accordingly it is
unnecessary to conclude specifically for it. But it is invariable practice to
include interest in the conclusions of an action, and there are dangers in
omitting to do so[2]. Where any divergence is sought in the interest craved in
respect of (1) date from which interest it to run, if not from date of decree; and
(2) rate of interest, if not that implied by legislation or rule of court, there
need to be specific conclusions with supporting averments. If compound
interest is sought, it must also be specifically concluded for[3], and the same
rule probably applies to conclusions for interest on interest[4].

1 *Dalmahoy and Wood v Magistrates of Brechin* (1859) 21 D 210. For the rule in actions of count and
  reckoning, see *Donaldson v Findlay, Bannatyne & Co* (1860) 22 D 937, (1864) 2 M (HL) 80;
  Project Contract Services Ltd v Fraioli 1980 SC 261.
2 See *Maclaren* p 298; *Macphail* p 300.
3 *Jolly v McNeill* (1829) 7 S 666 (rev 4 W & S 455); *Douglas v Douglas Trs* (1867) 5 M 827.
4 Compare *Nash Dredging (UK) Ltd v Kestrel Marine Ltd* 1986 SLT 67.

Date from which interest is due

1.32 Interest is deemed to run from the date of decree but there are many
recognised instances where an earlier date is allowed, including the date on
which the right of action arose, date of demand for payment, and date of
citation. There is no general rule and the question of the date from which
interest runs depends upon the particular area of law[1]. Where the parties have
expressly or by necessary implication agreed on a date, that date will be taken
as the appropriate date.

The rule concerning interest on damages (which applied to damages in
contract[2] and in delict) was that until date of decree no sum was due and
accordingly interest could run only from date of decree. This rule has been
superseded by statute[3], which gives the court power to award pre-decree
interest on damages from a date no earlier than that when the right of action
arose[4], and requires the court to award pre-decree interest in cases of damages
or solatium in respect of personal injuries unless there are reasons special to
the case why such interest should not be given[5].

1 See discussion in *Maclaren* pp 298–301; D M Walker *The Law of Civil Remedies in Scotland*,
  pp 367–369; W A Wilson *The Law of Scotland Relating to Debt* pp 154–155; W W McBryde
  The Law of Contract in Scotland pp 485–488.
2 See *McBryde* pp 485–488.
3 Interest on Damages (Scotland) Act 1958, as amended by the Interest on Damages (Scotland)
  Act 1971.

4 Interest on Damages (Scotland) Act 1958, s 1.
5 Ibid, s 1A. For discussion of operation of the 1958 Act, see *Wilson on Debt* pp 155–156; *McBryde* pp 488–489.

Rate of interest

1.33 There is no single fixed rate of interest which runs on decrees, and the general position is that the court has a discretion in fixing the rate[1]. The appropriate rate will depend on the branch of law in which the issue of interest arises and of the particular circumstances of the case[2]. In *Interplan (Joiners and Shopfitters) v Reid Furniture Co Ltd*[3], the sheriff principal held that sufficient averments had been made to allow a proof before answer where the pursuers claimed interest at 17 per cent on unpaid bills, this being the rate stated by them as that equal to or greater (but not less) than the rate of interest on a sum borrowed by the pursuers to replace the sum sued for.

1 For discussion of the historical bases of interest, see *Kearon v Thompson's Trustees* 1949 SC 287.
2 See *Maclaren* pp 302 et seq.
3 1984 SLT (Sh Ct) 42.

1.34 However, there are two important qualifications to the discretion enjoyed by the court as to rate of interest. The first is that interest payable under a decree will be deemed to be at a specified rate unless otherwise stated. At present this deemed rate is 15 per cent per annum[1].

1 RC 66 (in relation to any decree pronounced or extracted after 15 August 1985: SI 1985/1178; AS Interest on Sheriff Court Decrees or Extracts 1975, SI 1975/948, as amended with effect from 16 August 1985 by SI 1985/1179.

1.35 Secondly, where the parties have agreed on a rate of interest, that rate will be applied from the appropriate date (which is usually also regulated by the parties' agreement) until payment. At one time, it appeared to be the practice that courts would grant decree at the pactional rate only until the date of decree and at the deemed rate from that date[1]. Since the Inner House decision in *Bank of Scotland v Davis*[2], it is clear that the court should grant decree with interest on sums at a pactional rate until payment. In that case the court noted[3]:

> 'As a matter of principle, where there is a contract for the loan of money with an agreed rate of interest payable on the principal sum, we see no good reason why the court should refuse to grant a decree for payment in terms of that contract. The agreed rate of interest runs on the principal sum until payment. If repayment is not made voluntarily, the pursuer can enforce payment by obtaining a judicial decree and by taking such steps thereafter as may be necessary to enforce the decree. An action for repayment of a loan is the remedy afforded by law to the lender to enforce performance by the borrower of his or her contractual obligations. In principle, therefore, a decree for repayment of a loan should be granted in terms of the obligations undertaken by the borrower; and it should include interest on the principal sum at the agreed rate until payment of the principal sum together with the interest accrued thereon in terms of the contract. The proposition accepted by the sheriff that when decree is granted in an action for repayment the contract is at an end seems to us to be entirely wrong. If the crave or conclusion for payment is framed in terms of the contract the lender is asking the court to enforce the contract, not to terminate it.'

The court in *Davis* explicitly noted that pactional rates of interest were subject to the provisions of the Consumer Credit Act 1974 on extortionate credit bargains[4].

1 See eg *National Commercial Bank v Stuart* 1969 SLT (Notes) 52; *Avco Financial Services Ltd v McQuire* 1976 SLT (Sh Ct) 33; *Petroleum Industry Training Board v Jenkins* 1982 SLT (Sh Ct) 43.
2 1982 SLT 20; see also *Royal Bank of Scotland v Briggs* 1982 SLT (Sh Ct) 46. For discussion, see S A Bennett 'Bank debts: a matter of interest' 1983 SLT (News) 85.
3 *Bank of Scotland v Davis* 1982 SLT 20 at 20–21.
4 Consumer Credit Act 1974, ss 137–140. For discussion see *Wilson on Debt* pp 32–34; J J Pearson 'Consumer Credit' *The Laws of Scotland: Stair Memorial Encyclopaedia* vol 5, paras 932–933.

1.36 Where the court is awarding interest on decrees from a pre-decree date under the Interest on Damages (Scotland) Act 1958, the practice is to distinguish between damages for pre-decree and post-decree loss or injury and to award different rates of interest in respect of each[1]. The rate of pre-decree interest should reflect the 'deemed' rate or rates during the relevant period[2]. This pre-decree interest is included in the sum on which interest runs from the date of decree[3].

1 *Smith v Middleton* 1972 SC 30; *Picken v J Smart & Co (Contractors) Ltd* 1972 SLT (Notes) 12; *McMahon v J & P Coats (UK) Ltd* 1972 SLT (Notes) 16; *Cooper v Pat Munro (Alness) Ltd* 1972 SLT (Notes) 20; *McCuaig v Redpath Dorman Long* 1972 SLT (Notes) 42, (1972) 17 JLS 337, 338; *Ward v Tarmac Civil Engineering Ltd* 1972 SLT (Notes) 52; *Ross v British Railways Board* 1972 SC 154; *Orr v Metcalfe* 1973 SC 57; *Macdonald v Glasgow Corpn* 1973 SC 52; *McAllister v Abram* 1979 SLT (Notes) 6, 1981 SLT 85; *Plaxton v Aaron Construction (Dundee) Ltd* 1980 SLT (Notes) 6; *Prentice v Chalmers* 1985 SLT 168; *Wilson v Norman J Stewart & Co (1970) Ltd* 1986 SLT 469.
2 *Smith v Middleton* 1972 SC 30; *Starkey v NCB* 1987 SLT 103.
3 *Smith v Middleton* 1972 SC 30; *Mouland v Ferguson* 1979 SLT (Notes) 85.

1.37 A particular issue concerning rate of interest is statement of the rate in a variable manner. Many contracts for the loan of money from banks specify a rate of interest calculated at a stated percentage above lender's base-rate. When decree is sought to enforce the repayment of the loan at this rate of interest, a potential conflict arises between the principle that the courts should give effect to the terms of the contract between the parties[1], and the principle that courts 'should so express the decree that the defender shall be in no doubt regarding the obligation he has to discharge'[2]. A number of sheriff court decisions[3] have held that the conflict here is more apparent than real and that it is competent to grant decree requiring payment of a principal sum with interest thereon at n per cent per annum over the pursuer's base rate from time to time until payment. The view is taken that verification of the base rate of a bank from time to time is easily discoverable by a defender and by officers of court enforcing the decree. However, in one decision[4] a sheriff questioned the competency of such a decree and allowed the pursuers to amend their crave to read 'with interest thereon at the pursuer's base rate from time to time in force plus 7 per cent as same shall be determined at date of any extract of any decree to follow hereon or date of payment, whichever is the earlier'[5]. However, in *Geddes* the sheriff did not disapprove as such the competency of the original crave which was in the terms sought in other cases. The general practice is that if parties have agreed to a variable rate of interest, the decree for payment should conform exactly to that rate. The effect of the *Geddes* rule is not, as it might seem, to make more specific the rate of interest but rather to freeze the rate of interest at the time of payment or extract. But the rate of interest may have varied before either of those dates. In *Logie*, Sheriff Principal S E Bell said[6]:

> 'A calculation has to be done in every case. In particular, in cases where the *Geddes* formula is adopted, the calculation may involve one rate of interest from citation for a period and another rate thereafter until extract. When the formula in *Dunbar* and in the present case is used the calculation may involve a rate of interest from citation for a period, another rate thereafter until after extract, and another rate therafter until payment. In each case a calculation must be made. I understand that on any day the bank can immediately verify the amount of interest due. A defender for his part can ascertain changes in base rates and can check the bank's calculation.'

1 *Bank of Scotland v Davis* 1982 SLT 20; cp *Bank of Scotland v Forsyth* 1969 SLT (Sh Ct) 15.
2 *Middleton v Leslie* (1892) 19 R 801, 802 per Lord President Robertson.
3 *Bank of Scotland v Forsyth* 1968 SLT (Sh Ct) 83, 1969 SLT (Sh Ct) 15; *Royal Bank of Scotland plc v Dunbar* 1985 SLT (Sh Ct) 66; *Bank of Scotland v Logie* 1986 SLT (Sh Ct) 47.
4 *Royal Bank of Scotland plc v Geddes* 1983 SLT (Sh Ct) 32.
5 This was explicitly modelled on the conclusion approved on *Commerzbank AG v Large* 1977 SC 375. The sheriff also followed the *Commerzbank* rule in respect of the necessity of superseding extract until the pursuers provided a certified statement of the rate of interest prevailing at the date of extract decree. In the light of the comments in *Dunbar*, supra, it would appear to be more appropriate that the extract decree specifies *all* the interest rates throughout the relevant period.
6 1986 SLT (Sh Ct) 47, 49 referring to *Royal Bank of Scotland plc v Geddes* 1983 SLT (Sh Ct) 32, *Royal Bank of Scotland plc v Dunbar* 1985 SLT (Sh Ct) 66. In practice these calculations should be made by the creditor when instructing diligence.

EXPENSES

Expenses as part of process

1.38 It is not necessary, for expenses to be awarded in an action, that the written pleadings contain a conclusion or crave for expenses. However, a party seeking expenses must make a motion to the court for them. As expenses are part of a legal action, a separate action cannot in general be raised to recover the expenses of process[1].

1 *Young v Nith Commissioners* (1880) 7 R 891; *Wood v Wood's Trs* (1904) 6 F 640; *Cullen's Exors v Kilmarnock Theatre Co* 1913 1 SLT 290, 1914 2 SLT 334. A separate claim for expenses may be raised in the case of a *dominus litus*, and in a divorce action where the wife's solicitor claims her expenses from the husband: *MacPhail* p 643.

Nature of finding for expenses

1.39 There are two distinct stages as regards expenses of a court action, though in some situations both stages may take place at the same time[1]. Where expenses have been moved for, the first stage is for the court to make a finding that a party is liable to pay expenses to another party. The second stage is for the court to decern for the party so liable to pay a specified sum as expenses. As in many situations the amount of expenses due is not known to the court or has not been agreed by the parties, the finding of liability will continue the matter until decerniture for expenses can be made, which is only after taxation. It is the decerniture, and not the finding of liability, which is contained in the decree for expenses, which may accordingly be a separate decree from that decerning for the principal sum in the action.

1 J M Lees *Notes on the Structure of Interlocutors* (2nd edn 1915) pp 32–33; Report on Diligence and Debtor Protection (Scot Law Com Report no 95 (1985)) pp 81–82.

Procedure on award of expenses

COURT OF SESSION

1.40 In the Court of Session, the court will normally pronounce decree as to the principal matters of the action and where one party is found liable in expenses pronounce an interlocutor to that effect[1]. A remit is then made to the Auditor of Court for taxation of expenses. The Auditor, after hearing the parties at a diet of taxation, prepares a report on the taxation of the account of expenses, stating the amount of expenses as taxed[2]. Where no objection to the report has been made or upheld, the court decerns against the party found liable in expenses as taxed by the Auditor. It should be noted that separate extracts may be made of the separate decrees for principal sum and for expenses.

1 RC 348(1).
2 Procedure on the diet of taxation and on noting an objection to the Auditor's report is set out in RC 348–349.

SHERIFF COURT ORDINARY CAUSE ACTION

1.41 Decree for expenses is granted only after expenses have been taxed, unless the amount has been modified at a fixed amount[1]. Usually in the case of decree in absence, modified expenses are claimed and granted at the same time as decree for the principal sum[2]. Where a taxation of expenses is to be held, the sheriff clerk transmits the account and the process to the auditor of court[3]. A diet of taxation is fixed by the auditor, not earlier than seven days from the date he receives the account. At the diet the auditor, after considering any representations by the parties may make his decision or reserve consideration until later, in which case he must inform the parties who attended the diet of his ultimate decision. If no note of objection to the taxed account is made or upheld, the sheriff grants decree for the expenses as taxed[4].

1 OCR 97.
2 OCR 24.
3 Procedure is set out in OCR 98. See further D B White *Practice and Procedure in the Sheriff's Ordinary Court* pp 91–92.
4 Decree for expenses may be extracted in the name of the solicitor who conducted the cause: OCR 97.

SHERIFF COURT SUMMARY CAUSE ACTIONS

1.42 In summary cause actions, final decree dealing with the substantive issues of the action is not pronounced until the amount of any expenses to be awarded has been fixed by the sheriff clerk and approved by the sheriff[1]. A hearing on a claim for expenses takes place immediately after the decision on the substantive issue of the action. If that is not possible, a separate hearing on expenses is arranged, and the successful party must send his account of expenses to the sheriff clerk and to the other party or parties at least seven days before this hearing. At the hearing the sheriff clerk fixes the amount of expenses and reports to the sheriff. The parties may make further representations to the sheriff, who pronounces final decree including decree for payment of expenses as approved by him[2].

1 SCR 87, 88.
2 On application by a solicitor of any party to whom expenses may be awarded, the sheriff may when granting decree, grant decree for expenses in favour of that solicitor: SCR 88(7).

SHERIFF COURT SMALL CLAIMS ACTIONS

1.43 In small claims actions, decree on the main issue is pronounced along with any award of expenses[1]. There are limitations on the amount of expenses which may be awarded in small claims actions[2], but where these do not apply procedure for determination of expenses is the same as that in summary cause actions[3].

1 SMCR 25(3).
2 Sheriff Courts (Scotland) Act 1971, s 36B; Small Claims (Scotland) Order 1988, SI 1988/1999, para 4.
3 SMCR 26.

FOREIGN CURRENCY DECREES

Introduction

1.44 It is now clear that the Scottish courts have the power to grant a decree in a currency other than sterling[1]. What is not yet settled is the range of actions in which foreign currency decrees can be granted and the basis for considering the appropriate currency. In *Commerzbank AG v Large*, a Full Bench held that it was competent to grant a decree in West German Deutsch Marks where the action was for a debt, the money of account and the money of payment of which was West German currency, and which arose from a contract whose proper law was West German law. The court also held that for reasons of exchange control legislation (since suspended) and for the purposes of enforcement in Scotland, it was necessary to provide in such a decree for the conversion of the foreign currency into sterling. In that case the court accepted as competent the terms of the pursuer's conclusion 'for payment by the defender to the pursuer of the sum of . . . DM 7066.90 with interest thereon at the rate of 14.6 per centum per annum from 22nd November 1976 until payment or the sterling equivalent of the said sum and interest at the date of payment or at the date of extract whichever is the earlier.' The court expressly limited the force of its decision in *Commerzbank*, which was an undefended action, to actions having the characteristics of that case.

Shortly after that case, a decision of a sheriff principal in *L/F Foroya Fiskosola v Charles Mauritzen Ltd*[2] held that a decree could not be granted in Danish currency where sterling was the money of account and money of payment of a debt and where there was only a bare averment that the contract in question was governed by the law of Denmark, which averment was not supported by the rest of the pursuer's pleadings.

1 *Commerzbank AG v Large* 1977 SC 375. This decision was influenced by passages in Craig's *Jus Feudale* (1, 16, 22–23) and especially by the decision of the House of Lords in an English appeal, *Miliangos v George Frank (Textiles) Ltd* [1976] AC 443. The Full Bench decision in *Commerzbank* in effect disregarded the House of Lords decision of *Hyslops v Gordon* (1824) 2 Sh App 451, a Scottish case. For discussion of the issues of judicial precedent involved, see G Maher and T B Smith 'Judicial Precedent' *The Laws of Scotland: Stair Memorial Encyclopaedia* vol 22, paras 282, 354.
2 1978 SLT (Sh Ct) 27.

1.45 Since the decisions in *Commerzbank* and *L/F Foroya*, there have been no reported decisions of a Scottish court which deal expressly with the substantive principles of foreign currency decrees. In an Outer House case, *Worf v Western SMT Co Ltd*[1], the Lord Ordinary made awards of various heads of damages in US dollars in an action raised by the widow of a man who had died in a road accident in Scotland caused by the admitted fault of the defenders. The deceased and his family had been of Californian residence. No reference was made in the judgment as to the doctrinal basis for the currency of the awards but the implicit approach taken in this case is generally speaking consistent with that of English law on the currency to be applied in damages for tort, namely that damages should be awarded in the currency in which the loss was effectively borne or with which the loss had the closest connection[2].

In *North Scottish Helicopters Ltd v United Technologies Corporation Inc (No 2)*[3], the Lord Ordinary *obiter* accepted the approach of the House of Lords in *The Despina R* as to the appropriate basis for awards of damages for delict but no reference was made to any Scottish authority on foreign currency decrees. In this case, the pursuers sought recovery of sums of money which they claimed had been required to be paid by them as a result of the defender's fault. The sum of money expended had been in US dollars and that was the currency in which the pursuers claimed decree. However his Lordship held that on the facts of the case, the pursuers did not maintain trading accounts in US currency and that they would have been entitled only to payment of such sum in sterling as would have been required to purchase the US dollars used to meet the expenditure.

1 1987 SLT 317.
2 See *The Despina R* [1979] AC 685.
3 1988 SLT 778.

Procedure for enforcing decree

1.46 Where a pursuer wishes to obtain extract to enforce a foreign currency decree, the normal principle is that the foreign currency sum stated in the decree is converted into sterling at the date of extract, if payment has not already been made. (If payment has been made, conversion into sterling is at the date of such prior payment.) Extract is superseded until solicitors for the pursuer provide to the Extractor a certified statement of (1) the rate of exchange prevailing at the date of extract sought and (2) the sterling equivalent, at that rate, of the principal sum and interest. The Extractor endorses on the extract a docquet to the effect that in terms of this certificate the sterling equivalent of the principal sum and interest is at the date of extract £n[1]. Such a certificate will normally be obtained from one of the Scottish clearing banks and will specify the appropriate rate of exchange in London at the close of day prior to the day on which extract is sought[2].

In the sheriff court the procedure is for a minute to be endorsed on the initial writ or summons. This minute states the rate of exchange prevailing at close of business on the preceding day and the sterling equivalent at that rate of the sum decerned for in foreign currency and craves for extract in that form. This minute should be accompanied by an appropriate certificate[2].

1 *Commerzbank AG v Large* 1977 SC 375 at 383. See Court of Session Extract Department Regulations (Practice Note, 9 July 1980), Section A, reg 5A.
2 Compare the terms of the Practice Note in the Lothian and Borders Sheriffdom, which provides a model for such a certificate: Act of Court No 1 of 1978 (24 April 1978) (PH Book, D 1008).

Defender's option to pay once extract obtained

1.47 Once extract has been obtained in the form of conversion of the foreign currency sum into sterling at the date of extract, a question arises as to whether the defender may still make payment to the pursuer not in the converted sterling but in the foreign currency stated in the decree itself. This would be of advantage to the defender, and correspondingly to the disadvantage of the pursuer, where the foreign currency has declined in value against sterling subsequent to the date of extract. In *Commerzbank*[1], the court stated: 'For the purposes of this case the pursuers have deliberately chosen to fix the conversion date as the date of payment or at the date when the decree is extracted whichever is the earlier, and we can see no procedural obstacle in the way of pronouncing the decree now sought, or in enforcing payment under the decree if the defender does not voluntarily satisfy the judgment either in the currency of account or in the sterling equivalent at the time of payment. *The option must always be his.*' (Emphasis added.)

The meaning of this passage is by no means clear. The option referred to ('his' option) is clearly one belonging to the defender, not the pursuers, but a close reading of the passage suggests that the option available to the defender is to pay in the foreign currency of the decree or the sterling equivalent at the date of payment and that this option exists at the date of the payment *prior to extract*. However the general principle of the *Miliangos* decision suggests that if a particular foreign currency is the appropriate currency of the judgment, the pursuer is not entitled to refuse payment in that currency[2].

1 *Commerzbank AG v Large* 1977 SC at 383.
2 *Miliangos v George Frank (Textiles) Ltd* [1976] AC 443 at 466, per Lord Wilberforce: 'The creditor has no concern with pounds sterling: for him what matters is that a Swiss franc for good or for ill should remain a Swiss franc.' This passage is not cited in the Lord Ordinary's report or the judgment of the court in *Commerzbank*.

Pursuer's option to enforce payment

1.48 As a corollary to the right of the defender to make payment in the currency of the decree even if the cost in sterling of purchasing that currency falls subsequent to the date of decree, the creditor has the right where possible to enforce the decree in the foreign currency of the decree. In *Commerzbank*[1], the court noted: 'In our opinion justice requires that a foreign creditor who is entitled to payment of a debt due in the currency of his own country or the currency of a particular foreign country should not be bound to accept payment of the debt in the money of his debtor's country if any prejudice would be caused to him thereby.'

The court also specifically noted that the only reasons for converting the sum sought into sterling were because of exchange controls (subsequently suspended) and for enforcement in Scotland. But the possibility exists that the pursuer may be able to do diligence in Scotland to recover directly the sum due in the foreign currency rather than the sterling equivalent. For example, where the debtor holds a bank account in Scotland in the same foreign currency as that of the decree or in another currency other than sterling, an arrestment may be used to attach that account[2]. Similarly, the diligence of poinding and sale may be used where the defender possesses foreign currency (or traveller's cheques in a foreign currency) in his own premises[3].

1 1977 SC at 383.
2 For discussion see ch 5 below at para 5.07. Cp *Choice Investments Ltd v Jeromnimon* [1981] 1 QB 149.
3 See ch 7 below at para 7.53.

The possibility of a later conversion date

1.49   In *Commerzbank* the court expressly recognised that in circumstances other than those of that case a conversion date other than the earlier of the date of payment or of extract might be possible. The court quoted a passage from the speech of Lord Fraser of Tullybelton in *Miliangos* as stating the basic principle[1]: 'But there must be some provision for converting the foreign currency into sterling so that it can be enforced in this country. The question is what the conversion date should be. Theoretically, it should, in my opinion, be the date of actual payment of the debt. That would give exactly the cost in sterling of buying the foreign currency. But theory must yield to practical necessity to the extent that, if judgment has to be enforced in this country, it must be converted before enforcement. Accordingly, I agree with my noble and learned friend that conversion should be at the date when the court authorises enforcement of the judgment in sterling.'

In *Commerzbank*, the court accepted that the date of extract may well be the latest procedurally acceptable date of conversion in terms of practical necessity.

The question then arises whether a later conversion date is practically possible. The main practical problem is that of ensuring that the correct conversion is made, and it might be thought that responsibility for this should not rest with messengers-at-arms and sheriff officers. But against this objection there is the existing procedure whereby a certificate on exchange rate and conversion is completed by solicitors for the pursuer to pass to the extractor or the clerk of court. This procedure could be adapted so as to supply the officer of court with the relevant information on exchange rates as at the date of arrestment or charge. A definite sum is needed at each of these stages as the duties of the arrestee and debtor are fixed in relation to the sums arrested and charged for. Furthermore a number of sheriff court decisions[2] have held that it is competent to grant decree for payment of a sum of money with interest thereon at a variable rate. These cases take the view that rates of interest can be easily discovered by defenders and officers of courts and if that point of view is accepted, then there is little to distinguish most currency exchange rates from rates of interest. There remains the possibility of further fluctuation in currency values from these dates until the dates of furthcoming and warrant sale but no matter that fluctuation it still ensures that the pursuer is nearer to getting the equivalent for his foreign currency debt than allowed by the present precedure[3].

1 *Miliangos v George Frank (Textiles) Ltd* [1976] AC 443 at 502, cited in *Commerzbank AG v Large* 1977 SC 375 at 383.
2 See above at para 1.37.
3 The possibility of later conversion dates has been discussed by the Law Commission of England and Wales. See Private International Law. Foreign Money Liabilities (Law Com no 124) 1983, paras 3.12–3.15.

EXTRACT

Nature of extract

1.50 An extract has been described as a certificate by the proper officer that a decree in the terms stated exists in the records of the court[1]. A litigant, whether pursuer or defender, who has been granted decree in his favour is entitled to extract decree[2]. In the context of diligence the importance of extract is that it contains warrant for doing the appropriate types of diligence to enforce the decree.

1 *Inglis v McIntyre* (1862) 24 D 541, 544.
2 Where a person claims a right to extract decree which is derived from the successful litigant, procedure is governed by the 1987 Act, s 88. See below at para 1.64.

Court of Session decrees

RESPONSIBLE OFFICER

1.51 The responsibility for the issuing of extracts of Court of Session decrees lies with the Extractor of the Court of Session, who is a Depute Clerk of Session in charge of the Extracts Department of the Court[1].

1 RC 12; Public Records (Scotland) Act 1937, s 13.

WHEN EXTRACT MAY BE ISSUED

1.52 The court may, upon cause shown, and where justice so requires, grant warrant for the immediate extract of a decree or interlocutor[1]. Similarly the court has power to supersede extract until some condition has been fulfilled or for a specified period[2].

Where neither of these circumstances applies, decrees (other than decrees in absence) may be transmitted to the Extractor for extract on the eighth day after the date of the interlocutor[3]. Decrees in absence may be transmitted for extract on the eleventh day after the date of the interlocutor, but in most situations further periods must elapse before extract may be granted[4].

1 Extract Department Regulations (Practice Note, 9 July 1980), reg 1; *Gavin v Henderson* 1910 SC 357.
2 See eg *Thomson v Duncan* (1855) 17 D 1081; *Ballachulish Slate Quarries Co v Grant* (1903) 5 F 1105; *Wilson v Dick's Co-operative Institutions Ltd* 1916 1 SLT 312; *Bruce v McLellan* 1925 SC 103; *MacLean v Clan Line Steamers* 1925 SC 256; *Archibald v Archibald* 1989 SLT 199.
3 Extract Department Regulations, reg 1.
4 See above at para 1.10.

FORM OF EXTRACT

1.53 An extract may be partly or wholly written, typewritten, printed, engraved or lithographed[1]. Each page of the extract must be impressed with the Extractor's seal or stamp, and the last page must be signed by the Extractor. Any alteration must be authenticated by the initials of the Extractor or assistant Extractor. The place and date of extract are stated at the end[2].

1 RC 63.
2 *Maclaren* p 1100.

CONTENT OF EXTRACT

1.54 The extract sets forth the terms of the decree or interlocutor, the date of which is stated at the beginning of the extract[1]. The interest to run on any sum decerned for, will be set out as running from a stated date and at a stated rate[2]. The extract will also state the amount of expenses awarded[3]. Warrant for all lawful diligence will also be stated in the extract[4].

1 *Maxwell* p 623–624. The Extractor may look at the written opinion of the court in order to construe the interlocutor: *McKellar v Dallas's Ltd* 1928 SC 503. For decrees for sums in a foreign currency, see above at paras 1.44–1.49.
2 RC 66. See further at paras 1.31–1.37 above.
3 Where any interlocutor awards a lump sum as modified expenses, it is treated as also awarding the dues of any extract required to enforce the award. The Extractor includes the amount of those dues in the extract: RC 63A.
4 1987 Act, s 87(1); RC 64. See further below at para 1.57.

PROCEDURE FOR OBTAINING EXTRACT

1.55 Special provisions apply for obtaining extract of consistorial decrees. In other cases, extract is obtained by transmitting the whole process to the Extractor[1]. Where an interim decree is to be extracted, the process is returned to the court in due course. In the case of final extract, all steps of process must be returned and all productions borrowed before transmission.

Along with each process transmitted for extract, there must be lodged a note to the Extractor specifying (a) the names and addresses of the parties and (b) a copy of the interlocutor or interlocutors of which extract is required. This note must be signed by the solicitor ordering the extract, who must state the party for whom he acts.

No extract will be issued until the appropriate fee fund dues have been paid[2].

Once a process has been properly transmitted for extract, extract will be prepared and issued unless interdicted by the court or unless the clerk to the process intimates that a party to the cause desires to enrol a reclaiming motion[3].

In the case of a consistorial decree (including pecuniary provisions and expenses) pronounced on or after 23 September 1975, extract is sent free of charge to the solicitor for the pursuer or petitioner after the expiry of twenty-one days provided that no reclaiming motion has been made[4]. Additional extracts of such decrees may be obtained from the Extracts Office on payment of a fee[5].

1 See generally Extract Department Regulations; *Maxwell* pp 624–626.
2 The fee payable for extract decree following a summons or petition is currently £12; Court of Session etc Fees Order 1984, SI 1984/256, Sch, Pt I, G(1). Fee fund dues are paid in cash: SI 1976/184.
3 Review by the Inner House of an interlocutor of the Outer House is not prevented by reason only that extract has been issued before the expiry of the reclaiming days: RC 63B.
4 A copy of the extract is also sent to the defender or respondent. Procedure for the extract of a consistorial decree pronounced prior to 23 September 1975 is governed by Extract Department Regulations, Section B, regs 9, 10.
5 See Court of Session etc Fees Order 1984, SI 1984/256, Sch, Pt I, G(5). Currently the fee is £5.50.

WARRANT FOR EXECUTION

1.56 In every extract decree on which execution may proceed, there is included a warrant in the terms 'and the said Lords grant warrant for all lawful execution hereon'[1]. Where decree is granted by one of the superior courts[2] for payment of money, the warrant for execution in the extract has the effect of authorising[3]:
(i) in relation to a debt other than current maintenance, the charging of the debtor to pay to the creditor within the period specified in the charge the sum specified in the extract and any interest accrued on the sum and, in the event of failure to make such payment within that period, the execution of an earnings arrestment and the poinding of articles belonging to the debtor and, if necessary for the purpose of executing the poinding, the opening of shut and lockfast places;
(ii) in relation to a debt other than current maintenance, an arrestment other than an arrestment of the debtor's earnings in the hands of his employer; and
(iii) if the decree consists of or includes a maintenance order, a current maintenance arrestment in accordance with Part III of the 1987 Act.

1 RC 64. It is understood that the form of warrant in use continues to be that set out in this RC 64, as no Act of Sederunt has been made on this matter in terms of the 1987 Act, s 87(1). However such a warrant is treated in practice as the warrant referred to in s 87(2) of the Act, which sets out the diligences authorised by the warrant.
2 Ie the Court of Session, the High Court of Justiciary, and the Court of Tiends: 1987 Act, s 87(1).
3 Ibid, ss 73(1), (2), 87(2).

Sheriff Court

RESPONSIBLE OFFICER

1.57 The officer for the issuing of extracts of sheriff court decrees is the sheriff clerk[1].

1 Cp OCR 25.

1.58 The sheriff has a common law power to supersede extract[1]. In ordinary cause actions, the sheriff on cause shown may grant a motion to allow for early extract[2]. Such a motion must be made in the presence of the parties, or the sheriff must be satisfied that proper intimation of the motion had been made in writing to all other parties. There is no equivalent provisions for early extract in summary cause or small claims actions[3].

Where neither of these situations has occurred, the general rule is that extract of a decree or interlocutor in an ordinary cause defended action may be made after the expiry of the period for any party to mark or pursue an appeal or apply for leave to appeal[4]. A decree or interlocutor (unless unappealable) may be appealed within fourteen days of its date[5]. Where, following the pronouncement of decree, the sheriff has reserved any question of expenses, extract may be issued only after the expiry of fourteen days from the date of the interlocutor disposing of such expenses unless the sheriff directs otherwise[6].

Where decree in absence has been granted in an ordinary cause action, extract may be issued by the sheriff clerk on the expiry of fourteen days from the date it was granted[7]. However, the sheriff may on cause shown order the extract to be issued at an earlier date.

In summary cause and small claims actions, extract of decree may be issued only after the lapse of fourteen days from the granting of the decree. If an appeal has been lodged the extract must not be issued until the appeal has been disposed of[8].

1 Cp OCR 90(4).
2 OCR 90(3).
3 This is subject to an exception in the case of decree granted under SCR 68A (actions against persons in possession of heritable property without right or title) which gives the sheriff a discretion to shorten any time-period set out in the Summary Cause Rules. However the early issue of an extract in such a case does not prevent an appeal being made, but the lodging of a note of appeal does not sist diligence unless the sheriff directs otherwise: SCR 81A.
4 OCR 90(1).
5 OCR 91.
6 OCR 90(3).
7 OCR 25. The date of decree is the date upon which it is entered in the books of the court.
8 SCR 89; SMCR, App 3. This is subject to SCR 68A, discussed above.

FORMS OF EXTRACT

1.59 Forms of extract are set out in the Schedule to the Sheriff Courts (Scotland) Extracts Act 1892 and, in respect of various types of decree, also in the rules of court[1]. In ordinary cause actions, the extract is usually set out on a separate sheet of paper, and in summary cause and small claims the extract is filled in as part of the official form of summons.

1 See OCR Form 2; SCR Forms U-U14 (applicable also to small claims).

CONTENT OF EXTRACT

1.60 The extract sets out the essentials of the decree, including the principal sum decerned for, interest[1], and expenses. Where decree has been granted in absence that should be stated in the extract[2]. It is not necessary for the word 'decern' to be used in order to allow diligence to proceed on the extract[3]. The extract contains warrant for all lawful execution thereon[4].

The extract is signed by the sheriff clerk and the place and date of extract are stated.

1 For the rate of interest, see AS Interest on Sheriff Court Decrees or Extracts 1975, SI 1975/948, as amended. See discussion above at paras 1.33–1.37.
2 Sheriff Courts (Scotland) Extracts Act 1892, Sch 1; *Macphail* p 236.
3 Sheriff Courts (Scotland) Extracts Act 1892, s 4.
4 See further below at para 1.63.

PROCEDURE FOR OBTAINING EXTRACT

1.61 The general practice is that once a decree can be extracted[1], the sheriff clerk will forward an extract to the party entitled to it, or to that party's solicitor, without being requested to do so. The court fees payable in respect of the initial writ or summons of the action includes the issue of extract decree[2]. Where a further extract is required, application is made to the sheriff clerk with a fee of £3.

1 See above at para 1.59.
2 Sheriff Court Fees Order 1985, SI 1985/827, as amended, para 4(1).

WARRANT FOR EXECUTION

1.62 Extract of a sheriff court decree contains a warrant for all lawful execution thereon[1]. Where the decree requires the payment of money, such a warrant has the effect of authorising[2]:
(i) in relation to a debt other than current maintenance, the charging of the debtor to pay to the creditor within the period specified in the charge the sum specified in the extract and any interest accrued on the sum and, in the event of failure to make such payment within that period, the execution of an earnings arrestment and the poinding of articles belonging to the debtor and, if necessary for the purpose of executing the poinding, the opening of shut and lockfast places;
(ii) in relation to a debt other than current maintenance, an arrestment other than an arrestment of the debtor's earnings in the hands of his employer; and
(iii) if the decree consists of or includes a maintenance order, a current maintenance arrestment in accordance with Part III of the 1987 Act.

1 SCR 89(2); SMCR, App 3.
2 Sheriff Courts (Scotland) Extracts Act 1892, s 7(1) (as substituted by 1987 Act, s 87(3)). For special warrant in decrees for recovery of heritable property, delivery and sequestration for rent, see SCR 69, 71, 77, 78.

Acquisition of right to decree

1.63 The right to extract a decree and to do diligence upon it lies with the party named in the decree. Where another person acquires this right, eg by assignation from the original creditor which has been intimated to the debtor or by confirmation as the executor of the original creditor, special procedure exists which allows for the new creditor to extract the decree and proceed with diligence[1].

Application is made by the new creditor for a warrant which has the effect of authorising execution at his instance of any diligence authorised by the extract decree. Application is made to a clerk of court of the Court of Session in the case of a Court of Session decree, and to the appropriate sheriff clerk in the case of a sheriff court decree. With the application, there is submitted an extract of the decree and the assignation (along with evidence of its having been intimated to the debtor), confirmation as executor or other document establishing the applicant's right. The clerk on being satisfied of the applicant's right to the decree grants warrant.

Where a charge has already been served in pursuance of the decree and a certificate of execution of the charge is submitted with the application, the warrant granted by the clerk of court authorises further diligence by the new creditor on the basis of the charge.

1   1987 Act, s 88; SI 1988/2013, r 69. The same procedure, *mutatis mutandis*, applies in respect of a new creditor's right to obligations contained in documents registered for execution, and orders enforceable as if they were extract registered decrees arbitral bearing warrants for execution by a sheriff.

CHAPTER 2

BASIS OF DILIGENCE:
2. REGISTERED DEEDS, ETC

INTRODUCTION

2.01 As has been stated in the preceding chapter, diligence usually proceeds upon a court decree and the only courts which regularly issue decrees are the Court of Session and the sheriff court.

In this chapter, we shall deal with things which are at common law, or by statute, equivalent of decrees for the purposes of diligence. Probably the most common example is a deed which is registered in the Books of Council and Session (or the books of the sheriff court). It should be noted, however, that although these are equivalent to decrees, the provisions in the 1987 Act about time to pay directions do not apply[1]. However, in some instances, the provisions about time to pay orders do apply[2]. These will be noted at the appropriate places.

1 1987 Act, s 1 (time to pay directions) applies only to decrees: see further ch 3 below at para 3.04 et seq.
2 1987 Act, s 5 (time to pay orders) applies to a decree or other document which in terms of s 15(3) includes extracts of deeds registered for execution: see further ch 3 below at para 3.59 et seq.

DEEDS REGISTERED IN THE BOOKS OF COUNCIL AND SESSION (OR THE BOOKS OF THE SHERIFF COURT)

2.02 Unless statute provides otherwise, deeds may be registered for preservation and execution in either the Books of Council and Session, or those of the appropriate sheriff court[1]. However, less use is made of sheriff court books, and, because in some cases registration is competent only in the Books of Council and Session, the safer course is to use the Books of Council and Session. For example, a minute of resignation by trustees[2], and feu charters by subject superiors must be registered in the Books of Council and Session[3]. It is competent to apply for a time to pay order in respect of a debt due under such a document[4], and an extract is enforceable anywhere in Scotland[5]. Any document registered for execution in the Books of Council and Session or in sheriff court books comes within the scope of the provisions for the reciprocal enforcement of judgments between the different United Kingdom legal systems[6]. Such documents, however, are not judgments for purposes of the 1968 EC Convention on Jurisdiction and the Enforcement of

Judgments in Civil and Commercial Matters. However, special provision is made in the 1968 Convention for the enforcement between contracting states of 'authentic instruments', which are broadly equivalent to the Scots law concept of registered documents. The scheme for enforcing judgments under the Convention applies with certain modifications to the enforcement of authentic instruments[7].

1 The Registration Act 1698.
2 Trusts (Scotland) Act 1921, s 19.
3 Act 1693 (c 35) Anent Procuratories of Resignation and Precepts of Session.
4 1987 Act, s 15(3): definition of 'decree or other document'.
5 1987 Act, s 91(2).
6 Civil Jurisdiction and Judgments Act 1982, s 18(2)(c). See further ch 11 below at pp 292 et seq.
7 1968 Convention, arts 50, 51. For further discussion, see ch 11 below at pp 292 et seq.

Probative deeds

2.03   At common law, the deed has to be a probative deed[1] and must incorporate consent to registration for execution[2]. An extract of such a deed permits summary diligence to be done[3]. (It should be noted that it is not the diligence which is summary, but rather the process by which the equivalent of the decree is obtained)[4]. An extract of the deed will contain a warrant, the form of which is in the Schedule to the Writs Execution (Scotland) Act 1877[5]. Section 2 of the 1877 Act provides that the warrant should be in the form of the Schedule or as near to that as is possible. In practice, the form of the warrant is what appears in the Schedule. Section 3 in its amended form provides that where the debt is an ordinary debt[6], the debtor may be charged to pay and after the expiry of the days of charge, the creditor may execute an arrestment, an earnings arrestment, and a poinding[7]. Where the debt is a maintenance order[8], the creditor may use a current maintenance arrestment[9].

Despite that, however, there still remains doubt about whether other types of diligence are competent, in particular, inhibition. Gretton (in his book on Inhibitions) states that an inhibition is competent[10], whereas Professor Halliday notes that the diligences authorised by the 1877 Act are against the debtor's moveable estate and that if diligence is sought against the heritage of the debtor, further warrant would be required in the form of letters of inhibition[11]. In its amended form, the 1877 Act authorises the various diligences mentioned. That does not exclude others and, in practice, inhibition is used.

1 *Caroway v Ewing* (1611) M 14988.
2 *Erskine* (1710) M 14997; Titles to Land Consolidation (Scotland) Act 1868, s 138.
3 Ersk *Inst* II, 5, 54; Writs Execution (Scotland) Act 1877, ss 1, 2.
4 *Murray v McGuire* 1928 SC 647, SLT 430.
5 As amended by the 1987 Act, s 87(4).
6 Ie a debt including a fine, arrears of maintenance and the expense of a current maintenance arrestment, but *not* current maintenance (1987 Act, s 73(1)).
7 Writs Execution (Scotland) Act 1877, s 3(a), (b) (as amended).
8 As defined in the 1987 Act, s 106.
9 Writs Execution (Scotland) Act 1877, s 3(c); 1987 Act, s 106.
10 GL Gretton *The Law of Inhibition and Adjudication* (1987) p 8.
11 JM Halliday *Conveyancing Law and Practice in Scotland* vol I, para 4–67.

NATURE OF THE OBLIGATION

2.04 Frequently the obligation will be to pay a sum of money. In many instances, the sum which is due will appear *ex facie* of the document. If it does not, the deed must specify the method by which the sum due is to be ascertained[1]. For example, a standard security will usually provide that a certificate from an authorised officer of the lending institution will be conclusive of the amount due[2].

In other cases, the obligation may be an obligation *ad factum praestandum* and an essential requirement is that the obligation is precisely stated[3].

1 *Fisher v Syme* (1828) 7 S 97 (a certificate from the bank who was the creditor).
2 Halliday *The Conveyancing and Feudal Reform (Scotland) Act 1970* (2nd edn) para 10–05.
3 *Hendry v Marshall* (1878) 5 R 687.

Protests of negotiable instruments

2.05 This subject is dealt with under the heading of 'summary diligence' at paragraph 2.16.

Documents of debt

2.06 Inhibition is competent on documents of debt, provided they are probative. This topic is more fully dealt with in chapter 9.

Awards registrable in the Books of Council and Session

2.07 It should be noted that the statutory provisions relating to the awards of various bodies registrable in the Books of Council and Session make no mention of registration in the books of the appropriate sheriff court and it must therefore be assumed that this is not competent. It is competent to seek a time to pay order on such an award. The awards include decisions of the Lands Tribunal for Scotland[1], of the VAT Tribunal[2] those of a review board set up to consider the findings of an inspector of public inquiry in to an aircraft accident under the Civil Aviation (Investigation of Accidents) Regulations 1983[3] and the decision of a disciplinary committee of a board set up under the Agricultural Marketing Act 1958[4]. Other examples are mentioned in the footnote[5].

1 Conveyancing and Feudal Reform (Scotland) Act 1970, s 50(2).
2 Finance Act 1985, s 29.
3 SI 1983/511, reg 23.
4 Agricultural Marketing Act 1958, s 12.
5 Performing Right Tribunal Rules 1965, SI 1965/1504, r 23; Transport Act 1985, Sch 4 (order of Transport Tribunal); Energy Act 1983, s 9 (award of Secretary of State or arbiter about supply of electricity to private generators).

Awards treated as extract registered decrees arbitral

2.08 Awards of various bodies may be treated as if they were extract registered decrees arbitral; such awards either (1) bear a warrant for execution issued from the Books of Council and Session, or (2) bear a warrant for execution issued by the sheriff court of any sheriffdom in Scotland.

(1) Once again, no mention is made of the sheriff court. These awards are in the same category as any other writ which has been registered in the Books of Council and Session for execution, except that a time to pay order cannot be granted, because the 1987 Act refers only to 'an extract registered decree arbitral bearing a warrant for execution issued by the sheriff court'[1]. Two examples are an award of expenses by a body considering an appeal against a refusal by the Bank of England to grant recognition to a body under the Banking Act 1979[2] and expenses of an appeal against various determinations by the Director of Fair Trading, including an order prohibiting certain persons from acting as estate agents under the Estate Agents (Appeals) Regulations 1981[3].

1 1987 Act, s 15(3).
2 Banking Act 1979 (Scottish Appeals) Regulations 1980, SI 1980/348, reg 13.
3 Estate Agents (Appeals) Regulations 1981, SI 1981/1518 reg 25.

2.09 (2) Prior to the coming into force of the Debtors (Scotland) Act 1987, these awards were treated as if they were 'recorded' decrees arbitral, but the Act provides that they are now to be treated as registered decrees arbitral bearing a warrant for execution issued by the sheriff court of any sheriffdom in Scotland[1]. A time to pay order can be granted in respect of such awards[2]. Two important examples are awards of both industrial tribunals and employment appeal tribunals[3] and decisions of the Scottish Land Court[4]. Others are an award by the Minister of the expenses of a local inquiry under the Town and Country Planning (Scotland) Act 1972[5]; a similar award by the Secretary of State in respect of a local inquiry under the Education (Scotland) Act 1980[6], and an award against a claimant where an overpayment of social security has been made[7].

1 1987 Act, s 108(1), Sch 6, para 1.
2 Ibid, s 15(3).
3 Employment Protection (Consolidation) Act 1978, s 135(6), Sch 11, para 21A(2).
4 Crofting Reform (Scotland) Act 1976, s 17(1).
5 Town and Country Planning (Scotland) Act 1972, s 267(8).
6 Education (Scotland) Act 1980, Sch 1, para 8.
7 Social Security Act 1986, s 53.

ASSIGNATION

2.10 Where a creditor has acquired by assignation (a) an obligation contained in a document which is registered in the Books of Council and Session or in sheriff court books and the extract contains a warrant for execution, or (b) an order which is enforceable as if it were an extract registered decree arbitral bearing a warrant for execution issued by the sheriff, in order to enforce the obligation then, in the case of a document registered in the Books of Council and Session, he may apply to a clerk of the Court of Session, and in other cases to the sheriff clerk, in each case to do diligence in his own name[1].

1 1987 Act, s 88(1), (2), (6).

ARBITER'S AWARD

2.11 In a submission to arbitration, the parties usually agree that the arbiter's award may be registered for execution[1]. If that is done, the successful party may register the award either in the Books of Council and Session or in those of the appropriate sheriff court[2]. Where the registration is in the books of the sheriff court, a warrant of concurrence is no longer required before the award can be enforced in another sheriffdom[3]. If the parties have not consented to registration, the successful party would have to apply either to the Court of Session or the sheriff for a decree conform[4]. Once that has been obtained, the award would be enforceable in the same way as any other decree[5].

1 JM Halliday *Conveyancing Law and Practice in Scotland*, vol I, para 14–22.
2 *Halliday* para 14–22. That includes awards in arbitrations between subjects of different states: Arbitration Act 1950, s 40(1).
3 1987 Act, s 91(2).
4 *McCosh v Moore* (1905) 8 F 31, 11 SLT 112.
5 See ch 1 above.

SUMMARY WARRANTS

2.12 Summary warrants are obtained from the sheriff for the recovery of rates, charges for non-domestic and metered water supply, community charge, income tax, capital gains tax, corporation tax, development land tax, petroleum revenue tax, value added tax, and car tax. Where these are being recovered by summary warrant, there are significant differences from recovery by ordinary action. The recovery of debts by summary warrant is dealt with more fully in chapter 8.

ORDERS OF THE CRIMINAL COURTS

Fines

2.13 Section 411 of the Criminal Procedure (Scotland) Act 1975, provides that where civil diligence may be used to recover a fine by virtue of the Act, eg fines imposed upon companies, associations, incorporations, or bodies of trustees[1] or where a court of summary jurisdiction orders the fine to be recovered in this way, the finding of the court shall have added to it the words 'a warrant for civil diligence in a form prescribed by Act of Adjournal'. This permits charging the debtor, the execution of an earnings arrestment and a poinding, and an arrestment other than an arrestment of earnings. The warrant is to be enforced in the same way as the decree of a sheriff in a summary cause[2]. Under the Solicitors (Scotland) Act 1980, a fine imposed on a solicitor by the Scottish Solicitors' Discipline Tribunal shall be forfeit to the Crown[3] and is presumably recoverable in the same way as any other fine. If a solicitor is found liable for the expenses of the tribunal, the tribunal may apply to the Court of Session for a warrant for their recovery and if it is granted, it has the same effect as an extract decree[4]. If the case is appealed to the Court of Session, an award of expenses may be made against the solicitor, as well as a fine imposed[5].

1 Criminal Procedure (Scotland) Act 1975, s 333.
2 1987 Act, Sch 6, para 18.
3 Solicitors (Scotland) Act 1980, s 53(4).
4 Ibid, Sch 4, paras 20–21.
5 Ibid, s 54(1).

Compensation orders

2.14 The provisions of the 1975 Act relating to fines apply also to compensation orders[1].

It is not competent to grant either a time to pay direction or a time to pay order in respect of either fines or compensation orders[2]. That includes fines imposed in respect of professional misconduct, eg by the Scottish Solicitors' Discipline Tribunal. While the Criminal Procedure (Scotland) Act 1975[3] and the Criminal Justice (Scotland) Act 1980[4] contain provisions about payment of fines and compensation orders by instalments, the Solicitors (Scotland) Act 1980 does not contain any such provision and, in practice, the tribunal does not allow payment of fines by instalments.

1 Criminal Justice (Scotland) Act 1980, s 66.
2 1987 Act, s 15(3).
3 Criminal Procedure (Scotland) Act 1975, s 399.
4 Criminal Justice (Scotland) Act 1980, s 66.

Drug trafficking offences

2.15 Under the Criminal Justice (Scotland) Act 1987, if a restraint order has been granted[1], the Lord Advocate may apply to the Court of Session to grant a warrant for inhibition against any person to whom the order applies[2]. The inhibition may prevent the disposal of a particular property, or property in general[3]. Under the same Act, orders made by the High Court in England and Wales are enforceable in Scotland[4]. These matters are dealt with more fully in chapter 4 below.

Where a restraint order has been granted, the Lord Advocate may also apply to the Court of Session for a warrant of arrestment of the moveable realisable property of the person to whom the order applies. The warrant has effect as if it had been granted on the dependence of an action of debt at the instance of the Lord Advocate.

1 A restraint order prevents a person dealing with realisable property or making gifts of it (Criminal Justice (Scotland) Act 1987, s 9).
2 Ibid, ss 8, 9, 11.
3 Ibid, s 11.
4 Ibid, s 27.

SUMMARY DILIGENCE

2.16 Summary diligence is the term applied to the procedure by which a creditor obtains a warrant for diligence without obtaining a court decree. The term is misleading in that it is the procedure which is summary rather than the diligence[1]. Summary diligence is competent in two broad cases: (a) under statute, and (b) by agreement in certain documents, eg a standard security.

1 *Murray v McGuire* 1928 SC 647, SLT 430.

Statute

2.17 By statute, summary diligence is competent on (1) bills of exchange; promissory notes, bankers' notes (ie bank notes); (2) on exchequer bonds, and (3) under the Sheriff Courts (Scotland) Act 1907 in relation to leases.

BILLS OF EXCHANGE AND PROMISSORY NOTES

2.18 Although the Bills of Exchange Act 1882 codifies the law on bills of exchange and promissory notes, it expressly provides that the law on summary diligence has not been altered[1]. The relevant statutes on summary diligence are the Bills of Exchange Act 1681, the Inland Bills Act 1696 and the Bills of Exchange (Scotland) Act 1772[2]. It has been held that as these Acts apply only to bills and promissory notes, summary diligence cannot be done on a cheque[3].

A bill of exchange is defined in section 3 of the 1882 Act and a promissory note in section 89. For what constitutes a bill of exchange and a promissory note, see the standard text[4]. A bill of exchange will have at least three parties, the drawer, the drawee and the payee, but the payee may transfer or negotiate the bill to another, ie for payment. The parties who would be liable under the bill would be the drawer and any person who has accepted the bill, usually the drawee, and any endorser. A promissory note has only two parties, the granter (promisor) and the grantee (promisee). A promissory note has no drawee and therefore no acceptor.

Judging by the very small numbers of protests which are registered in the Register of Protests, it would seem that little use is made of bills and notes, at least domestically. Greater use is made of them in international mone markets. Apart from statutory provisions eg the Consumer Credit Act, there is no reason why a bill of exchange or promissory note cannot be granted for any debt. For example, a solicitor could ask for a promissory note for his fees. In our opinion, it would be incumbent on the solicitor to explain the consequences of non-payment, but if that were done, summary diligence could follow if his fee was not paid. The solicitor would be proceeding on the promissory note and not on his account and that would avoid having the account taxed as would be required if he were to sue for fees per his account.

1 Bills of Exchange Act 1882, s 98.
2 Bills of Exchange (Scotland) Act 1772 ss 42–43.
3 *Glickman v Linda* 1950 SC 18, SLT 9.
4 JB Byles *Law of Bills of Exchange* (26th edn) ch 2.

The nature of the bill or note

2.19 The bill or note must be complete and regular on the face of it which means that the liability of the party must be apparent and should not require proof by extrinsic evidence[1]. Any need for extrinsic evidence rules out summary diligence. However, summary diligence was held to be competent against a firm with a descriptive name where the bill was signed by all of the partners but the firm name did not appear on the bill[2].

1 *Summers v Marianski* (1843) 6 D 286.
2 *Rosslund Cycle Co v McCreadie* 1907 SC 1208, 15 SLT 271.

The amount

2.20   The bill or note must be for a sum certain in money, but may be payable with interest or by instalments[1]. A document which requires anything else to be done in addition to the payment of money, is not a bill of exchange[2] and the same applies to a promissory note. A promissory note, however, is not invalid merely because it also contains a pledge of collateral security[3]. Prior to the passing of the Consumer Credit Act 1974, it was common for a promissory note to be granted in security of a loan, but this facility is now severely restricted[4]. Except in a non-commercial agreement, a negotiable instrument cannot be taken as security under a regulated agreement, and the 1987 Act provides that summary diligence cannot be used to enforce a debt due under a regulated agreement or any related security[5].

Summary diligence can be used to recover not only the principal sum and instalments due, but also interest on these[6]. The 1882 Act does not say whether summary diligence is competent for an amount including interest if the bill or note does not mention interest or the rate. Graham Stewart, however, says that the practice is to do so, even if interest or the rate is not mentioned[7]. Presumably, only a reasonable rate of interest would be recoverable. Any other amount such as expenses of dishonouring, protesting etc must be sued for in a separate action.

1 Bills of Exchange Act 1882, ss 3, 9.
2 Ibid, s 3(2).
3 Ibid, s 83(3).
4 Consumer Credit Act 1974, s 123.
5 Ibid, s 93A added by 1987 Act, Sch 6, para 16.
6 Erskine *Institute* III, 2, 36.
7 Graham Stewart *The Law of Diligence* p 383.

The parties

2.21   Both the party seeking to do summary diligence and the party against whom it is sought, must appear *ex facie* of the bill. The party seeking to enforce the bill will usually be the payee, but it may also be an indorsee. The party liable will usually be the drawee but if the drawee has not accepted the bill, the drawer will be liable, as will any indorser. In the case of a promissory note, the person seeking to enforce it will usually be the promisee, and the person against whom enforcement is sought will usually be the promisor. A person cannot do summary diligence on a bill or note if he has raised an action for recovery of the sum due[1]. However, the party against whom summary diligence is sought must be subject to the jurisdiction of the Scottish courts[2].

1 *Denovan v Cairns* (1845) 7 D 348.
2 *Graham Stewart* p 401.

Procedure

2.22   Summary diligence is available only after the bill or note has been dishonoured and the dishonour noted. A bill of exchange is dishonoured by non-acceptance[1] and both a bill and a promissory note are dishonoured by non-payment[2]. The rules for presentment for acceptance and presentment for payment are set out in the Act[3]. It should be noted that in a case of a bill, if no specific place for payment is mentioned, the bill would have to be presented at the stated address of the drawee, or his place of business, or ordinary residence. If neither of these is known, presentment must be made at the last known place of business or residence[4]. In the case of both a bill and a note, if a place for payment is specified, in order to render the maker liable, presentment must be made there and not at any other place[5]. In any other case, presentment for payment is not necessary in order to render the maker liable but presentment for payment is necessary to render an indorser liable[6]. To avoid problems about presentment, a bill or promissory note should provide for payment to be made at some place which suits the creditor, bearing in mind that he will have to involve a notary public and two witnesses for any protest, since protest is necessary before summary diligence can be done[7]. The most suitable place would be either the creditor's place of business or his bank.

As a general rule, where a bill or note is dishonoured, notice of that dishonour must be given to the drawer and each indorser and if not, they are discharged[8]. The notice must be given within a reasonable time and the 1882 Act provides that the notice must be given or sent on the day of dishonour if the parties reside in the same place, or the day after if they reside in different places[9]. The details are set out in section 49 as applied to promissory notes by section 89. The Act does not specify the method of giving notice, but it would be prudent to send it by recorded delivery post (or fax) and where it is posted it will be deemed to have been given despite any miscarriage by the Post Office[10]. The notice should be sent to the place of business or the residence but if sent to the place of business that will always suffice[11]. The term 'protesting' applies to the noting on the bill of its dishonour.

1 Bills of Exchange Act 1882, s 43.
2 Ibid, ss 47, 87.
3 Ibid, ss 41, 45.
4 Ibid, ss 45(4).
5 Ibid, s 45(4).
6 Ibid, s 45(2).
7 Ibid, s 51.
8 Ibid, s 48.
9 Ibid, s 49(11).
10 Ibid, s 49(13).
11 *Beveridge v Fitzgerald* (1869) LR 4 QB 639.

2.23 *Protesting.* Protesting is done by the notary writing on the bill or note 'PNA' (Protested for Non-Acceptance) or 'PNP' (Protested for Non-Payment). The bill or note must be noted on the date of dishonour[1]. The notary puts the date of dishonour on the bill or note, adds his initials, and the witnesses add their names or initials also. A bill or note can be protested by a householder if there is no notary public available[2] but there is some doubt about whether such a protest permits summary diligence[3] and it is therefore best avoided.

The protest, ie the written document narrating the above, should be prepared as soon as possible. It must contain a copy of the bill or note including anything on the reverse side eg an endorsement. It should mention the party for whom the protest was made, and the party against whom it was made. If there is more than one party liable, eg in the case of a bill which has been indorsed, the protest must be made against them all. The protest should also state the reason for the protest, the demand which was made and any answer which was given. The protest must be registered in the Register of Protests or in the books of any competent sheriff court. This must be done within six months of the date of dishonour[4].

An extract of the registered bill or note is warrant for arrestment and a charge followed by poinding. The warrant authorises diligence against moveable property, and there is some doubt about whether other forms of diligence, eg inhibition, are competent[5]. The days of charge are fourteen in all but two cases. If the person to be charged is outside Scotland, or his whereabouts are unknown, the days of charge are twenty-eight[6].

1 Bills of Exchange Act 1882, s 51.
2 Ibid, s 94.
3 *Somerville v Aaronson* (1898) 25 R 254, 5 SLT 310.
4 Bills of Exchange Act 1681; *North British Bank v Thom* (1848) 10 D 1505.
5 See para 2.3 above.
6 1987 Act, s 90(3).

EXCHEQUER BONDS

2.24 All bonds and obligations granted in favour of the Crown may be registered for execution in the Books of Council and Session or those of the appropriate sheriff court, whether or not they contain a clause to that effect[1]. If the bond does not specify the sum which is due, the Inland Revenue may issue a certificate stating what is due. That certificate is sufficient evidence of stating what is due and permits a warrant to be granted for recovery of the sum stated in it, but the bond must expressly confer that privilege[1].

In practice, the Inland Revenue do not make any use of this procedure and any bond granted in favour of the Revenue contains a clause of consent to registration for execution and is treated as an ordinary bond. The same applies to HM Customs and Excise[2].

1 Exchequer Court (Scotland) Act 1856, s 38.
2 The authors are grateful to T H Scott Esq, Solicitor of Inland Revenue for Scotland and D I K MacLeod Esq, of Messrs Shepherd & Wedderburn for this information.

SHERIFF COURTS (SCOTLAND) ACT 1907

2.25 The provisions of sections 34 and 35 of the Sheriff Courts (Scotland) Act 1907 which permit a form of summary diligence in connection with removings were described by the Law Reform Committee for Scotland as 'so drastic and their operation so fraught with hazard . . . that they are seldom if ever used'[1]. The sections provide that, in certain circumstances, a lease, or the extract of a lease, or a letter, are the equivalent of a decree of removing and that, after the days of charge, the tenant can be ejected. As the Scottish Law Commission has recommended their repeal[2], it is thought unnecessary to expand on them here[3].

1 *Second Report of the Law Reform Committee for Scotland* (1957) Cmnd 114, para 5.
2 *Recovery of Possession of Heritable Property* (Scot Law Com no 118 (1989)) p 204.
3 For further details, see Paton and Cameron *The Law of Landlord and Tenant in Scotland* pp 261–262.

Deeds containing a clause consenting to registration for execution and other deeds capable of being registered

2.26 The deeds which commonly contain such clauses are personal bonds and standard securities. The Titles to Land Consolidation (Scotland) Act 1868, introduced short forms of clauses of consent to registration for preservation and execution[1]. The form is 'And I consent to registration hereof for preservation and execution'. In any deed, the statutory clause imports, unless specially qualified, 'a consent to registration and a procuratory of resignation in the Books of Council and Session, or other judges books competent, therein to remain for preservation; and also, if for execution, upon the issue of an extract containing a warrant for execution, all lawful execution shall pass thereon'[2].

The writs which may be registered must be probative[3], and with the exception of exchequer bonds, they must contain a clause of consent to registration for execution[4]. The writs so registered will usually contain an obligation to pay money but it is competent to register a writ containing an obligation *ad factum praestandum*. In each case, however, the obligation must be clear and precise. A personal bond will usually require payment of a principal sum with interest at a specified rate. That is sufficiently precise. In some cases, eg in a personal bond relative to a Form B standard security, the security may be for 'all sums due and to become due'. That, of itself, would not be specific enough, but the deed invariably contains a mechanism for ascertaining what is due, eg a statement under the hand of a specified officer of the creditor which is stated to be conclusive of the amount due[5]. In such a case, the bond or standard security would have to be presented for registration along with the certificate, although the latter itself need not be registered. The warrant will authorise summary diligence for recovery of the amount stated in the certificate. The debtor is not precluded, however, from demonstrating that some other sum is due[6].

Examples of writs containing obligations *ad factum praestandum* are feu contracts, feu charters, feu dispositions and leases. The obligation, however, must be specific. In *Hendry v Marshall*[7] a tenant obliged himself to maintain his farm in accordance with the rules of good husbandry. That was held not to be specific enough to justify a specific implement and hence, it would rule out summary diligence.

1 Titles to Land Consolidation (Scotland) Act 1868, s 138.
2 Ibid, Sch B, no 1.
3 The Registration Act 1698.
4 Exchequer Court (Scotland) Act 1856, s 38.
5 J M Halliday *The Conveyancing and Feudal Reform (Scotland) Act 1970* (2nd edn) para 10–05.
6 *Halliday* para 10–05.
7 (1878) 5 R 687.

ENFORCEMENT

2.27 If the deed or order or decision which is the equivalent of a decree is stated to be enforceable as if it were a decree, then the methods of enforcement are those applicable to Court of Session and sheriff court decrees respectively. Details of these are contained in the Rules of Court, the sheriff court rules and the summary cause rules. Thus the summary cause rules apply to the recovery of fines and compensation orders. Warrants of concurrence used to be required before a sheriff court decree could be enforced in another sheriffdom. The ordinary cause and summary cause rules dispensed with them[1] and the 1987 Act dispenses with warrants of concurrence in relation to writs registered in the books of the sheriff court or which are treated as if they were so registered[2].

The principal copy of a deed which is registered in the Books of Council and Session or the books of the sheriff court is retained, but an extract is issued and it is on the basis of the extract that diligence is done. The extract contains a copy of the whole deed and a warrant for diligence at the end. It is the extract which is sent to the officer of court.

The officer will enforce an extract, or other equivalent of a decree, only in accordance with its terms. If the document specifies a sum of interest and/or expenses, then the officer will do diligence to recover the principal sum and the interest/expenses. It may be, however, that the obligation includes an obligation to pay interest, but not at a fixed rate. For example, the personal obligation in a standard security may include an obligation to pay interest at a rate to be determined from time to time by the creditor, or the rate of interest may be what a particular bank charges on unsecured overdraft accounts. Although interest is due, the officer will not attempt to calculate the interest and those instructing him would require to specify the interest which is due. The same applies to expenses, eg of protesting a promissory note. Such expenses would not appear in the note itself and the officer would require details of the amount before he would execute diligence.

1 OCR r 16; SCR r 11.
2 1987 Act, s 91.

Obligations ad factum praestandum

2.28   A deed which imposes an obligation *ad factum praestandum* may be registered in the Books of Council and Session or in the books of the sheriff court. Under the 1987 Act, that, of itself, does not entitle the creditor to enforce that obligation by imprisonment[1]. If the creditor wishes to enforce his obligation in that way he will have to obtain an order from the court under the Law Reform (Miscellaneous Provisions) (Scotland) Act 1940.

1 1987 Act, s 100.

Changes in the debtor

2.29   If the original debtor has died, summary diligence cannot be done against his executors or other representatives and the debt must be constituted afresh by court action[1]. It is unlikely that the creditor would agree to an assignation by a debtor because that would probably require him to constitute the debt against the assignee. There are, however, special provisions which relate to heritable creditors[2].

1 *Kippen v Hill* (1822) 2 S 105.
2 See para 2.32 below.

CHANGES IN THE CREDITOR

2.30 The original creditor may have assigned his rights or died before registering the deed or he may have registered the deed and then assigned it or died.

ASSIGNATION OR DEATH PRIOR TO REGISTRATION

2.31 Where a creditor has acquired right by assignation or confirmation (in the case of a deceased creditor) to an obligation contained in a deed which has not been registered in the Books of Council and Session, he must register the deed and then apply to a clerk of the court for a warrant for execution. He may as an alternative, register the deed in the books of the sheriff court and obtain a warrant from the clerk of that court[1], which shall be in the form of a minute indorsed on the extract decree or other document[2].

When he acquires right to an order or decision which is enforceable as if it were an extract registered decree arbital bearing a warrant for execution issued by the sheriff court, he must again apply to the clerk of the appropriate court[3].

In all these circumstances the clerk will need to see either the extract decree of the document or a certified copy of the order or decision and the assignation or confirmation.

Where the creditor has already registered the deed before assigning it or before his death, the new creditor will apply to the courts in the same way. Whether the creditor has assigned the extract or the order, the assignation should refer to that and if the creditor's right is based on confirmation, the confirmation should mention the extract of the order.

The warrant granted will authorise in relation to 'an ordinary debt' charging the debtor followed by an earnings arrestment or a poinding or an ordinary arrestment and if the decree consists of, or includes a maintenance order, a current maintenance arrestment can be executed[4]. An 'ordinary debt' means any debt other than current maintenance and includes a fine or other order in criminal proceedings in respect of which a warrant for civil diligence has been issued[5].

Where the creditor has already charged the debtor, the execution of the charge should be produced to the clerk of the relevant court along with the other documentation referred to in the previous paragraph, in which event, the warrant issued will authorise the further steps of diligence mentioned above.

1 1987 Act, s 88(1).
2 AS (Proceedings in the Sheriff Court under the Debtors (Scotland) Act 1987) 1988, SI 1988/ 2013, r 69.
3 1987 Act, s 88(1).
4 Ibid, s 87(4).
5 Ibid, s 73(1).

Heritable securities

2.32 There are two exceptions to these rules about assignations in the case of heritable securities: (1) where a person has taken the security subjects by a conveyance which contains *in gremio* an agreement that the personal obligation in the security shall transmit against him and the conveyance has been signed by him; and (2) where a person has taken the security subjects by succession, gift or bequest and an agreement has been executed by that person to the transmission of the personal obligation against him. In the case of succession, a style of bond of corroboration is found in the Conveyancing (Scotland) Act 1924[1].

Where the obligation is transmitted against the new proprietor, the creditor may present a Minute to the Petition Department of the Court of Session or the appropriate sheriff court in the form prescribed in Schedule K to the 1924 Act for the Clerk to the Court or the sheriff clerk to append *fiat ut petitur* with the date and his signature. Summary diligence may proceed on that.

The following points are to be noted:

(1) It is not necessary that the original bond or standard security has been registered for execution, but it must contain consent for that.
(2) The procedure is available only against a person who has acquired the security subjects from the original debtor and is the proprietor of those subjects at the time the Minute is presented.
(3) The warrant craved in the Minute is only to charge and it is therefore doubtful whether arrestment or poinding would be authorised.
(4) The procedure is open to the assignee of the original creditor.
(5) When the procedure is used by the executor of the original creditor, the executor should have completed title by infeftment and the Minute should narrate the confirmation and notice of title.
(6) The original deed containing the security or extract from the Books of Council and Session or the Register of Sasines and any other writs which form the creditor's title to the security should be produced along with the Minute[2].

1 Conveyancing (Scotland) Act 1924, s 15, Sch A, form 2.
2 J M Halliday *Conveyancing Law and Practice In Scotland* vol I, para 4–74.

CHAPTER 3

EXTENSION OF TIME TO PAY DEBTS

INTRODUCTION

3.01 A requirement to pay a sum of money due under a court decree or its equivalent imposes a duty on the debtor to pay the whole sum due thereunder immediately, under threat of diligence proceeding against him. The Scottish Law Commission's research on the nature of debt and the circumstances of debtors revealed that for most consumer debtors who had been subjected to diligence, debts owing under a decree could be paid only by way of instalments rather than in a single payment[1]. The Commission also identified a number of defects in the operation of the scheme for instalment decrees in summary causes, which was then the only type of action in which an instalment payment could be made a part of a decree. Accordingly Part I of the 1987 Act introduced a general scheme giving debtors means for applying for extension of time in which to pay debts.

1 Report on Diligence and Debtor Protection (Scot Law Com no 95(1985)) pp 29–34.

Classification of time to pay provisions

3.02 The time to pay provisions of the 1987 Act can be classified in three ways.

Instalment decrees: time to pay directions. A debtor may apply for a court direction to be contained in a decree against him allowing him to pay the sums due under the decree by way of instalments. The amount and time-scale of the instalments are to be set out in the decree itself. The amount of the instalments and the period of the interval of time between payments need not be equal in size or length. Any such time to pay direction must be applied for before decree is granted and can be made in respect of decrees in actions in the sheriff court (in small claims, summary cause and ordinary cause actions) and in the Court of Session. However not all types of debt can be subject to time to pay directions. During the currency of the instalment arrangement set out in a time to pay direction the creditor is prevented from using certain specified diligences against the debtor to recover the debt in question.

Post-diligence instalment payments: time to pay orders. A debtor can apply for payment by means of instalments of debts constituted by decrees and other documents of debt, after certain stages of diligence to recover the debt have been used against him. Such time to pay orders are granted only in the sheriff court but may be applied for in respect of decrees of the Court of Session as well as of the sheriff court, and also in respect of various other bases of debt. As with time to pay directions (which are available only as part of decrees), time to pay orders have the effect of preventing the creditor from using certain specified diligences against the debtor to recover the debt in question.

Deferred lump sum payments. A debtor may apply to the court to be allowed to pay a debt by means of payment of a lump sum at a certain future date later than that which would be specified in the decree or expressed or implied in a document of debt. Such an order may be applied for as part of a time to pay direction (ie as part of a decree) or as a time to pay order (post-diligence). An order to pay by way of a lump sum is subject to the same limitations which apply to time to pay directions and time to pay orders respectively, and has the same effect in barring certain diligences by creditors.

Nature and scope of time to pay provisions

3.03 The precise nature and scope of the time to pay provisions of Part I of the 1987 Act should be noted.

(1) Time to pay provisions are available only in respect of certain types of debt. The categories of debt to which the time to pay provisions do not apply are examined in more detail later[1], but at this stage it can be noted that the time to pay provisions are inapplicable in respect of debts which already take into account the means of the debtor (for example maintenance debts) and also in respect of certain classes of privileged debt (eg collection of taxes).

(2) The scheme of Part I of the 1987 Act is aimed at consumer or non-commercial debtors. With certain exceptions the ability to apply for the various time to pay measures is restricted to individuals owing debts in a personal capacity.

(3) Reflecting the Act's aim of allowing individual debtors time to pay debts in an orderly fashion, the effect of time to pay measures is restricted in respect of the diligences which are barred during the currency of any such measure. Only those diligences expressly mentioned in Part I of the Act are stopped by the time to pay provisions. In general the prohibited diligences are those most commonly used against individual debtors (namely arrestment and furthcoming, earnings arrestment, poinding and sale, and adjudication). Part I of the Act does not affect the exercise of other diligences nor does it prevent creditors using other remedies open to them, including those remedies available against individual debtors (eg actions for recovery of heritable property, or for repossession of goods under a hire-purchase agreement).

(4) A final limitation on the time to pay provisions of the 1987 Act is practical in nature. Time to pay directions and time to pay orders require application by the debtor (or someone acting on his behalf[2]), and cannot be granted by a court *ex proprio motu*. Any such application must be accompanied by a proposal for payment, either on an instalment basis or as a deferred lump sum, and as a matter of practical effect any application must realistically

reflect the debtor's financial circumstances. Although variations to the terms of a time to pay direction or order can be made, a lapse in payment due under a time to pay measure can result in the debt being enforced by the full range of diligences and may also prevent the granting of a further time to pay measure. It is important therefore that debtors and those advising debtors put forward realistic proposals when applying for a time to pay measure.

1 See below at paras 3.24–3.32.
2 AS (Proceedings in the Sheriff Court under the Debtors (Scotland) Act 1987) 1988, SI 1988/2013 r 70; 1987 Act, s 97.

TIME TO PAY DIRECTIONS

3.04 A time to pay direction is an order of a court pronounced as a part of a decree which lays down a scheme for payment of the sums due under the decree by way of instalment or deferred lump sum payment.

Courts which may make a time to pay direction

3.05 A time to pay direction may be made, on application by the debtor or his representative, by the Court of Session or by the sheriff court. In the sheriff court, a time to pay direction may be made in all of ordinary cause, summary cause and small claims levels of action. However there are important restrictions on the types of action in which decree can be subject to time to pay directions[1]. The power to make a direction of this type applies where the court is 'granting decree'. This expression is wide enough to encompass the various ways which result in a court issuing a decree, eg where summary decree is granted in the Court of Session or where the court interpones its authority upon a minute of the parties settling an action. A time to pay direction is not available where there is no court decree and thus does not arise in respect of debts due under documents registered for execution or where parties settle an action without having the authority of the court interponed onto the agreement: in some of these cases however, a post-diligence time to pay order may be applied for[2].

1 See further paras 3.24–3.32 below.
2 See further para 3.64.

Title to apply for time to pay direction

3.06 A time to pay direction can be made only in relation to a debtor under a decree who is an individual rather than a corporate or quasi-corporate person. Furthermore, subject to certain exceptions, a time to pay direction is available only where an individual debtor is liable in a personal rather than in a representative or fiduciary capacity.

The matter of title to apply for a time to pay direction calls for some further comment.

3.07 (1) Time to pay directions apply in respect of an individual person liable under a decree for a principal sum of money, no matter the role played by the person in the litigation which resulted in the decree. Thus a party who was a defender, or one of a number of defenders, in an action, or a pursuer in a counter-claim, or a third-party minuter may apply for a time to pay direction.

3.08 (2) The 1987 Act allows individual debtors who are not liable in a personal capacity to apply for a time to pay direction in certain situations. All of these apparent exceptions are consistent with the scheme of the Act restricting time to pay measures to individuals liable in a personal capacity, for they all concern cases where one person is liable in a representative capacity for another individual person who is under a legal disability preventing him from making an application directly. The cases in which a time to pay direction may be made where an individual is liable in a representative capacity are[1]:
(a) a tutor of an individual person;
(b) a judicial factor *loco tutoris* on an individual person's estate;
(c) a curator bonis on an individual person's estate;
(d) a judicial factor *loco absentis* on an individual person's estate.
In these cases the person representing the debtor must have been acting in that capacity at the time the decree was granted and must have made the application for the time to pay direction in that capacity. As an application for a time to pay direction must be made prior to the granting of a decree, no time to pay direction by a person holding one of these representative positions can be made where the appointment occurred after the decree was granted[2]. If a time to pay direction has been made in respect of an individual debtor, any transmission of the obligation to pay the debt, either *inter vivos* or *mortis causa*, leads to the direction ceasing to have effect[3].

1 1987 Act, s 14(1).
2 On the question whether a time to pay order can be made in these circumstances, see below at para 3.61.
3 1987 Act, s 14(2).

3.09 (3) Apart from the exceptions noted above, time to pay directions can be made by a court only in respect of debts under decree owed by individual persons in a personal capacity. The concept of personal liability is not defined in the 1987 Act but its meaning can be understood by contrasting personal liability with representative or fiduciary liability. In this sense the ambit of personal liability is a wide one as personal liability can arise in a large range of circumstances. Whether liability is personal or not will normally be discovered from the terms of the decree itself, and it is the liability under a decree which determines whether a party has title to apply for a time to pay direction.

SEVERAL, AND JOINT AND SEVERAL, LIABILITY

3.10 Where liability is pronounced against several parties on a several or on a joint and several basis, the allocation of liability does not affect the nature of the liability as being either personal or representative (or fiduciary) in nature.

What the several, or the joint and several, liability determines is the proportion of liability which each party is allocated, but the liability is either a personal or non-personal one. Where a decree is pronounced on the basis of an allocated personal liability, any party so liable can apply for a time to pay direction in respect of a relevant type of debt. However, a time to pay direction pronounced against one debtor will not prevent a creditor doing diligence against other several or joint and several debtors to the extent of the respective liability of the debtors under the decree, unless those other debtors have also applied for a time to pay direction. In cases of several liability, if only one of the debtors has been granted a time to pay direction, the creditor can still do diligence against the other debtors but only in respect of the *pro rata* liability of those debtors. Where this situation arises in the cases of joint and several liability, the creditor can proceed to do diligence against the other debtors for the whole debt. In cases of delict where there is a finding of joint and several liability, the court must allocate the responsibility of each party[1]. Thus if one party pays the whole of the sum due he can recover from the other debtors their proportionate share of the shared debt. In this situation, as the duty to pay the contribution to a co-debtor is a debt arising under court decree, it would be appropriate for a co-debtor to apply for a time to pay direction which would be effective against any moves by the co-debtor to do diligence under the decree to recover his contribution.

Vicarious liability is a special instance of joint and several liability. Thus a person who is sued in a non-representative or non-fiduciary capacity and who is found liable on the basis of vicarious liability is still liable on a personal basis and would be entitled to apply for a time to pay direction. It should be remembered that only parties found liable in the decree can apply for a time to pay direction. Thus if the original wrongdoer is not sued and the decree is pronounced against the party vicariously liable, the original wrongdoer cannot use that decree as a basis for a time to pay direction should the person found vicariously liable proceed against him in a separate action for a right of relief. However, a decree in the action for the right of relief will result in the original wrongdoer's personal liability and this will provide the basis for a time to pay direction.

1 Law Reform (Miscellaneous Provisions) (Scotland) Act 1940, s 3; *Grant v Sun Shipping Co* 1948 SC (HL) 73; *Davidson v North of Scotland Hydro-Electric Board* 1954 SC 230.

PARTNERSHIPS

3.11 Decree pronounced against a partnership allows for diligence to proceed against partnership assets and also against any individual partner, whether or not the partner is named in the decree[1]. The liability of a partner, as contrasted with that of the partnership, in respect of debts due under decree against a partnership is a personal one, and as such can form the basis of an application by the partner for a time to pay direction. However, the partnership itself as a separate and non-individual legal entity lacks any title to apply for a time to pay direction. Accordingly where a decree is pronounced against a partnership in respect of a debt for which a time to pay direction can be made, each partner who is liable under the decree may apply for a time to pay direction in respect of his own personal liability. However any such direction will not prevent the creditor from doing diligence against the partnership property or property held by a partner not as his personal property but as trustee for the partnership.

1 Partnership Act 1890, ss 9, 12.

CLUBS AND UNINCORPORATED BODIES

3.12 A decree pronounced against a club or other unincorporated body will impose liability upon the club and its assets and may also impose liability upon the officials and members of the club in their personal capacities[1]. The exact scope of the personal liability of officials and members will depend upon the constitution and rules of the club, and the circumstances of each case. Where there is such personal liability, the official or member may apply for a time to pay direction but any such direction would be limited in its effect to the assets of the individual which he owns personally and would not extend to assets held by the official or member in a fiduciary capacity on behalf of the club or association.

1 *Thomson & Gillespie v Victoria Eighty Club* (1905) 13 SLT 399; *Cromarty Leasing Ltd v Turnbull* 1988 SLT (Sh Ct) 62. See further WA Wilson *The Law of Scotland Relating to Debt* pp 353–354.

SOLE TRADERS

3.13 A person carrying on a business under a trading or descriptive name may be sued in such a name alone[1]. However where decree is pronounced against any such business carried on by one person, the decree imposes liability on that person on a personal basis, that is in terms of diligence there is no distinction drawn between his business and non-business assets[2]. Accordingly, sole traders may apply for a time to pay direction which if granted will prevent the relevant diligences being used against all of his assets, including those used as part of his business.

1 OCR 14.
2 *Reid v Chalmers* (1826) 6 S 1120; *Road Haulage Executive v Elrick* 1953 SLT 112.

Methods of application for a time to pay direction

INTRODUCTION

3.14 A time to pay direction can be granted by the court only on the application of the debtor, not *ex proprio motu*. One of the major practical difficulties in bringing about sufficient use by debtors of their right to apply for a direction is ensuring that they are made aware of this right. The rules which implement the 1987 Act seek to achieve this aim by requiring service of various forms along with the service of the summons or initial writ of the action. These forms set out information on time to pay directions and also contain special sections for the debtor to complete if he wishes to apply to the court for a direction to be made.

However, some problems arise from this way of providing debtors with the means to apply for time to pay directions. First, it should be noted that generally speaking the forms are expressed in much more straightforward language than many other legal and court documents, but experience of the workings of the 1987 Act is required to show whether the plain language of the forms is plain enough.

A further point is that in the sheriff court the decision as to whether forms (and which forms) containing information on, and application sections for, time to pay directions is made by the sheriff clerk in granting warrant to cite. The warrant to cite will specify the form (if any) which the pursuer is authorised and required to serve with the initial writ or summons. But the situation may arise where the appropriate form is not mentioned in the warrant to cite. This situation may occur where a partnership is sued in the name of the partnership and the warrant to cite does not refer to the forms on time to pay directions (which the partners as individuals are entitled to apply for[1]). A similar point may arise where a sole trader is sued but the warrant to cite does not require service of the appropriate form for the defender to apply for a time to pay direction[2]. In such circumstances the pursuer has no authority to serve, as official documents, the appropriate forms beyond what is specified in the warrant to cite the defender. He could no doubt send, though necessarily by separate letter[3], a copy of the relevant form but he may have little incentive to take this step.

On the other hand, where the defender does not receive a form for application for a time to pay direction along with the summons or initial writ, he will still be able to attend court and make an oral application for a direction. But in many cases, the reality of the situation is that defenders do not dispute that the debt is owing[4] and even if they are aware of their rights to apply for a time to pay direction, many will be reluctant to attend court merely to make an application. Furthermore, in many cases where debtors are not provided with information on their rights to apply for a direction, they will not be in a position to take steps to make an application.

A further difficulty at a practical level is that where the debtor does apply for a direction by completing and submitting the appropriate form, his financial circumstances which are set out in the form will not be communicated to the pursuer, who is simply told that the defender has made proposals to pay at a certain level of instalment, or by lump sum after a certain period. As the pursuer may not be aware of the defender's financial circumstances, he may not be in a position to accept the defender's proposals for payment and will thus not intimate his acceptance of the defender's application. The net result of this situation is that a further stage of court procedure is required before a time to pay direction can be granted.

1 See above, para 3.11.
2 See above, para 3.13.
3 Unauthorised documents must not be sent with the service copy initial writ or summons: *Macphail* pp 218, 818; SMCR 32.
4 Scot Law Com Report no 95 (1985) pp 12–17.

SMALL CLAIMS

Payment actions

3.15 Where a defender in a small claims payment action admits the claim against him and wishes to make an oral application for a time to pay direction he must fill in the appropriate part of the form of response attached to the service copy summons. He must then lodge this response with the sheriff clerk on or before the return date specified in the summons[1]. The application is then dealt with at the preliminary hearing, the date of which is stated in the summons.

A preliminary hearing will also be held where the defender has completed the section in the service copy summons applying for a time to pay direction but the pursuer does not accept the proposals made in the application[2]. Where the defender makes such an application, the sheriff clerk sends a form to the pursuer which states the defender's proposals for payment and which allows the pursuer to reply by completing the appropriate box and returning the form to court. However this form does not contain the defender's financial circumstances, and it may not be easy for the pursuer to assess whether it is advisable to accept the defender's proposals.

At the preliminary hearing, the sheriff may deal with the defender's proposals to pay by making such an order as he considers appropriate[3].

Where the defender admits the claim against him and does not intend to appear but is seeking a time to pay direction, he makes his application by completing the appropriate part of the form of response attached to the service copy summons and lodging this with the sheriff clerk on or before the return date[4].

Where the pursuer accepts the proposals to pay made by the defender, he intimates his acceptance by lodging with the sheriff clerk a minute in Form 9 or Form 12, or by entering a minute in the Book of Small Claims that he does not object to the defender's proposals, and, for decree[5]. Such acceptance must be made before noon on the day prior to the date for the preliminary hearing. Where the pursuer intimates acceptance, the sheriff grants decree, including the time to pay direction, without the case calling in court.

Where a small claims payment action proceeds on a defended basis, the defender, at any time before decree is granted, may make a written or oral application to the sheriff for a time to pay direction[6].

1 SMCR 8(1)(d). The defender may also apply for an order to recall or restrict an arrestment on the dependence.
2 SMCR 12(1)(b).
3 SMCR 12(9).
4 SMCR 9.
5 SMCR 11(1).
6 SMCR 24. The defender may also apply for an order to recall or restrict an arrestment on the dependence.

OTHER SMALL CLAIMS ACTIONS

3.16 In small claims actions other than payment actions, the defender will in appropriate cases have been served with a copy summons which allows for the application for a time to pay direction. Where the defender does not wish to defend such an action, he may apply for a time to pay direction by (1) completing and returning the relevant part of the summons to the sheriff clerk at least seven days before the date for the preliminary hearing or (2) appearing at the preliminary hearing and moving for such a direction[1].

Where a non-payment action is defended, the defender at any stage before decree is granted may apply for a time to pay direction by written or oral application to the court[2].

Where decree in non-payment action has been granted but the defender has failed to comply with the decree, the pursuer may lodge with the sheriff clerk an incidental application for decree in terms of the alternative crave for payment[3]. As the incidental application must be intimated to the defender, he can appear at the hearing and move for a time to pay direction (and also for an order for the recall or restriction of an arrestment on the dependence).

1 SMCR 39(1). The defender may also apply for an order to recall or restrict an arrestment on the dependence.
2 SMCR 39(2). The defender may also apply for an order to recall or restrict an arrestment on the dependence.
3 SMCR 41.

SUMMARY CAUSE ACTIONS

Payment actions

3.17 Where a defender in a summary cause payment action admits the claim against him and wishes to make an oral application for a time to pay direction, he must lodge with the sheriff clerk a notice of intention to defend in accordance with Form Q on or before the return day specified in the form[1]. The application is then dealt with at the first calling of the case. A first calling will also be held where the defender has completed Form Q, applying for a time to pay direction but the pursuer does not accept the proposals made in the application[2].

At the first calling (including any continuation) the court must consider any application for a time to pay direction, whether or not the defender is present or represented[3].

Where the defender admits the claim against him and does not intend to appear but is seeking a time to pay direction, he makes his application by completing the appropriate part of Form Q and lodging it with the sheriff clerk on or before the return date[4].

Where the pursuer accepts the proposals to pay made by the defender, he intimates his acceptance by entering a minute in the Book of Summary Causes that he does not object to the defender's application[5]. Such acceptance must be made before noon on the day prior to the date for the first calling. Where the pursuer intimates acceptance, the sheriff grants decree, including the time to pay direction, without the case calling in court.

Where a summary cause payment action proceeds on a defended basis, the defender, at any time before decree is granted, may make a written or oral application to the sheriff for a time to pay direction[6].

1 SCR 51(d). The defender may also apply for an order to recall or restrict an arrestment on the dependence.
2 SCR 53(2).
3 SCR 53(4).
4 SCR 52.
5 SCR 54.
6 SCR 53(5). The defender may also apply for an order to recall or restrict an arrestment on the dependence.

Non-payment summary cause actions

3.18 In summary cause actions (other than payment actions) in which a time to pay direction may be applied for, the pursuer must serve on the defender the appropriate form (Form Bb) as part of, or together with, the summons. The defender may apply for a time to pay direction by[1]
(1) appearing at the first calling[2] and moving for such a direction;
(2) completing and returning the relevant part of Form Bb to the sheriff clerk.

This must be done at least seven days before the first calling (except where the period of notice has been reduced under SCR 4(2)).

(3) written or oral application at any stage prior to final decree being granted.

1 SCR 17A. The defender may also apply for an order to recall or restrict an arrestment on the dependence.
2 SCR 18(3)(c) allows for the first calling to be continued where the defender has applied for a time to pay direction.

ORDINARY CAUSE SHERIFF COURT ACTIONS

3.19   In ordinary cause actions in the sheriff court in which a time to pay direction may be applied for, the warrant of citation will require the service on the defender of a notice in Form B5 of the Ordinary Cause Rules[1]. Where the action proceeds as undefended, the defender may apply for a time to pay direction by completing the lodging with the sheriff clerk of the relevant part of Form B5 before the expiry of the period of notice[2].

If the pursuer does not object to the defender's application he minutes to that effect and for decree in terms of OCR 21. The sheriff then grants decree as appropriate. Where the pursuer does object to the application, he again minutes accordingly and also for decree in terms of OCR 21. The sheriff clerk then enrols for a hearing of the application. The hearing is intimated by the sheriff clerk to the defender and pursuer. At the hearing the sheriff may deal with the application as appropriate, whether or not any of the parties appear.

Where the action is defended, the defender may apply by motion for a time to pay direction at any time before decree is granted[3].

1 OCR 5(5)(b). Where the action proceeds by way of summary application, procedure is governed by OCR 5(4), (6), 21C.
2 OCR 21B. The defender may also apply for the recall or restriction of an arrestment on the dependence.
3 OCR 57A.

COURT OF SESSION ACTIONS

3.20   In an action in the Court of Session in which the defender may apply for a time to pay direction, the pursuer must when serving the summons also serve on the defender a notice in Form 65 and an application in Form 66[1]. Before service of these forms the pursuer must insert in Form 65 the date by which the defender must return Form 66 to court (which is the date of the expiry of the *induciae*). The pursuer must also have completed Part A of Form 66 before serving it on the defender.

1 RC 88B. These forms are also to be served where the pursuer serves on the defender pleadings as amended by minute of amendment calling him as a defender.

Application in undefended actions

3.21   Where the defender does not enter appearance but intends to apply for a time to pay direction, he does so by completing and returning Form 66 before the date specified in Form 65[1]. If the pursuer does not object to the application he may enrol to that effect for decree in absence under RC 89.

If the pursuer objects to the application, he enrols for decree in absence under RC 89 and lodges a copy of form 67. This form sets out the motion for decree in absence and the pursuer's grounds of objection, and must be intimated to the defender on an *induciae* of seven days. The motion enrolled by the pursuer is starred. The defender need not appear at the hearing of the motion and may choose instead to send to the Deputy Principal Clerk written representations in response to the pursuer's note of objections.

1 RC 88C. The defender may also apply for the recall or restriction of an arrestment on the dependence.

Application where appearance entered but defences not lodged

3.22 Where the defender enters appearance, does not lodge defences but intends to apply for a time to pay direction, such application is made by returning Form 66 not later than the date on which defences would have had to be lodged in process[1]. Thereafter the application is dealt with as if it had been made in an undefended action[2].

1 RC 88D. The defender may also apply for the recall or restriction of an arrestment on the dependence. Where appearance has been entered it does not matter that the date specified in Form 65 for making the application has expired or is due to expire before the date for lodging defences.
2 See above at para 3.21.

Application where defences lodged

3.23 Where defences to an action have been lodged, the defender, at any time before decree is granted, may apply for a time to pay direction by way of motion[1].

1 RC 88E. Applications in this way may also be made by a pursuer in a counter-claim or by a third party. Application may also be made for the recall or restriction of an arrestment on the dependence.

Debts in respect of which time to pay directions may and may not be made

3.24 A time to pay direction may be made only as part of a court decree. Furthermore a direction can be made only in respect of several categories of debt due under decree. Debts under decree which cannot be subject to a time to pay direction are as follows:

DEBTS DUE UNDER A DECREE NOT DECERNING FOR A PRINCIPAL SUM

3.25 A time to pay direction may be made only where a court grants decree for the payment of a principal sum of money[1]. Where there is more than one principal sum due under a decree, a time to pay direction may be made in respect of one or any or all of them. Where a decree contains no decerniture for a principal sum, eg as in actions of declarator, an award of expenses included in the decree cannot be the subject of a time to pay direction, although a post-decree time to pay order may be competent. However, where a decree contains decerniture for the payment of a principal sum of money as well as non-money provisions, a time to pay direction may be made in respect of any sum decerned for in the decree provided a direction can be made in respect of any of the principal sums. There are also special rules on claiming expenses and interest in respect of decrees containing a time to pay direction (discussed below).

1 1987 Act, s 1(1).

DEBTS IN EXCESS OF £10,000

3.26 It is not competent for a court to make a time to pay direction where the sum of money decerned for exceeds £10,000[1]. Where a decree decerns for separate principal sums, a time to pay direction can be made in respect of any such sum not exceeding £10,000 even if other principal sums are above that figure. In this context a principal sum due under a decree is exclusive of any interest and expenses also decerned for. However pre-decree interest which is quantified as a definite sum is to be treated as a separate principal sum.

1 1987 Act, s 1(5)(a). The Lord Advocate has power to vary the amount by regulations: 1987 Act, s 1(5)(a).

CAPITAL SUM DUE ON DIVORCE OR NULLITY OF MARRIAGE

3.27 A time to pay direction cannot be made where the decree contains an award of a capital sum on divorce or on the granting of a declarator of nullity of marriage[1]. The rationale for this exclusion is that a court in making an award of a capital sum on divorce or nullity has regard to the means of the debtor and can also order the payment to be made by way of instalments or a deferred lump sum[2].

1 1987 Act, s 1(5)(b).
2 See eg Family Law (Scotland) Act 1985, ss 12(2), (3), 17.

MAINTENANCE ORDERS

3.28 Debts in connection with a maintenance order cannot be made the subject of a time to pay direction[1]. The underlying rationale for this category of exclusion is similar to that of the case of capital sum awards, namely that the debtor's means are taken into account in assessing the amount to be paid. Furthermore with maintenance orders provisions exist in other statutes for the debtor making application for the variation and recall of such awards[2].

The idea of maintenance order in the 1987 Act is given a fairly extensive definition. Maintenance is defined as periodical sums payable under a maintenance order. Maintenance order is in turn defined in terms of the following list[3]:
(1) an order granted by a court in Scotland for payment of a periodical allowance on divorce or on the granting of a declarator of nullity of marriage[4];
(2) an order granted by a court in Scotland for aliment[5];
(3) an order under any of the following statutory provisions:
National Assistance Act 1948, section 43 or 44;
Ministry of Social Security Act 1966, section 23 or 24;
Social Work (Scotland) 1968, section 80 or 81;
Guardianship Act 1973, section 11(3);
Supplementary Benefits Act 1976, section 18 or 19;

Child Care Act 1980, section 50 or 51;

Social Security Act 1986, section 24 or 25.

(4) an order of a court in England and Wales or Northern Ireland registered in Scotland under Part II of the Maintenance Orders Act 1950;

(5) a provisional order of a reciprocating country which is confirmed by a court in Scotland under Part I of the Maintenance Orders (Reciprocal Enforcement) Act 1972;

(6) an order of a reciprocating country which is registered in Scotland under Part I of the Maintenance Orders (Reciprocal Enforcement) Act 1972;

(7) an order registered in Scotland under Part II, or under an Order in Council made in pursuance of Part III, of the Maintenance Orders (Reciprocal Enforcement) Act 1972;

(8) an order registered in Scotland under section 5 of the Civil Jurisdiction and Judgments Act 1982;

(9) an alimentary bond or agreement which has been (i) registered for execution in the Books of Council and Session or sheriff court books or (ii) registered in Scotland under an Order in Council made under section 13 of the Civil Jurisdiction and Judgments Act 1982. Included within the meaning of such an alimentary bond is a document providing for the maintenance of one party to a marriage by the other after the marriage has been dissolved or annulled.

1 1987 Act, s 1(5)(c).
2 Family Law (Scotland) Act 1985, ss 5, 13.
3 1987 Act, s 106.
4 At present these orders are governed by the provisions of the Family Law (Scotland) Act 1985, ss 8–17.
5 These are presently governed by the Family Law (Scotland) Act 1985, ss 1–7.

DEBTS SUBJECT TO A TIME ORDER UNDER THE CONSUMER CREDIT ACT 1974

3.29 By section 129(2)(a) of the Consumer Credit Act 1974, a court may provide for sums due under a regulated agreement under the 1974 Act to be paid by way of instalments[1]. Such orders may be made where the court makes an enforcement order under the 1974 Act, where a default notice has been served by the creditor on the debtor, and in an action by the creditor to enforce the agreement. The policy of the 1987 Act is to allow debtors time to pay debts but does not extend this power to allow frequent applications for instalment orders as this would frustrate the ability of the creditor to recover the debt. Accordingly, by section 14(3) of the 1987 Act, a time to pay direction cannot be made where a time order under the 1974 Act has been made previously. Furthermore, where a time to pay direction has been made a subsequent time order under the 1974 Act is not possible[2].

1 See further, Judith J H Pearson, 'Consumer Credit' in *The Laws of Scotland: Stair Memorial Encyclopaedia*, vol 5, para 926.
2 Consumer Credit Act 1974, s 129(3), added by 1987 Act, Sch 6, para 17.

ACTIONS FOR RECOVERY OF RATES AND COMMUNITY CHARGES

3.30   A decree in an action by a local authority for payment of
(1) rates,
(2) any community charge or community water charge within the meaning
of section 26 of the Abolition of Domestic Rates Etc (Scotland) Act 1987, or
(3) any amount payable under section 18(3) of the Abolition of Domestic
Rates Etc (Scotland) Act 1987[1], or
(4) any amount payable as a civil penalty under section 17(10) or 17(11) of the
Abolition of Domestic Rates Etc (Scotland) Act 1987[2]
cannot include a time to pay direction[3].

1 This provision deals with payment of community charges in respect of backdated period,
  with surcharge and interest.
2 These provisions deal with civil penalties imposed for failure to provide information to a
  community charge registration officer.
3 1987 Act, s 1(5)(e), (ee) (added by Abolition of Domestic Rates Etc (Scotland) Act 1987, s 33).
  For cases where arrears of rates or charges are recovered by means of summary warrant
  procedure, see below at para 3.32.

ACTIONS FOR RECOVERY OF TAXES

3.31   Decree in various actions for payment of taxes cannot contain a time to
pay direction[1]. These actions are
(1) actions by or on behalf of the Inland Revenue for payment of any sum
recoverable in respect of tax or as if it were tax;
(2) actions for payment of any duty due under the Betting and Gaming Duties
Act 1981;
(3) actions for payment of car tax due under the Car Tax Act 1983;
(4) actions for payment of value added tax under the Value Added Tax Act
1983 or any sum recoverable as if it were value added tax.

1 1987 Act, s 1(5)(d), (f). For cases where arrears of tax are recovered by summary warrant
  procedure, see para 3.32 below.

DEBTS DUE UNDER SUMMARY WARRANT

3.32   Arrears of taxes, rates and community charges may be collected by
means of special summary warrant procedure[1]. Although warrants are a
form of court judgement or order, a warrant is essentially in the form of an
order or permission addressed to an officer of court rather than a decree. In
cases of collection of taxes, rates and community charges, the warrant
provides for the authorisation of officers of court to apply the special
diligences which exist for those categories of debt. Section 1(1) of the 1987
Act empowers courts to grant a time to pay direction 'on granting decree for
payment of any principal sum of money', and it is clear that a summary
warrant is not a decree of this type. In any case, summary warrant procedure
does not involve the presence of the debtor, whose application, before decree
is made, is necessary for the making of a time to pay direction[2].

1 See ch 8 below at paras 8.01–8.20.
2 Scot Law Com Report no 95(1985) p 416.

Time to pay directions and recovery of expenses and interest

EXPENSES

Decree decerning for the payment of a principal sum of money

3.33 The question of expenses due in a court action is a distinct issue from that of the substantive point in the case. A decerniture for the payment of a specific sum as the expenses of an action requires a prior finding by the court that one party is liable to another party for expenses[1]. The two steps of the finding of liability and the decerniture for a specific sum do not necessarily occur at the same time. In the Court of Session, the court pronounces decree for payment of the principal sum together with a finding as to liability for expenses. At the same time, unless special cause is shown for not doing so, the court decerns, in a separate interlocutor, for the payment of expenses as they will be taxed by the Auditor of Court[2]. The extract of the interlocutor for expenses cannot be obtained until the Auditor has taxed the expenses. In defended ordinary cause actions in the sheriff court a similar practice is followed, ie a decree for payment of a principal sum will also contain a finding as to liability for expenses and a separate decree is issued for payment of expenses as taxed by the Auditor of Court[3]. However, in undefended ordinary cause sheriff court actions and summary cause actions, the decree dealing with the principal issues of the action also deals with liability for expenses and contains a decerniture for the expenses at a fixed amount[4].

1 Scot Law Com Report no 95 (1985), pp 81–92; J M Lees *Notes on the Structure of Interlocutors* (2nd edn) pp 32–33. For discussion see ch 1 above at paras 1.39–1.43.
2 RC 348.
3 OCR 97, 98.
4 SCR 87, 88; Scot Law Com Report no 95 (1985) p 82, fn 2. A similar procedure is adopted where expenses are awarded in a small claims action.

3.34 Because of the separate nature of the decernitures for principal sums and for expenses, special provisions apply to time to pay directions in respect of expenses where a decree decerns for payment of a principal sum of money:
(i) where decree for a principal sum contains a finding of liability for expenses, the payment of a sum as expenses may be the subject of a time to pay direction. The time to pay direction may be made in relation to both the principal sum and the expenses or in relation to only one of these sums[1].
(ii) a situation may arise where a time to pay direction is made in respect of expenses in a decree and the decree contains a finding as to liability for expenses but does not also decern for payment of the expenses or decerns for payment of expenses as taxed by the Auditor of Court without specifying the amount of those expenses. In these circumstances a time to pay direction takes effect in respect of the debtor's liability to obtemper its provisions only in relation to the extract of the subsequent decree decerning for payment of a sum as expenses[2].
(iii) where a decree for a principal sum contains a finding of liability for expenses but does not also contain a time to pay direction, it will not be possible to obtain a time to pay direction in relation to those expenses[3]. (However, a post-decree time to pay order may later be competent.)

1 1987 Act, s 1(1).
2 Ibid, s 1(4).
3 Ibid, s 1(3).

Decree not decerning for the payment of a principal sum

3.35 Where a decree contains no decerniture for the payment of a principal sum of money, no granting of a time to pay direction may be made in respect of any expenses due in relation to that decree[1]. This is so even where the expenses are quantified in the decree or where the decree contains a finding of liability for expenses.

1 1987 Act, s 1(1).

RECOVERY OF INTEREST

3.36 Where pre-decree interest is awarded as a quantified and specified sum in a decree, it is decerned for as a principal sum and may accordingly be made the subject of a time to pay direction.

A time to pay direction may apply to the principal sum alone or to the interest on that sum alone, or to both sums together. However, there are important restrictions on recovery of post-decree interest payable under a decree containing a time to pay direction. Interest on a principal sum decerned for in a decree is usually in the form of a specified rate from a certain date until the debt is paid[1]. From the perspective of the debtor such post-decree interest may cause problems in respect of calculating the amount due at any particular time after decree. Part I of the 1987 Act adopts the policy that if a decree contains a time to pay direction, post-decree interest may be recoverable only where the creditor gives specific intimation to the debtor of what is owing by way of interest. If such intimation is not given, the creditor may find that the post-decree interest is not recoverable at all.

Section 1(6) of the 1987 Act states that interest payable under a decree containing a time to pay direction cannot be recovered by the creditor except in accordance with the provisions on intimation laid out in section 1(7). However, this rule is subject to two provisos. The first proviso is that interest awarded as a specific sum in the decree itself is recoverable in the normal way. However, this sum may itself be the subject of a time to pay direction. The second proviso is important in that it brings out the very limited range of circumstances in which a creditor may recover interest where the section 1(7) procedures have not been used. Section 2(5) allows for any outstanding debt, including interest, to be recovered by the full range of competent diligences and remedies, where a time to pay direction has been recalled or has ceased to have effect. But this does not apply where the recall or cessation of effect of the order arises because the debt subject to the time to pay direction has been paid or extinguished, or because the debtor's estate has been sequestrated. The effect of these provisions is that a creditor can recover interest on a decree containing a time to pay direction only where
(1) the interest is quantified and specified in the decree as a principal sum; or
(2) the creditor has adopted the intimation procedures under section 1(7); or
(3) the time to pay direction has been recalled or has ceased to have effect for a reason other than payment or extinction of the debt or the sequestration of the debtor's estate.

To allow recovery of interest the creditor has to use the procedures set out in section 1(7). This requires the service of notice on the debtor claiming the interest and specifying the amount of interest claimed. Such notice must be served no later than fourteen days before the date on which the last instalment is due (or fourteen days before the last day of the period for payment by lump sum)[2]. Service may be made by recorded delivery post or by personal service by officer of court. Where interest is claimed under the section 1(7) intimation provisions, any payment made by the debtor under a time to pay direction is ascribed first to payment of the sum in respect of which the direction was made. Only when that debt has been discharged are payments ascribed to interest[3].

1 See ch 1 above at paras 1.31–1.37.
2 RC 88H; SI 1988/2013, r 3.
3 1987 Act, s 1(8), reversing in this context the common law rule that payments are ascribed first to interest and then to principal sum: see *Wilson on Debt* pp 169–170.

Effect of time to pay direction on diligence

3.37 The purpose of a time to pay direction as part of a court decree is to allow the debtor time in which to pay the sums due under the decree either by way of instalment payment specified in the decree or by a lump sum payment at a definite time in the future. To achieve this effect, the creditor cannot use diligence to enforce the debt under the decree during the currency of a time to pay direction. However, it must be stressed that the aim of Part I of the 1987 Act is restricted to providing time to pay debts in cases of non-commercial or consumer debts, and the Act does not rule out the use by creditors of all types of diligence[1].

1 A time to pay direction is set out in the decree issued by the court. Accordingly, an officer of court cannot execute any of the diligences affected by the direction on the basis of the extract decree unless he is instructed by the creditor that (1) the extract decree containing the direction has been intimated to the debtor and (2) the debtor has defaulted on the direction.

DILIGENCES IN EXECUTION BARRED BY A TIME TO PAY DIRECTION

3.38 In order to allow the debtor freedom from the pressure of diligence or the threat of diligence over his assets, a time to pay direction in a decree has the effect of preventing the creditor starting diligence in execution against the debtor's property. Accordingly, while a time to pay direction is in effect it is not competent to enforce payment of the debt concerned[1]
(1) by serving a charge for payment;
(2) by commencing or executing an arrestment and furthcoming, or arrestment and sale;
(3) by commencing or executing a poinding[2] and sale;
(4) by commencing or executing an earnings arrestment;
(5) by commencing or executing an action of adjudication for debt[3].
It must be stressed that only the diligences specified by section 2(1) of the 1987 Act are barred by a time to pay direction. Other diligences and remedies available to a creditor are unaffected.

1 Ie the sum or expenses to which the direction applies: 1987 Act, s 15(2); 1987 Act, s 2(1).
2 Poinding here is defined to include only personal poindings and to exclude poindings of the ground: 1987 Act, s 15(1).
3 In this context adjudication for debt does not include (a) an adjudication under a *debitum fundi* or (b) an adjudication under the Conveyancing (Scotland) Act 1924, s 23 (which deals with adjudication to recover arrears of ground annual): 1987 Act, s 15(1).
   It may also be noted that it is no longer possible for a creditor to use adjudication to enforce a

debt under a liquid document of debt without raising a prior court action to constitute the debt. By the 1987 Act, s 101 an action of adjudication for debt cannot be brought to enforce a debt payable under a liquid document of debt unless (a) the debt has been constituted by decree or (b) the debt is a *debitum fundi* or (c) the document of debt has been registered for execution in the Books of Council and Session or in sheriff court books. Where the document is a bill of exchange or a promissory note the relevant registration for execution is that of the protest of the bill or note. However, these provisions do not apply to actions of adjudication for debt under the Conveyancing (Scotland) Act 1924, s 23(5) (which deals with recovery of arrears of ground annual).

EFFECT OF TIME TO PAY DIRECTION ON DILIGENCE IN SECURITY AND DILIGENCES ON THE DEPENDENCE

3.39 Certain diligences may be used prior to a court action, either on the dependence of an action or in security of a debt, the major diligences in this respect being arrestment and inhibition[1]. Although inhibitions are used in security of debts and on the dependence of actions, inhibitions are not affected by time to pay directions.

In the case of arrestment on the dependence or in security, a potential problem could arise with its interaction with a time to pay direction. Where decree is granted to a creditor who has used arrestment on the dependence of an action or in security prior to the action, there is no need for that creditor to execute an arrestment in execution before he can complete the diligence by an action of furthcoming[2]. Accordingly, for a time to pay direction to have effect in barring diligence of arrestment in execution, it must prevent an arrestment on the dependence or in security from ripening into a diligence in execution. This is brought about by section 2(2) of the 1987 Act which lays down that while a time to pay direction is in effect, an arrestment on the dependence or in security, although remaining in force, cannot be followed by an action of furthcoming (or sale where that is the appropriate step for completing an arrestment).

1 See ch 4.
2 *Abercrombie v Edgar and Crerar* 1923 SLT 271.

3.40 Furthermore, instead of freezing an arrestment on the dependence or in security, a court when making a time to pay direction may recall or restrict the arrestment[1]. Such recall or restriction may be made subject to conditions requiring fulfilment by the debtor within a specified time[2]. If conditions are attached to recall or restriction, the court has power to postpone the granting of the decree containing the time to pay direction for a period to allow the debtor to fulfil the conditions. This power of the court to impose conditions on the recall or restriction of an arrestment on the dependence or in security is designed to protect the preference or security which the creditor obtains by use of the arrestment. The Scottish Law Commission Report gives the example of a court requiring a debtor to give the arrestee an irrevocable mandate for payment of the arrested funds to the creditor as a precondition to granting a time to pay direction in respect of the remaining debt[3]. However, it will not necessarily be in the creditor's interest to have an arrestment recalled, even on conditions, as he may lose the preference which the diligence attracts in competition with other creditors.

1 1987 Act, s 2(3). Any such recall does not prevent the creditor using the arrestment as a basis for a claim for *pari passu* ranking under the Bankruptcy (Scotland) Act 1985, Sch 7, para 24: 1987 Act, s 13(2).
2 1987 Act, s 2(4).
3 Scot Law Com Report no 95 (1985) p 87.

3.41   An arrestment on the dependence or in security may also be recalled or restricted, on application by debtor (or creditor), after the granting of a decree containing a time to pay direction[1]. As in the case of recall or restriction made at the time of making a time to pay direction, a post-decree recall or restriction of an arrestment on the dependence or in security may be made subject to conditions requiring fulfilment by the debtor.

The power of a court to impose conditions on the debtor before recalling or restricting an arrestment on the dependence or in security, either when granting a decree containing a time to pay direction or after such decree, does not detract from the powers of the court to recall or restrict an arrestment on more general grounds and conditions.

1   1987 Act, s 3(1)(b); RC 88F; SI 1988/2013, r 3. Any such recall does not prevent the creditor using the arrestment as a basis for a claim for *pari passu* ranking under the Bankruptcy (Scotland) Act 1985, Sch 7, para 24: 1987 Act, s 13(2).

RIGHT TO SEEK THE DEBTOR'S SEQUESTRATION

3.42   Although a time to pay direction affects only the rights and remedies of the creditor as specified in section 2(1) of the 1987 Act, it should be noted that a time to pay direction also prevents a creditor from founding on the debt to which a direction applies as a basis for presenting, or concurring in the presentation of, a petition for the sequestration of the debtor's estate[1]. For such a creditor to be able to bring about the debtor's sequestration on the basis of that debt, an existing time to pay direction would have to be recalled before the presentation of the petition for sequestration. However, creditors of the debtor whose debts are not subject to a time to pay direction are not barred from petitioning for the debtor's sequestration by the existence of a time to pay direction over other debts owing by the debtor.

1   1987 Act, s 12(1).

DILIGENCES AND REMEDIES UNAFFECTED BY A TIME TO PAY DIRECTION

3.43   A time to pay direction prevents the use of only those diligences and remedies specified in section 2(1) of the 1987 Act[1]. The diligences which are blocked by a time to pay direction are in general those most typically used against non-commercial debtors by unsecured creditors to attach and realise the debtor's property or funds in order to satisfy the debt. Many other available remedies and diligences are not inconsistent with giving the debtor time to pay a money debt. Furthermore, the general policy of Part I of the 1987 Act is that time to pay measures do not defeat any security which a creditor may enjoy in respect of a particular debt.

1   1987 Act, s 13(1).

Diligences not affected by a time to pay direction

3.44   *Current maintenance arrestment.* The category of debts owing as current maintenance, which can be collected only by means of a current maintenance arrestment, is identical with the range of maintenance debts which are excluded from the operation of time to pay directions[1].

1   1987 Act, ss 1(5)(c), 106.

3.45 *Inhibition.* The diligence of inhibition is prohibitory and personal in effect. Of itself an inhibition does not establish a nexus over any specific item of the debtor's property nor does it allow for a creditor to realise the debtor's property[1]. The Scottish Law Commission also noted that far from an inhibition being inconsistent with a time to pay direction, a debtor who had been granted the privilege of time in which to pay his debts should not be able to incur new debts to the prejudice of his creditors.

1 As a time to pay direction bars the use of both arrestment and adjudication but does not affect an inhibition, a problem may arise in the situation where property is sold by a heritable creditor and an inhibiting creditor seeks payment from the free proceeds. If a time to pay direction prevents the inhibiting creditor from using arrestment and adjudication, does he still have a title to make such a claim? See Scot Law Com Report no 95 (1985) p 86, n 1; G L Gretton *Inhibition and Adjudication* pp 97–101; *Halifax Building Society v Smith* 1985 SLT (Sh Ct) 25, 30.

3.46 *Adjudication in security.* This diligence, which has been described as unknown in modern practice, has been superseded in modern practice by the diligence of inhibition[1]. The Scottish Law Commission recommended that adjudication in security should not be affected by a time to pay direction on the grounds that pending a later review on the general law relating to adjudications it would be simpler to omit this specific diligence from the ambit of the 1987 Act provisions on time to pay debts[1].

1 Scot Law Com Report no 95 (1985) p 88.

3.47 *Sequestration for rent; poinding of the ground; maills and duties.* Although these measures are usually classified as types of diligence, they apply only in respect of certain categories of debt and as such more resemble security remedies than ordinary diligences.

Preservation of other remedies

3.48 Where a creditor has a security in respect of a debt to which a time to pay direction applies or possesses some other remedy against the debtor, apart from the diligences specified in section 2(1) of the 1987 Act, then these securities and remedies are unaffected by a time to pay direction[1]. As the rule is stated in terms of only those diligences specified in section 2(1) being barred by a time to pay direction, the ambit of unaffected remedies is very wide. The Scottish Law Commission Report in discussing the range of remedies unaffected by a time to pay direction notes that[2]:

'. . . a time to pay decree or order should not affect the other rights and remedies of the creditor for the recovery of the debt such as rights of set off, retention or lien; rights of recourse against cautioners or co-obligants of the debtor (who themselves would be entitled to apply for a time to pay decree or order if they were individuals); or the exercise of security rights over heritable or moveable property of the debtor, or of a cautioner, securing the debtor's personal obligation of payment, such as rights to call up the security on default or to realise or take possession of the secured property to satisfy the debt.'

1 1987 Act, s 13(1).
2 Scot Law Com Report no 95 (1985) p 112.

Alternative or additional remedies combined with a money debt

3.49 Special note should be made of particular types of remedy available to creditors where a time to pay direction has been made in respect of a debt.

Certain creditors may be able to combine an action against a debtor for payment of a sum of money with additional conclusions or remedies. Examples are a landlord raising an action for arrears of rent coupled with conclusions for a warrant to eject the tenant, or a building society seeking recovery of arrears of a loan along with the calling up of a standard security over the property, or a hire purchase company seeking arrears of sums due under the hire purchase agreement accompanied with repossession of the hired goods. A similar principle applies in respect of the power of fuel authorities to disconnect supply when there has been non-payment of charges by their customers[1].

The general principle that a time to pay direction operates only in respect of specified diligences has the effect that a decree with decerniture for payment of a sum of money coupled with warrant for ejection of a tenant or re-possession of hired goods or the like may be subject to a time to pay direction but only in respect of the money provisions of the decree. The various remedies such as repossession of heritable or moveable property, even if part of a decree subject to a time to pay direction, are unaffected by any such direction. This applies *a fortiori* to remedies which do not require a court decree for their operation (such as discontinuation of supply of fuel).

In the case of tenancies to which section 110 of the Rent (Scotland) Act 1984 applies, it should be noted that the amended version of that section confines its special provisions (namely that the sheriff must give leave before diligence can be done) to actions under the landlord's hypothec of sequestration for payment, or in security, of rent. However, other diligences enforcing arrears of rent may, if otherwise competent, be made subject to a time to pay direction. Moreover a sheriff in such actions under the landlord's hypothec has power to sist or adjourn the action to allow the tenant time to pay rent by instalments or otherwise. This power can be used at any time between first deliverance and the granting of warrant to sell the sequestrated goods[2].

1 Electric Lighting Act 1882, s 21; Electric Lighting Act 1909, s 18 (These two Acts are prospectively repealed by the Electricity Act 1989, Sch 18 which is not yet in force at the date of publication of this work.); Gas Act 1972, Sch 4, para 17; Code of Practice for Domestic Customers issued by the Electricity and Gas Industries, July 1982. See also Middleton, 'Paying the Poor Man's Fuel Bill' 1977 SCOLAG Bulletin 166; Neilands 'Electricity Accounts and Meters' 1982 SCOLAG Bulletin 141; Grimes 'Electricity Boards and the Consumer' 1982 SCOLAG Bulletin 154.
2 Rent (Scotland) Act 1984, s 110 as substituted by 1987 Act, Sch 6, para 26. For the combined workings of time to pay provisions and the right of the sheriff under the Tenants' Rights Etc (Scotland) Act 1980, Part II, to adjourn proceedings in cases of public sector tenancy rent arrears, see Scot Law Com Report no 95 (1985) pp 113–114.

Variation and recall of a time to pay direction

3.50 A time to pay direction sets out a scheme for payment of the debt concerned either by way of instalments or lump sum payment. The direction will normally reflect the scheme for payment suggested by the debtor in his application for the direction. From the debtor's point of view, it is important that the payment or payments specified in the direction are complied with, for failure to do so may result in the automatic lapse of the direction and may also prevent a later time to pay measure being granted to the debtor in respect of that debt.

Accordingly it is important that when debtors and their advisers are making an application for a time to pay direction, they set out proposals for payment by the debtor which are realistic in terms of his income, assets and other commitments. Research conducted for the Scottish Law Commission indicated that proposals for instalment payments under the former summary cause procedures were often set at levels which debtors could not afford to meet[1]. Furthermore, there may be changes in the debtor's circumstances after the direction has been granted which make it more difficult for the debtor to continue to make the payments due under the direction.

On the other hand, there may also be circumstances which justify the creditor seeking to have the terms of a time to pay direction modified or the direction recalled. For example, a creditor may discover that the debtor has assets, not previously disclosed or subsequently acquired, or that the debtor is removing assets from the jurisdiction.

To allow the court to deal with these sorts of circumstance, either the debtor or the creditor may apply to the court which granted a time to pay direction to have the direction varied or recalled. In respect of sheriff court decrees, application is made in Form 1 of the Sheriff Court Proceedings Act of Sederunt[2]. Where an application is lodged the sheriff clerk fixes a date for a hearing and makes intimation on the creditor and debtor. The hearing must be not less than seven days from the date of intimation. In the case of Court of Session decrees, the application is made by motion, which must be intimated by the applicant to the other party by recorded delivery letter on an *induciae* of fourteen days[3]. The motion must include a brief statement of the reason for the application. When the motion is enrolled, there must be lodged in process (1) a copy of the letter of intimation and certificate of posting and (2) any document to be relied on at the hearing of the motion. The court may grant the variation or recall if it is satisfied that it is reasonable to do so[4]. The clerk of court or sheriff clerk is under a duty to intimate a variation made to a time to pay direction to both the creditor and the debtor as soon as is reasonably practicable, and the variation does not have effect until such intimation is made[5]. No similar provision is made in respect of the recall of a time to pay direction, which takes effect from the date specified in the interlocutor recalling the direction.

1 Scot Law Com Report no 95 (1985) p 93.
2 SI 1988/2013, r 4, Form 1.
3 RC 88F.
4 1987 Act, s 3(1)(a).
5 Ibid, s 3(3).

3.51 It is not clear that where a time to pay direction is varied or recalled the court may impose conditions. Section 3(2) of the 1987 Act states that

'If an arrestment in respect of the debt concerned is in effect, the court may order that any variation, recall or restriction under subsection (1) above shall be subject to the fulfilment by the debtor of such conditions as the court thinks fit.'

Subsection (1) of section 3 refers to both variation and recall of a time to pay direction and also the recall or restriction of an arrestment on the dependence or in security. Accordingly, it would appear that where a time to pay direction is being varied or recalled, the court may impose conditions on the debtor only where there is an existing arrestment on the dependence or in security (whether or not the arrestment itself is also recalled or restricted).

Cessation of a time to pay direction

3.52 A time to pay direction can cease to have effect in five ways:
(a) recall, on application by debtor or creditor, by the court;
(b) default by the debtor in obtempering the direction;
(c) sequestration of the debtor's estate;
(d) transmission of the debt, *mortis causa* or *inter vivos*;
(e) payment or extinction of the debt.

RECALL OF A TIME TO PAY DIRECTION

3.53 See above at paras 3.50–3.51.

DEFAULT BY THE DEBTOR

3.54 A time to pay direction will lapse automatically if the debtor defaults in making payment as required by the direction. The modes of default which have this effect all relate to delay in making the appropriate payment or payments. The first step in determining whether there has been delay in payment is that of deciding on the commencement of the direction requiring payment. A defect in the previous summary cause scheme for instalment decrees was that there was no requirement for intimation to be made to the debtor that he was due to pay by way of instalments. As a result a debtor might not have discovered that he was to make payments until he had already defaulted in terms of the instalment decree[1]. To remedy this defect, the 1987 Act requires the creditor to make intimation to the debtor of an extract of the decree containing a time to pay direction. Until such intimation is made to the debtor the direction does not have effect in making the debtor liable to pay according to the terms of the direction. However, the requirement of intimation by creditor to debtor concerns the issue of determining the time at which the debtor starts to pay the debt under the decree according to the terms of a time to pay direction. Intimation is not necessary for the direction to have effect. A time to pay direction comes into force as soon as the court pronounces its interlocutor, even although its terms do not bind the debtor until the creditor makes the appropriate intimation. Thus a creditor cannot by delaying or refusing to intimate an extract of the decree to debtor, enable himself to use one of the diligences barred by a time to pay direction. A direction, though not intimated, still has effect on diligences in terms of section 2 of the 1987 Act.

Where the direction allows for payment by way of instalments, the first instalment becomes due after the expiry of the interval specified in the decree starting from the date of intimation[2]. In the case of a direction for payment by deferred lump sum, the debtor is liable to make the payment at the end of the period specified in the direction starting from the date of intimation[3]. Where a time to pay direction is part of a decree in relation to expenses but the expenses are specified in a subsequent decree the date of intimation is that of the intimation of the extract of the later decree decerning for or specifying the amount of the expenses[4].

1 Scot Law Com Report no 95 (1985) p 91.
2 1987 Act, s 1(1)(a).
3 Ibid, s 1(1)(b).
4 Ibid, s 1(4).

3.55 Default by the debtor of payment under a time to pay direction occurs in three different situations:

(1) where, on the date an instalment is due under a direction, there is still unpaid the sum of not less than the aggregate of two previous instalments[1];

(2) where any part of the debt remains outstanding at the end of the period of three weeks immediately following the day on which the last instalment was payable[2];

(3) in the case of payment by deferred lump sum, where any of the sum to be paid remains unpaid twenty-four hours after the end of the period specified in the direction[3].

Where a time to pay direction is made in relation to both a decree for a principal sum and a subsequent decree for expenses, default by the debtor in any of the above ways in making payment of a sum subject to the direction under one decree will result in the direction ceasing to have effect in respect of the sums covered by the direction under both decrees[4].

Where the debtor defaults in payment in any of the above-noted ways, the time to pay direction automatically ceases to have effect, without the need for prior recall by the court. On such automatic lapse the creditor can use any appropriate diligence or remedy to enforce the outstanding debt and also any interest on the debt, whether or not the interest was awarded in the decree as a specific, quantified sum[5].

1 1987 Act, s 4(1).
2 Ibid, s 4(2).
3 Ibid, s 4(3).
4 Ibid, s 4(4).
5 Ibid, s 2(5).

SEQUESTRATION OF THE DEBTOR'S ESTATE

3.56 A time to pay direction ceases to have effect[1]:

(1) on the granting of an award of sequestration of the debtor's estate;

(2) on the granting by the debtor of a voluntary trust deed whereby his estate is conveyed to a trustee for the benefit of his creditors generally; or

(3) on the debtor entering into a composition contract with his creditors.

The effect of a time to pay direction ceases automatically on the occurrence of any of these processes and does not require application by any party to the court for recall of the direction.

However, the effect of these various insolvency processes on time to pay directions differs in respect of their impact on the ability of creditors to do diligence. In the case of sequestration the creditor will not be able to use diligence to recover the remaining debt[2]. In the cases of trust deed for creditors, the use of subsequent diligence depends on whether the trust deed is or is not a protected one under the Bankruptcy (Scotland) Act 1985. A non-protected trust deed will bar acceding creditors from doing diligence unless a non-acceding creditor has gained a preference by diligence[3]. A non-acceding creditor is able to use diligence against the debtor's estate until, but not after, the trustee has completed title[4]. In the case of a protected trust deed the provisions of section 37 of the 1985 Act do not apply but a creditor who has not acceded to the trust deed has no higher right to recover the debt than has an acceding creditor[5].

An extra-judicial composition contract will normally bar diligence by creditors who are parties to it. It is an implied term of the contract that all creditors will be parties to it[6] and that no preferences will be given to any creditor[7]. A composition offer under Schedule 4 to the Bankruptcy (Scotland) Act 1985 can be made only after the issuing of the act and warrant to the permanent trustee[8]. Accordingly subsequent diligence by creditors is struck down by section 37(4) of the 1985 Act.

1 1987 Act, s 12(2).
2 1987 Act, s 2(5); Bankruptcy (Scotland) Act 1985, s 37(4).
3 *Jopp v Hay* (1844) 7 D 260; *Campbell & Beck v Macfarlane* (1862) 24 D 1097.
4 *Gibson v May* (1841) 3 D 974; *Ogilvie & Son v Taylor* (1887) 14 R. 399, 401; *Doughty v Wells* (1906) 14 SLT 299.
5 Bankruptcy (Scotland) Act 1985, Sch 5, para 6.
6 Bell *Comm* II, 400.
7 *Macfarlane v Nicoll* (1864) 3 M 237; *Bank of Scotland v Faulds* (1870) 42 Sc J 557; *Ironside v Wilson* (1871) 9 SLR 73.
8 Bankruptcy (Scotland) Act 1985, Sch 4, para 1(1).

TRANSMISSION OF THE DEBT

3.57 A time to pay direction lapses on the death of the debtor or on the transmission of the obligation to pay the debt to another person during the debtor's lifetime[1]. As the whole purpose of a time to pay measure is to give an extension of time to pay debts owed by someone personally liable, and as such is a privilege personal to the debtor under the decree, the transmission, *mortis causa* or *inter vivos*, of the debtor's liability to pay the debt makes the direction no longer appropriate. The direction in any of these circumstances lapses automatically and does not require to be recalled by the court. The creditor has the right, on death of the debtor or *inter vivos* transmission, to use any appropriate remedy or diligence to enforce the outstanding debt, including any interest on the debt whether or not that interest was specified in the decree[2]. Where a debt has been subject to a time to pay direction and has lapsed because of *inter vivos* or *mortis causa* transmission, it is not possible to make a subsequent time to pay order in respect of that debt[3].

1 1987 Act, s 14(2).
2 Ibid, s 2(5).
3 Ibid, s 5(4)(b).

PAYMENT OR EXTINCTION OF THE DEBT

3.58 Where the debt subject to a time to pay direction is paid in full or is extinguished in some other way, the direction ceases to have effect. A debt due under a decree may become extinguished inter alia[1] by way of discharge by the creditor; by compensation or set-off; or by novation or delegation; or by *confusio*; or by the running of the long negative prescription[2]. Where a direction ceases to have effect on this basis the creditor cannot recover any interest on the sum due on the debt unless he had previously used the procedures on intimation to the debtor of claims for interest[3].

1 For fuller discussion, see *Wilson on Debt* chs 13, 14.
2 Prescription (Scotland) Act 1973, Sch 1, para 2(a).
3 1987 Act, ss 1(6), (7), 2(5). See above at para 3.36.

TIME TO PAY ORDERS

3.59 A second type of court order which allows debtors an extension of time to pay debts is a time to pay order. Although certain categories of debt are excluded from the time to pay order provisions, the debts in respect of which a time to pay order may be made are not restricted to those based on a prior court decree. Such an order can be granted by a sheriff court only after diligence has started against the debtor and before the diligence has reached its final stage. As with a time to pay direction, a time to pay order may allow the debtor to pay the debts by way of specified instalments or as a lump sum at the end of a specified period. While a time to pay order is in force the creditor is prevented from using or completing certain specified diligences to recover the debt.

Courts with power to make a time to pay order

3.60 The power to make a time to pay order is restricted to the sheriff court[1]. The particular sheriff court with jurisdiction to deal with an application for a time to pay order depends on the basis of the debt to which the order is to apply[2]. Where the debt is constituted by a decree granted in a sheriff court, that court has exclusive jurisdiction to hear an application for a time to pay order. In other cases the sheriff court with jurisdiction to deal with time to pay orders is the court with jurisdiction in the place where the debtor is domiciled or, where the debtor is not domiciled in Scotland, the place in Scotland where he carries on a business. In this context domicile is to be determined in accordance with section 41 of the Civil Jurisdiction and Judgments Act 1982. Where the debtor does not carry on a business in Scotland, jurisdiction in respect of time to pay orders is also given to the sheriff court in any place where the debtor has property not exempt from diligence. In this last case, jurisdiction is possessed by the appropriate sheriff court or courts, whether or not the debtor has his domicile in Scotland in terms of the 1982 Act. In cases where the debt is not based on a sheriff court decree, accordingly, jurisdiction to pronounce a time to pay order may be shared between the sheriff court or courts in the place or places where the debtor has his domicile and (where he does not carry on business in Scotland) the place or places in Scotland where the debtor has assets not exempt from diligence. (These rules on allocation of jurisdiction to specific sheriff courts are without prejudice to the various rules of court which allow for transfer of cases[3].)

1 1987 Act, s 5(2).
2 Ibid, s 15(3).
3 OCR 19; SCR 22 (applicable to small claims actions).

Title to apply for a time to pay order

3.61 As with time to pay directions, time to pay orders may be made only in relation to a debtor who is an individual and only if he is liable for payment of the debt in a personal capacity[1]. An individual person may also be granted a time to pay order where he is liable to pay the debt as
(1) a tutor of an individual; or

(2) a judicial factor *loco tutoris* on an individual person's estate; or

(3) a curator bonis on an individual person's estate; or

(4) a judicial factor *loco absentis* on an individual person's estate.

These provisions are the same as those which apply to persons entitled to apply for a time to pay direction[2].

Moreover an applicant for a time to pay order must be a debtor 'under' certain categories of decree or document (discussed below). In some cases of transfer or transmission of a debt, the liability may arise under the mode of transmission rather than the original decree or document (eg where a debt due under a relevant type of decree or document is subject to novation or delegation, the resulting liability of the debtor arises under the novation or delegation and not the original decree or document).

1 1987 Act, s 14(1).
2 See above at paras 3.06–3.13.

Stage of diligence at which application for time to pay order is competent

3.62 An application for a time to pay order may be made only when diligence has been started to enforce the debt and before the diligence has reached its final stage. The underlying principle is that the debtor has most need of the protection of a time to pay order only when steps have been started against him to attach his property to recover the debt. An earlier application for a time to pay order, which need not relate to a debt due under a court decree, might lead to congestion of the resources of the sheriff court which has jurisdiction to deal with the application. On the other hand the debtor cannot delay in making an application for a time to pay order until a late stage in the diligence by which time the creditor can reasonably expect to realise or attach property of the debtor to satisfy the debt[1].

1 For the creditor's right to recover the expenses of diligence recalled as the result of a time to pay order, see 1987 Act, s 93(4), (5).

3.63 Accordingly, an application for a time to pay order may be made only in respect of a debt in which one (or more) of the following stages of diligence has occurred[1]:

(1) a charge for payment has been executed;

(2) an arrestment (whether an earnings arrestment or current maintenance arrestment or non-earnings arrestment) has been executed;

(3) an action for adjudiction of debt has been commenced.

An application may still be made even if any of these stages has been followed by further stages of the diligences provided that none of the following advanced stages of diligences has been reached[2]:

(1) in the case of a personal poinding, where a warrant of sale has been granted in respect of the poinded goods but has not yet been executed;

(2) where a non-earnings arrestment has been executed and a decree in an action of furthcoming has been granted but not yet enforced (or where appropriate a warrant to sell the arrested goods has been granted but not yet executed);

(3) where a decree in an action of adjudication for debt has been granted and the creditor has, with the debtor's consent or acquiescence, entered into

possession of any property adjudged by the decree or has obtained a decree of maills and duties, or a decree of removing or ejection, in relation to any such property.

Where any one of these advanced stages of a diligence has been reached, a time to pay order may not be made in respect of the debt which the diligence is seeking to recover until the diligence has been completed or ceases in some other way to have effect. However, these provisions do not prevent the parties from making voluntary arrangements for extending time to pay the debt[3].

When the diligence has been completed or loses effect, a time to pay order may be made in respect of any balance of the debt remaining due. The diligence of poinding and sale is completed on report of sale being made to the sheriff; and a non-earnings arrestment is completed when decree is granted in an action of furthcoming. An adjudication for debt is not a completed diligence until decree is granted in an action of declarator of expiry of the legal. The provisions which bar an application for a time to pay order where an advanced stage of a diligence has been reached do not apply to an earnings arrestment. Provided the first stage of this diligence (namely a charge and the service of a schedule of arrestment) has been executed, an application for a time to pay order may be made at any time while the debt is still due.

1 1987 Act, s 5(1).
2 Ibid, s 5(5).
3 For the effect of such voluntary arrangements on the time limits for applying for a warrant to sell poinded goods, see 1987 Act, s 27(2)(a).

Debts in respect of which time to pay orders may and may not be made

3.64 Subject to certain exceptions (discussed below) a time to pay order may be made in respect of a wide category of 'debts' due under a 'decree or document'. The idea of debt here includes principal sum, interest and expenses decerned for and also the expenses of the diligence so far used, provided that these expenses are chargeable to the debtor. Where there is more than one debt due under a relevant type of decree or document a time to pay order can be made in respect of one or more than one or all of the debts.

The notion of decree or other document is also given an extensive meaning. It does not apply to a maintenance order[1], or a summary warrant granted to recover arrears of rates, taxes and community charges[2]. However, 'decree or other document' does include[3]:

(1) a decree of the Court of Session or the sheriff court;
(2) an extract of a document which is registered for execution in the Books of Council and Session or the sheriff court books;
(3) an order or determination which by virtue of any enactment is enforceable as if it were an extract registered decree arbitral bearing warrant for execution issued by the sheriff;
(4) a civil judgment granted outside Scotland by a court, tribunal or arbiter which by virtue of any enactment or rule of law is enforceable in Scotland;
(5) a document or settlement which by virtue of an Order in Council made under section 13 of the Civil Jurisdiction and Judgments Act 1982 is enforceable in Scotland.

Certain categories of debts cannot be made subject to a time to pay order.

1 Defined in 1987 Act, s 106. See above at para 3.28.
2 Ibid, s 106.
3 Ibid, s 15(3).

OUTSTANDING DEBTS IN EXCESS OF £10,000

3.65 A sheriff cannot make a time to pay order where the amount of debt outstanding at the date of the application exceeds £10,000[1]. This sum is exclusive of any post-decree or post-extract interest but does include any interest which is quantified as a definite sum prior to extract where that is not decerned for as a separate principal sum. The relevant amount of debt is that outstanding at the time of application, not that amount originally due as a principal sum[2]. Accordingly, a time to pay order can be made where the amount due as a principal sum under a decree exceeded £10,000 (which would have prevented the making of a time to pay direction) provided the balance is not above that figure by the time of the application.

1 1987 Act, s 5(4)(a). The Lord Advocate has power to vary the amount by regulations: 1987 Act, s 5(4)(a).
2 By s 94 of the 1987 Act, payments made to account of the debt are applied firstly to the expenses of the diligence used to recover the debt, then to post-decree interest and then to the debt owing under the decree or document (including the expenses of any action and pre-decree interest).

DEBTS SUBJECT TO A PRIOR TIME TO PAY MEASURE

3.66 A time to pay order cannot be made in respect of any debt which has been subject to an earlier time to pay direction or time to pay order[1]. This is so whether or not the previous direction or order is still in force, and accordingly a time to pay direction or order which has been recalled will still prevent a later time to pay order in respect of the debt.

1 1987 Act, s 5(4)(b).

CAPITAL SUM DUE ON DIVORCE OR NULLITY OF MARRIAGE

3.67 A time to pay order cannot be made in respect of a debt due as a capital sum awarded on divorce or on the granting of a declarator of nullity of marriage[1]. The rationale for this exclusion is the same as that which applies to exclusions of these debts from the ambit of time to pay directions, namely that a court in making an award of a capital sum on divorce or nullity has regard to the means of the debtor and can also order the payment to be made by way of instalments or as a deferred lump sum[2].

1 1987 Act, s 15(3).
2 Family Law (Scotland) Act 1985, ss 12(2), (3), 17.

MAINTENANCE ORDERS

3.68 Debts in connection with a maintenance order cannot be made the subject of a time to pay order[1]. The underlying rationale for this category of exclusion is similar to that of the case of capital sum awards, namely that the debtor's means are taken into account in assessing the amount to be paid. Furthermore, with maintenance orders, provisions exist in other statutes for the debtor making application for the variation and recall of such awards.

The definition of maintenance in this context is the same as that which applies in the case of time to pay directions[2].

1 1987 Act, s 15(3).
2 Ibid, s 106. See above at para 3.28.

DEBTS DUE UNDER A SUMMARY WARRANT

3.69 Where a summary warrant has been granted to recover arrears of taxes, rates or community charges, a time to pay order cannot be made in relation to the debt concerned[1].

1 1987 Act, s 5(4)(c). The relevant summary warrants are those granted under or by virtue of the Local Government (Scotland) Act 1947, s 247; Taxes Management Act 1970, ss 63, 63A; Car Tax Act 1983, Sch 1, para 3; Value Added Tax Act 1983, Sch 7, para 6; Abolition of Domestic Rates Etc (Scotland) Act 1987, Sch 2, para 7: 1987 Act, s 106.

DEBTS OWING AS RATES AND COMMUNITY CHARGES

3.70 A time to pay order cannot be made in relation to the following categories for debt owing to a local authority as[1]
(1) rates;
(2) any community charge or community water charge within the meaning of section 26 of the Abolition of Domestic Rates Etc (Scotland) Act 1987;
(3) any amount payable under section 18(3) of the Abolition of Domestic Rates Etc (Scotland) Act 1987[2]; or
(4) any amount payable as a civil penalty under section 17 (10) or 17 (11) of the Abolition of Domestic Rates Etc (Scotland) Act 1987[3].

1 1987 Act, s 5(4)(e), (ee) (added by Abolition of Domestic Rates Etc (Scotland) Act 1987, s 33. For cases where arrears of rates or charges are recovered by means of summary warrant procedure, see above at para 3.69.
2 This provision deals with payment of community charges in respect of backdated period, with surcharge and interest.
3 These provisions deal with civil penalties imposed for failure to provide information to a community charges registration officer.

DEBTS OWING AS TAXES

3.71 Various debts owing as taxes cannot be made the subject of a time to pay order. These debts are
(1) any sums recoverable by or on behalf of the Inland Revenue in respect of tax or as if it were tax;
(2) any duty due under the Betting and Gaming Duties Act 1981;
(3) car tax due under the Car Tax Act 1983;
(4) value added tax under the Value Added Tax Act 1983 or any sum recoverable as if it were value added tax.

1 1987 Act, s 5(4)(d), (f). For cases where arrears of tax are recovered by summary warrant procedure, see para 3.69 above.

SUMS DUE UNDER ORDERS OF COURT IN CRIMINAL PROCEEDINGS

3.72 Any sum due under an order of court in criminal proceedings cannot be made the subject of a time to pay order[1]. This category covers all orders of courts in criminal proceedings and would extend not only to fines and criminal penalties but also to compensation orders and awards of expenses. An order of a court in criminal proceedings imposing a penalty for contempt of court is also excluded from the scope of time to pay orders under this heading.

However where an award of civil damages has been made in criminal proceedings in a foreign country and the foreign judgment has been registered in Scotland, a time to pay order may be made in respect of the registered judgment[2].

1 1987 Act, s 15(3).
2 See further ch 11 at para 11.118.

SUMS DUE AS CIVIL PENALTIES

3.73 A time to pay order cannot be made in respect of various debts owing as civil penalties[1]. These penalties are fines imposed:
(1) for contempt of court[2];
(2) under any enactment[3], for professional misconduct; or
(3) for failure to implement an order under section 91 of the Court of Session Act 1868 (orders for specific performance of a statutory duty).

1 1987 Act, s 15(3).
2 Where a civil court makes an order dealing with contempt of court, the order is treated as a civil decree rather than a criminal order: *Cordiner, Petr* 1973 SLT 125.
3 Eg Solicitors (Scotland) Act 1980, ss 53, 55; 1987 Act, s 80(5)(b).

DEBTS SUBJECT TO A TIME ORDER UNDER THE CONSUMER CREDIT ACT 1974

3.74 Where a time order under section 129(2)(a) of the Consumer Credit Act 1974 has been made, a later time to pay order in respect of the same debt cannot be made[1]. This is so whether or not the time order is still in effect. Conversely where a debt has at any time been subject to a time to pay order a subsequent time order under the 1974 Act is not possible[2].

Where a time to pay order is applied for, the applicant must specify in the application whether a time order under the 1974 Act has been made in relation to the debt[3].

1 1987 Act, s 14(3). See also above at para 3.29.
2 Consumer Credit Act 1974, s 129(3), added by 1987 Act, Sch 6, para 17.
3 SI 1988/2013, r 7.

Recovery of interest due under a decree for a debt subject to a time to pay order

3.75 As in the case of time to pay directions, special rules exist in regard to interest payable under a decree for payment of a debt which has been made subject to a time to pay order[1]. Where pre-decree interest is awarded as a quantified and specified sum in a decree, it is decerned for as a principal sum and may accordingly be made the subject of a time to pay order. A time to pay order may apply to the principal sum alone or the interest on that sum alone, or to both sums together. However, there are important restrictions on recovery of post-decree interest payable under a decree for a debt subject to a time to pay order. In general such post-decree interest may be recoverable only where the creditor gives specific intimation to the debtor of what is owing by way of interest. If such intimation is not given, the creditor may find that the post-decree interest is not recoverable at all.

3.76 Section 5(6) of the 1987 Act states that interest payable under a decree containing a time to pay order cannot be recovered by the creditor except in accordance with the provisions on intimation laid out in section 5(7). However, this rule is subject to two provisos. The first is that interest awarded as a specific sum in the decree itself is recoverable in the normal way. However, this sum may itself be the subject of a time to pay order. Secondly, section 9(12) allows for any outstanding debt, including interest, to be recovered by the full range of competent diligences and remedies, where a time to pay order has been recalled or has ceased to have effect. But this does not apply where the recall or cessation of effect of the order arises because the debt subject to the time to pay order has been paid or extinguished, or because the debtor's estate has been sequestrated. The effect of these provisions is that a creditor can recover interest on a decree containing a time to pay order only where

(1) the interest is quantified and specified in the decree as a principal sum; or
(2) the creditor has adopted the intimation procedures under section 5(7); or
(3) the time to pay order has been recalled or has ceased to have effect for a reason other than payment or extinction of the debt or the sequestration of the debtor's estate.

To allow recovery of interest the creditor has to use the procedures set out in section 5(7). This requires the service of notice, on the debtor, claiming the interest and specifying the amount of interest claimed. Such notice must be served no later than fourteen days before the date on which the last instalment is due to be paid (or fourteen days before the last day of the period for payment by lump sum)[1]. Where interest is claimed under the section 5(7) intimation provisions, any payment made by the debtor under a time to pay order is ascribed first to payment of the sum in respect of which the order was made. Only when that debt has been discharged are payments ascribed to interest[2].

1 SI 1988/2013, r 3.
2 1987 Act, s 5(8). Compare the effect of s 1(8), discussed above at para 3.36.

Applications for a time to pay order; interim order sisting diligence

METHOD OF APPLICATION FOR A TIME TO PAY ORDER

3.77 A time to pay order may be granted by a sheriff only on application by a debtor. Application is made by completing Form 2 of the Sheriff Court Proceedings Act of Sederunt and lodging it with the sheriff clerk[1]. The sheriff clerk is under a duty to give the debtor assistance in completing the application form for a time to pay order[2]. However this duty is confined to the question whether the application form is in the correct form and not with the substantive matter of what specific payments the debtor should offer. The sheriff clerk has immunity from action for breach of this duty[3].

1   SI 1988/2013, r 5(1).
2   1987 Act, s 6(2).
3   Ibid, s 96(2).

3.78   On receipt of an application for a time to pay order the sheriff clerk must, as soon as is reasonably practicable, serve on the creditor a copy of the application informing him that he may object to the granting of a time to pay order within a period of fourteen days after the date of service[1]. On receipt of an application in proper form, the sheriff, if satisfied that a time to pay order is competent, must make an interim order which sists the diligence already started against the debtor[2]. The sheriff clerk is under a duty to serve on the creditor a copy of any such interim order as soon as is reasonably practicable[3].

1   1987 Act, s 6(6)(a).
2   Ibid, s 6(3). See below at paras 3.81–3.86.
3   Ibid, s 6(4)(b).

3.79   If the creditor makes no objection to the granting of an application of a time to pay order within fourteen days of receiving a copy of the application, the sheriff must make a time to pay order in accordance with the terms of the debtor's application[1]. Where the creditor wishes to make objection to the application he does so by lodging with the sheriff clerk the appropriate portion of Form 2 (or a separate letter) setting out his objections, including any counter-proposals. Where such written objections are timeously made, the sheriff clerk fixes a date for the hearing of the application and intimates this date to the parties. The sheriff clerk also sends a copy of the written objections and counter-proposals to the applicant and advises him that he may accept the counter-proposals before the hearing. Any such acceptance is made by the applicant informing the sheriff clerk who intimates the acceptance to the creditor and cancels the hearing. The sheriff then makes a time to pay order in terms of the counter-proposals[2]. If the parties cannot agree on the making of an order or its terms, each party must be given an opportunity to be heard[3]. Once the parties have been heard, the sheriff may either refuse to make the order (in which case he must recall the interim order sisting diligence[4]) or grant the time to pay order. Any decision of the sheriff relating to an application for a time to pay order must be intimated by first class post by the sheriff clerk as soon as is reasonably practicable to both the debtor and the creditor. Where an order has been granted the sheriff clerk must also intimate to the creditor the date when he intimated that fact to the debtor[5], this information being relevant to the questions of possible default by the debtor[6] and making intimation in respect of interest on the debt[7].

1   1987 Act, s 7(1); SI 1988/2013, r 5(6).
2   SI 1988/2013, r 5(3), (5)–(8).
3   1987 Act, s 7(2)(b).
4   Ibid, s 7(3).
5   Ibid, s 7(4); SI 1988/2013, r 5(9).

6 1987 Act, s 5(2).
7 Ibid, s 5(7). See above at para 3.75.

3.80   The application must specify, to the best of the debtor's knowledge, the amount of the debt still outstanding at the date of the application. In cases where the debtor has retained copies of the decree and schedules given to him during diligence procedures, the calculation of overall debt less any sums paid to account should be relatively easy. Matters will be less straightforward where the debtor has little by way of records of the progress of payment of the debt. Where the debtor is unable to furnish the necessary information, the sheriff has power to make an order on the creditor to provide particulars of the decree or other document of debt within a specified period of time[1]. Such an order requires the creditor to furnish the following items of information:
(1) the date of the decree or other document of debt;
(2) the parties named in it;
(3) where appropriate, the court which granted it;
(4) details of the debt and any interest due; and
(5) any further information, relating to the decree or other document, which the sheriff considers necessary for determining the application.
If the creditor does not comply with such an order the sheriff, after giving the creditor an opportunity to make representations, has power to make an order recalling or extinguishing any existing diligence, and interdicting the creditor from executing any future diligence in respect of the debt[2].

The application for a time to pay order must include an offer to pay the outstanding debt either by way of specified instalments (payable at specified intervals) or by way of a lump sum at the end of a specified period[3]. In the case of instalment payments, there is no requirement that the amount of the instalment or the period of interval of time should be equal in size or length.

1 1987 Act, s 6(4); SI 1988/2013, r 5(2). The sheriff clerk must serve a copy of this order on the creditor as soon as is reasonably practicable: 1987 Act, s 6(6)(b); SI 1988/2013, r 5(3).
2 1987 Act, s 6(5); SI 1988/2013, r 5(4).
3 1987 Act, s 6(1).

EFFECT OF INTERIM ORDER SISTING DILIGENCE

3.81   A time to pay order can be granted only where diligence has already started but has not reached an advanced stage. An interim order is made on receipt of an application for a time to pay order. The purpose of the interim order is to prevent the creditor from reaching one of these advanced stages so as to make a time to pay order incompetent and from starting a new diligence. However, as it may be important for the creditor to reach a stage in a diligence which confers a preference in competition with other creditors, only the final stages in the affected diligences are excluded by an interim order. An interim order affects only those diligences and remedies specified in the 1987 Act and only to the extent set out.

An interim order comes into effect on intimation to the creditor by the sheriff clerk of the making of the order. It remains in force until the sheriff's decision on the application for a time to pay order has been intimated by the sheriff clerk to the creditor and the debtor[1].

1 1987 Act, s 8(2); SI 1988/2013, r 5(3).

Diligences affected by an interim order

3.82 *Poinding and sale.* While an interim order is in force, a creditor cannot apply for a warrant to sell poinded goods[1]. An application for a warrant of sale, which is pending when the interim order comes into effect, falls. An exception to this rule arises in the case of an application for warrant of sale under section 21(1)(b), which deals with the immediate sale or disposal of perishable goods. An application under section 21(1)(b), which is pending at the time an interim order comes into effect, can be continued but this exception does not apply where the application has not been made before the interim order comes into effect.

Moreover, the creditor is not prevented by the interim order from taking any step prior to that of application for a warrant of sale. Thus where a charge has been served on a debtor and an interim order comes into effect, the creditor can still have a poinding of the debtor's goods executed. An interim order does not prevent a charge being served on a debtor, and a creditor may serve a charge during the currency of an interim order. Provided the days of charge have expired without payment and a full time to pay order has not been pronounced, the creditor may also follow up the charge with a poinding. This will usually be possible only where the days of charge are fourteen[2] and the creditor has made objection to the application with the result that a hearing has been arranged to deal with the application.

1 1987 Act, s 8(1)(a). The period during which an interim order is in force is to be disregarded in calculating the period of 12 months during which a poinding remains valid for purposes of applying for a warrant of sale: 1987 Act, ss 8(3), 27.
   An interim order sisting diligence has no effect on a poinding of the ground executed against the debtor: ibid, s 15(1).
2 Days of charge are 14 where the debtor is within the United Kingdom: 1987 Act, s 90(3). Where the debtor is outside the United Kingdom or his whereabouts are unknown the days of charge are 28 days.

3.83 *Earnings arrestment.* A creditor cannot execute an earnings arrestment during the time an interim order is in effect[1]. However, an interim order does not affect the validity of any earnings arrestment or conjoined arrestment already in force, nor does it prevent a creditor from serving a charge on the debtor. An earnings arrestment is executed by service of the appropriate schedule of arrestment on the debtor's employer. As an earnings arrestment must be preceded by a charge[2], the debtor has the period of the days of charge to apply for a time to pay order to prevent an earnings arrestment being executed against him.

1 1987 Act, s 8(1)(b).
2 Ibid, s 47(2)(a).

3.84 *Arrestment (other than earnings arrestment).* An interim order does not prevent a creditor from executing a non-earnings arrestment in respect of the debt. Where a non-earnings arrestment has been executed, either before or after the making of an interim order, the interim order prevents the creditor from completing the diligence by raising an action of furthcoming (or sale)[1]. If an action of furthcoming (or sale) has been commenced when the interim order comes into effect, no decree can be granted in that action[2]. The period during which an interim order sisting diligence is in force is to be disregarded in computing the period of prescription of the arrestment[3].

1 1987 Act, s 8(1)(c).

2 Ibid, s 8(1)(c). In effect the action of furthcoming is sisted, as no decree whether for pursuer or any of the defenders can be granted.
3 Debtors (Scotland) Act 1838, s 22(2), added by 1987 Act, Sch 6, para 3.

3.85 *Action of adjudication for debt.* While an interim order is in effect, it is not competent to raise an action of adjudication for that debt[1]. Where such an action has been raised before the interim order comes into effect, the creditor cannot complete the diligence eg by raising an action of mails and duties and taking possession of the subjects, or collecting rents, or ejecting the debtor, or raising an action of declarator of expiry of the legal. However the creditor may take the steps of registering a notice of litigiosity in connection with the action, obtaining and extracting a decree in the action, registering an abbreviate of adjudication, and completing title to property adjudged by the decree.

1 1987 Act, s 8(1)(d). An interim order sisting diligence has no effect on an adjudication on a *debitum fundi* or on an adjudication under s 23 of the Conveyancing (Scotland) Act 1924 (adjudication to recover arrears of ground annual): s 1987 Act, 15(1).

Diligences and remedies unaffected by an interim order sisting diligence

3.86 An interim order sists only the diligences of poinding and sale, earnings and non-earnings arrestments, and adjudication for debt, and only to the extent set out by section 8(1) of the 1987 Act. Accordingly, all other diligences or steps in diligence available to a creditor (such as a charge, current maintenance arrestment, inhibition, poinding of the ground, sequestration for rent, etc) can still be used while an interim order is in force as can other remedies (such as calling up securities, taking possession of heritable or moveable property, disconnection of supply of fuel, etc). The existence of an interim order does not prevent the creditor using the debt to which an order applies as a basis for presenting a petition for the debtor's sequestration or for concurring in the presentation of such a petition[1].

1 1987 Act, s 12(1).

Effect of time to pay order on diligence

3.87 In order to achieve the purpose of granting the debtor an extension of time in which to pay his debt, a time to pay order prevents the creditor starting certain diligences to recover the debt. However, unlike a pre-decree time to pay direction, a time to pay order may be made only when certain diligences in execution have already started against the debtor in respect of the debt. To prevent these diligences defeating the purpose of the time to pay order, the court has power to make ancillary orders recalling or freezing any diligences already started.

DILIGENCES RENDERED INCOMPETENT BY A TIME TO PAY ORDER

3.88 Before a time to pay order can be granted, diligence must already have been used to recover the debt. One effect of a time to pay order is to prevent the creditor from using any fresh diligence in respect of the debt concerned. While a time to pay order is in effect it is not possible to enforce payment of

the debt by serving a charge for payment or by commencing or executing any of the following diligences[1]:
(1) arrestment and furthcoming (or sale),
(2) poinding and sale[2],
(3) earnings arrestment,
(4) an adjudication for debt[3].

1 1987 Act, s 9(1).
2 This applies only in respect of a personal poinding. A time to pay order has no effect on a poinding of the ground: 1987 Act, s 15(1).
3 A time to pay order does not apply to an adjudication on a *debitum fundi* or an adjudication under the Conveyancing (Scotland) Act 1924, s 23 (adjudication to recover arrears of ground annual).

EFFECT OF TIME TO PAY ORDER ON EXISTING DILIGENCES

3.89 Some diligences or steps of diligence which are in force when a time to pay order comes into effect, will be affected automatically by the order; others will be affected only when made subject to an ancillary order by the sheriff who grants the time to pay order.

Automatic lapse: charge

3.90 Where a charge for payment of a debt has been served prior to the granting of a time to pay order in respect of the debt, the charge automatically lapses without need for court order if the period of the charge has not expired[1]. If the period of the charge has expired when the time to pay order is made, neither the time to pay order nor any ancillary order has any effect on the expiry of the charge as a step in constituting the debtor's apparent insolvency under the Bankruptcy (Scotland) Act 1985, section 7[2].

It is to be noted that these effects of a time to pay order date not from the time the order is in effect but from the time of the making of the order.

1 1987 Act, s 9(10)(a).
2 Ibid, s 9(10)(b).

Compulsory recall of diligences

3.91 When making a time to pay order, the sheriff is under a duty to recall certain diligences if these have already been executed. The creditor can recover the expenses of the recalled diligences as part of the debt in respect of which the time to pay order is pronounced[1].

1 1987 Act, s 15(3).

3.92 *Earnings arrestment.* On making a time to pay order the sheriff must make an ancillary order recalling any existing earnings arrestment[1].

1 1987 Act, s 9(2)(a).

3.93 *Conjoined arrestment.* Where the debt is being enforced by a conjoined arrestment, the order affecting the diligence as it applies to the debt depends on which court made the conjoined arrestment order[1]. If the conjoined arrestment order was made in the same sheriff court (whether or not by the same sheriff) as the court making the time to pay order, the sheriff making the time to pay order must vary the conjoined arrestment order so as to exclude the debt from the order. Where no other debt is being enforced by the conjoined arrestment order or the only other debt is a maintenance debt, the sheriff must recall the conjoined arrestment order[1].

If a sheriff sitting in another sheriff court made the conjoined arrestment, the sheriff making the time to pay order must have intimation made on a sheriff in that other court. A sheriff in the other court is under a duty to vary or recall the conjoined arrestment order as above.

1 1987 Act, s 9(2)(b).

3.94 *Adjudication for debt.* Where an action of adjudication for debt has been commenced when a time to pay order is made, the sheriff must pronounce an ancillary order prohibiting the creditor from taking any further steps in carrying out the adjudication[1]. However such an order does allow the creditor to take the steps of registering a notice of litigiosity in connection with the action, obtaining and extracting a decree in the action, registering an abbreviate of adjudication, and completing title to the property adjudged by the decree[2].

1 This does not apply to an adjudication on a *debitum fundi* or an adjudication under the Conveyancing (Scotland) Act 1924, s 23 (adjudication to recover arrears of ground annual): 1987 Act, s 15(1).
2 1987 Act, s 9(2)(c).

3.95 Where a sheriff makes such an order in respect of an earnings arrestment, a conjoined arrestment or an adjudication for debt, the sheriff clerk is under a duty to make intimation of the order to the debtor and the creditor. This intimation should be made at the same time as the intimation of the time to pay order. The ancillary order does not come into effect until intimation has been made to the creditor[1]. In the case of an ancillary order relating to an earnings arrestment or a conjoined arrestment, intimation must also be made to the employer.

Where a sheriff fails to make an order recalling any of the above diligences, or makes an order but fails to specify the diligence in relation to which the order is made, the diligence remains in force[2]. However the diligence may be recalled under section 10(4) of the 1987 Act.

1 1987 Act, s 9(7).
2 Ibid, s 9(11).

3.96 *Recall or freezing of diligences.* Where a personal poinding or a non-earnings arrestment is in effect when a time to pay order is made, the sheriff may make an ancillary order recalling the diligence, which must be specified in the order[1]. No such ancillary order can be made without first giving the creditor an opportunity to make representations[2]. In making such a recall, the sheriff has power to order that the ancillary order or the time to pay order may be subject to conditions requiring fulfilment by the debtor[3]. The recall of any arrestment or poinding does not prevent the creditor claiming a *pari passu* ranking on the diligence under the debtor's sequestration[4].

If no such order is made recalling an existing poinding or non-earnings arrestment, the sheriff must make an order that no further steps can be taken by the creditor in the diligence concerned. The diligence must be specified in the order[5]. The effect of such an order is that a decree of furthcoming (or sale) of arrested property cannot be granted[6]. In the case of a poinding, a warrant to sell poinded goods cannot be granted[7]. However, the creditor can still make a report of the execution of the poinding or apply for a warrant to sell perishable poinded goods[8].

1 1987 Act, s 9(2)(d), (e).
2 Ibid, s 9(6).
3 Ibid, s 9(3).
4 Ibid, s 13(2); Bankruptcy (Scotland) Act 1985, Sch 7, para 24.
5 1987 Act, s 9(4), (5).
6 The period during which a time to pay order is in effect in relation to an arrestment is to be disregarded in computing the period of prescription of the arrestment: Debtors (Scotland) Act 1838, s 22(2), added by 1987 Act, Sch 6, para 3.
7 1987 Act, s 9(8).
8 Ibid, ss 9(4), 21(1), 22. The period during which a poinding is frozen by an ancillary order is to be disregarded in calculating the period of the duration of a poinding under s 27 of the 1987 Act.

3.97 Where a sheriff makes any such order in respect of a poinding or a non-earnings arrestment, the sheriff clerk is under a duty to make intimation of the order to the debtor and the creditor. This intimation should be made at the same time as the intimation of the time to pay order. The ancillary order does not come into effect until intimation has been made to the creditor[1].

Where a sheriff fails to make an order recalling or freezing any of the above diligences, or makes an order but fails to specify the diligence in relation to which the order is made, the diligence remains in force[2]. However the diligence may be recalled or restricted under section 10(4) of the 1987 Act.

1 1987 Act, s 9(7).
2 Ibid, s 9(11).

DILIGENCES AND REMEDIES UNAFFECTED BY A TIME TO PAY ORDER

3.98 A time to pay order prevents the use of only those diligences and remedies specified in section 9(1) of the 1987 Act, as do related ancillary orders made by sheriffs when making a time to pay order[1]. As with time to pay directions, the diligences which are blocked by a time to pay order are in general those most typically used against non-commercial debtors by unsecured creditors to attach and realise the debtor's property or funds in order to satisfy the debt. Many other remedies and diligences available are not inconsistent with giving the debtor time to pay a money debt. Further the general policy of Part I of the 1987 Act is that time to pay measures do not defeat any security which a creditor may enjoy in respect of a particular debt.

1 1987 Act, ss 9(11), 13(1).

Diligences not affected by a time to pay order

3.99 The following diligences remain unaffected by the existence of a time to pay order[1]:
(i)   current maintenance arrestment;
(ii)   inhibition;
(iii) adjudication in security;
(iv)   sequestration for rent;
(v)   poinding of the ground;
(vi)   maills and duties.

1 For general discussion of these categories of diligence which are unaffected by a time to pay order or an ancillary order see discussion of time to pay directions above at paras 3.43–3.49.

Preservation of other remedies

3.100 As is the case with time to pay directions, a time to pay order leaves untouched the right of the creditor to use any rights of security and other available remedies in respect of the debt.

1 For general discussion see above at paras 3.48–3.49.

3.101 However, a time to pay order does prevent a creditor from founding on the debt to which an order applies as a basis for presenting, or concurring in the presentation of, a petition for the sequestration of the debtor's estate[1]. For such a creditor to be able to bring about the debtor's sequestration on the basis of that debt, an existing time to pay order would have to be recalled before the presentation of the petition for sequestration. However, creditors of the debtor whose debts are not subject to a time to pay order are not barred from petitioning for the debtor's sequestration by the existence of a time to pay order over other debts owing by the debtor.

1 1987 Act, s 12(1).

Variation and recall of a time to pay order

3.102 A time to pay order sets out a scheme for payment of the debt concerned either by way of instalments or lump sum payment. The order will normally reflect the scheme for payment suggested by the debtor in his application for the order. From the debtor's point of view, it is important that the payment or payments specified in the order are complied with, for failure to do so may result in the automatic lapse of the order and will also prevent any subsequent time to pay measure being granted to the debtor in respect of that debt[1].

1 1987 Act, ss 5(4)(b), 14(3).

3.103 As is the case with a time to pay direction, it is important that when debtors and their advisers are making an application for a time to pay order, they set out proposals for payment by the debtor which are realistic in terms of his income, assets and other commitments. Changes in the circumstances of the case may also lead the debtor or creditor to seek to have the time to pay order recalled or varied.

On an application by the debtor or creditor, the court may grant the variation or recall if it is satisfied that it is reasonable to do so[1]. Application is made in Form 3 of the Sheriff Court Proceedings Act of Sederunt. When an application is lodged, the sheriff clerk fixes a date for a hearing and intimates this date to the debtor and creditor. The hearing must be held not less than seven days from the date of intimation. The sheriff may, where he considers it appropriate, make an order requiring any person in possession of a summons or writ or who holds an execution of diligence in respect of the debt to deliver it to the court.

The sheriff clerk is under a duty to intimate a variation made to a time to pay order to both the creditor and the debtor as soon as is reasonably practicable, and the variation does not have effect until such intimation is made[2]. No similar provision is made in respect of the recall of a time to pay order, which takes effect from the date specified in the interlocutor recalling the order.

1 1987 Act, s 10(1)(a); SI 1988/2013, r 6.
2 1987 Act, s 10(3).

3.104 As with time to pay directions, it is not clear that where a time to pay order is varied or recalled the court may impose conditions but it would appear that where a time to pay order is being varied or recalled, the court may impose conditions on the debtor only where there is an existing arrestment or poinding (whether or not the arrestment or the poinding itself is also recalled or restricted)[1].

1 1987 Act, s 10(2). See discussion above at para 3.51.

3.105 The court also has power, on application by the debtor or creditor, to make an order concerning any poinding or diligence frozen by an ancillary order issued with a time to pay order. The court has power to recall or restrict any such arrestment and to recall any such poinding. Such recall or restriction may be made subject to conditions requiring fulfilment by the debtor[1].

1 1987 Act, s 10(1)(b), (2); SI 1988/2013, r 6. Any such recall does not prevent the creditor using the arrestment or poinding as a basis for a claim for a *pari passu* ranking on the debtor's sequestrated estate: 1987 Act, s 13(2); Bankruptcy (Scotland) Act 1985, Sch 7, para 24.

3.106 Section 10 also allows for rectification of the situation where there has been a failure to recall or freeze an existing diligence when a time to pay order was made. If it comes to the knowledge of the sheriff, from any source and not only on application of one of the parties, that an earnings arrestment, a non-earnings arrestment, a poinding and sale, or an adjudication for debt, existed at the time of a time to pay order, the sheriff may make an order[1]
(a) recalling the time to pay order, or
(b) recalling or freezing the diligence, on the basis of orders similar to those under section 9[2].

1 1987 Act, s 10(4). S 9 applies to such orders under s 10(4)(b) with such modifications as are necessary.
2 Any such recall does not prevent the creditor using the arrestment or poinding as a basis for a claim for a *pari passu* ranking on the debtor's sequestrated estate: 1987 Act, s 13(2); Bankruptcy (Scotland) Act 1985, Sch 7, para 24.

Cessation of a time to pay order

3.107 A time to pay order can cease to have effect in five ways;
(a) recall by the court, on application by debtor or creditor;
(b) default by the debtor in obtempering the order;
(c) sequestration of the debtor's estate;
(d) transmission of the debt, *mortis causa* or *inter vivos*;
(e) payment or extinction of the debt.

RECALL OF A TIME TO PAY ORDER

3.108   See above at paras 3.102–3.106.

DEFAULT BY THE DEBTOR

3.109   A time to pay order will lapse automatically if the debtor defaults in making payment as required by the order. Generally speaking the modes of defaulting are the same as those applying to a time to pay direction.

A time to pay order comes into force following intimation of the order by the sheriff clerk to the debtor under section 7(4). Where the order allows for payment by way of instalments, the first instalment becomes due after the expiry of the interval specified in the decree starting from the date of intimation[1]. In the case of an order for payment by deferred lump sum, the debtor is liable to make the payment at the end of the period specified in the order starting from the date of intimation[2].

1 1987 Act, s 5(2)(a).
2 Ibid, s 5(2)(b).

3.110   Default by the debtor of payment under a time to pay order occurs in three different situations[1]:
(1) where, on the date an instalment is due under an order, there is still unpaid the sum of not less than the aggregate of two previous instalments;
(2) where any part of the debt remains outstanding at the end of the period of three weeks immediately following the day on which the last instalment was payable;
(3) in the case of payment by deferred lump sum, where any of the sum to be paid remains unpaid twenty-four hours after the end of the period specified in the order.

1 1987 Act, s 11(1)–(3).

3.111   Where the debtor defaults in payment in any of the above noted ways, the time to pay order automatically ceases to have effect, without the need for prior recall by the court. On such automatic lapse the creditor can use any appropriate diligence or remedy to enforce the outstanding debt and also any interest on the debt, whether or not the interest was awarded in the decree as a specific, quantified sum[1]. In these circumstances the creditor may use a poinding and sale even where he had previously used a poinding to recover the debt before the time to pay order was made[2].

1 1987 Act, s 9(12).
2 Cp ibid, s 25.

SEQUESTRATION OF THE DEBTOR'S ESTATE

3.112   A time to pay order ceases to have effect[1]:
(1) on the granting of an award of sequestration of the debtor's estate;
(2) on the granting by the debtor of a voluntary trust deed whereby his estate is conveyed to a trustee for the benefit of his creditors generally; or
(3) on the debtor entering into a composition contract with his creditors.

1 1987 Act, s 12(2).

3.113 The effect of a time to pay order ceases automatically on the occurrence of any of these processes and does not require application by any party to the court for recall of the order[1].

1 For the different effect of these processes on the creditor's ability to do diligence, see above at para 3.56.

TRANSMISSION OF THE DEBT

3.114 A time to pay order lapses on the death of the debtor or on the transmission of the obligation to pay the debt to another person during the debtor's lifetime[1]. As the whole purpose of a time to pay measure is to give an extension of time to pay debts owed by someone personally liable, and as such is a privilege personal to the debtor concerned, the transmission, *mortis causa* or *inter vivos*, of the debtor's liability to pay the debt makes the order no longer appropriate. The order in any of these circumstances lapses automatically and does not require to be recalled by the court. The creditor has the right, on death of the debtor or *inter vivos* transmission, to use any appropriate remedy or diligence to enforce the outstanding debt, including any interest on the debt whether or not that interest was specified in the decree[2]. Where a debt has been subject to a time to pay order and has lapsed because of *inter vivos* or *mortis causa* transmission, it is not possible to make a subsequent time to pay order in respect of that debt[3].

1 1987 Act, s 14(2).
2 Ibid, s 9(12).
3 Ibid, s 5(4)(b).

PAYMENT OR EXTINCTION OF THE DEBT

3.115 Where the debt subject to a time to pay order is paid in full or is extinguished in some other way, the order ceases to have effect[1]. Where an order ceases to have effect on this basis the creditor cannot recover any interest on the sum due on the debt unless he had previously used the procedures on intimation to the debtor of claims for interest[2].

1 For discussion of the ways in which a debt can be extinguished, see *Wilson on Debt* chs 13, 14.
2 1987 Act, ss 1(6), (7), 2(5). See above at para 3.75.

CHAPTER 4

DILIGENCE IN SECURITY

INTRODUCTION

4.01 It is a noticeable feature of the law of diligence that certain forms of diligence may be used not only to enforce a debt already due under a decree or other document of debt but as a protective measure for a debt not yet due or not yet duly constituted[1]. This chapter considers the two diligences which may be used for this purpose, arrestment and inhibition. It may be noted that on many points of procedure and competency (but not as to substantive effects) the law on arrestment and inhibition as protective measures is similar[2]. It should also be noted that there is no clear-cut division between many of the issues which concern these diligences as protective measures and as diligences in execution, and reference should therefore be made to the discussion of arrestment and inhibition in execution[3].

As diligences in security (or protective measures), arrestment and inhibition are used in two distinguishable but often overlapping situations. Each may be used on the dependence of an action for a debt presently due, and in special circumstances each may be used in security of a debt not yet due. Consideration is given in this chapter to both of these aspects of each diligence.

For the convenience of exposition, there is also a short discussion of the topic of arrestment to found jurisdiction.

1 J Graham Stewart *The Law of Diligence* p 1.
2 Compare G L Gretton *The Law of Inhibition and Adjudication* p 3.
3 See chs 5 and 9 below.

ARRESTMENT ON THE DEPENDENCE

Actions in which arrestment on the dependence may be used

COMPETENCY AND DEPENDENCY OF ACTION

4.02 An arrestment on the dependence of an action is competent only if the action is itself competent[1]. For example, if the defender in the action (ie the common debtor) is not subject to the jurisdiction of the Scottish courts, any warrant to arrest granted in respect of the summons or initial writ is invalid.

Where an action is originally incompetent and an arrestment is purported to be executed on the dependence of the action, an amendment which cures the competency at the action does not validate any arrestment already executed[2]. In these circumstances, a new arrestment must be executed on the basis of the warrant in the amended summons or initial writ.

An arrestment on the dependence of an action may be executed prior to service of the summons or initial writ[3]. Once an action is in dependence, an arrestment may be executed at any time until the case has been finally disposed of. If the process becomes asleep, an arrestment used while the action was in dependence remains good but a new arrestment on the dependence cannot be executed until the action is wakened[4].

1 *Fischer & Co v Anderson* (1896) 23 R 395; *Ellison v Ellison* (1901) 4 F 257.
2 *Fischer & Co v Anderson* (1896) 23 R 395.
3 In this situation the summons or initial writ must be served within fixed time-limits for the arrestment to remain good: see below at paras 4.16–4.19.
4 *Roughhead v Stephenson* (1842) 4 D 1406.

GENERAL PRINCIPLE: REQUIREMENT OF PECUNIARY CRAVE

4.03 The general principle is that an arrestment may be used on the dependence of an action only if the summons or initial writ of that action contains a pecuniary conclusion or crave[1]. A crave for the expenses of the action is not a pecuniary crave for this purpose[2].

This principle excludes arrestment on the dependence of actions in which the summons contains merely declaratory or reductive conclusions, or where the conclusions are for interdict or an order *ad factum praestandum*, or the action concerns only matters of status (eg divorce).

However, arrestment on the dependence may be used where the summons contains pecuniary conclusions which are alternative to or dependent upon non-pecuniary conclusions. For example, arrestment on the dependence is competent in respect of an action of decree *ad factum praestandum* with alternative conclusions for payment of damages[3], or an action for declarator of marriage with a crave for aliment[4].

1 *Graham Stewart* p 19; cp RC 70(2)(b).
2 *Stafford v McLaurin* (1875) 3 R 148; *Burns v Burns* (1879) 7 R 355.
3 *More v Stirling & Sons* (1822) 1 S 547; *Bell Princ* S 2275.
4 *Wylie v Smith* (1834) 12 S 903.

FUTURE AND CONTINGENT DEBTS

4.04 Arrestment on the dependence functions to provide the pursuer in an action with a measure of protection in respect of the debt owing to him and which is the subject-matter of the action. Even where the debt is constituted by decree, the normal rule is that the debt was in existence from the date when the right of action arose, not the date of decree[1].

However, debts instead of being presently due, may be future or contingent in nature. A future debt is one which comes into effect on the happening of a certain event in the future. A contingent debt is one which comes into existence on the happening of an uncertain future event[2]. The general rule is that where a debt is still only future or contingent, the creditor is not entitled to a protective remedy in respect of the debt in the form of arrestment or inhibition unless there are special circumstances to justify this. 'The general principle is that diligence cannot be used in respect of a future debt unless the defender is *in meditatione fugae* or *vergens ad inopiam* or the circumstances are such that it appears that he intends to remove his effects beyond the power of his creditors.[3]'

1 *Fisher v Weir* 1964 SLT (Notes) 99.
2 There are many shades of meaning to 'future' and 'contingent' in this context. For discussion, see WA Wilson *The Law of Scotland relating to Debt* pp 12–17.
3 *Tweedie v Tweedie* 1966 SLT (Notes) 89, 90. See also *Campbell v Cullen* (1848) 10 D 1496, 1498.

4.05 The special circumstances which permit the use of arrestment on the dependence of an action which has conclusions for payment of a future or contingent debt[1] are:

(1) that the defender is *vergens ad inopiam* (approaching insolvency). The notion of *vergens ad inopiam* is to be understood in a broad sense and does not require averments or proof that the defender is absolutely insolvent[2]. It is enough that the defender is in a sufficiently parlous financial standing that there is the possibility of imminent bankruptcy;

(2) that the defender is *in meditatione fugae* (with the intention of absconding) so as to make recovery of the debt impossible or more difficult[3]. It is not clear whether arrestment on the dependence would be justified on this basis if the defender is seeking to remove himself and his assets to a country where the pursuer could register the decree for enforcement, but it is submitted that facilities for enforcing a Scottish decree abroad do not bar the application of the special justifying ground for arrestment on the dependence that the defender is *in meditatione fugae*[4];

(3) other special circumstances. The category of special circumstances which allows the use of arrestment on the dependence of an action in respect of future or contingent debts has never been limited to the two grounds already examined, and special circumstances extend to any steps taken by the defender to remove his assets beyond the reach of the creditor[5]. In *Wilson v Wilson*[6], such special circumstances included the situation where the defender was seeking to frustrate the pursuer's claim for payment of a capital sum on divorce by attempting to sell the former matrimonial home and using the proceeds to buy another house in the name of a third party.

1 Special statutory provisions apply to consistorial actions. See below at para 4.07.
2 *Campbell v Cullen* (1848) 10 D 1496; *Pow v Pow* 1987 SCLR 290.
3 *Burns v Burns* (1879) 7 R 355; *James v James* (1886) 13 R 1153.
4 Cp *Zaeschmar v Shaw* 1988 SCLR 269 (on the requirement to sist a mandatory).
5 *Tweedie v Tweedie* 1966 SLT (Notes) 89.
6 1981 SLT 101.

4.06 The special circumstances justifying the use of arrestment on the dependence in relation to a future or contingent debt must be set out in the summons or motion which seeks warrant to arrest. Doubts have been expressed as to the competency of warrant being granted without judicial supervision or giving the defender an opportunity to contest the averments on special circumstances[1]. Such a situation occurs whenever warrant is granted when a summons in the Court of Session passes the Signet or a sheriff court summons or initial writ is presented to the sheriff clerk for warranting. However, the accepted practice is to grant warrant to arrest on the dependence provided the summons or initial writ contains appropriate averments setting out the special circumstances justifying the use of arrestment on the dependence[2].

1 *Symington v Symington* (1875) 3 R 205; *Wilson v Wilson* 1981 SLT 101.
2 *Campbell v Cullen* (1848) 10 D 1496, 1498; *Noble v Noble* 1921 1 SLT 57.

CONSISTORIAL ACTIONS

4.07 Claims for aliment and for financial provision on divorce are a form of contingent debt. The common law rules about the need to show special circumstances to justify arrestment on the dependence have been replaced by section 19 of the Family Law (Scotland) Act 1985, the effect of which is that in actions seeking payment of aliment or the making of an order for financial provision[1], the court may grant warrant to arrest on the dependence of the action 'on cause shown'. The court also has power to limit the arrestment to any particular property or funds not exceeding a specified value.

As the categories of special circumstances recognised by the common law are not fixed, this provision makes little change to the substantive law on the use of arrestment on the dependence. It has been argued that the main effect of section 19 of the 1985 Act is procedural in requiring warrant to be granted only after a motion or petition by the pursuer[2]. However, this view has not been adopted in practice, and warrant to arrest on the dependence in respect of aliment and claims for financial provision are granted where the summons or initial writ sets out appropriate averments to justify the arrestment.

1 As defined in the Family Law (Scotland) Act 1985, ss 8, 27(1).
2 *Gretton* p 14.

ACTION OF COUNT, RECKONING AND PAYMENT

4.08 The conclusion in an action of count, reckoning and payment is for payment of such sums as the accounting demonstrates to be due. As this crave is pecuniary in nature, arrestment on the dependence of the action is competent. Moreover, in such a case no special circumstances need to be averred before a warrant to arrest can be granted[1].

1 *Telford's Exor v Blackwood* (1866) 4 M 369; *Stafford v McLaurin* (1875) 3R 148, 149; *Fisher v Weir* 1964 SLT (Notes) 99.

ARRESTMENT ON THE DEPENDENCE IN ABSENCE OF SUBSTANTIVE PROCEEDINGS: CIVIL JURISDICTION AND JUDGMENTS ACT 1982, SECTION 27

4.09 By section 27 of the 1982 Act, the Court of Session may grant a warrant for the arrestment of any assets situated in Scotland[1] where proceedings have been commenced elsewhere in the United Kingdom or in another contracting state to the 1968 Judgments Convention. This power may be used only where:
(1) the foreign proceedings have not been concluded[2];
(2) the subject–matter of the proceedings is within the scope of the 1968 Convention[3]; and
(3) such a warrant could competently have been granted in equivalent proceedings before a Scottish court.
The exact meaning of this provision is not clear. It could be that the use of the word 'may' in describing the Court of Session's power implies that the court has some discretion in the granting of warrant for arrestment. This view was

taken by Lord Coulsfield in *Clipper Shipping Co v San Vincente Partners*[4] where his Lordship held that the court had power to refuse to grant a warrant under section 27 of the 1982 Act on the ground, inter alia, that granting it would be oppressive. It should be noted that that case concerned the arrestment of a ship and the competency of the arrestment of a ship on the dependence of a Scottish action depends upon there being a colourable case set out in the pleadings[5].

However, as the court's power arises only in connection with proceedings already commenced elsewhere and where warrant could be granted 'in equivalent proceedings' before a Scottish court, it is thought that grounds must be set out in the application to justify the granting of the warrant.

Procedure is by way of petition to the Outer House[6]. It is thought to be present practice that the petition must pray for intimation and ordaining of answers.

1 Whether a warrant to arrest granted by a Scottish court attaches assets furth of Scotland is considered in ch 5 below at para 5.06.
2 It is not necessary to show that any document has been served on the defender or notice given to him in order to establish that proceedings have been commenced: Civil Jurisdiction and Judgments Act 1982, s 27(2).
3 1968 Convention, art 1. For discussion of the scope of the Convention see ch 11 below at paras 11.37–11.47.
4 1989 SLT 204.
5 See below at para 4.32.
6 RC 189(a) (xxx).

DISPUTES TO BE RESOLVED BY ARBITRATION

4.10 An arrestment may be made on the dependence of an action even though the cause of action falls to be decided by separate arbitration proceedings. In *Motordrift A/S v Trachem*[1], arrestment was used on the dependence of an action concerning a contract between two parties, a clause of which referred any dispute between the parties to arbitration in England. The Lord Ordinary refused to recall the arrestment on the basis that the arbitration clause did not completely oust the jurisdiction of the Scottish courts. Moreover, if the pursuers were successful in the English arbitration, they might seek to enforce the arbitral award in Scotland and the arrestment would be effective in respect of enforcing the award against the defenders in Scotland.

1 1982 SLT 127. See also *Svenska Petroleum AB v HOR Ltd* 1986 SLT 513; *Mendok BV v Cumberland Maritime Corpn* 1989 SLT 192.

Procedure for obtaining warrant to arrest on the dependence

COURT OF SESSION

4.11 Warrant to arrest on the dependence of a Court of Session action may be obtained by filling in the appropriate part of the official form of summons[1]. The summons on passing the Signet is warrant for execution of the arrestment. In practice, there is very little scrutiny of the applications for warrant granted in this way, but good professional practice requires that appropriate averments are contained in the summons (eg where payment of a future or contingent debt is concluded for, the special justifying circumstances are detailed).

Where warrant is not sought when the summons is signeted, procedure to obtain warrant is by motion to the Lord Ordinary whose certified interlocutor is authority for service of the schedule of the arrestment[2]. The motion must set out the circumstances to justify warrant being granted.

1 RC 70(1), (2); Form 1; RC 74.
2 RC 74(d).

SHERIFF COURT

4.12 Warrant to arrest on the dependence of a sheriff court ordinary cause action is obtained by adding a crave or warrant in the initial writ. The warrant is included along with the warrant of citation[1]. Sheriff Macphail suggests that where the action is not one for payment of a sum of money then due, warrant for citation should be granted and warrant for arrestment granted only after service of the initial writ on the defender and a motion for warrant for arrestment has been intimated to the defender[2].

If warrant to arrest has not been granted with a warrant of citation, separate precepts of arrestment may be issued by the sheriff clerk on production to him of an initial writ with pecuniary craves[3] on which a warrant of citation has been granted[4].

Application for warrant to arrest may also be made at any stage of the action by motion.

In summary cause and small claims actions, warrant to arrest is obtained by requesting this when forwarding the summons to the sheriff clerk for warrant to cite the defender. As in ordinary cause actions, this will normally be granted as a matter of course, but in some cases the decision to grant warrant to arrest may be left for the sheriff[5].

Application for warrant to arrest may also be made at any stage of the action by incidental application.

1 If the warrant is not served before the case is tabled, a certified copy initial writ is used as warrant: OCR 42.
2 ID Macphail *Sheriff Court Practice* p 354.
3 It is submitted that this should be read as craves for payment of sums now due, not for future or contingent debts. A warrant in such cases should be by way of motion.
4 OCR 42 (not applicable to summary cause or small claims actions).
5 *Macphail* p 816.

Preventing warrant to arrest on the dependence

CAVEAT

4.13 Caveats directed at the granting of warrant to arrest on the dependence are not competent. In *Royal Bank of Scotland v Bank of Scotland*[1], the House of Lords overturned a decision of the Inner House which had allowed a procedure similar to, but not the same as, a caveat to prevent warrant to arrest being granted. The rule that caveats should not be accepted to prevent warrant to arrest on the dependence was stated in a sheriff court decision which gave full consideration to contemporary practices involved with caveats[2].

1 (1729) 1 Paton 14. Contrast the interpretation given to this case by *Gretton* (p 33) who does not note that the House of Lords overturned the decision of the Inner House, a point not

apparently noted in all reports of the decision: see *Scottish Revised Reports, House of Lords I 1707–1797*, p 169. See also (1989) 34 JLSS 318.
2 *Wards v Kelvin Tank Services Ltd* 1984 SLT (Sh Ct) 39.

INTERDICT

4.14 In situations where the defender to an action is aware that warrant to arrest his assets is being sought, he may use the remedy of interdict to prevent the granting of warrant. To justify the granting of interdict, malice and oppression in the use of the diligence must be capable of being instantly verified.

1 *Beattie & Son v Pratt* (1880) 7 R 1171; *Graham Stewart* p 195; S Scott Robinson *The Law of Interdict* p 25. Application for interdict must be made to the Court of Session: *Beattie & Son v Pratt* above.

Service of the arrestment

4.15 To bring the arrestment into effect, a schedule of arrestment must be served on the arrestee by an officer of court[1]. Service of the arrestment is important as (1) the date *and time* of the service of the arrestment, as set out in the report ('execution') of the arrestment, establishes the priority of the arrestment in certain situations of competition and (2) what is captured by the arrestment, by way of money or property, depends upon the date and time of service as the arrestment can attach only what is owing by the arrestee to the defender at the moment of service[2].

1 The 1987 Act, ss 77 and 91(2), clarifies which officers of court can serve which court's orders. See further ch 14 below at paras 14.21–14.23.
2 It can be noted that in some situations these two features may pull in different directions in deciding when the arrestment should be served.

SERVICE PRIOR TO CITATION OF THE DEFENDER

4.16 In order to minimise the possibility of the defender putting his debts or property beyond the reach of the pursuer, it is sometimes advisable to serve the warrant to arrest before serving the summons or initial writ. In this situation there are time-limits for the subsequent service of the summons or initial writ.

4.17 (1) In the Court of Session the warrant of citation must be served on the defender within twenty days after the date of execution of the arrestment[1]. The 1838 Act further requires that the summons be called in court within twenty days from the diet of compearance, but there is no such diet in modern practice, and it has been held sufficient that service on the defender is made within twenty days of the arrestment no matter when the action calls[2].

1 Debtors (Scotland) Act 1838, s 17.
2 *Brash v Brash* 1966 SC 56, SLT 157, 158.

4.18 (2) In sheriff court ordinary actions, arrestment made before service of the initial writ on the defender must be followed by citation within twenty days from the date of execution of the arrestment[1]. Moreover where the case is defended the cause must have been tabled within twenty days of the first court day occurring subsequent to the expiry of the induciae. In the case of undefended actions, decree in absence must also have been taken within twenty days of the expiry of the induciae.

Furthermore where there has been service of the arrestment prior to the service of the initial writ, the pursuer or officer must report the execution of the arrestment to the sheriff clerk as soon as possible[2]. Failure to follow this step renders the arrestment null, unless delay or failure to report the execution is not the fault of the pursuer or the officer[3].

1 OCR 112(1).
2 OCR 112(1); *Johnson v Johnson* (1910) 26 Sh Ct Rep 134; *Henley's Tyre & Rubber Co Ltd v Swan* 1929 SLT (Sh Ct) 48.
3 *Johnson v Johnson*, above; *Macphail* p 357.

4.19 (3) In summary cause and small claims actions, an arrestment used prior to the citation of the defender must be followed by such citation within forty-two days from the date of its execution[1]. The pursuer or officer must report the execution of the arrestment to the sheriff clerk immediately after its execution[2]. The certificate of execution must be on the same paper as the summons.

(4) In all cases where an arrestment on the dependence has preceded service of the summons or initial writ on the defender and the above-noted steps have not been taken, the arrestment becomes null. However this does not prevent any further arrestment being executed by virtue of the warrant to arrest[3].

1 SCR 47 (applicable also to small claims action).
2 For effect of failure to report the arrestment, see discussion of ordinary cause actions, above.
3 Debtors (Scotland) Act 1838, s 17.

MODES OF SERVICE OF ARRESTMENT

4.20 Service of the schedule of arrestment is made by officer of court in the presence of one witness[1]. The modes of service of warrant of arrestment are the normal modes used by officers in court in regard to service of courts writs, ie[2]:

(1) personal;
(2) 'dwelling house';
(3) in cases of arrestment on the dependence of sheriff court summary cause actions (including small claims actions), it is also competent to serve the schedule by means of registered letter or recorded delivery[3];
(4) edictal and other modes of service of persons furth of Scotland.

Edictal service does not have the effect of interpelling the arrestee from paying to the common debtor unless it is proved that he was in knowledge of the arrestment[4]. To achieve this intimation, edictal service is followed in practice by registered letter to the arrestee.

Where arrestment has not been executed by means of personal service, the arrestee is not bound to refund the debt arrested if he is without fault in ignorance of the arrestment and has paid away the arrested sum[5].

In sheriff court actions if a schedule of arrestment has not been personally served on the arrestee, the arrestment has effect only if a copy of the schedule is also sent in a registered or recorded delivery letter to the last known place of residence of the arrestee, or if such place of residence is unknown or the arrestee is a firm or corporation, to the arrestee's principal place of business or if this is not known, to any known place of business. In the report of execution the officer must certify that such a step has been done and specify the address in question[6].

1 The appropriate officer to serve the schedule of arrestment is discussed in ch 14 below at paras 14.21–14.23.
2 For fuller discussion of modes of service see ch 7 below at paras 7.06–7.12. Where it is anticipated that issues of competition with the arrestment may arise, personal service of the warrant should be used as this allows the officer to specify the exact time of service in his report of the service.
3 Execution of Diligence (Scotland) Act 1926, s 2(1), as amended; Sheriff Court (Scotland) Act 1971, s 35(2) (definition of summary cause to include small claim); SCR 10.
4 Debts Securities (Scotland) Act 1856, s 1.
5 *Laidlaw v Smith* (1838) 16 S 367.
6 OCR 111. This rule applies also to summary cause and small claims actions but presumably not where service has been effected by post under the 1926 Act.

ARRESTEES

4.21 The schedule of arrestment is served by the officer of court on the arrestee, ie the person who is under an obligation to account to the defender in respect of property or debt owing by him. The arrestee must be subject to the jurisdiction of the Scottish courts[1].

Some specialities should be noted as to the appropriate person on whom the service is to be made:

1 *Douglas Heron & Co v Palmer* (1777) Br's Supp 440; *Brash v Brash* 1966 SC 56.

4.22 *Limited companies:* the schedule of arrestment may be served by leaving it or sending it to the company's registered office[1]. However, this provision is not mandatory and service may also be made at a place of business of the company[2].

1 Companies Act 1985, s 725.
2 *Singh v Atombrook Ltd* [1989] 1 All ER 385; cp *Hopper & Co v Walker* (1903) 20 Sh Ct Rep 137.

4.23 *Partnerships; corporations:* service of the schedule is by service on one of the partners or 'servants' at a place of business[1]. In *Abbey National Building Society v Strang*[2], it was held that service of an arrestment had not been validly made where service was at the office of solicitors who acted as agents for the building society. On the facts of the case it was held that the relationship between the building society and the solicitors was such that the office could not be said to have been a 'place of business' of the building society.

1 Cp OCR 14 (applicable also to summary cause and small claims actions).
2 1981 SLT (Sh Ct) 4.

4.24 *Banks:* the exact position of service on a bank is not clear, at least as a matter of strict law. Service on a particular branch of the bank certainly operates to attach the account of the defender held there but may not be effective as regard accounts held at other branches. Practice is to serve the schedule at the head office and on branches where the defender is thought to have an account but probably service on the head office alone is sufficient to attach all accounts at the bank in Scotland as the bank will circulate details of the arrestment to all its branches.

It should be noted that it is the practice of the Scottish banks not to disclose whether arrestment on the dependence has attached anything[1].

Particular problems exist in respect of whether an arrestment served on a branch of a bank in Scotland operates so as to attach funds held in a branch situated furth of Scotland. This problem is discussed elsewhere[2].

1 WA Wilson on *The Law of Scotland relating to Debt* p 160; cp *Veitch v Finlay and Wilson* (1894) 10 Sh Ct Rep 13.
2 See ch 5 below at para 5.06.

4.25 *Representative capacity; trustees:* in all cases where the arrestee is holding funds or property in a special capacity, the practice is to specify that capacity in the schedule of arrestment but failure to do this does not invalidate the arrestment[1].

Service on a quorum of trustees is sufficient but the safer practice is to serve on all known trustees.

1 *Huber v Banks* 1986 SLT 58, which disapproved passages to contrary effect in *Graham Stewart*.

4.26 *Lord Advocate:* where an arrestment is to be served on the Lord Advocate as arrestee acting under the Crown Suits (Scotland) Act 1857, the arrestee should be designated as 'The Lord Advocate, Crown Office, Parliament Square, Edinburgh, as acting under the Crown Suits (Scotland) Act 1857'. The designation should also state on whose behalf the Lord Advocate is designated as arrestee, whether the Crown or a particular secretary of state, minister or department[1].

1 1980 SLT (News) 146.

REPORT OF EXECUTION OF ARRESTMENT

4.27 On completion of service of the schedule of arrestment, a report (also called an execution) of service is made out. The report sets out the essential features of the service, including the names of the officer and witness, both of whom must sign it. The report must also identify in whose hands the schedule of arrestment was left.

Any inaccuracy or omission in relation to the schedule or the report of the arrestment is fatal to the validity of the arrestment, unless the mistake is merely clerical and does not relate to any essential feature of the arrestment[1].

1 *Graham v Bell* (1875) 2 R 972 (error in date of decree held fatal to arrestment); *Pollock Whyte & Waddell v Old Park Forge Ltd* (1907) 15 SLT 3 (error in designation of common debtor does not cause prejudice to any party); *Baird v Baird* 1910, 1 SLT 95 (uncompleted correction to year of King's reign does not invalidate arrestment); *Lattimore v Singleton Dunn & Co* 1911 2 SLT 360 (ambiguity in designation of common debtor invalidated arrestment). See also *Marshall & Sons v Robertson* (1904) 21 Sh Ct Rep 243; *Grant v Rattray* (1906) 23 Sh Ct Rep 115; *Fraser-Johnston Engineering Co v Jeffs* 1920 SC 222; *Stirling Bonding Co v Great West Wine Co* 1927 SLT 579; *MacTaggart v Mackillop* 1938 SLT 100.

SERVICE OF ARRESTMENT OF SHIP

4.28 Arrestment of a ship is executed by the officer of court, in the presence of one witness, affixing the schedule of arrestment to the main mast of the ship (or if none, to the stern post[1]) and chalking the royal initials above it[2]. A copy of the schedule and also a copy of the execution of the arrestment are left with the owner or other person in charge of the ship. Copies are also left with the harbour master.

An arrestment of a ship may be executed only in a harbour or other safe place, such as an open roadstead[3]. A ship may not be arrested while at sea, even if the ship has set sail in breach of an earlier arrestment[4].

In most cases of arrestment of a ship, a warrant to dismantle is sought[5]. Warrant to dismantle is implied in a warrant to arrest on the dependence, and in an extract decree[6]. Warrant to dismantle does not authorise the removal of the ship to a safe harbour for the purpose of dismantling it[7]. A special warrant from a Lord Ordinary or sheriff in whose jurisdiction the vessel lies is necessary to authorise removal of the vessel[8]. The court will not, however, grant a warrant authorising the seizure of a ship on open seas to allow her to be dismantled[9].

Dismantling is effected by removing the sails and rudder from a sailing ship, and in the case of a power-driven vessel by the removal of a necessary part of the machinery.

1 *Balfour v Stein* 7 June 1808 FC.
2 Bell, *Comm on Statute* p 16; R Campbell *The Law and Practice of Citation and Diligence* p 158.
3 *Macpherson v Mackenzie* (1881) 8 R 706; *Petersen v McLean* (1868) 6 M 218.
4 *Carlberg v Borjesson* (1877) 5 R 188; 5 R (HL) 215.
5 RC 74. It is not clear that warrant to dismantle is to be read as implied in a sheriff court warrant to arrest.
6 *English's Coasting and Shipping Co Ltd v British Finance Co Ltd* (1886) 14 R 220, 224.
7 *Kennedy v McKinnon* (1821) 1 S 210.
8 See eg *Brodersen, Vaughan & Co v Falcks Rederiaktieselshabet* 1921, 1 SLT 60.
9 *JWA Upham Ltd v Torode* 1982 SLT 229.

REGISTRATION OF WARRANT TO ARREST FOR EXECUTION FURTH OF SCOTLAND

4.29 The arrestee must be subject to the jurisdiction of the Scottish courts at the time when the arrestment is executed[1].

Provided jurisdiction can be established against the arrestee, an arrestment may have two effects furth of Scotland. The first is whether the arrestment, served on the arrestee in Scotland[2], has any effect on property or debts owing by him to the defender which are situated furth of Scotland. This question is considered elsewhere[3]. A second concerns the registration of a warrant for arrestment granted by a Scottish court for enforcement elsewhere.

Many legal systems adopt a principle that foreign judgments will be enforced in that country, only if they are final rather than provisional in nature. This position is also adopted in the enforcement procedures used between the United Kingdom legal systems[4]. Accordingly, enforcing a warrant to arrest on the dependence of a Scottish action elsewhere in the United Kingdom is not possible but in this situation the pursuer has a remedy in the form of section 25 of the 1982 Act which allows for application to be made to the High Court in England and Wales and in Northern Ireland for the grant of interim relief in respect of actions commenced in Scotland[5].

Such application for interim protective measures may also be made to courts in other contracting states to the 1968 Convention[6]. In addition, the pursuer may use the enforcement procedures of the 1968 Convention to enforce the Scottish warrant in another contracting state. For purposes of the Convention, a judgment comes within the scope of the enforcement procedures if it is given by a court or tribunal of a contracting state whatever the judgment may be called, and includes a decree, order, decision or writ of execution[7]. A warrant to arrest on the dependence comes within this definition, and provisional measures have been held by the European Court to be within the scope of the Convention's enforcement procedures[8].

However, those procedures do not extend to *ex parte* orders and this excludes a warrant to arrest granted where the defender had no opportunity to be heard by the court. However, if the warrant was granted eg after an opposed motion by the pursuer, then such a warrant could be enforced in another contracting state under the 1968 Convention.

1 Stair III, 1, 24; *Coutts v Miln* (1733) Mor 4835; *Douglas, Heron & Co v Palmer* (1777) 5 Br's Supp 449; *O'Brien v A Davies & Son Ltd* 1961 SLT 85; *Brash v Brash* 1966 SC 56.
2 Ie one of the modes of service recognised by Scots law, whether or not the defender is in Scotland: see above at para 4.20.
3 See ch 5 at para 5.06.
4 Civil Jurisdiction and Judgments Act 1982, s 18(5)(d). See further ch 11 at para 11.139.
5 Ibid, s 25. The proceedings must concern a subject-matter within the scope of the 1968 Convention. For discussion see ch 11 at paras 11.37–11.47.
6 1968 Convention, art 24.
7 1968 Convention, art 25.
8 *De Cavel v De Cavel (No 1)* 143/78 [1979] ECR 1055, [1979] 2 CMLR 547.
9 *Denilauler v SNC Couchet Frères* 125/79 [1980] ECR 1553, [1981] 1 CMLR 62.

Subjects arrestable

GENERAL RULE

4.30 The general rule is that subjects may be arrested on the dependence of an action if they can be arrested in execution[1]. This rule is subject to exceptions in respect of earnings, pensions and various articles exempt from poinding. Some special cases of subjects exempt from arrestment on the dependence are examined below, as well as types of subjects which deserve special note in the context of arrestment on the dependence.

1 For fuller discussion see ch 5 below at paras 5.04–5.35.

EARNINGS: PENSIONS

4.31 The appropriate diligence in execution to be used against many categories of earnings and pensions is no longer arrestment and furthcoming but the new statutory diligences against earnings[1]. Furthermore by virtue of section 1 of the Law Reform (Miscellaneous Provisions) (Scotland) Act 1966, it is not possible to arrest earnings or pensions on the dependence of an action. For this purpose, earnings are defined as any sum payable by way of wages or salary under a contract of service or sums paid in addition to such wages or salary[2].

Pensions for this purpose include: (1) any annuity in respect of past services, whether or not the services were rendered to the person paying the annuity; (2) any periodical payment by way of compensation for the loss, abolition or relinquishment, or any diminution in the emoluments, of any office; and (3) any pension or allowance payable in respect of disablement or disability[3].

1 1987 Act, s 46. See further ch 6 below at para 6.03.
2 Law Reform (Miscellaneous Provisions) (Scotland) Act 1966, s 1(2)(a).
3 Ibid, s 1(2)(b).

SHIPS

4.32 Arrestment is the appropriate diligence to use against ships, even where they are in the hands of the common debtor[1]. However, by virtue of section 47 of the Administration of Justice Act 1956, a ship may be the subject of an arrestment on the dependence of an action only if:

(1) the action comes within one of the type of actions listed in section 47(2) of the 1956 Act permitting arrestment on the dependence. In general these actions relate to situations directly involving a ship; and

(2) the ship to be arrested is the ship with which the action is concerned, or all of the shares in the ship are owned by the defender against whom the conclusion of the action is directed[2].

However, a ship may be arrested, whatever the basis of the action, where (i) the action has been raised in another contracting state to the 1968 Convention, or elsewhere in the United Kingdom and (ii) section 27 of the Civil Jurisdiction and Judgments Act 1982 applies[3].

To permit the arrestment of a ship on the dependence, the summons or initial writ must disclose a 'colourable case', ie some intelligible and discernible cause of action[4].

Warrant to arrest a ship is usually also accompanied by warrant to dismantle the ship. It is preferable to seek a warrant to dismantle explicitly, though it may be implied in the warrant to arrest the ship[5].

1 See 1987 Act, Sch 6, which clarifies this position as regards a number of former exceptions under statute. See further below at paras 5.22, 7.54.
2 *West of Scotland Ship Owners' Mutual Protection & Indemnity Association (Luxembourg) v Aifanourious Shipping SA* 1981 SLT 233; *William Batey (Exports) Ltd v Kent* 1987 SLT 557.
3 *Clipper Shipping Co Ltd v San Vincente Partners* 1989 SLT 204. For discussion of the Civil Jurisdiction and Judgments Act 1982, s 27, see above at para 4.09.
4 *West Cumberland Farmers Ltd v Ellon Hinengo Ltd* 1988 SLT 294; *Clipper Shipping Co Ltd v San Vincente Partners* 1989 SLT 204.
5 Cp *JWA Upham Ltd v Torode* 1982 SLT 229. See above at para 4.28.

GOODS EXEMPT FROM POINDING UNDER SECTION 16 OF THE 1987 ACT

4.33 Section 16 of the 1987 Act exempts certain categories of goods from poinding, usually in circumstances where the goods are reasonably required for use by the person residing in the dwellinghouse where the goods are located[1]. By virtue of section 99(2) of the 1987 Act, goods exempt from poinding under section 16 of the Act are also exempt from arrestment, including arrestment on the dependence.

1 See further ch 7 below at paras 7.44–7.52.

LIABILITY TO ACCOUNT

4.34 In the case of arrestment on the dependence, where the initial aim of the diligence is to provide the pursuer in the action with a measure of security for payment of the sum found due to him by the defender, an important issue is the effect which follows from arresting an obligation to account. Indeed, all arrestments are directed not so much at the property of the defender which is in the physical possession of the arrestee, or the debt owing by the arrestee to the defender, but rather the arrestee's obligation to account to the defender. 'Arrestment can never be of anything but something of which there is a present liability to account[1].'

1 *Caldwell v Hamilton* 1919 SC(HL) 100, 109; Bell *Comm* II, 71; *Shankland & Co v McGildowny* 1912 SC 857, 862.

4.35 However, difficulties arise in relation to the arrestment of a liability to account:
(1) Many of the cases dealing with arrestment of obligation to account are in the context of arrestment to found jurisdiction, where, once jurisdiction had been established, it might not be crucial to the value of the arrestment that anything is found due in terms of the arrestment. (Arrestment to found jurisdiction does not of itself attach the arrested property.) But in the context of arrestment on the dependence the whole purpose of the arrestment is to provide the arrester with a measure of security; something must be attached at the moment of service of the arrestment to achieve this effect.

4.36 (2) However, in the context of competition, it is important that an obligation to account (for what it may prove to be worth) is arrestable. This is illustrated by the case of *Riley v Ellis*[1]. Here A claimed damages for wrongous dismissal against his employers. This claim was arrested by A's creditors at a time when no action had been raised against the employers and when no claim for damages intimated to them. After the arrestment A became bankrupt. In the particular circumstances if the arrestment was valid, it would defeat the claims of the trustee in bankruptcy. The court held that the liability of the employers to account to A in respect of his claim for damages was arrestable at the time the arrestment was made. Anything subsequently found to be due would therefore have priority over the claims of the trustee in bankruptcy. This proved to be of some point as the claim for damages was settled and the amount agreed to be paid under the settlement was captured by the arrestment[2].

1 1910 SC 934.
2 It can be noted that in *Riley v Ellis* 1910 SC 934 Lord President Dunedin accepted the general statement of law on the arrestability of a liability to account but took the view that in this case such liability arose only once the action for damages had been raised and on this particular point Lord Dunedin's view has been preferred in later cases. See further ch 5 below at para 5.14.

4.37 (3) It is unclear what counts as an obligation to account for this purpose. Graham Stewart noted that it 'is not, however, every obligation to account which may be arrested under these circumstances, and it is somewhat difficult to state a test for the validity of the arrestment which will be reconcilable with all the decided cases'[1].

Stewart's own analysis sets out the position in terms of a distinction between cases of trustees as arrestees (where the obligation to account is arrestable) and cases of agents as arrestees (where such an obligation is not arrestable). This distinction in turn depends upon (i) whether there is a continuing obligation to account even where no funds are presently held or (ii) the obligation to account arises only once funds or property come into the possession of the agent[2].

1 *Graham Stewart* p 71.
2 *Graham Stewart* pp 71–76.

4.38 Two cases since the time of Graham Stewart's treatise help to bring out the features of obligations to account which are arrestable. In *Shankland v McGildowny*[1], arrestment was used in an action against X in the hands of a sheriff clerk of a sum of money which X had consigned in court during an earlier, unrelated action. This earlier action was against X for payment or count and reckoning and X had counterclaimed, and was still proceeding at the time of the arrestment. It was held that arrestment always depended upon there being a present duty of accountability; the sheriff clerk had a duty to pay over and thus account for the consigned sum to the party successful in the action but until it was known who that party was (and this depended on the outcome of the action) there was no duty on the sheriff clerk to account to either party, and so no valid arrestment.

This case can be contrasted with that of *Boland v White Cross Insurance Association*[2]. Here an action resulted in decree for damages against the defender. The pursuer sought to arrest in the hands of the defender's insurers whatever was due by them to the defender in terms of a contract of insurance. However, the insurers claimed that there was nothing to be attached by the arresters as they were not liable to pay under the contract because of breach of the policy by the defender; and in any case any question of liability was to be determined by arbitration. It was held that all that the insurers' argument indicated was that any liability they might have to *pay* to the defender was dependent on the findings of arbitration. But the contract of insurance placed on them a duty to *account* to the defender, and it was this obligation (for what it was worth) which the arrestment attached.

1 1912 SC 857.
2 1926 SC 1066.

4.39 The nature of arrestment of the obligation to account is also illustrated in the cases of future and contingent debts[1]. A future debt (in the sense of a debt which will definitely be owing to the defender by the arrestee at some time in the future) is not arrestable at the present time as there is no current obligation to account in respect of it. However, arrestment of a 'termly' payment which is currently due, attaches the whole term's payment even though the future part of the payment is not yet due at the time of the arrestment[2]. On the other hand, a contingent debt, ie a debt which is vested in the defender at the time of the arrestment but which may be defeated by a later event or which requires a later event (eg a finding of damages) to indicate what is owing, is arrestable. However, a contingent debt is arrested *tantum et tale*, ie subject to all the conditions attaching to it as vested in the defender. Moreover, a debt may be a contingent one in the sense that until the occurrence of some future event, which may or may not happen (eg a *spes successionis*), there is no right vested in the debtor. In such a situation the arrestment does not attach anything[3].

1 For discussion of this distinction, see *Wilson on Debt* pp 12–17.
2 *Marshall v Nimmo & Co* (1847) 10 D 328, 329, 331 (arrestment of right to payment of price of a contract for work yet to be performed).
3 Stair III, 1, 31; Bell *Comm* II, 72; *Kerr v R & W Ferguson* 1931 SC 736; cp *Leggat Bros v Gray* 1908 SC 67, 76.

Cessation of arrestment on the dependence

OUTCOME OF ACTION

4.40   Arrestment on the dependence of an action, unless otherwise ended, endures until the action has been finally disposed of[1]. Where the party who has used the arrestment is unsuccessful in the action, the arrestment flies off as soon as the period for appeal against the award of decree has passed without an appeal being applied for[2]. Where the arrester obtains decree in his favour, the arrestment remains valid and in effect becomes an arrestment in execution. It may be completed by action of furthcoming without the need to execute a further arrestment in execution[3].

1 *Graham Stewart* p 21. Actions are finally disposed of once the period for appealing has expired without an appeal being applied for.
2 *Creswell v Colquhoun & Co* 1987 SLT 329.
3 *Abercrombie v Edgar and Crerar* 1923 SLT 271. *Graham Stewart* (p 231) describes the opposing view as 'contrary to principle, practice and precedent'.

FAILURE TO CITE THE DEFENDER TIMEOUSLY

4.41   Where an arrestment on the dependence of an action is executed before service on the defender of the summons or initial writ in the action, special rules provide for steps to be taken for citation of the defender and other steps in the action within specified time-limits. Failure to observe these requirements nullifies the arrestment[1].

1 See above at paras 4.16–4.19.

PRESCRIPTION

4.42   An arrestment on the dependence prescribes after three years from the date of decree in the action[1]. The raising of an action of furthcoming or an action of multiplepoinding by the arrester or arrestee interrupts the prescriptive period[2]. An arrestment on the dependence in relation to a 'future or contingent' debt prescribes after three years from the date when the debt becomes due and the contingency is purified unless there has been a relevant interruption of the period[3].

   Where an arrestment on the dependence of an action secures a debt which is subject to a time to pay measure under Part I of the 1987 Act, the period in which the time to pay measure is in effect is disregarded in computing the period of the prescription[4].

1 Debtors (Scotland) Act 1838, s 22(1).
2 *Graham Stewart* p 223.
3 It has been argued that future and contingent debt in this context means simply contingent debt: *Wilson on Debt* p 13. See also *Jamieson v Sharp* (1887) 14 R 643.
4 Debtors (Scotland) Act 1838, s 22(2). On time to pay measures, see ch 3 above.

RECALL

General

4.43   An arrestment on the dependence may cease to have effect by being recalled. Recall in a strict sense is to be distinguished from the loosing of an arrestment. A loosing has effect by allowing the arrestee to make over the subjects to, or to pay, the defender. However in a loosing the position of the pursuer is still protected by caution being provided. Furthermore, if the goods or funds are still in the hands of the arrestee when the pursuer obtains decree, they remain subject to an action of furthcoming[1].

In addition to an arrestment on the dependence being recalled or loosed, it may also be restricted. Restriction is appropriate where it is shown that the pursuer's interest in a protective measure is still adequately served by a lesser sum or few items of property being subject to the arrestment.

As arrestment on the dependence of an action is an important protective measure available to a litigant, recall or restriction should not be granted where doing so would defeat the pursuer's legitimate interests in his protective measure[2].

1 Bell *Comm* II, 67; *Ballinten v Connon* (1848) 11 D 26, 33; *Graham Stewart* pp 195–197.
2 *Svenska Petroleum AB v HOR Ltd* 1986 SLT 513, 518.

Extrajudicial recall

4.44 An arrestment may be recalled without any judicial order by means of the parties agreeing to a recall[1]. Where the arrester fails to grant an extrajudicial recall in circumstances in which there is no longer any justification in the continuation of the arrestment, such as where the sum sued for has been paid in full, he will be liable for the expenses of any application to the court for recall[2].

1 *Ewing v Wight* (1829) 7 S 618; *Simpson v Fleming* (1857) 20 D 77.
2 JA Maclaren *Expenses in the Supreme and Sheriff Courts of Scotland* p 117.

Grounds for judicial recall

4.45 *On caution.* Recall of an arrestment may be granted where the defender offers caution for the sum covered by the arrestment or the whole sum sued for. Caution for the whole debt (including expenses) is more commonly used, in that it relieves all existing arrestments and prevents further arrestments[1]. Where caution is offered or ordered for a lesser sum, the amount of caution depends on the circumstances of each case[2]. Caution for the full amount will not normally be ordered where the action is for payment of a random sum, eg damages for defamation[3]. The factors to be considered are the nature of the action, the amount arrested and the circumstances of the common debtor. In *Fisher v Weir*[4], a warrant to arrest on the dependence of an action of count, reckoning and payment was refused on the condition that the defender consigned in joint names with the pursuer the principal sum admitted to be due by him, together with interest to the date of consignation.

Where application is made to recall an arrestment on the dependence in an action where decree for payment includes a time to pay direction, recall will be granted usually only on the debtor making caution or securing the pursuer's position in some way[5].

1 *Macphail* p 361.
2 Bell *Comm* II, 66. Examples are set out in *Graham Stewart* at pp 203–204.
3 *Manson v Macara* (1839) 2 D 208; cp *Farrell v Willox* (1849) 11 D 565; *Marsh v Millar* (1849) 12 D 172; *Cullen v Buchanan* (1862) 24 D 1280; *Burns v Burns* (1879) 7 R 355; *James v James* (1886) 13 R 1153.
4 1964 SLT (Notes) 99.

5 1987 Act, ss 2, 3; RC 88C–88E; OCR 21C, 57A; SCR 17A; SMCR 8–11, 24, 39. See further, ch 3 above at paras 3.39–3.41.

4.46 *Without caution.* Arrestment on the dependence may be recalled without caution or consignation where (A) use of the arrestment is nimious or oppressive or (B) where the arrestment is invalid.

(A) Arrestment nimious or oppressive. The underlying idea as to nimious or oppressive use of arrestment is not that it is legally incompetent for the diligence to be used, but that in the circumstances its use or continued use is unfair or prejudicial to the defender.

Examples include cases: where the conclusions of the action are extravagant, or the sum arrested is disproportionate to what is being sued for[1]; where the arrester acted in bad faith in using the arrestment[2]; where there are ample funds to meet the pursuer's claim and no prospect of his being defeated by other creditors[3]; where there has been excessive delay in proceeding with the action[4]; where the purpose of the arrestment is to embarrass the defender rather than protect the legitimate interests of the pursuer as a litigant[5]; where the pursuer is sufficiently secured by other diligence[6].

1 *Shanks v Thomson* (1838) 16 S 1353; *Levy v Gardiner* 1964 SLT (Notes) 68.
2 *Alexander v Graham* (1842) 5 D 218; *Rintoul, Alexander & Co v Bannatyne* (1862) 1 M 137.
3 *Graham Stewart* p 199; *Magistrates of Dundee v Taylor & Grant* (1863) 1 M 701.
4 *Telford's Exor v Blackwood* (1866) 4 M 369; *Radford & Bright Ltd v DM Stevenson & Co* (1904) 6 F 429; *Mowat v Kerr* 1977 SLT (Sh Ct) 62.
5 *Svenska Petroleum AB v HOR Ltd* 1986 SLT 513.
6 *Hamilton v Bruce's Trs* (1857) 19 D 745; *Macintosh v Miller* (1864) 2 M 452.

4.47 (B) Arrestment invalid. An arrestment which is or becomes invalid is null and strictly speaking no recall is necessary. However, unless the invalidity of the arrestment is clear, the safest course is to seek extrajudicial or judicial recall. The arrestment may be invalid in a wide range of circumstances. These include cases: where special circumstances are not averred in respect of arrestment on the dependence of an action for a future or contingent debt[1]; where there has been a procedural irregularity in the execution of the arrestment[2]; where the arrestment was used against property which is not arrestable[3]; where the action has become null by supervening event[4].

1 *Symington v Symington* (1875) 3 R 205; *Burns v Burns* (1879) 7 R 355; *James v James* (1886) 13 R 1153.
2 *MacTaggart v MacKillop* 1938 SLT 100; *Richards & Wallington (Earthmoving) Ltd v Whatlings* 1982 SLT 66; *F J Neale (Glasgow) Ltd v Vickers* 1973 SLT (Sh Ct) 88.
3 *Lord Ruthven v Drummond* 1908 SC 1154; *Gatoil International v Arkwright-Boston Manufacturer's Mutual Insurance Co* 1985 SLT 68.
4 Cp *Van Uden v Burrell* 1916 SC 391.

4.48 Difficulties may arise where the ground of the invalidity of the arrestment being alleged is that the arrested property did not belong to, or that there was no duty on the arrestee to account to, the defender. One difficulty is the stage of procedure at which a third party may seek recall. If a third party is claiming property as his own, he is not able to seek recall by motion in an action to which he is not a party[1], though exceptionally this has been allowed where a ship owner used the procedures under Court of Session RC 74(g) to have recall of the arrestment of cargo on board his ship[2]. In the circumstances of that case the arrested subject (the cargo) could not have been discharged from the ship and stored in a place within the jurisdiction of the court. In effect, the arrestment of the cargo had the effect of also arresting the ship. In these circumstances, it was held that the ship owner had sufficient interest to seek recall under RC 74(g).

1 *Tait v Main* 1989 SCLR 106.
2 *Svenska Petroleum AB v HOR Ltd* 1982 SLT 343; see also *West Cumberland Farmers Ltd v Director of Agriculture of Sri Lanka* 1988 SLT 294.

4.49 Accordingly, recall sought by a third party must be made by some procedure other than by motion in the action. Where the arrestment is of a debt, the arrestee (or other party) may dispute that the debt was owing to the defender in the action, only at the stage of the action of furthcoming[1]. However, if the arrested subjects are other forms of moveable property, whether corporeal or incorporeal, a third party may raise the issue of ownership of the arrested goods in a petition for recall[2].

1 *Vincent v Chalmers & Co's Tr* (1877) 5 R 43.
2 *Barclay Curle & Co Ltd v Sir James Laing & Sons Ltd* 1908 SC 82; *Blade Securities Ltd, Petr* 1989 SLT 246.

4.50 Where the issue of the ownership of the arrested goods is raised at the stage of motion for recall (ie if raised by the defender) or in a petition for recall, the general rule is that a proof will not be allowed[1]. Unless the pursuer's own pleadings do not aver that the property is that of the defender's, the arrestment will be recalled only if the defender or third party demonstrates that the property was not the defender's by instantly verifiable and conclusively verified averments[2]. Exceptionally, however, the court may be prepared to allow a proof of averments as to ownership of arrested property[3].

1 *Vincent v Chalmers & Co's Tr* (1877) 5 R 43.
2 *Barclay Curle & Co Ltd v Sir James Laing & Sons* 1908 SC 82; *William Batey (Exports) Ltd v Kent* 1987 SLT 557.
3 *Schultz v Robinson and Niven* (1861) 24 D 120; *Blade Securities Ltd, Petrs* 1989 SLT 246.

Procedure

4.51 *Court of Session.* Application for the recall of an arrestment on the dependence of a Court of Session action is made by motion. Where the action has not yet called, application is made by letter to the Deputy Principal Clerk craving that the court should grant an application for recall and enclosing a copy of the summons. The letter is intimated to the pursuer. The application is dealt with by a Lord Ordinary in chambers[1].

Written answers to a motion or letter of application are not normally used[2].

The decision of a Lord Ordinary may be reclaimed without leave within seven days[3].

Where recall is sought by way of petition, the petition is presented to the Outer House[4].

1 RC 74(g).
2 *Noble v Noble* 1921 1 SLT 57.
3 RC 74(h).
4 RC 189(a)(xv); compare *Blades Securities Ltd, Petrs* 1989 SLT 246. See further at para 4.49 above.

4.52 *Sheriff court.* Where recall is sought by a party to an action, procedure is by way of motion, intimated to the other party (and possibly also to the arrestee)[1]. When motion cannot be used, application for recall is made by summary application[2]. The motion or application is normally dealt with without the need for written answers[3].

When an arrestment is recalled or restricted, the practice is for the sheriff clerk to issue a certificate which sets out the consequences of the order.

1 *Mowat v Kerr* 1977 SLT (Sh Ct) 62.
2 Debtors (Scotland) Act 1838, s 21; *Johnson v Johnson* (1910) 26 Sh Ct Rep 134, 136.
3 *Uden v Burrell* (1914) 30 Sh Ct Rep 224; *Macphail* p 363.

4.53 *Time to pay directions: time to pay orders.* When a court pronounces decree containing a time to pay direction, it may recall or restrict an arrestment used on the dependence of an action. If there is no such recall or restriction, it is not possible for the creditor to raise an action of furthcoming (or sale) while the direction remains in force[1].

When recall or restriction of the arrestment is to be made, the court may order that the making of a time to pay direction is to be postponed to the debtor fulfilling conditions, normally so as to ensure the continued protection of the creditor's position[2].

Furthermore while the direction is in effect, application may be made to have an arrestment on the dependence recalled or restricted[3]. As at this stage the creditor has decree in his favour, recall or restriction will normally be granted only on caution or other similar condition.

1 1987 Act, s 2(2), (3). See further ch 3 above at paras 3.39–3.41.
2 Ibid, s 2(4).
3 Ibid, s 3(1), (2); RC 88F AS (Proceedings in the Sheriff Court under the Debtors (Scotland) Act 1987) 1988, SI 1988/2013, r 4, Form 1.

4.54 Similarly when a sheriff has made an interim time to pay order, it is not competent to follow up an arrestment on the dependence with an action of furthcoming or sale[1]. When a sheriff makes a full time to pay order he may make an order recalling or restricting such an arrestment, and this recall or restriction may be made subject to conditions[2]. Where a sheriff does not order the recall or restriction of an arrestment on the dependence when making a time to pay order, he must grant an order that the creditor can take no further steps to complete the arrestment[3].

1 1987 Act, s 8(1).
2 Ibid, s 9(2)(e).
3 Ibid, s 9(3).

Expenses

4.55 An award of expenses for recall of an arrestment does not depend upon the merits of the main action, as recall is looked upon as a separate process[1]. However, in modern practice, the question of expenses for recall is reserved until the merits of the action have been disposed of[2]. The general rule as regards expenses of recall is that the expenses fall on the party seeking recall except where recall is granted:
(a) on the ground that the use of the arrestment was nimious or oppressive[3];
(b) the arrestment was null as proceeding upon an improper warrant or a fundamental irregularity in execution[4];
(c) the pursuer should have granted an unconditional extrajudicial recall[5].

1 *Graham Stewart* p 212; *Clark v Loos* (1855) 17 D 306.
2 Cp *Muir & Co v United Collieries* 1908 SC 768.
3 *Magistrates of Dundee v Taylor and Grant* (1863) 1 M 701; *Macintosh v Miller* (1864) 2 M 452; *Radford & Bright Ltd v DM Stevenson & Co* (1904) 6 F 429.

4 *Clark v Loos* (1855) 17 D 306.
5 Maclaren *Expenses in the Supreme and Sheriff Courts of Scotland* p 117; *Graham Stewart* pp 212–213; cp *Robertson v Park Dobson & Co* (1896) 24 R 30.

SEQUESTRATION: INSOLVENCY

4.56 Arrestments on the dependence may be struck down by the insolvency and sequestration of the common debtor where he is an individual person, and where the common debtor is a company, by its liquidation. These matters are discussed in chapter 10[1].

1 See further ch 10 below at paras 10.36, 10.40.

ARRESTMENT IN SECURITY OF LIQUID DEBT

4.57 Arrestment as a protective measure may also be used in respect of a liquid debt based on a document of debt (such as a registered document or bill) where the term of payment has not yet come, but the debtor is *vergens ad inopiam, in meditatione fugae,* or otherwise threatening to dissipate his funds or property so as to defeat the creditor receiving payment[1]. In these circumstances, warrant to arrest is obtained by application by way of petition for letters of arrestment[2]. The application must set out the basis of debt and specify the special circumstances justifying the granting of the warrant. The warrant is authority to arrest the debtor's moveable property until caution is found.

Once warrant has been obtained, further procedure is the same as for arrestment on the dependence of an action.

1 See further *Graham Stewart* pp 22–23.
2 See also OCR 42.

ARRESTMENT TO FOUND JURISDICTION

4.58 Brief consideration will now be given to the subject of arrestment to found jurisdiction. Although this form of arrestment is not strictly speaking a diligence[1], but rather a mode of founding jurisdiction, in practice where it is used it is often coupled with arrestment on the dependence of the action concerned.

The points of speciality about this form of arrestment are noted.

1 *Fraser-Johnston Engineering Co v Jeffs* 1920 SC 222, 228; *Alexander Ward & Co v Samyang Navigation Co Ltd* 1975 SC (HL) 26, 54.

Competency of using arrestment to found jurisdiction

4.59 Founding jurisdiction by means of arrestment of the defender's property has long been regarded as an anomalous and exorbitant basis of jurisdiction and its scope is not to be extended[1]. An important set of restrictions on the use of this form of arrestment is to be found in the provisions of the Civil Jurisdiction and Judgments Act 1982. Where the defender in the action is domiciled[2] in a contracting state other than the United Kingdom and the action concerns a matter within the scope of the 1968 Convention, jurisdiction cannot be founded on arrestment of the defender's property[3].

Where the defender is domiciled[4] in any part of the United Kingdom, including Scotland, arrestment can be used to found jurisdiction only where the subject-matter of the action is outwith the scope of the 1968 Convention and of Schedules 4 and 8 to the 1982 Act[5].

Where an action is within the scope of Schedule 8 to the 1982 Act and the defender is not domiciled anywhere in the United Kingdom or in any contracting state to the 1968 Convention, jurisdiction may be founded in a court for the place where any moveable property[6] belonging to the defender has been arrested. In any such sheriff court action it is no longer necessary that jurisdiction could not be based on any other ground.

Where the subject-matter of the action is beyond the scope of the 1968 Convention and Schedules 4 and 8 to the 1982 Act, arrestment may used to found jurisdiction no matter the domicile[7] of the defender. It should be noted, however, that in such circumstances not all types of action may be based on this ground of jurisdiction. This basis of jurisdiction cannot be used in actions which cannot lead to a decree in money terms (eg decrees of declarator, reduction, status)[8]. Where an action has mixed petitory and non-petitory conclusions, arrestment may be used to found jurisdiction.

In actions beyond the scope of the 1968 Convention and Schedules 4 and 8 to the 1982 Act, jurisdiction in a sheriff court action may be founded on arrestment only if the defender is not otherwise subject to the jurisdiction of the Scottish courts[9].

1 *Baines & Tait v Compagnie Generale des Mines d'Asphalte* (1879) 6 R 846, 850; *Parnell v Walter* (1889) 16 R 917, 924; *Craig v Brunsgaard, Kjosterud & Co* (1896) 23 R 500, 504; *Brower's Exor v Ramsay's Trs* 1912 SC 1374; *Shankland & Co v McGildowny* 1912 SC 857, 861, 869; *Alexander Ward & Co v Samyang Navigation Co Ltd* 1975 SC (HL) 26.
2 Ie as determined by the Civil Jurisdiction and Judgments Act 1982, ss 41–46.
3 1968 Convention, art 3.
4 Ie as determined by the Civil Jurisdiction and Judgments Act 1982, ss 41–46.
5 Ibid, Sch 8, r 2(8). Sch 9 sets out the proceedings excluded from Sch 8.
6 Ibid, Sch 8, r 2(8). The term 'property' is probably to be read as including debts owing to the defender: see Anton *Civil Jurisdiction in Scotland* p 188.
7 Ie as determined by the Civil Jurisdiction and Judgments Act 1982, ss 41–46.
8 *Graham Stewart* pp 249–254; AE Anton *Private International Law* pp 112–114.
9 Sheriff Courts (Scotland) Act 1907, s 6(c).

Warrant to arrest

4.60 Warrant to arrest to found jurisdiction is obtained in the same manner as warrant to arrest on the dependence of an action, except that in the nature of things such a warrant cannot be granted once an action has commenced against the defender. In the Court of Session, the summons once signeted is warrant to arrest to found jurisdiction provided application has been made by filling in the blank in the appropriate part of the summons form[1].

Where the summons contains warrant for both arrestment to found jurisdiction and arrestment on the dependence of the action, it is not necessary to serve separate schedules of arrestment[2].

In the sheriff court, warrant, if craved for, is granted along with the warrant to cite the defender[3]. Averments to justify the granting of the warrant must be included in the condescendence of the initial writ[4].

1 RC 74. See also RC 74(f) (minute of amendment calling additional or substitute defender).
2 RC 74(c).
3 OCR 5, Form B; SCR 3(2); SMCR 3(6).
4 OCR 6. There is no equivalent rule in respect of summary cause and small claims actions, but the same practice is followed: *Macphail* pp 125–126, 816.

Subjects arrestable

4.61 In general, subjects which can be arrested in execution can be arrested to found jurisdiction[1]. Thus arrestment of property of small value, provided the value is not merely elusory, is sufficient to found jurisdiction[2]. The arrestment of a liability to account suffices unless it is immediately verifiable that no balance is due by the arrestee at the time of the arrestment[3].

1 *Graham Stewart* pp 254–262; AE Anton *Private International Law* pp 108–112.
2 *Shaw v Dow and Dobie* (1869) 7 M 449; 455.
3 *Napier, Shanks & Bell v Halvorsen* (1892) 19 R 412; *J & C Murray v Wallace, Marrs & Co* 1914 SC 114; *Mitchell & Muil v Feniscliffe Products Co* 1920 1 SLT 199.

Effect of arrestment to found jurisdiction

4.62 It is a clearly-established principle in modern times that arrestment to found jurisdiction creates no *nexus* over the property arrested[1]. The arrestment is a mode of founding jurisdiction rather than a diligence strictly speaking. Jurisdiction founded in this way remains good even if the property or debt is later delivered or paid to the defender or if the property is subsequently removed from the court's territorial jurisdiction[2].

1 *North v Stewart* (1890) 17 R (HL) 60. See discussion in *Graham Stewart* pp 269–272. A *nexus* is, of course, put over the subjects when they are also arrested on the dependence of the action.
2 *North v Stewart* (1890) 17 R (HL) 60 at 63, per Lord Watson; *Craig v Brunsgaard, Kjosterud & Co* (1896) 23 R 500.

INHIBITION AS A DILIGENCE IN SECURITY

4.63 This section of the present chapters deals with inhibition as a diligence in security and chapter 9 deals with inhibition in execution. The main features of inhibition are dealt with in chapter 9 and only the special features of inhibition on the dependence and in security are covered here.

Inhibition on the dependence

4.64 An inhibition may be granted on the dependence of either a Court of Session or sheriff court action. Some doubt exists about whether it is competent to inhibit on the dependence of summary cause, small claims or summary application types of action. The forms attached to the summary cause and small claims rules mention only arrestment on the dependence[1]. However, there is no doubt that inhibition can be used on the dependence of an ordinary cause action[2], but the form of initial writ annexed to the ordinary cause rules again mentions only arrestment on the dependence[3]. In practice, inhibitions have been granted on the dependence on summary cause actions[4], and there is no reason why the same approach should not apply to small claims actions.

Summary applications are competent in a number of situations[5], and the application is commenced by an initial writ framed in accordance with that annexed to the ordinary cause rules[6]. Although the availability of inhibition on the dependence is in some doubt, it does appear that inhibition on the dependence has been granted in respect of some summary applications under the Conveyancing and Feudal Reform (Scotland) Act 1970. Given that the applicant is likely to be a heritable creditor, there will often be little point in seeking an inhibition where the creditor already has a preference by virtue of the standard security. However, an inhibition may be of some value where the debtor owns other heritable property.

Inhibition is not competent on the dependence of proceedings before an industrial tribunal or the Employment Appeal Tribunal or on the dependence of any other such proceedings. In these cases, because the relevant statutes provide that the decision is to be treated as a registered decree arbitral or that it can be registered in the Books of Council and Session or in the books of the appropriate sheriff court, they exclude the possibility of inhibition on the dependence[7].

1 SCR Forms A, B etc; SMCR Form 1.
2 *Macphail* pp 364–368.
3 Form A.
4 W W McBryde and N J Dowie *Petition Procedure in the Court of Session* (1st edn, 1980) p 47.
5 *Macphail* ch 26.
6 *Macphail* p 879.
7 Employment Protection (Consolidation) Act 1978, Sch 11, Pt I; Banking Act 1979 (Scottish Appeals) Regulations 1980, SI 1980/481, reg 13.

Inhibition in security

4.65 The term 'inhibition in security' is sometimes used to mean inhibition on the dependence but in its strict use, inhibition in security is an inhibition used in respect of a debt which is future or contingent. It follows therefore that such an inhibition may be used in execution, or on the dependence, or on a document of debt.

This use of inhibition is an exception to the general rule that diligence may be used only in respect of debts which are presently due[1]. Before it can be used, there must be special circumstances and at one time the special circumstances were limited to the fact that the debter was *vergens ad inopiam* or was *in meditatione fugae*. More recently[2], Lord Maxwell extended the notion of inhibition in security and granted a warrant to inhibit where there was an averment in a divorce action that the defender intended to sell the family home and buy one in the name of his mistress. If there are special circumstances, these must be sufficiently set out in the application for inhibition[3]. If this is not done, the warrant will not be granted. (For the problems which may arise in this connection see Gretton on Inhibitions[4].) One case which is worth mentioning is a consistorial action. In terms of the Family Law (Scotland) Act 1985, an inhibition may be used in actions for aliment or divorce provided cause is shown[5]. The opinion has been expressed that it will be easier to obtain an inhibition (and an arrestment) under the 1985 Act than previously[6]. In the discussions of inhibition on the dependence and in execution, inhibition in security should be borne in mind.

1 *Dove v Henderson* (1865) 3M.339.
2 *Wilson v Wilson* 1981 SLT 101.
3 For a recent case, see *Pow v Pow* 1987 SLT 127, 1987 SCLR 290.
4 *Gretton* pp 12–13.
5 Family Law (Scotland) Act 1985, s 19.
6 HRM Macdonald *A Guide to the Family Law (Scotland) Act 1985* p 61.

Nature of claim

4.66   As a general rule, the conclusions of the action must be pecuniary and so it would not be competent to inhibit on the dependence of actions of reduction or declarator and it is not possible to get round that by claiming that the inhibition is in respect only of expenses[1]. However, once expenses have been awarded, inhibition would be competent[2].

There are some exceptions to the need for a pecuniary claim. There is some authority for the view that inhibition is competent in an action relating to the defender's heritage, eg, an action to implement a contract of sale or of lease[3]. Another exception arises under the Family Law (Scotland) Act 1985 which provides that it is competent to inhibit in respect of a property transfer order but the court can restrict the inhibition to the specific property[4]. The safe course would be to resort to inhibition in such a case because the property transfer order is not registrable in either the Register of Sasines (Land Register) or the Register of Inhibitions and Adjudications.

1 *Weir v Otto* (1870) 8M 1070.
2 See opinion of Lord Cowan in *Weir v Otto* (1870) 8M 1070 at 1071.
3 *Barstow v Menzies* (1840) 2 D 611; *Seaforth's Trs v Macaulay* (1844) 7 D 180. Whether inhibition
  may be used in respect of an action enforcing a standard security, see above at para 4.64.
4 Family Law (Scotland) Act 1985, s 19(1).

Procedure

4.67   The principal methods by which a warrant to inhibit may be obtained are by: (1) Bill and Letters; (2) summons, and; (3) motion[1].

At one time, the only competent procedure was by Bill and Letters. Even today, there is only one exception and that is where there is a depending cause in the Court of Session where the warrant to inhibit may be incorporated in the summons of sought in a separate motion. In other cases, the procedure must be by Bill and Letters, ie where the inhibition is used in execution of a Court of Session decree where inhibition was not granted on the dependence, or where it is used on a document of debt, or on the dependence of an action in or in execution of a decree of, the sheriff court.

1 W W McBryde and N J Dowie *Petition Procedure in the Court of Session* (1st edn, 1980)
  pp 45–49.

BILL AND LETTERS

4.68   A Bill has to be prepared narrating the grounds on which inhibition is sought, ie the decree, or the action, or the document of debt. If the inhibition is in security, the special circumstances must also be set out and if used under the Family Law (Scotland) Act 1985, 'cause' must be shown. The Bill must be signed by the solicitor for the applicant and presented to the General Department of the Court of Session along with the supporting documentation referred to, namely, the decree, or a certified copy of the summons or of the initial writ together with the execution of service, or the service copy of the summons in a summary cause with the execution of service.

If the Bill is in order, it will be granted, but if there is some doubt, the matter will be referred to the Lord Ordinary[1]. There is no appeal from a refusal by the Lord Ordinary, but in exceptional circumstances, he can refer the matter to the court. Whenever the Bill is granted, the Clerk will write on it 'Fiat ut Petitur,' which is authority for the Letters to pass the Signet. The Letters are then prepared by the applicant's solicitor. They run in the name of the Crown and the Titles to Land Consolidation (Scotland) Act 1868 provides that the Letters 'may be in the form or as nearly as may be' of Schedule QQ to that Act. The signeted Letters contain the warrant to inhibit. The old form of letters still appears to be competent but is never used in practice.

1 Court of Session Act 1988, s 49(2).

SUMMONS

4.69 By rule 74 of the Rules of Court, the signeting of a summons which includes an application for a warrant to inhibit has the same effect as signeted Letters.

MOTION

4.70 By rule 74(d), the Lord Ordinary may grant warrant to inhibit on the basis of a motion only where the cause is still depending and the original summons did not contain the necessary application. The certified copy interlocutor in such a case is the equivalent of signeted Letters[1]. In addition, a warrant to inhibit may be applied for in a minute of amendment citing additional defenders, or a substitute defender[2] in an order authorising a third party notice[3], in a counterclaim[4]: and in an application by the Lord Advocate under the Criminal Justice (Scotland) Act 1987. In terms of section 11 of that Act, the Lord Advocate may apply to the Court of Session for warrant to inhibit any person who is the subject of a restraint order, the effect of which is to prevent a person who is suspected of drug trafficking from disposing of property[5]. The warrant for inhibition, if granted, has the same effect as a warrant granted on the dependence of an action for debt.

1 *Fisher v Weir* 1964 SLT (Notes) 99.
2 RC 74(f).
3 RC 85(1)(b).
4 RC 84(c).
5 Drug trafficking is defined in the Criminal Justice (Scotland) Act 1987, s 11(1).

Notice

4.71 As a general rule, an inhibition takes effect only from the date of recording in the Register of Inhibitions and Adjudications[1] but there is one exception which is by recording a notice of inhibition which is provided for in section 155 of the 1868 Act[2]. Such a notice should be in the form set out in Schedule PP to the Act[2] or as nearly as may be, and should conform with the terms of the warrant, either the Letters or the summons. The terms of section 155 exclude the use of a notice of inhibition where the warrant is other than Letters or a summons. The notice may be recorded in the Register of Inhibitions and Adjudications prior to the recording of the inhibition, and even prior to service. If having done that, the inhibiting creditor records his inhibition within twenty-one days, the inhibition will take effect from the date of the notice. The purpose of recording a notice is to give the inhibiting creditor an advantage where a delay or a warning to the debtor might mean that the inhibition did not have the desired effect. If the notice is used, the debtor could therefore be inhibited without being aware of the fact.

1 Criminal Justice (Scotland) Act 1987, s 11(1).
2 Titles to Land Consolidation (Scotland) Act 1868.

Service

4.72 Inhibition must be served on the debtor and it must be served by a messenger-at-arms. If there is no resident messenger, or service has to be in one of the Islands, a sheriff officer who is authorised to practice in any part of the sheriff court district may serve it[1]. Service may be personal, or at the debtor's dwellinghouse, or it may be done edictally[2]. The terms of RC 74(a) do not make it clear whether postal service is competent, but in practice, inhibitions are not served by post. The person effecting service will serve the warrant and also a schedule of inhibition and then return it to the inhibiting creditor with an execution of service which is essential for the recording of the inhibition. The Keeper can refuse to accept an inhibition if he does not consider it valid, but he runs the risk of being made liable in damages if he is proved wrong[3]. Once it is recorded, the inhibition is deemed to have been intimated to all persons, because the Register of Inhibitions and Adjudications is a public register, not only in the sense that it is open to the public but also in the sense that the public are deemed to have knowledge of its contents.

Unlike arrestment on the dependence, inhibition on the dependence cannot be served prior to the service of the summons or initial writ of the action[4].

1 Execution of Diligence (Scotland) Act 1926, s 1.
2 RC 74–75.
3 *Davidson v Mackenzie* (1856) 19 D 226.
4 See above at para 4.02.

Extinction of inhibitions

4.73 Inhibitions on the dependence are extinguished if the creditor fails to obtain decree in the action. All inhibitions are extinguished by: (a) payment; (b) discharge; (c) recall; (d) death; (e) prescription. The extinction may be total which is usual, or partial, either restricted to a particular property or a particular transaction.

FAILURE TO OBTAIN DECREE

4.74 'If the action shall not terminate in decree, the inhibition has no effect',[1]. In such circumstances, the debtor is entitled to a discharge at the inhibiting creditor's expense, and the debtor would probably be entitled to recover his own agent's expenses as well[2].

1 Bell *Comm* II, 138.
2 *Graham Stewart* p 573 (recall); *Gretton* p 44.

PAYMENT

4.75   In exchange for payment, the debtor is entitled to a discharge, but he must meet the expense of that[1].

1 *Graham Stewart* p 573.

DISCHARGE

4.76   A discharge is a formal document evidencing the extinction usually because payment has been made. Normally the discharge will be required by the debtor, in which event the debtor will be liable for the expenses[1]. If, however the reason for the discharge is the failure to obtain decree, the inhibitor pays the expenses. The discharge should be recorded in the Register of Inhibitions and Adjudications because the debtor will wish that, and a purchaser would be entitled to reject the title as unmarketable if an apparently undischarged inhibition appears on the search[2]. There is no mechanism for registering the discharge on the title sheet of the Land Register but the Keeper can note such other information as he thinks fit[3] and a discharge would be noted in this way.

1 *Graham Stewart* p 573.
2 *Dryburgh v Gordon* (1896) 24 R 1, 4 SLT 173; *Newcastle Building Society v White* 1987 SLT (Sh Ct) 81.
3 Land Registration (Scotland) Act 1979, s 6(1)(g).

RECALL

4.77   An inhibition on the dependence can be recalled on payment, caution, consignation, on evidence of nimiety and oppression, or if there has been a procedural irregularity. Of these grounds, the first is obvious.

Caution, consignation and nimiety

4.78   These justify recall on the basis that it would be inequitable to continue with the inhibition. It seems clear from the authorities that in considering whether to recall where there is caution or consignation, the courts will assess the likelihood of success[1] and the rules of court permit the judge to determine the amount to be consigned and the adequacy of the caution[2].

1 *Turnbull Tr v Turnbull* (1823) 2 S 450; *Hay v Morrison* (1838) 16 S 1273.
2 RC 238; *David McAlpine Properties Ltd v Jack Jarvis (Kirkcaldy) Ltd* 1987 GWD 10–620; *Arch Joinery Contracts Ltd v Arcade Building Services* 1989 GWD 8–352.

Nimiety or oppression

4.79   This notion is incapable of definition, but a number of examples are given by Gretton of where the courts have permitted recall on this ground[1]. He suggests that local authorities, state corporations and 'blue chip' organisations might be regarded as having such sufficient financial standing that the pursuer would not require the interim security of an inhibition on the dependence.

1 *Gretton* p 36.

Irregularity

4.80 An inhibition will be recalled if the warrant for it is missing or defective or where it has been executed irregularly eg where a copy of the inhibition was left for the defender at a house where he stayed for a few days prior to emigrating[1].

1 *Morton v Smith* (1902) 9 SLT 396.

Procedure

4.81 Inhibitions may be recalled by petition, or motion or a letter of application.

While an inhibition on the dependence may be recalled by petition, it may also be recalled by motion in a Court of Session action which is still depending[1]. However where the cause has not called, the procedure is to apply to the Deputy Principal Clerk by letter. He will arrange a hearing before a Lord Ordinary[2].

1 RC 74(i).
2 RC 74(g).

Expenses of recall

4.82 The expenses of recall are usually determined not by the outcome of the action, but by the circumstances surrounding recall. If the reason for the recall is some fault on the part of the inhibiting creditor eg that the inhibition is nimious or oppressive, or irregular, the expenses of the recall must be met by the inhibitor[1]. That would also be the result if the inhibitor failed in the principal action[2]. However, the issue of expenses is uncertain in other cases such a recall on caution, or consignation, or settlement[3].

1 *Graham Stewart* p 573.
2 *Graham Stewart* p 573.
3 *Graham Stewart* p 573, cf *Gretton* pp 39–40.

DEATH

4.83 The effect of death of the debtor has already been discussed[1].

1 See above at para 4.73.

PRESCRIPTION

4.84 An inhibition prescribes five years from the day on which it is recorded in the Personal Register or five years from the date of the notice (if the inhibition is recorded within twenty-one days)[1]. The present provision repeats that in the 1874 Act[2]. Inhibitions are not now renewable, but re-inhibition is competent[3].

1 Conveyancing (Scotland) Act 1924, s 44.

2 Conveyancing (Scotland) Act 1874, s 42.
3 Conveyancing (Scotland) Act 1924, s 44(6).

Prescription and reduction

4.85 One matter which remains unresolved is whether on the expiry of inhibition by prescription, any deeds or debts granted in contravention of the inhibition cease to be voidable. If the inhibition prescribes and that has the effect of validating otherwise voidable transactions, there would be a strange result. If A inhibited B in January 1984 and B granted a disposition in February 1984, the inhibition prescribes in January 1989 and the disposition once voidable is now valid. A disposition granted in December 1988 would also become valid in January 1989. Although this may be the result of section 44 of the Conveyancing (Scotland) Act 1924, that has been questioned[1].

1 See *Gretton* pp 46–48; D J Cusine 'Further Thoughts on Inhibitions' (1987) 32 JLSS 66.

CHAPTER 5

NON-EARNINGS ARRESTMENT

INTRODUCTION

5.01 Arrestment is a diligence used against moveable property of the debtor which is not in his possession. It is a diligence involving three parties. A creditor may use arrestment against the debtor where the debtor is himself owed money by a third party, or where the third party is in possession of property of the debtor's. The creditor is known as the arrester; the third party who owes a debt to the debtor or who is in possession of the debtor's property is the arrestee; and the debtor is termed the common debtor[1].

By using an arrestment in the hands of the arrestee, the arresting creditor achieves the effect of preventing the arrestee from making payment of his debt to the common debtor or returning the common debtor's property to him. However, arrestment is an incomplete or inchoate diligence. Although it establishes a nexus or attachment over the arrested goods or funds, it does not of itself give the arresting creditor any title to the goods or funds. To achieve such a title the arrestee must take a further step by way of an action of furthcoming, though in most circumstances in practice a more informal arrangement is made among the parties concerned.

1 For an explanation of this somewhat confusing terminology, see Bell *Comm* II, 63.

WARRANT TO ARREST IN EXECUTION

5.02 Warrant to execute an arrestment in execution (other than an arrestment of earnings) is contained in an extract of decree for payment of money pronounced by the Court of Session, the High Court of Justiciary, the Court of Teinds and the sheriff court[1]. Extract of a document registered in the Books of Council and Session or in sheriff court books which contains an obligation to pay a sum of money is also warrant for arrestment in execution[2].

Any such warrant also implies a warrant to dismantle a ship in the case of an arrestment of a ship[3].

A reference in any enactment to an order being enforceable in like manner as a recorded decree arbitral is to be construed as a reference to such an order being enforceable in like manner as an extract registered decree arbitral bearing a warrant for execution issued by the sheriff court of any sheriffdom in Scotland[4].

1 1987 Act, s 87(1), (2); Sheriff Court (Scotland) Extracts Act 1892, s 7(1). See discussion in ch 1 above at paras 1.57, 1.63.

2 Writs Execution (Scotland) Act 1877, s 3.
3 *English's Coasting & Shipping Co Ltd v British Finance Company Ltd* (1886) 14 R 220, 223, 224.
4 1987 Act, Sch 6, para 1.

SERVICE OF ARRESTMENT

5.03 An arrestment in execution is made by service of a schedule of arrestment on the arrestee. Service is made by officer of court in the presence of one witness[1]. The modes of service are:
(i)   personal;
(ii) 'dwelling house';
(iii) postal in the case of certain types of summary cause and small claims decrees;
(iv) service on persons furth of Scotland, including edictal service.
These modes of service are considered in more detail elsewhere[2].

1 Debtors (Scotland) Act 1838, s 32.
2 See ch 7 below at paras 7.06–7.12.

SUBJECTS ARRESTABLE AND NON-ARRESTABLE

Subjects arrestable

GENERAL; OBLIGATION TO ACCOUNT

5.04 All debts owing by the arrestee to the common debtor and all moveable property of the common debtor held by the arrestee may be arrested in the hands of the arrestee provided that at the time of the arrestment the arrestee is under an obligation to account for the debt or moveable property to the common debtor. The crucial aspect of this principle is the existence of an obligation to account which is truly what is attached by an arrestment[1].

As concerns debts as the subject of an arrestment, the 'debts may be pure or conditional, constituted or unconstituted, liquid or illiquid, in short, every claim of a moveable nature, though its extent or validity depends on the issue of a suit may be arrested'[2].

This section examines some examples of subjects which are or are not arrestable on the basis of the general principle as stated above[3]. There is also some discussion of various categories of debts or moveable property which are exempt from arrestment.

1 *Shankland v McGildowny* 1912 SC 857, 862; *Caldwell v Hamilton* 1919 SC (HL) 100, 119.
2 *Graham Stewart* p 44.
3 See ch 4 above at paras 4.34–4.39 for a more detailed discussion of arresting an obligation to account.

BANK, BUILDING SOCIETY ACCOUNTS

5.05 Funds held on an account with a bank or building society are commonly-used subjects of arrestment. The practice in serving the schedule of arrestment is to deliver the schedule to the head office of the bank with a copy sent to the local branch where it is believed the common debtor has his account. The head office then circularises details of the arrestment to its branches. The Scottish banks will reveal the extent to which an arrestment in execution has attached funds belonging to the debtor but will not divulge any information as to whether an arrestment on the dependence has attached anything.

Two particular points about arresting bank accounts may be noted:

Location of the account

5.06 Whether an arrestment served in Scotland has effect on property or debts outside Scotland may be considered in the present context, as in practice these difficulties most typically arise for arrestees such as banks and building societies with branches in more then one legal system. In particular, complex issues arise concerning the effect of an arrestment served on a bank or building society in Scotland on an account held by the common debtor/customer at one of its English branches[1].

General principle suggests that an arrestment is effective where at the time of the service of the arrestment, the common debtor could have established jurisdiction against the arrestee and taken steps to enforce payment in Scotland. Accordingly, much depends on the particular terms of the contract between the common debtor and the arrestee. In *Ewing v McLelland*[2], it was held that an arrestment of a claim under a contract of insurance, served on the insurer's Scottish office, was ineffectual where the insurer was an English company with its head office in England, the insured property was situated in Ireland, and the mode of payment was through the agent who effected the insurance. In that case the agent was based in Ireland. Similarly, in *J Verrico & Co Ltd v Australian Mutual Provident Society*[3], it was held that it was a term of a contract of insurance between the common debtor and arrestees that sums due under policies were payable only at the London office of the arrestees. Accordingly, an arrestment served on the arrestee's Glasgow branch was ineffectual.

On the other hand there are several decisions which clearly establish the principle that provided the common debtor could have established jurisdiction and sued for payment in Scotland, an arrestment served on the arrestee in Scotland attaches funds due even if the account is held in England or somewhere else furth of Scotland[4].

The problems which exist for the arrestee in this situation are a possible double jeopardy in that by giving effect to the arrestment, as required by Scots law, the arrestee may be open to action by the customer in England. This could arise where the courts in England hold that the proper law of the contract of an account located in England is English law[5], and that no recognition is to be given in England to a Scottish arrestment served in Scotland in respect of such an account[6].

---

1 Where the arrested subject is a corporeal moveable, it must be located in Scotland for an arrestment to have effect over it: *Clan Line Steamers Ltd v Earl of Douglas Steamship Co Ltd* 1913 SC 967, 972.
2 (1860) 33 Sc J 1.
3 1972 SLT (Sh Ct) 57.
4 See *Rae v Neilson* (1742) Mor 716; *Dunn's Exor v Canada Investment and Agency Co Ltd* (1898, unreported); *Wallace & McNeil on Banking Law* (9th edn) p 205; *Hopper & Co v Walker* (1903) 20 Sh Ct Rep 137; *McNairn v McNairn* 1959 SLT (Notes) 35; *O'Brien v A Davies & Son Ltd* 1961 SLT 85; *Brash v Brash* 1966 SC 56; *Graham Stewart* p 34.

5 *Joachimson v Swiss Bank Corporation* [1921] 3 KB 110; *Richardson v Richardson* [1927] P 228; *Libyan Arab Foreign Bank v Manufacturers Hanover Trust Co* [1989] 4 CL § 48.
6 Cp *Rossano v Manufacturers Life Insurance Co Ltd* [1963] 2 QB 352; *Power Curber International Ltd v National Bank of Kuwait SAK* [1981] 1 WLR 1233. For discussion of English law on this point, see Dicey & Morris *Conflict of Laws* (11th edn), pp 966–968.

Foreign currency account

5.07 Where the common debtor holds a foreign currency account in Scotland, the bank owes to the common debtor a duty to account in respect of it, and it is clearly arrestable by the creditors of the common debtor. Where decree is granted for a sum in a non-sterling currency, a conversion of the sum due into sterling is normally made at the date of extracting the decree[1]. However, this conversion is made solely for the purpose of enforcing the decree and if the foreign currency account is in the same currency as the currency of the decree, it is submitted that there is no need to convert the sum as stated in the decree[2].

The situation is less clear where the decree is for payment of a sum in sterling or in a sum in a different foreign currency from that of the foreign currency account. Again the need to convert is a purely practical one and it is submitted that any such extract decree can be the basis of an arrestment served on a bank for arrestment of the sum specified in the extract, as converted if needs be into any foreign currency in which the account is kept[3]. The rate of conversion will be that applicable as at the date of the service of the schedule of the arrestment.

1 *Commerzbank AG v Large* 1977 SC 375. For further discussion see ch 1 above at para 1.48.
2 Cp *Commerzbank* at p 383, citing *Miliangos v George Frank (Textiles) Ltd* [1976] AC 443 at 502.
3 Cp *Choice Investments Ltd v Jeromnimon* [1981] 1 QB 149.

DEPOSIT RECEIPT

5.08 Where money is deposited on terms such as 'in the name of A for B' much depends on the circumstances as to whether A or B is the customer to whom the bank owes an obligation to account, and accordingly whether it is the creditor of A or B who may arrest the funds in the hands of the bank[1].

The range of circumstances is illustrated in a number of cases. In *Union Bank of Scotland v Mills*[2], it was held that where money was deposited in the name of 'A in trust' but without there being any beneficiary specified, A was the customer and that the unnamed beneficiary could not be a common debtor in respect of an arrestment served on the bank[3]. Even where money is deposited by one person in trust for a *named* party, it is not always the case that the named party is the bank's customer to whom the bank owes a duty to account[4].

A deposit receipt may be put in so-called 'joint' names. This does not mean that the funds become a species of joint property. The fact that the deposit receipt is in 'joint' names of 'A and B' does not prevent the arrestment of the funds where only one or other of the parties A and B is the common debtor[5].

1 See *Royal Bank of Scotland v Skinner* 1931 SLT 382, 386. In this case a bank passbook was in the name of 'J M Skinner for Mrs Duncan Cameron'. It was held that Mrs Cameron was the customer of the bank and Skinner merely her agent.
2 (1926) 42 Sh Ct Rep 141.
3 Where money is held in the name of a solicitor under the heading of 'client account', the solicitor and not the client is the bank's customer and the funds are arrestable by the solicitor's creditors: *Plunkett v Barclays Bank* [1936] 2 KB 107, 118–119.

4 *Rigby v Fletcher* (1833) 11 S 256; *Lindsay v London and North West Railway Company* (1860) 22 D
   571. In *McAdam v Martin's Trustees* (1872) 11 M 32, a solicitor was sent funds by a client in
   respect of a particular transaction. The solicitor put the funds into an account in his own name
   until the transaction was completed. The solicitor was then sequestrated. The court held that
   as the money had been given to the solicitor for a specific purpose and was still distinguishable
   from his own funds, it did not come within the sequestration of his estate. In this case the court
   put some emphasis on the fact that the purpose and ultimate destination of the money appeared
   clearly from the various papers of the parties, including the entries in the books of the bank (see
   Lord Ardmillan at p 37). See also *National Bank v MacQueen* (1881) 18 SLR 683; *Clark v
   National Bank of Scotland* (1890) 27 SLR 628.
5 *Allan's Exor v Union Bank of Scotland* 1909 SC 206.

NATIONAL SAVINGS BANK DEPOSITS

5.09   Funds in a deposit account in the National Savings Bank, which at one
time were exempt from arrestment, may now be arrested[1].

1 Crown Proceedings Act 1947, s 46; Law Reform (Miscellaneous Provisions) (Scotland) Act
   1985, s 49; *Brooks Associates Incorporation v Basu* [1983] QB 220.

FEES, COMMISSIONS

5.10   Payments due as fees or commission for work done or to be done
under a contract for services (*locatio operis faciendi*) are arrestable[1]. The view is
taken that as the parties' contract is complete, the duty to pay is arrestable
even though the actual payment may be conditional upon satisfactory
execution of the works to be done[2].

Where the relationship between the parties is one of employer–employee
under a contract of employment (*locatio operarum*), payment due as earnings
under the contract are attachable only by means of an arrestment against
earnings[3].

1 *Marshall v Nimmo & Co* (1847) 10 D 328; *MacLaren v Preston* (1893) 1 SLT 75 (sum of money
   due as commission for sale of a ship, arrested before sale concluded).
2 'When a contract is made to perform work for a price to be paid on the completion of it to the
   satisfaction of the employer, the rights of the contractor to the stipulated price is no doubt
   conditional on the completion on the work to the employer's satisfaction; but, subject to that
   condition, the right is established or vested in the contractor by the conclusion of the contract':
   Park Dobson & Co v Wm Taylor & Son 1929 SC 571 at 579, per Lord President Clyde.
3 1987 Act, Part III. For further discussion see below at para 5.30 and ch 6 at para 6.03.

RENTS, PERIODICAL PAYMENTS, ANNUITIES

5.11   Rents and other periodical payments may be arrested in respect of
what is due (including interest) at the time of the arrestment[1]. Arrestment
will also catch any arrears owing at the time of service of the arrestment.
Where the rents etc have been paid in advance of the time when they are due, a
subsequent arrestment will not catch them unless it can be shown that the
advance payment was not made in good faith[2].

Similarly an annuity may be arrested in respect of what is due as arrears and
for the current term[3]. If arrangements have been made to pay the annuity in
advance, an arrestment will attach only unpaid arrears[4].

1 Bell's *Comm* II 72; *Livingston v Kinloch* (1795) Mor 769; *Smith & Kinnear v Burns* (1847) 9 D
   1344.
2 *Graham Stewart* pp 50–51.

3 *Corse v Masterton* (1705) Mor 767; *Clunie's Creditors v Sinclair* (1739) Mor 772; *Seton v Caithness* (1761) Mor 772; *Graham Stewart* pp 52–53.
4 *Smith & Kinnear v Burns* (1847) 9 D 1344; *Davidson v Mackay & Skene* (1887) 4 SLR 100.

BONDS AND DEBENTURES

5.12   Personal bonds and debentures are arrestable for the principal sum and interest[1]. Heritable bonds which have not been followed by infeftment may also be arrested for principal and interest. Where a heritable bond has been duly constituted by infeftment, an arrestment attaches only past due and current interest[2].

1 *Stuart v Stuart* (1705) Mor 140, 703. See generally *Graham Stewart* pp 46–49.
2 *Simpson v White* (1633) Mor 698.

INSURANCE POLICIES

5.13   Where payments of proceeds under an insurance policy depend upon claims made on the basis of the occurrence of an event before any payment is due, an arrestment cannot attach anything until the insurer's liability arises[1]. In the case of life assurance, the proceeds of the policy may be arrested while the insured is still alive, even if further premiums are paid subsequent to the arrestment[2].

1 *Kerr v R & W Ferguson* 1931 SC 736; cp *Boland v White Cross Insurance Association* 1926 SC 1066.
2 *Strachan v McDougle* (1835) 13 S 954; *Bankhardt's Trustees v Scottish Amicable Assurance Society* (1871) 9 M 443. For the mode of disposal of the policy at the furthcoming see *Clark v Scottish Amicable Assurance Company* (1922) 38 Sh Ct Rep 170.

CLAIMS FOR AND AWARDS OF DAMAGES

5.14   Awards of damages may be arrested in the hands of the party found liable to pay, by the creditor of the successful party to the action for damages[1]. As an award of damages has effect as finding the damages due as at the date of raising the action for damages[2], claims of damages may be arrested before any award is made, provided the action for damages has been raised[3].

A similar principle applies in respect of court awards under other headings, for example redundancy payments and orders of industrial tribunals[4].

Awards of compensation by the Criminal Injuries Compensation Board under the Criminal Injuries Compensation Scheme may not be arrested in the hands of the Board[5].

1 *Alexander Mather & Sons v John Wilson & Co* (1908) 15 SLT 946 (where the arrestment was defeated by the defenders' insurers paying a sum in settlement, after motion for a new jury trial had been granted).
2 *Wardrop v Fairholm & Arbuthnot* (1744) Mor 4860.
3 *Riley v Ellis* 1910 SC 934 at 944–945, per Lord President Dunedin; see *Caldwell v Hamilton* 1919 SC (HL) 100.
4 Cp 1987 Act, s 73(3)(g).
5 Criminal Justice Act 1988, s 117.

EXPENSES

5.15   An award of expenses against a litigant to be paid to another litigant is arrestable by the creditors of that other party[1]. Expenses may be arrested even if the amount to be paid is not ascertained[2].

1 *Donoghue v Stevenson* 1932 SLT 520; *Agnew v Norwest Construction Company* 1935 SC 71.
2 *Agnew v Norwest Construction Company* 1935 SC 71.

SHARES

5.16 Shares held in a company represent a duty on the company to account to the shareholder[1]. Accordingly, creditors of the shareholder may arrest shares in the hands of the company, provided it is a company which is registered in Scotland[2]. As the duty of accountability is owed by the company to the registered shareholder, arrestment of the shares cannot be made by a creditor of another party unless the arrester can show that there is a direct accountability by the company to that other party. In *Blade Securities Ltd Petr*[3], arrestments were declared incompetent where a pursuer sought to arrest on the dependence of an action shares, which were averred to be held by the registered owners as mere nominees for the defender in the action.

Although in general a subsidiary company cannot hold shares in its holding company[4], a subsidiary company creditor may arrest shares in its holding company in respect of a debt owing by the registered shareholder[5]. In such a case a subsequent furthcoming must conclude for the sale of the shares rather than their transfer to the subsidiary company.

1 *American Mortgage Company of Scotland Ltd v Sidway* 1909 SC 500, 505.
2 *Sinclair v Staples* (1860) 22 D 60; *American Mortgage Company of Scotland Ltd v Sidway* 1909 SC 500.
3 1989 SLT 246; see also *Lindsay v L & N W Railway Company* (1860) 22 D 571.
4 Companies Act 1985, s 23.
5 *Stenhouse London Ltd v Allwright* 1972 SC 209.

CALLS ON SHARES

5.17 Where a company has made a call on a shareholder, the amount due by the shareholder may be arrested by the creditor of the company[1]. As the amount due on subscribed shares is a contingent debt until called up, such uncalled capital is not arrestable[2].

1 *Hill v College of Glasgow* (1849) 12 A 46; cp *Queensland Mercantile & Agency Ltd v Australian Investment Company Ltd* (1888) 15 R 935.
2 *Lindsay v La Martona Rubber Estates Ltd* 1911 2 SLT 468.

PARTNERSHIP INTEREST

5.18 The creditor of an individual who is also a partner in a partnership may arrest the debtor's interest in the partnership[1]. However, while the partnership continues, the debtor remains a partner and his interests are still regulated by the terms of the partnership agreement[2]. The arrestment cannot be followed by a furthcoming until the partnership is dissolved[3]. A creditor of an individual partner cannot arrest in respect of claim against the debtor as an individual funds in the hands of a third party due to the partnership itself[4].

1 *Cassells v Stewart* (1879) 6 R 936, 956.
2 *Rae v Neilson* (1742) Mor 716.
3 Ersk *Inst* III, 3, 24.
4 *Parnell v Walter* (1889) 16 R 917.

TRUST FUNDS

5.19   The right of a beneficiary under a trust is arrestable if it is of a moveable nature at the time of the arrestment[1]. The beneficiary may have an interest in the trust of a moveable nature, even if the trust estate itself is heritable[2].

The creditors of the truster may arrest any right of reversion of a moveable nature[3].

1 *Smith's Trustees v Grant* (1862) 24 D 1142; *Chamber's Trustees v Smiths* (1878) 5 R (HL) 151.
2 *Grierson v Ramsay* (1780) Mor 759; *Douglas v Mason* (1796) Mor 16213; *Learmonts v Shearer* (1866) 4 M 540.
3 *Cameron v McEwen* (1830) 8 S 440; *Renton v Girvan* (1833) 12 S 266; *Graham Stewart* pp 60–61, 65.

LEGITIM; TESTAMENTARY BEQUESTS

5.20   A non-vested *spes successionis* cannot be arrested. However, the right to legitim, once vested from the death of the person from whom it is claimed, may be arrested in the hands of the deceased's executor or trustee[1]. Testamentary bequests once vested may also be arrested in the hands of the executor by the creditors of the beneficiary[2].

1 *Waddell v Waddell's Trustees* 1932 SLT 201.
2 For a useful discussion as to the rules of vesting, see R B M Howie 'Vesting' in *The Laws of Scotland: Stair Memorial Encyclopaedia* vol 25, paras 906 et seq.

CORPOREAL MOVEABLES

5.21   Corporeal moveables belonging to the common debtor may be arrested when they are in the hands of someone other than the common debtor or the arresting creditor[1] who has an obligation to account in respect of them to the common debtor[2]. In most cases this obligation to account will reflect a recognised form of contract between the common debtor and the third party[3].

Examples of arrestment in the hands of parties who owe an obligation to account to the common debtor in respect of goods belonging to the common debtor include goods in the possession of: a carrier[4]; a factor[5]; a depositary[6]; a custodier[7]; an auctioneer[8]; a banker[9]; a solicitor[10] and a trustee[11].

On the other hand, where a third party is merely holding the goods for the common debtor, such as with an innkeeper[12], or hotel owner[13], the goods are treated as being still in the possession of the common debtor and the appropriate diligence is poinding, not arrestment[14].

1 The anomalous right of an unpaid seller to arrest goods of the debtor in his own hands under s 40 of the Sale of Goods Act 1979 has been abolished by the 1987 Act, Sch 8.
2 But not where the obligation to account is owed to someone else: *Young v Aktiebolaget Ofverums Bank* (1890) 18 R 163; *Heron v Winfields Ltd* (1894) 22 R 182.
3 *Graham Stewart* pp 107–108.
4 *Matthew v Fawns* (1842) 4 D 1242; *Lindsay v L & N W Railway Company* (1860) 22 D 571; *N B Railway v White* (1881) 9 R 97; *Frederick Braby & Co Ltd v Edwin Danks & Co* (1907) 15 SLT 161.
5 *Dunlop v Weir* (1823) 2 S 167.
6 *Appin's Creditors* (1760) Mor 749; *Bridges v Ewing* (1830) 15 S 8.
7 *Inglis v Robertson & Baxter* (1898) 25 R (HL) 70; *Moore & Weinberg v Ernsthausen Ltd* 1917 SC (HL) 25.

8 *Mackenzie & Co v Finlay & Ors* (1868) 7 M 27.
9 *Graham v Macfarlane* (1869) 7 M 640.
10 *Brown v Blaikie* (1850) 13 D 149; *Telford's Executor v Blackwood* (1866) 4 M 369.
11 *Graham Stewart* p 108.
12 *Hume v Baillie* (1852) 14 D 821.
13 *Hutchison v Hutchison* 1912 1 SLT 219.
14 A special case where the common debtor retains civil possession arises where his goods have been stolen and come in to the hands of the police or procurator fiscal: *Stuart v Cowan & Co* (1883) 10 R 581; *Jopp v McHardy* (1890) Guthrie's Sh Ct Ca 2, 145; *Guthrie v Morren* (1939) 55 Sh Ct Rep 172. Whether the goods of a landlord in the possession of his tenants may be arrested is discussed in ch 7 below at para 7.29.

SHIPS

5.22 Arrestment, rather than poinding, is the appropriate diligence against a ship, even where the ship is in the hands of the debtor or his agent[1]. The arrestment of a ship covers all the immediate machinery in the ship and all instruments which are essential to its functioning[2]. A share of a ship may be arrested.

A ship in the course of construction may be arrested as a maritime subject provided that at the time of arrestment it has acquired the identity of a ship[3].

The arrestment of a ship does not attach freight, which may be arrested as a debt in the normal way[4]. Nor does arrestment of a ship arrest cargo which must be separately arrested[5].

1 *Barclay Curle & Co Ltd v Sir James Laing & Son Ltd* 1908 SC 82 at 89. See further ch 7 below at para 7.54.
2 *The Dundee* (1823) 1 Hagg. Adm 109; *Armstrong & Co v MacGregor & Co* (1875) 2 R 339.
3 *Balfour v Stein* 7 June 1808 FC; *Mill v Hoar* FC 18 December 1812. The ship, of course, must belong to the common debtor at the time of the arrestment. See below at para 5.25.
4 *Ranking & Co v Tod* (1870) 8 M 914; *The Norsoen v Mackie, Koth & Co* 1911 SC 172.
5 *Kellas v Brown* (1856) 18 D 1089; *Svenska Petroleum AB v HOR Ltd* 1983 SLT 493, 1986 SLT 513.

Subjects not arrestable

HERITABLE PROPERTY

5.23 Arrestment is a diligence which can be used against debts or property which are of a moveable, rather than heritable, nature at the time of the arrestment[1]. The question of the appropriate diligence to use against fixtures is considered elsewhere[2].

1 *Grierson v Ramsay* (1780) Mor 759; *Douglas v Mason* (1796) Mor 16213; *Learmonts v Shearer* (1866) 4 M 540.
2 See ch 7 below at para 7.28.

PROPERTY IN THE HANDS OF THE CREDITOR, OR THE DEBTOR

5.24 The arrester cannot arrest property in his own hands. Schedule 8 to the 1987 Act abolishes the anomalous situation under section 40 of the Sale of Goods Act 1979 which allows a seller of goods to arrest goods in his own hands.

Nor may goods be arrested which are in the common debtor's actual or deemed possession. In such circumstances the appropriate diligence to use against the property is poinding[1].

However, ships may be arrested in whosoever's hands they are at the time of the arrestment[2].

1 See ch 7 below at para 7.29.
2 See further above at para 5.29.

PROPERTY, DEBTS, NOT THE COMMON DEBTOR'S

5.25 An arrestment can attach only property belonging to, or debts owing to, the common debtor as at the time of the service of the schedule of arrestment. Thus it is incompetent to arrest a debt not owing directly by the arrestee to the common debtor but by the debtor of the arrestee to the arrestee[1]. A debt due to a limited company or a partnership may not be arrested in respect of a debt owed by an individual member or partner[2].

Goods, ownership of which has not yet passed to the debtor[3], or the ownership of which has already passed from the debtor to someone else[4], may not be arrested by the creditor of the debtor.

1 *J & C Murray v Wallace Marrs & Co* 1914 SC 114; cp *Heron v Winfields Ltd* (1894) 22 R 182.
2 *Hay v Dufourcet & Co* (1880) 7 R 972; *Parnell v Walter* (1889) 16 R 917.
3 *Sir James Laing & Sons v Barclay Curle & Co* 1908 SC (HL) 1.
4 *Hope's Trustees v Hope* (1904), 11 SLT 625.

JOINT AND COMMON PROPERTY

5.26 Where property is held by more than one person jointly, ie where the entire property is held indivisibly by all the owners, such property cannot be arrested in respect of debts of any of the owners as individuals[1]. However where property is held on a common basis, ie each owner has a separate title to a specific share in the whole property, the separate interest of each co-owner may be arrested[2].

1 *Fleming v Twaddle* (1828) 7 S 92; *Lucas's Trustees v Campbell & Scott* (1894) 21 R 1096; *Lord Ruthven v Pulford* 1909 SC 951; cp *Smith v Wilson* (1890) 7 Sh Ct Rep 58.
2 Cp *Byng v Campbell* (1893) 1 SLT 371 (overruled on facts of particular terms of lease); *Malcolm v Cook* (1853) 16 D 262; *Graham Stewart* p 197. (This is one case in which an arrestment in execution may be loosed or recalled. The loosing or recall will be on caution.)

SUBJECTS SPECIALLY APPROPRIATED

5.27 Goods or funds which have been appropriated to a particular purpose cannot be arrested by the depositor's creditors so as to defeat the object of the appropriation. However goods or funds not required for the purpose of the appropriation may be arrested[1].

The appropriation of the property of funds must have been made prior to the service of the arrestment[2].

1 *Mackenzie & Co v Finlay* (1868) 7 M 27. For fuller discussion see *Graham Stewart* pp 82–92; W A Wilson *The Law of Scotland relating to Debt* p 221.
2 *National Bank of Scotland v MacQueen* (1881) 18 SLR 683; *British Linen Co v Kansas Investment Co* (1895) 3 SLT 138, 202.

BILLS AND NEGOTIABLE INSTRUMENTS

5.28 Bills and negotiable instruments as mere physical objects are merely documents or vouchers for debt and as such are not arrestable[1]. Where the common debtor is the payee in the bill, the sum in the bill may be attached by arrestment by his creditors in the hands of the acceptor. However, any such arrestment will not prevail against a subsequent indorsement of the bill made to a bona fide indorsee for value[2].

1 *Jamieson v Leckie* (1792) Mor 74; *Dunlop v Jap* (1752) Mor 741; *Graham Stewart* pp 78–80.
2 *Smith v Home* (1712) Mor 711; *Buchanan v Cochrane* (1764) Mor 14208.

DOCUMENTS OF NO INTRINSIC VALUE

5.29 Documents such as writs, evidents, papers, plans, business books etc which are of no intrinsic mercantile value are not arrestable[1].

1 *Trowsdale's Trustee v Forcett Rly Co* (1870) 9 M 88; *Millar & Lang v Poole* (1907) 15 SLT 76.

EARNINGS

5.30 The diligence of arrestment and furthcoming cannot be used to attach the category of earnings set out in section 73(2) of the 1987 Act, to which the new diligences provided for by Part III of the 1987 Act apply[1].

Earnings of serving members of the armed forces are also exempt from arrestment[2]. However, by virtue of sections 150–152 of the Army Act 1955 and Air Force Act 1955, the Defence Council has power to make deductions from the earnings of members of those forces to satisfy maintenance debts. A similar scheme applies to members of the naval forces[3]. The Armed Forces Act 1971 widens the scope of deductions which the Defence Council may make to cover most types of civil debts[4]. There are also restrictions on the use of diligence, including arrestment, against the earnings and property of the reserve and auxiliary forces called out for service or extended training[5].

The position concerning the arrestment of earnings of merchant seamen is not clear. Prior to the 1987 Act the position was that earnings of fishermen were open to the diligence of arrestment and furthcoming. The earnings of non-fishermen were open to arrestment for maintenance debts but not in respect of other types of debt[6]. The intention of the Scottish Law Commission's recommendations was that a similar arrangement should apply to the new diligences against earnings[7]. Certainly the earnings of seamen come within the definition of earnings as set out in the 1987 Act, section 73(2). Moreover section 73(3) of the 1987 Act states that in relation to the enforcement by an earnings arrestment of a debt other than maintenance, the wages of a seaman (other than a member of the crew of a fishing boat) are not to be treated as earnings. What these various definitions leave is the following position. The diligence of current maintenance arrestment may be used against the earnings of both fishermen and non-fishermen seamen. A similar position holds in respect of the use of earnings arrestment for arrears of maintenance. As regards the use of earnings arrestment for a non-maintenance debt the diligence may be used as against the earnings of fishermen but not as against the earnings of non-fishermen.

It is to be noted, however, that the 1987 Act does not exempt, for the purposes of earnings arrestment for a non-maintenance debt, the earnings of non-fishermen seamen from diligence. Rather what it states is that for such purposes such earnings do not count as earnings, and as a consequence do not fall within the provisions of Part III of the 1987 Act which abolishes the common law diligence of arrestment and furthcoming against earnings. This gives rise to a possibility that an old-style diligence of arrestment and furthcoming may be used against the earnings of non-fishermen seamen. Such a possibility would seem to be precluded by the provisions of the Merchant Shipping Acts mentioned above. However Schedule 8 to the 1987 Act specifically repeals both provisions as they apply to arrestment, and accordingly it follows that the diligence of arrestment and furthcoming may be used against the earnings of seamen other than fishermen where the debt to be recovered is not one within the definition of maintenance under section 106 of the 1987 Act. It can also be noted that abolition of the *beneficium competentiae* by section 46(2) of the 1987 Act will not extend to the arrestment of the earnings of non-fishermen where the arrestment is used to recover a debt other than maintenance.

Payments owing as fees or commission to self-employed persons for contract work, although 'earnings' in a loose sense, are not earnings for purposes of section 46 of the 1987 Act, and the new forms of diligence under Part III of the 1987 Act do not apply to them. Arrestment and furthcoming is the appropriate diligence to use to attach such fees[8].

1 See further ch 6 below at paras 6.01–6.03.
2 Army Act 1955, s 203; Air Force Act 1955, s 203.
3 Naval Forces (Enforcement of Maintenance Liabilities) Act 1947.
4 Armed Forces Act 1971, ss 59, 61.
5 Reserve and Auxiliary Forces (Protection of Civil Interest) Act 1951, ss 8, 9.
6 Merchant Shipping Act 1970, s 11(1)(a); Merchant Shipping Act 1979, s 39.
7 Report on Diligence and Debtor Protection (Scot Law Com no 95 (1985)) pp 337–338.
8 See above at para 5.10.

ALIMENTARY PAYMENTS

5.31 Payments made for alimentary purposes, ie in respect of the support and maintenance of the recipient, are not open to arrestment by the creditors of the recipient[1]. A fund is not alimentary merely if it declares that it is not open to the diligence of creditors[2].

Some qualification should be noted to this general rule that alimentary payments are free from arrestment:
(a) the exemption applies only to what is truly alimentary, ie what is needed for the upkeep and maintenance of the recipient. Anything in excess of what is truly alimentary is arrestable[3]. The appropriate level of maintenance and upkeep is to be determined according to the individual circumstances of each case (eg in respect of age, social position, ability of the recipient to keep himself or herself). In the case of alimentary payments made under court order these factors will already have been considered by the court which made the order, and unless there has been a subsequent change in the circumstance of the recipient without a variation of the court order, alimentary court orders are exempt from arrestment;
(b) alimentary payments in arrears may be arrested, the basis of this rule being that if the recipient has taken no steps to recover arrears, they are in excess of what he needs for his maintenance[4];

(c) where the debt for which the arrestment is used is itself an alimentary one, an alimentary provision is open to arrestment[5].

1 *E Buchan v His Creditors* (1835) 13 S 1112; *Lord Ruthven v Pulford & Sons* 1909 SC 951.
2 *Douglas, Gardiner & Mill v Mackintosh's Trustees* 1916 SC 125.
3 *Livingstone v Livingstone* (1886) 14 R 43; *Cuthbert v Cuthbert's Trustees* 1908 SC 967.
4 *Drew v Drew* (1870) 9 M 163; *Muirhead v Miller* (1877) 4 R 1139.
5 *Waddell v Waddell* (1836) 15 S 151; *Lord Ruthven v Pulford & Sons* 1909 SC 951; *Baird v Baird* 1910 1 SLT 95; *Turnbull & Son v Scott* (1899) 15 Sh Ct Rep 268; *Officers' Superannuation and Provident Fund v Cooper* 1976 SLT (Sh Ct) 2.

SOCIAL SECURITY BENEFITS; STATE PENSIONS

5.32 Social security benefits and state pensions are in general subject to a prohibition on any 'assignment or charge', which has the effect of exempting them from diligence[1].

Benefits exempted on this basis include:
unemployment benefit[2]
sickness benefit[2]
invalidity benefit[2]
maternity benefit[2]
widow's allowance and pension[2]
retirement pension[2]
guaranteed minimum pension[3]
child benefit[4]
housing benefit[5]
income support[5]
family credit[6].

Similarly most state-paid pensions are exempt from arrestment, or may be arrested only in certain circumstances, usually where the 'assignment or charge' is made for the benefit of the recipient of the pension[6].

1 *Mulvenna v The Admiralty* 1926 SC 854, 856; *Macfarlane v Glasgow Corporation* (1934) 50 Sh Ct Rep 247; *Sinton v Sinton* 1976 SLT (Sh Ct) 95. Any pension, allowance or benefit payable under any enactment relating to social security does not come within the scope of the new diligences against earnings introduced by Part III of the 1987 Act: 1987 Act, s 73(3)(d), (f).
2 Social Security Act 1975, s 87.
3 Social Security Pensions Act 1975, s 48.
4 Child Benefit Act 1975, s 12.
5 Social Security Act 1986, Sch 10, para 48.
6 Pensions affected include police pensions (Police Pensions Act 1976, s 9); firemen's pensions (Firemen's Pension Scheme Order 1971, SI 1971/145; Fire Services Act 1947, s 26); teachers' pensions (SI 1969/77, reg 75; SI 1969/78, reg 76); local government employees' pensions (SI 1974/812, reg L13); customs and excise officers' pensions (Customs and Excise Act 1952, s 2(2); parliamentary pensions (Parliamentary and other Pensions Act 1987, Schs 1(9), 2(1)). It should also be noted that the new diligences against earnings do not apply to any occupational pension payable under any enactment which precludes the assignation of the pension or excludes it from diligence: 1987 Act, s 73(3)(d).

ARTICLES EXEMPT FROM POINDING UNDER SECTION 16 OF THE 1987 ACT

5.33 Section 16 of the 1987 Act exempts from poinding various goods of the debtor. Where such goods are in the possession of someone other than the debtor, and as such may be open to arrestment, they cannot be arrested if they are exempt from poinding under section 16[1]. Section 16(1) exempts from poinding, and thus also from arrestment, various types of goods of the debtor's, no matter where they are situated but in most cases only where they are reasonably required for the use of the debtor or any member of his household. Section 16(2) exempts from poinding, and also from arrestment, various items of furniture and plenishings belonging to the debtor provided they are situated in a dwellinghouse and are reasonably required for people residing there. Accordingly, household furniture belonging to the debtor which is stored in a warehouse would not be exempt from poinding under section 16, nor from arrestment under section 99, of the 1987 Act.

1 1987 Act, s 99(2).

ROLLING–STOCK OF PRIVATE RAILWAYS

5.34 Rolling-stock and plant of private railways which are open for public traffic are exempt from arrestment in execution[1]. However, this exemption does not apply to arrestment on the dependence[2].

1 Railway Companies (Scotland) Act 1867, s 4; cp *Haldane v Girvan & Portpatrick Railway Company* (1881) 8 R 669. See also below para 7.57.
2 *Graham Stewart* p 104.

CONTINGENT AND FUTURE DEBTS

5.35 Whether debts which are contingent or future in nature may be arrested is discussed in the context of arrestment on the dependence[1].

1 See ch 4 above at para 4.39.

EFFECT OF ARRESTMENT

General effect

5.36 Arrestment is an inchoate diligence and does not operate to transfer any real rights to the arresting creditor, for which an action of furthcoming (or sale) or the informal device of a mandate, is required[1]. One effect of an arrestment is to interpel the arrestee from paying over the debt to the common debtor or handing over the arrested property to him. Where moveable property has been arrested, the arrestee may continue to use it, provided that the goods are not removed from where they have been arrested[2]. The arrestee is under no duty to earmark or invest arrested funds nor to account for interest on the funds[3].

Arrestment has the effect of rendering the arrested subjects litigious, but this does not prevent the common debtor from authorising the arrestee to pay over the funds or property to the arresting creditor[4].

1 *Lord Advocate v Royal Bank of Scotland* 1977 SC 155.
2 Cp *Carlberg v Borjesson* (1877) 5 R 188, 195. For breach of arrestment see below at para 5.39.
3 *Glen Music Co Ltd v City of Glasgow DC* 1983 SLT (Sh Ct) 26.
4 The practice of mandating the release of funds or property to the creditor has been recognised by statute: Bankruptcy (Scotland) Act 1985, s 36(2)(d); Insolvency Act 1986, s 243(2)(d).

Arrestment attaches tantum et tale

5.37 As far as the arresting creditor is concerned, the extent of the right or preference which he obtains by the arrestment is exactly equivalent to the right in the property or debt which the common debtor enjoyed at the time of the arrestment[1]. The creditor takes the inchoate preference secured by the arrestment *tantum et tale* as it stood in the common debtor, and any qualifications to the right of the common debtor in respect of the arrested subject apply also as against the arresting creditor.

A leading illustration of the doctrine of *tantum et tale* in this context is *Chamber's Trs v Smiths*[2] where a trust fund was arrested in the hands of trustees in respect of a debt owed by a legatee who had a vested right to the legacy. However, at the time of the arrestment the trustees retained a power to restrict the extent of the legacy payable to the common debtor. It was held that the trustees could, subsequent to the arrestment, exercise their power so as to prevent the entire legacy being transferred to the creditor in a furthcoming.

Similarly, an arrestment was held not to bar the operation of a subsequent English 'charging order' which had the effect of transferring the debt to the charger[3]; an arrestment may be made of a debt which has already been arrested, but is subject to the preference secured by the prior arresting creditor[4]; an arrestment of a debt is subject to a claim of compensation open to the arrestee as against the common debtor[5].

1 *Chamber's Trustees v Smiths* (1878) 5 R (HL) 151; *Hunter v Hunter's Trustees* (1848) 10 D 922; *Trapp v Meredith* (1871) 10 M 38; *National Bank of Scotland v Adamson* 1932 SLT 492.
2 (1878) 5 R (HL) 151.
3 *North v Stewart* (1890) 17 R (HL) 60.
4 *W H Hill v Mannings Trustees* 1951 SLT (Sh Ct) 29.
5 *Lennie v Mackie & Co* (1907) 23 Sh Ct Rep 85.

Fee for operating arrestment

5.38 As the arrestee's duties in respect of the arrested funds or property are essentially negative, no practice or rule has evolved of allowing the arrestee to recover any expenses which he incurs in processing and maintaining the arrestment in his hands[1]. It may be that where the arrestee is put to great expense or inconvenience in keeping the arrested property, he can seek to have the arrestment recalled on that basis. However, in practice the expense involved as far as concerns arrestees is with processing the service of arrestment, especially where arrestments are served on the head office of banks. In the absence of any express contractual term, a bank cannot deduct a charge against a customer/common debtor[2], and no such remedy would arise where the arrestment proved fruitless as the common debtor was not a customer. It might be that the position of an arrestee is analogous to that of a haver who is entitled to a fee from the party citing him for searching out the documents called for and for copying extracts from them[3]. However, it is uncertain whether this analogy can be pressed far enough to justify an arrestee making a claim against the arrested funds.

1 Section 71 of the 1987 Act allows an employer operating an arrestment against earnings to deduct a fee from the employee's protected earnings. However there is no common law basis for such a charge.

2 Cp *Tai Hing Cotton Mill Ltd v Liu Chong Hing Bank* [1986] AC 80.
3 *Cuthbertson v Elliot* (1860) 22 D 389; *MacKinnon v Guildford* (1894) 2 SLT 309; *Forsyth v Pringle Taylor & Lamond Lawson* (1906) 14 SLT 658.

BREACH OF ARRESTMENT

5.39 If during the validity of an arrestment the arrestee voluntarily pays the debt or delivers the goods arrested to the common debtor or other party, he commits a breach of arrestment. A breach of arrestment is a form of contempt of court but it is unlikely that an arrestee would be held liable for civil contempt, and *a fortiori*, criminal contempt, except in extreme circumstances[1].

An arrestee who is in breach of arrestment by paying over the sum or handing over the property to the common debtor or some other party than the arrester is liable to pay the arrester the value of the arrested sum or property[2]. However, the arrestee has a defence to such a claim if he is unaware that an arrestment has been served[3]. A similar statutory rule applies in respect of an arrestee furth of Scotland[4].

While an arrestment continues in effect, the arrestee may not hand over the arrested funds or property to the arresting creditor except where (1) the common debtor has granted a mandate authorising this transfer or (2) the creditor has obtained decree in an action of furthcoming or multiple-poinding. Where the creditor accepts arrested funds or subjects in the knowledge that their transfer to him is in breach of arrestment, he commits an illegal act and will be requested by the court to return the funds or subjects to the arrestee[5]. The possible prejudice to the common debtor from this situation is obvious in the case of an arrestment on the dependence, but it may be that a less strict view would be taken of unauthorised transfer of arrested goods to the arresting creditor in the case of arrestment in execution unless the common debtor could aver prejudice to him.

The only person who is not liable to repay arrested funds or goods on breach of arrestment is someone who has received them in ignorance of the arrestment[6].

1 *Inglis & Bow v Smith and Aikman* (1867) 5 M 320; *Harvie v Ross* (1887) 24 SLR 250.
2 Breach of Arrestment Act 1581(c 23); *Grant v Hill* (1792) Mor 786. If the value of the arrested subject cannot be ascertained the arrestee is liable for the whole debt due to the arrester: *Macarthur v Bruce* (1760) Mor 803.
3 *Laidlaw v Smith* (1838) 16 S 367, (1841) 2 Rob 490.
4 Debts Securities (Scotland) Act 1856, s 1.
5 *High-Flex (Scotland) Ltd v Kentallen Mechanical Services Company* 1977 SLT (Sh Ct) 91.
6 *High-Flex (Scotland) Ltd v Kentallen Mechanical Services Company* 1977 SLT (Sh Ct) 91, 94.

CESSATION OF ARRESTMENT

5.40 An arrestment is an inchoate diligence and requires completion by way of an action of furthcoming[1]. However, an arrestment may cease to have effect in a number of ways prior to a furthcoming.

1 *Lord Advocate v Royal Bank of Scotland* 1977 SC 155. See further below at paras 5.45–5.51.

Mandate

5.41 Although arrestment has effect in making the arrested subject litigious[1], it has been for long accepted that it is permissible for the common debtor to authorise by mandate (which need not be but invariably is in writing) the arrestee to hand over the arrested subjects or funds to the arresting creditor[2]. Indeed, failure to mandate the payment of the arrested subjects will render the common debtor liable in expenses in a subsequent action of furthcoming[3], and in the vast majority of cases a furthcoming is not in practice required in order to complete the arrestment.

1 Bell *Comm* II, 63–64; *Graham Stewart* p 125; *High-Flex (Scotland) Ltd v Kentallen Mechanical Services Co* 1977 SLT (Sh Ct) 91.
2 This practice has been recognised by statute: Bankruptcy (Scotland) Act 1985, s 36(2)(d); Insolvency Act 1986, s 243(2)(d).
3 See below at para 5.50.

Recall

5.42 As an arrestment in execution proceeds in respect of a debt found to be due, the general rule is that such an arrestment will be recalled only on payment of the debt, including the expenses of the arrestment itself[1].

1 *Graham Stewart* pp 196–197 mentions a number of instances where an arrestment in execution may be loosed or recalled on caution. These are cases where there is some doubt about the debt being presently due or ever becoming due, ie where the decree is under suspension or reduction, in certain types of debt under the registered mutual contracts, and where the debt is future or contingent.

Prescription

5.43 Arrestments in execution prescribe after a period of three years from the date of the service of the arrestment[1]. In the case of an arrestment used for a contingent debt, the period begins at the time the contingency becomes purified, but in the case of a future debt from the date of the arrestment[2]. The prescriptive period will be interrupted by the raising of an action of furthcoming or multiplepoinding.

Any period during which the arrestment is subject to an interim or full time to pay order is to be disregarded in calculating the prescriptive period[3].

1 Debtors (Scotland) Act 1838, s 22; *Graham Stewart* p 223.
2 *Jamieson v Sharp* (1887) 14 R 643; W A Wilson *The Law of Scotland relating to Debt* p 13.
3 Debtors (Scotland) Act 1838, s 22(2). On time to pay measures see ch 3 above.

Insolvency

5.44 For the effect on an arrestment of the insolvency and sequestration or liquidation of the common debtor, see discussion in chapter 10 below[1].

1 Ch 10 below at paras 10.36, 10.40.

ACTION OF FURTHCOMING

Nature of action; parties

5.45 Arrestment operates to attach property and thus secures a measure of preference for the arresting creditor. However, it is merely an inchoate diligence and by itself does not adjudge property or debts to the arrester[1]. In order to achieve this, some further step must be taken. In practice the step most commonly taken is the informal one whereby the common debtor gives authority by written mandate for the property or funds held by the arrestee to be handed over or transferred to the arresting creditor.

However, where no such mandate can be made, eg because the common debtor is not willing to do so or he is no longer traceable, the more formal step of raising an action of furthcoming must be taken by the arresting creditor in order to complete the diligence[2].

An action of furthcoming craves for the arrestee to make furthcoming, payment and delivery of the sum owed by the arrestee to the common debtor, and arrested in his hands by the pursuer, or of so much thereof as will pay the debt and expenses of the diligence[3]. Where the arrested goods are corporeals the action may conclude for warrant to sell the arrested goods and to apply the proceeds in extinction of the debt and the expenses.

The parties to the action of furthcoming are the arresting creditor as pursuer and the arrestee and common debtor as first and second defenders respectively. Where arrestment has been used on the dependence of an action against a number of defenders, only those defenders found liable in the decree in the action may be called as common debtors in the furthcoming[4]. It is open to any interested party to appear and state defences in the action, but where there are competing claims to ownership of property a more appropriate remedy is an action of multiplepoinding rather than a conjoined furthcoming[5]. If there are any such competing claims, the furthcoming may be sisted pending the raising of an action of multiplepoinding[6].

1 *Lucas's Trustees v Campbell & Scott* (1894) 21 R 1096.
2 An arrestment not followed by a furthcoming is not an effectually exected diligence for purposes of competition where a receiver has been appointed by virtue of a floating charge: *Lord Advocate v Royal Bank of Scotland* 1977 SC 155.
3 Expenses are considered below at para 5.50.
4 *Creswell v Colquhoun & Co* 1987 SLT 329.
5 *Paterson & Son v McInnes* (1950) 66 Sh Ct Rep 226; *Macphail* pp 700–701 but contrast *Graham Stewart* p 239.
6 *Ross v Brunton* (1914) 30 Sh Ct Rep 141.

Jurisdiction

5.46 An action of furthcoming is not competent if the arrestee is not subject to the jurisdiction of the Scottish courts. As the arrestee must also be subject to the jurisdiction of the Scottish courts at the time of the arrestment[1], the effect of rule 2(9) of Schedule 8 to the 1982 Act is that in most cases the arrestee will continue to be subject to the jurisdiction of the Scottish courts even if only on the basis of that rule[2].

However this rule will not found jurisdiction against an arrestee as a defender in an action of furthcoming where the defender is domiciled in a contracting state to the 1968 Convention other than the United Kingdom[3].

But in most cases of an arrestee with a domicile in such a contracting state, another ground of jurisdiction will be available. Jurisdiction in respect of a furthcoming may be based on article 6(1) of the 1968 Convention, where the common debtor is domiciled in Scotland and possibly also on article 16(5) of the Convention[4].

Similarly, the common debtor must also be called as a defender to the action of furthcoming. Provided the debt has been competently constituted against him, either by decree or document of debt registered for execution in Scotland, it does not matter if the common debtor is not otherwise subject to jurisdiction, as rule 2(9) of Schedule 8 to the 1982 Act will usually provide a basis for jurisdiction in the furthcoming[5]. Again, however, in most cases some other basis of jurisdiction will be present.

Where the action of furthcoming is to be raised in a sheriff court[6], the following courts have jurisdiction:
(a) the sheriff court where the arrestee has his domicile[7];
(b) the sheriff court where the common debtor has his domicile[8];
(c) the sheriff court where the arrested property is situated[9].

1 See above at pp 94–95.
2 Civil Jurisdiction and Judgments Act 1982, Sch 8, r 2(9) gives jurisdiction to the court in the place where property is situated in proceedings 'brought to assert, declare or determine proprietory or possesory rights or rights of security in or over moveable property, or to obtain authority to dispose of moveable property'. Of course, if the property has been removed from the place of arrestment this ground of jurisdiction may not apply.
3 Ibid, s 20(1), (4).
4 Article 16(5) of the 1968 Convention gives exclusive jurisdiction in proceedings concerned with the 'enforcement of judgments' to the courts of the contracting state which the judgment has been or is to be enforced. Two points should be noted here. The first is whether an action of furthcoming should be classified as proceedings concerned with the enforcement of judgments. The second is whether if such a classification can be adopted, it applies where the basis of debt for which the arrestment has been used is a registered document of debt.
5 Cp discussion at text on footnotes at 3 and 4 above.
6 This is subject to the points made above concerning defenders who have a domicile in a contracting state other than the United Kingdom. It should also be noted that action of furthcoming is a separate action from that which led to decree. Accordingly, the various rules about jurisdiction as between the Court of Session and sheriff courts, and rules on privative jurisdiction apply.
7 Civil Jurisdiction and Judgments Act 1982, Sch 8, rr 1, 2(15)(a).
8 Ibid.
9 Ibid, Sch 8, r 2(9).

Basis of action

5.47 The summons or initial writ of the action must contain appropriate averments as to[1]:
(a) the basis of the debt which is being enforced by an arrestment and furthcoming. The extract of the decree or document of debt should be produced. Averments should also state the total sum due by the common debtor to the pursuer as at the raising of the action of furthcoming.

An action of furthcoming is incompetent on the basis of an arrestment on the dependence of an action before decree has been granted in that action[2].
(b) the arrestment served in the hands of the arrestee. The execution of the arrestment is to be produced. Where an arrestment has been used on the dependence of an action, an action of furthcoming may be raised without the pursuer having to use an additional arrestment in execution[3]. The arrestment prescribes if not followed up by an action of furthcoming within three years[4].

Where the sum arrested is a future or contingent debt the action of furthcoming will be sisted until such time as the arrested debt becomes due[5]. Alternatively, though less commonly, decree in the furthcoming may be granted but extract superseded[6].

1 W J Dobie *Styles for Use in the Sheriff Courts in Scotland* pp 167–174; S A Bennett *Style Writs for the Sheriff Court* pp 144–145.
2 *Creswell v Colquhoun & Co* 1987 SLT 329; cp *Gordon v Hill* (1841) 3 D 517.
3 *Abercrombie v Edgar and Crerar* 1923 SLT 271.
4 Debtors (Scotland) Act 1838, s 22. See above at para 5.43.
5 *Boland v White Cross Insurance Co* 1926 SC 1066; cp *Fergusson & Co v Brown & Tawse* 1918 SC (HL) 125.
6 *Graham Stewart* pp 229, 235.

Defences to action

ARRESTEE

5.48 As a defence to the action of furthcoming, the arrestee may not dispute the debt due by the common debtor to the arresting pursuer[1]. However, the arrestee may raise a defence that:
(i) the arrestment was invalid[2];
(ii) the action of furthcoming is procedurally irregular, eg because the common debtor has not been called[3];
(iii) the arrestment attached nothing in his hands;
(iv) he has a defence against the common debtor in respect of the arrested debt or property. As the arrester attaches the common debtor's right *tantum et tale*, the 'arrestee may therefore plead against the arrester all defences which he could have pleaded in an action at the instance of the common debtor for the debt or goods arrested'[4]. Such defences include a right of real security[5], or extinction of the debt, prior to the furthcoming; or that the goods have been attached by a sequestration for rent, or a complete poinding[6]; or that any question of liability by the arrestee to the common debtor depended upon arbitration (in which case the furthcoming is sisted to await the outcome of the arbitration)[7].

Where the common debtor has a defence against the arrestee and the arrestee is seeking to deny or restrict his liability to the common debtor the arresting creditor may use this defence against the arrestee in a furthcoming[8].

1 *Houston v Aberdeen Town & Country Banking Co* (1849) 11 D 1490.
2 Stair III, 1, 37, Bell *Comm* II, 64; *Oliphant v Douglas* (1663) Mor 15002 (defence that arrestment was executed on a Sunday).
3 *Anderson, Child & Child v Pott* (1829) 7 S 499.
4 *Graham Stewart* p 233.
5 *Brodie v Wilson* (1837) 15 S 1195; *Macpherson v Wright* (1885) 12 R 942.
6 *Borthwick v North British Railway Company* (1892) 9 SLR 60; *Graham Stewart* pp 234–235.
7 *Palmer v South East Lancashire Insurance Co Ltd* 1932 SLT 68; *Cant v Eagle Star Insurance Co Ltd* 1937 SLT 444.
8 *Neil v South East Lancashire Insurance Co Ltd* 1929 SN 8.

COMMON DEBTOR

5.49 The common debtor may make objection to the validity of the arrestment or in respect of any procedural irregularity in the action of furthcoming. He may not make any objection to the debt said to be owing to the arresting pursuer, unless the debt is based on a document of debt rather than upon a decree[1].

1 *Donaldson v Orb* (1855) 17 D 1053.

Expenses

5.50 In most cases an action of furthcoming is required where the common debtor refuses to sign a mandate authorising the release of funds or property by the arrestee to the creditor. Accordingly, a crave for expenses is made against the arrestee only in the event of his offering any opposition to the action[1]. Normally also there are averments as to the failure by the common debtor to sign a mandate to justify an award for expenses against him.

The expenses of the arrestment and the expenses of the action of furthcoming are recoverable out of the arrested fund[2]. In so far as these expenses are not recovered from the arrested funds, the court grants decree in the furthcoming for payment of the outstanding balance of the expenses. Decree is warrant for further diligence to recover the unpaid balance of expenses.

1 *Wightman v Wilson* (1858) 20 D 779.
2 1987 Act, s 93(2).

Sale of ship

5.51 Where the subject of the arrestment is a ship the diligence is completed by means of an action of sale rather than an action of furthcoming[1]. All parties having an interest in a ship are entitled to appear and enter claims in the action. Unlike the case of an action of furthcoming, in an action of sale it is possible to have conclusions to establish the validity of the debt due to the arrester by the common debtor[2]. Sale is by way of public roup, with the clerk of court or sheriff clerk officiating as the clerk of sale. The price paid for the ship is consigned in court, and upon a minute being presented to the Lord Ordinary or sheriff, decree is granted to give a title to the ship to the purchaser.

1 Cp *Munro v Smith* 1986 SLT (Sh Ct) 26.
2 *Taylor v Williamson* (1831) 9 S 265; *Graham Stewart* p 243.

CHAPTER 6

ARRESTMENT OF EARNINGS

ABOLITION OF ARRESTMENT OF EARNINGS

Criticism of the diligence of arrestment and furthcoming as used against earnings

6.01   Part III of the 1987 Act sets out provisions on the new diligences against the earnings of a debtor in the hands of his employer, which the 1987 Act introduced to replace the diligence of arrestment and furthcoming. Although the use of arrestment and furthcoming against earnings had not attracted the same degree of criticism and controversy as had been raised against poinding and sale, the Scottish Law Commission identified a number of defects in the law on arrestment and furthcoming as it applied to earnings[1].

In particular, the Commission identified two major problems in the application of arrestment to earnings. The first was that as arrestment attaches only what is due to the common debtor (the employee) at the time of the arrestment, many creditors required to repeat arrestments against the same source of earnings in order to clear their debts. Secondly, the level of subsistence which the common debtor/employee could claim from the arrested earnings was often too low. The Commission considered a number of different models for reform of the law and recommended that the diligence of arrestment and furthcoming should be abolished and replaced by a system of continuous diligence against earnings, which would continue until the debt was paid off and which would provide the debtor with a more realistic level of subsistence[2].

The Commission also noted that various studies had identified problems faced by maintenance creditors in enforcing their debts[3]. A particular feature of maintenance is that the creditor is usually seeking an amount which falls due over regular periods of time. The Commission recommended that a new diligence against the debtor's earnings should be introduced which would attach in each pay period, not default debts in the form of arrears of maintenance, but the current maintenance due in respect of that pay period.

As the new diligences against earnings would, unlike arrestment and furthcoming, continue in operation until the debt was cleared or ceased to exist, a problem might arise where later creditors wished to use diligence against the same earnings but found themselves shut out by a prior diligence against those earnings. To overcome these difficulties, the Scottish Law Commission recommended that there should be a procedure for conjoining creditors who seek to do diligence against the earnings of the same debtor and for a proportionate sharing-out of the sums deducted from the earnings.

These various recommendations were implemented by Part III of the 1987 Act.

1 Report on Diligence and Debtor Protection (Scot Law Com no 95 (1985)) pp 68–71, 323–332, 364–367, 391–393.
2 The diligence of earnings arrestment introduced by the 1987 Act is modelled more closely on the system of enforcement against earnings used in Australia, Canada and the USA than on the English system of attachment of earnings. For discussion of the differences between the Scottish and English systems, see Scot Law Com Report no 95 (1985), pp 329–332.
3 Scot Law Com Report no 95 (1985), pp 364–369.

New diligences against earnings

6.02 Section 46(1) of the 1987 Act abolishes the diligence of arrestment and furthcoming as it applies to the earnings[1] of a debtor and replaces it with three new diligences:
(1) *earnings arrestment*, which is used to enforce payment of (default) debt due as at the date of the execution of the diligence[2];
(2) *current maintenance arrestment*, which is used to enforce the payment of current maintenance[3]; and
(3) *conjoined arrestment order*, which is used to enforce the payment of two or more debts owing to different creditors against the same earnings[4].

Although the word 'arrestment' is used in the names of each of these new diligences, they should not be seen as mere modifications of the diligence of arrestment and furthcoming but as new types of diligence.

1 For the meaning of 'earnings' see 1987 Act, s 73(2) and discussion below at para 6.03.
2 See below at paras 6.05–6.31.
3 See below at paras 6.32–6.51.
4 See below at paras 6.52–6.74.

Scope of the new diligences; meaning of 'earnings'

6.03 The diligence of arrestment and furthcoming has been abolished and replaced by the new diligences only in respect of 'earnings' as that term is itself defined in Part III of the 1987 Act. It is important to realise that if a payment does not come within the scope of earnings as defined, the new diligences do not apply and such a payment is open, unless otherwise exempt, to the diligence of arrestment and furthcoming. It should also be noted that the idea of earnings for this purpose is in some senses narrower than earnings in ordinary language (eg earnings within Part III of the 1987 Act do not include the earnings of the self-employed) and in some senses is wider (eg by including occupational pensions).

The first point to note is that earnings are within the scope of Part III of the 1987 Act only if they are paid to the debtor by an employer under a contract of service or apprenticeship[1]. Thus, sums due to the debtor under a contract for services are not covered by the new diligences but are open to arrestment and furthcoming[2].

Further, earnings extend only to 'sums' of money payable by an employer to the debtor[3]. Thus, benefits in kind, even if taxable, are not covered by Part III of the 1987 Act[4], nor are sums payable directly to a third party, even if for the benefit of the debtor.

Subject to these points the following sums are earnings for purposes of Part III of the 1987 Act:

(1) wages or salary;

(2) fees, bonuses, commissions, or other emoluments, payable under the contract of service or apprenticeship;

(3) pensions[5]. This term includes a pension declared to be alimentary, an annuity in respect of past services (whether or not the services were rendered to the person paying the annuity), and any periodical payments of compensation for the loss, abolition, relinquishment, or diminution in earnings of any office or employment.

(4) statutory sick pay.

However, the following are not to be treated as earnings:

(1) a pension or allowance payable in respect of disablement or disability;

(2) any sum the assignation of which is precluded by section 203 of the Army Act 1955 or section 203 of the Air Force Act 1955, or any like sum payable to a member of the naval forces of the Crown, or to a member of any women's service administered by the Defence Council[6];

(3) in relation to the enforcement by an earnings arrestment of a debt other than maintenance, the wages of a seaman (other than a member of the crew of a fishing boat)[7];

(4) any occupational pension payable under any enactment which precludes the assignation of the pension or exempts it from diligence;

(5) a pension, allowance or benefit payable under any enactment relating to social security;

(6) a guaranteed minimum pension within the meaning of the Social Security Pensions Act 1975;

(7) a redundancy payment within the meaning of section 8(1) of the Employment Protection (Consolidation) Act 1978.

These payments, unless otherwise exempt will be open to arrestment and furthcoming. In fact, most of the above categories are exempt from diligence.

1 1987 Act, ss 46(1), 73(1) (definition of 'employer'). An exception arises in the case of a pension. Unless exempted, a pension is treated as earnings and the person who pays the pension is treated for this purpose as the employer of the recipient.

2 Although the legal distinction between a contract of service and a contract for services is fairly clear, the determination as to which category any particular case falls can be far from straightforward. A considerable body of case-law has arisen on this issue. For discussion see 'Employment' in *The Laws of Scotland: Stair Memorial Encyclopaedia* vol 9, para 19.

Prior to the 1987 Act this issue did not present problems for creditors or officers of court, as the same documents were lodged with the 'employer' no matter which legal category was involved. Now, however, the creditor must decide whether to instruct a prior charge and the diligence of earnings arrestment on the one hand, or on the other to instruct an arrestment and furthcoming.

3 1987 Act, s 73(2).

4 They may, of course, be subject to the diligence of arrestment and furthcoming.

5 Many pensions are exempt from diligence, including diligence against earnings. See further ch 5 above at para 5.32.

6 See ch 5 above at para 5.30.

7 See ch 5 above at para 5.30.

Abolition of the common law *beneficium competentiae*

6.04 In respect of earnings to which Part III of the 1987 Act applies[1], the common law *beneficium competentiae*, whereby a reasonable amount is exempted from arrestment for the subsistence of the debtor and his dependants[2], is abolished[3]. The various statutory provisions on limitations of the amount of wages arrestable have also been swept away by the 1987 Act and replaced by the provisions applicable to the new diligences against earnings[4].

1 See above at para 6.03.
2 See *Shanks v Thomson* (1838) 16 S 1353; *Thomson v Cohen* (1915) 32 Sh Ct Rep 15; *Caldwell v Hamilton* 1919 SC (HL) 100; *Young v Turnbull* 1928 SN 46; *Webster v Douglas* (1933) 49 Sh Ct Rep 294; *Birrell's Tr v Birrell* 1957 SLT (Sh Ct) 6; *Cochran's Tr v Cochran* (1958) 74 Sh Ct Rep 75. For discussion of the common law rule, see G Maher *A Textbook of Diligence* pp 39–42.
3 1987 Act, s 46(2).
4 Wages Arrestment Limitation (Scotland) Act 1870 (as amended), repealed by 1987 Act, Sch 8. For the limitations on the amount deductible under the new diligences against earnings see below at paras 6.13–6.18, 6.43, 6.61–6.62.

EARNINGS ARRESTMENT

Debts recoverable by earnings arrestment

6.05 An earnings arrestment can be used to enforce a debt (other than one of current maintenance) which is due at the date of the service of the schedule of arrestment on the employer[1]. The diligence cannot be used on the dependence of an action or in security of a future or contingent debt.

Included within a debt recoverable by an earnings arrestment are[2]:
(a) the principal sum, interest and expenses due under the decree or other document of debt;
(b) any subsequent interest on these sums which has accured as at the date of service of the schedule of arrestment; and
(c) the expenses incurred in executing the earnings arrestment and charge which preceded it.
In order to be recoverable by an earnings arrestment, any or all of the above sums must be specified in the earnings arrestment schedule[3].

A single earnings arrestment may be used to enforce more than one debt due by the same debtor to the same creditor, provided the various procedural steps have been taken in respect of each debt[4].

1 1987 Act, s 46(1)(a).
2 Ibid, s 48(1).
3 Ibid, s 48(3). See further below at para 6.07.
4 1987 Act, s 48(4).

Commencement of earnings arrestment

SERVICE OF PRIOR CHARGE

6.06 An earnings arrestment may be executed only after the service of a charge for payment on the debtor and expiry of the period of charge without payment being made[1]. The period of charge is fourteen days where the person being charged is within the United Kingdom, and twenty-eight days if he is outside the United Kingdom or his whereabouts are unknown.

A prior charge is not necessary for the execution of an earnings arrestment in pursuance of a summary warrant[2].

A charge lasts for a period of two years, but a creditor may serve a further charge, within or after the two-year period[3].

1 1987 Act, s 90(1), (3). For modes of service of a charge see ch 7 below at paras 7.06–7.12.
2 1987 Act, s 90(2).
3 Ibid, s 90(5)–(7). For further discussion, see ch 7 below at para 7.13.

SERVICE OF SCHEDULE OF EARNINGS ARRESTMENT

6.07 An earnings arrestment is executed by an officer of court serving on the employer of the debtor an earnings arrestment schedule[1]. This schedule is in Form 30 of the Sheriff Court Proceedings Act of Sederunt and must state:
(1) the name, designation and address of the creditor, the debtor, the employer and any person residing in the United Kingdom to whom payment under the arrestment is to be made;
(2) the decree or other document constituting the debt and when, where and by whom it was granted or issued;
(3) the date on which any charge for payment was served; and
(4) the debt outstanding and the manner of its calculation.
Attached to the schedule are copies of the terms of section 49(1)–49(6) of the 1987 Act, and of Schedule 2 to the Act[2].

When making service of the schedule, the officer must also intimate a copy of it to the debtor, but failure to make this intimation does not by itself invalidate the arrestment[3].

The mode of service is by registered or recorded delivery post[4]. Where such service cannot be made, the officer may use any other competent mode of service, but such service cannot be executed on Sunday, Christmas Day, New Year's Day or Good Friday[5]. Where service is by means other than post, it is not clear whether a witness need be present. Section 70(3) of the 1987 Act states that where service by post cannot be effected, service is to be made 'by any other competent mode of service'. Section 32 of the 1838 Act provides that more than one witness shall not be required for the service of execution of schedules. However, the requirement of a witness laid down by section 32 is a condition for the validity of a service rather than a mode of service. Moreover, section 70(4) requires the certificate of execution to be signed only by the officer who effected the service[6], and it seems odd that a witness should be required for the service of a document but not to sign the certificate of execution[7]. Despite this, practice appears to be that a witness is present when an earnings arrestment schedule is executed by means other than service by post.

1 1987 Act, s 70(1); AS (Proceedings in the Sheriff Court under the Debtors (Scotland) Act 1987) 1988, SI 1988/2013, r 38, Form 30.
2 These provisions deal with the deductions which the employer is to make from the employee's earnings in operating the earnings arrestment.
3 1987 Act, s 70(1), (2).
4 Ibid, s 70(3); SI 1988/2013, r 66.
5 1987 Act, s 70(3), (5).
6 Ibid, s 70(4); SI 1988/2013, r 67, Form 60.
7 Cp Stair III, 3, 10 and *Graham Stewart* p 328, who suggest that where a witness is to be present, his subscription on the certificate of execution is essential.

LOCATION OF EMPLOYER

6.08 Where the debtor is an employee who is an officer of the Crown, his employer is the chief officer in Scotland of the relevant department or other body[1].

An earnings arrestment schedule may be served on an employer who is subject to the jurisdiction of the Scottish courts. In the case of a company incorporated and registered in the United Kingdom or whose central management and control is exercised in the United Kingdom, a place of business in Scotland suffices to give that company a domicile in Scotland and accordingly that company will be subject to Scottish jurisdiction[2]. Thus where the debtor is an employee of a United Kingdom company, an earnings arrestment may be used against that employee's earnings following service and expiry of a charge on the debtor, and following service of an earnings arrestment schedule at the Scottish branch or place of business of the company. This is so, no matter where the debtor has his residence or place of work and no matter where the company's wages department is situated.

1 1987 Act, s 73(1), (5).
2 Civil Jurisdiction and Judgments Act 1982, s 42.

COMMENCEMENT OF OPERATION OF EARNINGS ARRESTMENT

6.09 It is not necessary for an earnings arrestment schedule to be served at the head office of the wages department of the employer. Moreover, there is considerable variation in the practice of employers in respect of administering wages and salaries. To allow for the practicalities and administrative problems which may ensue as a consequence of these features, the 1987 Act does not provide for an earnings arrestment necessarily to become fully operational as soon as it is served on the employer. Although generally an earnings arrestment comes into effect when the schedule is served on the employer[1], the employer is not bound to operate the arrestment until the next pay day occurring seven days after the service of the schedule[2]. However, the employer may, if he so wishes, give effect to an earnings arrestment on any day occuring within seven days after the service of the schedule.

1 1987 Act, s 47(2)(a).
2 Ibid, s 69(2), (3).

Operation of earnings arrestment

GENERAL EFFECT

6.10 The general effect of an earnings arrestment is to require the employer of the debtor, while the arrestment is in effect, to deduct from the debtor's net earnings on every pay day, a sum determined in accordance with the provisions of the 1987 Act. The employer is further required to pay any sum so deducted to the arresting creditor as soon as is reasonably practicable[1].

1 1987 Act, s 47(1).

DEDUCTIONS TO BE MADE BY EMPLOYER

Service on employer of statutory tables

6.11 The sums to be deducted by an employer in giving effect to an earnings arrestment are calculated by reference to tables set out in Schedule 2 to the

1987 Act. Copies of these tables must be included in the schedule of the earnings arrestment served on the employer[1].

1 SI 1988/2013, r 38(3). These tables may be varied by regulations. Any regulations so made must also be intimated to the employer: 1987 Act, s 47(7), (8); SI 1988/2013, r 39, Form 31.

Net earnings

6.12 The deduction which the employer is to make is from the net earnings of the employee. In arriving at net earnings the employer must first disregard whatever payments to the employee do not count as 'earnings' for purposes of Part III of the 1987 Act[1]. Thereafter net earnings are what remains after the deduction of any sums in respect of[2]
(i) income tax;
(ii) primary class 1 contributions under Part I of the Social Security Act 1975;
(iii) amounts deductible under any enactment, or in pursuance of a requirement in writing by the debtor, for the purposes of a superannuation scheme within the meaning of the Wages Councils Act 1979.

1 See above at para 6.03.
2 1987 Act, s 73(1).

Weekly-paid earnings

6.13 Where the debtor's earnings are payable weekly, the employer deducts the appropriate sum from his net earnings as set out in Table A of Schedule 2 to the 1987 Act[1]. It has for long been a principle of Scots law that a debtor whose wages are being arrested is entitled to retain a reasonable amount for his own subsistence[2]. This principle is continued by the 1987 Act in respect of the new diligences against earnings. As regards earnings arrestment the debtor is always entitled to keep at least £35 per week of his net earnings and no deductions under any earnings arrestment may be made from any net earnings not exceeding £35 per week. A similar level of protection for the debtor is provided in respect of earnings paid at other levels[3].
   Where the employer makes a nil deduction, the earnings arrestment does not cease to have effect but rather continues in force until such time as appropriate deductions can be made and the debt is cleared.

1 1987 Act, s 49(1)(a).
2 'There is no doubt that it was the law of Scotland, long before Queen Victoria or any of her race sat upon the throne of these kingdoms, that labourers' wages could not be arrested except as to what was over and above a necessary aliment': *Shanks v Thomson* (1838) 16 S 1353, 1362.
3 It is to be noted that the same subsistence level is provided, no matter the type of debt being recovered by the earnings arrestment, and so the normal rules on deductions apply in respect of recovery of arrears of maintenance, rates, community charges and taxes.

Monthly-paid earnings

6.14 Where the debtor's earnings are paid monthly, the employer deducts the appropriate sums from net earnings as set out in Table B of Schedule 2 to the 1987 Act[1].

1 1987 Act, s 49(1)(b).

Earnings paid at intervals of weeks or months

6.15 Where the debtor's earnings are paid at regular intervals of a whole number of weeks or months, the employer makes the appropriate deduction by: (i) calculating the net earnings paid on the basis of a single week or month, as the case may be; (ii) making the deduction as set out in Table A or (in the case of monthly-paid earnings, Table B); and finally, (iii) multiplying that sum by the number of weeks or months in question[1].

For example, where a debtor is paid at intervals of six weeks and his net earnings on a pay day come to £540, the employer divides that sum by six to obtain the weekly 'rate' of pay (ie £90), consults Table A and makes the appropriate deduction (ie £11) and multiplies that sum by six, to give the total deduction of £66.

Similarly where a debtor is paid every three months and his net earnings on a pay day are £3,600, the monthly 'rate' is £3,600 divided by three (ie £1,200). The deduction for that level of monthly net earnings, as set out in Table B, is £312, and the total deduction made by the employer is £312 × 3 (ie £936).

1 1987 Act, s 49(1)(c).

Earnings paid at other regular intervals

6.16 Where the debtor is paid at regular intervals other than weekly or monthly (or multiples of weeks or months), the appropriate deduction is made by calculating the daily net earnings[1]. This is done by dividing the net earnings payable at the pay day by the number of days in the interval. The next step is to make a deduction in respect of this sum in terms of Table C in Schedule 2 to the Act, and then multiplying that sum by the number of days in the interval[2].

1 Where payment is by two or more payments at regular intervals the appropriate deductions are governed by 1987 Act, s 49(6).
2 1987 Act, s 49(2). Examples of this situation may not be common but would apply to eg contracts of employment where earnings are paid every forty days.

Earnings paid at irregular intervals

6.18 Where the earnings are paid to the debtor at irregular intervals, deductions are made in terms of a notional daily rate of earnings[1]. To arrive at this rate, the employer divides the net earnings payable at the pay day by the number of days since the last pay day[2]. The appropriate deduction is made against this sum in accordance with Table C in Schedule 2 to the 1987 Act, and that deduction is then multiplied by the number of days since the last pay day to give the total deduction.

For example, where it is fifty-five days since the last pay day and the debtor's net earnings are £770, the daily net earnings are £770 divided by fifty-five ie £14. The appropriate deduction to make against this sum is £1.80 and the total deduction is £1.80 × 55, ie £99.

1 1987 Act, s 49(3).
2 If the earnings are the first earnings to be paid to the debtor, the earnings are divided by the number of days since the commencement of employment: 1987 Act, s 49(3)(a)(ii).

Additional payments as earnings

6.18 Where the debtor is paid additional payments as earnings, such as overtime, bonuses, or commission, the deduction to be made depends upon whether or not the additional payments are paid on the same pay day as the payment of regular earnings. If they are so paid, the additional earnings are aggregated to the earnings and are treated as regular earnings for purposes of making the deduction[1]. If the additional payments are paid on a different pay day from that of regular earnings, the employer deducts a flat-rate 20 per cent from the additional payments[2].

1 1987 Act, s 49(4).
2 Ibid, s 49(5).

Power to vary level of deductions

6.19 The amount of the deductions to be made from the debtor's earnings and the level of subsistence provided for the debtor, as set out in the various statutory tables, are in terms of fixed sums. To prevent the level of these sums becoming out-of-date, the Lord Advocate is given power to vary the levels of deduction by regulation[1].

Where an earnings arrestment is already in force and variations are made by regulations, the regulations do not apply to that earnings arrestment unless and until the making of the regulations is intimated to the employer[2].

1 1987 Act, s 49(7).
2 Ibid, s 49(8); SI 1988/2013, r 39, Form 31.

MODE OF PAYMENT

6.20 Once the employer has calculated the appropriate deduction to be made from the debtor's net earnings, he must as soon as is reasonably practicable, pay the deducted sum to the creditor. Payment to the creditor may be made by cheque, but if a cheque tendered for payment has been dishonoured (or payment by cheque is for any reason ineffectual), the creditor may insist that payments, including all future payments, must be made in cash[1].

1 1987 Act, s 57(2), (3).

FEE FOR OPERATING EARNINGS ARRESTMENT

6.21 An employer is entitled to deduct from the debtor's earnings, a sum in respect of a fee for operating an earnings arrestment[1]. It should be noted that the amount chargeable is only really a token sum and the current level of fee is fifty pence[2] for each occasion the employer is required to make a deduction in operating the earnings arrestment. The fee is deducted from what is left of the debtor's net earnings after a deduction has been made in giving effect to the arrestment. No fee is chargeable where no deduction falls to be made, eg because the net earnings of the debtor are within the protected subsistence level.

1 1987 Act, s 71. A similar fee may be charged by the employer in respect of a current maintenance arrestment or a conjoined arrestment order.
2 This sum may be varied by regulations by the Lord Advocate.

FAILURE BY THE EMPLOYER TO OPERATE EARNINGS ARRESTMENT

6.22 Where an employer fails to comply with an earnings arrestment, he becomes liable to pay to the creditor the sum which would have been paid if the earnings arrestment had been complied with[1]. Furthermore, in these circumstances the employer is not entitled to recover from the debtor any sum paid to him which should have been deducted in operating the earnings arrestment.

1 1987 Act, s 57(1). However, this rule is subject to s 69(4) of the 1987 Act: see below at para 6.23.

RESTRICTIONS ON EMPLOYER'S LIABILITY

6.23 A claim against the employer for failure to give effect to an earnings arrestment by making the appropriate deduction from the debtor's net earnings or for failure to pay over to the creditor the amount deducted, expires after one year from the date when the deduction or payment has, or ought to have, been made[1].

1 1987 Act, 69(4). A similar principle applies in respect of claims for failure by the employer to operate a current maintenance arrestment or a conjoined arrestment order.

Duration of earnings arrestment

GENERAL RULE

6.24 The general rule as concerns the duration of an earnings arrestment is that it remains in effect until[1]:
(1) the debt recoverable by it[2] has been paid (or is otherwise extinguished);
(2) the debtor has ceased to be employed by the employer;
(3) the arrestment has been recalled; or
(4) the arrestment has been abandoned by the creditor.
In addition there are other ways in which an earnings arrestment may cease to have effect[3].

1 1987 Act, s 47(2)(b).
2 See above at para 6.05.
3 See below at paras 6.25–6.30.

REVIEW

6.25 There are two forms of review of an earnings arrestment, which may be made to the sheriff having jurisdiction over the place where the earnings arrestment was executed. If that place is not known to the applicant, application is made to the sheriff with jurisdiction over an established place of business of the debtor's employer[1].

1 1987 Act, ss 50, 73(1).

6.26 In the first place, an application may be made to the sheriff by the debtor or the person on whom an earnings arrestment schedule was served, for a declaration that an earnings arrestment is invalid or has ceased to have effect[1]. Such an application is in Form 32 of the Sheriff Court Proceedings Act of Sederunt and must state:
(1) the name and address of the creditor, the debtor, the officer of court who served the earnings arrestment schedule and the person on whom the schedule was served:

(2) the court which granted the original decree and the date of that decree, or details of the summary warrant or other document, upon which the earnings arrestment proceeded;
(3) the date of service of the earnings arrestment schedule;
(4) the form of the order sought;
(5) the reasons for the application; and
(6) any competent crave for expenses.
A copy of the earnings arrestment schedule is to be attached to the application. On the lodging of an application, the sheriff clerk fixes a date for a hearing and makes intimation as appropriate.

Where the sheriff is satisfied that a declarator should be granted as applied for, he may also make such consequential order as appears necessary in the circumstances[2].

The making of any such declarator is not subject to appeal[3].

1 1987 Act, s 50(1); SI 1988/2013, r 40, Form 32.
2 Any such consequential order is to be intimated by the sheriff clerk to the debtor, the creditor and the person on whom the earnings arrestment schedule was served.
3 1987 Act, s 50(2).

6.27 Secondly, an application may also be made to the sheriff by the debtor, creditor or employer for the determination of any dispute as to the operation of an earnings arrestment[1]. An application must be in Form 33 of the Sheriff Court Proceedings Act of Sederunt and must state:
(1) the name and address of the creditor, the debtor, the officer of court who served the earnings arrestment schedule and the employer;
(2) the court which granted the original decree and the date of that decree, or details of the summary warrant or other document, upon which the earnings arrestment proceeded;
(3) the date of service of the earnings arrestment schedule;
(4) the subject-matter of the dispute;
(5) the form of the order sought, including any sum sought to be reimbursed or paid;
(6) any claim for interest and the date from which such interest should run; and
(7) any competent crave for expenses.
A copy of the earnings arrestment schedule is to be attached to the application. On the lodging of an application, the sheriff clerk fixes a date for a hearing and makes intimation as appropriate.

In dealing with an application the sheriff may make an order for the payment of a sum which mistakenly has not been paid under the earnings arrestment, and for the reimbursement of a sum which mistakenly has been paid. Any such sum is to be paid with interest from the date specified in the order[2].

1 1987 Act, s 50(3); SI 1988/2013, r 41, Form 33.
2 1987 Act, s 50(4), (5). On the rate of interest, see 1987 Act, s 73(1).

PRESCRIPTION

6.28 Section 22 of the 1838 Act (by which arrestments prescribe in three years) does not apply to an earnings arrestment, a current maintenance arrestment or a conjoined arrestment order[1].

Claims against the employer or failure to operate a diligence against earnings lapse after one year[2].

1 Debtors (Scotland) Act 1838, s 22(3), added by 1987 Act, Sch 6, para 3.
2 1987 Act, s 69(4). See further above at para 6.23.

INSOLVENCY; SEQUESTRATION

6.29 As conjoined arrestment orders provide a means for different creditors to share in diligence against the same earnings of the debtor, the provisions of the Bankruptcy (Scotland) Act 1985 on equalisation of diligences on the apparent insolvency of the debtor[1] do not apply in respect of an earnings arrestment, a current maintenance arrestment or a conjoined arrestment order[2].

However, any such diligence against the debtor's earnings ceases to have effect on the date of the debtor's sequestration[3]. Moreover, a creditor may not use the diligence of earnings arrestment or current maintenance after the date of the debtor's sequestration where he can claim for the debt in the sequestration[4].

Deductions under a diligence against earnings made prior to the date of the debtor's sequestration may be paid over to the creditor but any such deductions made after that date are recoverable by the trustee in sequestration. However, a sum deducted before the date of sequestration under a conjoined arrestment order may be disbursed by the sheriff clerk after that date[5].

1 Bankruptcy (Scotland) Act 1985, Sch 7, para 24(8).
2 1987 Act, s 67.
3 Ibid, s 72(2). The date of sequestration is the date on which sequestration is awarded where the petition for sequestration is presented by the debtor. Where the petition is presented by a creditor or trustee acting under a trust deed, it is the date on which the court grants warrant to cite the debtor: Bankruptcy (Scotland) Act 1985, s 12(4); 1987 Act, s 72(5).
4 1987 Act, s 72(4).
5 Ibid, s 72(3).

TIME TO PAY ORDER

6.30 When a sheriff makes a time to pay order, he must also make an order recalling any existing earnings arrestment[1], and while a time to pay order is in effect it is not competent to commence or execute an earnings arrestment in respect of the debt concerned[2].

In respect of an interim time to pay order, section 8(1) of the 1987 Act states that it shall not be competent to 'execute' an earnings arrestment to recover the debt. An earnings arrestment is executed on the date of service of an earnings arrestment schedule on the employer[3], and it would appear that an interim order under section 6(3) of the 1987 Act does not prevent the continued operation of an already existing earnings arrestment.

1 1987 Act, s 9(2)(a). See also 1987 Act, s 9(2)(b) for the effect of a time to pay order on the operation of a conjoined arrestment order.
2 Ibid, s (9)(1)(b).
3 Ibid, s 47(2)(a).

EFFECT OF TERMINATION OF EARNINGS ARRESTMENT

6.31 Where the debt being recovered by an earnings arrestment is paid in full, or is otherwise extinguished or is no longer enforceable by diligence, the creditor must make intimation in writing of this fact to the employer as soon as is reasonably practicable[1]. Where the creditor fails to make such intimation, the employer is not liable for any deductions made unless and until he does receive intimation from the creditor[2], but the debtor may recover from the creditor any sum paid by the employer in excess of the debt. The debtor is entitled to interest on this sum.

Furthermore, the debtor may make an application for an order requiring the creditor to pay a sum not exceeding twice such an amount, including interest[3]. Application is made to the sheriff court with jurisdiction over the place where the arrestment was executed, or where that place is not known to the applicant, over the place where the debtor's employer has an established place of business[4]. Application is to be in Form 41 of the Sheriff Court Proceedings Act of Sederunt and must specify:

(1) the name and address of the debtor, the creditor, the officer of court who served the arrestment and the employer:

(2) the court which granted the original decree and the date of that decree, or details of the summary warrant or other document, upon which the arrestment proceeded;

(3) the amount of the debt or the sum to be deducted from the debtor's earnings;

(4) where appropriate, the expenses of diligence;

(5) where appropriate, whether the debt recoverable under the earnings arrestment is paid or otherwise extinguished and, if so, from what date and in what circumstances;

(6) where appropriate, whether the current maintenance arrestment has ceased to have effect and, if so, from what date and in what circumstances;

(7) where appropriate, whether the debt being enforced by the earnings arrestment has ceased to be enforceable by diligence and, if so, from what date and in what circumstances;

(8) the calculation showing the sum alleged to have been received by the creditor in excess of entitlement;

(9) the sum sought from the creditor and the grounds for seeking such sum; and

(10) any competent crave for expenses.

A copy of the arrestment schedule is to be attached to the application. On the lodging of an application, the sheriff clerk fixes a date for a hearing and makes intimation to the applicant and the creditor. The sheriff has a discretion to grant the application. This provision is meant to act as a penalty on creditors for failure to make intimation and is over and above the debtor's right to repayment with interest of sums in excess of the debt[5].

1   1987 Act, s 57(4); SI 1988/2013, r 50.
2   1987 Act, s 69(5).
3   Ibid, s 57(6); SI 1988/2013, r 51, Form 41.
4   1987 Act, s 73(1).
5   Report on Diligence and Debtor Protection (Scot Law Com no 95 (1985)) p 356.

CURRENT MAINTENANCE ARRESTMENT

Debts enforceable by current maintenance arrestment

NATURE OF CURRENT MAINTENANCE

6.32 The 1987 Act defines current maintenance only circularly by reference to the type of maintenance for which a current maintenance arrestment may be used[1]. However, the underlying idea of a current maintenance arrestment is that it is a diligence against earnings used to recover maintenance as it falls due, and as such is as much a collecting device than a diligence in the traditional sense[2].

However, the idea of maintenance is defined by the 1987 Act. Maintenance is defined as periodical sums payable under a maintenance order. Maintenance order is in turn defined in terms of the following list[3]:

(1) an order granted by a court in Scotland for payment of a periodical allowance on divorce or on the granting of a declarator of nullity of marriage[4];

(2) an order granted by a court in Scotland for aliment[5];

(3) an order under any of the following statutory provisions:

National Assistance Act 1948, section 43 or 44;

Ministry of Social Security Act 1966, section 23 or 24;

Social Work (Scotland) Act 1968, section 80 or 81;

Guardianship Act 1973, section 11(3);

Supplementary Benefits Act 1976, section 18 or 19;

Child Care Act 1980, section 50 or 51;

Social Security Act 1980, section 24 or 25;

(4) an order of a court in England and Wales or Northern Ireland registered in Scotland under Part II of the Maintenance Orders Act 1950;

(5) a provisional order of a reciprocating country which is confirmed by a court in Scotland under Part I of the Maintenance Orders (Reciprocal Enforcement) Act 1972;

(6) an order of a reciprocating country which is registered in Scotland under Part I of the Maintenance Orders (Reciprocal Enforcement) Act 1972;

(7) an order registered in Scotland under Part II, or under an Order in Council made in pursuance of Part III, of the Maintenance Orders (Reciprocal Enforcement) Act 1972:

(8) an order registered in Scotland under section 5 of the Civil Jurisdiction and Judgments Act 1982;

(9) an alimentary bond or agreement which has been (i) registered for execution in the Books of Council and Session or sheriff court books or (ii) registered in Scotland under an Order in Council made under section 13 of the Civil Jurisdiction and Judgments Act 1982. Included within the meaning of such an alimentary bond is a document providing for the maintenance of one party to a marriage by the other after the marriage has been dissolved or annulled.

---

1 1987 Act, s 73(1).
2 Report on Diligence and Debtor Protection (Scot Law Com no 95 (1985)) pp 364–369.
3 1987 Act, s 106.
4 At present these orders are governed by the provisions of the Family Law (Scotland) Act 1985, ss 8–17.
5 These are presently governed by the Family Law (Scotland) Act 1985, ss 1–7.

6.33   As a current maintenance arrestment may be used only to recover maintenance as it falls due, it cannot be used to recover:
(1) arrears of maintenance which have accrued prior to the service of the current maintenance arrestment[1];
(2) arrears of maintenance arising from a shortfall between what is due as maintenance and the sum deducted from earnings in the operation of a current maintenance arrestment[2];
(3) expenses of the action or process which resulted in the maintenance order;
(4) the expenses of the current maintenance arrestment itself[3].
However, these sums all count as so-called 'ordinary' debts and may be recovered by other appropriate diligence, including earnings arrestment[4].

1 1987 Act, s 73(1). Interest on any such arrears may be recovered as an 'ordinary' debt by appropriate diligence.
2 No interest accrues on any arrears of maintenance arising while a current maintenance arrestment is in effect: Ibid, s 51(6).
3 Ibid, ss 51(3), 73(1).
4 For the combined use of earnings arrestment and current maintenance arrestment, see ibid, s 58, discussed below at para 6.53.

ENFORCEMENT OF TWO OR MORE MAINTENANCE OBLIGATIONS TO THE SAME
PERSON

6.34   A single current maintenance arrestment may be used against the debtor's earnings to recover current maintenance owing under one or more maintenance orders and payment is due by the same debtor to the same person[1]. The maintenance due must be in respect of more than one individual.

1 1987 Act, s 52. It does not matter whether the maintenance due is for the benefit of the payee under the order or for another person.

DIVERSION OF ARRESTED EARNINGS TO THE SECRETARY OF STATE

6.35   The situation may arise where the maintenance creditor is in receipt of income support. If the creditor is also using a current maintenance arrestment[1], she may authorise the Secretary of State on behalf of the Department of Social Security to receive any sums payable under the arrestment[2]. The Secretary of State intimates this authorisation to the employer who directs the payments due to the maintenance creditor to the Secretary of State. This arrangement continues until the current maintenance arrestment loses effect[3], or the maintenance creditor withdraws the authorisation or ceases to be in receipt of income support.

1 Or a conjoined arrested order.
2 Social Security Act 1986, s 25A (added by 1987 Act, s 68). The authorisation must be in writing.
3 See below at paras 6.45–6.51.

Commencement of current maintenance arrestment

PRIOR DEFAULT BY DEBTOR

6.36   A current maintenance arrestment may not be used by a maintenance creditor until there is unpaid by the debtor a sum not less than the aggregate of three instalments of maintenance[1]. This requirement does not apply in respect of a maintenance order which varies or supersedes an earlier order which is being enforced by a current maintenance arrestment[2].

1 1987 Act, s 54(1)(c). For non-Scottish orders see below at para 6.38.
2 Ibid, s 56.

INTIMATION TO THE DEBTOR

6.37 No prior charge need be served on the debtor to allow a current maintenance arrestment to be used[1]. However, a broadly similar effect is achieved by the requirement that the creditor must make appropriate intimation to the debtor of the making, registration or confirmation of the maintenance order[2]. Furthermore, a current maintenance arrestment may be executed only after the lapse of four weeks since the date of such intimation[3].

1 1987 Act, s 90(1).
2 Exactly what is to be intimated depends on the type of maintenance order in question: 1987 Act, s 54(1)(a); SI 1988/2013, r 45, Form 37.
3 1987 Act, s 54(1)(b).

NON-SCOTTISH ORDERS

6.38 The prerequisites for use of a current maintenance arrestment noted above, ie default by the debtor, intimation by the creditor, and the lapse of four weeks do not apply in respect of certain non-Scottish orders[1]. The orders in question are those registered in Scotland as set out in the 1987 Act, section 106, categories (c), (e), (f) and (g) of the definition of maintenance order[2]. The above-mentioned prerequisites do not apply where there has been produced to the court in Scotland which registered the order, a certificate of arrears[3] to the effect that at the time of the issue of the certificate the debtor was in arrears in his payment of instalments under the order.

1 1987 Act, s 54(2).
2 Ibid, s 106. See above at para 6.32, categories (4), (6), (7) and (8).
3 Maintenance Orders (Reciprocal Enforcement) Act 1972, s 21.

FURTHER CURRENT MAINTENANCE ARRESTMENT

6.39 The prerequisites to using a current maintenance arrestment noted above[1] also do not apply where the creditor has previously used a valid current maintenance arrestment which has ceased to have effect[2]. This is so, provided the reason for the cessation of the previous current maintenance arrestment is other than recall under section 55(2) of the 1987 Act. The further current maintenance arrestment must be used within three months after the date on which the prior arrestment ceased to have effect.

It is to be noted that it need not be the same maintenance order which is being enforced by the earlier and later current maintenance arrestments. Indeed, the purpose of this provision is to deal with the situation where a maintenance order, which is being enforced by a current maintenance arrestment, is varied or superseded by a new maintenance order.

1 Ie default by the debtor, intimation by the creditor, and the lapse of four weeks.
2 1987 Act, s 54(3).

SERVICE ON EMPLOYER

6.40 A current maintenance arrestment is brought into effect by service of a current maintenance arrestment schedule on the debtor's employer[1]. The details of the service of the schedule and intimation of copies are the same as for earnings arrestment, discussed above[2].

A current maintenance arrestment schedule which is served on the employer and a copy intimated to the debtor is to be in the form of Form 34 of the Sheriff Court Proceedings Act of Sederunt and must state[3]:

(1) the name, designation and address of the creditor, the debtor, the employer and any person residing in the United Kingdom to whom payment under the arrestment is to be made;

(2) the maintenance order constituting the current maintenance, when and by whom it was granted or issued, and, where appropriate, details of its registration or confirmation;

(3) the maintenance payable under the maintenance order by the debtor expressed as a daily rate;

(4) where appropriate, the date of intimation made to the debtor under section 54(1) of the 1987 Act and particulars of default; and

(5) whether or not income tax falls to be deducted from the maintenance payable by the debtor[4].

For purposes of paragraph (3), the daily rate of maintenance is calculated (i) where the maintenance is paid monthly, by multiplying the monthly rate by twelve and dividing by 365; (ii) where it is paid quarterly, by multiplying the quarterly rate by four and dividing by 365[5]; (iii) in other cases, by dividing the amount due by the number of days in the interval between payments.

The terms of section 53(1) and (2) of the 1987 Act (which set out the deductions to be made from the debtor's net earnings) are to be attached to or reproduced on the current maintenance schedule and on the copy intimated to the debtor[6].

1 1987 Act, s 51(2)(a).
2 Ibid, s 70. See above at para 6.07.
3 SI 1988/2013, r 42, Form 34.
4 The effect of the Finance Act 1988, ss 36, 37 is that no deductions in respect of income tax are made for maintenance payments.
5 1987 Act, s 51(4), (5).
6 SI 1988/2013, r 42(3).

COMMENCEMENT OF OPERATION OF CURRENT MAINTENANCE ARRESTMENT

6.41 As is the case with earnings arrestment, a current maintenance arrestment comes into effect when the current maintenance arrestment schedule is served on the employer[1]. However, the employer is not bound to operate the arrestment until the next pay day occuring seven days after the service of the schedule[2]. The employer may, if he so wishes, give effect to an earnings arrestment on any day occurring within seven days after the service of the schedule.

1 1987 Act, s 51(2)(a).
2 Ibid, s 69(2), (3).

Operation of current maintenance arrestment

GENERAL

6.42 A current maintenance arrestment has the effect of requiring the employer of the debtor to deduct a sum from the debtor's net earnings on every pay-day while the arrestment is in effect[1]. As soon as is reasonably practicable the employer must pay any sum deducted to the creditor[2].

1 1987 Act, s 51(1).
2 For the mode of payment to the creditor, see ibid, ss 57(2), (3) discussed above at para 6.20.

DEDUCTIONS

6.43 In operating a current maintenance arrestment, the employer deducts from the debtor's net earnings[1] a sum arrived at by multiplying the daily rate of maintenance[2] by the number of days (including non-working days) since the last pay-day when a deduction was made in respect of the arrestment. However, the debtor must be left, from his net earnings, with a sum equal to £5 per day for the number of days since the last pay (or since service of the current maintenance arrestment schedule, if there was no prior deduction made[3]). A deduction under a current maintenance arrestment must be modified to allow for the debtor's subsistence level of £5 per day.

The following example is given by the Scottish Law Commission Report to illustrate the operation of the rules on deductions[4]:

> 'A man liable to pay £50 per week aliment for his wife and three children normally earns £100 per week net. His employer deducts £50, remits it to the wife and pays the balance of £50 to the man. One week the man earns only £80 net. The employer cannot deduct the full £50 due that week since this would leave the man only £30 which is below the £35 per week exemption level. Instead the employer pays the man his exempt earnings of £35 and remits the balance of £45 to the wife.'

The daily subsistence level for the debtor may be varied by regulation by the Lord Advocate. Any such regulations do not apply to an existing current maintenance arrestment unless and until the creditor or debtor intimates the making of the regulations to the employer[5].

As all maintenance payments are now made gross of income tax[6], the employer does not make any further deductions in respect of tax from the amount deducted under the current maintenance arrestment.

The employer is also entitled to charge the debtor a fee of fifty pence per deduction for operating a current maintenance arrestment. The fee is deductible from the amount of the debtor's net earnings after the deduction under the current maintenance arrestment[7].

1 For net earnings, see 1987 Act, s 73(1) and discussion above at para 6.12.
2 Ie the rate as specified in the current maintenance arrestment schedule.
3 1987 Act, s 53(1), (2). Where no previous deduction has been made under the current maintenance arrestment, the daily rate of maintenance is multiplied by the number of days since the date of service to the schedule of the arrestment.
     What is not clear is the calculation to be made when there have been a number of deductions made under the current maintenance arrestment but on the last pay-day the debtor's earnings did not exceed a daily rate of £5 per day. It is submitted that in respect of that day the employer is treated as having made a nil deduction (rather than not having made a deduction at all) and he

calculates the relevant number of days from that day when operating the current maintenance arrestment on the next pay day.

4 Scot Law Com Report no 95 (1985), p 374.

5 1987 Act, s 53(3), (4); SI 1988/2013, r 43, Form 35.

6 Finance Act 1988, ss 36, 37, Sch 14, Pt IV, superseding 1987 Act, s 53(5), (6).

7 1987 Act, s 71. It can be noted that where the employer chooses to charge this fee, the debtor will not retain all of the £5 per day subsistence where the deduction under the current maintenance arrestment leaves only the amount of that level.

FAILURE BY EMPLOYER TO OPERATE CURRENT MAINTENANCE ARRESTMENT; RESTRICTION ON LIABILITY OF EMPLOYER

6.44   The provisions on the failure of an employer to operate a current maintenance arrestment and restrictions on the employer's liability are the same as those applying in the case of an earnings arrestment, and reference is made to discussion of these matters above[1].

1 See above at paras 6.22–6.23.

Duration of current maintenance arrestment

GENERAL RULE

6.45   Once a current maintenance arrestment comes into effect it remains in effect until the debtor has ceased to be employed by the employer or it has been recalled or has been abandoned by the creditor[1]. A current maintenance arrestment also ceases to have effect[2]

(1) on the obligation to pay maintenance under the maintenance order ceasing or ceasing to be enforceable in Scotland[3]; or

(2) on the coming into effect of an order or decree which varies, supersedes or recalls the maintenance order which is being enforced by the current maintenance arrestment[4]. Where such a later order is made by a court in Scotland, it may include a condition that it shall not come into effect until the earlier of

(i) expiry of a period, specified in the later order, to allow notice to be given to the employer that the earlier order has been varied or superseded; or

(ii) service of a new current maintenance arrestment schedule in pursuance of the later order[5].

This power to postpone the coming into effect of the later order does not apply where it is an award for periodical allowance on divorce or nullity or marriage, which supersedes an earlier decree for aliment for the benefit of a spouse[6].

1 1987 Act, s 51(2)(b).

2 Ibid, s 55(8).

3 Where a maintenance order pronounced outwith Scotland and registered in a sheriff court for enforcement in Scotland ceases to have effect because the debtor no longer resides in Scotland, the sheriff clerk of that court shall intimate those facts to the person upon whom the current maintenance arrestment was served: SI 1988/2013, r 49.

4 In the case of a non-Scottish order which has this effect on a maintenance order being enforced by a current maintenance arrestment, the relevant date is the date of registration of the later order in Scotland: 1987 Act, s 55(9).

5 Ibid, s 56(1).

6 Ibid, s 56(2).

REVIEW OF CURRENT MAINTENANCE ARRESTMENT

6.46 There are three forms of review of a current maintenance arrestment. These modes of review are made by application to the sheriff having jurisdiction over the place where the current maintenance arrestment was executed. If that place is not known to the applicant, application is made to the sheriff with jurisdiction over an established place of business of the debtor's employer[1].

1 1987 Act, ss 55, 73(1).

6.47 In the first place, an application may be made to the sheriff by the debtor or the person on whom the current maintenance arrestment schedule was served for a declaration that the current maintenance arrestment is invalid or has ceased to have effect[1]. Such an application is to be in the form of Form 38 of the Sheriff Court Proceedings Act of Sederunt and must state:
(1) the name and address of the creditor, the debtor, the officer of court who served the current maintenance arrestment schedule and the person on whom the schedule was served;
(2) the maintenance order and when, where and by whom it was granted or issued and, where appropriate, details of its registration or confirmation;
(3) the date of service of the current maintenance arrestment schedule;
(4) the reasons for the application;
(5) the form of the order sought; and
(6) any competent crave for expenses.
A copy of the current maintenance arrestment schedule is to be attached to the application. On the lodging of an application, the sheriff clerk fixes a date for a hearing and makes intimation as appropriate.

Where the sheriff is satisfied that a declarator should be granted as applied for he may also make such consequential orders as appears necessary in the circumstances[2].

The making of any such declarator is not subject to appeal[3].

1 1987 Act, s 55(1); SI 1988/2013, r 46, Form 38.
2 Any such consequential order under s 55(1) is to be intimated by the sheriff clerk to the debtor, the creditor and the person on whom the current maintenance arrestment schedule was served: 1987 Act, s 55(3).
3 Ibid, s 55(4).

6.48 Secondly, application may be made by the debtor for recall of the current maintenance arrestment on the ground that he is unlikely to default again in making payment of maintenance[1]. Application is in Form 39 of the Sheriff Court Proceedings Act of Sederunt and must specify:
(1) the name and address of the creditor, the debtor, the officer of court who served the current maintenance arrestment schedule and the employer;
(2) the maintenance order and when, where and by whom it was granted or issued and, where appropriate, details of its registration or confirmation;
(3) the date of service of the current maintenance arrestment schedule;
(4) such information as the applicant considers appropriate to satisfy the sheriff that he will not default again in paying maintenance;
(5) the order sought; and
(6) any competent crave for expenses.

Further procedure is as with an application for declarator or invalidity of a current maintenance arrestment.

1 1987 Act, s 55(2); SI 1988/2013, r 47, Form 39.

6.49   Thirdly, an application may also be made to the sheriff by the debtor, creditor or employer for the determination of any dispute as to the operation of a current maintenance arrestment[1]. An application is to be in the form of Form 40 of the Sheriff Court Proceedings Act of Sederunt and must state:
(1) the name and address of the creditor, the debtor, the officer of court who served the current maintenance arrestment schedule and the employer:
(2) the maintenance order and when, where and by whom it was granted or issued and, where appropriate, details of its registration or confirmation;
(3) the date of service of the current maintenance arrestment schedule;
(4) the subject-matter of the dispute;
(5) the form of the order sought, including any sum sought to be reimbursed or paid;
(6) any claim for interest and the date from which such interest should run; and
(7) any competent crave for expenses.
A copy of the current maintenance arrestment schedule is to be attached to the application. On the lodging of an application, the sheriff clerk fixes a date for a hearing and makes intimation as appropriate.
   In dealing with an application the sheriff may make an order for the payment of a sum which mistakenly has not been paid under the current maintenance arrestment, and for the reimbursement of a sum which mistakenly has been paid. Any such sum is to be paid with interest from the date specified in the order[2].

1 1987 Act, s 55(5); SI 1988/2013, r 48, Form 40.
2 1987 Act, s 55(6), (7). For the rate of interest, see 1987 Act, s 73(1).

PRESCRIPTION; INSOLVENCY, SEQUESTRATION

6.50   The application of the rules on prescription to current maintenance arrestments, and the effect on current maintenance arrestments of the insolvency and sequestration of the debtor, are the same as those in respect of earnings arrestments. These matters are discussed above[1].

1 See above at paras 6.28–6.29.

EFFECT OF TERMINATION OF CURRENT MAINTENANCE ARRESTMENT

6.51   The rules on this matter are the same as those applying to earnings arrestment, discussed above[1].

1 See above at para 6.31.

CONJOINED ARRESTMENT ORDERS

General rule on multiple use of diligences against earnings

6.52   The general rule is that more than one diligence against earnings may not be in operation against the same earnings at the same time. This general rule is subject to one exception noted below[1]. Thus, while one earnings arrestment is in effect, any other earnings arrestment against the same earnings of the debtor is not competent. Similarly, while a current maintenance arrestment is in effect, any other current maintenance arrestment against the same earnings of the debtor is incompetent[2].

Where two or more schedules of the same type of arrestment are served on the employer on the same day, the employer is to give effect to the arrestment, the schedule of which he received first. If the employer cannot determine the time he received the schedules, he has a choice as to which arrestment he gives effect to[3].

It should be noted that the provisions on equalisation of poindings and arrestments within certain time-limits from apparent insolvency of the debtor, do not apply to diligences against earnings[4]. The remedy of the creditor who is shut-out from using diligence against earnings by the provisions of the 1987 Act is to apply for a conjoined arrestment order. To assist such a creditor in applying for a conjoined arrestment order, the employer must provide him with certain items of information as soon as possible after the service of the schedule of the frustrated arrestment[5]. The items of information in question are:

(1) the name and address of the creditor using diligence against the debtor's earnings;

(2) the date and place of execution; and

(3) the debt recoverable specified in the earnings arrestment schedule or, as the case may be, the daily rate of maintenance specified in the current maintenance schedule.

If the employer fails to give this information, the second creditor may make an application to the sheriff for an order ordaining the employer to do so[6].

1 See para 6.53 below.
2 1987 Act, s 59(1), (2). An earnings arrestment and current maintenance arrestment come into effect on the day of service of the schedule of arrestment: 1987 Act, ss 47(2)(a), 51(2)(a).
3 Ibid, s 59(3).
4 Bankruptcy (Scotland) Act 1985, Sch 7, para 24; 1987 Act, s 67, Sch 6, para 28(b).
5 1987 Act, s 59(4).
6 Ibid, s 59(5); SI 1988/2013, r 52, Form 42. Application is made to the sheriff having jurisdiction over the place where the creditor serves the schedule of the arrestment affected by s 59: 1987 Act, s 73(1).

Simultaneous operation of earnings and current maintenance arrestment

6.53 The exception to the general rule stated above is that one earnings arrestment and one current maintenance arrestment may be operated at the same time against the same earnings of the debtor[1]. In such circumstances, a conjoined arrestment order is neither necessary nor competent. The creditor using the earnings arrestment may be the same person as, or a different person from, the creditor using the current maintenance arrestment.

Where the employer finds that he cannot make sufficient deductions from the debtor's net earnings[2] on any pay-day to give full effect to both arrestments he must give priority to operating the earnings arrestment[3]. The current maintenance arrestment is then operated against any balance of the net earnings.

1 1987 Act, s 58(1).
2 Ibid, s 73(1). See above at para 6.12.
3 Ibid, s 58(2).

Conjoined arrestment order: application

6.54 An application for a conjoined arrestment order may be made by a 'qualified' creditor, ie a creditor who would be entitled but for the operation of section 59(1) or 59(2) of the 1987 Act to enforce his debt by an earnings arrestment or a current maintenance arrestment[1].

It should be noted that to be 'entitled' to use an earnings arrestment a creditor (other than a creditor proceeding on a summary warrant) must have had a charge served on the debtor and the period of charge expired without payment[2].

An application for a conjoined arrestment order may not be made[3]:

(1) where there is no arrestment in effect against the debtor's earnings;

(2) where all the debts are maintenance debts payable by the same debtor to the same person such that they could be enforced under section 52(5)(a) of the 1987 Act; or

(3) where there are two debts which could be enforced together under section 58(1) of the 1987 Act.

Application for a conjoined arrestment order is made to the sheriff court with jurisdiction over the place where the existing arrestment was executed. Where there are both an earnings arrestment and a current maintenance arrestment in existence, application may be made to the sheriff court where either was executed[4]. The application is in Form 43 of the Sheriff Court Proceedings Act of Sederunt and must specify[5]:

(1) the name and address of the applicant, the debtor, the employer and any person residing in the United Kingdom to whom payment is to be made in respect of the applicant's debt;

(2) such information relating to the debt due to the applicant as would require to be specified in an earnings arrestment schedule or, as the case may be, a current maintenance arrestment schedule;

(3) in respect of each earnings arrestment or current maintenance arrestment already in effect against the debtor in the hands of the same employer –

(i) the name and address of the creditor;

(ii) the date and the place of the execution of such arrestments; and

(iii) the debt recoverable specified in the earnings arrestment schedule or, as the case may be, the daily rate of maintenance specified in the current maintenance schedule; and

(4) the expenses of the application.

On the lodging of the application, the sheriff clerk sends a form to the debtor and any other creditor already using diligence against the debtor's earnings. If the debtor or any such creditor wishes to object to the application he must complete and return the form. If necessary, a hearing is arranged for considering the application. However, a sheriff may refuse an application for a conjoined arrestment order only if an order cannot be made competently[6]. The decision of the sheriff making a conjoined arrestment order is not subject to appeal[7].

Once a conjoined arrestment order is made, the sheriff clerk must serve a copy of the order on the applicant, the employer, the debtor, and the creditor in the arrestment or arrestments existing prior to the making of the order[8].

1 1987 Act, s 60(1)(b).
2 Ibid, s 90(1). See above at para 6.06.
3 Ibid, s 60(1)(a), (4).
4 Ibid, s 73(1).

5 SI 1988/2013, r 53, Form 43.
6 1987 Act, s 60(2).
7 Ibid, s 60(8).
8 Ibid, s 60(7); SI 1988/2013, r 54(3).

Effect of conjoined arrestment order

6.55 A conjoined arrestment order is in the form of Form 45 of the Sheriff Court Proceedings Act of Sederunt[1]. The order has the effect of recalling the arrestment against the debtor's earnings in force prior to the making of the order. A further effect is that the order requires the employer to make deductions from the debtor's net earnings in accordance with section 63 of the 1987 Act[2].

The conjoined arrestment order itself must[3]:

(1) specify any earnings arrestment or current maintenance arrestment in effect against the earnings of the debtor in the hands of the same employer;

(2) notify the employer that he must deduct a sum calculated in accordance with section 63 of the 1987 Act from the debtor's net earnings on any pay-day and to pay the sum deducted to the sheriff clerk as soon as is reasonably practicable for so long as the order is in effect;

(3) specify, as appropriate, the amount recoverable in respect of the debt or debts and the maintenance, expressed as a daily rate or aggregate of the daily rates;

(4) state the address of the sheriff clerk to whom payments are to be sent and, where appropriate, a court reference number; and

(5) if appropriate, include an award of expenses.

1 SI 1988/2013, r 54(1).
2 1987 Act, s 60(3).
3 Ibid, s 60(6); SI 1988/2013, r 54(2).

6.56 While the conjoined arrestment order is in force, a creditor may not use an earnings arrestment or a current maintenance arrestment against the earnings affected by the order. Nor may a further conjoined arrestment order be granted against those earnings[1]. A creditor who seeks to serve a schedule of arrestment in these circumstances must be informed by the employer that there is a conjoined arrestment order and which court made the order[2]. If the employer refuses to give this information, the creditor may apply to the sheriff for an order requiring the employer to provide it[3].

1 1987 Act, s 62(1). Provision is made by s 62(3) of the 1987 Act for the situation where between the application for a conjoined arrestment order and its being granted a further arrestment becomes operative under s 58(1).
2 Ibid, s 62(2).
3 Ibid, s 62(4); SI 1988/2013, r 56, Form 48. Application is made to the sheriff court having jurisdiction over the place where the creditor serves the schedule of arrestment affected by s 62: 1987 Act, s 73(1).

6.57 Only the sums specified in the conjoined arrestment order may be recovered by it. These sums are set out in the application by the qualified creditor or in the arrestment which is recalled by the conjoined arrestment order[1]. In the case of a creditor for a debt other than one of current maintenance, the conjoined arrestment order may recover (1) all sums (including expenses) due under the decree or other document of debt[2] and (2) any interest on that sum accrued at the date of making the conjoined arrestment order.

A creditor who has used an earnings arrestment which is recalled by the conjoined arrestment order, may recover the outstanding principal sum and interest as at the date of the execution of the arrestment. He may also recover the expenses of the arrestment and the charge which preceded it[3].

Where arrears of maintenance are to be enforced by a conjoined arrestment order, no interest on such arrears accrues while the order is in effect[4].

A creditor who makes an application for a conjoined arrestment order is entitled to recover under it the expenses of making the application provided these are set out in the application[5].

1 1987 Act, s 61(1), (2).
2 This includes, as ordinary debts, the expenses of executing a current maintenance arrestment: ibid, s 51(3).
3 Ibid, s 61(1)(c).
4 Ibid, s 61(3).
5 Ibid, 61(4). He is not entitled to recover the expenses of any earnings arrestment or current maintenance arrestment executed after the date of application: ibid, s 61(5).

Application for variation of a conjoined arrestment order

6.58 Provision is made for a creditor who is not part of a conjoined arrestment order but who is unable to use diligence against the debtor's earnings because of a conjoined arrestment order, to apply to the sheriff for an order varying the terms of the conjoined arrestment order so that it includes the debts of that creditor in its operation[1]. Application is made to the sheriff court in which the conjoined arrestment order was made[2]. The applicant creditor (unless a current maintenance creditor) must have served a prior charge on the debtor, which has expired without payment at the time of the application.

The application is in the form of Form 49 of the Sheriff Court Proceedings Act of Sederunt and must specify:
(1) the name and address of the applicant, the debtor, the employer and any person residing in the United Kingdom to whom payment is to be made in respect of the applicant's debt;
(2) the date of the conjoined arrestment order;
(3) such information relating to the debt due to the applicant as would require to be specified in an earnings arrestment schedule or, as the case may be, a current maintenance arrestment schedule;
(4) the expenses of the application.
On the lodging of the application, the sheriff clerk sends various forms to the debtor, the employer and the other creditors whose debts are being enforced by the conjoined arrestment order. These forms allow for any of these persons to object to the application for variation. If objection is made, a hearing is held; otherwise the sheriff grants the application[3]. A copy of the order varying the conjoined arrestment order is served by the sheriff clerk on each party to whom the application was intimated.

The varied order will set out the debts covered by it in the same manner as a conjoined arrestment order. It comes into effect seven days after a copy has been served on the employer[4].

1 1987 Act, s 62(5); SI 1988/2013, r 57, Form 49.
2 1987 Act, s 73(1).

3 It appears that a sheriff must grant a competently-made application, if necessary after hearing the other parties. See 1987 Act, s 62(5): 'The sheriff on an application by a creditor . . . *shall* make an order varying the conjoined arrestment order'. Contrast the terms of SI 1988/2013 r 57(6). A decision of the sheriff granting an application is not subject to appeal: 1987 Act, s 62(9).

4 1987 Act, s 62(6), (7).

Operation of a conjoined arrestment order

GENERAL EFFECT

6.59   The service of a copy of the conjoined arrestment order on the employer has the effect of requiring him to deduct a sum calculated in accordance with section 63 of the 1987 Act from the debtor's net earnings[1] on any pay day while the order is in effect[2]. The employer then makes over the deduction to the sheriff clerk who in turn disburses the various shares of the deducted sum to the creditors whose debts are covered by the conjoined arrestment order.

A conjoined arrestment order comes into effect seven days after a copy has been served by the sheriff clerk on the employer[3]. It remains in force until the debtor ceases to be employed by the employer or until a copy of an order recalling the conjoined arrestment order has been served on the employer[4].

1 For the meaning of net earnings, see 1987 Act, s 73(1) and discussion above at para 6.12.
2 Ibid, s 60(3).
3 Ibid, s 60(5)(a). This is subject to the provisions of the 1987 Act, s 69(2)–(3), discussed above at para 6.09.
4 Ibid, s 60(5)(b).

FAILURE BY EMPLOYER TO OPERATE A CONJOINED ARRESTMENT ORDER

6.60   Where an employer fails to comply with a conjoined arrestment order, he is liable to pay to the sheriff clerk any sum that would have been deducted under the order[1]. The employer is not entitled to recover any sum he has paid to the debtor in contravention of the order.

1 1987 Act, s 60(9). Any claim by the sheriff clerk must be made within one year from the date when the deduction or payment should have been made. The sheriff clerk may proceed by applying for a warrant for diligence against the employer: SI 1988/2013, r 55.

SUMS DEDUCTIBLE BY THE EMPLOYER OPERATING A CONJOINED ARRESTMENT ORDER

All debts non-maintenance debts

6.61   Where all the debts subject to a conjoined arrestment order are debts other than current maintenance, the employer makes deductions on a pay-day as if the debts were one debt being enforced by an earnings arrestment[1].

1 1987 Act, s 63(2). See above at paras 6.13–6.18. Similar provision exists in respect of intimation to the employer of regulations changing the tables in Sch 2 to the 1987 Act. In the case of a conjoined arrestment order, intimation is made by the sheriff clerk: 1987 Act, s 63(7); SI 1988/2013, r 58, Form 52.

All debts current maintenance

6.62 Similarly, where all the debts are for current maintenance, the deduction made by the employer is the same as if he were operating a current maintenance arrestment in respect of the aggregate daily rates of maintenance[1].

1 1987 Act, s 63(3), (4). See above at para 6.43. Similar provision exists in respect of intimation to the employer of regulations changing the amount of the debtor's daily subsistence level. In the case of a conjoined arrestment order, intimation is to be made by the sheriff clerk: 1987 Act s 63(6), (7); SI 1988/2013, r 58, Form 52.

Mixture of ordinary and current maintenance debts

6.63 Where one or more of the debts are 'ordinary' debts and one or more are for current maintenance, the sum to be deducted by the employer is the aggregate of[2]
(i) the sum deductible in operating an earnings arrestment in respect of the ordinary debt or total of all the ordinary debts; and
(ii) the sum deductible in operating a current maintenance arrestment in respect of the current maintenance debt or all the current maintenance debts. However, this deduction is made only from the balance of the debtor's net earnings once the deduction in (i) above has been made.

1 1987 Act, s 63(5).

Payment to sheriff clerk

6.64 Once the employer has made the deductions under a conjoined arrestment order, he must make payment of the deduction to the sheriff clerk as soon as is reasonably practicable. Payment to the sheriff clerk may be by cheque unless previously a cheque making payment has been dishonoured, in which case the sheriff clerk can insist on payment being made in cash[1].

1 Ibid, s 63(10), (11).

DISBURSEMENT BY SHERIFF CLERK OF SUMS RECEIVED FROM EMPLOYER

6.65 Once the sheriff clerk receives deductions from an employer operating a conjoined arrestment order, he is responsible for making disbursement of the proportionate share of the deduction to the creditor whose debts are being enforced by the conjoined arrestment order[1].

The disbursement is made in accordance with the following rules set out in Schedule 3 to the 1987 Act:
(1) Where all the debts are ordinary debts, in every disbursement by the sheriff clerk each creditor shall be paid the same proportion of the amount of his debt.
(2) Where all the debts are current maintenance, in any such disbursement, if the sum available for disbursement is –
    (i) sufficient to satisfy every creditor in respect of the amount of maintenance to be deducted in respect of his debt on that pay day, each creditor shall be paid that amount;
    (ii) insufficient to satisfy every creditor in respect of the amount of maintenance specified in (i) above, each creditor shall be paid the same proportion of that amount.

(3) Subject to paragraph 4 below, where the debts comprise both ordinary debts and current maintenance, in any such disbursement –

(i) if only one of the debts is an ordinary debt, the creditor in that debt shall be paid the sum which would be payable to him if the debt were being enforced by an earnings arrestment;

(ii) if more than one of the debts is an ordinary debt, each of the creditors in those debts, out of the sum which would be payable to a creditor if the debt were a single debt being enforced by an earnings arrestment, shall be paid the same proportion of the amount of his debt;

(iii) if only one of the debts is current maintenance, the creditor in that debt shall be paid the sum which would be payable to him under section 51 of the 1987 Act if the debt were being enforced by a current maintenance arrestment;

(iv) if more than one of the debts is current maintenance, each of the creditors in those debts shall receive a payment in accordance with paragraph 2 above.

(4) If the sum available for any disbursement is insufficient to enable the provisions of paragraph 3 above to operate both in relation to the ordinary debts and the current maintenance, priority shall be given in the disbursement to the ordinary debts.

(5) For the purposes of Schedule 3 to the 1987 Act, the amount of an ordinary debt –

(i) of a creditor whose debt was being enforced by an earnings arrestment which was recalled under section 60(3) of the 1987 Act, shall be the amount specified in the earnings arrestment schedule;

(ii) of any other creditor, shall be the amount specified in the conjoined arrestment order or the order under section 62(5) of the 1987 Act.

1 1987 Act, s 64.

EXTINCTION OF DEBT BEING ENFORCED BY CONJOINED ARRESTMENT ORDER

6.66 The creditor whose debt is being enforced by a conjoined arrestment order must inform the sheriff clerk that the debt is extinguished or is no longer enforceable by diligence. If the creditor fails to make due intimation as soon as is reasonably practicable, any sum he thereafter receives under the conjoined arrestment order is recoverable by the sheriff clerk with interest. All such amounts recovered in this way are disbursed by the sheriff clerk to the remaining creditors in accordance with the provisions of Schedule 3 to the 1987 Act[1].

Furthermore, where a creditor has failed to make due intimation to the sheriff clerk of the extinction of his debt, the debtor may apply to the sheriff for an order for payment of a sum of money by the creditor to the debtor. This sum cannot exceed twice the amount recoverable by the sheriff clerk in respect of overpayment[2].

1 1987 Act, s 65(5), (6), (8).
2 Ibid, s 65(7); SI 1988/2013, r 60, Form 55. Compare discussion above at para 6.31.

DISPUTES AS TO OPERATION OF CONJOINED ARRESTMENT ORDER

6.67 An application may be made to the sheriff by the debtor, creditor, employer or the sheriff clerk for the determination of any dispute as to the operation of a conjoined arrestment order[1]. An application is in Form 54 of the Sheriff Court Proceedings Act of Sederunt and must state:

(1) the name and address of the applicant, the debtor, the creditors whose debts are being enforced by the conjoined arrestment order, the employer and the sheriff clerk;

(2) the date of the conjoined arrestment order and the court which made the order;

(3) the subject-matter of the dispute;

(4) the order sought, including details of any sum for which reimbursement or repayment is sought;

(5) any claim for interest and the date from which such interest should run; and

(6) any competent crave for expenses.

On the lodging of an application, the sheriff clerk fixes a date for a hearing and makes intimation as appropriate.

In dealing with an application the sheriff may make an order for the payment of a sum which mistakenly has not been paid under the conjoined arrestment, and for the reimbursement of a sum which mistakenly has been paid. Any such sum is to be paid with interest from the date specified in the order[2].

1　1987 Act, s 65(1); SI 1988/2013, r 59, Form 54.
2　1987 Act, s 65(2), (3). For the rate of interest, see 1987 Act, s 73(1).

Cessation of conjoined arrestment order

GENERAL

6.68　A conjoined arrestment order once in effect remains so until the debtor ceases to be employed by the empoyer or an order recalling the conjoined arrestment order has been served on the employer under section 66(7) of the 1987 Act[1].

1　1987 Act, s 60(5).

RECALL; VARIATION

Recall under section 66(1)(a)

6.69　The following persons may make an application for recall of a conjoined arrestment order[1]:

(i) the debtor;

(ii) any creditor whose debt is being enforced by the order;

(iii) the person on whom a copy of the order or an order varying the order was served;

(iv) the sheriff clerk;

(v) if the debtor's estate has been sequestrated, the interim trustee appointed under section 13 of the Bankruptcy (Scotland) Act 1985 or the permanent trustee in sequestration.

Application is made to the sheriff court in which the conjoined arrestment order was granted. Application is in Form 56 of the Sheriff Court Proceedings Act of Sederunt and must specify[2]:

(i) the name and address of the debtor, the creditors whose debts are being enforced under the conjoined arrestment order, the person on whom a copy of the order or order varying the order was served under section 60(7) or 62(6) of the 1987 Act, any trustee in the debtor's sequestration and the sheriff clerk to whom payment is made under the order;

(ii) the date of the conjoined arrestment order and the court which made the order;

(iii) if appropriate, that the conjoined arrestment order is invalid and why it is claimed to be invalid;

(iv) if appropriate, that all ordinary debts enforced by the order have been paid or otherwise extinguished or have ceased to be enforceable and in each case when and how this occurred;

(v) if appropriate, that all obligations to pay current maintenance enforced by the order have ceased or have ceased to be enforceable by diligence and in either case when and how this occurred;

(vi) if appropriate, that the debtor's estate has been sequestrated and when this occurred;

(vii) the order sought and any consequential order; and

(viii) any competent crave for expenses.

Where an application has been lodged the sheriff clerk fixes a hearing and makes appropriate intimation.

The sheriff must make an order recalling the conjoined arrestment order if he is satisfied:

(i) that the conjoined arrestment order is invalid;

(ii) that all the ordinary debts enforced by the order have been paid or otherwise extinguished or have ceased to be enforceable by diligence and that all the obligations to pay current maintenance being so enforced have ceased or have ceased to be enforceable by diligence[3]; or

(iii) that the debtor's estate has been sequestrated.

The sheriff may also make such consequential order as appears necessary.

1 1987 Act, s 66(2).
2 SI 1988/2013, r 61, Form 56.
3 In this case intimation or a hearing is not always necessary: see SI 1988/2013, r 61(4).

Recall under section 66(1)(b)

6.70 Application to the sheriff for recall of a conjoined arrestment order may also be made by all the creditors whose debts are being enforced by the order. The application is in Form 57 of the Sheriff Court Proceedings Act of Sederunt and must specify:

(i) the name and addresses of the applicants and the debtor;

(ii) the date of the conjoined arrestment order and the court which made the order;

(iii) the reasons for the application; and

(iv) any consequential order sought.

On the lodging of such an application the sheriff may grant it immediately or may make such other order as he considers appropriate.

Variation on extinction of debt

6.71 Where a debt being enforced by a conjoined arrestment order is extinguished or is no longer enforceable[1], an application may be made to the sheriff[2] for an order to vary the conjoined arrestment order to take account of this fact. The application may be made by the debtor, any creditor whose debt is being enforced by the conjoined arrestment order, the employer or the sheriff clerk[3]. The application is in Form 58 of the Sheriff Court Proceedings Act of Sederunt and must specify[4]:

(i) the name and address of the debtor, the employer, the creditors whose debts are being enforced by the conjoined arrestment order and the sheriff clerk;

(ii) the date of the conjoined arrestment order and the court which made the order;

(iii) if appropriate, that any ordinary debt being enforced by the order has been paid, otherwise extinguished or has ceased to be enforceable by diligence and in each case when and how this occurred;

(iv) if appropriate, that an order or decree varying, superseding or recalling any maintenance order has come into effect and when and by whom the order or decree was granted;

(v) if appropriate, that an obligation to pay maintenance has ceased or has ceased to be enforceable in Scotland and in either case when or how this occurred;

(vi) the order sought; and

(vii) any competent crave for expenses.

1 For the case of a current maintenance debt, see 1987 Act, s 66(4)(b), (5).
2 See 1987 Act, s 73(1).
3 1987 Act, s 66(4).
4 SI 1988/2013, r 63, Form 58.

Request by creditor to cease enforcement of the debt

6.72 A creditor whose debt is being enforced by a conjoined arrestment order may make an application to the sheriff[1] for an order to vary the conjoined arrestment order to exclude his debt from the order[2]. Any such application must be in writing[3].

1 1987 Act, s 73(1).
2 Ibid, s 66(6).
3 See further SI 1988/2013, r 64.

Service of sheriff's decision on recall or variation

6.73 Where an order for the recall or variation of a conjoined arrestment order has been made, the sheriff clerk must as soon as is reasonably practicable thereafter serve a copy of the order for recall or variation on[1]:
the debtor
the employer
any creditor whose debt is being enforced by the conjoined arrestment order
(where the recall is on the ground of the debtor's sequestration), the interim or permanent trustee in sequestration.
In general, service of the copy of the order is necessary for the order to have effect[2].

1 1987 Act, s 66(7); SI 1988/2013, r 65.
2 1987 Act, s 66(8)–(10).

TIME TO PAY ORDER

6.74 Where a debt is being enforced by a conjoined arrestment order and a time to pay order is made in respect of that debt, the sheriff making the time to pay order must vary the conjoined arrestment order so as to exclude the debt from it. If no other debt or maintenance is being enforced by the conjoined arrestment order, the sheriff must recall that order.

The sheriff has these powers only where the time to pay order and the conjoined arrestment order were made in the same sheriff court. Where these orders were made in different sheriff courts, the sheriff making the time to pay order must intimate that order to the sheriff in the court which made the conjoined arrestment order. That sheriff must vary, or if appropriate recall, the conjoined arrestment order[1].

1 1987 Act, s 9(2)(b).

PRESCRIPTION: INSOLVENCY, SEQUESTRATION

6.75 The application of the rules on prescription to conjoined arrestment orders, and the effect on such orders of the insolvency and sequestration of the debtor, are the same as in respect of earnings arrestments. These matters are discussed above[1].

1 See above at paras 6.28–6.29.

CHAPTER 7

POINDING AND SALE

INTRODUCTION

7.01 The diligence of poinding and sale gave rise to considerable controversy and criticism during the period of consultation held by the Scottish Law Commission on reform of the law of diligence[1]. Most of the criticism focused on the social injustice in the situation where a debtor could be deprived of necessary household goods by the diligence, on the humiliation experienced by debtors in the public and publicised sale of their goods for debt, and the expense involved in a multi-staged diligence.

The strategy of the Commission was to reject calls for the total abolition of the diligence as being too undiscriminating and not placing attention on the aspects of the existing law which most needed reform. The Commission favoured retaining the diligence in its multi-staged form (prior charge, valuation of goods, application for warrant to sell the goods, the sale), although recognising that this did lead to the possibility of considerable expenses where the diligence proceeded to all its stages[2]. To strike a proper balance between the diligence operating as an effective mode of enforcing debt and protecting the debtor from unnecessary harshness the Commission proposed that:

(1) all items of household goods and various other types of goods which the debtor and members of his household reasonably required should be exempt from poinding;

(2) the debtor should be given a variety of rights throughout the stages of the diligence to have the goods released from the poinding;

(3) strict time-limits for executing the diligence were to be introduced;

(4) in general, creditors were not to be allowed to execute more than one poinding in the debtor's premises to enforce the same debt;

(5) the debtor was to be given protection in the form of judicial supervision by way of the creditor or officer of court making reports to the court at various stages of the diligence;

(6) warrant to sell goods should require separate application at which the debtor is entitled to appear and make objection.

These recommendations were implemented in Part II of the 1987 Act.

1 Report on Diligence and Debtor Protection (Scot Law Com no 95 (1985)), pp 60–68, 238–239.
2 By far the majority of poindings do not reach the stage of warrant sale: Scot Law Com Report no 95 (1985), pp 17–20.

THE CHARGE

Nature of charge

7.02 A charge is a formal request in writing served on the debtor and demands payment by him of sums due within a specified time, and which warns the debtor that specified diligences may proceed against him if payment of the sum stated as due in the charge is not made[1]. A charge for payment is a necessary prerequisite of executing the diligences of poinding and sale, and earnings arrestment, unless these diligences proceed on a summary warrant[2].

In general terms, a prior charge has been a necessary preliminary to poinding since the Poinding Act 1669[3], and the Scottish Law Commission recommended its retention despite the effect which the charge has of adding to the expenses of executing the diligence of poinding and sale[4]. The charge has a significant role in informing the debtor that he is due to make payment under a court decree (or other document of debt) and in most cases provides the debtor with a point of contract with the creditor in the shape of the officer of court who serves the charge[5]. Furthermore, service of a charge is one of the steps which triggers the right of the debtor to make an application for a time to pay order[6]. Service of a charge by an officer of court also allows the officer to advise the instructing creditor on the prospects for recovering the debt by a poinding at the debtor's premises.

1 Charges are also required in relation to other types of diligence, eg civil imprisonment or the delivery of goods.
2 1987 Act, s 90(1), (2). In practice in summary warrant poindings, the officer of court sends an informal notice of the poinding to the debtor.
3 Poinding Act 1669, c 5 (repealed by the 1987 Act, Sch 8). A prior charge was not necessary under the former small claims procedures in certain circumstances, but is required in respect of the existing summary cause and small claims actions.
4 Scot Law Com Report no 95 (1985), pp 239–240.
5 The officer has a presumed authority to collect the sums specified in the charge on behalf of the creditor. AS (Messengers-at-Arms and Sheriff Officers Rules) 1988, SI 1988/2097, r 16(1)(a).
6 1987 Act, s 5(1)(a). See ch 3 above at para 3.63.

Warrant to charge

7.03 Warrant to serve a charge on a debtor is contained in the extract decree or extract document of debt[1]. Such warrants may be executed anywhere in Scotland without the need for a warrant of concurrence[2]. The right to serve a charge based on a decree prescribes after the lapse of a period of twenty years unless the creditor has taken steps to enforce the debt by other diligence or the debtor has acknowledged the debt within that period[3].

1 1987 Act, s 87. Procedure where title to enforce the debt has been acquired from the party in whose favour the decree or document of debt was granted is now governed by s 88 of the 1987 Act. Letters of horning, horning and poinding, poinding, and caption have been abolished: s 89.
2 1987 Act, s 91.
3 Prescription and Limitation (Scotland) Act 1973, ss 7, 9, 10; Sch 1, para 2(a).

Form of charge

7.04 The form of a charge for payment is set out in an Act of Sederunt[1]. It should be noted that the charge must specify the various items of the total sum due as at the time of serving the charge. These items include the principal sum, interest on that sum to date, expenses[2], and expenses of the charge, and are usually stated less any sum paid to account. Only payment of, or tender to pay, this total sum by the debtor acts to terminate the poinding and sale[3].

A schedule of charge may note any payments already made to account. However, where the charge specifies a sum in excess of what is actually, or remains, due, it is nonetheless good in respect of what is due, and there is no duty to account for payments already made by the debtor[4]. To justify having a charge suspended, the debtor must be able to aver and prove that all of the sums specified in the charge have been paid in full[5].

The charge must also correctly set out the names (and any special capacities) of the party charging and the party being charged. The addresses of the parties must also be included[6]. The rationale of setting out the address of the party charging was that the debtor must be given sufficient information to allow him to pay the sum charged. However, under the existing law the officer executing the charge now has an implied authority to act as the agent of the creditor as regards collecting debts due under the diligence. It may therefore be sufficient if the name and address of the officer is stated in the charge without also stating the address of the creditor, but the safe practice is to include this last item of information.

1 AS (Form of Charge for Payment) 1988, SI 1988/2059; Act of Adjournal (Consolidation Amendment No 2) (Forms of Warrant for Execution and Charge for Payment of Fine or Other Financial Penalty) 1989, SI 1989/1020.
2 In the case of judgments registered under the Civil Jurisdiction and Judgments Act 1982, Schs 6, 7 interest may also run on the court costs (Civil Jurisdiction and Judgments Act 1982, Sch 6, para 8(3); Sch 7, para 7(2)).
3 1987 Act, s 95.
4 *Wilson v Stronach* (1862) 24 D 271; *Thiem's Trustees v Collie* (1899) 7 SLT 4; *Haughhead Coal Company v Gallocher* (1903) 11 SLT 156; *Dickson v United Dominions Trust Ltd* (No 2) 1983 SLT 502.
5 *Dickson v United Dominions Trust Ltd* (No 2), above.
6 *Dunbar & Co v Mitchell* 1928 SLT 225.

Days of charge

7.05   Prior to the 1987 Act there was a confusing variety in the days of charge, ie the period within which the charge requires the debtor to make payment of the sums due[1]. By virtue of section 90(3), the days of charge are fourteen days if the person on whom the charge is served is within the United Kingdom and twenty-eight days if he is outside the United Kingdom or his whereabouts are unknown. It should be noted that this rule states the appropriate days of charge in terms of the debtor either being within or not within the United Kingdom rather than his having residence or domicile there. Accordingly, where the debtor is resident or domiciled in the United Kingdom but is not personally present anywhere in the United Kingdom when the charge is served, the days of charge are twenty-eight days.

It should also be noted that the courts are not in general empowered to lengthen or shorten the days of charge.

1 Scot Law Com Report no 95 (1985), p 241.

Modes of service of charge

7.06   Generally speaking, a charge must be served by an officer of court[1] by means of personal service or one of its accepted equivalents. These modes of service require the presence of a witness in addition to the officer of court[2].

Unlike the position as regards the execution of a poinding or warrant sale, there is no provision in respect of the time of day or night when a charge may be made. However, a charge cannot be executed on a Sunday or day of public holiday[3], and the safest practice seems to be that a charge should wherever possible be executed at the times and on the days when the poinding may be executed[4].

The provisions of the Citation Amendment (Scotland) Act 1882 (which allows service of citations by means of post by solicitors) do not apply to a charge to pay[5]. Service by post is possible only in relation to certain summary cause sheriff court actions.

1 Charges based on a warrant of a sheriff clerk may be executed only by a sheriff officer, not by a messenger-at-arms: 1987 Act, s 77(2). See further ch 14 below at paras 14.21–14.23.
2 Debtors (Scotland) Act 1838, s 32.
3 Stair IV, 47, 27; *Montieth v Hutton* (1900) 8 SLT 250.
4 1987 Act, s 17.
5 *Gow & Sons v Thomson* (1895) 1 Adam 534.

PERSONAL SERVICE

7.07 Personal service is effected by means of the officer delivering the schedule of the charge to the debtor in person wherever he can be found[1]. Where the debtor is thought to be within his house or premises, the officer should attempt to make personal service, rather than use one of its alternatives[2].

Personal service is executed when the schedule of charge is tendered to the debtor, and does not require that the debtor should accept the service[3]. However, if the debtor refuses to accept the schedule, this fact should be mentioned in the report of service[4].

1 RC 74A; OCR 10; SCR 6.
2 *Bruce v Hall* (1708) Mor 3696.
3 Stair IV, 38, 15; J Graham Stewart *The Law of Diligence* p 320.
4 Cp *Busby v Clark* (1904) 7 F 162.

SERVICE AT DWELLINGHOUSE OR PLACE OF BUSINESS OF THE DEBTOR

7.08 Where the debtor cannot be found so as to allow personal service, the charge may be served at the debtor's dwellinghouse. For this purpose the dwellinghouse is the place where the debtor is ordinarily resident[1], but not eg where he is merely the owner of leased property. The officer on being admitted to the house should ask for the debtor; if the debtor is present, personal service on him should be made. If the debtor is not present, the schedule of the charge may be left in the hands of a resident in the house with directions to give it to the debtor. It is unsuitable for the schedule to be left with children or with others who are unable to understand the officer's directions[2].

Where the debtor's place of residence is not known, or where the debtor is being charged in relation to a business or commercial debt, this mode of service may be made at the debtor's place of business by leaving the schedule in the hands of an employee[3].

1 *Corstorphine v Kasten* (1898) 1 F 287. If the debtor has more than one place of residence, service
  may be made at any one of them: *Macdonald v Sinclair* (1843) 5 D 1253.
2 Cp *South of Scotland Electricity Board v Brogan* 1981 SLT (Sh Ct) 8.
3 OCR 10(1); SCR 6(1).

'KEYHOLE' SERVICE

7.09 Where personal service or service by way of leaving the schedule with
an inmate of the debtor's dwellinghouse or place of business has been
attempted unsuccessfully, the officer may deposit the schedule through the
letter-box of the premises or by fixing it to the door of the debtor's premises.
Prior to service by this means, the officer should satisfy himself that the
premises are empty by making six audible knocks[1] on the door of the
premises and he should also make any further inquiries as are necessary to
establish the whereabouts of the debtor or any inmates of the premises[2].

Where such 'keyhole' service has been made after unsuccessful attempts at
personal or dwellinghouse service, the officer must send a copy of the
schedule to the debtor at the address where he thinks it most likely the debtor
is to be found[3].

1 This is not a flexible requirement. In *Duff v Gordon* (1707) Mor 3775, the court declared invalid
  a report of service of a charge which narrated that three audible knocks had been given. The
  court opined: 'it seems that the messenger had been dreaming of the three oyesses.' See further
  Graham Stewart p 321.
2 OCR 10(2), (3); SCR 6(2).
3 The copy is sent by ordinary post: OCR 10.

SERVICE BY POST

7.10 Service of a charge by means of post is possible only in the case of a
charge following upon a decree for payment of money granted in a sheriff court
summary cause or small claims action where (i) the place of executing the
charge is in any of the islands of Scotland or (ii) the place of executing the
charge is in any sheriff court district for which there is no resident sheriff
officer; or (iii) the place of executing the charge is more than twelve miles
distant from the seat of the court where the decree was granted[1].

Service is by means of registered letter or first class recorded delivery post[2].

Where a charge is served by post the days of charge start to run at the end of
the day of service[3].

1 Execution of Diligence (Scotland) Act 1926, s 2(1)(b), as amended by the 1987 Act, Sch 6, para
  12.
2 Recorded Delivery Service Act 1962, s 1; SCR 10(1).
3 SCR 10(2); *McCormick v Martin* 1985 SLT (Sh Ct) 57.

SERVICE ON A DEBTOR FURTH OF SCOTLAND

Court of Session

7.11 Service on a debtor in a country furth of the United Kingdom may be
made by any of the following methods of service if permitted under a
convention providing for service in that country or insofar as permitted by
the laws of that country[1].
(a) By post. Where service is by post it is executed by a messenger-at-arms

posting a copy of the charge by registered or recorded delivery letter addressed to the debtor.

On being executed, there must be lodged a certificate of execution in Form 3 (with such modification as may be necessary) together with a certificate of delivery or such evidence of actual delivery to the debtor or to his place of residence as the court may require.

(b) Through the central, or other appropriate, authority of the country in which the debtor is to be found, at the request of the Foreign Office. Where service is by this method the messenger must –

  (i)   send a copy of the charge, with a request for execution by the method indicated in the request, to the Secretary of State for Foreign and Commonwealth Affairs; and

  (ii) lodge a certificate signed by the authority serving the charge that it has been, and stating the manner in which it was, executed, together with, where appropriate, a translation into English.

(c) Through a British consular officer in the country in which the debtor is to be found, at the request of the Foreign Office. Where service is by this method the messenger must –

  (i)   send a copy of the charge, with a request for execution by the method indicated in the request, to the Secretary of State for Foreign and Commonwealth Affairs; and

  (ii) lodge a certificate signed by the authority serving the charge that it has been, and stating the manner in which it was, executed, together with, where appropriate, a translation into English.

(d) By an huissier, other judicial officer or competent official in the country in which the defender is to be found, at the request of a messenger-at-arms. In this case the messenger sends a copy of the charge with a request for service of the charge by the method indicated in the request, to the official in the country in which the charge is to be served. There must be lodged a certificate signed by the official serving the charge that it has been, and stating the manner in which it was, executed, together with, where appropriate, a translation into English.

(e) Personal service. The messenger must lodge a certificate of execution, together with, where appropriate, a translation into English, and the service is to be witnessed by a witness who signs the certificate of execution (which must state his occupation and address).

Where service is to be executed in a country where English is not an official language the copy of the charge shall be served together with a translation in an official language of that country[2].

Where the place where the debtor resides cannot be ascertained or service under any of the above methods has proved unsuccessful, service may be made by the methods set out in RC 75 on edictal service and service by advertisement[3].

1 RC 74B.
2 Any translation must be certified as a correct translation by the person making it; and the certificate must contain the full name, address and qualification of the translator.
3 RC 75 refers to citation but it is understood that in practice the rule also applies to other Court of Session writs.

Sheriff Court

7.12 A charge or warrant may be served outwith Scotland on any person[1] –
(a) at a known residence or place of business in England and Wales, Northern Ireland, the Isle of Man, the Channel Islands or any country with

which the United Kingdom does not have a convention providing for service
of writs in that country –
> (i) in accordance with the rules for personal service under the domestic
> law of the place in which service is to be effected; or
> (ii) by posting in Scotland a copy of the document in question in a
> registered or recorded delivery letter or the nearest equivalent which the
> available postal services permit addressed to the person at his residence or
> place of business;

(b) in a country which is a party to the Hague Convention on the Service
Abroad of Judicial and Extra-Judicial Documents in Civil or Commercial
Matters dated 15 November 1965 or the European Convention on
Jurisdiction and Enforcement of Judgments in Civil and Commercial Matters
as set out in Schedule 1 to the Civil Jurisdiction and Judgments Act 1982 –
> (i) by a method prescribed by the internal law of the country where
> service is to be effected for the service of documents in domestic actions
> upon persons who are within its territory;
> (ii) by or through a central authority in the country where service is to be
> effected at a request of the Foreign Office;
> (iii) by or through a British Consular authority at the request of the
> Foreign Office;

Where service is effected by either of methods (ii) or (iii) the officer of the
court must –
> send a copy of the document, with a request for service to be effected by
> the method indicated in the request to the Secretary of State for Foreign
> and Commonwealth Affairs; and
> lodge in process a certificate of execution of service signed by the authority
> which has effected service.
> (iv) where the law of the country in which the person resides permits, by
> posting in Scotland a copy of the document in a registered or recorded
> delivery letter or the nearest equivalent which the available postal services
> permit addressed to the person at his residence; or
> (v) where the law of the country in which service is to be effected
> permits, service by an huissier, other judicial officer or competent official
> of the country where service is to be made. Where service is effected by
> this method the officer of court must –
>> (1) send to the official in the country in which service is to be effected a
>> copy of the document, with a request for service to be effected by
>> delivery to the debtor or his residence; and
>> (2) lodge in process a certificate of execution of service by the official
>> who has effected service.

(c) in a country with which the United Kingdom has a convention on the
service of writs in that country other than the conventions in (b) above, by
one of the methods approved in the relevant convention.
A document which requires to be posted in Scotland for the purposes of this
rule is to be posted by an officer of court, and on the face of the envelope used
for postal service under this rule there shall be written or printed a notice in
the same or similar terms as that required in the case of ordinary service under
OCR 10.
  Where service is effected in accordance with paragraph (a)(i) or (b)(i), the
officer must lodge a certificate by a person who is conversant with the law of
the country concerned and who practises or has practised as an advocate or
solicitor in that country or is a duly accredited representative of the

government of that country, stating that the form of service employed is in accordance with the law of the place where the service was effected. It is not necessary to lodge such a certificate where service has taken place in another part of the United Kingdom, the Channel Isles or the Isle of Man.

Every document and any notice on the face of the envelope referred to above must be accompanied by a translation in an official language of the country in which service is to be executed unless English is an official language of that country[2].

Although the Sheriff Court Rules contain provisions on the citation of defenders whose whereabouts are unknown[3], in practice there appears to be no means under the Rules to serve a charge on a debtor in these circumstances. It is understood, however, that some sheriff courts may allow publication on the walls of court to act as the equivalent to service of a charge where the debtor's whereabouts are unknown to the creditor.

1 OCR 12; SCR 9; SMCR, App 9.
2 A translation must be certified as a correct translation by the person making it and the certificate must contain full name, address and qualifications of the translator and be lodged along with the execution of such service or certificate of service.
3 OCR 11; SCR 8; SMCR 6.

Duration of charge; second charges

7.13 A charge for payment once served gives the creditor the right to proceed with the diligences of poinding and sale and earnings arrestment on the basis of that charge for a period of up to two years from the date of its service on the debtor[1]. However a creditor may reconstitute his right to execute these diligences by having a further charge for payment served on the debtor[2]. Provided the warrant to charge is still valid, a second charge may be served at any time, either during or after the two-year period of duration of the first charge. However, no expenses incurred in the service of a further charge within the period of two years from service of the first charge can be claimed from the debtor[3].

What is not clear is how often a further charge for payment may be made. Section 90(6) refers to the debtor reconstituting his right to do diligence on a charge for payment by 'service of *a further* charge for payment'. Section 90(7) reflects the above-noted rule on expenses in terms of '*a further* charge' served during the duration 'of *the first* charge'. This language seems more consistent with the view that the creditor is allowed to serve only one further charge for payment after the service of the first such charge. However, this interpretation does cause considerable restrictions on the right of the creditor to do diligence which requires a charge for payment, or to use a charge as a basis for the debtor's sequestration. For example, a debtor who executed a poinding on the basis of a second charge could find that he would be able to execute an earnings arrestment against the debtor in respect of any remaining balance of the debt only if the schedule of the earnings arrestment was served within two years of the second charge. But in these circumstances, the creditor would still be able to execute a non-earnings arrestment, even if the duration of the second charge had elapsed. A contrary interpretation of the provisions, which allows as many subsequent charges as the creditor wishes to serve, at least has the advantage of avoiding these somewhat arbitrary distinctions. Furthermore the protection afforded to the debtor by the provisions of the 1987 Act which prohibit second poindings of the same goods or in the same premises for the same debt, and prohibit second warrant sales in respect of the same debt, remain unaffected by allowing the creditor to make more than one further charge[4].

It should be noted that during the duration of a charge, a creditor may proceed to execute either one or both of diligences of poinding and sale and earnings arrestment. There is no need for a separate charge for payment in respect of each type of diligence.

1 1987, Act, s 90(5).
2 Ibid, s 90(6).
3 Ibid, s 90(7).
4 See below at paras 7.85–7.96.

Parties charged

7.14 It is essential that the charge correctly identifies the name, designation, and where appropriate the special capacity of the person or persons being charged. Generally speaking, the party to be charged will be charged with the same name, designation and capacity as set out in the extract decree or registered document. Where there is a mistake in any of these matters in the extract decree, a charge in the same terms will not be valid unless the debtor has barred himself from objecting, eg by using a name in trading or by entering appearance in an action and not objecting[1].

Some specialities about debtors to be charged should be noted:

1 *Spalding v Valentine & Co* (1883) 10 R 1092; *Brown v Rodger* (1884) 12 R 340; *Cruickshank v Gow & Sons* (1888) 15 R 326.

DEBTOR LIABLE IN REPRESENTATIVE CAPACITY

7.15 Where the debtor is liable under the decree or document in a representative rather than personal capacity, he can be charged only in that representative capacity and is liable only to the extent of the estate or funds which he holds in that capacity[1].

1 *Craig v Hogg* (1896) 24 R 6; *Drummond v Carse's Executors* (1881) 8 R 449; *Graham Stewart* p 294.

MULTIPLE DEBTORS

7.16 Where the debtors are joint obligants, the decree will in most cases specify whether each debtor is liable jointly and severally (which involves each being charged for the whole debt) or merely for a pro rata share of the total debt[1]. The charge must correctly reflect the extent of the debtor's liability to pay under the decree or document. An extract registered protest of a bill of exchange may be in force jointly and severally against each debtor[2].

1 *Zuill v McMurchy* (1842) 4 D 871. For the special case of partnerships, see below at para 7.18.
2 *Graham Stewart* pp 295–296.

SOLE TRADERS

7.17 A sole trader must be charged in his own name, although the name of his business may be added. This is so no matter the designation in which the debtor was sued[1]. As a sole trader enjoys no separate legal personality, his liability is always a personal one and diligence against him is not restricted to his business assets[2].

1 OCR 14 (applicable also to summary cause and small claims decrees).
2 Bell _Comm_ II, 514.

PARTNERSHIPS

7.18 There exist a variety of ways in which a partnership may be designated as a defender to a court action[1]. However, the extract decree is warrant to charge the partnership and also any or all of the partners, even if they are not named in the decree[2]. Where some but not all of the partners are named in the decree, a charge may be served on the partners not named as well as those named[3]. However, a person who is not a partner cannot be charged in respect of a partnership debt, even if he is liable on the basis of having held himself out as a partner[4].

1 _Antermony Coal Company v Wingate_ (1866) 4 M 1017; OCR 14; _McNaught v Milligan_ (1885) 13 R 366. For the place of service of charge see OCR 14(2).
2 Partnership Act 1890, s 4(2); _Ewing v McClelland_ (1860) 22 D 1347. It should be noted that in respect of Court of Session decrees, a charge on a partnership with a descriptive name (as opposed to a social name) cannot be served only on the partnership at its place of business but must also be served on at least three partners: _Graham Stewart_ p 325.
3 _Knox v Martin_ (1847) 10 D 50.
4 _Brember v Rutherford_ (1901) 4 F 62.

CORPORATIONS

7.19 Corporations are charged in their corporate names, without any office holders or members being specified in the charge[1]. The constitution of the corporation may also specify a representative who is authorised to accept a charge as a charge against the corporation[2].

The extent to which members of a corporation are liable for the corporation's debts is established by the mode of corporation.

1 _Graham Stewart_ pp 299–300.
2 Cp _National Exchange Company of Glasgow v Drew_ (1840) 11 D 179; _N B Banking Company v Allan_ (1850) 12 D 966.

UNINCORPORATED ASSOCIATIONS

7.20 Certain unincorporated associations and public bodies are authorised by statute or custom to charge and be charged by the holder or holders of a particular office in the association or body as its representative[1]. Special provision exists for raising actions in the sheriff court against voluntary associations carrying on a business under a trade or descriptive name[2]. However, a charge may be made against only those officials or members of the association called in the action[3].

1 _Graham Stewart_ pp 301–304.
2 OCR 14(1); _Borland v Lochwinnoch Golf Club_ 1986 SLT (Sh Ct) 13.
3 _Aitchison v McDonald_ 1911 SC 174.

Report of Charge

7.21 After service of charge, the officer must submit a report of the charge to the court. (It is not clear how long after the charge the report must be submitted.) The report of the charge is the only evidence which can be admitted that the charge was served[1]. The report must set out all the matters which are set out in the schedule of charge, and must be signed by both the officer and the witness to the service of the charge[2]. Any error, apart from a merely clerical one, will vitiate the report[3].

1 *McCalla v Magistrates of Ayr* (1679) Mor 12632; *McKean* (1694) Mor 3784; *Haswel v Magistrates of Jedburgh* (1714) Mor 11733, 12270.
2 A form of report for Court of Session charges is set out in RC Form 44.
3 In *Paterson v Scottish Insurance Commissioners* 1915 2 SLT 178, a charge was held to be invalid where the name of the sheriff officer who executed it was omitted from the report. Contrast *Henderson v Rollo* (1871) 10 M 104.

POINDING

Prerequisites to poinding

WARRANT TO POIND

7.22 As with any diligence, a poinding may proceed only where there is a warrant to execute it. A warrant to poind is contained in inter alia:
(a) extract decree for payment of money pronounced by the Court of Session, the High Court of Justiciary, sheriff court and the Court of Teinds[1];
(b) extract of a document registered in the Books of Council and Session or in sheriff court books which contains an obligation to pay a sum of money[2];
(c) a summary warrant granted by a sheriff for collection of taxes, rates or community charges[3].
    It should be noted that a warrant to poind cannot be granted on the dependence of an action or in security of a debt, but only as a diligence in execution.

1 1987, Act, s 87(1), (2); Sheriff Courts (Scotland) Extracts Act 1892, s 7(1) (as amended by 1987 Act, s 87(3)).
2 Writs Execution (Scotland) Act 1877, s 3 (inserted by 1987 Act, s 87(4)).
3 Taxes Management Act 1970, s 63; Car Tax Act 1983, Sch 1, para 3(4); Value Added Tax Act 1983, Sch 7, para 6(6); Local Government (Scotland) Act 1947, s 247 (as amended by 1987 Act, Sch 4, para 1); Abolition of Domestic Rates Etc (Scotland) Act 1987, Sch 2, para 7(3).

EXPIRY OF THE DAYS OF THE CHARGE

7.23 A poinding may be executed only after the days of charge have expired[1] and before the expiry of the charge itself[2]. In calculating whether the days of the charge have expired the day on which the charge is served is excluded. A poinding may thereafter not take place until the day after the last day of charge[3].
    The expiry of the days of charge for payment of the debt, not followed by payment, constitutes the apparent insolvency of the debtor unless it is shown that the debtor was able and willing to pay the debt[4].

1 A prior charge is not necessary in the case of a poinding under summary warrant.

2 See above at paras 7.05, 7.13.
3 Cp *Graham Stewart* at p 338: 'In other words the day on which the charge is given, the days of charge and the day on which the poinding is executed must make up [at least] two days more than the days of charge.'
4 Bankruptcy (Scotland) Act 1985, s 7(1)(c).

CONTINUING LIABILITY OF DEBTOR

7.24 A poinding may be executed only where there is a continuing liability to pay on the part of the debtor. A debtor will have such continuing liability unless he has paid in full the sum or sums charged for, including the expenses of the charge itself[1].

1 See above at para 7.04.

Time and days of poinding; powers of entry

7.25 No poinding may be executed on a Sunday, Christmas Day, New Year's Day or Good Friday[1].

At common law a poinding could not take place outwith the hours of daylight. This rule was abolished by the 1987 Act which instead prohibits the execution of a poinding from being commenced before 8 am or after 8 pm, or its being continued after 8 pm[2]. However, the officer of court may apply to the sheriff for permission to commence or continue a poinding beyond these times. Such an application is made by endorsing a minute on the extract decree, summary warrant or other document on which the poinding has proceeded[3]. The minute, which need not be intimated to the debtor or to any other party must specify the extension sought and the reason or reasons for the extension. The sheriff has a discretion to grant or refuse the application and may do so without a hearing.

The warrant to execute a poinding also authorises the officer, if necessary for the purpose of executing the poinding, to open shut and lockfast places[4]. In the case of a poinding at commercial premises, the practice is for the officer to post a letter to the debtor, or to leave a note for him, informing him that a poinding is to be carried out and requesting that the premises are open on the date of the poinding. If access to the premises still cannot be gained, the officer uses the services of a locksmith (whose fee is chargeable to the debtor).

However the position as regards poinding in a dwellinghouse is now regulated by section 18 of the 1987 Act. This section places restrictions on the power of an officer, notwithstanding the warrant to open shut and lockfast places, to enter the dwellinghouse to execute a poinding there if, at the time of intended entry, it appears to the officer that no one or only children under the age of 16 are present there. In these circumstances, the officer may enter the dwellinghouse only if he has served notice on the debtor of the date of intended entry at least four days before that date. However, where such notice is likely to prejudice the execution of the poinding, the sheriff may dispense with the requirement of its service. The sheriff may exercise this power on application by the officer of court made by minute specifying the reason or reasons why notice might prejudice execution of the poinding. This application does not require to be intimated to the debtor[5].

1 1987 Act, s 17(1). Other days on which a poinding may not be executed may be prescribed by Act of Sederunt. No such Act of Sederunt has yet been made.

2 1987 Act, s 17(2).
3 AS (Proceedings in the Sheriff Court under the Debtors (Scotland) Act 1987) 1988, SI 1988/ 2013, r 9(1), (3).
4 1987 Act, s 87(2)(a); Sheriff Courts (Scotland) Extracts Act 1892, s 7(1)(a); Writs Execution (Scotland) Act 1877, s 3(a); SI 1988/2013, Forms 61–63.
5 1987 Act, s 18(2); SI 1988/2013, r 10.

Goods poindable and non-poindable; exempt goods

GENERAL PRINCIPLE

7.26 The general principle is that a poinding may be used only against the corporeal moveable property belonging to the debtor which is in the debtor's possession at the time of the poinding. This section examines the component elements of this general principle and considers various categories of goods which are poindable and non-poindable in terms of it. There is also consideration of certain categories of property which though poindable in terms of this general principle are rendered exempt from that diligence. It should be noted that in the case of non-commercial debtors, the single most significant category of exempt goods is that provided for by section 16 of the 1987 Act[1].

1 See below at paras 7.44–7.52.

CORPOREAL PROPERTY; INCORPOREAL PROPERTY

7.27 The diligence of poinding is completed by sale under sheriff's warrant, and title to the goods does not pass to the creditor or other party until the sale. Accordingly, property which cannot be sold is not poindable: 'the essence of poinding is that the goods poinded may be taken to the market-cross and sold'[1].

On this basis incorporeal property is not open to the diligence of poinding, but most types of incorporeal moveable property may be arrested[2]. Arrestment is the proper diligence to attach debts or claims for the payment of money[3].

1 *Trowsdale's Trustee v Forcett Railway Company* (1870) 9 M 88, 95 (a case which held that on this criterion business books, papers, writs and certificates cannot be poinded). See also Bell *Prin* § 2289.
2 See ch 5 above.
3 Bell *Comm* II, 59, 60; Bell *Prin* § 2289; *Mackenzie & Co v Finlay* (1868) 7 M 27.

MOVEABLE PROPERTY; HERITABLE PROPERTY

7.28 A poinding may be used against only the moveable property of the debtor, not against his heritable property. In many cases the distinction between these two categories of property is clear-cut, or where difficulties exist, they do not occur in the context of the diligence of poinding. Problems may arise, however, as regards the matter of fixtures, ie moveable property which is connected with or attached to heritable property in such a way that it is to be treated as having itself become heritable.

Unfortunately, this topic has given rise to a considerable body of judicial decision, which is not altogether consistent. Although various factors have been identified as requiring consideration on whether a particular piece of property is, or is not, a fixture, this question is to be treated as a question of fact to be decided in the circumstances of each case[1]. The factors to be considered include the degree and nature of the attachment, whether the goods or the land (or building) have been specially adapted, the object and the purpose of the attachment, and the context in which the issue arises.

In conveyancing practice the following items are usually treated as heritable in nature[2]:
(i)   electricity systems (including meters, wall sockets, wiring);
(ii) gas meters and piping;
(iii) central heating systems (electrical, gas or oil-fired);
(iv) built-in kitchen units, cupboards, wardrobes etc;
(v)   fitted bathroom units.

The following items are usually treated as moveable property:
(i)   electrical apparatus such as fires, washing machines, cookers, refrigerators, televisions (including TV aerials);
(ii) carpets and other floor coverings;
(iii) curtains;
(iv) gas fires, cookers;
(v)   mirrors and pictures.

It should also be noted that certain items (eg the keys of a house) are held to be constructive fixtures[3].

Property which is heritable may become moveable. For example, minerals, trees or crops are heritable until cut or separated from land, when they become moveable. Thus corn which has been cut and stacked can be poinded[4]. Moreover, an exception to the general rule exists in that growing corn may be poinded, provided it is of such ripeness or maturity that an approximate estimate of the value of the crop can be made, and there is a traceable link between the identity of what is poinded and what is afterwards sold[5].

1 *Howie's Trustees v McLay* (1902) 5 F 214, 216; *Scottish Discount Co Ltd v Blin* 1986 SLT 123. For discussion of the various factors to be considered, see Rankine *The Law of Landownership in Scotland* (4th edn) pp 116 et seq; DM Walker *Principles of Scottish Private Law* vol 3 (4th edn), pp 11–15; WM Gloag and RC Henderson *Introduction to the Law of Scotland* (9th edn) pp 612–616.
2 See JM Halliday *Conveyancing Law and Practice in Scotland* vol 2 (1986) pp 23–26.
3 *Barr v McIlwham* (1821) 1 S 124; *Fisher v Dixon* (1845) 4 Bell's App 286; *Brand's Trustees v Brand's Trustees* (1876) 3 R (HL) 16.
4 *Lord Hatton* (1677) Mor 10515; *Hay v Hay* (1679) Mor 10517; *Skene v Lord Carloury* (1688) Mor 10523; *Erskine v Boswell* (1707) Mor 10525.
5 *Ballantine v Watson* (1709) Mor 10526; *Dun v Johnston* (1818) Hume 451; *Elders v Allan* (1833) 11 S 902 (poinding in December of braided corn invalid).

GOODS IN THE DEBTOR'S POSSESSION

7.29   A poinding may be held only in respect of goods in the debtor's own possession[1]. However, possession may be either actual or 'civil', ie possession through an intermediary[2]. Goods of the debtor which are physically in the hands of a third party may pose problems as to whether they can be said to be in the 'civil' possession of the debtor (in which case they may be poinded) or are not so (in which case they may be open to arrestment in the hands of the third party)[3].

An approximate criterion for determining this issue is whether the owner of the goods could demand to take immediate and physical possession of the goods, or whether the person with physical possession has some basis for resisting this claim. This could arise where he is in the possession of the goods not as a mere agent (in a non-technical sense) of the owner, but under a contract which imposes on him a liability to account. Thus in *Hutchison v Hutchison*[4], it was held that where a guest in a hotel had left luggage and golf clubs in the hands of the hotel keeper, the guest had remained in the possession of the goods and thus an arrestment in the hands of the hotel keeper was invalid.

This question may arise where goods of a landlord are in premises let to a tenant. Where the goods are part of the subjects let, as with furnished premises, the goods are deemed to remain in the possession of the landlord and may be poinded by the landlord's creditors[5]. However, if the goods are in the hands of a tenant under a contract such as deposit, the appropriate diligence by the landlord's creditors is that of arrestment in the hands of the tenant[6].

1 A creditor may poind goods of the debtor in his own possession: see below at para 7.30.
2 Bell *Prin* § 1312; *Union Bank of Scotland v Mackenzie* (1865) 3 M 765; *Moore v Gledden* (1869) 7 M 1016; *Mitchell's Trustees v Gladstone* (1894) 21 R 586.
3 For discussion see *Graham Stewart* pp 107–112.
4 1912, 1 SLT 219; cp *Heron v Winfields Ltd* (1894) 22 R 182.
5 *Hunter v Lees* (1733) Mor 136; *Davidson v Murray* (1784) Mor 761. However such goods may be exempt from poinding under s 16 of the 1987 Act.
6 Cp *Appin's Creditors* (1760) Mor 749, but note section 99(2) of the 1987 Act which extends s 16 of that Act to the arrestment of goods.

GOODS IN THE CREDITOR'S POSSESSION

7.30 Goods belonging to the debtor which are in the creditor's possession may be poinded by that creditor[1]. Where goods are poinded which are not in the possession of the debtor, the officer of court who carries out the poinding must serve a copy of the poinding schedule by post on the debtor[2].

1 *Lochhead v Graham* (1883) 11 R 201; *Tillicoultry v Lord Rollo* (1678) Mor 10517. It should be noted that Sch 8 to the 1987 Act repeals s 40 of the Sale of Goods Act 1979, which contained an anomalous provision allowing the seller of goods to arrest and poind goods still in his possession.
2 1987 Act, s 20(6)(c).

GOODS NOT IN THE OWNERSHIP OF THE DEBTOR

General principle

7.31 Goods may be poinded only if they are owned by the debtor. A later section examines the situation where goods are owned by the debtor in common with another person or persons. This section is concerned with the issues which arise in connection with goods which the debtor does not own at all (at least in the capacity in which he is liable to pay the debt).

A major source of difficulty is the wide range of contexts in which the issue of ownership of moveable property can arise. For example, goods owned by the debtor jointly with another person cannot be poinded in respect of the debtor's individual debt[1]. Goods held by the debtor on trust cannot be poinded, even if the trust is latent[2]. Partnership property is not poindable in respect of the debts of the partners as individuals[3]. Goods in which a person has a merely temporary interest (eg liferent) cannot be poinded by the creditor of that person[4], but such goods may be poinded by the creditor of the owner though they cannot be sold until the possessor's right of possession has terminated[5].

In cases of domestic poindings especially, problems exist in relation to goods supplied to the debtor on a legal basis other than a sale but which involves the immediate transfer of possession. Contracts with similar economic functions, and to the non-lawyer similar content, have different effects on whether ownership of goods has transferred to the debtor and the goods are thus subject to poinding by his creditors. Thus goods subject to a current hire-purchase agreement are not poindable nor are goods sold under a conditional sale agreement. However, goods supplied under a credit (or instalment) sale will normally pass title and so will be subject to poinding.

These features cause difficulties for officers of court who execute poindings. Officers do not have a detailed knowledge of the law of property. Moreover, fraudulent claims of third-party ownership would frustrate the possibility of executing poindings in many situations. However, the basic principle remains that only the property of the debtor can be used as the basis of a poinding against that debtor. The 1987 Act tends to reconcile these conflicting interests by, first, setting out a code of procedure for the officer who executes the poinding where goods may belong to a third party, and, secondly, providing for remedies for a third party whose goods have been included in a poinding.

1 *Fleming v Twaddle* (1820) 7 S 92. See further below at para 7.34.
2 *Graham Stewart* pp 67–68; WA Wilson *The Law of Scotland relating to Debt* p 204.
3 *Dawson v Cullen* (1825) 4 S 39.
4 *Scott v Price* (1837) 15 S 916.
5 *Graham Stewart* p 340, gives the example of furniture let to a tenant: *Davidson v Murray* (1784) Mor 761.

Officer's duties when poinding goods which may not belong to the debtor

7.32 Prior to commencing a poinding, the officer must make inquiry of any person present as to the ownership of the articles proposed to be poinded[1]. This duty does not arise when no one is present at the poinding. The Act does not specify the effect of the failure of the officer to fulfil this duty. However, the language of the section is mandatory, and it is submitted that any such failure invalidates the poinding[2]. If a claim is made by or on behalf of a third party that the goods belong to him rather than to the debtor, the officer must make further inquiries as to the ownership of the goods[3].

In determining a question of ownership of goods the officer is guided by section 19(2) of the 1987 Act which lays down a presumption that any article in the possession of the debtor is owned by him unless the officer knows or ought to know that the contrary is the case. This presumption is not rebutted merely by an assertion by any person that the article is not owned by the debtor. Clearly, more by way of proof of ownership is called for. Nor is the presumption overcome solely by virtue of the fact that the article is of a type which is commonly held under a limited title of possession, such as hire, hire purchase or conditional sale agreement.

In determining a question of claim of ownership by a third party of goods which are in the possession of the debtor, the officer has to consider a wide range of factors. These include the nature of the premises themselves. For example in certain types of commercial premises (eg auctioneers, garages)[4], the weight to be given to the presumption that possession infers ownership is less than in relation to other types of premises. The general position is stated by the Scottish Law Commission in their report in the following terms[5]:

'The officer has to be given a discretion in view of the wide variety of circumstances that may be encountered; whether the article should be poinded or excluded will depend on the nature of the claim, the credibility of the person making it, the nature of the goods, and whether satisfactory documentary or other corroborative evidence is available.'

The position seems to be that the officer should include goods that are in the possession of the debtor in a poinding unless there is clear and convincing proof that the goods belong instead to someone else. An officer's liability in damages would arise in such circumstances only if there was such clear proof. However, the officer would not be protected where the facts of the claim were clear but he misunderstood the legal effect of the claim (eg the difference between a credit and a conditional sale agreement). But in most cases where there is any doubt as to the factual or legal basis of a claim of ownership, the safest course for the officer is to include the goods in the poinding. This approach is reinforced by the provisions which prohibit second poindings. If goods on the debtor's premises are not included in the poinding, these goods may not be poinded later for the same debt even if it is later shown that they did and still do belong to the debtor. However, where goods are poinded but later released on the basis that they belong to a third party, in most cases a further poinding can be held[6].

Any claim that a poinded article does not belong to the debtor must be noted by the officer in his report of the poinding[7]. Failure to make such a note has the effect of invalidating the poinding[8].

1 1987 Act, s 20(2)(c). The officer must in particular ask such person whether there are any persons who own any articles in common with the debtor. See below at para 7.63.
2 Cp the effect of failure to note a claim that goods belonged to a third party: *Maxwell v Controller of Clearing House* 1923 SLT (Sh Ct) 137; *Cameron v Cuthberston* 1924 SLT (Sh Ct) 67.
3 It is no longer competent for the officer in executing the poinding to examine a person on oath as to the ownership of goods: 1987 Act, s 21(3).
4 Compare Scot Law Com Report no 95 (1985), p 311.
5 Scot Law Com Report no 95 (1985), p 314.
6 1987 Act, s 40(5).
7 Ibid, s 22(2); SI 1988/2013, r 15, Form 9.
8 *Maxwell v Controller of Clearing House* 1923 SLT (Sh Ct) 137; *Cameron v Cuthbertson* 1924 SLT (Sh Ct) 67.

Remedies of third party

7.33 Where an article has been included in a poinding which it is claimed belongs to a third party and not to the debtor, the third party has a number of remedies open to him.

(1) Application to the officer of court. The officer who executed the poinding has power to release an article from poinding where the poinding has been completed and the warrant sale not yet taken place. He may do so if satisfied that the article belongs to a third party and the debtor, or other person in possession of the article, does not deny that the third party owns it[1].

The release of an article on this basis must be reported by the officer to the sheriff[2]. Where the officer releases an article on this basis, he may proceed to poind other articles belonging to the debtor in the same premises[3]. There is no need for the sheriff to give authority for this further poinding.

(2) *Application to the sheriff.* A third party may apply to the sheriff for a poinded article to be released from the poinding. The application may be made at any time after the execution of the poinding and before the sale under warrant[4]. The application is in the form of Form 27 of the Sheriff Court Proceedings Act of Sederunt[5], and must specify

(a) where known, the name and address of the creditor, the debtor, the officer of court who executed the poinding and any person other than the debtor having possession of the poinded article;

(b) where known, the court which granted the original decree and the date of that decree or details of the summary warrant or other document, upon which the poinding proceeded;

(c) the date and place of execution of poinding;

(d) if appropriate, where and when the warrant sale is to be held;

(e) the article which is sought to be released;

(f) any competent crave for expenses.

When the application is lodged the sheriff clerk fixes a date for the hearing and intimation is made on the applicant, the creditor, the debtor, the officer of court who executed the poinding, and the person having possession of the article in question. The officer is required to lodge a copy of the poinding schedule prior to the hearing[6].

If the sheriff is satisfied that the poinded article belongs to the applicant he orders its release from the poinding. The sheriff clerk intimates the sheriff's decision to any person to whom intimation of the application was made but who was not present when the application was determined[7].

As is the case when a poinded article has been released by an officer of court under section 40(1), where the sheriff releases goods from the poinding on the basis that goods belong to a third party, a further poinding of the debtor's goods in the same premises may be held[8].

The making of any such application to the sheriff by a third party does not prejudice that party's right to take other proceedings for the recovery of the poinded article. Whatever decision the sheriff makes in determining an application is not binding in those other proceedings[9].

(3) *Other remedy.* A person who claims that goods belonging to him and not to the debtor have been poinded may raise an action of interdict together with an action for the delivery of the goods. Depending upon the stage of diligence reached, the interdict may seek to prevent a warrant of sale being granted[10] or a warrant sale taking place[11].

It should be noted that sale under sheriff's warrant passes title in the goods sold under the usual rules for the sale of goods. The general principle is *nemo dat quod non habet*, subject to recognised exceptions[12]. Accordingly, the true owner of goods sold under sheriff's warrant can raise an action for delivery of the goods from a purchase at sale[13] and from the creditor where the goods have been adjudged to him[14].

Depending upon the circumstances which led to the goods being included in the poinding, the true owner of the goods may be able to claim damages from the officer or creditor. However, the mere inclusion of goods of a third party i . a poinding is not sufficient to make the officer or creditor liable in damages to the third party. This would arise only if it was clear that the goods should not have been included in the poinding[15].

---

1 1987 Act, s 40(1).

2 The release of the goods is reported, depending upon the stage the diligence has reached, in

the application for a warrant of sale, a separate report after grant of warrant and before the sale, or in the report of the sale: ibid, s 40(4).
3 Ibid, s 40(5), which overrides ibid, s 25, which generally prohibits second poindings in the same premises for the same debt.
4 Ibid, s 40(2).
5 SI 1988/2013, r 34(1), (2).
6 Ibid, r 34(4).
7 Ibid, r 34(5).
8 See above at para 7.33.
9 1987 Act, s 40(3).
10 H Burn-Murdoch, *Interdict in the Law of Scotland* p 189.
11 *Jack v Waddell's Trustees* 1918 SC 73. A sheriff may grant interdict against the sale of poinded goods notwithstanding that he granted the warrant of sale: *Jack v Waddell's Trustees*.
12 Sale of Goods Act 1979, s 21. For discussion of the exceptions see D M Walker *Principles of Scottish Private Law* Vol 3 (4th edn) pp 423–429. At p 429, *Walker* states that the sale under sheriff's warrant always confers good title on the purchaser, but he cites no authority for this view.
13 *Carlton v Miller* 1978 SLT (Sh Ct) 36.
14 *George Hopkinson Ltd v N G Napier & Sons* 1953 SC 139.
15 See *Nelmes v Gillies* (1883) 10 R 890; *McLean v Boyek* (1893) 10 SLR 10; *Macintyre v Murray & Muir* (1915) 31 Sh Ct Rep 49; *Boyle v James Miller & Partners Ltd* 1942 SLT (Sh Ct) 33.

JOINT PROPERTY

7.34 A special instance of the rule that only goods of the debtor may be included in a poinding is that of joint property. Property is owned jointly where there is one indivisible title to the property by two or more persons. In contrast to common property, where the co-owners each have a determinate share of the property, in the case of joint property there are no separate shares in the property[1]. An example of joint property is estate vested in trustees, but property may also be gifted or bequested to persons in such a way that they hold the property jointly rather than in common. As each of the joint owners cannot dispose of any share in the joint property, it follows that joint property cannot be poinded in respect of the debts of the owners as individuals[2]. However, where joint owners are found liable in the same capacities as that in which they hold the property (eg as trustees, members of a club), diligence in respect of such liability is used against joint property, not the property held as individuals.

The situation is confused by the terminology often used to refer to joint and common property. The term joint property (eg as in joint bank account, joint tenancies) is frequently used when the term 'common' property is technically the more correct. Furthermore, where two or more persons are found to be jointly, or jointly and severally, liable the term joint in this context has a different meaning. Where parties are liable jointly, each party is liable only for a pro rata share of the total sum due[3]. Where parties are liable jointly and severally, each party is liable to pay the whole sum to the creditor, though he may have a right of relief against his fellow debtors[4]. The point to note is that in each of these situations the liability of each debtor is an individual one (unless he has been sued in some special capacity) and accordingly diligence proceeds against the individual property of the debtor (including property which he holds in common with others).

1 For discussion of this distinction, see K G C Reid 'Common Property' 1985 SLT (News) 57.
2 *Fleming v Twaddle* (1828) 7 S 92.
3 *Coats v Union Bank of Scotland* 1928 SC 711, 1929 SC (HL) 114; W A Wilson *The Law of Scotland relating to Debt* p 319.
4 *Fleming v Gemmil* 1908 SC 340.

GOODS OWNED BY THE DEBTOR IN COMMON WITH ANOTHER PERSON

7.35 In contrast to the case of joint property, property is owned in common when each of two or more persons has a separate title to a determinate share of the property. As the share of each co-owner transmits separately, in principle goods owned in common can be poinded for the debt of one co-owner only, at least as far as concerns that owner's share in the property. However, the practice developed that goods owned in common by a debtor and another person were not poinded for the debts of the debtor, and this practice appears to have developed into a rule that such goods were not poindable[1].

This rule led to problems in situations where goods were typically owned, or presumed to be owned, in common. Such a situation could arise in relation to goods situated in domestic premises. By virtue of the presumption in section 19(2) of the 1987 Act, namely that ownership is presumed from possession, common ownership would fall to be presumed in relation to goods in domestic premises owned in common or subject to a so-called 'joint' (ie common) tenancy. Furthermore, the Family Law (Scotland) Act 1985 creates further presumptions as to common ownership in respect of certain types of property of a married couple. Section 25 creates a presumption of common ownership of household goods. Such goods included decorative or ornamental goods and are defined as goods kept or used at any time during the marriage in the matrimonial home for joint [sic] domestic purposes of the parties to the marriage. However, this principle does not arise in relation to:
(i) money or securities;
(ii) motor car, caravan or other road vehicle;
(iii) a domestic animal;
(iv) goods acquired by gift or succession from a third party;
(v) goods not obtained in prospect of, or during, the marriage.
Section 26 of the 1985 Act creates a presumption of common ownership in relation to property derived from house-keeping allowance.

All of these presumptions are rebuttable by proof that the goods belong to one or other of the parties, or to a third party. But unless there is some such proof the officer at a poinding would have to continue to presume common ownership. In such circumstances the continuation of the common law rule (as that rule was typically understood) would frustrate poindings in many, if not in most, domestic premises.

To avoid these problems, section 41(1) of the 1987 Act provides that goods owned in common by the debtor and another person may be poinded in respect of the debts of that debtor. However, the 1987 Act also provides various measures to protect the co-owner's position where goods owned in common with the owner have been poinded.

1 Cp Scot Law Com Report no 95 (1985), pp 317–318. The report refers to a passage in *Graham Stewart* at p 346. However this passage deals explicitly with the case of joint property and the cases referred to by *Graham Stewart* are also restricted to joint property.

7.36 *Information about poinding during the poinding procedure.* Before the officer commences a poinding he must make inquiries of any person present as to the ownership of goods which he proposes to poind, and in particular he must inquire whether any article is owned in common by the debtor and another person[1].

At the completion of the valuation the officer must inform any person present who owns any poinded article in common with the debtor of his right to redeem the poinded goods under sections 41(2) and 41(3)(a) of the 1987 Act, and of his right to have goods released under sections 16(4) and 41(3)(b) of the Act[2].

1 1987 Act, s 20(2)(c).
2 Ibid, s 20(6)(e), (f).

7.37 *Application for release of exempt article.* A person who owns a poinded article in common with the debtor may apply to the sheriff to have the article released from the poinding on the ground that the article is exempt from poinding in terms of section 16 of the 1987 Act[1]. Such an application must be made within fourteen days after the date of the execution of the poinding. In the context of the 1987 Act, the term 'execution' appears to mean the carrying out of the poinding, not its report.

1 1987 Act, s 16(4); SI 1988/2013, r 8.

7.38 *Application for release of poinded goods on grounds of undue harshness.* At any time after the execution of a poinding and before the warrant sale, the third party who owns goods with the debtor which have been included in the poinding may apply to the sheriff to have the goods released from the poinding on the grounds that the continued poinding or sale of the co-owned goods would be unduly harsh to the third party in the circumstances[1]. This power of the sheriff to release co-owned goods is similar to that available to him when dealing with applications by the debtor under section 23[2].

Where goods are released by the sheriff on this basis, the officer of court may without express authorisation of the sheriff poind other articles belonging to the debtor in the same premises as those where the poinding was executed[3].

1 1987 Act, s 41(3)(b). The form of application is set out in SI 1988/2013, r 35, Form 28. The application must state the basis of the undue harshness to the applicant.
2 See below at para 7.77.
3 1987 Act, s 41(6).

7.39 *Application to the officer to redeem the goods.* The co-owner of poinded goods may apply to the officer of court who executed the poinding to redeem the goods[1]. This application may be made at any time after the execution of the poinding and before the warrant sale. The officer may release co-owned goods from a poinding, where a third party claims that a poinded article is owned in common by the debtor and himself and where he pays to the officer a sum equal to the value of the debtor's interest in the article. Before the officer can release the goods on this basis he must be satisfied of the truth of third party's claim, including the extent of the debtor's own interest in the goods. He may not release the goods if the debtor (or if a different person, the person in possession of the goods), denies the third party's claim that the third party is a co-owner with the debtor (but not apparently if the debtor merely denies the extent of his co-ownership as claimed by the third party).

A release granted by the officer does not become effective until the officer issues a receipt for the payment made by the third party. The effect of issuing the receipt is to transfer the debtor's interest in the released article to the third party[2]. The officer of court must report the release of the goods to the sheriff[3].

1 1987 Act, s 41(2).

2 Ibid, s 41(4).
3 Ibid, s 41(5). The mode of making this report depends upon the stage of diligence which has been reached.

7.40 *Application to the sheriff to redeem the goods.* Instead of applying to the officer to allow redemption of the goods, where the officer is unable to release the goods because the debtor (or possessor of the goods) disputes co-ownership, the third party may apply to the sheriff[1]. Application may be made at any time after the execution of a poinding and before the warrant sale, and is made in accordance with the Sheriff Court Proceedings Act of Sederunt, rule 35 and Form 28.

On receiving the application the sheriff clerk fixes a date for the hearing and makes intimation of the hearing to the applicant, the creditor, the debtor, the officer of court who executed the poinding, any person named in the application who owns or claims to own the article in common with the debtor, and any person having possession of the poinded article[2].

If the sheriff is satisfied that the poinded article is owned in common by the debtor and the third party who has made the application, he may order the release of the article from the poinding if the third party undertakes to pay to the officer of court a sum equal to the value of the debtor's interest in the article. Intimation of the sheriff's decision is made by the sheriff clerk to any person to whom intimation of the application was made but who was not present when the application was determined[3].

The release of the goods is not effective until the officer issues a receipt for payment by the third party[4]. The issuing of the receipt transfers to the third party the debtor's interest in the goods.

1 1987 Act, s 41(3). It is not clear that the application may be made when what is at issue is not the fact of co-ownership, but the respective interests of the co-owners.
2 Whether or not he appears at the hearing, the officer of court must lodge with the court a copy of the poinding schedule before the date of the hearing: SI 1988/2013, r 35(4).
3 Ibid, r 35(5).
4 1987 Act, s 41(4).

7.41 *Payment of proceeds of warrant sale.* Special provision is made for the situation where a third party claims that the poinded article is owned in common by the debtor and himself but he does not seek the release of the article from the poinding[1]. If the claim is not admitted by the creditor and debtor, the third party may apply to the sheriff for a finding of common ownership of the poinded articles[2].

In this situation, the interests of the co-owner of the poinded goods are protected by his receiving from the creditor a fraction of the proceeds of the sale of goods at the warrant sale which corresponds to the co-owner's interest in the article[3]. Where goods are sold at a warrant sale for less than their appraised value, or the goods are adjudged to the creditor in default of sale, the co-owner receives from the creditor the fraction of the appraised value of the goods which corresponds to his interest in those goods.

1 1987 Act, s 41(7), (8).
2 SI 1988/2013, r 36. It is not clear that application may be made when what is at dispute is not the fact of co-ownership but the respective interests of the co-owners.
3 A co-owner may purchase the goods at a warrant sale: 1987 Act, s 37(5).

GOODS SUBJECT TO REAL SECURITY

7.42   Goods which are already subject to a right of real security in favour of one creditor may be poinded by another creditor but not to the extent of prejudicing the security[1]. Such a security may be constituted by hypothec, pledge or lien[2]. Goods which have been arrested by another creditor may be poinded before the arrester has obtained a decree of furthcoming. However, in almost all cases of poinding, the debtor is insolvent by virtue of the fact that there has been an expired charge for payment or summary warrant without payment of the debt[3], and the extent of any priority established by poinding in these circumstances is effected by the provisions on equalisation of diligences[4].

1 Stair I, 13, 11; Bell *Comm* II, 60; *Graham Stewart* pp 340–341.
2 For poinding of goods subject to the landlord's hypothec, see *Graham Stewart* pp 483–485; *Wyllie v Fisher* 1907 SC 686.
3 Bankruptcy (Scotland) Act 1985, s 7(c)(ii), (iii). Apparent insolvency is *not* constituted by a poinding following upon a summary warrant for recovery of a community charge.
4 Bankruptcy (Scotland) Act 1985, Sch 7, para 24. For further discussion, see ch 10 below at para 10.34.

7.43   The categories of goods examined above all illustrate the types of goods which are, or are not, poindable and the extent to which such goods may be poinded. Certain goods which are in principle poindable are exempt from poinding.

GOODS EXEMPTED BY SECTION 16 of the 1987 act

7.44   Section 16 of the 1987 Act provides for the exemption from poinding of a variety of types of goods. A number of preliminary points may be noted. First, in most cases goods are exempted from poinding by section 16 only if the goods are 'reasonably required' for the use of the debtor or a member of his household. This expression is by its very nature difficult to give precise definition to, and indeed is used in the Act to cater for the variety of circumstances in which debtors and their households may find themselves. In applying this criterion officers must therefore look to the particular circumstances of each debtor (and where relevant his household)[1].
A second preliminary point concerns the location of the exempted goods. In the cases of clothing, tools of trade, medical equipment, educational goods, toys and articles for the upbringing of a child, the exemption applies to goods belonging to the debtor no matter where they are situated[2]. In the case of domestic furniture and plenishings, the exemption applies only to goods of the debtor which at time of the poinding are in a dwellinghouse, a term which includes a caravan, a houseboat and any structure adapted for use as a residence[3]. However, the dwellinghouse need not be the debtor's own place of residence and the exemption applies in respect of persons who are resident in the dwellinghouse even if not the debtor himself.
Thirdly, the exemptions under section 16 apply in respect of articles reasonably required for use by the debtor and any member of his household (and in the case of furniture and plenishings, the resident of the

dwellinghouse where the goods are located and any member of his household). The term household is not defined but it is wider than the spouse of the debtor and their children. In this context, household is to be given a wide meaning and would include cohabiting couples and their family.

Fourthly, it can also be noted that all goods exempt from poinding under section 16 of the 1987 Act are also exempt from (non-earnings) arrestment by the creditor[4].

Finally, property which is exempted from poinding for the purpose of protecting the debtor and his family does not vest in the debtor's trustee in sequestration[5]. This would apply to most exemptions under section 16 of the 1987 Act, except in the case where furniture and plenishings are exempt under section 16(2) as being reasonably required for the use of a resident in the household other than the debtor and his own family.

1 See *Dumfries & Galloway RC v Ronald* (unreported, Stranraer Sheriff Court, 27 January 1989), where it was held by the sheriff that a three-piece suite and two wardrobes were reasonably required for the use of a single man.
2 1987 Act, s 16(1).
3 Ibid, ss 16(2), 45.
4 Ibid, s 99(2).
5 Bankruptcy (Scotland) Act 1985, s 33.

Debtor's goods exempt from poinding (under section 16) in respect of debts due by him

7.45 *Clothing.* Items of clothing belonging to the debtor which are reasonably required for his own use or use by any member of his household are exempt from poinding[1].

1 1987 Act, s 16(1)(a).

7.46 *Tools of trade.* Implements and tools of trade, including books and other equipment, which are reasonably required for use by the debtor for the practice of his profession, trade or business are exempt from poinding. Also exempt are such tools of trade etc in respect of the trade, business or profession carried on by a member of the debtor's household[1].

These provisions are much more extensive than those allowed by the common law, which they replace[2]. However, there is an upper limit to the amount which can be exempted under this heading. Tools of trade etc are exempt only to an aggregate value of £500[3], the aggregate comprising tools etc used by the debtor as well as members of his household.

The £500 upper limit to this exemption presents a number of problems. The value of tools of trade etc probably refers to the value which the officer fixes for the appraisal of the goods at the poinding, ie the value which the goods would be likely to fetch if sold on open market[4]. Accordingly, where there are a number of such goods, the officer at the poinding is required to appraise all, or enough, of them before allocating £500 worth of these goods as to the category of the exempt goods. Difficulties may arise where the tools of trade etc are not easily divisible but where their total value is more than £500. For example an officer may be able to exempt the first £500 worth of a solicitor's library by specifying the volumes covered by the poinding and by implication specifying those parts of the library not so covered. But where there is, for example, one item with the value of £1,000 and a poinding is held for a debt of £400, the officer is placed in a difficult situation. Where goods are of a nature that they cannot be broken down into constituent parts without rendering them unworkable, the exemption would seem to apply to the whole article and not simply to the first £500 of it. The safer course for the officer, however, is to include the article in the poinding and let the debtor make an appeal to the sheriff against the inclusion of the article and to seek its release from the poinding[5].

1 1987 Act, s 16(1)(b). This provision applies generally to tools of trade, including those used for agricultural purposes. The Diligence Act 1503 (c 45) which exempted goods for ploughing during the plough season is repealed by the 1987 Act, Sch 8.
2 Scot Law Com Report no 95 (1985), pp 253–255.
3 This amount may be varied by regulation made by the Lord Advocate.
4 1987 Act, s 20(4).
5 Ibid, s 16(4). See below at para 7.52.

7.47 *Medical aids and equipment.* Medical aids and medical equipment which are reasonably required for use of the debtor or any member of his household are exempt from poinding[1].

1 1987 Act, s 16(1)(c).

7.48 *Books and educational articles.* Also exempt from poinding are the debtor's books and other articles which are reasonably required for the education or training of the debtor or any member of his household[1]. There is an upper limit to this exemption of an aggregate of £500[2], as regards such articles by the debtor *and* members of his household. Similar difficulties may arise in this context as those considered in the exemption of tools of trade[3].

1 1987 Act, s 16(1)(d).
2 This amount may be varied by regulations made by the Lord Advocate.
3 See above at para 7.46.

7.49 *Children's toys.* Toys for the use of any child who is a member of the debtor's household are exempt from poinding[1]. Toys are not defined, and it should be noted that there is no criterion of reasonable requirement for this category of exempt goods[2]. However there is a limitation in that the exemption applies only where there is a child who is a member of the household, rather than applying to all children's toys belonging to the debtor.

The term child is not defined but probably applies to any child, legitimate or illegitimate, under the age of 18[3]. Provided that the child is a member of the debtor's household, it does not matter that he does not reside with the debtor.

1 1987 Act, s 16(1)(e).
2 Dr Nichols comments: 'The effect is that not only teddies, Lego and doll's houses are exempt but also BMX bikes, electric train sets, computers and possibly even micro computers and snooker tables' (*The Debtors (Scotland) Act 1987* p 18–24).
3 Cp Law Reform (Parent and Child) (Scotland) Act 1986, s 8.

7.50 *Articles for the upbringing of children.* Articles reasonably required for the care or upbringing of a child who is a member of the debtor's household are exempt from poinding[1]. As with the exemption of children's toys, this exemption applies only where there is a child who is a member of the debtor's household, though the child need not reside with the debtor.

1 1987 Act, s 16(1)(f). For the meaning of 'child' see above at para 7.49.

7.51 *Domestic furniture and plenishings.* Section 16(2) of the 1987 Act specifies a list of types of furniture and plenishings belonging to the debtor which are exempt from poinding provided (1) at the time of the poinding they are in a dwellinghouse (which need not be the debtor's dwellinghouse); (2) they are reasonably required for use in the dwellinghouse by the person who resides there or a member of his household. (These persons need not be the debtor or a member of the debtor's household.)

The types of articles covered by this exemption are[1]:

(a)   beds or bedding;
(b)   household linen;
(c)   chairs or settees;
(d)   tables;
(e)   food;
(f)   lights or light fittings;
(g)   heating appliances;
(h)   curtains;
(j)   floor coverings;
(k)   furniture, equipment or utensils used for cooking, storing or eating food;
(l)   refrigerators;
(m) articles used for cleaning, mending, or pressing clothes;
(n)   articles used for cleaning the dwellinghouse;
(o)   furniture used for storing –
    (i)   clothing, bedding or household linen;
    (ii) articles used for cleaning the dwellinghouse;
    (iii) utensils used for cooking or eating food;
(p)   articles used for safety in the dwellinghouse;
(q)   tools used for maintenance or repair of the dwellinghouse or of household articles.

1 The Lord Advocate has power by regulations to add to this list, or to delete or vary any of the items contained in it: 1987 Act, s 16(3).

7.52 *Application for release of poinded goods.* Where an officer includes in a poinding, goods which the debtor considers should have been exempt from poinding under section 16 of the 1987 Act, the debtor may apply to the sheriff to have the articles in question released from the poinding[1]. Such an application may also be made by any person who owns the poinded article in common with the debtor, and by any person in possession of the poinded article. The application, in Form 4 of Sheriff Court Proceedings Act of Sederunt[2], must be made within fourteen days after the date of the 'execution' of the poinding. In the 1987 Act, official reports of diligence are referred to as reports rather than as 'executions', and the time-limit for making an application under section 16(4) of the 1987 Act runs from the date on which the poinding was carried out rather than the date of the report of poinding made under section 22 of the Act.

An application for release of the poinded articles under section 16 must specify:
(a) the name and address of the applicant, the creditor, the officer of court who executed the poinding and any person whom the applicant claims owns the poinded article in common with him and any person having possession of the poinded article;
(b) the court which granted the original decree and the date of that decree upon which the poinding proceeded;
(c) the date and place of execution of the poinding;

(d) the poinded article sought to be released;

(e) the reasons for seeking the release of the poinded article; and

(f) any competent claim for expenses.

Once the application has been received, the sheriff clerk fixes a date for a hearing and makes intimation to the various parties. A copy of the poinding schedule must be lodged by the officer before the date of the hearing. If the sheriff is satisfied that the article is exempt from poinding under section 16 of the 1987 Act, he must make an order releasing the article from the poinding. The sheriff clerk intimates the sheriff's decision to any person to whom intimation of the application was made but was not present when the application was determined.

The release of an article from poinding on this ground does not allow a second poinding to take place in the same premises in respect of the same debt[3].

1 1987 Act, s 16(4).

2 SI 1988/2013, r 8. This rule also applies to the release of an article exempt under s 99 of the 1987 Act from arrestment and from sequestration for rent.

3 1987 Act, s 25.

MONEY

7.53 It is not clear whether money in the form of coins and banknotes may be poinded[1], but the accepted practice is to excluded money from poinding[2]. There are several bases which support this practice. First, banknotes (as well as other forms of negotiable instruments) are incorporeal rather than corporeal moveable property[3] which are not subject to the diligence of poinding. Secondly, notes and coins which circulate as currency are not goods which can be sold[4].

However, where notes and coins do not circulate as currency (as with eg antiques, foreign currency), they can be sold and as such are poindable.

1 Bell *Comm* II, 60; *Graham Stewart* p 40; *Alexander v McClay* (1826) 4 S 439. Under section 32 of the Exchequer Court (Scotland) Act 1856, the Crown could poind banknotes, money and bills but this section has been repealed by the 1987 Act, Sch 8.

2 Scot Law Com Report no 95 (1985), pp 257–258.

3 D J Cusine 'Money and Means of Exchange' in *The Laws of Scotland: Stair Memorial Encyclopaedia* vol 14, para 1806.

4 Sale of Goods Act 1979, s 61(1); *Cusine* above, paras 1807–1808.

SHIPS

7.54 Ships, boats and goods on board cannot be poinded[1]. There is no obvious rationale for this rule, which is contrary to principle, but is firmly established as a long-accepted practice. Indeed the 1987 Act amends a number of statutory provisions by substituting the diligence of arrestment and sale instead of poinding and sale as the correct diligence to use against ships.

1 *Graham Stewart* p 344. The correct diligence to use is arrestment and sale. See ch 5 above at para 5.22.

2 1987 Act, Sch 6, amending Harbours, Docks and Piers Clauses Act 1847, s 57; Sea Fisheries Act 1883, s 20(2); Merchant Shipping Act 1894, s 693; Sea Fisheries Act 1968, s 12(2)(a); Prevention of Oil Pollution Act 1971, s 20(1); British Fishing Boats Act 1983, s 5(2)(a); Inshore Fishing (Scotland) Act 1984, s 8(2)(a).

GOODS PREVIOUSLY POINDED

7.55 Goods which have been previously poinded and sold and brought back for the debtor cannot be poinded again for the same debt[1]. In many cases the statutory rules on prohibition of second poinding in the same premises will give the same result[2], but the common law rule has application where the goods were poinded on premises other than the debtor's and also where ownership of poinded goods has reverted to the debtor under section 37(7) of the 1987 Act[3].

1 *Anderson v Buchanan* (1848) 11 D 270; Bell *Comm* II, 58; *Graham Stewart* p 347.
2 1987 Act, s 25. See below at paras 7.85–7.96.
3 See below at para 7.131.

GOODS AFFECTED BY THE RESERVE AND AUXILIARY FORCES (PROTECTION OF CIVIL INTERESTS) ACT 1951

7.56 Where the debtor is a person within the scope of the protection provided by the Reserve and Auxiliary Forces (Protection of Civil Interests) Act 1951[1], a poinding may proceed against the debtor's property only with the leave of the appropriate court[2]. The leave of the court is not required in respect of a poinding to enforce certain types of debt[3].

1 For a general discussion of the 1951 Act, see J S Campbell ' "A Lawyer's Purgatory". The Reserve Etc Forces Act' 1951 SLT (News) 99. The persons covered by the 1951 Act are set out in the Reserve and Auxiliary Forces (Protection of Civil Interests) Act 1951, Sch 1.
2 Reserve and Auxiliary Forces (Protection of Civil Interests) Act 1951, s 8(2). The appropriate courts are those which pronounced the decree or in whose books a non-Scottish judgment has been registered for enforcement: SI 1952/117.
3 Reserve and Auxiliary Forces (Protection of Civil Interests) Act 1951, s 8(2), proviso.

ROLLING STOCK OF PRIVATE RAILWAYS

7.57 Rolling stocks and plant of private railways which are opened for public traffic are exempt from poinding[1].

1 Railways Companies (Scotland) Act 1867, s 4. Cp *Haldane v Girvan and Portpatrick Railway Company* (1881) 8 R 669. There are still a number of such private railways in Scotland.

GOODS SITUATED IN THE PALACE OF HOLYROODHOUSE

7.58 It has been held by the House of Lords in a case decided in 1826 that goods situated in the Palace of Holyroodhouse cannot be poinded[1]. This is so even if the monarch is not resident there at the time the poinding is attempted to be executed.

1 *Earl of Strathmore v Laing* (1826) 2 W & S 1. It should be noted that this decision reversed the decision of the Court of Session and was given by the House of Lords after argument for the appellant only.

MOBILE HOMES

7.59 Depending upon the degree of fixation, a mobile home may be heritable or moveable property[1]. If the mobile home is moveable property it is open to the diligence of poinding and sale. However the effect of that diligence on a mobile home may be to render the debtor homeless, and poinding and sale is a swifter diligence than those normally used to recover possession of heritable property (eg removings and ejections, adjudications).

Accordingly, section 26 of the 1987 Act provides protection for the debtor whose only or principal residence is a caravan, houseboat or other moveable structure. Such property is not exempt from poinding but at any time after the execution of the poinding and before the granting of a warrant of sale, the debtor may apply to the sheriff for a sist of the poinding[2]. The purpose of the sist is to allow the debtor time in which to find alternative accommodation.

The duration of the sist is within the discretion of the sheriff, and it appears that an application may be made for an extension of a sist already granted or for a further sist[3].

The period of any sist granted on such an application is to be disregarded in calculating the duration of the poinding[4].

1 *Renfrewshire Assessor v Mitchell* 1965 SC 271; *Redgates Caravan Parks v Ayrshire Assessor* 1973 SLT 52.
2 1987 Act, s 26(1); SI 1988/2013, r 18. Where a poinded mobile home is the only or principal residence of a person other than the debtor, that other person may make an application for a sist.
3 D I Nichols *The Debtors (Scotland) Act 1987* p 18–33.
4 1987 Act, ss 26(2), 27(1), (2).

Poinding procedure

7.60 The procedure to be followed in executing a poinding is governed by sections 20 and 21 of the 1987 Act.

The various stages are as follows:

EXHIBITION OF WARRANT

7.61 Before executing the poinding the officer must exhibit to any person present in the premises the extract of decree (or other warrant to poind) and the certificate of execution of the charge in respect of that warrant. It is no longer necessary for the officer to make a public proclamation of the poinding nor to read publicly the extract decree or execution of the charge[1].

1 1987 Act, s 20(2).

DEMAND OF PAYMENT

7.62 The next stage is for the officer to demand payment from the debtor of the sum due, if the debtor is present. Payment may also be demanded from any other person who appears to the officer to be authorised to act for the debtor. The sum due includes the total amount outstanding under the decree (or other document on which the poinding proceeds) and the expenses of the charge[1].

1 1987 Act, ss 2(2), 45. The sum due may also include any sum owing under s 93(5) of the 1987 Act.

INQUIRIES AS TO THE OWNERSHIP OF GOODS TO BE POINDED

7.63 The officer must, prior to the poinding, make inquiry of any person present as to the ownership of the goods which he proposes to poind. In particular, he must inquire whether there are any persons who own any such goods in common with the debtor[1].

1 1987 Act, s 20(2). See above at paras 7.32–7.36.

PRESENCE OF WITNESS

7.64 One witness must accompany the officer of court at the poinding[1]. The stages noted above[2] are strictly speaking stages prior to the poinding, which begins with the valuation of the goods, and no witness is required in respect of these stages. In practice, the witness will be present throughout the entire procedure.

1 1987 Act, s 20(3).
2 Ie exhibition of the warrant, demand of payment and inquiries as to ownership of the goods.

VALUATION OF GOODS

7.65 The poinding, strictly speaking, begins when the officer values the goods[1]. The goods must be valued at the price which they would be likely to fetch if sold on the open market. Where the officer considers that the goods are such that a professional valuer should make the valuation, he may arrange for such a valuation.

1 1987 Act, s 20(4). For further details see below at paras 7.72–7.76.

PREPARATION AND HANDING OVER OF POINDING SCHEDULE

7.66 The officer is to prepare a poinding schedule which must be in Form 5 of the Sheriff Court Proceedings Act of Sederunt[1]. This form specifies inter alia:
(a) the identity of the creditor and the debtor;
(b) the goods poinded and their respective values;
(c) the sum recoverable;
(d) the place where the poinding was executed.
The schedule also warns the debtor that any unauthorised removal of the poinded goods or any wilful damage or destruction of them shall be treated as a breach of poinding and may be dealt with as a contempt of court.

On completion of the poinding the officer and witness sign the poinding schedule. The officer must then deliver the schedule to any person in possession of the goods[2] and if that person is not the debtor he also serves a copy of the schedule by post on the debtor. The date on which the poinding schedule is delivered or left with the debtor is deemed to be the date on which the poinding was executed[3].

The officer must also provide various items of information relating to the rights of the debtor and other parties[4]. This information is set out in the poinding schedule. The appropriate steps which the officer must execute in this regard are to[5]:
(a) inform the debtor (if present at the poinding) of his right to redeem the poinded goods under section 21(4) of the 1987 Act;
(b) inform any person present who owns any poinded goods in common with the debtor of his right to redeem the goods under section 41(2) and 41(3)(a) of the 1987 Act;
(c) inform the debtor (if present) and any person present who owns any poinded article in common with the debtor, or who is in possession of any poinded article, of his right to apply for an order releasing articles from poinding under sections 16(4), 23(1), or 41(3)(b) of the 1987 Act.

1 1987 Act, s 20(5); SI 1988/2013, r 11.
2 He may instead leave the poinding schedule in the premises, where the poinding was executed in a dwellinghouse or other premises, or alternatively deliver the schedule to premises occupied by the person in possession of the poinded goods: 1987 Act, s 20(6)(b).
3 Ibid, ss 20(6)(b); 21(7).
4 Ibid, s 20(6)(d)–(f).
5 In practice the handing over or delivery of the poinding schedule to the debtor means that the provision of this information is not a separate or further stage of the poinding. It also means that the debtor is provided with this information even when he is not present at the poinding. It is also to be noticed that the information is to be given to any co-owner of the goods only if that person is present at the poinding, and presumably this information may be given orally.

CONJOINING OF POINDING CREDITORS

7.67 At any time before the poinding schedule is handed over or delivered under section 20(6)(b) of the 1987 Act, the officer of court may be requested by another creditor to conjoin that creditor in the poinding[1]. The officer must conjoin the other creditor if that creditor delivers to him a warrant to poind (including a certificate of execution of a charge)[2]. However, it is not competent to conjoin one creditor who is poinding in respect of a debt based on a decree or other document of debt and another creditor poinding for a debt for which he holds a summary warrant[3].

Where two poinding creditors are conjoined, the officer must poind sufficient goods to satisfy the debts of both creditors[4]. However, the conjoining of creditors is necessary only where there are insufficient goods to meet the claims of both creditors, and in this situation the conjoined creditors rank rateably in proportion to their debts in the poinding[5].

The conjoining of another creditor must be mentioned in the poinding schedule.

1 1987 Act, s 21(8). This provision permits an officer to accept instructions from different creditors to poind against one debtor. Two separate poindings may also be conjoined prior to the granting of the warrant of sale of the first poinding. See 1987 Act, s 43; SI 1988/2013, r 37. Application under r 37 is made by indorsing a minute on the report of the later poinding.
2 Where a creditor is unable to be conjoined (eg days of charge have not expired) he may still have a claim under the equalisation provisions of the Bankruptcy (Scotland) Act 1985, Sch 7, para 24.
3 1987 Act, s 21(9). Two creditors holding summary warrants may be conjoined: 1987 Act, Sch 5, para 6(8).
4 *Graham Stewart* p 356.
5 *Graham Stewart* p 366.

STEPS TO ENSURE SAFETY OF GOODS

7.68 After the execution of the poinding a number of steps are available to ensure the security of the poinded goods.

Immediate removal

7.69 In general terms, the officer of court must leave the poinded goods at the place where they have been poinded[1]. If it is thought that to do this might threaten the security of the goods, the normal course is to make an application to the sheriff for an appropriate order[2]. However, if the officer considers there is not sufficient time to obtain such an order, he may remove them provided[3]:
(i) the poinding did not take place at a dwellinghouse or similar premises;
(ii) the officer considers the removal necessary for the security of the goods or the preservation of their value; and
(iii) the goods are removed to the nearest convenient premises belonging to the debtor or the person in possession of the article (or where there are no such premises to the nearest suitable secure premises).
The expense of such immediate removal is borne by the creditor.

1 1987 Act, s 20(7).
2 Ibid, s 21(1)(a).
3 Ibid, s 20(7).

Application to sheriff for order of the security of goods

7.70 At any time after the execution of the poinding[1], the creditor, the officer on behalf of the creditor, or the debtor may apply to the sheriff to make an order for the security of any of the poinded goods[2]. The application must state the reasons why such an order should be made and the proposed security arrangements. On the lodging of an application, the sheriff decides on what procedure is appropriate. He may dispose of the application without a hearing or without intimation being made to any party, including the applicant[3]. Intimation will not be made on a party where the reason alleged in the application why an order should be made is that that party might seek to remove or destroy the goods.

Where the sheriff considers that a hearing should be held to dispose of the application, the sheriff clerk must make intimation on the applicant, and any other party on whom intimation is to be made[4]. The sheriff clerk will also intimate the sheriff's decision on the application to any person to whom intimation of the application was made but who was not present at the hearing. There is no need to intimate the decision on a party to whom intimation of the application was not made.

1 For the date of execution of a poinding see 1987 Act, s 21(7). See further above at para 7.66.
2 1987 Act, s 21(1)(a); SI 1988/2013, r 12(1), Form 6.
3 SI 1988/2013, r 12(2).
4 Ibid, r 12(3). Whether or not intimation has been made to him the officer who executed the poinding must lodge with the court a copy of the poinding schedule before the date of the hearing. This requires that the sheriff clerk informs the officer of this date, even where no formal intimation is to be made.

Application to sheriff of the immediate disposal of poinded goods

7.71 At any time after the execution of the poinding[1], the creditor, the officer on his behalf, or the debtor may apply to the sheriff to make an order for the immediate disposal of certain types of poinded goods[2]. An order may be made in respect of goods which are of a perishable nature or are likely to deteriorate substantially and rapidly in their condition or value. The latter category is intended to cover items such as Christmas cards or magazines whose value might be considerably lessened by the time they were sold under a warrant sale[3]. If the sheriff grants an order for the immediate disposal of such goods he must also order that once the goods are sold, the proceeds of sale are to be paid to the creditor or are to be consigned in court until the diligence comes to an end. The latter course is appropriate where only part of the poinded goods are disposed of under such an application.

Where such an application is made by the creditor or officer of court, the applicant must intimate the application to the debtor when making the application. Application by a debtor is intimated to the creditor (or to the officer of court) by the sheriff clerk[4].

Once the sheriff is satisfied that appropriate intimation has been made he determines further procedure as he considers appropriate. The sheriff's determination of the application is not subject to appeal.

1 1987 Act, s 21(7). See above at para 7.66.
2 1987 Act, s 21(1)(b); SI 1988/2013, r 13, Form 7.
3 Scot Law Com Report no 95 (1985), p 276.
4 SI 1988/2013, r 13(2).

Valuation of goods

7.72 The most significant step in the diligence of poinding and sale is that of the valuation of goods made at the poinding. Among the various functions which the appraised value of poinded goods plays are the following:
(a) A poinding may be recalled or a warrant of sale refused on the basis of a substantial aggregate undervaluation of poinded goods[1];
(b) The debtor has the right to redeem the poinded goods by paying their appraised value[2];
(c) Where goods are unsold after an auction sale or are sold below their valuation, the debt is reduced by the amount of the valuation[3];
(d) Goods in co-ownership may be released from the poinding by the co-owner paying the debtor's interest in the article in terms of the article's valuation[4];
(e) The amount of the valuation of goods acts as the upper reserve price of the goods at a subsequent warrant sale[5];
(f) The debtor may have the remaining goods released from poinding when goods of sufficient value in terms of their valuation have been removed to an auction room for sale[6].

1 1987 Act, ss 24(3), 30(2).
2 Ibid, ss 21(4), 33(2).
3 Ibid, s 37(9).
4 Ibid, s 41.
5 Ibid, s 37(3), (4).
6 Ibid, s 33(1).

WHO MAKES THE VALUATION?

7.73 The valuation of the poinded goods is made by the officer of court who executes the poinding[1]. However, where the officer considers that a proper valuation calls for the skills of a professional valuer or other suitable person, he may arrange for the valuation to be carried out by such a person. A valuation may be made by a professional valuer in any poinding, but the extra expense of this procedure is chargeable against the debtor only if such a step is advisable (eg because of the unusual nature of the articles to be poinded).

1 1987 Act, s 20(4).

EXTENT OF VALUATION

7.74 The officer (or where appropriate the professional valuer) is entitled to poind goods only to the extent necessary to ensure the recovery of the total sum due if the goods were sold at their appraised value[1]. The total sum due includes the outstanding principal sum (including interest and court expenses), and the expenses of the charge and the entire diligence of poinding and sale chargeable against the debtor under Schedule 1 to the 1987 Act[2].

This provision may pose problems where goods subject to a poinding are not easily divisible. For example, a poinding may be held to recover a total debt of £500. The only goods of the debtor which are poindable is a motor car whose valuation under section 20(4) of the 1987 Act is £1,000. To poind the whole car worth £1,000 for a debt of £500 would breach section 19(1) of the 1987 Act. However, there is no legal barrier to goods being owned by more than one person nor to part ownership of goods being offered for sale. It is submitted that in this situation, the officer should value the car at £1,000 and poind it to the extent of £500. Since a sheriff's warrant can authorise only the sale of goods which have been previously poinded, a half-share of the car is offered at any subsequent warrant sale.

1 1987 Act, s 19(1); cp *McKinnon v Hamilton* (1866) 4 M 852; *Hamilton v Emslie* (1860) 7 M 173, 176.
2 1987 Act, s 45.

AMOUNT OF VALUATION

7.75 Poinded goods must be valued at the price they would be likely to fetch if sold on open market[1]. Although the 1987 Act does not expressly state so, the time of sale on open market for purposes of fixing the valuation is that at the poinding, not a subsequent sale under sheriff's warrant[2]. In other words, the risk of deterioration in the condition of the goods between the poinding and the warrant sale lies with the creditor.

Where the goods are valued on an unusual basis (eg a car valued not as a motor vehicle but only as scrap), the special basis of the valuation must be set out in the schedule and the report of the execution of the poinding[3].

It is not a justification of goods being undervalued at a poinding that this would result in lower fees being charged against the debtor[4].

1 1987 Act, s 20(4).
2 Cp D I Nichols *The Debtors (Scotland) Act 1987* p 18–29.
3 *Lombard North Central Ltd v Wilson* (unreported, Glasgow Sheriff Court, 7 October 1980).
4 *Scottish Gas Board v Johnstone* 1974 SLT (Sh Ct) 65.

REVALUATION OF POINDED GOODS

7.76 The general rule is that once an article has been poinded, the revaluation of that article in the same poinding is incompetent[1]. This rule is expressly subject to section 29(2)(b) of the 1987 Act which permits the sheriff, on application by the creditor or the officer on his behalf, to authorise the revaluation of poinded goods which have been damaged or destroyed. The damage or destruction need not have been the fault of the debtor[2].

It should be noted that goods once valued cannot be revalued where the poinding is suspended by the granting of an interim or full time to pay order. However, the prohibition on revaluation applies to goods already poinded in the same poinding, and not the goods previously poinded in a prior poinding where a second poinding for the same debt is permissible[3].

1 1987 Act, s 21(6).
2 Ibid, s 29(2)(b). Application is governed by SI 1988/2013, r 24, Form 18.
3 Ie, under 1987 Act, ss 9(12), 28(2).

Redemption of goods: release of goods on grounds of undue harshness

7.77 If the debtor is present at a poinding he must be informed by the officer of his right to redeem poinded goods under section 21(4) of the 1987 Act[1]. This provision confers on the debtor the right to redeem poinded goods by paying to the officer of court a sum equal to the appraised value of the goods. This right may be exercised by the debtor within fourteen days after the date of execution of the poinding[2]. Goods redeemed by the debtor in this way cannot be poinded again for the same debt[3].

Where the officer of court receives payment by the debtor for redemption of the goods, he must grant a receipt which operates to release the goods from the poinding. The redemption must be mentioned in the report of the execution of the poinding[4]. If the officer has already submitted this report, the officer must report the redemption to the sheriff as soon as is reasonably practicable.

1 1987 Act, s 20(6)(d). See above at para 7.66.
2 1987 Act, s 21(4).
3 _Fiddes v Fyfe_ (1791) Bell's Oct Cas 355.
4 1987 Act, s 21(5); SI 1988/2013, r 14, Form 8.

7.78 Furthermore, within the same period (ie fourteen days after the execution of the poinding), the debtor or any person in possession of a poinded article may apply to the sheriff for the release of the poinded article on the ground that its continued inclusion in the poinding or its sale under warrant would be unduly harsh in the circumstances[1]. The idea of what is unduly harsh is not defined in the 1987 Act, but the Scottish Law Commission Report envisaged that an application might be granted not only in respect of articles of merely sentimental value to the debtor but also articles essential to the applicant's business[2].

An application must specify:
(a) the name and address of the applicant, the creditor, the officer of court who executed the poinding and, as appropriate, the debtor or the person having possession of the poinded article;
(b) the court which granted the original decree and the date of that decree, upon which the poinding proceeded;
(c) the date and place of the execution of the poinding;
(d) the poinded article sought to be released;
(e) the reasons for seeking release of the poinded article; and
(f) any competent crave for expenses.
When an application has been lodged the sheriff clerk fixes a date for a hearing and makes intimation to the various parties[3]. The sheriff clerk also intimates the sheriff's decision on the application to any person to whom intimation of the application was made but who was not present when the application was determined.

Where application for release of a poinded article on the ground of undue harshness is granted, the sheriff may authorise the poinding of other articles belonging to the debtor on the same premises following an application to that effect by the creditor or by the officer on his behalf. This latter application may be made orally at the time of granting the earlier application for release of the article or by indorsing a minute on the order granted[4].

1 1987 Act, s 23(1); SI 1988/2013, r 16, Form 10.
2 Scot Law Com Report no 95 (1985), pp 256–257.
3 The officer must lodge with the court a copy of the poinding schedule before the date of the hearing. This is so whether or not the officer intends to appear at the hearing: SI 1988/2013, r 16(4).
4 1987 Act, s 23(2); SI 1988/2103, r 16(6).

Report of execution of poinding

7.79 The officer must submit a report of the execution of the poinding to the sheriff within fourteen days after the date of execution[1]. The officer may apply for an extension of this period by indorsing a minute to that effect on the extract decree (or other document of debt) upon which the poinding proceeded. The minute must set out the reasons for the extension[2].

1 1987 Act, s 22(1). The date of the execution of the poinding is determined by 1987 Act, s 21(7). See above at para 7.66.
2 SI 1988/2013, r 15(3).

7.80 A report of the execution of a poinding must be in Form 9 of the Sheriff Court Proceedings Act of Sederunt[1]. In the report the sheriff officer must note:
(a) the court which granted the original decree and the date of that decree, or details of the document upon which the poinding proceeded, and the date of any charge;
(b) that he did, before executing the poinding:
(i) exhibit to any person present the warrant to poind and the certificate of execution of charge;
(ii) demand payment of the sum reoverable from the debtor, if he was present, or any person present appearing to the officer to be authorised to act for the debtor; and
(iii) make enquiry of any person present as to the ownership of the articles proposed to be poinded, and in particular whether there were any persons who own any article in common with the debtor;
(c) if appropriate, that he informed the debtor of his right to redeem poinded articles and whether any articles have been redeemed;
(d) if appropriate, that he informed any person present who owns any poinded article in common with the debtor of his right to redeem poinded articles;
(e) if appropriate, that he informed the debtor and any person present who owns any poinded article in common with the debtor, or who is in possession of the poinded article, of his right to apply for an order releasing articles from poinding under sections 16(4), 23(1) or 41(3)(b) of the 1987 Act;
(f) whether he has carried out any of the actions mentioned in section 20(7) of the 1987 Act;
(g) the articles poinded and their respective values;
(h) the sum due by the debtor, including the fees, mileage charges or outlays which have been incurred in serving the charge and executing the poinding, and the amount of each; and
(i) in the case of a further or second poinding, the circumstances justifying the poinding.
The officer must also note any assertion made before the submission of the report that any poinded article does not belong to the debtor[2].
The report must be signed by the officer of court and the witness who attended the poinding.

1 SI 1988/2013, r 15(1).
2 1987 Act, s 22(2).

REFUSAL TO RECEIVE A REPORT

7.81 The only grounds on which the sheriff may refuse to receive a report of the execution of a poinding are (1) that the report had not been submitted timeously, and (2) that the report has not been signed by the officer and the witness[1]. If a sheriff refuses to receive the report on one of these grounds, the effect is that the poinding thereupon ceases to have effect. A second poinding in the same premises in respect of the same debt is incompetent[2].

A refusal to receive a report of the execution of a poinding is to be intimated by the sheriff clerk to the debtor and if that is a different person also to the person in possession of the poinded goods[3].

1 1987 Act, s 22(3), (5).
2 Ibid, s 25.
3 Ibid, s 22(4).

Challenges to poinding

INVALIDITY OR CESSATION OF POINDING

7.82 The sheriff has power to declare a poinding as invalid or as having ceased to have effect[1]. This power may be exercised on his own initiative or on application by the debtor[2], at any time before the sale of the poinded goods. If the sheriff is satisfied that the poinding is invalid or has ceased to have effect, he must make an appropriate order and may also make such consequential orders as appear necessary in the circumstances. If the sheriff intends to use this power *ex proprio motu* he must give the creditor and the debtor an opportunity to make representations and to be heard[3].

A poinding which is valid ceases to have effect by extinction of the debt which it seeks to recover. A poinding ceases by payment of the debt only where the full amount recoverable by it is paid to the creditor (or the creditor's agent, including the officer) or this amount is tendered by the debtor and the tender is not accepted within a reasonable time[4]. The full amount is the principal sum (including the principal sum, interest and court expenses) and the full expenses of the diligence[5]. Furthermore, a valid poinding may cease to have effect by the expiry of the period of one year from its date of execution, unless the period of poinding has been extended[6].

There are many grounds on which a poinding is invalid. In short any fundamental irregularity in the carrying out of the charge and poinding will lead to the poinding being invalid. Dr Nichols notes the following examples: a poinding executed before expiry of the days of a charge, the officer entering an empty dwellinghouse without following the procedure laid down by section 18 of the 1987 Act, and a Court of Session decree executed by someone not holding a commission as a messenger-at-arms[7]. Further illustrations include a poinding proceeding without a proper warrant to poind, or a poinding executed by an officer in respect of a debt in which the officer has a disqualifying interest[8].

Where goods which are non-poindable or are exempt from poinding have been included in a poinding, the poinding remains good in respect of any other goods included in it but is otherwise invalid. However, the poinding of goods which are exempted from poinding solely by virtue by section 16 of the 1987 Act does not form the basis for a sheriff declaring a poinding invalid[9]. (The debtor's remedy in this situation is to appeal against the poinding of the goods under section 16(4) of the 1987 Act.)

It is not clear to what extent the wrongful valuation of poinded goods leads to the invalidity of the poinding. Substantial undervaluation of the poinded goods in aggregate terms is a ground for the debtor seeking recall of the poinding under section 24(3) of the 1987 Act. Where there has been no serious attempt to appraise the goods or the goods have been valued lumped together, the poinding is invalid[10].

1 1987 Act, s 24(1).
2 Application is made in accordance with SI 1988/2013, r 17, Form 11, discussed below at para 7.83.
3 1987 Act, s 24(5). Where the sheriff makes such an order *ex proprio motu* the order is intimated to the debtor by the sheriff clerk: 1987 Act, s 24(6). Procedure where an order in respect of the invalidity or cessation of the poinding is made on an application by the debtor is the same as that following an application for recall of the poinding. See below at para 7.83.
4 1987 Act, s 95.
5 Ibid, ss 93; 45.
6 Ibid, s 27(1). See below at paras 7.97–7.107.
7 D I Nichols *The Debtors (Scotland) Act 1987* p 18–32.
8 1987 Act, s 83. See further ch 14 at paras 14.26–14.28.
9 1987 Act, s 24(2).
10 *Le Conte v Douglas* (1880) 8 R 175; *McKnight v Green* (1835) 13 S 342. However, where one or some articles have been improperly valued, the poinding may remain good in respect of other goods which have been properly poinded: *McKnight v Green*, above.

RECALL OF POINDING

7.83 The sheriff also has power at any time before an application is made for a warrant of sale to recall a poinding on certain grounds[1]. This power cannot be exercised on his own initiative but only following an application by the debtor[2]. The application must specify:
(a) the name and address of the creditor, the officer of court who executed the poinding and any other person having an interest;
(b) the court which granted the original decree and the date of that decree upon which the poinding proceeded;
(c) the date and place of execution of the poinding;
(d) the reason for the application and the order sought; and
(e) if appropriate, any competent crave for expenses.
On the lodging of such an application the sheriff clerk must fix a date for a hearing, and make intimation to the applicant, the creditor and any other party having an interest. The sheriff clerk also intimates the application to the officer of court who executed the poinding with an order that the officer delivers a copy of the poinding schedule to the court before the date of the hearing.

There are three grounds on which the sheriff may recall a poinding:
(a) that it would be unduly harsh in the circumstances for a warrant of sale of the poinded goods to be granted. It should be noted that the undue harshness in this context is a general reference to the poinding being completed by a warrant sale, not to the inclusion of individual articles among the poinded goods. (In this last respect an application may be made under section 23(1) of the 1987 Act[3].) The Scottish Law Commission Report envisaged that this

ground for recalling a poinding involves something beyond mere hardship to the debtor and that the use of this ground would apply only in exceptional cases[4];

(b) that the aggregate values placed on the poinded goods at the poinding was substantially below the aggregate of the prices which they would have been likely to fetch if sold on the open market[5]. It should be noted that this ground applies only in terms of the overall or aggregate undervaluation of the poinded goods, and so mistakes in the appraisal of individual items (provided the mistakes were not so serious as to invalidate the poinding of these articles[6]) might even, or balance each other, out. A further point is that the language of section 24(3)(b) of the 1987 Act makes clear that the substantial undervaluation refers to the valuation made at the time of the poinding in terms of prices the goods would be likely to fetch if sold at that time, and not at the time of the application for recall;

(c) that the likely aggregate proceeds of the sale of the poinded goods would not exceed the likely expenses of the sale[7]. The likely expenses of the sale are those likely to be incurred in the application for warrant of sale and in any steps required to execute that warrant, on the assumption that the application and such steps are unopposed. The expenses of sale do not include the expenses of the charge and poinding. The likely aggregate proceeds of the sale will be determined by the aggregate appraisal of the poinded goods, unless it can be shown that their current condition or the nature of the market is such that it is likely that a different price will be realised. Accordingly, this ground for recalling a poinding is applicable where it is likely that the sale of the goods will realise very little or nothing at all, even though if such a sale did proceed the debt would still be reduced by the amount of the appraised values. This ground may not be used for recalling a poinding where a second poinding in the same premises for the same debt has been authorised or is competent under the 1987 Act[8].

The sheriff's decision on an application for recall of a poinding is intimated by the sheriff clerk to any person to whom intimation of the application was made but who was not present when the application was determined[9].

1 1987 Act, s 24(3).
2 Application must be made in accordance with SI 1988/2013, r 17 and Form 11.
3 See above at para 7.78.
4 Scot Law Com Report no 95 (1985), p 288. An example cited by the Commission is where the debtor's spouse is dying in hospital.
5 Cp *Scottish Gas Board v Johnstone* 1974 SLT (Sh Ct) 65.
6 See above at para 7.82.
7 Cp *South of Scotland Electricity Board v Carlyle* 1980 SLT (Sh Ct) 98.
8 1987 Act, s 24(4). See below at paras 7.85–7.96.
9 SI 1988/2013, r 17(4).

CHALLENGE TO POINDING BY PROTECTED SPOUSE UNDER THE MATRIMONIAL
HOMES (FAMILY PROTECTION) (SCOTLAND) ACT 1981

7.84 Where a protected spouse has been granted an order under section 3(3) or 3(4) of the Matrimonial Homes (Family Protection) (Scotland) Act 1981 conferring the right to use or possess furniture and plenishings in the matrimonial home, such a spouse may challenge a poinding of such furniture and plenishings carried out against his or her spouse as debtor[1]. On application by a protected spouse the sheriff has power, where satisfied that the main or sole purpose of the poinding was to prevent the protected spouse's statutory rights of use and possession of the poinded goods, to (i) declare the poinding null, or (ii) make such order as appropriate to protect the use or possession of the goods by the protected spouse.

An application must be made by the protected spouse within forty days of the execution of the poinding.

1 The right of the protected spouse in this case is in addition to his or her right to have furniture and plenishings declared exempt from the poinding under section 16(4) of the 1987 Act. See also Family Law (Scotland) Act 1985, s 14(5).

Second poinding in same premises for same debt

7.85 One of the central provisions of the 1987 Act in relation to the diligence of poinding and warrant sale is that regulating the time-limits in which a creditor must apply for a warrant to sell poinded goods[1]. The protection afforded to debtors by these provisions would be easily evaded if creditors could proceed to use a second poinding to recover the same debt as that pursued by a prior poinding which had elapsed without a warrant of sale being granted. Accordingly, section 25 provides that where articles have been poinded another poinding in the same premises to enforce the same debt is not competent[2]. It is important to note that this prohibition on second poinding applies even where the first poinding is invalid (eg where there has been no prior charge, or the poinding is invalidated by the officer's disqualifying interest in the debt).

1 See 1987 Act, s 27. See discussion below at paras 7.97–7.102.
2 1987 Act, s 25. A further poinding is always competent where the debtor has other property kept in premises other than the premises where the first poinding was held. This is so even in respect of property which was at the premises of the original poinding but which was not poinded there.

EXCEPTIONS

7.86 There are various exceptions to this general rule. In a number of the exceptions, a further poinding in the same premises is directly permitted by the 1987 Act:

Goods subsequently brought on to the premises

7.87 Section 25 of the 1987 Act allows a further poinding for the same debt in the same premises where goods have been brought onto the premises subsequent to the poinding. However, the further poinding may be used only in respect of those goods and not against goods which were on the premises at the time of the original poinding but were not poinded then.

Time to pay order recalling poinding with later default by the debtor

7.88 Where a time to pay order has been made and has resulted in a poinding being recalled or a poinding being made subject to no further steps being taken and there has been subsequent default on the order on the part of the debtor, the creditor may use a further poinding in the same premises as those where the poinding had been executed prior to the making of the time to pay order[1].

1 1987 Act, ss 9(12), 11. The same effect follows where the time to pay order ceases to have effect following the debtor's granting a composition contract or granting a voluntary trust deed for his creditors. The right to execute a further poinding arises even where the time to pay order involves only the freezing rather than the recall of the original poinding.

Authorised removal of goods to new premises

7.89 Where the creditor gives written consent, the debtor or person in possession of the goods may remove them to another location[1]. Alternatively, goods may be removed if the sheriff has given authorisation, following upon an application by the debtor or person in possession of the goods[2]. Such authorised removal of poinded goods to another location leaves the poinding in existence in respect of both the removed goods and those remaining in the original premises[3].

However, where goods have been removed to a new location in a different sheriffdom or sheriff court district there are practical problems in continuing both poindings from the original sheriff court district. Accordingly, where goods have been removed with the authorisation of the sheriff or creditor, those goods may be repoinded in their new premises[4]. This is so whether or not the new location of the poindings is in the same sheriffdom or sheriff court district. Furthermore, a further poinding may be used in respect of goods remaining in the original premises, whether or not they were previously poinded. In the case of either (or both) such repoindings, the original poinding is deemed to have been abandoned[5].

1 1987 Act, s 28(1)(a). Written consent may be given by the officer of court on behalf of the creditor.
2 1987 Act, s 28(1)(b). Applications are made in accordance with SI 1988/2013, r 20, Form 14. The applicant must state reasons for seeking the removal of the goods.
3 1987 Act, s 18(7).
4 Ibid, s 28(2).
5 The debtor is liable for the expense of the further poinding or poindings but not for the expenses of the original poinding deemed to have been abandoned: 1987 Act, Sch 1, para 5. However it may be made a condition of the authorisation granted by the creditor or sheriff that the debtor also pays the expenses of the original poinding: 1987 Act, Sch 1, para 6.

Release of goods belonging to a third party

7.90 Where goods belonging to a third party have been released by an officer of court or sheriff from the poinding the officer may poind other articles belonging to the debtor in the same premises[1].

1 1987 Act, s 40(5). See above at para 7.33.

Release of goods in common ownership on basis of undue hardship

7.91 Where a sheriff grants a release from the poinding of goods in the common ownership of the debtor and another person on the grounds of undue harshness[1], the officer of court may poind other articles belonging to the debtor in the same premises[2].

1 1987 Act, s 41(3)(b). See above at para 7.38.
2 1987 Act, s 41(6).

SECOND POINDINGS AUTHORISED BY A SHERIFF

7.92 In the following cases a second poinding in the same premises may be executed in respect of the same debt but only if the sheriff so authorises the second poinding after application by the creditor or officer.

Release of goods of the debtor on grounds of undue harshness

7.93 Where the sheriff has granted an order for the release of a poinded article belonging wholly to the debtor on the ground that its continued inclusion in the poinding or its sale would be unduly harsh in the circumstances[1], the sheriff may authorise the poinding of other articles belonging to the debtor on the same premises[2].

1 1987 Act, s 23(4). See above at para 7.78.
2 1987 Act, s 23(2). Application for a further poinding is made by the officer or the creditor either orally at the time of the granting of the application for release of the article, or by indorsing a minute on the order granted: SI 1988/2013, r 16(6).

Unauthorised removal of poinded goods

7.94 Where poinded goods have been removed to another location without authorisation, the poinding of those goods remains in force[1]. Where unauthorised removal of goods takes place through the fault of the debtor[2], the sheriff may grant an application authorising the poinding of other articles belonging to the debtor in the same premises[3].

1 1987 Act, s 28(7).
2 The debtor would be at fault where the removal resulted from his failure to look after the goods properly but not eg where his premises have been broken into and the goods stolen. Cp Scot Law Com Report no 95 (1985), p 279.
3 1987 Act, s 28(6). The application is made by the creditor or officer on his behalf and may be made by oral motion in proceedings relating to the poinding or by using Form 17. See SI 1988/2013, r 23.

Poinded goods destroyed or damaged

7.95 Where poinded goods have been destroyed or damaged in circumstances in which the debtor is at fault[1], the sheriff may grant an application by the creditor or officer on his behalf authorising the poinding of other articles belonging to the debtor in the same premises as those of the original poinding[2].

1 Cp above at para 7.94, n 2.
2 1987 Act, s 29(2); SI 1988/2013, r 24, Form 18.

7.96 Where a further poinding has taken place on any of the grounds mentioned in paragraphs 7.88–7.95 above, the creditor or officer may apply to the sheriff to have the further poinding conjoined with the original poinding[1]. The sheriff cannot make such an order until after fourteen days from the date of the execution of the further poinding, nor may such an order for conjoining be made where a warrant of sale has been granted in respect of either poinding[2].

1 1987 Act, s 43(1); SI 1988/2013, r 37.
2 1987 Act, s 43(2).

Duration of poinding

GENERAL RULE OF TWELVE MONTHS DURATION

7.97 A poinding ceases to have effect after one year from the date of the execution of the poinding unless there has been an application made for a warrant of sale of the poinded goods[1]. Thus where a poinding was executed on 26 March in one year, it will cease to have effect unless there has been an application for warrant of sale at any time prior to midnight of the day of 26 March the following year[2].

1 1987 Act, s 27(1). This is subject to the further provisions of s 27, discussed below. The date of the execution of a poinding is determined in accordance with the 1987 Act, s 21(7).
2 See D C Coull 'Time' *The Laws of Scotland: Stair Memorial Encyclopaedia* vol 22, paras 821–823.

EXTENSION OF PERIOD OF DURATION OF POINDING

7.98 Any time before an application is made for a warrant of sale, the creditor or officer on his behalf may apply to the sheriff to have the period of the duration of the poinding extended[1]. The application is made in Form 13 and must specify:
(a) the name and address of the debtor, and where appropriate, the creditor and the officer of court who executed the poinding;
(b) the court which granted the original decree and the date of that decree, or details of the summary warrant or other document, upon which the poinding proceeded;
(c) the date and place of execution of the poinding;
(d) the period of extension sought;
(e) the reasons for making the application; and
(f) where appropriate, any competent crave for expenses.
On the lodging of an application the sheriff clerk fixes a date for a hearing and makes intimation on the applicant, the debtor and where appropriate the officer of court[2].

There are two grounds on which the sheriff may grant an extension of the poinding[3]:
(1) The first is that, if granted, the debtor is likely to comply with an agreement between himself and the creditor to pay off the sums due[4].
(2) The second ground is that the extension is needed to allow the creditor to complete the diligence where he is not responsible for the circumstances giving rise to the need for the extension and he would be prejudiced by the poinding coming to an end.
Where an extension is granted, an application may be made before the expiry of the period of extension for a further extension on either of these grounds[5]. A further extension may be granted more than once.

While any such application is pending, the poinding continues in force until the application has been disposed of. If the application is on the basis of an agreement to pay by the debtor and the date of the hearing is later than fourteen days before the poinding is due to end, the poinding continues to have effect until fourteen days after the disposal of the application[6].

A decision of the sheriff on an application for extension, or further extension of the period of the poinding is not subject to appeal[7].

1 1987 Act, s 27(2); SI 1988/2013, r 19.
2 The officer who executed the poinding must lodge with the court a copy of the poinding schedule before the date of the hearing: SI 1988/2013, r 19(4).
3 1987 Act, s 27(2)(a), (b).
4 The 1987 Act does not require that the agreement between the parties has already been made, but in almost all cases this will be necessary before the sheriff can be satisfied that the debtor will comply with any agreement to pay. Any agreement may be to pay by way of instalments or otherwise.

5 1987 Act, s 27(3).
6 Ibid, s 27(5)(a).
7 Ibid, s 27(4). The decision of the sheriff on any such application is to be intimated to the debtor
   by the sheriff clerk.

APPLICATION FOR WARRANT OF SALE

7.99 Where an application has been made for a warrant to sell poinded goods during the period in which a poinding is in force, the poinding remains effective, both where the warrant of sale is granted and where it is refused[1].

Where the warrant of sale is granted, the poinding continues to have effect until the date of the sale of the goods or the date on which ownership of the goods passes to the creditor under section 37(6) of the 1987 Act. Where warrant is granted but the goods are not sold nor ownership passes to the creditor, the poinding remains in force until the expiry of the period specified for the sale in the warrant.

Where an application for warrant sale is refused, the poinding remains in force for a period of seven days unless an application is made for leave to appeal against the refusal in which case it continues until leave has been refused or the application withdrawn. Where leave to appeal has been granted, the poinding remains in effect until the period of appeal has expired without an appeal being made, or where the appeal is made, until the appeal is determined or abandoned[2].

1 1987 Act, s 27(5)(b), (c).
2 Ibid, s 27(5)(b). Application for leave to appeal against a decision refusing a warrant of sale
   must be made within seven days of the decision. Appeal may be made only on a question of
   law, which must be specified in the application for leave: 1987 Act, s 103; SI 1988/2013, r 72.
   An application must be made within a period of fourteen days from the date when leave to
   appeal is granted: 1987 Act, s 103(2).

PAYMENT AGREEMENTS AFTER WARRANT OF SALE

7.100 Where a report is made to the court that after the granting of a warrant of sale, the creditor and debtor have entered into an agreement for the debtor to pay the sums due, the poinding is extended by a period of six months from the date of the latest such report[1].

1 1987 Act, s 27(6). See below at para 7.122. This provision is without prejudice to 1987 Act,
   s 27(7) discussed below.

ALTERATION OF ARRANGEMENTS OF SALE

7.101 Section 35 of the 1987 Act permits the creditor or officer to apply for variation of the arrangements for sale specified in the warrant of sale[1]. Where the variation is allowed, the poinding continues in effect as if the original warrant had contained the terms of the variation[2]. If the variation is refused the sheriff may issue an order as to when the poinding ceases to have effect, but in doing so he must allow at least the period for application for leave to appeal against the refusal of the variation to elapse or any such application to be dealt with in the period for making any appeal or the disposal of any such appeal[3].

1 1987 Act, s 35. See below at paras 7.125–7.128.

2 1987 Act, s 27(7)(b).
3 Ibid, s 27(7)(a). For appeals see ibid, s 103; SI 1988/2013, r 72.

INTERRUPTION OF DURATION OF POINDING

7.102   Certain periods of interruption of the duration of a poinding or of the extension of its duration, are disregarded when determining whether a poinding has ceased to have effect. These are:
(i)   any period during which an interim time to pay order is in effect[1];
(ii) any period during which a time to pay order is in effect[2];
(iii) any period during which an order is in effect sisting a poinding in respect of a mobile home[3].

1 1987 Act, s 8(3).
2 Ibid, s 9(9).
3 Ibid, s 26(2).

Use, removal of, and interference with poinded goods

GENERAL EFFECT

7.103   Where goods have been poinded, the debtor (or party in possession of them) may continue to use the goods in the normal way, as the risk of depreciation in the value of the goods through such fair wear and tear is for the creditor to carry[1].

However, the goods may not be used in such a way as to cause their damage or destruction (unless normal use of the goods leads to them being used up or consumed) nor in general may the goods be removed from the premises where the poinding took place. A breach of poinding is committed by the unauthorised removal of the goods but also by the wilful damage or destruction of them committed by the debtor or by any person (other than the creditor or any officer of court) who knows that the goods are subject to a poinding[2]. Such a breach of poinding may be dealt with as a contempt of court.

1 See above at para 7.75.
2 1987 Act, ss 28(3), 29(1).

AUTHORISED REMOVAL OF POINDED GOODS

7.104   The debtor or person in possession of poinded goods may seek permission to remove the goods to another location[1]. If so removed the goods remain poinded but may be repoinded[2].

1 1987 Act, s 28(1); SI 1988/2013, r 20. See above at para 7.89.
2 1987 Act, s 28(7), (2). See above at para 7.89.

UNAUTHORISED REMOVAL OF POINDED GOODS

7.105   Where poinded goods have been removed from the premises of poinding without authorisation the goods still remain subject to the poinding[1]. The creditor may apply to have further goods of the debtor repoinded in the original premises[2]. The creditor may also apply to the sheriff for an order requiring the person in possession of the removed goods to restore them to the original premises within a specified time[3]. The application for the order must specify, inter alia the present whereabouts of the goods in question if these are known. Where a location for the present whereabouts is specified in the application and an order is granted and not complied with, the sheriff may grant warrant to officers of court to search for the goods in those premises and to restore the goods to their original premises (or take other measures as directed). The warrant is authority to open shut and lockfast places. Procedure for obtaining the warrant is made by indorsing an appropriate minute on the form of application for order for restoration[4].

However an order for restoration of removed goods cannot be made where it would prejudice the rights of bona fide purchasers for value[5]. Where it appears to the sheriff that poinded goods which have been removed in an unauthorised way have been acquired for value without knowledge of the poinding by the purchaser, he must refuse to make an order for their restoration (or if an order has already been made he must recall it)[6]. The sheriff must also in these circumstances make an order releasing the article in question from the poinding.

1 1987 Act, s 28(7).
2 Ibid, s 28(6). See above at para 7.94.
3 1987 Act, s 28(4)(a). Application is made in accordance with SI 1988/2013,r 21 and Form 15.
4 1987 Act, s 28(4)(b); SI 1988/2013, r 21(8), (9).
5 *Arnot v Dowie* (1863) 2 M 119; *Graham Stewart* p 358.
6 1987 Act, s 28; SI 1988/2013, r 22 and Form 16.

DAMAGE AND DESTRUCTION OF POINDED GOODS

7.106 There are four main consequences which follow from the damage to, or the destruction of, poinded goods:
(a) where the damage or destruction is wilful, a breach of poinding has occurred which may be dealt with as a contempt of court[1];
(b) following an application by the creditor or officer on his behalf, the sheriff may authorise the revaluation of any damaged goods[2]. The revaluation is made on the same criterion as set out in section 20(4), ie the price the goods would be likely to fetch if sold on open market at the time of revaluation;
(c) where the debtor is at fault in respect of the damage or destruction, the sheriff may authorise a further poinding of the debtor's goods[3];
(d) where a third party in the knowledge of the poinding, wilfully damages or destroys a poinded article, or where a third party removes a poinded article in breach of poinding and the article is then either lost, stolen, damaged or destroyed, the sheriff may order the third party to consign a sum in court[4]. Such an order may be made where the effect of a third party removing poinded goods is that the goods are acquired for value by another person without knowledge of the poinding. The sum to be consigned is the appraised value of the article, or if the article still has value and is still available for poinding, the difference in its appraised value and its current value[5]. A consigned sum is paid to the creditor (with any surplus going to the debtor) on completion of the warrant sale[6].

1 1987 Act, s 29(1).
2 Ibid, s 29(2)(b); SI 1988/2013, r 24, Form 18.

3 1987 Act, s 29(2)(a); SI 1988/2013, r 24, Form 18. See above at para 7.95.
4 1987 Act, s 29(3); SI 1988/2013, r 25 Form 19.
5 1987 Act, s 29(4).
6 Ibid, s 29(5). The consigned sum is also to be paid to the creditor where the poinding 'otherwise ceases to have effect' but it is not clear that this payment is made where a poinding ceases to have effect because of the expiry of the twelve-month period of its duration.

Expenses

7.107 The expenses recoverable in connection with serving a charge and in the process of poinding and warrant sale are set out in Schedule 1 to the 1987 Act[1]. These are discussed in chapter 13 below.

1 1987 Act, s 44, Sch 1.

WARRANT SALE

Application for warrant of sale: grounds for refusal

REQUIREMENT OF WARRANT OF SALE

7.108 In order to complete the diligence of poinding the poinded goods must be sold. Warrant to poind does not of itself include a warrant to sell the goods, which is granted by the sheriff as a separate warrant following application by or on behalf of the creditor[1].

1 1987 Act, s 30(1). However, summary warrants for recovery of taxes, rates, community charges etc include both a warrant to poind and a warrant to sell poinded goods: 1987 Act, Sch 5, para 14. See ch 8 below at paras 8.10–8.11.

APPLICATION FOR WARRANT

7.109 An application to the sheriff for a warrant to sell poinded goods is to be made by the creditor (or officer on his behalf) in accordance with rule 26 of the Sheriff Court Proceedings Act of Sederunt[1]. The application in Form 20 must specify:
(a) the name and address of the applicant, the creditor, any person in possession of the poinded article, the debtor and the auctioneer or officer of court or other person who is to conduct the sale;
(b) the date of the report of execution of poinding to the sheriff;
(c) the name and address of the officer of court who will make the arrangements for the sale in accordance with the warrant;
(d) the intended location of the sale. Where this location is a dwellinghouse, there must have been obtained prior to the application, the written consent of the debtor and (if a different person) of the occupier. The consent is to be in Form 22. Where the intended location is premises other than a dwellinghouse or an auction room, there must have been obtained written consent, in Form 22, of the occupier of the premises. Where such written consent is required, the duly completed form must accompany the application for warrant;
(e) the applicant's proposals for public notice of the sale where it will not be held in an auction room;
(f) the applicant's proposals for the period within which the sale is intended to take place; and

(g) any release or redemption of a poinded article.

When making an application, the creditor or officer must serve on the debtor a copy of the application (and of any accompanying documents) and also a notice in Form 21[3]. This Form sets out the rights of the debtor to make objections within fourteen days after the date of the application on a number of specified grounds. Service on the debtor of these forms and documents must be by recorded delivery post or by officer of court, and an execution of service must be completed and returned to the court.

The debtor may object to an application for a warrant of sale either by completing the appropriate portion of Form 21 and returning it to the sheriff or submitting written objections to the sheriff clerk. An objection in either of these forms must be served on the sheriff clerk within fourteen days after the date of the making of the application. Where an objection is made by the debtor, the sheriff clerk fixes a date for a hearing and intimates it to the creditor and debtor.

Where the debtor does not make timeous objection, the sheriff may dispose of the application without a hearing. However, where the sheriff intends to refuse to grant a warrant of sale on his own initiative, both parties must be given an opportunity to be heard on the application. This is so even if the debtor has not made any objection to the application[4].

Where the sheriff refuses to grant a warrant of sale, this decision is intimated by the sheriff clerk to the debtor and, if a different person, also to the person in possession of the poinded goods[5].

1 SI 1988/2013, r 26, Form 20.
2 1987 Act, s 32(1), (4); SI 1988/2013, r 27, Form 22. See below at paras 7.118–7.120.
3 1987 Act, s 30(3); SI 1988/2013, r 26(3).
4 1987 Act, s 30(4); SI 1988/2013, r 26(10).
5 1987 Act, s 30(6).

GROUNDS FOR REFUSING TO GRANT APPLICATION FOR WARRANT

7.110 The 1987 Act states four grounds on which the sheriff may refuse to grant application for warrant of sale[1]. It appears that unless one of these grounds applies the sheriff must grant the warrant[2].

The sheriff may refuse to grant a warrant of sale, either _ex proprio motu_ or on objection by the debtor, on the ground that[3]:

(a) the poinding is invalid or has ceased to have effect[4]. It is _not_ a ground for refusing a warrant that any poinded article is exempt from poinding by virtue of section 16 of the 1987 Act[5];

(b) the aggregate of the appraised values of the poinded goods was substantially below the aggregate of the prices which they would be likely to fetch if sold on the open market[6]; or

(c) the likely aggregate proceeds of the sale of the poinded goods would not exceed the expenses to be incurred in applying for a warrant of sale and in executing the terms of the warrant[7]. In making this calculation, it is to be assumed that the application and further steps are unopposed.

Furthermore, the sheriff may refuse to grant a warrant on objection made by the debtor on the ground that[8]

(d) the granting of the warrant would be unduly harsh in the circumstances.

1 1987 Act, s 30(2).
2 Cp _Clark v Clark_ (1824) 3 S 143; _Clark v Hinde Milne & Co_ (1884) 12 R 347; _Jack v Waddell's Trs_ 1918 SC 73.

3 1987 Act, s 30(2)(a).
4 Cp above at para 7.82.
5 1987 Act, s 30(5).
6 Cp above at para 7.83.
7 Cp above at para 7.83.
8 1987 Act, s 30(2)(b). Cp above at para 7.83.

Provisions of the warrant of sale

7.111 The warrant of sale granted by the sheriff sets out the various arrangements for the sale. The warrant must specify the following:

MODE OF SALE

7.112 A sale under warrant must be by public auction[1]. A private sale of the poinded goods cannot be held while the poinding continues.

1 1987 Act, s 31(1).

APPOINTMENT OF OFFICER TO MAKE ARRANGEMENTS

7.113 An officer of court must be appointed with the duty of making arrangements for carrying out the terms of a warrant[1]. These duties include the removal of goods to the location of the sale, intimation of the sale to the debtor and person in possession of the poinded goods, attendance at and supervision of the sale, disposal of proceeds of the sale, and the report of the sale to the court. Where possible the officer who executed the poinding should be appointed in the warrant[2].

1 1987 Act, s 31(2)(a).
2 Scot Law Com Report no 95 (1985), p 296.

PERIOD FOR HOLDING SALE

7.114 As sales of poinded goods in many cases will be held in public auction rooms rather than the debtor's own premises[1], it will not always be possible at the time of granting the warrant to fix a date for the sale. The necessary flexibility is achieved by the requirement that the warrant must specify a period within which the sale is to take place[2].

1 See below at paras 7.118–7.120.
2 1987 Act, s 31(2)(b). The warrant extends the period of poinding until the sale is executed or the warrant expires unexecuted at the end of the specified period: 1987 Act, s 27(5)(c).

APPOINTMENT OF AUCTIONEER

7.115 Where the sale is to take place in an auction room, the auction will be conducted by an auctioneer there, who accordingly need not be specifically appointed in the warrant. However, where the sale is to take place in premises other than an auction room, if the appraised value of the poinded goods is £1,000[1] or less, the warrant appoints as auctioneer the officer appointed to make the arrangements of sale[2]. However where there is to be a sale, not in an auction room, of poinded goods with appraised value of more than £1,000[3], there must be appointed as the auctioneer of the sale a person who carries on business as an auctioneer. However, no auctioneer who is an employee or partner of the officer should be appointed[4]. If no such person is available the officer acts as auctioneer[5].

Where an officer is not appointed as auctioneer he must attend the sale and keep a record of the goods sold and the price at which they were sold[6]. He must also make a record of any unsold goods the ownership of which passes to the creditor. If the sale is held in premises other than an auction room, the officer also supervises the sale.

Where the officer is appointed as auctioneer, he is attended at the sale by one witness[7].

1 This figure may be altered by Act of Sederunt: 1987 Act, s 31(3)(a).
2 1987 Act, s 31(3)(a).
3 This figure may be altered by Act of Sederunt: 1987 Act, s 31(3)(a).
4 *Cantors Ltd v Hardie* 1974 SLT (Sh Ct) 26; see also *Allison's (Electrical) Ltd v McCormick* 1982 SLT (Sh Ct) 93.
5 1987 Act, s 31(3)(b).
6 1987 Act, s 37(1). In this situation no witness is required.
7 1987 Act, s 37(2).

WARRANT TO OPEN SHUT AND LOCKFAST PLACES

7.116 The warrant of sale empowers the officer of court appointed under it to open shut and lockfast places for the purpose of executing the terms of the warrant[1].

1 1987 Act, s 31(2)(c).

DETAILS OF PUBLIC NOTICE OF SALE

7.117 Where the sale is to take place in premises other than an auction room, the warrant must set out the details (such as timing and form of the sale[1]).

1 1987 Act, s 34(4).

LOCATION OF SALE

7.118 The warrant must specify a location for the sale[1]. Different considerations apply in respect of sales to be held in a dwellinghouse[2] (whether or not the debtor's) and those to be held in other types of premises.

1 1987 Act, s 31(1).
2 See 1987 Act, s 45 for the meaning of dwellinghouse.

Sales in a dwellinghouse

7.119 A warrant cannot provide for a sale to take place in a dwellinghouse unless all of the occupiers and, if he is not an occupier, the debtor have given written consent in Form 22[1].

Where any such consent is not given the sale must take place in an auction room to be specified in the warrant[2]. Moreover, where consent is required but not given the sheriff must refuse to grant a warrant where the likely proceeds of the sale would not exceed the expenses of applying for and carrying out the sale (including the cost of removal[3]). A warrant may be granted in these circumstances, however, when a creditor is able to offer suitable premises for holding the sale. However if the place proposed by the creditor is another dwellinghouse, the consent in writing must be given by the occupiers of that dwellinghouse and by the debtor[4].

1 1987 Act, s 32(1); SI 1988/2013, r 27, Form 1. The Act does not define what is meant by an occupier in these circumstances and it may be that all occupiers of any age must give written consent or such consent be given on their behalf.
2 1987 Act, s 32(2).
3 Ibid, s 32(3). In making this calculation it must be assumed that the application for the warrant and the steps in executing it are unopposed. Cp 1987 Act, s 24(3)(c), discussed above at para 7.83.
4 1987 Act, s 32(3). Where the creditor proposes premises other than a dwellinghouse, the conditions set out in s 32(4) and (5) must be met. See discussion below at para 7.120.

Sales in premises other than a dwellinghouse or an auction room

7.120 A warrant can provide for a sale to be held in premises other than a dwellinghouse or an auction room which are occupied by someone other than the debtor or creditor, only if the occupier or occupiers give his or their written consent in Form 22[1]. The refusal of an occupier to give consent can be overridden by the sheriff only where such premises[2] are those where the poinded goods are situated and the sheriff considers that it would be unduly costly for the goods to be removed to other premises for sale[3].

1 1987 Act, s 32(4); SI 1988/2013, r 27.
2 Ie premises other than a dwellinghouse or auction room.
3 1987 Act, s 32(5).

Redemption or release of goods after warrant

7.121 As the application for warrant of sale marks a crucial stage in the diligence of poinding, the policy of the 1987 Act is to allow the parties to make arrangements to prevent a sale taking place. One way in which this is achieved is by section 33(2), which allows the debtor to redeem the poinded goods within seven days after the day of service on him of a copy of an application for warrant of sale[1]. The goods are redeemed by the debtor paying their appraised value to the officer of court who is to grant a receipt in Form 23[2]. This receipt acts as a release of the goods from the poinding.

Goods may also be released by the parties agreeing to do so[3].

A further mode of releasing goods from the poinding arises where a warrant sale is to be held in premises other than those where the goods are situated. When the officer removes the goods for sale, he need take only such goods the appraised values of which equal the total sum still owing[4]. Where there are goods not so removed, the officer must release them from the poinding.

Any redemption or release of goods in any of these ways must be reported to the sheriff[5].

1 1987 Act, s 33(2). However, the debtor does not have this right where the application is for the immediate sale of perishable or similar goods under the 1987 Act, s 21(1).
2 1987 Act, s 33(2); SI 1988/2013, r 28.
3 1987 Act, s 33(4).
4 Ibid, s 33(1). The total sum still owing is to be calculated with reference to ibid, s 45.
5 Ibid, s 33(5). The specific mode of reporting the redemption or release will depend on which stage the poinding has reached.

Payment agreements after warrant of sale

7.122 After the grant of a warrant of sale, the creditor may cancel the arrangements of the sale for the purpose of giving effect to an agreement between the creditor and the debtor for payment of the total debt (by instalments or otherwise)[1]. Where any such agreement has been made the creditor or officer on his behalf must report it to the sheriff as soon as is reasonably practicable[2]. The effect of such a report is to extend the date of sale in the original warrant by six months[3] from the date of the report.

If the debtor becomes in breach of the agreement to pay, a sale under the terms of the warrant may be held if the warrant as extended by six months from the report to the court still allows this. If the warrant does not allow this a sale may be held only if the creditor or officer applies for a variation of the warrant[4]. Such application must be made within six months after the date of the report of the agreement in court, and must show that the reasons for not holding the sale under the original warrant (as extended by six months) were not the responsibility of the creditor or of the officer[5].

These procedures for cancelling the arrangements of sale may be adopted by the creditor on not more than two occasions[6]. Where a report of a second payment agreement is made, it must be done within the period of the warrant (as extended). The date of sale is then further extended by another six months from the date of the second report. Similarly, if an application for variation of the warrant is required, this must be made within six months of the second report.

For example, if the original warrant sets a date for sale by May, where an agreement to pay is reported to court in April, that provision of the warrant is extended until October. If the debtor is in breach of the agreement, the original warrant may be applied until October, and any application for variation must also be made by October. If a second report of agreement is made in August, the warrant is then further continued until February of the following year. Again, if there is a breach of the agreement by the debtor, sale under the original warrant may be held until February. An application for variation must also be made before that date.

1 1987 Act, s 36(1).
2 Ibid, s 36(2).
3 Ibid, s 36(4).
4 Variation of a warrant is granted under ibid, s 35(1): see below at paras 7.125–7.128.
5 1987 Act, s 36(3)(b); SI 1988/2013, r 30, Form 24.
6 1987 Act, s 36(1).

Intimation of warrant and arrangements for sale

7.123 The officer appointed in the warrant to make the arrangements of sale must intimate a copy of the warrant on the debtor and, if a different person, the person in possession of the poinded goods. When he has fixed the date for sale, the officer must intimate this to the debtor (and to the person in possession of the goods[1]). Intimation is usually made by means of recorded delivery post, but a fee for hand service by an officer may be allowed on cause shown[2]. Intimation of the warrant may be made at any time after it is granted but not later than the date of intimation of the date of sale.

Where the goods are to be removed to premises for sale, the officer of court must make appropriate intimation to the debtor (or if a different person, the person in possession of the goods), not less than seven days before the date fixed for the removal of the goods[3]. Such intimation must set out the date arranged for the removal and the place where the sale is to be held.

1 1987 Act, s 34(1).
2 Citation Amendment (Scotland) Act 1882, ss 3, 6; *Lochhead v Graham* (1883) 11 R 201.
3 1987 Act, s 32(5).

Publication of sale

7.124 As sale under warrant will in most cases be held in public auction rooms there is no need to make any advertisement of the sale which indicates that the sale is a warrant sale or which identifies the debtor[1]. The sale, however, must be advertised by public notice and if the premises where the sale is to be held do not 'belong' to the debtor, the notice must not name the debtor nor disclose that the goods for sale are poinded goods[2]. Where the sale is to take place in premises other than an auction room, the form and timing of the public notice are regulated by the warrant of sale[3]. Where sale is to be held in premises other than the debtor's premises or an auction room, the public notice must state that the goods to be sold do not belong to the occupier of the premises[4].

Formal public notice of the details of the sale is given by the sheriff clerk arranging to have a copy of the warrant of sale displayed on the walls of the court which granted it[5]. The displayed copy of the warrant on the walls of the court continues until the sale has been concluded.

1 See Scot Law Com Report no 95 (1985), pp 66–67, 294–295 for an account of the distress to debtors which was caused by the former practice of public advertisement of warrant sales in newspapers and by handbills.
2 1987 Act, s 34(5). This provision is curiously worded. It would appear to allow for the practical necessity for naming the debtor as a way of identifying the location of the sale when the sale is to take place in the debtor's dwellinghouse or other premises of the debtor. The subsection refers not to the debtor's premises (contrast s 34(6)) but to premises belonging to the debtor. Where a sale has to be held in the debtor's dwellinghouse, he cannot be named in the notice if he occupies it as a tenant but he can be so named if he is an owner-occupier.
3 1987 Act, s 34(4).
4 Ibid, s 34(6).
5 Ibid, s 34(3); SI 1988/2013, r 29(1). The rationale of this provision is to allow third party owners of poinded goods (eg goods on hire purchase) an opportunity to discover that their goods are to be sold: see Scot Law Com Report no 95 (1985), pp 294–295.

Variation in terms of warrant and arrangements for sale

VARIATION IN TERMS OF THE WARRANT

7.125 Where it proves impossible to implement the sale in terms of the warrant, the creditor or officer on his behalf may apply to have the terms of the warrant varied[1]. The reason why the sale cannot be implemented must not be one for which the creditor or officer is responsible.

1 1987 Act, s 35(1).

APPLICATION FOR VARIATION

7.126 An application for variation of a warrant of sale must be made in

Form 24[1]. The application must be accompanied by the original warrant of sale and must specify:

(a) the name and address of the applicant, the creditor, the debtor, and any person in possession of the poinded article, and the auctioneer or officer of court who is to conduct the sale;

(b) the date of the original warrant of sale;

(c) details of any steps of diligence taken;

(d) the applicant's proposals for variation and his reasons for seeking such variation;

(e) any release or redemption of a poinded article;

(f) details of any agreement between creditor and debtor to pay the debt by instalments or otherwise and any breach of it;

(g) details of any cancellation of warrant sale; and

(h) any additional powers sought by the applicant in the event of the application being granted.

When making the application the creditor or officer must also serve on the debtor a copy of the application and a notice in Form 25[2]. An execution of service of this notice must be lodged along with the application and the original warrant. The debtor may object to the application by lodging written objections with, or returning a completed Form 25 to, the sheriff clerk within seven days of service on him. Where the debtor does object, the sheriff clerk fixes a date for the hearing which he intimates to the parties. If the debtor does not object, the sheriff may dispose of the application without a hearing, but must always allow the parties an opportunity to be heard where he seeks to refuse the application *ex proprio motu*[3].

Where the sheriff refuses to grant an application of variation the sheriff clerk intimates that decision to the debtor and to any other person in possession of the poinded articles[4].

1 SI 1988/2013, r 30.
2 Service may be by recorded delivery post or by officer of court. A copy of the application must also be served on the person in possession of the poinded goods, if not the debtor: 1987 Act, s 35(5)(b).
3 Ibid, s 35(6).
4 Ibid, s 35(8).

DETERMINATION OF THE APPLICATION

7.127 A sheriff may refuse to grant an application for variation only on the ground that[1] (i) the poinding is invalid or ceased to have effect, or (ii) the proposed variation is unsuitable.

The sheriff may refuse an application on one or other of these grounds either *ex proprio motu* or following an objection by the debtor. It is not a ground for refusing an application merely that a poinded article is exempt from poinding under section 16 of the 1987 Act[2].

Where a variation is made in the location of the sale, section 32 governs the consents which must be obtained[3]. Where any variation is granted the sheriff may make such consequential orders as he thinks fit[4].

1 1987 Act, s 35(2). Cp s 24(1), discussed above at para 7.82.
2 1987 Act, s 35(3).
3 Ibid, s 35(4).
4 Ibid, s 35(7).

VARIATION IN DATE OF REMOVAL OF GOODS, DATE OF SALE

7.128 The date for removal of the goods to the place of sale and the date of the sale itself, are not specified in the warrant of sale[1]. Where the officer has made arrangements for either or both of these matters but there has been no intimation of them to the debtor[2], the officer may vary the date provided the terms of the warrant are observed as to the date by which the sale must take place. The officer may make such changes even if intimation has been made on the person in possession of the goods if that is a different person from the debtor himself[3].

However, if intimation has been made on the debtor of the date of sale or the date of removal of the goods, a new date cannot be arranged unless the reason for not being able to proceed on the date as intimated is one for which the creditor or officer is not responsible[4]. If a new date can be arranged it must be not less than seven days after the date on which it is intimated to the debtor. A new date fixed for a warrant sale must conform to the terms of the warrant as to the date by which a sale must take place[5].

1 1987 Act, s 31(2)(b). See above at para 7.114.
2 Ie under s 34(1) or 34(2). See above at para 7.123.
3 1987 Act, s 35(9).
4 Ibid, s 35(10).
5 Ibid, s 35(11). The new date must also be intimated to the person in possession of the poinded goods, if that is not the debtor.

The warrant sale

RESERVE PRICE FOR BIDDING

7.129 The warrant sale proceeds in the same manner as any other sale by auction[1]. There is no need to have any upset price (ie the price at which bidding commences) nor any reserve price (ie the price at which goods are not sold if bidding does not reach it). However, the creditor may choose to have a reserve price, and this can be set at any price at or below the appraised values placed on the goods at the poinding[2]. There is no need to disclose any reserve price[3].

The normal rule of auction sales is that owners of the goods being auctioned cannot bid[4], nor may he arrange for others to bid with a view to putting up the price. In the context of a warrant sale these practices apply to the debtor. Furthermore an officer of court who has acted in a poinding or sale as part of his official functions may not, directly or indirectly through an agent, purchase the goods at the warrant sale[5]. However, the 1987 Act makes clear that the creditor may bid, as may any person who owns the article in common with the debtor[6].

1 See T G Wright 'Auction' 2 *Encyclopaedia of the Laws of Scotland* (ed Lord Dunedin and J Wark 1927) pp 18–26.
2 1987 Act, s 37(3). Where goods have been revalued under the 1987 Act, s 29(2), a reserve price at the sale cannot exceed that revaluation.
3 Ibid, s 37(4).
4 *Shiell v Guthrie's Trustees* (1874) 1 R 1083; *Wright v Buchanan* 1917 SC 73. See also the Mock Auctions Act 1961.
5 AS (Messengers-at-Arms and Sheriff Officers Rules) 1988, SI 1988/2097, r 31. Nor may the officer share with the purchaser any profit made reselling the goods bought at a warrant sale.
6 1987 Act, s 37(5).

GOODS UNSOLD OR SOLD FOR LESS THAN THEIR APPRAISED VALUE

7.130 Where goods remain unsold at the sale[1], or the goods are sold at a price below their appraised value, the debt is nonetheless reduced by the amount of the appraised value[2]. Where goods are sold for more than their appraised value the price paid is put towards payment of the debt[3].

1 For transfer of ownership of such goods, see below at para 7.131.
2 Where such goods have been revalued under the 1987 Act, s 29(2), the amount to be credited to the debtor is the original appraisal, not the revaluation, provided that (1) the damage to the goods was not caused by the debtor's fault and (2) no sum has been consigned in court by a third party under the 1987 Act, s 29(3). See further above at para 7.106.
3 See further below at para 7.132.

OWNERSHIP OF UNSOLD GOODS

7.131 Where the sale reaches a stage where it realises the total sum due the sale should stop, and any remaining unsold goods remain the property of the debtor[1]. If the sum due has not been realised by the sale, the ownership of any poinded goods remaining unsold after the sale passes to the creditor[2]. This is without prejudice to any rights of a third party in the property[3].

Special rules apply where goods have passed into the ownership of the creditor after a warrant sale which had been held in premises 'belonging' to the debtor[4]. In this situation, the ownership of the goods passes back to the debtor unless the creditor takes appropriate steps to uplift the goods from the debtor's premises. If the premises are the debtor's dwellinghouse, the goods must be uplifted by 8 pm on the day the sale is completed. If the sale was held in other premises of the debtor, goods must be uplifted by 8 pm[5] on the third working day[6] following the day of sale. To enable the creditor to uplift the goods the officer is empowered to remain on the premises and to re-enter them[7].

1 1987 Act, s 37(6).
2 Ibid, s 37(6). For the definition of the sum due, see 1987 Act, s 45.
3 Compare *George Hopkinson Ltd v Napier & Sons* 1953 SC 139; see discussion above at para 7.33.
4 1987 Act, s 37(7). The use of the words 'belonging to the debtor' appears to exclude cases where the debtor occupies premises as a tenant under a lease. See discussion above at para 7.124.
5 This time may be varied by Act of Sederunt; 1987 Act, s 37(7). No variation has yet been made.
6 'Working day' excludes: Saturday, Sunday, 1st January, 2nd January, 25th December, 26th December, Good Friday, Easter Monday, and a day of public holiday in the area in which the premises are situated: 1987 Act, s 37(8).
7 If necessary, the officer has power to open shut and lockfast premises: 1987 Act, s 37(7)(b).

DISPOSAL OF PROCEEDS OF SALE

7.132 Once the sale is completed, it is the responsibility of the officer of court appointed under the warrant to pay from the proceeds of sale[1] such sum as will meet the outstanding debt[2]. The creditor and the officer may agree that the officer is entitled to deduct his fees and outlays from the sum to be remitted to the creditor. If there is any surplus after payment of all sums due by the debtor to the creditor, the officer is to pay the surplus to the debtor. If the debtor cannot be found, any surplus is to be consigned in court[3].

Consignation of the proceeds of the sale may also occur where the sheriff so directs. Such direction may be given when another creditor has lodged a claim to a share in the proceeds of sale under the equalisation provisions of the Bankruptcy (Scotland) Act 1985[4].

1 Proceeds of sale include any sums consigned in court by a third party under s 29(3): see the 1987 Act, s 29(5).
2 Ibid, s 38(a). The total sum due is calculated in terms of the 1987 Act, s 45.
3 Ibid, s 38(b).
4 Bankruptcy (Scotland) Act 1985, Sch 7, para 24; cp *Gillion & Co Ltd v Christison* (1909) 25 Sh Ct Rep 283.

Report of warrant sale

WARRANT GRANTED BUT NO SALE HELD

7.133 A report of sale by the officer to the court and examination of the report by the auditor and the sheriff are important measures of checking that the warrant has been properly carried out. However, where a warrant has been granted but no sale held, there is no report to the court[1]. It should be noted that Part V of the 1987 Act provides for various modes of inspecting the work of an officer of court and these measures do provide some degree of control over poindings that do not reach the stage of sale[2].

1 1987 Act, s 39(1).
2 See ch 14 below at para 14.43.

FORM OF REPORT OF WARRANT OF SALE

7.134 A report of a warrant sale must be in Form 26 of the Sheriff Court Proceedings Act of Sederunt[1]. The report must specify:
(a) the name and address of the creditor, the debtor and any person, other than the debtor, who had possession of the poinded article;
(b) the date of the decree, summary warrant or other document, upon which the sale proceeded, the date of issue of any extract decree and the prior steps of diligence;
(c) details of the warrant of sale and any variation of it;
(d) any intimation, service and notices given by the officer of court in respect of the sale;
(e) when and where the sale took place and the persons who arranged and conducted the sale;
(f) the articles which have been sold and the amount for which they have been sold;
(g) any articles which were not sold and whether their ownership passed to the creditor or reverted to the debtor;
(h) the sum which was due by the debtor and the expenses chargeable against the debtor under Schedule 1 to the 1987 Act;
(i) the amount of any surplus paid or to be consigned in court;
(j) any balance of the debt due by the debtor;
(k) any release or redemption of a poinded article whether or not otherwise reported to the court or specified in a warrant of sale or for variation of it; and
(l) any article damaged, destroyed, lost or stolen, any sum consigned by a party in connection with it and any balance of that sum due to the creditor or debtor.

With the report there is lodged the extract decree (or other document of debt), the original warrant of sale and any variation of it, any executions or certificates of intimation, service, copies of public notices. There must also be included vouchers for outlays.

The report must be signed by the officer of court[2].

1 1987 Act, s 39(1); SI 1988/2013, r 31.
2 1987 Act, s 39(2). If a witness was required to attend the sale under 1987 Act, s 37(2), the witness must also sign the report.

DATE OF SUBMISSION OF REPORT

7.135 The officer must submit the report of the warrant sale to the sheriff within fourteen days after the date of completion of the sale[1]. However, the report must still be received by the sheriff even if it is submitted late[2]. Where the officer submits the report late without reasonable excuse or where he wilfully refuses or delays to make a report timeously, the sheriff may order that the officer is liable for all or part of the expenses of diligence[3]. The sheriff may also report the officer for misconduct in such circumstances[4].

1 1987 Act, s 39(1).
2 Ibid, s 39(10).
3 Ie all expenses chargeable against the debtor under the 1987 Act, Sch 1, including those of the charge, poinding and sale.
4 1987 Act, s 79(1)(b). See further ch 14 below at paras 14.44–14.47.

REMIT TO AUDITOR

7.136 When the report of sale is received, it is remitted to the auditor of court. The auditor taxes the expenses chargeable against the debtor under Schedule 1 to the 1987 Act[1]. He also certifies the balance due to or by the debtor following the poinding and sale. If the auditor proposes to alter the figures for these items, he must give all interested parties an opportunity to make representations. The auditor then makes a report on all these matters to the sheriff. The auditor may also draw to the sheriff's attention any other matter which seems to call for investigation[2].

No fee is charged by the auditor in respect of his report[3].

1 1987 Act, s 39(4).
2 *Lombard North Central Ltd v Wilson* (unreported, Glasgow Sheriff Court, October 1980) (apparently unrealistic valuation of poinded goods); Scot Law Com Report no 95 (1985), p 308.
3 1987 Act, s 39(7).

POWERS OF SHERIFF

7.137 On receiving the auditor's report, the sheriff makes an order declaring the certified balance due by or to the debtor[1]. If he proposes to modify the balance as certified by the auditor, he must fix a date for a hearing which is intimated by the sheriff clerk to interested parties[2].

The sheriff may also declare the poinding and sale to be void. He may do so if satisfied that there has been a substantial irregularity in the poinding and sale[3]. However, an order to this effect may be made only after a hearing which has been intimated by the sheriff clerk to the interested parties. If an order is made, the sheriff may also make whatever consequential orders are necessary but no order or consequential order affects the title of any person to any goods acquired by him at the warrant sale, or subsequently, in good faith and for value[4].

Any order made by the sheriff upholding the certified balance, modifying that balance, or declaring the poinding and sale void is intimated to the debtor by the sheriff clerk[5].

1 1987 Act, s 39(5).
2 SI 1988/2013, r 32(1).
3 Substantial irregularity does not include failure or delay by the officer to make a report of the sale: 1987 Act, s 39(5).
4 1987 Act, s 39(9).
5 Ibid, s 39(5). See also SI 1988/2013, r 32(2).

INSPECTION OF REPORT

7.138 The report of sale is retained by the sheriff clerk for a period of five years from its being lodged with the court[1]. During this period it may be inspected by any interested person on payment of the prescribed fee[2].

1 1987 Act, s 39(8); SI 1988/2013, r 33.
2 Ie, as prescribed in an order made under the Courts of Law Fees (Scotland) Act 1895, s 2.

CHAPTER 8

MISCELLANEOUS DILIGENCES

RECOVERY OF TAXES, RATES, COMMUNITY CHARGES

Summary warrant and court actions

GENERAL

8.01 Central government authorities may raise court actions in respect of various types of tax[1]. Similarly, local authorities may raise court actions to recover unpaid rates and community charges[2]. Such actions proceed in the normal way, and decree in favour of the taxing or local authority is warrant for diligence in the normal way [3]. However, in most cases of arrears of taxes, rates and community charges, the taxing and local authorities may proceed by way of summary warrant procedure. This involves the authority obtaining, by non-contentious application, warrant authorising the recovery of the arrears in question by diligence. Summary warrant procedure differs from the use of court action in two respects:

(1) the application for a summary warrant does not allow for the participation of the debtor. However, when a summary warrant has been granted, the relevant authorities often intimate this fact to the debtor in order to promote informal settlement of the arrears[4];

(2) the diligences authorised by summary warrant, though similar to those authorised by decree in a court action, are in some cases more streamlined in nature[5].

1 Taxes Management Act 1970, ss 67, 68 (income tax, capital gains tax, corporation tax, development land tax); Car Tax Act 1983, Sch 1, para 3(1); Value Added Tax 1983, Sch 7, para 6(1).
2 Local Government (Scotland) Act 1947, s 247(1)(b); Abolition of Domestic Rates Etc (Scotland) Act 1987, Sch 2, para 7(1)(b).
3 A levying authority obtaining decree for arrears of community charge may also apply for deductions to be made from income support payable to the debtor. See further below at para 8.12.
4 Report on Diligence and Debtor Protection (Scot Law Com no 95) (1985)), p 417.
5 See below at paras 8.06–8.11.

OPTION TO USE BOTH PROCEDURES

8.02 In most cases of arrears of taxes, rates and community charges, the appropriate authorities have an option to use a court action or summary warrant procedure[1]. The practice is to proceed by way of action where there is any dispute as to the liability for the tax, rates or charge or the amount owing[2]. The tax authorities have a power to proceed by way of both summary warrant and court action, and may, for example, raise a court action and then apply for a summary warrant, even if decree is obtained in the action. Similarly, the tax authorities may obtain a summary warrant, which can be abandoned at any time and a court action raised[3].

However, there are restrictions on the power of local authorities proceeding by way of *both* summary warrant and court action[4]. A summary warrant for arrears of rates and community charges may not be granted if an action has been raised to recover the arrears. An action for arrears of rates etc may not be raised where any of the diligences authorised by a previously-granted summary warrant in respect of the arrears has been executed. Where a summary warrant has been granted but no diligence executed on its authority, a subsequent court action for the arrears causes the summary warrant to cease to have effect.

1 Local authorities have such an option even in respect of arrears of community charge owing on a joint and several basis by a spouse under the Abolition of Domestic Rates Etc (Scotland) Act 1987, s 8(7). See Abolition of Domestic Rates Etc (Scotland) Act 1987, Sch 2, para 7, as amended by the Local Government Finance Act 1988, Sch 13, Pt IV.
  No summary warrant procedure exists in respect of unpaid inheritance tax, which must be recovered by court action: Inheritance Tax Act 1984, ss 242–244.
2 Scot Law Com Report no 95 (1985), p 417.
3 *Wight v Craig* (1919) 35 Sh Ct Rep 22; Scot Law Com Report no 95 (1985), p 418.
4 Local Government (Scotland) Act 1947, s 247(4), (5); Abolition of Domestic Rates Etc (Scotland) Act 1987, Sch 2, para 7.

Summary warrant procedure

POWER TO GRANT

8.03 A summary warrant for recovery of taxes, rates and community charges may be granted only by a sheriff[1]. Application is normally made to a sheriff in the sheriffdom or sheriff court district where the debtor resides but a summary warrant granted by a sheriff may be executed anywhere in Scotland[2].

1 Taxes Management Act 1970, s 63(1); Car Tax Act 1983, Sch 1, para 3(3); Value Added Tax Act 1983, Sch 7, para 6(5); Local Government (Scotland) Act 1947, s 247(2); Abolition of Domestic Rates Etc (Scotland) Act 1987, Sch 2, para 7(2).
2 1987 Act, s 91(1)(c).

WHO MAY APPLY

8.04 Application for a summary warrant in respect of income tax, capital gains tax, corporation tax and development land tax is made by a collector of taxes[1]. In the case of car tax and VAT, application is made by the Commissioners of Customs and Excise, who may by regulation provide for application to be made by officers of the Commissioners holding a specified rank[2]. Applications for a summary warrant in respect of arrears of rates are made by the rating authority[3], and by the levying authority in respect of unpaid community charges[4].

1 Taxes Management Act 1970, s 63(1).
2 Car Tax Act 1983, Sch 1, para 3(3), (7); Value Added Tax Act 1983, Sch 7, para 6(5), (9).
3 Local Government (Scotland) Act 1947, s 247(2).
4 Abolition of Domestic Rates Etc (Scotland) Act 1987, Sch 2, paras 1(1), 7(2).

FORM OF APPLICATION

8.05 An application for a summary warrant is made by the appropriate person presenting to the sheriff a certificate[1]:

(1) stating that none of the persons specified in the application has paid the tax, rates or community charge due;

(2) stating that appropriate demand for payment of the amount due from each person has been made. In the case of income tax, capital gains tax and development land tax, demand for payment under section 60 of the Taxes Management Act 1970 must have been made. In the case of rates and community charge, the relevant authority must have given written notice to each person on the application list requiring payment within fourteen days from the date of such notice;

(3) stating that the period of notice for payment has expired without payment being made[2]; and

(4) specifying the amount due and unpaid by each person on the application list.

Provided the application is in the correct form, the sheriff must grant a summary warrant in the appropriate form[3]. The procedure for obtaining a summary warrant is *ex parte*, but if the certificate in the application is mistaken in terms of what it set out, the creditor authority incurs strict liability for wrongous diligence[4]. In the case of summary warrant for arrears of community charge, no mistake in the name of a person or place, or informality in any notice or communication, prejudices the recovery of the sum claimed[5]. However, these provisions must not be read as implying an excuse for any wrongful diligence.

The summary warrant granted is authority for certain specified diligences to be used to recover the sum due and unpaid[6]. In the case of rates and community charge, the summary warrant also authorises such diligence to be used to collect a surcharge of 10 per cent of the amount remaining due and unpaid[7]. There is no equivalent surcharge authorised by summary warrant in connection with unpaid tax.

1 Taxes Management Act 1970, s 63(1); Car Tax Act 1983, Sch 1, para 3(3); Value Added Tax Act 1983, Sch 7, para 6(5); Local Government (Scotland) Act 1947, s 247(2); Abolition of Domestic Rates Etc (Scotland) Act 1987, Sch 2, para 7(2).
2 There is no equivalent requirement to include this matter in an application for amounts due for deductions of PAYE or under the 'lump' or applications under the Car Tax Act 1983 or the Value Added Tax Act 1983.
3 AS (Proceedings in the Sheriff Court under the Debtors (Scotland) Act 1987) 1988, SI 1988/2013, Forms 61, 63.
4 Scot Law Com Report no 95 (1985), p 416.
5 Abolition of Domestic Rates Etc (Scotland) Act 1987, Sch 2, para 7(8).
6 See below at paras 8.06–8.12.
7 Local Government (Scotland) Act 1947, s 247(2); Abolition of Domestic Rates Etc (Scotland) 1987, Sch 2, para 7(2). The percentage may be varied by regulation.

Diligence under summary warrant

POWER TO EXECUTE

8.06 A summary warrant granted by a sheriff may be executed only by a sheriff officer. The warrant may be executed by a sheriff officer of the court which granted it, or of the sheriff court district in which it is to be executed[1].

1 1987 Act, s 91. The warrant may be executed by an appropriate sheriff officer anywhere in
   Scotland. No warrants of concurrence are necessary.

DILIGENCES AUTHORISED BY SUMMARY WARRANT

8.07 A summary warrant granted to recover arrears of taxes, rates and
community charges is authority to execute
(1) an arrestment and action of furthcoming or sale;
(2) an earnings arrestment;
(3) a poinding and sale in accordance with Schedule 5 to the 1987 Act.

Arrestment and furthcoming

8.08 The law governing the diligence of arrestment and furthcoming (or
sale) authorised by a summary warrant is in all respects the same as that
governing the diligence following on an extract decree or other document of
debt[1].

1 See ch 5 above.

Earnings arrestment

8.09 A summary warrant also authorises the diligence of earnings
arrestment under Part III of the 1987 Act, and where appropriate a conjoined
arrestment order[1]. The only significant difference between an earnings
arrestment following on a summary warrant and other earnings arrestments
is that an earnings arrestment on a summary warrant does not require a prior
charge to have been served on the debtor and may accordingly proceed as
soon as the warrant is granted[2].

1 See ch 6 above.
2 1987 Act, s 90(2).

Poinding and sale

8.10 A poinding and sale under summary warrant follows the provisions of
Schedule 5 to the 1987 Act[1]. Schedule 5 to a considerable extent resembles the
provisions on poinding and sale contained in Part II of the 1987 Act. The
major variations are that in the case of a summary warrant poinding no prior
charge is necessary and the summary warrant is itself warrant to sell poinded
goods. In general, summary warrant procedure involves less judicial
supervision by way of reporting to the sheriff. The more particular variations
between the two sets of provisions are consequential upon these points.

1 1987 Act, s 74(2).

8.11 The chief differences between summary warrant poinding and sale and
other instances of the diligence are summarised in the following list:
(i) in summary warrant procedure a poinding may proceed without a charge
having been served on the debtor (1987 Act, s 90(2));
(ii) there are no provisions for report of the execution of a summary warrant
poinding to the sheriff (contrast 1987 Act, s 22);
(iii) application by the debtor for recall of a summary warrant poinding may
be made at any time before intimation of the date of removal of goods or of
the date of sale (contrast 1987 Act, Sch 5, para 8(3) and s 24(3));

(iv) in summary warrant procedure there are no provisions for extending the duration of poinding during the period of application for warrant to sell the goods (contrast 1987 Act, s 27(5)–(7));

(v) in summary warrant procedure, there is no need for a separate application for warrant of sale nor is there any such separate warrant (contrast 1987 Act, ss 30, 31);

(vi) there are no provisions in respect of summary warrant poindings for refusal to grant warrant of sale (contrast 1987 Act, s 30(2));

(vii) where goods have been released or redeemed from a summary warrant poinding, the officer need not report this to the sheriff (contrast 1987 Act, s 33(5));

(viii) the officer of court to whom the summary warrant is granted (as the officer with responsibility for arranging the sale), must intimate both the date and place of the sale to the debtor. However, there is no need to serve any warrant on the debtor (contrast 1987 Act, Sch 5, para 16(1)(a) and s 34(1));

(ix) in a summary warrant poinding intimation of removal of the goods for sale must be made not less than fourteen days before the date arranged for their removal (contrast 1987 Act, Sch 5, para 16(1)(b) and s 34(2));

(x) a poinding under summary warrant procedure has different provisions for alteration of the arrangement of sale (contrast 1987 Act, Sch 5, para 17 and ss 35, 36);

(xi) in summary warrant procedure, there are no special provisions for the appointment of an auctioneer, the duties of the officer or the presence of a witness at the sale (1987 Act, s 37(1), (2));

(xii) a report of sale in summary warrant procedure is made by the officer to the creditor, not to the sheriff (contrast 1987 Act, Sch 5, para 20(1) and s 39(1));

(xiii) in summary warrant procedure, there are no provisions dealing with the failure by the officer to submit a report of sale (1987 Act, s 39(3));

(xiv) the procedure for taxing the report of sale is more simplified in summary warrant procedure (contrast 1987 Act, Sch 5, para 20(3) and s 39(4)–(8));

(xv) in summary warrant procedure, there is no need for the officer to report a release from the poinding of goods belonging to a third party (1987 Act, s 40(4));

(xvi) in summary warrant procedure, there is no need for the officer to report the release from poinding of goods of the debtor owned in common with a third party (1987 Act, s 41(5)).

ARREARS OF COMMUNITY CHARGE: DEDUCTIONS FROM INCOME SUPPORT

8.12 Where a levying authority has obtained a decree or summary warrant against a debtor in respect of arrears of community charge, and the debtor is entitled to income support within the meaning of the Social Security Act 1986, the authority may apply to the Secretary of State for deductions to be made from income support towards the arrears[1]. This power is without prejudice to the right of the levying authority to recover the arrears by any other means. Procedure for making and determining an application has been prescribed[2].

1 Abolition of Domestic Rates Etc (Scotland) Act 1987, Sch 2, para 7A, added by Local Government Finance Act 1988, Sch 12, para 36(10).

2 Community Charges (Deductions from Income Support) (Scotland) Regulations 1989, SI 1989/507.

8.13   The sheriff officer's fees and necessary outlays in connection with executing a summary warrant are chargeable against the debtor[1]. However, no fee is chargeable by the sheriff officer against the debtor for collecting or accounting to the creditor for any sums paid by the debtor in respect of the amount owing. These provisions are without prejudice to paragraphs 25–34 of Schedule 5 to the 1987 Act, which regulate the expenses of poinding and sale chargeable against the debtor[2].

1 Taxes Management Act 1970, s 63A; Car Tax Act 1983, Sch 1, para 3(5), (6); Value Added Tax Act 1983, Sch 7, para 6(7), (8); Local Government (Scotland) Act 1947, s 247A; Abolition of Domestic Rates Etc (Scotland) Act 1987, Sch 2, para 8.
2 On the expenses of diligence, see further ch 13 below.

Excise, betting and gaming duties

RECOVERY OF EXCISE DUTIES

8.14   A specialised summary warrant procedure exists in respect of arrears of payment by a revenue trader of excise duty (other than duty chargeable on imported goods)[1]. A sheriff, on application, by the proper officer[2], which contains a certificate that excise duty remains unpaid by the trader after the time within which it is payable, may grant a warrant authorising a sheriff officer:
(1) to take into possession, by force if necessary, anything liable to execution under section 117 of the Customs and Excise Management Act 1979. For this purpose the sheriff officer has authority to open shut and lockfast places; and
(2) to sell by public auction anything so taken into possession, after giving six days notice of the sale.
The goods which may be taken into possession by the officer under such a warrant are goods in the possession of the debtor or his agent which are
(i) all goods liable to a relevant excise duty, whether or not that duty has been paid;
(ii) all materials for manufacturing or producing any such goods; and
(iii) all apparatus, equipment, machinery, tools, vessels and utensils for, or for preparing any such materials for, such manufacture or production, or by which the trade in respect of which the duty is imposed or carried on[3].
Such goods may be taken into possession by an officer under the sheriff's warrant when they come into the subsequent possession of a third party, unless that third party is a bona fide purchaser for value[4].
Proceeds of the sale of such goods are applied first towards the expenses incurred in the taking into possession and sale and then towards payment of the duty due from the trader. Any surplus is paid to the trader[5].

1 Customs and Excise Management Act 1979, s 117.
2 Ibid, ss 1, 8(2).
3 Ibid, s 117(1).
4 Ibid, s 117(2)–(4).
5 Ibid, s 117(7).

BETTING AND GAMING DUTIES

8.15 Another summary warrant procedure exists in respect of unpaid general betting duty or bingo duty or any sum owing by virtue of section 12(1) or section 14 of, or Schedule 2 to, the Betting and Gaming Duties Act 1981. A sheriff, on application, by the proper officer, which contains a certificate that a person has failed to pay such duty after written demand on him, may grant a warrant authorising a sheriff officer[1]:

(1) to take into possesion, by force if necessary, any of that person's corporeal moveables not exempt from poinding. For this purpose the sheriff officer has authority to open shut and lockfast places; and

(2) to sell by public auction anything so taken into possession, after giving six days notice of the sale.

In some circumstances the officer may also take into possession and sell corporeal moveables, whether or not belonging to the debtor, which are found on premises on which is conducted the gaming or playing of bingo giving rise to the duty[2].

The proceeds of the sale go towards the expenses of taking the goods into possession and sale of the goods and then to the payment of the amount due. Provision is made for the return of any surplus to the debtor[3].

1 Betting and Gaming Duties Act 1981, s 29(1).
2 Ibid, s 29(2).
3 Ibid, s 29(3).

Priority of claim for tax

NATURE OF PRIORITY

8.16 Section 64 of the Taxes Management Act 1970 provides that before a creditor may use diligence against his debtor's moveable goods and effects, he must pay to the Inland Revenue up to one year's arrears of various sums owing by the debtor to the Revenue[1]. If the creditor fails to pay his debtor's tax arrears and proceeds with diligence against his debtor's moveable goods and effects, the Inland Revenue may use a summary warrant poinding under Schedule 5 to the 1987 Act against the property to recover the sums due to it. The creditor's own diligence is postponed to the Inland Revenue's poinding[2].

The Scottish Law Commission recommended that the Revenue's priority should be abolished completely[3], but no changes were made by the 1987 Act. However section 154 of the Finance Act 1989 restricted the types of tax to which the priority applies and this has modified but not eliminated many of the practical difficulties which the Commission had identified with these provisions[4].

1 Taxes Management Act 1970, s 64(1).
2 Ibid, s 64(2).
3 Scot Law Com Report no 95 (1985), pp 444–450. The recommendation of the Commission that a similar privilege available to local authorities in respect of rates debts should be abolished was implemented by the 1987 Act: Local Government (Scotland) Act 1947, s 248, repealed by 1987 Act, s 74(4), Sch 8.
4 In its previous form, s 64 of the Taxes Management Act 1970 gave the Inland Revenue a priority in respect of a wide range of taxes. In effect this made the creditor liable for the tax debts of his debtor, even though the creditor would be unaware of his debtor's tax liabilities and even though the creditor would be unable to require the Inland Revenue to disclose the debtor's tax arrears.

TAXES TO WHICH THE PRIORITY APPLIES

8.17   The 1987 Act made no change to the taxes to which the priority of section 64 of the 1970 Act applies. However that section was amended by the Finance Act 1989 with the effect that the priority extends only to[1]
(1) sums due for deductions of PAYE under section 203 of the Income and Corporation Taxes Act 1988; and
(2) sums due in respect of deductions to be made by the debtor under section 559 of that Act (sub-contractors in the construction industry).
In both cases the priority covers only payments due in the twelve months before the date of the poinding.

   Since the 1987 Act no priority is given in respect of arrears of rates[2], and it may be noted that there is no such priority in respect of arrears of community charge.

1 Taxes Management Act 1970, s 64 (as amended by Finance Act 1989, s 155).
2 Local Government (Scotland) Act 1947, s 248, repealed by 1987 Act, s 74(4) and Sch 8.

DILIGENCES AFFECTED

8.18   Section 64 of the 1970 Act operates to postpone the effect of diligences by the creditor against the debtor's moveable property and effects. In terms of the statute itself, these diligences include poinding and sequestration for rent and have been held to extend poinding of the ground[1], arrestment of funds[2], and the attachment of rents under a decree of maills and duties[3]. The priority does not affect diligences against the heritable property of the debtor.

   Where any such diligence has been commenced and the Inland Revenue uses summary warrant procedure to recover the arrears due to it, the creditor's diligence is not nullified but is postponed to the Revenue's claim. However, the practicalities of many situations are that the debtor may not have any or sufficient assets to attach once the tax priority has been taken.

1 *Campbell v Edinburgh Parish Council* 1911 SC 280.
2 *Wood v Glasgow Corporation* (1912) 28 Sh Ct Rep 91, 93; *Wood v Glasgow Corporation* (1916) 2 SLT (Sh Ct) 171; *Cameron v Neil* (1926) 42 Sh Ct Rep 171.
3 *Bow v Shaw* (1914) 30 Sh Ct Rep 138. However the priority does not affect the remedy of the holder of a standard security to attach rents: Scot Law Com Report no 95 (1985), p 448.

USE OF SUMMARY WARRANT POINDING BY INLAND REVENUE

8.19   Where a creditor fails to pay the debtor's arrears owing to the Revenue but commences one of the diligences affected by section 64, the Inland Revenue may use summary warrant procedures to execute a poinding and sale to recover those arrears. It appears that the Revenue may use poinding and sale even against goods of the debtor which have been sold in a warrant sale at the instance of the creditor to a purchaser for value who had no notice of the tax arrears[1].

1 Scot Law Com Report no 95 (1985), pp 448–449.

EXPENSES FOR FRUSTRATED DILIGENCE

8.20   Where the Inland Revenue use summary warrant procedure after a creditor has already executed diligence, the Revenue are under no obligation to meet the expenses of the creditor's diligence which has been blocked by the statutory preference. However, the Inland Revenue by extra-statutory concession do allow the creditor to recoup the expenses of frustrated diligence[1].

1 Report of the Committee on Diligence (Chairman, Sheriff H McKechnie) Cmnd 456 (1958), para 117.

Imprisonment for non-payment of taxes, rates, community charges

8.21 Section 74(3) of the 1987 Act enacts that no person shall be imprisoned for failure to pay rates or any tax. There are no provisions in the Abolition of Domestic Rates Etc (Scotland) Act 1987 authorising the imprisonment of community charge defaulters[1].

1 For fuller discussion of civil imprisonment for debt, see below at paras 8.32–8.43.

Abolition of special Exchequer diligence

8.22 Sections 28–34, 35, and 42 of the Exchequer Court (Scotland) Act 1856 provided special modes of diligence and various preferences to the Crown in respect of Crown debts constituted by decree of the Court of Session sitting as the Court of Exchequer[1]. These provisions have been repealed by section 74(5) of the 1987 Act. Diligence on Exchequer decrees are now the ordinary diligences in normal form.

1 For background discussion, see Scot Law Com Report no 95 (1985), pp 440–443.

ACTIONS FOR DELIVERY

8.23 Actions for delivery may be raised in respect of (a) specific items of moveable property and (b) children.

Delivery of moveables

8.24 Actions for delivery of moveables can be raised in a variety of circumstances, but there is a broad distinction to be drawn between situations in which delivery is sought from a person who has possession of the goods without ever having had any title to them, and those in which the possessor was at one time entitled to have possession but is no longer entitled. Recovery of goods from a thief would be in the first category; recovery of goods from a custodier would be in the second.

An action of delivery, as a form of diligence, covers both. It is an action *ad factum praestandum* which concludes for delivery where the defender is in possession of moveables which the pursuer is entitled to possess. The obligation to deliver may arise because the goods have been purchased under a contract of sale[1] or hire purchase[2] or exchanged under a contract of barter[3]. It will also arise where the goods have been stolen[4], or otherwise wrongfully withheld eg on the termination of a hire purchase contract[5]. If the debtor in a hire purchase or conditional sale agreement is in breach of contract but has paid one-third or more of the purchase price, the goods are 'protected goods' and can be recovered by the creditor only by court action[6], which would be an action inter alia for delivery. When the action is raised it is normally continued to give the defender an opportunity to implement[7].

1 *Sutherland v Montrose Shipbuilding Co* (1860) 22 D 665.
2 *Rudman v Jay* 1908 SC 552, 15 SLT 853.
3 *Widenmeyer v Burn, Stewart & Co* 1967 SC 85, SLT 129.
4 *Dalhanna Knitwear Co v Ali* 1967 SLT (Sh Ct) 74.
5 *English v Donnelly* 1958 SC 484, 1959 SLT 2.
6 Consumer Credit Act 1974, s 90.
7 I D Macphail *Sheriff Court Practice* para 25–164.

REMEDIES FOR NON-IMPLEMENT

8.25 Where a person seeks delivery of an item of moveable property, the action may conclude for damages if the contract is not implemented. That is specifically provided for in the Sale of Goods Act[1], but specific implement will be granted only when the contract is for the sale of some specific item and the buyer can demonstrate that there is something special about the item which he has bought eg that it is unique[2].

However if specific implement is granted, the defender who fails to obtemper the decree may be imprisoned. Imprisonment is competent only in the case of wilful refusal and even then, the maximum period of imprisonment is six months. Imprisonment does not extinguish the obligation[3].

Prior to the 1987 Act, an extract of a document containing an obligation *ad factum praestandum* was warrant for imprisonment. Under the 1987 Act there will have to be an action based on the obligation and only in the event of non-compliance with that decree may imprisonment be ordered[4].

However the court may 'on any application' (which in most cases will be that of the defender) recall the decree and instead of granting warrant to imprison the defender, substitute an order for payment, or make any other order including a warrant to search any premises for corporeal moveables which the defender has been ordered to deliver to the pursuer[5]. The warrant includes authority to open shut and lockfast places[6].

Where the action for delivery is a summary cause, the warrant to open shut and lockfast premises applies only to the defender's premises and a charge must be served following decree of delivery[7].

1 Sale of Goods Act 1979, s 52.
2 *Union Electric Co v Holman* 1913 SC 954, 2 SLT 5.
3 Law Reform (Miscellaneous Provisions) (Scotland) Act 1940, s 1.
4 1987 Act, s 100.
5 Law Reform (Miscellaneous Provisions) (Scotland) Act 1940, s 1(2).
6 Ibid, s 1(3).
7 SCR 71: The position regarding small claims is unclear in that the rules provide for payment as an alternative should the decree not be implemented. AS (Small Claim Rules) 1988, SI 1988/1976, r 4(1).

Delivery of children

GENERAL

8.26 An order of a Scottish, or foreign court[1] granting custody of a child is not of itself a sufficient warrant to obtain delivery of the child[2], but, as a general rule, a person who has the right of custody (whether by virtue of a court order or not) may raise an action for delivery against anyone wrongfully withholding the child[3]. In contrast to the order for custody, the warrant for delivery is one *ad factum praestandum*[4].

1 *Kelly v Marks* 1974 SLT 118.
2 *Caldwell v Caldwell* 1983 SC 137, SLT 610.
3 *Leys v Leys* (1886) 13 R 1223; *Campbell v Campbell* 1920 SC 31, 1919 2 SLT 227. Parents, eg, who are entitled to custody could raise an action for delivery without first having a decree granting them custody.
4 *Brown v Brown* 1948 SC 5, SLT 129; *Guthrie v Guthrie* 1954 SLT (Sh Ct) 58; *Thomson v Thomson* 1979 SLT (Sh Ct) 11.

JURISDICTION

8.27 An order for delivery of a child may be sought in proceedings to enforce a custody order or in an independent cause[1]. The proceedings are competent both in the Court of Session and in the sheriff court[2].

1 *Muir v Milligan* (1868) 6 M 1125.
2 *Guthrie v Guthrie* 1954 SLT (Sh Ct) 58.

WHO MAY APPLY

8.28 At one time, an action for delivery would have been competent only to a parent[1], but now anyone who can show an interest may be awarded custody[2] and hence would be entitled to raise an action for delivery. Under the Social Work (Scotland) Act 1968[3], a local authority may resolve that the parental rights in a child in its care or in the care of a voluntary organisation should vest in it. Accordingly, the local authority would be entitled to raise an action for delivery of the child. Where parental rights have been so assumed, a parent has no right to raise an action for custody[4].

1 *Begbie v Nicol* 1949 SC 158, SLT 131.
2 Law Reform (Parent and Child) (Scotland) Act 1986, ss 2, 3.
3 Social Work (Scotland) Act 1968, s 16.
4 *Beagley v Beagley* 1984 SC (HL) 69, SLT 202.

DISCRETION

8.29 Even if a person *ex lege* has the right to custody or the court has made an award of custody in his favour, the court will not automatically grant a warrant for delivery[1]. In the following situations, such a warrant has been refused: where this would be prejudicial to the child's health and welfare[2]; where the custody order is being challenged or where it is likely to be suspended[3].

1 *Thomson Petr* 1980 SLT (Notes) 29.
2 *Hood v Hood* (1871) 9 M 449.
3 *Fowler v Fowler* (No 2) 1981 SLT (Notes) 78.

ENFORCEMENT

8.30 An order for delivery of a child is enforced by either messengers-at-arms or sheriff officers. They may be given power to search for the child, enter premises by force[1] and to take the child and deliver it to the person entitled to custody. The enforcement is therefore a civil matter and so neither the procurator fiscal nor the police have a duty to assist the officers of court[2]. However, the police may become involved if there is a threat of a breach of the peace. Failure to comply with an order amounts to contempt of court[3] and is enforceable by imprisonment.

1 SCR 71.
2 *Caldwell v Caldwell* 1983 SC 137, SLT 610.
3 *Leys v Leys* (1886) 13 R 1223.

CHILD ABDUCTION AND CUSTODY ACT 1985

8.31   The object of this Act is to assist those who have custody rights to have abducted children returned to them. It does so by implementing the Hague Convention on the Civil Aspects of International Child Abduction and the European Convention on Recognition and Enforcement of Decision concerning Custody of Children and on Restoration of Custody of Children. The Hague Convention requires the child to be returned immediately to its country of habitual residence and the European convention deals with the recognition and enforcement of custody orders. The Child Abduction Act 1984 imposes a criminal penalty on abducters. This Act provides the civil procedures for securing their return[1].

1 RC 260 H–L; OCR 132B.

CIVIL IMPRISONMENT

Introduction

8.32   The theory behind civil imprisonment is that a debtor who failed to pay his debts or perform his obligations after being charged to do so in the name of the Sovereign, was in rebellion[1]. Limited use was made of the remedy, probably because the debtor would not be able to comply while he was in prison. The Debtors (Scotland) Act 1880 abolished imprisonment for debt, except where the debt was a fine or other penalty due to the Crown, taxes, rates and sums due as aliment[2]. The Law Reform (Miscellaneous Provisions) (Scotland) Act 1940 altered the law in relation to imprisonment for failure to obtemper a decree *ad factum praestandum*[3], but the 1987 Act abolished imprisonment for failure to pay fines or penalties due to the Crown[4], except as undernoted. It also abolished imprisonment for failure to pay rates and taxes[5] and it is incompetent to imprison anyone for failure to pay the community charge[6]. The 1987 Act made further changes to the 1940 Act[7]. As a result, civil imprisonment is now available only where there is (a) a failure to pay a fine imposed for contempt of court; (b) a breach of an order made under the Court of Session Act 1868; (c) a failure to pay aliment; or (d) a failure to obtemper a decree *ad factum praestandum*.

1 Stair IV, 47.
2 Debtors (Scotland) Act 1880, s 4.
3 Law Reform (Miscellaneous Provisions) (Scotland) Act 1940, s 1.
4 1987 Act, s 74(5).
5 Ibid, s 74(3).
6 Abolition of Domestic Rates Etc (Scotland) Act 1987, Sch 2, para 7.
7 1987 Act, s 100.

CONTEMPT OF COURT

8.33 Contempt of court is dealt with at common law and under the Contempt of Court Act 1981, as amended[1], but it is the Act which imposes penalties. It is, however, the 1987 Act[2] (altering the Debtors (Scotland) Act 1880) which provides that imprisonment is competent for a failure to pay a fine imposed for contempt.

1 See J Ross Harper 'Contempt of Court' in *The Laws of Scotland: Stair Memorial Encyclopaedia* vol 6, paras 310–400.
2 1987 Act, Sch 6, para 8.

BREACH OF AN ORDER UNDER THE COURT OF SESSION ACT 1868

8.34 Under section 91 of the 1868 Act, the court may, on summary petition, order the restoration of possession of property of which the petitioner has been violently or wrongfully deprived, and order specific implement of a statutory duty[1]. Failure to comply can result in imprisonment[2].

1 See eg *Adamson v Edinburgh Street Tramway Co* (1872) 10 M 533.
2 Court of Session Act 1868, s 91; 1987 Act, Sch 6, para 8.

FAILURE TO PAY ALIMENT

Introduction

8.35 The general power to imprison a person for non-payment of aliment was abolished in 1882, but despite that, the sheriff may imprison someone if he wilfully fails to pay sums awarded as aliment and the expenses of the relevant action[1]. Only the sheriff has this power[2].

1 Civil Imprisonment (Scotland) Act 1882, s 4.
2 *Strain v Strain* (1886) 13 R 1029.

Aliment

8.36 The term 'aliment' is construed strictly and it does not include:
(1) a periodical allowance granted on divorce[1];
(2) sums due under an extract registered bond of aliment[2], because it is not due under a court decree. Thus, sums agreed as aliment in a separation or divorce agreement which are not part of the decree cannot be enforced by civil imprisonment;
(3) sums paid by a third party to the person entitled to the aliment[3];
(4) arrears, where the right to aliment has ceased[4].

1 *White v White* 1984 SLT (Sh Ct) 30.
2 *McGeekie v Cameron* (1897) 13 Sh Ct Rep 357.
3 *Tevendale v Duncan* (1883) 10 R 852.
4 *Glenday v Johnston* (1905) 8 F 27, 13 SLT 467.

How to proceed

8.37 Subject to the statutes which confer rights on other persons to apply for imprisonment, the application must be made by the creditor. Thus an assignee of a decree cannot enforce it by civil imprisonment[1].

However, the holder of a decree for an alimentary debt cannot have the debtor imprisoned automatically on default. The creditor requires a warrant from the sheriff, but the procedure is summary and there are no written pleadings[2]; the usual procedure is to apply to the sheriff by minute craving warrant to imprison[3]. However, the sheriff has a discretion whether or not to grant the warrant. There is no appeal against the sheriff's decision and the creditor is liable for the expenses of the application whether or not it is successful[4] and also for the expenses of implementing the warrant.

1 *Cain v McColm* (1892) 19 R 813.
2 Civil Imprisonment (Scotland) Act 1882, s 4; *Cook v Wallace and Wilson* (1889) 16 R 565.
3 W J Dobie *Law and Practice of the Sheriff Courts in Scotland* p 282.
4 *Strain v Strain* (1886) 13 R 1029.

Failure to pay

8.38 Because imprisonment for a civil debt is the penalty for failure to obtemper a decree, the sheriff must be satisfied that the refusal to pay is wilful. The 1882 Act specifically excludes cases where the debtor does not have the means to pay[1]. In determining means, certain state benefits, namely any increase of injury benefit or disablement benefit in respect of a child, or of industrial death benefit, is ignored[2].

Warrant has been refused in the following situations: (i) where the debtor has been sequestrated[3], (ii) where the debtor's wages were arrested after the application for warrant for imprisonment[4] and (iii) where the debtor's offer to maintain the pursuer was refused and the debtor then fell into arrears[5].

1 Civil Imprisonment (Scotland) Act 1882, s 4, proviso 3.
2 Social Security Act 1975, s 87(3).
3 *Strain v Strain* (1886) 2 Sh Ct Rep 320.
4 *Renwick v Blair* (1911) 27 Sh Ct Rep 210.
5 *Cassells v Cassells* 1955 SLT (Sh Ct) 41, 71 Sh Ct Rep 113.

Implement of the Warrant

8.39 The warrant for imprisonment must be implemented by officers of the court and cannot be implemented by the police[1]. That is done by personal service on the defender to pay under pain of imprisonment.

The defender can be imprisoned for not more than six weeks[2], but imprisonment does not extinguish the debt, nor does it prevent the creditor using other remedies to recover it[3]. The debtor may be imprisoned on a subsequent occasion provided at least six months have elapsed since his release from prison[4].

1 Sheriff Courts (Scotland) Extracts Act 1892, s 8.
2 Civil Imprisonment (Scotland) Act 1882, s 4.
3 Ibid, s 4, proviso 5.
4 Ibid, s 4, proviso 4.

FAILURE TO IMPLEMENT A DECREE AD FACTUM PRAESTANDUM

8.40 Although the 1880 Act abolished civil imprisonment for debt, it specifically left unaltered the courts' power to imprison for failure to obtemper a decree *ad factum praestandum*[1]. This power is now regulated by the Law Reform (Miscellaneous Provisions) (Scotland) Act 1940[2] and the 1987 Act[3].

The 1940 Act applied only to decrees, but the 1987 Act provides that an obligation *ad factum praestandum* which is contained in a document registered in the Books of Council and Session or sheriff court books cannot automatically be enforced by imprisonment. Now the creditor will have to bring an action based on the obligation, obtain a decree and apply to the court for an order under the 1940 Act[3]. Under the 1940 Act, the debtor may be imprisoned for up to six months if his failure to comply with a decree is wilful[4].

It is desirable that the decree should state a time within which it has to be implemented, even if there is no conclusion or crave to that effect[5]. If the decree does not specify a time, the charge is on an *induciae* of seven days[6].

1 Debtors (Scotland) Act 1880, s 4.
2 Law Reform (Miscellaneous Provisions) (Scotland) Act 1940, s 1.
3 1987 Act, s 100.
4 Law Reform (Miscellaneous Provisions) (Scotland) Act 1940, s 1.
5 *Macdonald v Mackessack* (1886) 16 R 168; *Johnstone v Harris* 1977 SC 365, 1978 SLT (Notes) 81.
6 *McLintock v Prinzen and Van Glabbeek* (1902) 4 F 948, 10 SLT 157.

Procedure

8.41 The pursuer normally lodges a minute setting out his claim that the defender is wilfully refusing to obtemper the decree. The defender is cited to appear at a diet at which the pursuer must substantiate his claim. The court may order that the defender be imprisoned, but it also has the power to recall the original decree and substitute for the obligation an order for payment of a specified sum, or, make any other order which it thinks appropriate[1]. That order is authority to search premises and to open shut and lockfast premises[2]. Even where the defender has been imprisoned, he may be liberated if he has complied with the decree, or is no longer wilfully refusing to obtemper it[3].

1 In *Edgar v Fisher's Trs* (1893) 21 R 59, 1 SLT 301, the defender's estates were sequestrated.
2 Law Reform (Miscellaneous Provisions) (Scotland) Act 1940, s 1(2)(3).
3 Ibid, s 1(1).

Nature of the obligation

8.42 An obligation of a positive nature, eg to deliver something, is enforced by specific implement, whereas an obligation which is negative in nature, eg not to build on another person's ground, is enforced by interdict. Failure to comply with a decree of specific implement or interdict may result in imprisonment.

Specific implement will not be granted in the following cases:
(1) where the obligation is to pay money[1]. However, by statute, a decree of specific implement will be granted in a contract to pay for and take up shares in a company[2];
(2) where the relationship is an intimate one eg a partnership[3];
(3) where compliance with the decree would be impossible, eg where, in order to execute a contract, access is required to land, where no right of access exists[4];
(4) where the court cannot enforce the decree eg where the obligant is a juristic (non-natural) person[5];
(5) where there is no *pretium affectionis*, ie where there is nothing special about the goods which the obligant is obliged to deliver[6];
(6) where the obligation is not specific[7];

In all of these cases, imprisonment will not be available and some other remedy, frequently damages, must be sought.

1 W M Gloag *The Law of Contract* pp 635–636.
2 Companies Act 1985, s 195.
3 *Macarthur v Lawson* (1877) 4 R 1134 at 1136 per Lord President Inglis.
4 *Sinclair v Caithness Flagstone Co* (1898) 25 R 705, 5 SLT 364.
5 *Gall v Loyal Glenbogie Lodge* (1900) 2 F 1187, 8 SLT 140; *Macleod v Alexander Sutherland Ltd* 1977 SLT (Notes) 44.
6 *Union Electric Co v Holman* 1913 SC 954, 2 SLT 5.
7 *Hendry v Marshall* (1878) 5 R 687.

Interdict

8.43 While interdict is the method of enforcing an obligation not to do something and breach is punishable by imprisonment[1], it has been stated that breach of interdict is not contempt of court[2].

1 *The Laws of Scotland: Stair Memorial Encyclopaedia* vol 6, para 322.
2 *Johnston v Grant* 1923 SC 789, SLT 501.

SEQUESTRATION FOR RENT

Introduction

8.44 In addition to the ordinary remedies available to a landlord for recovery of rent, including summary diligence on a lease which contains a clause of consent to registration for execution, he may have a right in security, known as a hypothec, over moveable property on the leased subjects. That hypothec is enforced by the process of sequestration for rent. Before the right can exist, there must be the relationship of landlord and tenant and not, for example, a security transaction disguised as a lease[1]. It is unusual to find an express requirement in a commercial lease that the tenant should provide goods of sufficient value to cover the rent, but the remedy of sequestration is still used, and may be useful provided the tenant is still solvent.

1 *Heritable Securities Investment Association v Wingate's Tr* (1880) 7 R 1094.

Types of lease covered

8.45 The landlord's hypothec was abolished in relation to all subjects over two acres which are let for agriculture or pasture[1]. The phrase 'agriculture or pasture' does not cover market gardens, or nurseries[2]. It therefore extends to all other subjects eg warehouses, factories, houses, shops, mines, quarries and fisheries[3].

1 Hypothec Abolition (Scotland) Act 1880, s 1.
2 J Rankine *The Law of Leases in Scotland* (3rd edn) pp 382–383.
3 *Rankine* pp 373–380.

Goods covered

8.46 The subjects covered are known as the *invecta et illata* and that encompasses, in general, ordinary stock-in-trade, furnishings in a house, and ordinary equipment. The hypothec covers goods which have been brought on to the premises by the tenant, even although they do not belong to him, eg items on hire[1] and goods belonging to a sub-tenant may be sequestrated for rent due by the principal tenant and also for rent due by the sub-tenant[2]. Goods which have been sold, but not removed, are also subject to the hypothec[3].

1 *Dundee Corpn v Marr* 1971 SC 96, SLT 218.
2 *Stewart v Stables* (1878) 5 R 1024.
3 *Ryan v Little* 1910 SC 219, 1909 2 SLT 476. In that case, it was pointed out that the Sale of Goods Act 1893 did not alter the law on the landlord's hypothec (s 61(5) now s 62(5)).

Goods not covered

8.47 The following are exempted: items which are exempted from poinding under section 16 of the 1987 Act are also exempted from sequestration for rent[1]; goods which are on hire-purchase, or the subject of a conditional sale agreement[2]; money, bonds and bills[3]; the tenant's clothes[3]; goods which are on the premises merely temporarily[4]; goods which belong to a member of the tenant's family, or a lodger[5].

1 1987 Act, s 99(1).
2 Consumer Credit Act 1974, s 104.
3 Bell *Prin* § 1276.
4 *Jaffray v Carrick* (1836) 15 s 43; *Dundee Corpn v Marr* (supra).
5 *Bell v Andrews* (1885) 12 R 961.

Goods removed

8.48 The landlord may interdict the removal of goods, or, if they have been removed, he may be granted a warrant to have them brought back. The writ may crave warrant for the recovery of goods removed but this can be done by a separate minute, or a minute endorsed on the writ. If good cause can be shown, the sheriff may grant the warrant, but in most instances, he will order intimation to the tenant and any other party involved and give them an opportunity to be heard[1]. If the tenant removes goods which have been sequestrated, he is liable for breach of the sequestration. The landlord may seek the return of the goods, or ask for consignation of, or caution for the amount due and failing that, a fine, or imprisonment[2].

1 I D Macphail *Sheriff Court Practice* para 23–17.
2 *Macphail* para 23–22.

Rents covered

8.49 The hypothec secures rent for one year, but not the arrears[1], but if the landlord does not enforce his right by sequestration within one month of the date when the rent was due, the hypothec is unenforceable for that term's rent[2].

1 *Young v Welsh* (1883) 12 S 233.
2 Bell *Comm* II, 33.

To whom the remedy is available

8.50 Apart from the landlord, the remedy is available to a heritable creditor under an *ex facie* valid disposition, or a bond and disposition in security, provided the creditor has entered into possession, or by an adjudger who is infeft and has entered into possession[1]. It is also available to a tenant who has granted a sub-lease[2].

1 W M Gloag and J M Irvine *Rights in Security and Cautionary Obligations* p 421.
2 Bell *Comm* II, 32.

Competition

8.51 This is dealt with in chapter 10.

Sequestration

8.52 This is probably competent only in the sheriff court[1]. It may proceed as an ordinary cause, or as a summary cause[2], and may be for payment of the rent due, or in security of rent to become due, but the action is usually for both[3]. When the rent does not exceed £1,500, the action must be a summary cause[4]. The practice is to sequestrate for the rent due and for a future term or terms, but not exceeding one year in total. The crave will seek warrant to sell and for payment to the pursuer of, or from, the proceeds. If they are insufficient, decree will be sought for the balance. The pursuer will also seek warrant to have the premises replenished and failing that, authority to relet them[5].

In the first deliverance on the writ, the sheriff may sequestrate the goods and grant warrant to have them inventoried but not valued, and if necessary made secure[6]. The fact that the officer does not appraise goods of sufficient value to cover the rent means that the process may be more expensive than poinding. The warrant will include authority to open shut and lockfast premises[7] and the warrant must be signed by the sheriff personally[8]. The tenant may also be interdicted from removing goods which are subject to the hypothec.

1 *Duncan v Lodijensky* (1904) 6 F 408, 11 SLT 684.
2 The ordinary cause procedure is described here. The summary cause procedure is contained in SCR 72–78 and is described in *Macphail* paras 25–166—25–171.
3 W J Dobie *Styles for use in the Sheriff Courts in Scotland* pp 486–471.
4 Sheriff Courts (Scotland) Act 1971, s 35(1)(b).
5 *Macphail* para 23–14.
6 *Macphail* para 23–15; OCR 102.
7 OCR 100.
8 OCR 8(2).

Inventory and care of the goods

8.53 The warrant will be executed by the sheriff officer and he will inventory the goods in the presence of a witness. He need not appraise the goods[1] and so he will inventory all the goods on the premises, no matter how much is due by way of rent[2]. At any time, the sheriff may appoint someone to take charge of the sequestrated effects, or may require the tenant to find caution for their preservation. In addition, he may grant warrant to sell perishable articles[3].

1 *Lochgilphead Town Council v McIntyre* (1940) 59 Sh Ct Rep 179.
2 *Marquis of Breadalbane v Toberonochy Slate Quarry Co* (1916) 33 Sh Ct Rep 154.
3 *Macphail* para 23–18.

Recall

8.54 The sequestration may be recalled upon payment, or caution, but failing that, decree will be granted[1].

1 *Macphail* para 23–19.

The effect of decree

8.55 The pursuer will make a motion to the sheriff to grant warrant to sell whatever amount of the goods is necessary to meet the amount due including the interest and expenses. The sale is reported and once the accounts have been taxed, the balance is paid to the landlord. If a balance remains due by the tenant, the decree will be extracted and diligence done on it[1].

1 *Macphail* para 23–20.

POINDING OF THE GROUND

8.56 This is a process available to a creditor in a *debitum fundi* whereby he can poind moveables on lands over which the *debitum fundi* is constituted[1]. The action may be raised by a superior in respect of his feuduty[2], the creditor in a real burden secured over land[3], and a heritable creditor under either a standard security[4] or a bond and disposition in security[5], the creditor in a ground annual[6], and one who has a decree of maills and duties[7]. It is not, however, open to a creditor under an *ex facie* absolute disposition[8], nor to a creditor under a bond and assignation in security of a long lease[9]. The action may be raised either in the Court of Session or the sheriff court. Because those who can competently raise such an action have other and more effective remedies, such actions are rare. The form of the warrant in the extract decree will be laid down by Act of Sederunt[10].

1 *Graham Stewart* p 493.
2 Stair IV, 23, 5; *Stewart v Gibson's Tr* (1880) 8 R 270.
3 Ersk *Inst* IV, 1,1; *Graham Stewart* p 493.
4 J M Halliday *Conveyancing Law and Practice in Scotland* vol III, para 39.68.
5 *Halliday* vol III, para 33.16.
6 *Bell's Trs v Copeland* (1896) 23 R 650, 3 SLT 324.
7 *Henderson v Wallace* (1875) 2 R 272.
8 *Scottish Heritable Security Co v Allan Campbell & Co* (1876) 3 R 333.
9 *Luke v Wallace* (1896) 23 R 634, 3 SLT 325.
10 1987 Act, s 87(5).

Competency

8.57 At the time the action is raised, the debt must actually be due[1]. An action for poinding of the ground is not affected by either a time to pay direction, or a time to pay order[2]. The action is competent only in respect of arrears of rent and the rent for the present term[3].

1 *Graham Stewart* pp 493–496.
2 1987 Act, ss 2, 9, 13(1).
3 Bell *Comm* II, 56.

Subjects attached

8.58 The warrant in the action is authority to poind all moveables belonging to the debtor, or his tenants, or to other possessors of the lands[1]. Moveables belonging to third parties cannot be poinded[2]. The restrictions on what may be poinded under an ordinary poinding apply to a poinding of the ground[3].

1 *Graham Stewart* pp 501–503.
2 *Thomson v Scoular* (1882) 9 R 430.
3 For further details, see ch 7.

Procedure

8.59 The action will crave warrant to poind and distrain the moveables and to have them inventoried and made secure[1]. Service of the writ creates a *nexus* over the goods[2]. The officer of court will inventory the goods but will not appraise them.

1 W J Dobie *Styles for Use in the Sheriff Courts in Scotland* pp 372–374.
2 *Lyons v Anderson* (1880) 8 R 24.

Effect

8.60 Mere service of the summons or initial writ does not prevent the tenants from paying rent to the proprietor[1]. The right to poind has been compared to a floating charge, in that the right, of itself, does not create any *nexus* over particular items, and so any moveables removed before the action is raised are not attached. Service of the action creates a *nexus*, perfecting the creditor's preferable right to them, or to their proceeds if they have been sold. This preference arises from infeftment[2].

1 *Royal Bank of Scotland v Dixon* (1868) 6 M 995.
2 *Athole Hydropathic Co Ltd v Scottish Provincial Assurance Co* (1886) 13 R 818.

Decree

8.61 The decree is a warrant to poind and a poinding may take place without a charge. A sale can then proceed in the same way as with a personal poinding[1].

1 *Macphail* para 23–26.

Competition

8.62 This is dealt with in chapter 10.

Liability of poinder for taxes

8.63 Prior to the 1987 Act the local rating authority and the Inland Revenue had a preference for one year's arrears over the goods belonging to the debtor. These could be recovered from the poinding creditor[1]. The preference for rates has been abolished and the preference afforded to the Revenue has been modified[2].

1 Local Government (Scotland) Act 1947, s 248; Taxes Management Act 1970, s 64.
2 1987 Act, s 74(4); Finance Act 1989, s 150.

Reform

8.64 The Scottish Law Commission's Discussion Paper on Adjudication for Debt and Related Matters[1] recommends the abolition of the diligence.

1 Adjudication for Debt and Related Matters (Scot Law Com Discussion Paper no 78 (November 1988)), vol 2, p 238.

MAILLS AND DUTIES

8.65 This is an action whereby the creditor in a heritable security may attach rents due by tenants of the subjects over which the security has been granted[1]. The action is available to the creditor in a bond and disposition in security[2], but not a standard security[3]. The creditor in a ground annual may also raise the action[4]. It is not open to the creditor in a real burden[5] because he has no right to enter into possession. For that reason, it is not open to a superior[6]. It is not open to the creditor in an assignation in security of a recorded lease because there is a special statutory procedure which allows him to enter into possession[7]. The creditor in an *ex facie* absolute disposition has a direct right to the rents and so the action is not necessary and may be incompetent[8]. Like poinding of the ground, such actions are rare and for the same reasons. An action of maills and duties is not affected by either a time to pay direction or a time to pay order[9].

1 *Graham Stewart* p 511.
2 The clause of assignation of rents in the bond and disposition in security gives the creditor the right to the rents in the event of the debtor's default. *Aberdeen Corpn v British Linen Bank* 1911 SC 239, 1910 2 SLT 348.
3 The creditor now has the right to enter into possession if the debtor has failed to comply with a calling up notice (Conveyancing and Feudal Reform (Scotland) Act 1970, s 20(1)) or if has obtained a decree under s 24 of the 1970 Act, or as provided for in the standard security.
4 *Somerville v Johnstone* (1899) 1 F 726, 6 SLT 365; J M Halliday *Conveyancing Law and Practice in Scotland* vol III, para 35.03.
5 Stair IV, 35, 24.
6 *Prudential Assurance Co v Cheyne* (1884) 11 R 87.
7 Registration of Leases (Scotland) Act 1857, ss 6, 20.
8 *Scottish Heritable Security Co v Allan Campbell & Co* (1876) 3 R 333.
9 1987 Act, s 13(1).

Competency

BOND AND DISPOSITION IN SECURITY

8.66 An action of maills and duties can be raised in three situations (a) default in payment of the principal sum; (b) default in payment of the interest; and

(c) apparent insolvency of the proprietor (not the debtor) and where the proprietor grants a trust deed for creditors[1].

1 Conveyancing (Scotland) Act 1924, s 25(1)(a).

GROUND ANNUAL

8.67 The action may be raised where the debtor has failed to make payment[1].

1 *Somerville v Johnstone* (1899) 1 F 726, 6 SLT 365.

Procedure

8.68 When such actions are raised, the procedure adopted is that laid down by the Heritable Securities (Scotland) Act 1894. The action is raised against the proprietor of the subjects and it is not necessary to call the tenants as defenders. However, notice of the raising of the action may be given to the tenants (by registered letter) in the form laid down in Schedule B of the 1894 Act or as near to that as is possible and the effect of receipt of the notice is to prevent them from paying their rents to the proprietor[1].

1 Heritable Securities (Scotland) Act 1894, s 3.

Decree

8.69 Once decree is obtained, the creditor may serve notice (again by registered letter) and when the tenant receives that, he must pay the rents to the creditor[1]. It is not clear from the Act what the tenant must do with rent in the interval between the raising of the action and the giving of notice of the decree.

1 Heritable Securities (Scotland) Act 1894, s 3.

Obtaining possession

8.70 If the landholder wishes to enter into possession of the security subjects, he may raise an action of ejection against the proprietor as an occupant without title if the proprietor is in default of payment of interest or capital[1]. The bondholder who assumes possession may administer the property and grant leases[2]. However, as an occupier, he will be liable as such[3], and therefore may incur liability under the Occupiers Liability (Scotland) Act 1960.

1 Heritable Securities (Scotland) Act 1894, s 5.
2 Ibid, ss 6, 7.
3 *Baillie v Shearer's Factor* (1894) 21 R 498, 1 SLT 496.

Competition

8.71 This is dealt with in chapter 10.

CHAPTER 9

DILIGENCE AGAINST
HERITABLE PROPERTY

INHIBITION IN EXECUTION

9.01 This section deals with the general aspects of inhibition as a diligence in execution. Special features of inhibition on the dependence are discussed in chapter 4[1].

1 See ch 4 above at paras 4.64 et seq.

Nature of inhibition

9.02 An inhibition may prevent a person who has an interest in heritable property from disposing of that interest to the prejudice of his creditors. As such, it can be used in addition to other diligences such as poinding and arrestment but it may be that the number of articles which are exempted from poinding may make that diligence less worthwhile and, of course, an arrestment depends upon the creditor knowing in whose hands to arrest. Inhibition may therefore be an effective alternative to other diligences.

Erskine defines inhibition as 'a personal prohibition, prohibiting the party inhibited to contract any debt or grant any deed by which any part of his lands may be alienated or carried off, to prejudice of the creditor inhibiting'[1]. A fuller definition is given by Graham Stewart, 'Inhibition is merely a negative or prohibitory diligence. It strikes against subsequent debts and posterior voluntary conveyances, gratuitous or onerous, by the person inhibited which are in any way prejudicial to the inhibitor. It gives a title to challenge only voluntary acts and is no bar to what the debtor is bound to perform. It in no way operates as a transfer of the possession or property of the subject to the inhibitor, vests no real right and gives no title to rank with those who have acquired a real right by voluntary security or adjudication'[2]. These definitions make it clear that inhibition is no more than a personal or prohibitory diligence which does not create any *nexus* over the property. If the inhibition fails to have the desired effect, the creditor would have to resort to further action or diligence to make his right real. Having said that, inhibition is probably effective in most cases.

1 Ersk *Inst* II, 11, 2.
2 J Graham Stewart *The Law of Diligence* p 551.

248

Bases

9.03 Inhibition may proceed on the basis of: (1) a decree for payment – inhibition in execution; (2) an action which is pending – inhibition on the dependence; and (3) a document of debt.

9.04 Inhibition in execution can proceed on the basis of a decree of the Court of Session, or of the sheriff court[1]. Foreign decrees which have been registered for execution in Scotland under the 1982 Act or other provisions are also a basis for inhibition[2]. A decree of the Scottish Land Court can be registered in the Books of Council and Session[3], but an order or determination can be enforced as if it were a decree of the sheriff in the jurisdiction in which enforcement will take place[4].

1 Inhibition was incompetent on an old-style small debt decree (*Lamont* (1867) 5 M 84). However, the reasoning in that case does not apply to present-day summary cause and small claims decrees.
2 See further ch 11 below.
3 Lord Elliot 'The Scottish Land Court' *The Laws of Scotland: Stair Memorial Encyclopaedia* vol 6, para 977.
4 Crofting Reform (Scotland) Act 1976, s 17(1).

9.05 Orders of the Tribunal can be recorded for execution in the Books of Council and Session and enforced accordingly[1]. They may be the basis for inhibition.

1 Lands Tribunal Act 1949, s 3(12)(d).

9.06 They are enforced as if they were an extract registered decree arbitral bearing a warrant for execution in any sheriffdom in Scotland[1]. If they are awards for payment, they may be a basis for inhibition.

1 Employment Protection (Consolidation) Act 1978, s 135(6), Sch 9, para 7, Sch 11, para 21(1).

9.07 Documents which are registered or which can be registered, or which are to be regarded as the equivalent of ones registered and which contain an obligation to pay money may be a basis for inhibition.

Gretton states this without reservation[1], but the opinion was expressed on the basis of the original wording of the Writs Execution (Scotland) Act 1877 that the warrant of execution permitted only diligence against moveables eg arrestment and poinding[2]. However, in its amended form, the 1877 Act *authorises* certain specified diligences against moveables[3], but it does not exclude others.

1 G L Gretton *The Law of Inhibition and Adjudication* p 8.
2 J M Halliday *Conveyancing Law and Practice in Scotland* vol I, para 4–67. For further comment, see ch 2.
3 Writs Execution (Scotland) Act 1877, s 3, as amended by the 1987 Act, s 87(4).

SUMMARY WARRANTS

9.08 The legislation permitting summary warrants permits only the diligences of arrestment and poinding[1].

1 Local Government (Scotland) Act 1947, s 247; Taxes Management Act 1970, s 63; Value Added Tax Act 1983, Sch 7, para 6; Car Tax Act 1983, Sch 1, para 3(2).

Inhibition on the dependence

9.09 This is discussed in chapter 4 above[1].

1 See ch 4 at paras 4.64 et seq.

INHIBITION ON A DOCUMENT OF DEBT

9.10 In the usual case, inhibition proceeds on a decree or the equivalent, or on a depending action. However, an inhibition may proceed on a document of debt. There is some doubt, about what is a 'document of debt' for this purpose[1], but Gretton[2] suggests that it is any probative document whereby a debtor binds himself to pay. The doubt probably arises from the two different senses in which 'probative' is used, ie as equivalent of 'attested', or in the sense of 'self-proving'[3]. A personal bond would be an obvious example since it will usually be probative in both senses, but there is some doubt about bills of exchange and promissory notes, as it has been held that a bill of exchange is not probative in the second sense because if the signature is challenged, the person founding on the bill must prove that it is genuine[4]. A similar doubt surrounds an IOU. However, despite that doubt, it is the practice to grant inhibition on bills and promissory notes[5]. There is no need for the debt to be liquid[6].

In most instances, the creditor will register the document for execution, in which event, he will do summary diligence on the extract and not on the document of debt itself. However, if the document does not contain the necessary consent to registration, or the debt is not yet due, or summary diligence is prohibited, eg under the Consumer Credit Act 1974[7], it will be necessary to inhibit on the document of debt itself. Inhibition is obtained in such a case by Bills and Letters.

1 *Graham Stewart* p 527; Ersk *Inst* II, 11, 3.
2 *Gretton* p 9.
3 Report on Requirements of Writing (Scot Law Com no 112 (1988)) para 5.1.
4 *McIntyre v National Bank of Scotland* 1910 SC 150, 1 SLT 63.
5 *Gretton* p 9.
6 *Graham Stewart* pp 528–530.
7 S 93A of the Consumer Credit Act 1974 added by the Debtors (Scotland) Act 1987.

The Land Register

9.11 A problem arises in connection with the Land Register. The Land Registration (Scotland) Act 1979 requires the Keeper to enter on any title sheet 'any subsisting entry in the Register of Inhibitions and Adjudications adverse to the interest'[1]. The practice at Meadowbank House is not to insert a reference to the inhibition immediately, but only when the title sheet is updated. For the problems to which this may give rise, the reader is referred to Gretton[2].

1 Land Registration (Scotland) Act 1979, s 6(1)(c).
2 *Gretton* pp 23–27.

Expenses

9.12 In theory, the expenses of using inhibition cannot be recovered from the debtor[1], but in practice an inhibiting creditor will refuse to recall or discharge his inhibition unless he is repaid in full, including expenses.

1 *Graham Stewart* p 554–555.

Effect

9.13 Graham Stewart describes the effects of inhibition as follows:

'Inhibition is merely a negative or prohibitory diligence. It strikes against subsequent debts and posterior voluntary conveyances, gratuitous or onerous, by the person inhibited which are in any way prejudicial to the inhibitor. It gives a title to challenge only voluntary acts and is no bar to what the debtor was bound to perform. It no way operates as a transfer of the possession or property of the subject to the inhibitor, vests no real right, and gives no title to rank with those who have acquired a real right by voluntary security or adjudication'[1].

There are therefore three effects. The first is that voluntary disposal of the heritage is challengeable. The second is that any voluntary security which is granted is challengeable and the third is that any debts which are contracted after the inhibition, are postponed to the inhibitor's claims[2]. The inhibition has no effect on debts contracted previously, and that common law position has been restated in statute[3]. Each of these effects will be discussed in detail. It should be noted that an inhibition is not effected by either a time to pay direction or a time to pay order[4].

1 *Graham Stewart* p 551.
2 Bell *Comm* II, 139; *Graham Stewart* pp 551, 559.
3 Bell *Comm* II, 139; Titles to Land Consolidation (Scotland) Act 1868, s 155.
4 1987 Act, ss 2, 9.

The first and second effects

VESTS NO REAL RIGHTS

9.14 To say that inhibition vests no real right is merely to emphasise that it is negative or prohibitory. It can therefore strike only at future voluntary acts, and those whose debts have been contracted prior to the inhibition can proceed as if the inhibition did not exist[1]. In addition, however, the inhibition does not give the creditor any right to the heritage or to payment out of the proceeds of any sale of the heritage and he must either use further diligence (adjudication to acquire a real right to the heritage or arrestment of the proceeds) or rank in the debtor's sequestration or liquidation. By virtue of section 31(2) of the Bankruptcy (Scotland) Act 1985 and section 185 of the Insolvency Act 1986, a trustee in sequestration or liquidation can sell free of any inhibition, but must give effect to it in the ranking process.

1 *Baird and Brown v Stirrat's Tr* (1872) 10 M 414.

FUTURE ACTS

9.15 An inhibition will strike only at deeds or debts entered into or contracted after its date. As has been said, that was the position at common law and is now expressly stated in section 155 of the Titles to Land Consolidation (Scotland) Act 1868: '[N]o inhibition shall have any effect against any act or deed done, committed, or executed prior to the registration' of the notice of inhibition, or the execution of the inhibition where the notice procedure was not used.

In *Halifax Building Society v Smith*[1], the court held that in the case of a debt, the relevant date is the date of the contract. If the deed which is challenged is a conveyance, it is the date of missives and not that of the conveyance which is relevant. This case is one of three recent cases[2] dealing with the preference of an inhibitor, and they restate the view that the inhibition has no effect on debts contracted previously. There are, however, other recent cases[3] which take the opposite view and they must therefore be of doubtful authority on this point.

1 1985 SLT (Sh Ct) 25.
2 The other cases are *McGowan v Middlemas* 1977 SLT (Sh Ct) 41 and *Ferguson & Forster v Dalbeattie Finance Co* 1981 SLT (Sh Ct) 53.
3 *George M Allan Ltd v Waugh's Trs* 1966 SLT (Sh Ct) 17; *Bank of Scotland v Lord Advocate* 1977 SLT 24; *Abbey National Building Society v Shaik Aziz* 1981 SLT (Sh Ct) 29.

VOLUNTARY ACTS

9.16 Inhibition strikes against the voluntary debts or deeds of the inhibited person ie those to which he was not bound prior to the inhibition[1]. If therefore, the act is one which the debtor was or can be obliged to perform, it is not struck at, nor is an act of a third party. A good example of an act which the debtor can be obliged to perform is the granting of a conveyance in implement of missives[2]. On the same reasoning, an inhibition will prevent the debtor granting a security whether in the form of a heritable (fixed) security or a floating charge. An act by a third party would include an adjudication by another creditor or the sale by a heritable creditor under a pre-existing heritable security[3].

One issue which remains unclear is the position of persons such as executors, liquidators, and judicial factors. As Gretton points out[4], there are two problems. One is whether an inhibition registered against the person represented eg the deceased, is effective against the representative. In relation to a deceased, Graham Stewart's view was that it was not effective against the heir[5], but the position of the executor is unclear. Gretton's view, which we share, is that where the representative's appointment is a judicial one, eg an executor's confirmation, or the act and warrant of a trustee in bankruptcy, he is not affected by the inhibition[6]. That, however, still leaves the question whether the inhibitor retains any preference which he might have had in any competition. Gretton's view is that 'it may still be effectual'[7]. He does not provide any reason. Our view is that, if the inhibition is ineffective against the representative, who is then free to sell the property, it would seem to follow logically that the inhibition is not effectual in relation to the free proceeds.

There is clear authority for the proposition that the debtor is not prevented by the inhibition from carrying out 'acts of ordinary administration'[8], but in that connection, the granting of leases requires special mention. Bell says 'it does not annul a lease of ordinary duration and at a fair rent'[9]. However, although the notion of fair rent was previously enshrined in the legislation dealing with domestic property[10], that notion is replaced by an 'open market' rent under the Housing (Scotland) Act 1988[11]. It is difficult at present to know what a fair rent is in a commercial or industrial lease, and in all leases 'ordinary duration' would be virtually impossible to define. The safe course of action for a person inhibited is to treat all leases as being struck at.

1 Ersk *Inst* II,11,11.
2 *Grant v Mansfield* (1774) M 7007; see also *Graham Stewart* pp 563–564.
3 *McGowan v Middlemas* 1977 SLT (Sh Ct) 41.
4 *Gretton* p 59.
5 *Graham Stewart* p 554.
6 *Gretton* p 59.
7 *Gretton* p 59.
8 Bell *Comm* II, 142.
9 Bell *Prin* § 1185.
10 Rent (Scotland) Act 1984; Housing Rents and Subsidies (Scotland) Act 1975.
11 Housing (Scotland) Act 1988, s 25.

THE THIRD EFFECT

9.17   Debts contracted after the inhibition are postponed to the claims of the inhibitor where the debtor's property is sold and the proceeds are being distributed. That is derived from Bell's Canons of Ranking[1] which were approved in *Baird and Brown v Stirrat's Tr*[2].

Gretton explains clearly how this works. In brief, the inhibitor is to rank as if the post-inhibition debt did not exist ie he is to be neither benefited nor prejudiced by it, while the pre-inhibition creditors are to rank as if the inhibition did not exist ie they are to be neither benefited nor prejudiced by it. This is done by dividing the ranking into two (imaginary) rounds. In the first round, the parties are ranked as if the inhibition did not exist. In the second round, the pre-inhibition creditors simply carry forward their first-round ranking unaltered, but the inhibitor draws back from the post-inhibition creditor sufficient funds to put him (the inhibitor) in the same position he would have been in had the post-inhibition debt not existed[3]. Gretton also provides a worked example in his chapter on ranking[4].

1 Bell *Comm* II, 143; *Gretton* pp 78–79.

2 (1872) 10 M 414.
3 *Gretton* p 75.
4 *Gretton* pp 78–91.

TO THE PREJUDICE OF THE CREDITOR

9.18 As the quotation[1] from Graham Stewart makes clear, the acts must be to the prejudice of the inhibiting creditor. This matter will be considered more fully in relation to enforcement.

1 See para 9.13 above.

PROPERTY AFFECTED

9.19 Originally, an inhibition struck at the debtor's estate, both heritable and moveable, but it is now settled that only heritable estate is affected[1]. There is a division of views on the basis for determining whether property is heritable or moveable for the purposes of an inhibition[2], but the majority view is that it is the law on adjudication and not the law of succession which is relevant[3]. The test is whether the property can be the subject of an adjudication.

The debtor need not be infeft in the property[4], but a problem arises with a purchaser under missives. It has recently been decided[5] that his right is moveable and so the purchaser would be able to sell unaffected by the inhibition. The correctness of this decision has been questioned[6] principally because the inhibition would not be effective against either the seller or the purchaser, the purchaser because his right is moveable and the seller because the conveyance granted in implement of the missives would not be a voluntary act. The right of a purchaser under missives is heritable for succession purposes[7] and the authorities on that point do not appear to have been cited in the recent cases. An inhibition may be restricted to a particular item of heritable property. This is usually done by having an inhibition partially recalled[8]; the inhibition may be restricted at the outset[9], under the Criminal Justice (Scotland) Act 1987[10].

1 Stair IV, 50, 5; Titles to Land Consolidation (Scotland) Act 1868, s 156, Sch QQ.
2 *Graham Stewart* pp 547–548.
3 *Gretton* p 49.
4 *Dryburgh v Gordon* (1896) 24 R 1, 4 SLT 173; *George M Allan Ltd v Waugh's Trs* 1966 SLT (Sh Ct) 17 (*ex facie* absolute disposition).
5 *Leeds Permanent Building Society v Aitken Malone & MacKay* 1986 SLT 338.
6 *Gretton* p 50.
7 *Ramsay v Ramsay* (1887) 15 R 25.
8 *McInally v Kildonnan Houses Ltd* 1979 SLT (Notes) 89.
9 *Pow v Pow* 1987 SLT 127, 1987 SCLR 290.
10 Criminal Justice (Scotland) Act 1987, s 11.

Corporeal heritable property

9.20 The most obvious example of corporeal heritable property is land, usually a house. Thus, the debtor can be prevented from disposing of his house, or if he does purport to dispose of it, the disposal can be reduced. It is however, fairly common for houses to be owned 'jointly', for example, by a husband and wife. In that event, an inhibition against the husband will affect only his share, but the practical effect is that the property cannot be sold, because it is unlikely that anyone would wish to purchase the wife's *pro indiviso* share. If, however, one of the 'joint' owners of the heritable property raises an action for division and sale, it is arguable that any subsequent sale is the result of a judicial act and not a voluntary act of the debtor and hence an inhibition has no effect. However, this matter is undecided. The problem of a purchaser under missives has already been discussed.

Incorporeal heritable property

9.21 The most obvious example is a lease and so an inhibition may strike at the interest of either a lessor or a lessee.

9.22 *Lessor.* The general rule is that an inhibition will prevent the granting of a lease because the lease may be an alienation of the heritable property to the prejudice of the inhibiting creditor. As has been noted, there is authority for the view that this does not prevent the lessor granting a lease at a fair rent and of ordinary duration[1], on the basis that such a lease does not diminish the value of the lessor's heritable property. Although that is probably still the law, the problems which can arise are considerable, and so, it would be best to assume that the granting of any lease could be struck at by an inhibition, because the lease could operate to the prejudice of the inhibiting creditor.

1 Bell *Comm* II, 142; *Graham Stewart* p 562.

9.23 *Lessee.* An inhibition would strike at a lessee's interest only if the lease is assignable. If the lease cannot be assigned, there is no disposal and nothing which can be adjudged and so nothing which can be the subject of an inhibition.

The general principle is that the interest of a tenant cannot be assigned because of the element of *delectus personae*. It may be, however, that the lease is of such duration as to imply assignability[1]. Two situations require special mention. One is where the lease provides that it cannot be assigned without the landlord's consent and the other is where it provides that it cannot be assigned without the landlord's consent, but adds something like 'which consent shall not be unreasonably withheld'. In the first case where the lease cannot be assigned without consent, the lease is no different from one which cannot be assigned[2]. In the second case, where consent is required, but it is not to be unreasonably withheld, the position is less certain. Gretton's view is that such a lease is adjudgeable, provided the adjudger would be someone to whom the landlord would not object[3]. That would make its 'adjudgeability' conditional upon an adjudication and the landlord finding the adjudger acceptable. If Gretton's reasoning is accepted, the lessee in such a lease can be inhibited. Professor Halliday does not deal with the point specifically, but says that where an assignation requires consent, there is no right in the tenant which can be adjudged[4]. Paton and Cameron is to the same effect[5]. In our opinion, that is the preferable view, but it might be worth having an inhibition against a lessee in the hope that it would be effective. An inhibition has no effect on the renunciation of a lease[5].

1 See J M Halliday *Conveyancing Law and Practice in Scotland* vol III, para 31.02.
2 G C H Paton and J G S Cameron *The Law of Landlord and Tenant in Scotland* p 153.
3 *Gretton* p 52.
4 *Halliday* vol III, para 25–25.
5 *Paton and Cameron* p 59.

Acquirenda

9.24 At common law, an inhibition affected the debtor's property no matter when he acquired it. That position was altered by the 1868 Act which makes it clear that no inhibition 'shall have any force or effect as against any lands to be acquired by the person or persons against whom such inhibition is used after the date of recording such inhibition or of recording the previous notice thereof prescribed by this Act'[1]. The words 'to be acquired' require some explanation. Does one 'acquire' heritable property on the conclusion of missives, or on delivery of the conveyance, or on recording? There is no doubt that once the conveyance is recorded, the property is acquired and so it would be affected by any subsequent inhibition. Conveyancing practice, however, has been to regard someone who purchases under the missives as inhibitable in respect of that property, but in the *Leeds Permament Building Society* case[2] the court took the view that delivery of the conveyance was the operative moment. The safe course would be not to regard property as *acquirenda* unless the inhibition pre-dates the missives.

1 Titles to Land Consolidation (Scotland) Act 1868, s 157.
2 1986 SLT 338.

Securities

9.25 Another very important effect of an inhibition is that it prevents the debtor from granting heritable securities. In most instances, the debtor will be inhibited after he has granted the security. In that event, the inhibition has no effect on the security and it follows therefore that the heritable creditor can exercise all of his remedies and, in particular, the power of sale. The creditor's ranking is not affected either. The inhibition may, however, strike at future advances obtained by the debtor, if they are contracted for after the inhibition, but not at future advances made after the inhibition if the creditor was contractually obliged to make them. Furthermore, the inhibition will not strike at the security in so far as it covers interest on advances made prior to the inhibition[1]. We shall return, in dealing with ranking, to the exercise by a heritable creditor of his power of sale.

1 *Scottish Waggon Co v Hamilton's Tr* (1906) 13 SLT 779.

9.26 *Floating charges.* At this stage, it is important to mention the floating charge which can also affect heritable property. In principle, an inhibition should strike at a subsequent floating charge, but that statement is difficult to reconcile with the decisions in *Lord Advocate v Royal Bank*[1] and *Armour and Mycroft Petrs*[2]. If the floating charge antedates the inhibition, it will not be affected by it. In both instances, the operative date is the date of the charge and not the date of crystallisation.

1 1977 SC 155, 1978 SLT 38.
2 1983 SLT 453.

Trusts and executries

9.27 There is no doubt that an inhibition is effective against trustees and executors, but the inhibition must be directed against the person in his representative capacity. There is, however, doubt about whether an inhibition directed against a deceased is effective against the representatives[1].

The safe course would therefore be to inhibit the representatives. An inhibition can also be directed against a beneficiary if the beneficiary's interest is heritable. Thus, if there is a specific bequest of heritage to the beneficiary, that can be inhibited. On that basis, an inhibition can probably affect a surviving spouse's prior rights to heritage under the Succession (Scotland) Act 1964 and indeed against anyone who would succeed to the heritage on intestacy. Other instances are dealt with more fully by Gretton[2].

1 *Gretton* pp 59–60.
2 *Gretton* ch 4.

Enforcement

9.28   As has been noted, inhibition has no effect on pre-existing deeds or debts[1], and if there are no post-inhibition deeds and debts, no preference is created. Even if there are deeds or debts which contravene the inhibition, as it does not confer any real rights, the inhibiting creditor must usually take other steps to enforce his right. These steps are reduction, adjudication, arrestment and sequestration or liquidation.

1 *Scottish Waggon Co v Hamilton's Tr* (1906) 13 SLT 779.

REDUCTION

9.29   In many instances, the voluntary deed in contravention of the inhibition will be a conveyance, but if the inhibited debtor purports to enter into missives, they are struck at also. That is the first effect of inhibition noted above. The second effect is that a security is also struck at and that means a standard security and probably also a floating charge. The third effect is that debts contracted after the inhibition are postponed to it in any ranking. Reduction is not usually needed until a post-inhibition debtor adjudicates[1].

The inhibiting creditor is entitled to reduce any deed or debt only to the extent to which he is prejudiced by it[2]. The deed or debt is null only vis-à-vis the inhibitor, but as regards others, the deed or debt is valid[3]. Thus if A inhibits B, and B, in contravention of the inhibition, dispones to C, A can reduce the disposition by A to B. However, the title in the Register of Sasines or Land Register stands in C's name and he remains the owner. The reduction, however, allows A, the inhibitor, to proceed as if B was still the owner and so he can adjudge the property.

Should the inhibiting creditor need to reduce a deed or debt, the extract decree should be recorded in the Register of Sasines or registered in the Land Register[4]. Reduction does not operate harshly against C because he is deemed to have knowledge of the inhibition. In most instances, the purchaser will refuse to settle the transaction unless the inhibition is discharged and the search cleared. The inhibitor is, however, in a strong position and can threaten to reduce the sale[5].

In practice, reduction is used only when the inhibition is in execution. According to Erskine, decree of reduction cannot be granted when inhibition is used on the dependence because at that stage, it has not been determined whether 'the inhibitor be truly creditor to the party inhibited'[6]. It is probably open to the inhibitor to raise an action of reduction but sist it until the outcome of the principal action[7].

The right to reduce something done in the teeth of an inhibition is linked with prescription of inhibitions. This matter will be dealt with under extinction.

1 Stair IV, 35, 21; Ersk *Inst* II, 11, 11.
2 Ersk *Inst* II, 11, 14.
3 W Ross *Lectures on the History and Practice of the Law of Conveyancing and Legal Diligence* (2nd edn, 1822) 1, 488.
4 Conveyancing (Scotland) Act 1924, s 46; Land Registration (Scotland) Act 1979, s 29(2).
5 'Inhibition' in *Encyclopaedia of the Laws of Scotland* vol 8, para 435.
6 Erskine *Inst* II, 11, 3.
7 *Gretton* p 96.

ADJUDICATION

9.30 If the inhibition does not have the desired effect, the only way by which the inhibitor can obtain a real right to the debtor's heritage is by adjudication. The right does not become real until after the expiry of the 'legal' of ten years during which time the debtor can redeem[1]. For that reason alone, adjudication is rare.

1 *Graham Stewart* p 654.

ARRESTMENT

9.31 Where the subjects have been sold, other than by the debtor, the funds are moveable and the inhibitor may attach these only by arrestment. This normally happens after a heritable creditor has exercised his power of sale under an *ex facie* absolute disposition, or a standard security. The law is somewhat confused by the existence of several conflicting decisions[1] but the position is probably still as stated by Bell[2]. '[T]he inhibitor has not . . . without adjudication or other diligence any active title on which he can demand payment.' An inhibitor must therefore adjudge before the sale, or arrest the proceeds afterwards.

1 *George M Allan Ltd v Waugh's Trs* 1966 SLT (Sh Ct) 17; *Bank of Scotland v Lord Advocate* 1977 SLT 24; *Abbey National Building Society v Shaik Aziz* 1981 SLT (Sh Ct) 29; cp *McGowan v Middlemas* 1977 SLT (Sh Ct) 41; *Ferguson & Forster v Dalbeattie Finance Co* 1981 SLT (Sh Ct) 53; *Halifax Building Society v Smith* 1985 SLT (Sh Ct) 25.
2 Bell *Comm* II, 139.

Bankruptcy and liquidation

9.32 Under this head we shall consider inhibitions in relation to sequestration, trust deeds and liquidation.

SEQUESTRATION

9.33 The Bankruptcy (Scotland) Act 1985, section 31(2) provides that the title of the trustee in sequestration is not challengeable on the ground that there is a pre-existing inhibition. The trustee can therefore sell the property without having to discharge the inhibition unless of course, he is obliged himself to provide a clear search. However, the inhibitor's rights are transferred to the proceeds of sale because section 31(2) says 'reserving any effect of such inhibition on ranking'.

How this is done in practice will be discussed under the heading of ranking. That was the law under the earlier legislation. The Bankruptcy (Scotland) Act 1985 has, however, altered the law in relation to inhibitions which take effect within sixty days of sequestration. They are nullified and the trustee is given the right to challenge anything done in contravention and also to receive payment for the discharge of the inhibition[1].

1 Bankruptcy (Scotland) Act 1985, s 37(2).

TRUST DEEDS

9.34 If the trust deed is voluntary, the inhibitor may challenge it but his right of challenge will be lost if he has acceded to the trust deed.

Under the 1985 Act, there may be a 'protected trust deed'[1] and all creditors are deemed to be acceding. It follows therefore that any inhibiting creditor cannot reduce the trust deed, but the inhibitor's rights are transferred to the proceeds of sale.

1 Bankruptcy (Scotland) Act 1985, Sch 5.

LIQUIDATION

9.35 A floating charge is a voluntary security and as it may affect the company's heritable property, it may be struck at by an inhibition. In theory, if the inhibition pre-dates the floating charge, the floating charge would be in violation of it, but a floating charge granted prior to the inhibition would not be affected by it. That is the position in relation to standard securities and there is no reason in principle for distinguishing the two as far as the effect of inhibition is concerned.

Ranking

9.36 The ranking which an inhibiting creditor is entitled to outwith bankruptcy and upon bankruptcy is dealt with in chapter 10.

ADJUDICATION

9.37 There are three main uses of the term 'adjudication', namely (a) adjudication in execution; (b) adjudication in security; and (c) adjudication in implement. The last is not a diligence for debt.

It should be noted that the 1987 Act has several important provisions dealing with adjudication for debt. In the first place, it is not competent to commence or execute an action of adjudication for debt if either a time to pay direction or a time to pay order is in force[1]. Secondly, the creditor in a liquid document of debt cannot bring an action for adjudication unless the debt has been constituted by a decree, or the debt is a *debitum fundi*, or the document of debt, or the protest of a bill of exchange, or promissory note has been registered for execution in the Books of Council and Session or those of the sheriff court[2]. The exception is an action for adjudication of a ground annual[3]. The object of this provision is to ensure that the debtor is not given the facility of time to pay.

1 1987 Act, ss 2, 9.
2 Ibid, s 101.
3 Conveyancing (Scotland) Act 1924, s 23(5).

Adjudication in execution

9.38 This is a Court of Session action directed against specific heritable property. If the pursuer in the action succeeds, he must record the extract decree in the Register of Sasines or register it in the Land Register, and on the expiry of ten years, 'the legal', the creditor may raise an action of declarator of expiry of the legal and the decree in that action converts the right in security into an unencumbered title to the subjects. While the creditor will normally have inhibited, inhibition is not a necessary precursor[1].

1 *Gretton* p 157.

PROCEDURE

9.39 The summons must identify the subjects by a description which can be recorded or registered. A full particular description or statutory description by reference is desirable, and in the case of a registered title, the reference number[1].

1 *Gretton* p 157.

BASIS

9.40 The basis for an adjudication will be either a decree for payment, or a document of debt. If the document of debt is not liquid, the creditor may adjudicate in security. If he has neither a decree nor a liquid debt, he would have to raise an action of constitution (to establish the indebtedness) and adjudication[1].

1 *Gretton* p 157.

NOTICE OF LITIGIOSITY

9.41 Once the summons has been signeted, the creditor may register a notice of summons of adjudication in the Register of Inhibitions and Adjudications[1]. The effect of that is to render the subjects litigious and so voluntary deeds will be reducible if they are to the prejudice of the creditor[2]. The mere raising of the action does not render the subjects litigious[3]. The notice must sufficiently identify the subjects and so a proper conveyancing description is desirable[4]. The notice requires to be intimated to other creditors, who may be conjoined as pursuers[5].

1 The form is to be found in the Titles to Land Consolidation (Scotland) Act 1868, Sch RR.

2 Conveyancing (Scotland) Act 1924, s 44(2).
3 Ibid, s 44.
4 Titles to Land Consolidation (Scotland) Act 1868, s 159.
5 *Graham Stewart* pp 610–611.

PROPERTY AFFECTED

9.42 With the exception of rights in heritage which are not assignable, all heritable property can be adjudged. This matter has been discussed in connection with inhibition[1]. However, property held in common requires special mention. In most instances, this will be the matrimonial home. However, the matrimonial home may be owned by one spouse with the potential for occupancy rights in the other or it may be owned jointly.

Where the title to a matrimonial home is in the name of both spouses, a creditor of either spouse may adjudge. Gretton adds the proviso that the proceedings are not conclusive and he refers to section 12 of the Matrimonial Homes (Family Protection) (Scotland) Act 1981[1]. With respect, the Act does not apply in the case of joint ownership[2], but it does apply where the title is in the name of one spouse only. Occupancy rights cannot be adjudged but a creditor of the entitled spouse can adjudge and can remove both spouses unless there was collusion between the entitled spouse and the creditor.

In all cases where the title stands in the name of more than one person, a creditor who adjudges a share cannot do anything against the wishes of the other proprietor(s) and, as a security holder, could not raise an action for division and sale. As Gretton rightly says he will have to wait until the expiry of the legal which makes his right one of ownership[3].

1 *Gretton* p 163.
2 Matrimonial Homes (Family Protection) (Scotland) Act 1981, s 12.
3 *Gretton* p 163.

DECREE AND COMPLETION OF TITLE

9.43 If the action succeeds, the pursuer can obtain an extract decree or an abbreviate of the decree. The extract must be recorded in the Register of Sasines or registered in the Land Register. The abbreviate is registered in the Register of Inhibitions and Adjudications. An abbreviate would be required where the subjects which have been adjudged are not held on a recordable or registerable title eg a lease of less than twenty years.

Where the subjects are so held and the debtor is infeft, the extract decree of adjudication once recorded or registered gives the creditor a heritable security, but the debtor remains the heritable proprietor. Where the debtor is not infeft, eg a person to whom the subjects have been transferred by a docket under the Succession (Scotland) Act 1964, completion of title in the Sasine Register is done by recording a notice of title, which should have as the links in title, the confirmation, the docket and the decree. In the case of a registered interest, it is not necessary to register a notice of title, but the links mentioned above would have to be produced to the Keeper[1].

1 *Gretton* pp 158–159; *Graham Stewart* pp 614–615.

EXPIRY OF THE LEGAL

9.44 If the decree of adjudication has existed for ten years without payment having been made, the creditor may raise an action in the Court of Session for declarator of expiry of the legal[1]. He then becomes the full owner, but should record his decree in the Register of Sasines or present it to the Keeper so that the title sheet can be altered. Even if the creditor does not raise an action of declarator, he will become the true owner by the operation of prescription[2]. Actions of declarator of the expiry of the legal are rare because the creditor will usually be paid on the sale of the property, perhaps by the debtor, more likely by the holder of a standard security, or on sequestration or liquidation.

1 *Graham Stewart* pp 654–664.
2 G L Gretton 'Prescription and the Foreclosure of Adjudications' 1983 JR 177.

COMPETITION

9.45 Competition is dealt with in chapter 10.

Adjudications rank in accordance with the dates of infeftment following upon decrees in favour of the adjudgers, but the Diligence Act 1661 provides that adjudications within a year and a day of each other rank *pari passu*. The problems of this provision are dealt with by Gretton[1].

1 *Gretton* p 166.

RECEIVERSHIP

9.46 The attachment of a floating charge is subject to 'effectually executed diligence'. While there is probably no doubt that an adjudication could be effectually executed diligence, it is not clear whether decree would be sufficient, or whether completion of title would be required[1].

1 See *Gretton* pp 166–167.

Adjudication on the dependence

9.47 This concept does not exist, but a creditor in a liquid document of debt can adjudge without constituting his debt.

Adjudication in security

9.48 This is available on documents of debt where the time of payment has not yet arrived. The creditor would have to aver special circumstances, such as that the debtor is *vergens ad inopiam*, but the category of 'special circumstances' for the purposes of inhibitions will apply[1].

1 See ch 4 above.

Adjudication in implement

9.49 This action is one raised by a purchaser of heritable property where the seller fails or refuses to grant a conveyance. The seller would normally raise an action for implement and failing implement he will resile and claim damages. Decree of specific implement, however, will not transfer the property to him and only if the seller refuses to execute the conveyance despite the decree, will the court order the clerk to execute the deed instead of the seller. Adjudication in implement operates as a conveyance to the purchaser and it is not subject to the general law on adjudication and in particular, the 'legal' does not apply[1].

1 *Graham Stewart* pp 667–669.

Reform

9.50 The Scottish Law Commission has produced a Consultative Memorandum on adjudication for debt[1].

1 Adjudications for Debt and Related Matters (Scot Law Com Discussion Paper no 78 (1988)) vols 1, 2.

REMOVINGS AND EJECTIONS

Introduction

9.51 The terminology in relation to these processes has been confused since the passing of the Sheriff Courts (Scotland) Act 1907. Each of the terms 'removing' and 'ejection' has two meanings and it is essential to set these out first in the hope that the confusion may be dispelled, or least reduced. The term 'removing' has a general meaning which covers any surrender of heritable property and it is usually applied to the surrender of a lease by a tenant. However, it has the more specific meaning of an action by which a landlord seeks to recover possession of property from a tenant. The tenant's right is terminated by a judicial process. By contrast, 'ejection' is used of an action whereby the owner or possessor of heritable property seeks to recover possession from someone who has no right or title, the typical example being a squatter. It is also used in another sense to denote the last stage in an action of removing (or its equivalent) whereby the court grants warrant for the eviction of the occupants by officers of court.

Removings

9.52 There are two broad types of removing. The first is called an 'extraordinary removing' where the tenant incurs an irritancy, and the other is removing at the expiry of a lease. Unless the context indicates otherwise, 'removing' in this chapter means the latter.

EXTRAORDINARY REMOVING

9.53 Irritancies in leases may be legal or conventional. The only legal irritancy is non-payment of rent for two years[1] or, in the case of an agricultural holding, for six months[2]. The irritancy may often be expressly provided in the lease, but if not it will be implied. A conventional irritancy is one expressed in the lease itself and can take a variety of forms. It may relate to non-payment of rent, or a failure on the part of the tenant to perform some other obligation in the lease, or it may arise in the event of the tenant's bankruptcy or on entering into a trust deed for creditors. A legal irritancy (and probably also a conventional one which is no more than an expression of the legal one) is purgeable at any time prior to decree being granted[3]. Under the Law Reform (Miscellaneous Provisions) (Scotland) Act 1985, a landlord's right to irritate a lease is restricted[4]. Where the breach consists of a failure to pay rent or some other sum, the landlord must give notice[5]. Where the breach arises for some other reason, he cannot terminate the lease unless a fair and reasonable landlord would do so[6].

Although extraordinary removings are usually dealt with in the context of leases, it is submitted that the process is applicable when a superior irritates a feu. In that context, the legal irritancy is a failure to pay feuduty for five years[7], but that is purgeable at any time prior to the recording of the extract decree in the Register of Sasines or the Land Register[8]. Where the irritancy is conventional, the court has a discretion whether or not to allow the irritancy to be purged[9].

1 Ersk *Inst* II, 6, 44.
2 Agricultural Holdings (Scotland) Act 1949, s 19.
3 Ersk *Inst* I, 5, 27.
4 Law Reform (Miscellaneous Provisions) (Scotland) Act 1985, ss 4–7.
5 Ibid, ss 4, 6, 7.
6 Ibid, ss 5, 6, 7.
7 Feu Duty Act 1597 as amended by Land Tenure Reform (Scotland) Act 1974, s 15.
8 Conveyancing Amendment (Scotland) Act 1938, s 6.
9 *Precision Relays Ltd v Beaton* 1980 SC 220, SLT 206.

ORDINARY REMOVINGS: HISTORY

Pre 1907

9.54 Prior to the Sheriff Courts (Scotland) Act 1907 ('the 1907 Act'), the processes of removing and ejection were distinct, but in relation to removing alone, there were five forms of procedure. These were: (i) an action under the Act of 1555 (c 12) which could be raised in either the Court of Session or the sheriff court against agricultural tenants; (ii) An action under the Act of Sederunt 14 December 1756, which was available where tenants had not undertaken to remove without warning; (iii) Letters of Horning might be obtained by the landlord under the Act of Sederunt 1756. These were available where tenants had undertaken to remove without warning; (iv) an action for declarator or irritancy and removing eg at the instance of a superior, or a landlord; (v) a common law action for removing, or declarator and removing, which might be brought in either the Court of Session or the sheriff court[1]. The action for ejection was not governed by any statutes and proceeded as an ordinary action to recover possession from someone who occupied *aut vi, aut clam, aut precario*[2].

1 J Rankine *The Law of Leases in Scotland* (3rd edn) p 50–558.
2 See para 9.87 below.

The 1907 Act

9.55 Under the 1907 Act, five other procedures were added without affecting any of the procedures mentioned above. As Lord Johnston said in *Campbell's Trs v O'Neill*[1], 'The result has been, I am persuaded, to throw the whole matter which was by no means devoid of confusion at any rate, into still greater confusion'[2].

1 1911 SC 188, 1910 2 SLT 392.
2 1911 SC 188 at 192, 1910 2 SLT 392 at 394.

PRESENT POSITION

The 1971 Act

9.56 The Sheriff Courts (Scotland) Act 1971 applies the summary cause procedure to actions for the recovery of heritable property, unless the action has an additional or alternative crave for payment of a sum exceeding £1,500[1]. This was thought to remove the difficulty of deciding between an action of removing and use of ejection. However, the 1971 Act has been interpreted as being restricted to those cases where the pursuer or his predecessor in title had been in possession of the subjects[2]. The Act does not apply to proceedings under Part II of the Conveyancing and Feudal Reform (Scotland) Act 1970 where it is expressly provided that proceedings are to be by summary application[3]. It does not apply to an action under section 9 of the Land Tenure Reform (Scotland) Act 1974 where there has been a contravention of the requirement that subjects under a long lease may not be used as a private dwellinghouse[4]. The lessor's action of removing is an ordinary action in either the Court of Session or the sheriff court[5]. Lastly, extraordinary removings following upon an irritancy may be raised in either the Court of Session or the sheriff court[6].

1 Sheriff Courts (Scotland) Act 1971, s 35.
2 *Prestwick Investment Trust v Jones* 1981 SLT (Sh Ct) 55.
3 Sheriff Courts (Scotland) Act 1971, s 29(2).
4 Conveyancing and Feudal Reform (Scotland) Act 1970, s 8.
5 Land Tenure Reform (Scotland) Act 1974, s 9.
6 Sheriff Courts (Scotland) Act 1907, s 5(4).

NOTICE TO QUIT

9.57 A notice to quit can be served for two reasons. One is to prevent the operation of tacit relocation and the other is as a preliminary to an action of removing.

FORM AND PERIOD OF NOTICE

Form

9.58 Because, as a general rule, any lease may be continued by tacit relocation[1], a lease can be brought to an end only by notice from the landlord to the tenant. In practice, formal notice should be given, despite some doubt about the degree of formality required in a notice served to prevent the lease from continuing by the operation of tacit relocation[2].

1 Stair II, 9, 3; Rankine *The Law of Leases in Scotland* p 598; G C H Paton and J G S Cameron *The Law of Landlord and Tenant in Scotland* pp 221–222.
2 *Paton and Cameron* p 225.

Notice by the landlord

9.59 The basic common law requirement is that the notice must be definite and unconditional[1]. However, the 1907 Act, the Agricultural Holdings (Scotland) Act 1949, the Succession (Scotland) Act 1964, the Housing (Scotland) Act 1987, the Rent (Scotland) Act 1984 and the Housing (Scotland) Act 1988 impose stricter requirements.

1 *Paton and Cameron* p 278.

THE SHERIFF COURTS (SCOTLAND) ACT 1907

9.60 Where a landlord raises an action of removal of a tenant where the subjects exceed two acres in extent, but the tenant does not have a lease, the notice to be given must be in accordance with Form L in Schedule 1 of the Act[1]. Where the landlord raises an action for removal under section 37[2] the form of notice must be in accordance with Form N.

1 Sheriff Courts (Scotland) Act 1907, s 36, Sch 1, r 104.
2 Applicable to leases with or without land not exceeding two acres and lands (without houses, mills, fishings and shootings) not exceeding two acres.

THE AGRICULTURAL HOLDINGS (SCOTLAND) ACT 1949: AGRICULTURAL HOLDINGS

9.61 Under the Agricultural Holdings (Scotland) Act 1949[1], the landlord must give written notice either in the form of notice laid down in section 6 of the Removal Terms (Scotland) Act 1886 or that prescribed by the Sheriff Courts (Scotland) Act 1907.

1 Agricultural Holdings (Scotland) Act 1949, s 27(1).

THE SUCCESSION (SCOTLAND) ACT 1964: NOTICE BY THE LANDLORD OR THE EXECUTOR

9.62 This is dealt with below at paragraph 9.81.

THE HOUSING (SCOTLAND) ACT 1987: PUBLIC SECTOR TENANCIES

9.63 The 1980 Act governs only tenancies of dwellinghouses in the public sector which are secure tenancies[1]. The landlord must serve a notice of intention to bring an action for recovery of possession[2]. The notice must state the ground upon which the action will be raised and the date after which it may be raised[3]. The form of notice is laid down by statutory instrument[4].

1 Housing (Scotland) Act 1987, s 44.
2 Ibid, s 47(2).
3 Ibid, s 47(3).
4 Secure Tenancies (Proceedings for Possession) (Scotland) Order 1980, SI 1980/1389.

THE RENT (SCOTLAND) ACT 1984: NON-PUBLIC SECTOR TENANCIES

9.64 This applies to the tenancy of dwellinghouses other than public sector tenancies. The notice must be in writing[1] and in a prescribed form[2].

1 Rent (Scotland) Act 1984, s 112.
2 Notices to Quit (Prescribed Information) (Protected Tenancies and Part VII Contracts) (Scotland) Regulations 1980, SI 1980/1667.

THE HOUSING (SCOTLAND) ACT 1988: ASSURED AND SHORT ASSURED TENANCIES

9.65 As from 2 January 1989, under the Housing (Scotland) Act 1988, new lets of houses from private landlords or housing associations will, as a general rule, be in the form of either an assured tenancy, or a short assured tenancy[1].

1 Housing (Scotland) Act 1988, ss 12–15 (assured tenancy), ss 32–35 (short assured tenancy); Housing (Scotland) Act 1988 (Commencement) Order 1988, SI 1988/2036.

Recovery of possession: (a) assured tenancy

9.66 The Act provides that the sheriff will not grant an order for possession of a house let under an assured tenancy unless the landlord can bring himself within one of the grounds specified in the Act[1]. These grounds are similar to those which currently exist under the 1984 Act and include where the tenant is in arrears with the rent, or persistently delays to pay the rent, where the tenant damages the property, or creates a nuisance, where the landlord wishes to redevelop the property, and where suitable alternative accommodation is available[2]. However, before applying to the court, the landlord must (1) serve a notice to quit and (2) serve a notice of intention to raise proceedings for recovery of possession (unless the sheriff feels that there are circumstances which permit the landlord to dispense with the latter)[3].

1 Housing (Scotland) Act 1988, s 18, Sch 5.
2 Ibid, Sch 5.
3 Ibid, s 19.

Recovery of possession: (b) short assured tenancy

9.67 On the expiry of the period of the short assured tenancy, the landlord is entitled to have possession restored to him but he must serve a notice to quit which gives the tenant two months' notice (or any longer period set out in the tenancy agreement) of his intention to resume possession[1].

1 Housing (Scotland) Act 1988, s 33.

Recovery of possession: (c) under the Housing (Scotland) Act 1987

9.68 The court shall make an order for possession if the landlord can establish any of the grounds in paragraphs 1–7 and 16 of Part I of Schedule 3, eg rent not paid, house being neglected and if any of the grounds set out in paragraphs 8–15 can be established then the court shall make an order if it appears to the court that other suitable accommodation will be available for the tenant[1].

1 Housing (Scotland) Act 1987, s 48; *City of Glasgow DC v Brown* 1988 SCLR 433.

NOTICE BY THE TENANT

9.69 The general requirement that notice should be definite and unconditional applies also to notice by the tenant[1]. However, although stricter statutory requirements have been imposed on landlords, these do not apply to tenants. Thus, when giving notice under the 1907 Act, the tenant may use Forms L or M but is not obliged to do so[2]. A special case exists under the Succession (Scotland) Act 1964[3].

1 *Paton and Cameron* p 278.
2 Sheriff Courts (Scotland) Act 1907, Sch 1, rr 104–105.
3 Succession (Scotland) Act 1964, s 16(3)(4). See para 9.82 below.

WRITTEN NOTICE

9.70   At common law, notice may be given orally[1] but there is doubt about the types of lease to which that rule applies[2]. By statute, the lease of a dwellinghouse can be terminated only by written notice[3], and that would be the prudent course to adopt in all leases. Because some statutes[4] specify the information which the notice must contain[5], it would be possible to have one document which gives both the notice and the requisite information[6].

1 *Gilchrist v Westren* (1890) 14 R 363.
2 *Paton and Cameron* p 272.
3 Rent (Scotland) Act 1984, s 112; Housing (Scotland) Act 1987, s 47; Housing (Scotland) Act 1988, ss 19, 33.
4 Eg Agricultural Holdings (Scotland) Act 1949, Rent (Scotland) Act 1984, Housing (Scotland) Act 1988.
5 Eg Agricultural (Miscellaneous Provisions) Act 1968, s 11(1).
6 For the problems which can arise from separate documents, see *Barns Graham v Lamont* 1971 SC 170, SLT 341.

NOTICE IN AGRICULTURAL HOLDINGS

9.71   Although notice must be in writing, the 1949 Act does not lay down the form which the notice must take. However, there are some specialities about agricultural holdings: (a) different dates may apply to different parts of the holding[1]; (b) the landlord may serve a notice to quit in respect of a part[2]; and (c) the notice must contain certain things if the landlord wishes to avoid or reduce his liability for compensation[3].

1 *Milne v Earl of Seafield* 1981 SLT (Sh Ct) 37.
2 Agricultural Holdings (Scotland) Act 1949, s 32.
3 Ibid, s 6(1).

PERIOD OF NOTICE

9.72   What period of notice is required depends in part on the subjects and in part on the period of the lease. It is convenient to categorise subjects into non-agricultural and agricultural.

Non-agricultural

9.73   (i) A lease of lands of more than two acres for a duration of more than three years, the notice is not less than one year and not more than two years[1].
(ii) A lease of lands of more than two acres for a duration of less than three years or held from year to year by the operation of tacit relocation, the notice is not less than six months[2].

(iii) Houses let with or without land attached not exceeding two acres let for one year or more, the notice is not less than forty days[3].

(iv) Land not exceeding two acres with houses and mills, fishing, shootings and all other heritable subjects except those exceeding two acres let for one year or more, the notice is not less than forty days[4].

(v) Houses or other heritable subjects let for less than one year but more than six months, the notice, in the absence of express stipulation, is forty days[5].

(vi) Houses or other heritable subjects let for less than four months, the notice is a minimum of twenty-eight days[5].

(vii) Under the Rent (Scotland) Act 1984, a minimum of twenty-eight days is required[6] but special rules apply to a furnished or service letting (Part VII Contracts)[7].

(viii) Under the Housing (Scotland) Act 1987, a minimum of four weeks' notice is required[8].

(ix) Under the Housing (Scotland) Act 1988, at least twenty-eight days' notice is required[9].

There is some doubt in those cases under the 1907 Act whether the provisions of the Act apply generally or only where some court process is involved[10], and whether the statutory provisions supplant any conventional provision or vice versa[11].

The Removal Terms (Scotland) Act 1886 contains a curious provision that removal at the term of Whitsunday and Martinmas means noon on 28 May and 28 November respectively, but that forty days' notice must be given prior to 15 May and 11 November respectively[12].

In two types of lease mentioned in the 1907 Act no notice is required[13]. These are rarely, if ever, used.

1 OCR 103.
2 OCR 103.
3 OCR 103.
4 Sheriff Courts (Scotland) Act 1907, s 37, OCR 103.
5 Sheriff Courts (Scotland) Act 1907, s 38.
6 Rent (Scotland) Act 1984, s 112; *Hamilton District Council v Maguire* 1983 SLT (Sh Ct) 76.
7 Rent (Scotland) Act 1984, ss 71–76.
8 Housing (Scotland) Act 1987, s 47.
9 Housing (Scotland) Act 1988, ss 18–19.
10 *Craighall Cast Stone Co v Wood* 1931 SC 66, SLT 67 (restricted to court proceedings); cp *Duguid v Muirhead* 1926 SC 1078 at 1082–1083 per Lord Constable.
11 *Duguid v Muirhead* 1926 SC 1078 at 1082–1083 per Lord Constable; cp *Viscountess Cowdray v Ferries* 1918 SC 210 at 219, 1918 1 SLT 152 at 154, per Lord Johnston.
12 Removal Terms (Scotland) Act 1886, s 4.
13 Sheriff Courts (Scotland) Act 1907, ss 34, 35; see para 9.85 below.

Agricultural holdings

9.74 The Agricultural Holdings (Scotland) Act 1949 provides that to terminate a lease, either party must give not less than one year and not more than two years' notice in writing[1]. It also provides that 'unless the context otherwise provides' in a lease entered into after 1 November 1948, 'Whitsunday' means 28 May and 'Martinmas' means 28 November[1]. That provision applies only to references to these terms in the Act and a reference in a lease to 'Whitsunday' still means 15 May and, to 'Martinmas', 11 November[2]. There is therefore some doubt whether, if 'Whitsunday' and 'Martinmas' are not defined in the lease, a notice to quit at 'Whitsunday' means 15 or 28 May and at 'Martinmas' means 11 or 28 November[3].

1 Agricultural Holdings (Scotland) Act 1949, s 93(1).
2 B Gill *The Law of Agricultural Holdings in Scotland* para 179.
3 *Stirrat v Whyte* 1967 SC 205, 1968 SLT 150; cp *Austin v Gibson* 1974 SLT (Land Ct) 12.

CHALLENGE OF NOTICE

9.75 As a general rule, if a landlord in the exercise of his statutory or contractual rights serves a notice to quit, it is not open to the tenant to argue that the landlord should have exercised his discretion and not served the notice[1]. However, under the Agricultural Holdings (Scotland) Act, when a notice is served on the tenant, he may within one month serve a counter notice which has the effect of requiring the landlord to obtain the consent of the Land Court except in special circumstances[2].

1 *City of Aberdeen District Council v Christie* 1983 SLT (Sh Ct) 57.
2 Agricultural Holdings (Scotland) Act 1949, s 25.

SERVICE OF NOTICE

9.76 The method of service of notice varies with the type of subjects.

Verbal leases of urban subjects (other than houses) for not more than a year

9.77 Notice in these circumstances may be given verbally[1].

1 J Rankine *The Law of Leases in Scotland* p 574.

Other urban subjects

9.78 The 1907 Act provides that any removal notices under sections 34–38 may be served by an officer of court or by registered letter[1]. The Removal Terms (Scotland) Act 1886 permits service by registered letter for all tenancies of houses which are not being let with agricultural land for agricultural purposes[2], and recorded delivery service is also competent[3]. However, it is not clear whether these provisions which apply to notice by the landlord apply equally to notice by the tenant. Although the 1907 Act uses the term 'may', which suggests that the language is permissive, the courts have taken the view that the only competent methods of service are those set out in rule 106[4]. A tenant could therefore claim that the notice had not been properly served even although he admitted receiving it.

1 OCR 106.
2 Removal Terms (Scotland) Act 1886, s 6.
3 Recorded Delivery Service Act 1962.
4 *Department of Agriculture v Goodfellow* 1931 SC 556, SLT 338 (the rule was then 113).

Agricultural holdings

9.79 The 1949 Act provides that where notice has to be given to a landlord, it must be delivered to him, or left at his proper address, or be sent to him by registered letter[1]. When the landlord is giving notice, he must use the methods prescribed by the 1886 Act or the 1907 Act[2].

1 Agricultural Holdings (Scotland) Act 1949, s 90(1).
2 Ibid, s 24(4).

Part owners

9.80 A part owner who is one of several landlords cannot, in the absence of a provision in the lease, give notice to terminate the lease[1] nor can such a person bring an action of removal[2]. However, one joint tenant can give notice of termination and hence exclude tacit relocation[3].

1 *Gates v Blair* 1923 SC 430, SLT 257.
2 *Aberdeen Station Committee v N B Railway Co* (1890) 17 R 975.
3 *Smith v Grayton Estates* 1960 SC 349, SLT 38.

The effect of the death of one of the parties

9.81 *Death of the landlord.* The problems which arise relate to serving of a notice to quit on the tenant and the service of such a notice by the tenant. In each case it is probably correct to say that the executor, albeit unconfirmed, steps into the landlord's shoes[1].

1 *Garvie's Trs v Garvie's Tutors* 1975 SLT 94.

9.82 *Death of the tenant.* Unless a lease expressly states that it will come to an end on the tenant's death, the lease will vest in the executor[1] who can transfer the tenant's interest to a person to whom it has been bequeathed or to the person entitled to succeed to it on intestacy[1]. That power must be exercised within one year of the tenant's death, except that in an agricultural tenancy it must be exercised within that period or within one year of the outcome of a dispute about the validity of a bequest[2]. The subsequent issue of confirmation in favour of the executor will validate acts done prior to confirmation[3]. If the power is not exercised within the period, the landlord may give notice terminating the lease. The period of notice is six months or any shorter period presented by statute, or in an agricultural tenancy, not less than one year and not more than two[4].

If there is no executor or one has not been appointed on time, the lease probably terminates without any need for notice[5].

1 Succession (Scotland) Act 1964, s 16(2).
2 Ibid, s 16(3).
3 *Garvie's Trs v Garvie's Tutors* 1975 SLT 94.
4 Succession (Scotland) Act 1964, s 16(4).
5 *Lord Rotherwick's Trs v Hope* 1975 SLT 187; *Coats v Logan* 1985 SLT 221.

TITLE TO SUE

9.83 To establish a title to sue, the pursuer must be infeft, at the latest, by the time at which decree is granted[1]. Thus, it has been held that a purchaser under missives cannot competently give a tenant notice to quit[2], and if the seller has given notice, but the purchaser wishes to raise an action, he must obtain an assignation from the seller of the notice[3]. That applies equally where the landlord serves a notice of irritancy and then sells. The purchaser must have the original notice assigned to him[4]. Those who are in the position of trustee may raise such actions[5]. The problems arising in some other cases are dealt with more fully elsewhere[6], but the position of heritable creditors is dealt with later in the chapter.

1 *Walker v Hendry* 1925 SC 855, SLT 592.
2 *Alexander Black & Sons v Paterson* 1968 SLT (Sh Ct) 64.

3 *Grant v Bannerman* (1920) 36 Sh Ct Rep 59.
4 *Life Association of Scotland v Black's Leisure Group plc* 1988 SCLR 172 upheld by Second Division on 28 February 1989 (1989 GWD 10–444).
5 Trusts (Scotland) Act 1921, ss 2, (4)(1)(c) as amended.
6 A G M Duncan *Research Paper on Actions of Ejection and Removing* (Scot Law Com (1984)).

TITLE TO DEFEND

9.84 There is some doubt about whether service of a notice to quit on a party infers a right or title to defend an action. That has largely been avoided by the introduction of the summary cause for recovery of possession of heritable property which applies to former tenants and to unauthorised occupants.

A difficulty which still remains is where the identity of the occupiers is unknown eg sub-tenants, or squatters.

While the Summary Cause Rules provide for the situation in which the address of the defender is unknown[1], they do not provide for the situation in which his identity is unknown. That creates problems where there are sub-tenants whose identity is not known to the landlord. A similar problem arises in trying to eject squatters whose identity is not known, eg at a sit-in at a factory. Under the Rent (Scotland) Act 1984, a tenant is obliged to give certain information about a sub-tenancy to the landlord[2], but in other cases, there is no obligation.

1 SCR 6.
2 Rent (Scotland) Act 1984, s 100.

DECREE AND ENFORCEMENT

9.85 While the extract decree in a summary cause normally requires to be followed by a charge of fourteen days[1], no days of charge are required on a decree for the recovery of possession[2]. A decree in an ordinary action of removing is followed by a charge of forty-eight hours[3], and summary diligence for the removal of a tenant under sections 34 and 35 of the 1907 Act where the lease or a letter consenting to remove are the equivalent of a decree of removing, requires a charge of forty-eight hours[4]. Summary removings under section 38 of the 1907 Act do not require any days of charge[5]. It appears still to be the law that a Court of Session decree for the recovery of possession is not a warrant for diligence[6]. After the execution and registration of the necessary charge, letters of ejection from the signet have to be obtained and these are directed to the sheriff of the district in which the property is located[7]. Where a charge is required, it cannot be served by post[8]. Notwithstanding what has just been said, the practice is to give notice in all cases.

1 SCR 91.
2 SCR, Form U3.
3 Sheriff Courts (Scotland) Extracts Act 1892, s 2.
4 Because the documents are the equivalent of decrees of removing.
5 1907 Act, Form L.
6 'Ejection' in *Encyclopaedia of the Laws of Scotland* vol 6, para 266.
7 *Encyclopaedia of Scottish Legal Styles* vol 4, p 253.
8 Section 2(1)(b) of Execution of Diligence (Scotland) Act 1926 applies only to decrees for payment of money.

The action of ejection

9.86   The remedy of ejection as a form of action must be distinguished from the action of removing and the ancillary warrant of ejection attached to the decree in an action of removing.

GROUNDS

9.87   The remedy is competent where a possessor of heritable property does not have, and never has had, either right or title to possess[1], in other words, the possession is *aut vi, aut clam, aut precario*, violent, fraudulent or precarious[2]. The best example is that of a squatter. The action is not incompetent merely because a point of law is in issue[3]. If a person had a title or right to possess and it has come to an end, the appropriate remedy is removing[4]. Thus, someone who fails to pay the purchase price of heritable property can be dispossessed only by an action of removing[5]. There is some authority for the view that a possessor who has no title and hence someone against whom an action of ejection could be raised, can be summarily ejected 'by force' and 'without legal process'. These brave words came from Lord Traynor in *Dunbar's Trs v Bruce*[6], but it is not clear whether his Lordship had had any practical experience.

1 *Dunbar's Trs v Bruce* (1900) 3 F 137, 8 SLT 276.
2 *Cairns v Innes* 1942 SC 164, SLT 129, per Lord President Normand.
3 *Cairns v Innes* 1942 SC 164, SLT 129.
4 *Lowe v Gardiner* 1921 SC 211, 1 SLT 44.
5 *Cook v Wylie* 1963 SLT (Sh Ct) 29.
6 *Dunbar's Trs v Bruce* (1900) 3 F 137, 8 SLT 276.

PURSUERS

9.88   The action may be raised by an owner, including a *pro indiviso* proprietor[1] but one owner in common can probably not bring an action against the other, the correct course being to raise an action for division and sale[2], after which an occupant would have to have an action of removing or perhaps ejection raised against him. In principle, an action or ejection would be available to a bona fide possessor whose right is challenged by someone with no right to possess. By statute, if a proprietor is in personal possession of security subjects and is in default in that he has failed to make punctual payment of interest, or after being requested to repay the capital fails to do so, he is deemed to be an occupant without a title and the creditor may raise an action of ejection[3].

1 *Warrand v Watson* (1905) 8 F 253, 13 SLT 727.
2 *Price v Watson* 1951 SC 359, SLT 266.
3 Heritable Securities (Scotland) Act 1894, s 5.

DEFENDERS

9.89   The following are examples of those who have been held to possess without right, or title, namely: (a) the sequestrated owner of heritage[1], but that is now subject to the protection in respect of the matrimonial home conferred by the Bankruptcy (Scotland) Act 1985[2]; (b) a squatter[3]; (c) a debtor who has failed to pay interest or capital under a standard security[4]; (d) the executor of a liferenter[5]; and (e) an employee who has a service tenancy and whose contract of employment has come to an end[6].

A sub-tenant in possession as of right cannot be ejected on termination of the main tenancy if he has not received notice[7]. Furthermore, the Rent (Scotland) Act 1984 provides for a sub-tenant who remains, to become the tenant[8], and the statutory provisions on interposed leases provide that where the interposed lease comes to an end, the original relationship of landlord and tenant is re-established[9].

1 *White v Stevenson* 1956 SC 84, SLT 194.
2 Bankruptcy (Scotland) Act 1985, ss 40–41.
3 *Hutchison v Alexander* (1904) 6 F 532, 11 SLT 729; *Plessey Co plc v Wilson* 1983 SLT 139.
4 Heritable Securities (Scotland) Act 1894, s 5.
5 *Gordon v Michie's Reps* (1794) M 13853.
6 *Sinclair v Tod* 1907 SC 1038, 15 SLT 113.
7 *Robb v Brearton* (1895) 22 R 885, 3 SLT 81; cp *South Western Farmers Ltd v Gray* 1950 SLT (Sh Ct) 10.
8 Rent (Scotland) Act 1984, s 19.
9 Land Tenure Reform (Scotland) Act 1974, s 17.

CAUTION FOR VIOLENT PROFITS

9.90 In the most recent case, it has been held that it is incompetent to seek caution from the defender for violent profits[1], but consignation of arrears of rent may be required[2].

1 *Mackays v James Dean & Son Ltd* 1977 SLT (Sh Ct) 10.
2 *Simpson v Goswani* 1976 SLT (Sh Ct) 94.

EXECUTION OF THE DECREE

9.91 The defender may be ejected without notice[1], but the sheriff may require notice to be given.

1 *Reid v Anderson* (1920) 36 Sh Ct Rep 11.

HERITABLE CREDITORS UNDER THE 1970 ACT

9.92 Under the Conveyancing and Feudal Reform (Scotland) Act 1970, there are a number of situations in which the debtor will be in default and which will permit the heritable creditor to exercise his power of sale[1]. There are two situations in which he may exercise his power without reference to the court and these are (a) where the debtor has failed to comply with a calling-up notice[2] and (b) where a notice of default has been served and either not objected to, or upheld despite the objection or varied, but the debtor has failed to comply with the notice[3]. In one other case, the creditor must apply to the court for the power to sell ie where the proprietor is insolvent[4]. The Act also provides that where there is default within the meaning of standard condition 9(1)(b) or 9(1)(c), the creditor may apply to the court for the exercise of any of the powers in standard condition 10 which includes the most important remedy ie sale of the security subjects. There is a considerable degree of uncertainty about how to remove the debtor who is still in occupation. The 1970 Act provides that any application to the court (ie the sheriff court) for the exercise of these remedies must be by summary application[5]. Some sheriffs have taken the view that it is incompetent to seek a warrant for ejection of the debtor in such a summary application and that, if ejection is required, there must be a separate application in the form of an ordinary action. Because of the importance of this issue, the various decisions are listed below with a summary of their findings, but until the matter is settled by a higher court, heritable creditors would be advised not to apply to the court for the exercise of the power of sale and, if possible to rely on the terms of section 5 of the 1894 Act which would permit them to raise an action of ejection where the debtor has failed to pay interest or capital which will be the most common reason for wishing to exercise the power of sale. The decisions referred to above are as follows: (i) *Prestwick Investment Trust v Jones*[6] (Sheriff Grant, Ayr) – ejection may proceed as a summary application (the action was brought under the 1894 Act) (ii) *Provincial Building Society v Menzies*[7] (Sheriff Principal Taylor) – remedies under the Act could be sought as an ordinary action and ejection could be part of that; (iii) *National and Provincial Building Society v Riddell*[8] (Sheriff Kelbie, Dumbarton) – ejection is a normal and necessary part of an application for power of sale under the Act; (iv) *Mountstar Metal Corporation v Cameron*[9] (Sheriff Principal Bell, Aberdeen) – ejection could not be part of summary application under the Act, but remedies under the Act could be sought in ordinary action and ejection could be part of that; (v) *Bradford & Bingley Building Society v Roddy*[10] (Sheriff Risk, Aberdeen) – applied Mountstar; (vi) *Bradford & Bingley Building Society v Walker*[11] (Sheriff Kelbie, Aberdeen) – followed *Mountstar* (reluctantly) but expressed the opinion that remedies under the Act could not be sought in an ordinary action. In this respect, he did not think himself bound by the decision in *Mountstar*; (vii) *Cedar Holdings Ltd v Mahmood Iyyaz*[12] (Sheriff Principal Caplan, Paisley) – crave for ejection could be combined with summary application under the Act; (viii) *Hill Samuel & Co Ltd v Haas*[13] (Sheriff Principal Caplan, Paisley) – where the heritable creditor already has power of sale by virtue of default, an application to dispossess the debtor is not an application under the 1970 Act and hence the debtor may be dispossessed by the ordinary action of ejection; (ix) *Clydesdale Bank Plc v Finlay & Co*[14] (Sheriff Principal O'Brien, Edinburgh) – applications under the Act must be summary, but warrant to eject cannot be part of that.

1 Conveyancing and Feudal Reform (Scotland) Act 1970, ss 20(1), 23(2), 24(1).
2 Ibid, s 20(1).
3 Ibid, s 23(2).
4 Ibid, s 24(1).
5 Ibid, s 29(1).
6 1981 SLT (Sh Ct) 55.
7 1984 SLT (Sh Ct) 84.
8 1986 SLT (Sh Ct) 6.
9 1987 SLT (Sh Ct) 107. There were two decisions in this case but only the first has been reported. The two parts are discussed in *Bradford & Bingley Building Society v Walker* 1988 SLT (Sh Ct) 33.
10 1987 SLT (Sh Ct) 109.
11 1988 SLT (Sh Ct) 33.
12 1989 SLT (Sh Ct) 71.
13 1989 SLT (Sh Ct) 68.
14 1989 SLT (Sh Ct) 77.

Execution of diligence following decree of removing or ejection

9.93 The diligence must be carried out without undue delay[1], but it cannot be done at night[2]. The practice is for officers of court to give warning of their intention to execute the decree[3]. To this end, the officer must ensure that the subjects are cleared and the practice is to secure them against re-entry and if necessary to have new locks fitted. The royal initials are chalked on the outside of doors, together with the date of ejection and the officer's initials[4]. Although the police are not competent to execute diligence[5], their assistance may be sought if the officer of court anticipates that a crime may be committed while he is attempting to enforce the decree.

1 *Taylor v Earl of Moray* (1892) 19 R 399 (three weeks were held not to be undue delay).
2 *Macgregor v Earl of Strathallan* (1864) 2 M 339.
3 G Maher *A Textbook of Diligence* p 134.
4 A G M Duncan *Research Paper on Actions of Ejection and Removing* (Scot Law Com (1984)), para 8.4.
5 *Caldwell v Caldwell* 1983 SC 137, SLT 610.

Law reform

9.94 The Scottish Law Commission have published a Report on Scottish Term and Quarter Days[1] and a Report on the Recovery of Possession of Heritable Property[2]. The implementation of the recommendations in these documents will make significant changes to the foregoing.

1 Report on Scottish Term and Quarter Days (Scot Law Com no 108 (1987))
2 Recovery of Possession of Heritable Property (Scot Law Com no 118) (1989)).

CHAPTER 10

COMPETITION OF DILIGENCES

INTRODUCTION

10.01 Diligences compete both within and outwith the bankruptcy of the debtor. In general, where the debtor is not bankrupt, preference is given to the diligence done earlier in time over one done later in time. However, where the debtor is bankrupt, there is a system for equalising diligences.

OUTWITH BANKRUPTCY

10.02 Although in some contexts diligences may be equalised outwith bankruptcy processes, the present section will consider issues of competition other than equalisation.

Issues of preferences in respect of tax claims by the Inland Revenue are considered elsewhere[1].

It is also important to bear in mind the possible existence of charging orders which can be made under various statutes and may affect the debtor's heritable property even in bankruptcy[2].

1 See ch 8 above.
2 Eg Buildings (Scotland) Act 1959, s 16; Housing (Scotland) Act 1987, Sch 9; Water (Scotland) Act 1980, s 65; Civil Legal Aid (Scotland) Regulations 1987, SI 1987/381, reg 40. Much will depend on the terms of the particular statute: see *Sowman v City of Glasgow District Council*, 1984 SC 91, 1985 SLT 65.

Arrestments

ARRESTMENTS INTER SE

10.03 Priority among arrestments, whether they are arrestments on the dependence, or in execution, is determined by the date of service of the arrestment, and not by the date of decree in any action of furthcoming[1]. Arrestments served on the same day will rank *pari passu*[2], unless the execution of service shows the time at which service took place, in which event the earlier will be preferred or the one showing the time will be preferred[3]. The preference formerly given to Crown arrestments[4] has been abolished[5]. However, the possible existence of a time to pay decree or order has to be borne in mind.

1 *Wallace v Scot* (1583) M 807.
2 *Sutie v Ross* (1705) M 816.
3 *Hertz v Itzig* (1865) 3 M 813.
4 Exchequer Court (Scotland) Act 1856, ss 30, 42.
5 1987 Act, s 74.

ARRESTMENTS AND OTHER DILIGENCE AND RIGHTS

Poinding

10.04 Where an arrestment is in competition with a poinding, priority is determined by whichever is the earlier of the date of the decree of furthcoming, or the date of completion of the poinding, ie when the report of the sale is lodged with the clerk of the court[1].

1 Ersk *Inst* III, 6, 21; J Graham Stewart *The Law of Diligence* p 365. There is some divergence in the authorities as to the date when the poinding is complete. Another view is that it is complete when the poinding has been done. (See *New Glenduffhill Coal Co Ltd v Mair & Co* (1882) 10 R 372; cp 1987 Act, s 21(7).)

Assignations

10.05 Priority is determined by the date of the arrestment compared with the date of intimation of the assignation[1]. If the arrestment is effected prior to the date of intimation, it will be preferred – otherwise, the assignation will be preferred[2]. In *Executive Council for the City of Glasgow v T Sutherland Henderson Ltd*[3], a doctor granted a mandate to the pursuers to pay to the defenders all fees due to him. An attempt was subsequently made to arrest sums due to the doctor in the hands of the pursuers. It was held that, upon intimation, the mandate was an effectual assignation. The intimation of a transfer of shares in a limited company will prevail over a subsequent arrestment even although the transfer has not yet been registered[4].

In the common situation where a seller of heritable property has obtained overdraft facilities to purchase another property and grants a mandate to his solicitor to pay the free proceeds of sale to the bank and that is intimated to the bank, any subsequent arrestment in the hands of the solicitor will not be effectual.

1 *Graham Stewart* p 141.
2 Stair III, 1, 43.
3 1955 SLT (Sh Ct) 33.
4 *National Bank of Scotland Glasgow Nominees Ltd v Adamson* 1932 SLT 492.

Heritable creditor's right to rents

10.06 Under a standard security, the creditor is entitled in certain circumstances to enter into possession and uplift the rents. That is merely a personal right and it does not prevent the rents being attached by diligence. If the heritable creditor's infeftment is prior to the arrestment, it is thought, on the analogy of an action of maills and duties, that the arrester will be preferred if he has obtained a decree of furthcoming prior to the heritable creditor being entitled to enter into possession[1]. The heritable creditor will be entitled to enter into possession if there has been a failure to comply with a calling-up notice[2], or a failure to comply with any other requirement arising out of the security and the court has granted warrant to the heritable creditor to enter into possession, or where the proprietor is insolvent and the court has granted warrant[3].

1 *Graham Stewart* pp 163–165.
2 Conveyancing and Feudal Reform (Scotland) Act 1970, s 20(1).
3 Ibid, s 24(1).

Landlord's hypothec

10.07 A landlord's hypothec is preferable to the diligence of ordinary creditors[1] and he retains his preference even although he does not sell the goods over which his right exists[2].

1 *Graham Stewart* p 483.
2 *Young v Welsh* (1833) 12 S 233.

Earnings arrestments

10.08 An earnings arrestment comes into force on the date of execution[1] which is the date when the appropriate schedule is served. When the employer receives two or more earnings arrestment schedules on the same day and he knows the respective times of receipt, the earlier has preference[2]. If he does not know the times, he can choose which he will implement[3]. The only way in which this can be avoided is for the officer of court to mark the date and time on the execution of any subsequent postal service on the employer. When an earnings arrestment is in force, no other earnings arrestment can be[4], but a conjoined arrestment order is competent[5].

1 1987 Act, s 47(2).
2 Ibid, s 59(3)(a).
3 Ibid, s 59(3)(b).
4 Ibid, s 59(1).
5 Ibid, s 60.

Current maintenance arrestment

10.09 A current maintenance arrestment comes into force when it is served[1] and competition between maintenance arrestments is determined in the same way as priority between earnings arrestments[2]. Again, not more than one maintenance arrestment is competent[3], but there may be a conjoined arrestment order[4]. When an earnings arrestment and a current maintenance arrestment are in force, the employer operates the earnings arrestment first[5].

1 1987 Act, s 51(2).
2 Ibid, s 59(3).
3 Ibid, s 59(2).
4 Ibid, s 60.
5 Ibid, s 58(2); for details, see ch 6 above.

Conjoined arrestment order

10.10 The general rule that an employer may not operate more than one earnings arrestment or more than one current maintenance arrestment, is modified by the availability of a conjoined arrestment order. This is competent where an employer is operating an earnings arrestment, or a current maintenance arrestment, or both, and there is another creditor who, but for these arrestments, would be entitled to recover his debt by an arrestment[1]. The details are contained in chapter 6.

1 1987 Act, s 60.

Poindings

10.11 As Graham Stewart observes, the effect of poindings in a competition is governed by the same rules as apply to arrestments[1].

1 *Graham Stewart* p 363.

WITH ANOTHER POINDING

10.12 The first poinding which is followed by a sale is preferred[1].

1 *Graham Stewart* p 366.

WITH AN ARRESTMENT

10.13 Priority is determined by comparing the date of furthcoming with the date of the report of the sale, and the earlier will be preferred. Where neither a furthcoming nor a sale has followed, the respective dates of the poinding and the arrestment determine priority[1].

1 *Graham Stewart* pp 159, 366. The date of the poinding is established in accordance with the 1987 Act, s 21(7).

WITH AN ASSIGNATION

10.14 The assignation must be completed by intimation to make it complete, and that date has to be compared with the date of execution of the poinding. The earlier of the two will be preferred[1].

1 *Graham Stewart* p 366.

WITH A SALE

10.15 If the property in the goods passes to the purchaser before the execution of the poinding, the purchaser will be preferred[1]. If the sale takes place after that date, but the goods have been delivered to a bona fide purchaser, the purchaser will be preferred[2]. Graham Stewart expresses the view that where the price has been paid but the goods have not been delivered, the goods may be poinded[3]. Under the Sale of Goods Act 1979 the property in the goods may have passed to the buyer and accordingly would not be the property of the seller and hence would not be available for poinding in respect of a debt due to him. If the purchaser becomes aware of the poinding, he should not pay the purchase price to the debtor (seller), but hold it for the poinding creditor[4]. Any unauthorised removal of goods by a person who knows about the poinding is punishable under the 1987 Act[5].

1 *Turner v Mitchell & Rae* (1884) Guthrie's Sh Ct Cas (Second Series) 152.
2 *Graham Stewart* p 366.
3 *Graham Stewart* pp 127, 366.
4 *Turner v Mitchell and Rae* (1884) Guthrie's St Ct Cas (Second Series) 152.
5 1987 Act, s 28.

WITH A POINDING OF THE GROUND

10.16 The position of a heritable creditor who poinds the ground is determined not only by his infeftment, but also by the service of the action of poinding of the ground[1]. If the infeftment precedes the sale in the ordinary poinding, the poinder of the ground will be preferred if service of his action is before the sale of the other poinder[2]. If the date of the infeftment is after the date of the poinding, Graham Stewart expresses the opinion that the preference is to be determined by the dates of the respective poindings, since the poinder of the ground has no preference arising from his infeftment[2].

1 *Tullis v Whyte* 18 June 1817 FC.
2 *Graham Stewart* p 366.

WITH A LANDLORD'S HYPOTHEC FOR RENT

10.17 A landlord who has a hypothec is preferred to the diligence of ordinary creditors[1].

1 *Graham Stewart* p 483.

Inhibitions

WITH ANOTHER INHIBITION

10.18 Priority is determined according to dates of decrees in actions of adjudication following upon the inhibitions[1]. If the inhibiting creditors adjudge within a year and a day of each other, the adjudications rank *pari passu*[2].

1 *Graham Stewart* p 561.
2 Diligence Act 1661; Adjudications Act 1672.

WITH OTHER CREDITORS

10.19 The ranking which an inhibiting creditor receives where there are other creditors, is governed by the principles of ranking set out in Bell's Commentaries[1]. These Canons of Ranking, as he called them, were approved by the First Division in *Baird and Brown v Stirrat's Tr*[2]. According to these Canons, the position of the inhibitor is as follows: Those whose debts were contracted *prior* to the inhibition rank as if the inhibition did not exist, the inhibiting creditor ranks as if the post-inhibition debts do not exist. The most satisfactory way of explaining this is to assume that there are two rounds of ranking and these are best illustrated by an example which appears in George Gretton's work on Inhibitions in which he gives fifteen examples of ranking which should be looked at for the detail[3].

EXAMPLE

The debtor has no moveable estate, but has heritable property worth £24,000.

Creditor A's debt is £24,000 (pre-inhibition)
Creditor B's debt is £12,000 (the inhibiting creditor)
Creditor C's debt is £12,000 (post-inhibition)

Total   £48,000

ROUND 1		ROUND 2	
Creditor A	£12,000	Creditor A	£12,000
Creditor B	£ 6,000	Creditor B	£ 8,000
Creditor C	£ 6,000	Creditor C	£ 4,000
Total	£24,000	Total	£24,000

The explanation for the ranking is that in Round 1 the parties are ranked equally because the assumption is made that the inhibition does not exist. Therefore A gets £12,000, B gets £6,000 and C gets £6,000. In Round 2, however, the inhibiting creditor is entitled to assume that the post-inhibition creditor does not exist. The inhibiting creditor is therefore entitled to recover from the post-inhibition creditor whatever amount would be necessary to put the inhibitor in the position he would have been if the post-inhibition creditor had not existed. If creditor C had not existed, A would have taken £16,000 and B would have taken £8,000. B therefore takes £8,000 and C's claim is reduced to £4,000. A's claim as a pre-inhibition creditor is not, however, increased to £16,000, because he should be neither advantaged nor disadvantaged by the existence of the inhibiting creditor and accordingly he carries forward the same amount from Round 1 to Round 2.

1 Bell *Comm* II, 413.
2 (1870) 10 M 614.
3 G L Gretton *The Law of Inhibition and Adjudication* ch 7.

WITH A HERITABLE CREDITOR EXERCISING HIS POWER OF SALE

10.20 With the possible exception of bankruptcy, this is probably the most common situation in which the position of an inhibiting creditor will have to be considered. As his right is not real, he may adjudge before the sale by the heritable creditor. If he does so, that will create a *nexus* over the property[1]. According to Bell[2], the inhibiting creditor would not have any preference over the free proceeds of sale without doing further diligence ie arresting. This issue is fully discussed by Gretton[3] in relation to some recent decisions which cannot be reconciled. The cases are *George M Allan Ltd v Waugh's Tr*[4]; *Bank of Scotland v Lord Advocate*[5]; *McGowan v Middlemas*[6]; *Abbey National Building Society v Shaik Aziz*[7]; *Ferguson & Forster v Dalbeattie Finance Co*[8] and *Halifax Building Society v Smith*[9]. With the exception of the *Bank of Scotland* case, an Outer House decision, the cases are all sheriff court cases. In each of the cases, the facts were similar. There was a heritable creditor and later another creditor inhibited the debtor. The heritable creditor exercised his power of sale and the question which then arose was how the inhibiting creditor should rank on the proceeds of the sale. In *George M Allan Ltd v Waugh's Tr*, there was a sequestration, whereas the other cases involved an action of multiplepoinding. The only case which raised the issue of the inhibiting creditor's right to the free proceeds was *Halifax Building Society v Smith* where the sheriff decided that the inhibitor secured a preference without the need to arrest.

1 *Graham Stewart* pp 613 *et seq.*
2 Bell *Comm* II, 139.
3 *Gretton* pp 104–111.
4 1966 SLT (Sh Ct) 17.
5 1977 SLT 24.
6 1977 SLT (Sh Ct) 41.
7 1981 SLT (Sh Ct) 29.
8 1981 SLT (Sh Ct) 53.
9 1985 SLT (Sh Ct) 25.

WITH A FLOATING CHARGE

10.21 A floating charge which pre-dates an inhibition is not struck at by the inhibition, but there is some doubt about the effect of an pre-existing inhibition on a subsequent floating charge. Graham Stewart says that an inhibition will strike at a posterior real security[1] and that view is shared by Gretton[2], but, as the latter rightly points out, the position is not clear because of the decision in *Lord Advocate v Royal Bank*[3] where the court was faced with the interpretation of the Companies (Floating Charges and Receivers) (Scotland) Act 1972, now repealed, but re-enacted[4]. It was decided that an arrestment was not 'effectually executed diligence' and thus not effective against a crystallised floating charge. That decision has been much criticised[5], but standing it, it would seem to follow that an inhibition will not strike at a posterior floating charge, at least where it has crystallised[6].

1 *Graham Stewart* p 557.
2 *Gretton* pp 125–126.
3 1977 SC 155, 1978 SLT 38.
4 Companies Act 1985, s 462; Insolvency Act 1986, ss 55, 60.
5 G L Gretton 'Diligence, Trusts and Floating Charges' (1981) 26 JLSS 57, 102; W A Wilson 'Effectively Executed Diligence' 1978 JR 253; A J Sim 'The Receiver and Effectually Executed Diligence' 1984 SLT (News) 25; cp JADH 'Inhibitions and Company Insolvencies: A Contrary View' 1983 SLT (News) 177.
6 Gretton's view, which is shared by most of those referred to in fn 5, is that an inhibition is to be preferred to a subsequent floating charge on the basis that the latter is a voluntary deed (*Gretton* p 126).

WITH A RECEIVER

10.22 On the basis of the *Royal Bank* case, the inhibiting creditor will not be able to challenge the receiver. If, however, the inhibition is to be considered an effectually executed diligence, the receiver may apply to the court for authority to sell the property free of diligence, should the inhibitor attempt to obstruct the receiver in the sale[1].

1 Insolvency Act 1986, s 61.

WITH MISSIVES

10.23 It is not unusual to find that a seller is inhibited after the conclusion of missives, but before delivery of the conveyance in favour of the purchaser. As the inhibition strikes only at future voluntary acts, it will not prevent completion of the transaction because the seller was obliged to fulfil the contract prior to the inhibition[1]. However, the existence of the inhibition may give rise to the suggestion that the search is not clear and hence that the seller who has undertaken to provide a clear search must have the inhibition removed because the title is not marketable. Views differ on what is a clear search and discussion of the point is outwith the scope of this book[2]. In our view, however, the question whether a search is clear is a matter of law and the mere existence of an inhibition in a search does not *ipso facto* mean that the search is not clear[3].

Where, however, the inhibition is on the record before the conclusion of missives, the transaction will be struck at. The transaction will probably proceed, but there will be an obligation on the seller to have the inhibition discharged[4] and the search cleared, because in that case, the search is, without doubt, not clear.

1 Stair IV, 20, 29; Bell *Comm* II, 141–142.
2 See *Gretton* pp 149–151; *Dryburgh v Gordon* (1896) 24 R 1, 4 SLT 173; *Cameron v Williamson* (1895) 22 R 293, 2 SLT 450.
3 *Newcastle Building Society v White* 1987 SLT (Sh Ct) 81; K G C Reid 'Good and Marketable Title' (1988) 33 JLSS 162–165 esp at 165.
4 *Graham Stewart* p 557 and authorities cited there.

WITH A STANDARD SECURITY

10.24 In most cases, the debtor will be inhibited after he has granted the standard security, and clearly, the security is not affected by it. The inhibiting creditor will undoubtedly wish payment from the free proceeds of sale and he should therefore follow his inhibition with an arrestment of the fund in order to secure any preference. As inhibition strikes only at the debtor *qua* his heritable property, it must be doubted whether the inhibitor has any preference over the free proceeds if he has not done diligence on them. However, in *Halifax Building Society v Smith*[1], it was held that the inhibitor did have such a preference without the need for further diligence[2].

If, on the other hand, the debtor is inhibited prior to his granting a standard security, that will be struck at by the inhibition[3].

It may be, however, that the inhibition post-dates the standard security, but the heritable creditor makes a further advance to the debtor after the inhibition. There does not seem to be any reported case on this point, but the opinion expressed by Graham Stewart[4] and Gretton[5], which would seem to be correct, is that the inhibition will, in general, strike at such an advance. That would appear to be subject to the qualification that the inhibition will not strike at interest on the pre-inhibition advance[6], nor at expenses incurred thereanent, nor at further advances which the creditor had obliged himself to make prior to the inhibition, even although the advance was made afterwards[7].

1 1985 SLT (Sh Ct) 25.
2 For a criticism on this point, see *Gretton* p 108.
3 *Graham Stewart* p 557; *Gretton* p 111.
4 *Graham Stewart* p 565.
5 *Gretton* p 112.
6 *Scottish Waggon Co v Hamilton's Tr* (1906) 13 SLT 779.
7 On the analogy of the ranking of standard securities, see the Conveyancing and Feudal Reform (Scotland) Act 1970, s 13.

10.25 Unless the inhibiting creditor accedes to the trust deed, he may reduce the conveyance of any heritable property to the trustee because the act is voluntary. The trust deed may be protected within the meaning of the Bankruptcy (Scotland) Act 1985, in which event all creditors are deemed to be acceding[1].

1 Bankruptcy (Scotland) Act 1985, Sch 5, paras 5–7.

Landlord's hypothec for rent

10.26 The landlord makes his hypothec good by the process of sequestration for rent, but the landlord's preference is determined by his hypothec and not by the sequestration[1]. His hypothec has preference over the diligence of ordinary creditors, but ranks after the superior's hypothec for feuduty[2], a remedy which is rarely used. He may find, however, that in some circumstances it is not worthwhile pursuing a sequestration, because he will have to pay certain arrears of tax which might render his sequestration of little value, unless some accommodation can be reached with the Inland Revenue.

Apart from the position of the Inland Revenue, the landlord is most likely to face competition with a poinding creditor. If the poinding is done before the rent is due, the landlord may interdict the poinder, unless he gives security for the whole rent covered by the hypothec. If the poinding is done after the rent is due, the hypothec attaches plenishings equivalent in value to a year's rent and so the poinding creditor can poind the remaining effects[3].

If the goods have been sold but not delivered, it has been held that they are still available to the landlord[4]. The case in which this was held, referred to an old case[5], but the judges also observed that the Sale of Goods Act[6] does not alter the law on the landlord's hypothec.

1 *Graham Stewart* p 485.
2 Ersk *Inst* II, 6, 63.
3 *Graham Stewart* p 484.
4 *Ryan v Little* 1910 SC 219, 1909 2 SLT 476.
5 *Kinneil v Menzies* (1790) M 4973.
6 Sale of Goods Act 1893, s 61(5) (now Sale of Goods Act 1979, s 62(5)).

Poinding of the ground

10.27 The date of service of the action of poinding of the ground makes real the preference which a heritable creditor has by virtue of his infeftment[1].

1 *Royal Bank v Bain* (1877) 4 R 985 at 991 per Lord Deas; *Athole Hydropathic Co v Scottish Provincial Assurance Co* (1886) 13 R 818.

10.28 In a competition with a personal poinding, the date of service has to be compared with the date of the report of the sale under the personal poinding, and the earlier of the two will prevail[1].

1 *Tullis v Whyte* 18 June 1817 FC.

WITH AN ARRESTMENT

10.29 The date of service has to be compared with the date of the decree of furthcoming, and, again, the earlier of the two will prevail[1].

1 *Graham Stewart* p 506.

WITH A PURCHASER

10.30 The date of service has to be compared with the date of completion of the sale[1]. Under the Sale of Goods Act 1979, property in the goods passes when it is intended to pass[2], whereas at common law property passed on delivery, which is a much clearer notion.

1 *Graham Stewart* p 506.
2 Sale of Goods Act 1979, s 18.

WITH ANOTHER POINDING OF THE GROUND

10.31 In any competition, the dates of infeftment determine the preference and the earlier infeftment will prevail[1]. Because the superior's infeftment ante-dates all others, he will be preferred to any subsequent poinder of the ground.

1 Stair II, 5, 12; *Royal Bank v Bain* (1877) 4 R 985.

Maills and duties

10.32 This action is open only to a heritable creditor whose right depends upon infeftment, but he makes his preference real by this action. Competition is determined in the same way as competition in poindings of the ground[1]. Where, however, the heritable creditor is the holder of a standard security, it is submitted that priority is determined by the date upon which he became entitled to enter into possession.

1 *Graham Stewart* p 524.

Adjudication

10.33 As a general rule, adjudications rank in accordance with their dates of recording in the Register of Sasines, or registering in the Land Register. However, where creditors adjudge within a year and a day of an effectual adjudication (ie recording, or registering in the appropriate Register), they rank *pari passu*[1].

1 Diligence Act 1661; Adjudications Act 1672.

EQUALISATION AND APPARENT INSOLVENCY

10.34 Apart from the equalisation of adjudications already notice, all arrestments and poindings which have been executed within sixty days prior to apparent insolvency (formerly notour bankruptcy) or with four months thereafter are ranked *pari passu*, as if they had been executed on the same date[1]. Furthermore, any creditor wishing to challenge the preference can produce a decree or liquid grounds of debt and, if he does, he is entitled to rank as if he had executed either a poinding, or an arrestment[2]. If a creditor who has arrested has obtained a decree of furthcoming, or a poinding creditor has proceeded to a sale, and has obtained payment of his debt, he must account to other creditors who rank *pari passu* by virtue of the Bankruptcy (Scotland) Act 1985, but he is entitled to deduct his expenses[3]. This applies to companies also[4]. If a debtor grants a trust deed while he is practically insolvent, that constitutes apparent insolvency and so arrestments and poindings executed within sixty days prior to the granting of the trust deed also rank *pari passu*[5].

The advantage of equalisation under section 10 is that it excludes the claims of preferential creditors who would be given their preference in a sequestration.

1 Bankruptcy (Scotland) Act 1985, Sch 7, para 24; see also G L Gretton 'Multiple Notour Bankruptcy' (1983) 28 JLSS 18.
2 Bankruptcy (Scotland) Act 1985, Sch 7, para 24(1).
3 Ibid, Sch 7 para 24(3); *Stewart v Stewart's Trs* (1916) 32 Sh Ct Rep 43.
4 Insolvency Act 1986, s 185.
5 Bankruptcy (Scotland) Act 1985, s 7(1).

BANKRUPTCY

10.35 The Bankruptcy (Scotland) Act 1985 preserves the prior law, with only minor amendments in respect of inhibitions.

Arrestments and poindings

10.36 Sequestration is the equivalent of an arrestment in execution followed by a decree of furthcoming, or warrant of sale, and a completed poinding[1]. The Act provides that the trustee ranks *pari passu* with all arrestments and poindings carried out within sixty days before or four months after apparent insolvency[2]. Furthermore, no arrestment or poinding carried out within sixty days before sequestration, and on, or after, sequestration, can create a preference and so that has the effect that, where there has been apparent insolvency within four months prior to sequestration, the sequestration is equalised with an arrestment or poinding done within the sixty-day period prior to apparent insolvency[3]. In *Johnston v Cluny Trs*[4], it was held that where an arrestment was executed within the sixty day period and the funds were handed over to the arrester following on a decree of furthcoming obtained prior to sequestration, the arrester could retain the funds. By analogy, that reasoning could have been applied to the proceeds of a sale following upon a poinding. That decision has effectively been reversed by section 37(4), which provides that no arrestment or poinding will be effectual whether or not it still subsists at the date of sequestration. However, an arresting, or poinding, creditor whose diligence has been cut down may recover his expenses[5]. It has been decided that an arrestment which has executed prior to the sixty days but is not followed by a furthcoming is not effectual against a trustee in sequestration, but that the arrester's preference is preserved[6]. However, in a more recent case, it was decided that an arrestment in these circumstances is not struck at by a subsequent liquidation[7]. There is, therefore, a difference between sequestration and liquidation which does not seem justified given that the provisions of the Bankruptcy (Scotland) Act 1985 apply to companies[8].

1 Bankruptcy (Scotland) Act 1985, s 37(1)(b).
2 Ibid, s 37(4).
3 Ibid, s 37(4).
4 1957 SC 184; SLT 293.
5 Bankruptcy (Scotland) Act 1985, s 37(5).
6 *Gordon v Millar* (1842) 4 D 352.
7 *Commercial Aluminium Windows Ltd v Cumbernauld Development Corpn* 1987 SLT (Sh Ct) 91. *Gordon v Millar* was not preferred to but the sheriff pointed out that the bankrupt's property vests in the trustee but not in the liquidator.
8 Insolvency Act 1986, s 185.

Inhibitions

10.37   In a sequestration, or where a voluntary trust deed is granted, or in a liquidation, two issues arise. The first is what effect does the inhibition have on the appointment of the trustee or liquidator, and the second is how does the inhibitor rank.

SEQUESTRATION

10.38   Section 31(2) of the Bankruptcy (Scotland) Act 1985 provides that the title of a trustee is not challengeable on the ground of any prior inhibition. The trustee is therefore free to sell, and, from a conveyancing point of view, the purchaser cannot object to the existence of such an inhibition. Although that is so, the sub-section provides that the inhibitor's rights are preserved. The assumption is that the inhibition takes effect more than sixty days prior to the sequestration. Once again, the example given by George Gretton on page 84 is instructive.

Sequestration. Heritable estate worth £18,000.

Creditor A's debt is £12,000 (pre-inhibition)
Creditor B's debt is £12,000 (inhibitor)
Creditor C's debt is £12,000 (post-inhibition, but secured)

Total	£36,000

ROUND I

C gets paid in full. A ranks as if the inhibition did not exist.

Therefore A gets	£ 3,000
B	£ 3,000
C	£12,000
Total	£18,000

ROUND 2

A still ranks as if the inhibition did not exist, but the inhibitor, B draws back from C enough to put him in the same position as he would have been had C's claim not existed. Had that been so, A would have got £9,000 and so would B, the inhibitor.

Therefore A gets	£ 3,000	
B	£ 9,000	
C	£ 6,000	
Total	£18,000	

The 1985 Act also provides that where the inhibition takes effect within sixty days before the sequestration, it does not create any preference. Any right of challenge is vested in the trustee and he has the right to receive payment and grant the discharge[1].

In the last example, if the inhibition and hence C's debt took effect within the sixty days, the Act provides that the money due to the inhibitor in round 2 is not paid to him, but becomes a general fund[1].

The total claims are £36,000 and so the divided is one quarter.

A gets ¼ of £12,000 ie	£3,000	
B	£3,000	
C	£3,000	
Total	£9,000	

ROUND 3

In round 3, the position becomes

A gets £3,000 (round 2)	+ £2,000	Total	£ 5,000
B gets £9,000 (round 2)	− £6,000 + £6,000 / 3		£ 5,000
C gets £6,000 (round 2)	+ £2,000		£ 8,000
		Total	£18,000

1 Bankruptcy (Scotland) Act 1985, s 37.

VOLUNTARY TRUST DEED

10.39 Since this is a voluntary act by the debtor, it is reducible by the inhibitor so far as the trust deed covers heritage. That is, of course, unless the inhibitor had acceded to the trust deed. If the trust deed is protected under the Act[1], a non-acceding creditor has no greater right than an acceding creditor, but he may petition for sequestration[2].

1 Bankruptcy (Scotland) Act 1985, s 70.
2 Ibid, Sch 5.

Liquidation

10.40 The Insolvency Act 1986 applies the provision of section 37 of the Bankruptcy (Scotland) Act 1985 to companies[1]. Section 37(1)(a) places the liquidator in the position of having a recorded decree of adjudication and that gives him preference over anyone whose diligence is not complete. He can therefore proceed to sell despite the inhibition, but if he has undertaken to provide 'clear searches' which he will probably not do, he will be forced to discharge the inhibition[2]. The existence of the inhibition is not 'prejudicial' to the liquidation and so an obligation to exhibit or deliver a search showing nothing prejudicial to the seller is not affected by the existence of the inhibition[3].

Section 37 alters the previous law by providing that no inhibition which takes effect within sixty days of the winding-up order can create a preference for the inhibitor[4], and any payment made thereafter for the discharge of the inhibition is to be made to the liquidator[5] who must grant a discharge. Furthermore, the liquidator has the same rights as the inhibiting creditor would have had to challenge any voluntary disposal by the company[6]. If the inhibition is put on more than sixty days prior to the winding-up order, the liquidator's position is governed by section 37(1).

1 Insolvency Act 1986, s 185.
2 *Dryburgh v Gordon* (1896) 24 R 1, 4 SLT 173; see also *Newcastle Building Society v White* 1987 SLT (Sh Ct) 81.
3 See para 10.22 above.
4 Bankruptcy (Scotland) Act 1985, s 37(2).
5 Ibid, s 37(3).
6 For further discussion see *Gretton* pp 125–133.

Receivership

10.41 Section 61 of the Insolvency Act 1986 provides that where a receiver wishes to sell property which is affected or attached by 'effectual diligence' and he cannot obtain the consent of the person who carried out the diligence, he may apply to the court for authority to sell or dispose of the property free of the diligence. The notion of 'effectually executed diligence' has been discussed earlier[1], but it would seem that arrestments and probably also poindings, inhibitions and the landlord's hypothec for rent are not 'effectually executed diligence', nor presumably are they 'effectual diligence'. The receiver would not therefore be affected by them, but, in any event, he may seek the permission of the court to sell property free of these diligences even if they are 'effectually executed' or 'effectual'.

1 See above at para 10.21.

Administration

10.42 Administration is governed by the Insolvency Act 1986. Sections 10 and 11 provide that creditors cannot use diligence after the making of an administration order, and that operates retrospectively to the date of the petition for the appointment of the administration. An inhibition after that date is therefore incompetent. As Gretton notes[1], there are at least two unresolved matters. The first is whether an inhibition which exists at the date of petition, which would otherwise be struck at, revives if the petition is not granted. Section 10 suggests that it does not, unjust as that may seem. The second is whether a creditor who has obtained a warrant to inhibit, but has not registered it, can register it despite a petition for the appointment of an administrator. Gretton suggest that sections 10 and 11 would prevent him from doing so. That would seem to apply also where a notice of inhibition has been registered, but the inhibition itself has not.

1 *Gretton* pp 134–136.

Adjudication

10.43 Sequestration is the equivalent of a decree of adjudication for debt in respect of the debtor's heritable estate[1] and so the trustee representing the general body of creditors ranks *pari passu* with those who have adjudged within a year and a day of the sequestration, and all those who have adjudged within that period also rank *pari passu* with each other.

1 Bankruptcy (Scotland) Act 1985, s 31.
2 Ibid, s 37(1)(a).
3 Insolvency Act 1986, s 185.

Poinding of the ground and mails and duties

10.44 A poinding of the ground which has not been followed by a sale of the poinded items outwith sixty days prior to sequestration, is cut down by sequestration, except for interest on the current half-year's instalment and the interest for the previous year[1]. The remedy of mails and duties is not affected by sequestration because the creditor is merely enforcing his already-existing preference[2]. The same applies to companies[3].

1 Bankruptcy (Scotland) Act 1985, s 37(6).
2 *Graham Stewart* p 524.
3 Insolvency Act 1986, s 185.

Landlord's hypothec for rent

10.45 A landlord's hypothec for rent is not affected by sequestration, on the theory just mentioned in connection with mails and duties, that he is merely enforcing his existing preference[1]. However, it has been held that a receiver will prevail over a landlord who sequestrated for rent after his appointment[1]. The decision turned on the meaning of the phrase 'fixed security' in the Companies (Floating Charges and Receivers) (Scotland) Act 1972[2] which provides that a creditor can prevail against the receiver only if he has effectually executed diligence or has a fixed security or is the holder of a pre-existing floating charge. Because the sequestration took place after the appointment, the landlord had not 'effectually executed diligence', but the sheriff held that a hypothec for rent was not a fixed security, nor was it in the nature of a floating charge[3]. This decision has been criticised in that it leaves the exact nature of the landlord's hypothec in a state of considerable uncertainty[4].

1 *Cumbernauld Development Corporation v Mustone Ltd* 1983 SLT (Sh Ct) 55.
2 Companies (Floating Charges and Receivers) (Scotland) Act 1972, s 15(2)(a), now s 462 of the Companies Act 1985, ss 55, 60 of the Insolvency Act 1986.
3 Companies (Floating Charges and Receivers) (Scotland) Act 1972, s 31.
4 W G Simmons 'A Legal Black Hole' (1983) 28 JLSS 352; G L Gretton 'Receivership and Sequestration for Rent' 1983 SLT (News) 277; Halliday *Conveyancing Law and Practice in Scotland* vol III, para 41–24.

Law reform

10.46 The Scottish Law Commission produced a discussion paper on Equalisation of Diligence, in November 1988[1].

1 Equalisation of Diligence (Scot Law Com Discussion Paper no 79 (1988)).

CHAPTER 11

ENFORCEMENT OF FOREIGN JUDGMENTS

INTRODUCTION

11.01 Diligence is regulated by the law of the country in which it is to be executed and the enforcement of foreign decrees by way of diligence in Scotland requires appropriate authority from a Scottish court. By the common law, the method of obtaining such authority is to raise an action in the Court of Session for a decree conform. Although the common law provides a number of fundamental principles in this area of law, its relative uncertainty and the need to use a court action in Scotland has resulted in the introduction of statutory rules giving effect to international conventions on enforcement of foreign judgments. The general scheme of many of these conventions is that a judgment pronounced by a court of one contracting state is registered in the court of another contracting state, and the court of the place of registration then pronounces an order authorising the enforcement of the judgment in that legal system.

This chapter examines the statutory schemes for enforcement of foreign judgments which are most commonly used. Reference should be made to discussion elsewhere of the common law procedures and of specialised statutory schemes in respect of various types of judgments[1].

1 See G Maher 'Recognition and Enforcement of Non-Scottish Judgments' in Diligence and Enforcement of Judgments, *The Laws of Scotland: Stair Memorial Encyclopaedia* vol 8.

ADMINISTRATION OF JUSTICE ACT 1920

Geographical extent of the 1920 Act scheme

11.02 The Administration of Justice Act 1920, Part II provides for a scheme for the reciprocal enforcement of judgments of the superior courts of various legal systems. The scheme of the 1920 Act extends to 'Her Majesty's Dominions' to which it is made applicable by Order in Council. At present the Act has been extended to the following legal systems[1]:

Anguilla
Antigua and Barbuda
Bahamas
Barbados
Belize

Bermuda
Botswana
British Indian Ocean Territory
British Virgin Islands
Cayman Islands

Christmas Islands	Papua New Guinea
Cocos (Keeling) Islands	Queensland
Cyprus	St Christopher and Nevis
Dominica	St Helena
Falkland Islands	St Lucia
Fiji	St Vincent and the Grenadines
The Gambia	Saskatchewan
Ghana	Seychelles
Gibraltar	Sierra Leone
Grenada	Singapore
Guyana	Soloman Islands
Hong Kong	South Australia
Jamaica	Sovereign Base Areas of Akrotiri
Kenya	and Dhekelia (Cyprus)
Kiribati	Sri Lanka
Lesotho	Swaziland
Malawi	Tanzania
Malaysia	Tasmania
Malta	Trinidad and Tobago
Mauritius	Turks and Caicos Islands
Montserrat	Tuvalu
Newfoundland	Uganda
New South Wales	Victoria
New Zealand	Western Australia
Nigeria	Zambia
Territory of Norfolk Island	Zimbabwe
Northern Territory (Australia)	

1 Reciprocal Enforcement of Judgments (Administration of Justice Act 1920, Pt II) (Consolidation) Order 1984, SI 1984/129, amended by SI 1985/1994.

Scope of the 1920 Act

11.03 The scheme for reciprocal enforcement of judgments under Part II of the 1920 Act applies in respect of judgments or court orders:
(a) which have been obtained in a superior court of a legal system to which the Act applies. In the United Kingdom the appropriate judgments are those of the Court of Session in Scotland, and of the High Court of England and Wales and in Northern Ireland[1]; and
(b) which require payment of a sum of money[2].

In addition, the 1920 Act applies to awards in arbitration proceedings for payment of sums of money which have become enforceable in the legal system of origin in the same manner as a judgment of a superior court in that legal system[3].

1 Administration of Justice Act 1920, ss 9(1), 10(1).
2 Ibid, s 12(1).
3 Ibid, s 12(1), 9(1).

11.04 Judgments requiring payment of multiple damages, as defined by section 5(1) of the Protection of Trading Interests Act 1980, cannot be registered in the United Kingdom under Part II of the 1920 Act[1]. These judgments are:

(i) judgments for multiple damages, ie a judgment for an amount arrived at by doubling, trebling or otherwise multiplying a sum assessed as compensation for loss or damage by the person in whose favour the judgment was given. The expression 'or otherwise' must be read as *ejusdem generis* with the words preceding it, and a judgment is not struck at where multiplying has the effect of decreasing the sum awarded, eg multiplying by half because of 50 per cent contributory negligence;

(ii) a judgment based on a provision or rule of law specified in an order by the Secretary of State. The Secretary of State has power to make such an order in respect of foreign laws restricting or distorting commercial competition;

(iii) a judgment for contribution, where a judgment of type (i) or (ii) has been made against a third party.

Section 5 of the 1980 Act is aimed primarily at limiting the effect in the United Kingdom of United States anti-trust laws[2]. It should be noted that any judgment within the scope of section 5 is unenforceable here in its entirety and not simply in respect of that part in excess of genuine compensation.

1 See also RC 248(b) which requires the Lord Ordinary to satisfy himself that a judgment is not within the scope of s 5 of the Protection of Trading Interests Act 1980 before he can exercise his discretion to register the judgment under the Administration of Justice Act 1920 in the Court of Session.
2 G C Cheshire and P M North *Private International Law* (11th edn 1987), pp 375–376.

Procedure for registration of a 1920 Act judgment in Scotland

COMMON LAW ACTION FOR DECREE CONFORM

11.05 Instead of using the 1920 Act procedures, a creditor may use the common law action for decree conform to enforce a foreign judgment in Scotland. However, where a common law action is raised in respect of a judgment within the scope of the 1920 Act, the creditor cannot recover any expenses of the action unless there has been a previous unsuccessful application for registration under the Act[1].

1 Administration of Justice Act 1920, s 9(5). The court has power to award expenses in a common law action even where there has been no previous application under the 1920 Act but it is unlikely that expenses would be awarded except in highly unusual circumstances.

TITLE TO MAKE APPLICATION

11.06 Title to apply for registration of a 1920 Act judgment lies with the person in whose favour the judgment was granted and also his successors and assignees[1].

1 Administration of Justice Act 1920, s 12(1). It is not clear which legal system determines the validity of any question of succession or assignation but as a matter of general principle this is a question for Scots law, including its rules of international private law.

TIME-LIMIT FOR APPLICATION

11.07 An application for registration of a 1920 Act judgment must be made within twelve months of the date of the judgment. The court to which application for registration is made has power to extend the period during which an application may be presented[1]. A judgment which is no longer open to registration under the 1920 Act may be enforced in Scotland by means of a common law action for decree conform but this would normally result in the expenses of the action being unrecoverable by the pursuer[2].

1 Administration of Justice Act 1920, s 9(1).
2 See above at para 11.05.

PROCEDURE IN THE COURT OF SESSION

11.08 Procedure for registration of a 1920 Act judgment is regulated by RC 248. Application is by way of petition presented to the Outer House. The petition specifies the full name, title, trade or business, and usual or last place of abode of both the judgment creditor and the judgment debtor. The judgment, or a certified copy, is produced with the petition, along with an affidavit to the effect that the application meets the requirements of the 1920 Act. The Lord Ordinary, in the exercise of his discretion (see below), may then grant warrant for registration of the judgment[1].

1 RC 248(a), (b).

11.09 At this stage no notice is given to the judgment debtor of the application for registration of the judgment. However, the warrant granted by the Lord Ordinary for registration of the judgment has to specify a date before which the judgment debtor is entitled to apply to the Lord Ordinary to have the registration set aside. After the warrant has been granted the procedure is then for the petitioner to produce a certified copy of the warrant and the judgment (or certified copy) to the Keeper of the Registers[1]. Once the registration has been made by the Keeper in the Register of Judgments in the Books of Council and Session, the petitioner must immediately make intimation on the judgment debtor. The terms of the intimation are set out in RC 248(e)[2]. The execution of the intimation is then lodged in process.

1 RC 248(d).
2 Ie: 'I hereby give you notice that a judgment [*specifying name*] has been registered in the Register of Judgments in the Books of the Lords of Council and Session, and that if you intend to apply to have the registration set aside you must do so before [*specify date*].'

11.10 The warrant for registration specifies a date before which the judgment debtor may apply to the Lord Ordinary to have the registration set aside[1]. If the judgment debtor makes no application within the specified time to have the registration set aside, or where such application has been made and refused, the Deputy Principal Clerk must grant a certificate to that effect[2]. Until such a certificate has been granted, extract of the registered judgment cannot be obtained[3].

1 RC 248(c). In fixing this date, regard is to be had to the judgment debtor's place of residence.
2 RC 248(f).
3 RC 248(d). Note also RC 248(g) which deals with procedure where registration is to be cancelled following application by a judgment debtor.

Grounds for refusing registration or for setting aside registration

11.11   A Lord Ordinary in dealing with a petition for warrant to register a judgment under Part II of the 1920 Act has a discretion whether or not to grant the warrant, the Act empowering (but not requiring) the court dealing with the application to issue a warrant if in all the circumstances of the case it thinks 'it is just and convenient that the judgment should be enforced in the United Kingdom[1]'.

1 Administration of Justice Act 1920, s 9(1).

11.12   Furthermore, there are a number of grounds which require the court to refuse to grant warrant for registration of a 1920 Act judgment, or which require it on application by the judgment debtor to cancel a registration of a judgment[1].

These grounds are:

(1) The court in which the judgment was given acted without jurisdiction. It is not clear what tests are to be applied in determining jurisdiction in this context though it is likely that the Scottish courts would apply the common law criteria for international jurisdiction[2].

(2) The judgment debtor, being a person who was neither carrying on business nor ordinarily resident within the jurisdiction of the original court, did not voluntarily appear or otherwise submit or agree to submit to the jurisdiction of that court.

(3) The judgment debtor, being the defender in the proceedings, was not duly served with the process of the original court and did not appear, notwithstanding that he was ordinarily resident or was carrying on business within the jurisdiction of that court or agreed to submit to the jurisdiction of that court.

(4) The judgment was obtained by fraud.

(5) The judgment debtor has satisfied the Lord Ordinary either that an appeal is pending, or that he is entitled and intends to appeal, against the judgment.

(6) The judgment was in respect of a cause of action which for reasons of public policy or for some other similar reason could not have been entertained by the registering court.

(7) The judgment is one to which section 32 of the Civil Jurisdiction and Judgments Act 1982 applies. This section renders unenforceable in the United Kingdom, judgments of overseas courts[3] given in proceedings where the bringing of the proceedings was contrary to an agreement that the dispute in question would be settled otherwise than by proceedings in the courts of that country[4].

1 Administration of Justice Act 1920, s 9(2).
2 See A E Anton *Private International Law* pp 574–583.
3 Ie courts of a country or territory outside the United Kingdom.
4 A E Anton *Civil Jurisdiction in Scotland* pp 203–204; see *Fracomin SA v Sudan Oil Seeds Co Ltd* [1983] 1 WLR 1026.

Effect of registration

11.13   Once registration of a judgment has been completed without recall, the judgment becomes enforceable as if it had been given by the registering court[1]. The reasonable expenses involved in the registration (which include the expenses of obtaining a copy of the judgment from the original court, and the expenses of application for registration) are recoverable as if they were sums due under the judgment[2].

1 Administration of Justice Act 1920, s 9(3)(a). The provisions of RC 248(f) that the days of charge on registered judgments are 15 days appear to have been superseded by the 1987 Act, s 90 which lays down days of charge of 14 days (or 28 days where the defender is resident furth of the United Kingdom or his whereabouts are unknown).
2 Administration of Justice Act 1920, s 9(3)(c).

Registration elsewhere of judgments of the Court of Session

11.14   Where a judgment 'obtained' in the Court of Session is to be enforced elsewhere under the scheme which the 1920 Act gives effect to in the United Kingdom, procedure is by way of petition to the Outer House[1]. A judgment obtained in the Court of Session includes an extract of a document which has been registered for execution in the Books of Council and Session[2]. Lodged with the petition are (a) an extract decree setting forth the judgment to be enforced and (b) an affidavit that the judgment debtor is resident in a legal system to which the 1920 Act scheme applies[3]. The Lord Ordinary then pronounces an interlocutor ordering the Deputy Principal Clerk to issue a certified copy of the judgment in the appropriate form.

1 Administration of Justice Act 1920, s 10.
2 *Taylor, Petr* 1931 SLT 260.
3 RC 248(h). If the judgment debtor has such a residence it does not matter that he is present in Scotland: *Bank of West Africa* 1931 SLT 83.

FOREIGN JUDGMENTS (RECIPROCAL ENFORCEMENT) ACT 1933

Extent of reciprocal enforcement of judgments under the 1933 Act

11.15   The Foreign Judgments (Reciprocal Enforcement) Act 1933 provides a scheme for the recognition and enforcement within the United Kingdom of certain types of judgment of courts and tribunals in legal systems of other states. The Crown is empowered to make Orders in Council extending the application of the scheme of the Act to countries which afford substantial reciprocity of treatment to similar judgments of United Kingdom courts[1].

1 Foreign Judgments (Reciprocal Enforcement) Act 1933, s 1(1). Orders in Council may also extend the scheme of the Act to Commonwealth countries. The 1933 Act scheme supersedes the scheme of the 1920 Act in respect of any country to which both Acts have been extended.

11.16   To date the 1933 Act has been extended to cover judgments of courts of the following countries[1].

Australian Capital Territory	France
Austria	Federal Republic of Germany
Bangladesh	Guernsey
Belgium	India
British Columbia	Isle of Man

Israel	Nova Scotia
Italy	Ontario
Jersey	Pakistan
Manitoba	Saskatchewan
The Netherlands	Surinam
New Brunswick	Tonga
Norway	Yukon Territory

1 The Act also extends to the judgments of the Federal Court of Canada. For a list of the Orders in Council and Statutory Instruments extending the Foreign Judgments (Reciprocal Enforcement) Act 1933, see Parliament House Book, B 44/1.

11.17   Where a judgment of a country which is or is part of a contracting state to the Brussels Judgments Convention of 1968 comes within the scope of both the 1968 Convention and the scheme of the 1933 Act, the 1968 Convention supersedes the scheme of the 1933 Act[1].

Judgments are within the scope of the 1933 Act only if they were made after the coming into force of the Order in Council extending the Act to the court making it[2].

1 1968 Convention, art 55.
2 Foreign Judgments (Reciprocal Enforcement) Act 1933, s 1(2)(c).

Judgments to which the 1933 Act applies

11.18   As far as recognition and enforcement in Scotland are concerned, the provisions of the 1933 Act apply only in respect of certain types of judgment made by courts or tribunals specified as recognised for that purpose in the Order in Council which extends the Act to the relevant country. A judgment which is the result of arbitration is within the scope of the Act if under the law in force in the place where it was made it has become enforceable in the same manner as a judgment given by a court in that place[1].

1 Foreign Judgments (Reciprocal Enforcement) Act 1933, s 10A.

11.19   For a judgment to be within the scope of the 1933 Act it must be both (a) final and conclusive between the parties or require interim payment by the judgment debtor to the judgment creditor, and (b) require payment of a sum of money other than a sum payable as a tax, fine or penalty[1]. A judgment given by a court in criminal proceedings may be within the scope of the 1933 Act where it is for payment of a sum of money in respect of compensation or damages to an injured person[2].

A judgment which has been partly satisfied may be registered under the Act in respect of the balance still due[3]. Judgments which have been wholly satisfied or which cannot be enforced by execution in the country of the original court, cannot be registered under the Act[4].

Where a foreign judgment contains different provisions and only some of these are within the scope of the 1933 Act, the judgment may be registered under the Act but only in respect of those provisions[5].

1 Foreign Judgments (Reciprocal Enforcement) Act 1933, s 1(2). See also s 1(3) for the definition of 'final and conclusive'. The idea of fine or penalty was considered in *SA Consortium General Textiles v Sun and Sand Agencies Ltd* [1978] QB 279, 299–300, 305–306.
2 Foreign Judgments (Reciprocal Enforcement) Act 1933, s 11(1).

3 Ibid, s 2(4).
4 Ibid, s 2(1).
5 Ibid, s 2(5).

11.20 The scheme of the 1933 Act applies in approximately modified form to foreign judgments within the scope of various international Conventions[1].

Although these international Conventions generally follow the procedure of the 1933 Act, each of the Acts which implements the various Conventions lays down rules as to whether the original court had jurisdiction as a basis for setting aside registration. Furthermore the ground for setting aside registration that a judgment is in breach of section 32 of the Civil Jurisdiction and Judgments Act 1982 does not apply in cases of judgments under most of these international Conventions[2].

1 See Carriage of Goods by Road Act 1965, ss 4, 11(2); Nuclear Installations Act 1965, s 17(4); Merchant Shipping (Oil Pollution) Act 1971, s 13(3); Carriage of Passengers by Road Act 1974, s 5; Carriage by Railway Act 1972, s 5(1), (3); Merchant Shipping Act 1974, s 6(4), (5); Merchant Shipping Act 1979, s 14; Civil Aviation (Eurocontrol) Act 1983, s 1; International Transport Conventions Act 1983, s 6.
2 Civil Jurisdiction and Judgments Act 1982, s 32(4)(b).

Procedure for registration

11.21 A foreign judgment to which the 1933 Act applies can be enforced in Scotland only by means of the procedure under the Act and not by a common law action[1].

1 Foreign Judgments (Reciprocal Enforcement) Act 1933, s 6.

11.22 Procedure for enforcement in Scotland is for the judgment creditor (or his assignée or successor[1]) to make application by petition to the Outer House[2]. Application must be made within six years after the date of the judgment (or the date of the last judgment where there has been an appeal). Application must be accompanied by a certified copy of the judgment issued by the original court and authenticated by its seal. If necessary, there must also be a certified translation of the judgment into English.

1 Foreign Judgments (Reciprocal Enforcement) Act 1933, s 6.
2 Ibid, s 2(1); RC 249(1).

11.23 With the application there is presented also an affidavit stating to the best of the information and belief of the deponent:
(i) that the applicant is entitled to enforce the judgment;
(ii) as the case may require, either that at the date of the application the judgment has not been satisfied, or, if the judgment has been satisfied in part, what the amount is in respect of which it remains unsatisfied;
(iii) that at the date of the application the judgment can be enforced by execution in the country of the original court;
(iv) that if the judgment were registered, the registration would not be, or be liable to be, set aside under section 4 of the 1933 Act;
(v) that the judgment is not a judgment to which section 5 of the Protection of Trading Interests Act 1980 applies.
The affidavit must also
　(a) specify the amount of interest (if any) which under the law of the

country of the original court has become due under the judgment up to the time of the registration;

(b) state the full name, title, trade or business, and the usual or last known place of abode or business of both the judgment creditor and judgment debtor, so far as known to the deponent;

(c) where the judgment is in respect of different matters not all of which are within the scope of the 1933 Act, the provisions in respect of which it is sought to register the judgment[1].

1 RC 249(2)(2) states a requirement for the affidavit to convert a judgment in foreign currency into sterling at the rate of exchange at the date of the judgment. However, this rule seems to have been rendered inapplicable by the Administration of Justice Act 1977, Sch 5, repealing section 2(3) of the Foreign Judgments (Reciprocal Enforcement) Act 1933 which required such conversion.

11.24 Procedure on application is for the Lord Ordinary to satisfy himself that the judgment is one which meets the requirements of the 1933 Act. On being so satisfied, the Lord Ordinary grants warrant for registration of the judgment. Thereafter the warrant is registered in the Register of Judgments of the Books of Council and Session but extract is superseded until such time as the applicant has notified the judgment debtor of the registration and either the judgment debtor has made no objection to the registration or any such objection has been considered and rejected[1].

1 RC 249(5)–(11).

11.25 Objection to registration may be made either on the basis that the Lord Ordinary was mistaken in being satisfied that the application for registration fell within the requirements of the 1933 Act; or that some factual basis of the applicant's case was unfounded (eg where the judgment was wholly satisfied). An application to have a registration set aside is made by petition to the Outer House. On any such application the Lord Ordinary may order such inquiry as thought necessary.

If an application is made to have registration set aside on the basis that an appeal against the original judgment is pending or imminent, the Lord Ordinary may sist the registration for a period allowing the appeal to be heard[1]. If the ground of objection to registration is that the judgment is not yet enforceable by execution in the country of origin, a further application for registration may be made once the judgment becomes enforceable there[2]. If a judgment has been registered in respect of a whole sum payable under it and it has been partly satisfied, the judgment creditor may apply to have the judgment registered for the remaining balance[3].

1 Foreign Judgments (Reciprocal Enforcement) Act 1933, s 5(1).
2 Ibid, s 5(2).
3 Ibid, s 5(3).

Grounds for setting aside registration of a 1933 Act judgment

11.26 On application by the judgment debtor or by any other person liable under the law of the legal system of origin to have the judgment enforced against him, registration of the judgment may be or must be set aside in certain circumstances.

The court may set aside registration if satisfied that the subject-matter of the proceedings in the original court had previously been dealt with by a full and conclusive judgment given by a court of competent jurisdiction[1].

1 Foreign Judgments (Reciprocal Enforcement) Act 1933, s 4(1)(b); cp *Vervaeke v Smith* [1983] AC 145, 156, 159.

11.27 Registration *must* be set aside where the court is satisfied that[1]:
(1) The judgment is not one within the scope of the 1933 Act.
(2) The registration of the judgment did not follow the procedure set out in the 1933 Act and RC 249.
(3) The judgment debtor, as the defender in the original proceedings, did not receive notice of the proceedings in sufficient time to defend the proceedings. The question of what is sufficient time is for the registering court to determine and it does not matter for this purpose that by the law of the country of the original proceedings, there was due service on the defender. However, this ground does not apply if the defender entered appearance in the original proceedings.
(4) The judgment was obtained by fraud.
(5) The enforcement of the judgment would be contrary to the Scots law conception of public policy.
(6) The rights under the judgment are not vested in the person who made the application for registration.
(7) The judgment is struck at by section 5 of the Protection of Trading Interests Act 1980.
(8) The judgment is struck at by section 32 of the Civil Jurisdiction and Judgments Act 1982.
(9) The courts of the country of the original court had no jurisdiction in the circumstances of the case. The wording of the relevant provision of the 1933 Act suggests that what is at issue here is not whether the original court itself had jurisdiction but whether *any* court of that country had jurisdiction. (The original court itself must be a recognised court for its judgments to be registered under the Act.) Criteria for determining whether courts of the country of the original court possessed, or lacked, jurisdiction are set out in the 1933 Act.

1 Foreign Judgments (Reciprocal Enforcement) Act 1933, s 4(1)(a).

11.28 Under the Act a court has jurisdiction for this purpose[1]:
(i) In the case of a judgment given *in personam*, in the circumstances as set out below. However, actions *in personam* do not include any matrimonial cause or any proceedings in connection with matrimonial matters, administration of estates and deceased persons, bankruptcy, winding-up of companies, lunacy or guardianship of 'infants'[2].

The circumstances in which there exists jurisdiction in actions *in personam* are where:
(a) the judgment debtor, as the defender in the original court, submitted to the jurisdiction of that court by voluntarily appearing in the proceedings;
(b) the judgment debtor was the pursuer in, or counterclaimed in, the proceedings in the original court;
(c) the judgment debtor, as the defender in the original court, had before the commencement of the proceedings agreed, in respect of the subject matter of the proceedings, to submit to the jurisdiction of that court or of the courts of the country of that court;

(d) the judgment debtor, as the defender in the original court, was at the time when the proceedings were instituted resident in, or being a body corporate had its principal place of business in, the country of that court; or

(e) the judgment debtor, as defender in the original court, had an office or place or business in the country of that court and the proceedings in that court were in respect of a transaction effected through or at the office or place.

(ii) In the case of a judgment given in an action of which the subject matter was immoveable property or in an action *in rem* of which the subject matter was moveable property, the original court has jurisdiction if the property in question was at the time of the original proceedings situated in the country of the court of those proceedings.

(iii) In cases other than those within (i) and (ii), the original court has jurisdiction where the law of the registering court recognises it as having jurisdiction.

On the other hand courts of the country of the original court are deemed not to have had jurisdiction[3]:

(i) if the subject matter of the proceedings was immoveable property outside the country of the original court; or

(ii) if the judgment debtor, as the defender in the original proceedings, was a person whom under the rules of public international law was entitled to immunity from the jurisdiction of the courts of the country of the original court and did not submit to the jurisdiction of that court[4].

1 Foreign Judgments (Reciprocal Enforcement) Act 1933, s 4(2).
2 Ibid, s 11(2).
3 Ibid, s 4(3).
4 See generally, Lewis *State and Diplomatic Immunity* (2nd edn, 1985).

Effect of registration under the 1933 Act

11.29   Once a foreign judgment has been registered in Scotland under the 1933 Act it has the same effect as far as concerns execution as a judgment given by the Court of Session[1]. Diligence on a registered judgment is, of course, not possible until such time as the extract is issued, and extract must be superseded until expiry of the time limit for application to have the registration of the judgment set aside or the disposal of any such application[2].

1 Foreign Judgments (Reciprocal Enforcement) Act 1933, s 2(2).
2 RC 249(11). Diligence requiring a charge upon such an extract is stated by RC 249(11) as being fifteen days or such other period as the Lord Ordinary thinks fit. This must now be read in the light of the 1987 Act, s 90, which lays down days of charge of fourteen days (or twenty eight days where the debtor resides outside the United Kingdom or his whereabouts are unknown).

11.30   Section 2(2) of the 1933 Act also provides that a registered judgment is to carry interest on the sum due as if the judgment was one given by the Court of Session. This has effect so that a contractual rate, or a judicial rate as stated in the registered judgment, will continue to be the rate after registration. Such a rate certainly runs up to the time of registration[1] and Scots law accepts that such a rate should usually run after decree is given[2]. If no such rate is stated in the judgment, the normal deemed rate will apply from the date of registration[3].

1 Foreign Judgments (Reciprocal Enforcement) Act 1933, s 2(6).
2 *Bank of Scotland v Davis* 1982 SLT 20. See further ch 1 above at para 1.35.
3 RC 66.

11.31   Also recoverable on the basis of the extract of a judgment registered under the 1933 Act are the reasonable expenses of, and incidental to, registration, including the expenses of obtaining a certified copy of the judgment from the original court[1].

1 Foreign Judgments (Reciprocal Enforcement) Act 1933, s 2(6).

11.32   A further and more general effect to be given in Scotland to judgments within the scope of the 1933 Act arises by virtue of section 8 of the Act. Such judgments, or judgments which would be within the scope of the Act if they required payment of a sum of money, are to be recognised as conclusive of the issues between the parties thereto. This effect arises whether or not the judgment has been registered under the Act. However this effect does not apply to such judgments, registration of which has been set aside, or would have been set aside, on grounds other than[1]
(i)   that a sum of money was not payable under the judgment; or
(ii) that the judgment had been wholly or party satisfied; or
(iii) that at the date of the application, the judgment could not be enforced by execution in the country of the original court.
    It is not clear whether section 8 applies in respect of all types of action *in personam*[2].

1 Foreign Judgments (Reciprocal Enforcement) Act 1933, s 8(2)(a).
2 *Vervaeke v Smith* [1981] Fam 77, [1983] AC 145.

Scottish judgments

11.33   Scottish judgments of a type within the scope of the 1933 Act may be registered for enforcement in a country to which the scheme of the Act extends. Application for enforcement in such a country of a judgment of the Court of Session is made by petition to the Outer House[1]. With the petition there is lodged an extract decree setting forth the judgment. Before the relevant certificates can be issued by the Deputy Principal Clerk, the Lord Ordinary must be satisfied, usually on the basis of an appropriate affidavit lodged with the petition, that the requirements of the Act have been complied with.
    In respect of sheriff court judgments to be enforced under the 1933 Act, application is made by minute lodged in the process in which the judgment was obtained. With the minute there is lodged (i) an extract decree setting forth the judgment or a copy of the judgment, and (ii) an affidavit as to the purpose for which the application is made[2].

1 RC 249(13).
2 AS (Enforcement Abroad of Sheriff Court Judgments) 1962, SI 1962/1517.

RECIPROCAL ENFORCEMENT OF EEC CIVIL AND COMMERCIAL JUDGMENTS

Extent of the EEC Judgments Convention

11.34   The reciprocal recognition and enforcement of judgments in civil and commercial matters given by courts in member states of the European

Community are governed by the 1968 Brussels Convention on Jurisdiction and Enforcement of Judgments in Civil and Commercial Matters, along with the associated Annexed Protocol, a 1971 Protocol, and various Accession Conventions. These documents will be referred to collectively as the '1968 Convention'. The 1968 Convention came about to implement the obligation on member states of the European Community imposed by article 220(4) of the EEC Treaty:

> 'Member States shall, so far as is necessary, enter into negotiations with each other with a view to securing for the benefit of their nationals:
>
> . . .
>
> – the simplification of formalities governing the reciprocal recognition and enforcement of judgments of courts or tribunals . . .[1].'

1 Art 220(4) of the EEC Treaty also requires member states to take steps to simplify procedures for reciprocal recognition and enforcement of arbitration awards. Arbitration awards are not within the scope of the 1968 Convention and no EEC Convention on arbitration awards has yet been made.

11.35   The method of the 1968 Convention is to allow the 'free movement' of judgments within the European Community by requiring member-States to adopt a common set of rules on jurisdiction on civil and commercial matters, as detailed in the Convention itself[1].

Article 63 of the 1968 Convention requires new member-States of the European Community to accept the Convention, with any modifications as appropriate, as a way of implementing its obligation under article 220(4) of the EEC Treaty. Such an Accession Convention was made in 1978 on the entry of the United Kingdom, Republic of Ireland, and Denmark into the European Community. This was followed by an Accession Convention in 1982 on the entry of Greece into the European Community. A further Accession Convention will be required in due course to cover the obligations of Spain and Portugal under article 220(4) of the EEC Treaty.

Not all of the above Accession Conventions have yet been ratified in full. The United Kingdom gave effect to the Convention by the Civil Jurisdiction and Judgments Act 1982, the relevant provisions of which were brought into force on 1 January 1987. As of July 1989, the 1968 Convention is in force between the six original contracting states (ie Belgium, France, West Germany, Italy, Luxembourg and the Netherlands) and also the United Kingdom, Denmark and the Republic of Ireland[2].

1 Cp Case 125/79 *Denilauler v SNC Couchet Frères* [1980] ECR 1553, [1981] 1 CMLR 62; case 166/80 *Klomps v Michel* [1981] ECR 1593, [1982] 2 CMLR 773.
2 For discussion of the territorial units to which the 1968 Convention extends in each contracting state, see AM, 'The Civil Jurisdiction and Judgments Act 1982' 1987 SLT (News) 29.

11.36   It should also be noted that negotiations have been held between the member states of the European Community and countries in the European Free Trade Association (EFTA) with a view to a Convention, parallel to the 1968 Convention, being adopted by the two groups of states. The effect of any such parallel convention between the European Community and EFTA states would be to widen considerably the extent of judgments subject to common provisions for reciprocal recognition and enforcement.

Scope of the Judgments Convention

11.37   Only judgments within the scope of the Judgments Convention can be recognised and enforced according to the special provisions set out in the Convention. Article 1 of the Convention declares that the Convention shall apply 'in civil and commercial matters whatever the nature of the court or tribunal. It shall not extend, in particular, to revenue, customs or administrative matters'.

The core idea here is that of 'civil and commercial matters', but this expression is not defined except negatively by the topics which are explicitly excluded from the scope of civil and commercial matters. The phrasing of the types of excluded matters is not exhaustive and other general categories of exclusion may fall to be implied. What is covered by the ideas of revenue, customs and administrative matters is to based on 'independent', Convention-based criteria and not on purely national criteria.

What is of particular significance in determining the scope of civil and commercial matters covered by the Convention is the approach taken by the European Court in interpreting the Convention. The court has held that the Convention is to be interpreted as a body of law independent of the legal systems of the contracting states, although notice may be taken of general principles which are shared by the national legal systems[1]. As a consequence, where a court of one contracting state has made a decision on whether a particular action is within the scope of the Convention, and subsequently the judgment in that action is to be recognised or enforced in another contracting state, the courts of the other contracting state are not bound by the earlier decisions on the scope of the Convention but must apply independent Convention principles and if necessary make a reference to the European Court[2].

1 Case 29/76 *LTU v Eurocontrol* [1976] ECR 1541, [1977] 1 CMLR 88; Case 33/78 *Somafer v Saar-Ferngas* [1978] ECR 2183, [1979] 1 CMLR 490; Case 33/81 *Ivanel v Schwab* [1982] ECR 1891, [1983] 1 CMLR 538; Case 814/79 *Netherlands v Ruffer* [1980] ECR 3807, [1981] 3 CMLR 293; Case 34/82 *Peters v ZNAV* [1983] ECR 987, [1984] 2 CMLR 605.
2 See eg Case 143/78 *De Cavel v De Cavel (No 1)* [1979] ECR 1055, [1979] 2 CMLR 547, Case 29/76 *LTU v Eurocontrol* [1976] ECR 1541, [1977] 1 CMLR 88; Case 120/79 *De Cavel v De Cavel (No 2)* [1980] ECR 731, [1980] 3 CMLR 1.

11.38   It should also be noted that the scope of the Convention is defined in terms of the subject-matter of the proceedings rather than the nature of the court or tribunal issuing the judgment. Thus the Convention applies to civil and commercial judgments made by eg criminal courts and administrative tribunals[1].

1 Reports by P Jenard on the 1968 Convention and the 1971 Protocol p 9. For the weight to be given to the official Reports on the 1968 Convention by Mr P Jenard and Report on the Accession Convention by Professor Peter Schlosser, see Civil Jurisdiction and Judgments Act 1982, s 3(3).

11.39   The key to the idea of civil and commercial matters is a distinction between public and private law which is drawn in the legal systems of the original contracting states but which has no precise equivalent in the United Kingdom legal systems[1]. In *LTU v Eurocontrol*[2], the European Court of Justice held that an action to recover charges payable by a company to an international body which was governed by public law was an exercise of a power under public law and thus was beyond the scope of the Convention. The court said:

'Although certain judgments given in actions between a public authority and a person governed by private law may fall within the area of application of the Convention, this is not so where the public authority acts in the exercise of its powers.'

In *The Netherlands v Ruffer*[3], the European Court applied this criterion to an action by the State of the Netherlands to recover the costs of removing a wreck from a public waterway. It held that the state was acting in the exercise of its public power and thus the action was not within the range of article 1 of the Convention.

1 A E Anton *Civil Jurisdiction in Scotland* pp 37–38.
2 Case 29/76, [1976] ECR 1541, [1977] 1 CMLR 88.
3 Case 814/79, [1980] ECR 3807, [1981] 3 CMLR 293.

11.40 Article 1(2) of the Convention also provides for certain topics which although civil or commercial in nature are excluded from the scope of the Convention. As the European Court has stressed the importance of the Convention being given an independent interpretation, it is important to bear in mind that the excluded topics must be understood in terms of the general scheme of the Convention rather than in terms of concepts of national legal systems. The civil and commercial topics expressly excluded are as follows.

STATUS OR LEGAL CAPACITY OF NATURAL PERSONS

11.41 Schlosser[1] states that the following matters are included within the idea of status:
(i) voidability and nullity of marriage;
(ii) judicial separation;
(iii) dissolution of marriage;
(iv) death;
(v) status and capacity of minors;
(vi) legal representation of a mentally disordered person;
(vii) nationality and domicile;
(viii) care, custody and adoption of children.
However, maintenance judgments are clearly within the scope of the Convention[2], as are judgments concerning the status or capacity of legal persons[3].

1 Professor P Schlosser *Report on the Accession Convention* para 51.
2 Case 120/79 *De Cavel v De Cavel (No 2)* [1980] ECR 731, [1980] 3 CMLR 1.
3 P Jenard *Report on the 1968 Convention and the 1971 Protocol* p 11.

RIGHTS IN PROPERTY ARISING OUT OF A MATRIMONIAL RELATIONSHIP

11.42 The idea of matrimonial property regimes or relationships is not known to Scots law as a specific legal concept, unlike the position in the legal systems of the original contracting states. In *De Cavel v De Cavel (No 1)*[1], the European Court held that the matrimonial property rights excluded from the Convention covered not only property arrangements specifically and exclusively envisaged by certain national legal systems in the case of marriage but also any proprietary relationships resulting directly from a matrimonial relationship or its dissolution. It continued:

> 'Disputes relating to the assets of spouses in the course of proceedings for divorce may therefore, depending on the circumstances, concern or be closely connected with:
> (1) questions relating to the status of persons; or
> (2) proprietary legal relationships between spouses resulting directly from the matrimonial relationship or the dissolution thereof; or
> (3) proprietary legal relationships existing between them which have no connection with the marriage.
> Whereas disputes of the latter [*sic*] category fall within the scope of the Convention, those relating to the first two categories must be excluded therefrom.'

It has been noted that these categories are not easy to apply and that in particular the distinction between (2) and (3) may be a fine one in practical application[2]. A particular problem concerns a judgment ordering payment by one spouse to another of a lump sum of money on the dissolution of a marriage. If the judgment is classified as one concerning a property right, it will be outwith the scope of the Convention; whereas if it is classified as concerning maintenance, it will be within the scope of the Convention.

1 Case 143/78, [1979] ECR 1055, [1979] 2 CMLR 547. See also Case 25/81 *CHW v GJH* [1982] ECR 1189, [1983] 2 CMLR 125.
2 A E Anton *Civil Jurisdiction in Scotland* p 41.

11.43   In the context of enforcement of judgments, a further problem is that the court of origin may not make clear when delivering a judgment concerning a property matter between spouses whether the judgment is or is not connected with the marriage or its dissolution (ie whether it is in category 2 or 3 in terms of the *De Cavel* judgment). Anton notes that a consequence may be that the court dealing with the application for enforcement may require to investigate the financial and property dealings of the spouses before and during the marriage to determine into which *De Cavel* category the judgment falls, and that such a process of investigation is inappropriate in the course of application for enforcement, which is intended to be summary in nature[1].

1 A E Anton *Civil Jurisdiction in Scotland* p 41.

WILLS AND SUCCESSION

11.44   Excluded from the Convention procedures on enforcement and recognition are judgments relating to wills and succession. This expression is wide enough to cover all questions concerning the administration of estates, rights on intestacy, and the validity and interpretation of wills. Where a trust is created by a will, judgments on matters concerning the creation, the validity or the interpretation of the will are also excluded. However, a judgment on a dispute between a trustee under the will and someone other than a beneficiary under the trust is not excluded by this provision[1].

1 *Schlosser* para 89.

BANKRUPTCY AND INSOLVENCY

11.45 Judgments on matters of bankruptcy and insolvency of natural and legal persons are excluded from the scope of the Convention. Article 1(2) specifies the following processes as within this exclusion:

bankruptcy
winding-up of insolvent companies or other legal persons
judicial arrangements
compositions
analogous proceedings.

Judgments are excluded under this heading only when they relate directly to natural or legal persons who are bankrupt or insolvent. Thus, proceedings equivalent to a voluntary winding-up of a company or a winding-up subject to the supervision of the court are not excluded[1]. However, where the judgment does not make clear whether a company has been wound-up because of its insolvency, the court to which application for enforcement has been made will have to make inquiries as to the state of the company's solvency before it can process the application[2].

1 Cp Case 133/78 *Gourdain v Nadler* [1979] ECR 733, [1979] 3 CMLR 180.
2 *Schlosser* para 57.

SOCIAL SECURITY

11.46 The idea of social security is not defined in the Convention. However, Jenard states that the exclusion of judgments in matters of social security does not apply to judgments in actions between social security authorities and third parties against whom a right or recourse exists by operation of law or subrogation[1].

1 *Jenard* p 13.

ARBITRATION

11.47 In general, arbitration is excluded from the scope of the Convention. A particular problem arises where a court of a contracting state gives a judgment on a matter despite the parties having agreed to submit any dispute on that matter to arbitration. It is not clear whether such a judgment is a judgment relating to arbitration and thus outwith the scope of the Convention[1].

1 A E Anton *Civil Jurisdiction in Scotland* pp 44–45.

Range of types of judgment subject to the 1968 Convention

11.48 A judgment on a matter within the scope of the Convention which is made by a court or tribunal of one contracting state may be enforced in another contracting state by means of the special procedures specified by articles 25 and 31–51 of the Convention. The enforcement provisions of the Convention are not limited to judgments given by the higher or superior courts or tribunals of contracting states. Moreover, the nature and terms of the judgment are not relevant to its enforceability in another contracting state: article 25 states that '"judgment" means any judgment given by a court or tribunal of a Contracting State, whatever the judgment may be called, including a decree, order, decision or writ of execution, as well as the determination of costs or expenses by an officer of court.'

Accordingly the Convention scheme for enforcement applies to both money and non-money judgments, and also applies to both final and interlocutory judgments[1]. However, the enforcement provisions apply only to interlocutory orders which govern the legal relationships of the parties, not those dealing with procedural steps of the litigation[2].

1 Case 143/78 *De Cavel v De Cavel (No 1)* [1979] ECR 1055, [1979] 2 CMLR 547.
2 *Schlosser* paras 184, 187.

11.49 It is less clear whether a judgment can be enforced under the Convention where it is a judgment of the court which gives effect to enforcing a judgment of a foreign court[1]. The scheme of the Convention, as well as of other conventions for enforcing foreign judgments, is that the court of the country where enforcement is sought pronounces an interlocutor 'internalising' the terms of the foreign judgment. As the Convention scheme for enforcement of judgments in different contracting states is to a considerable extent based on the same code of rules in jurisdiction in civil and commercial actions in all contracting states, it is unlikely that where a judgment of a court in a non-contracting state has been subject to an order of a court of a contracting state for enforcement in that state, the order will be subject to the Convention's enforcement procedures for enforcement in another contracting state. The position is less clear whether an order of a court in one contracting state to enforce a judgment from a court of a second contracting state can be enforced directly in another contracting state. This issue may have practical relevance where the original judgment is no longer enforceable in the state of origin but the order internalising the judgment in the second state still allows for execution of the judgment in that state.

1 For discussion, see A E Anton *Civil Jurisdiction in Scotland* p 130.

11.50 Documents which are registered in the books of a court for execution do not come within the provisions of enforcement of judgments under the Convention. However, special provision is made for enforcement between contracting states of so-called 'authentic instruments' (which are broadly equivalent to registered documents) and court settlements[1]. The scheme for enforcing such instruments and settlements is broadly similar to the general scheme for enforcing judgments.

1 1968 Convention, arts 50 & 51. See below at paras 11.130–11.134.

Exclusion of other modes of enforcement

11.51 When a judgment has been given on a matter within the scope of the Convention by a court of a contracting state, it is not possible to raise an action on the same matter involving the same parties in another contracting state as an alternative to enforcing the judgment in the other contracting state. In *De Wolf v Cox*[1], such a step was attempted in circumstances where it was less expensive to raise a second action in the Netherlands than to enforce in the Netherlands a judgment of a court in Belgium on the same matter. The

European court held that the second action was incompetent. A clear implication of this decision is that where a judgment can be enforced under the provisions of the Convention, no other mode of enforcing the judgment is permissible. Thus a judgment which is enforceable in Scotland under the terms of the Convention, cannot be the basis for an action for decree conform.

1 Case 42/76, [1976] ECR 1759, [1977] 2 CMLR 43.

11.52 It should be noted that the scheme of the Foreign Judgments (Reciprocal Enforcement) Act 1933 extends to Belgium, France, West Germany, Italy and the Netherlands. By articles 55 and 56 of the Convention, the scheme of the 1933 Act is superseded by that of the Convention itself as far as concerns reciprocal enforcement of judgments between the United Kingdom and those five other contracting states. However, the 1933 Act scheme still applies in respect of judgments within its scope and outwith the scope of the 1968 Convention[1].

1 Cases 9/77 and 10/77 *Bavaria Fluggesellschaft Schwabe and Germanair v Eurocontrol* [1977] ECR 1517, [1980] 1 CMLR 566.

Grounds for refusing to enforce a foreign judgment

11.53 Judgments within the scope of the Convention given by a court in one contracting state can be enforced in another contracting state by following a specified procedure which involves the party who is seeking to enforce the judgment making application to a specified court in that other state[1]. The court to which application for enforcement is made has only very limited grounds for refusing to accept the judgment as one capable of enforcement under the Convention.

1 See further below at paras 11.75 et seq.

11.54 The Convention itself specifies the grounds for refusing to enforce a judgment of a court of another contracting state. Among grounds which are *not* open to a court to which application for enforcement has been made are:
(1) In general a court to which application has been made for the enforcement of a judgment of a court of another contracting state has no power to review the substance of the foreign judgment[1]. However, this prohibition on review of substance is subject to the requirement that in certain circumstances the court of the country of enforcement must satisfy itself that the judgment is one within the scope of the Convention (eg whether a judgment in a dispute between spouses concerns an issue of general property law or of matrimonial property law).
(2) The provisions of the Convention on recognition and enforcement of the judgments of courts of other contracting states are closely linked to the provisions of the Convention which set out a common code of jurisdiction on civil and commercial matters. At common law and in many conventions for the enforcement of foreign judgments, a requirement of equivalence of grounds of jurisdiction between the state of origin and state of enforcement is fundamental. One effect of a common code on jurisdiction set out by the Convention is that it allows for the 'free movement of judgments' between contracting states. Furthermore, the process of enforcing a judgment given in

one contracting state in another contracting state is intended to be summary in nature[2], and as a consequence the court of the country of enforcement is in general not permitted to review the jurisdiction of the court in which the judgment was given. However, article 28 does allows certain cases where review of jurisdiction by the court of enforcement is permitted and indeed required[3].

1 1968 Convention, art 34(3).
2 Cp 1968 Convention, art 34(1); Case 198/85 *Carron v West Germany* [1987] 1 CMLR 838 at 844.
3 See further below at paras 11.68–11.69.

11.55 A further consequence of the general prohibition on review of jurisdiction is that a judgment within the scope of the Convention can be enforced in another contract state *whatever* the basis of jurisdiction of the court of origin of the judgment. Where the defender is domiciled in a contracting state, the jurisdictional rules will ensure that the Convention's code of jurisdiction will be applied by the court of origin. Where, however, the defender is not a domicillary of a contracting state, a judgment on a Convention matter will be enforced in another Contract State even where the court of origin assumed jurisdiction on a ground not recognised under, or forbidden by, the Convention. This is subject to the provisions of article 59 of the Convention[1].

1 See below at paras 11.70–11.73.

11.56 Grounds for not enforcing a judgment of a court of a contracting state in another contracting state are of two types: the first set of grounds relate to the procedural prerequisites for a valid application for the enforcement of a judgment given in another contracting state. These are considered below at paragraphs 11.75–11.116. The second set of grounds for refusing enforcement of a judgment of a court of another contracting state are specified in articles 27 and 28, and these are intended to be the only reasons for refusing a validly-made application for enforcement of a judgment in another contracting state. The grounds set out in articles 27 and 28 (which relate to the questions of recognition of foreign judgments and are extended to enforcement of foreign judgments by article 34(2)) are mandatory in nature and fall to be applied by the court in the contracting state where enforcement is sought *ex proprio motu*, if necessary[1].

1 Refusal to enforce a Convention judgment on the basis of article II of the Annexed Protocol is not mandatory for a court to which application is made for enforcement. See further below at para 11.74.

GROUNDS REQUIRING NON–ENFORCEMENT OF A CONVENTION JUDGMENT OF A
COURT OF ANOTHER CONTRACTING STATE

Public policy (article 27(1))

11.57 A judgment is not to be enforced where such enforcement would be contrary to the public policy in the contracting state in which enforcement is sought. What is prohibited by public policy is the *enforcement* of the judgment in the state of enforcement, not the substance of the judgment itself. It is for the court of the state where enforcement is sought to apply the principle of public policy of that legal system but it has been suggested that such national criteria for public policy must be appropriate to the general scheme of the Convention and that the European Court of Justice may have a general supervisory role over the approaches adopted by the national courts[1].

No definition of public policy is provided by the Convention or in the 1982 Act. The Maxwell Report in its discussion of the concept of 'ordre public' in the laws of the original contracting states notes that the idea refers to 'those mandatory rules of law which a State considers so fundamental to its moral, social or economic order that they should prevent the application of foreign laws and judgments which conflict with them'[2].

Whatever the scope of public policy in this context, it cannot be used as a basis for reviewing the jurisdiction of the court of origin of the judgment, even in those limited cases where review of jurisdiction is permissible[3]. It has also been suggested that public policy does not allow refusal to enforce a judgment on grounds of procedural irregularity or breach of natural justice (which are dealt with by article 27(2)), nor does public policy allow refusal to enforce a judgment merely because the court of origin did not apply the rules of international private law of the legal system of the court of enforcement[4]. On the other hand public policy may allow non-enforcement in cases of a judgment obtained by fraud (though this may be subject to certain limitations)[5] and judgments for multiple damages[6].

1 A E Anton *Civil Jurisdiction in Scotland* p 134.
2 *Report of the Scottish Committee on Jurisdiction and Enforcement* (Chairman, Lord Maxwell) (1980), p 117.
3 1968 Convention, art 28(3).
4 *Jenard* p 44.
5 Cp *Schlosser* para 192. Cheshire and North in *Private International Law* at p 417 suggest that 'it would be best to confine the public policy defence in cases of fraud to the situation in which (i) there is evidence of fraud which was unavailable and unexamined earlier in the proceedings and (ii) the evidence arises at such a late stage that it cannot be raised on appeal in the State which granted the judgment, and the only court in which the fraud can be considered is the recognising court.'
6 A E Anton *Civil Jurisdiction in Scotland* p 135; Stone (1983) 32 ICLQ 477, 480–481.

Rights of the defender where judgment pronounced in absence (article 27(2))

11.58 A judgment of a court of one contracting state shall not be enforced in another contracting state where the judgment was 'given in default of appearance, if the defendant was not duly served with the document which instituted the proceedings or with an equivalent document in sufficient time to enable him to arrange for his defence.' What constitutes due service of the document instituting the proceedings is to be determined in accordance with the law of the state of origin of the judgment and with any convention on service of documents existing between that state and the state where service is effected (eg the 1965 Hague Convention on Service of Documents Abroad, which has been ratified by all the member states of the European Community except Spain and the Republic of Ireland.) The court to which application for enforcement is made must satisfy itself that due service was made on the defender in the case of a judgment in absence, even where the court of origin of the judgment has already held that proper service on the defender has been effected[1].

1 Case 288/81 *Pendy Plastic v Pluspunkt* [1982] ECR 2723, [1983] 1 CMLR 665.

11.59 There is no requirement that service of the initiating document must have been personal in nature. What is required is that the mode of service allows the defender to take steps to defend his interests[1]. What is sufficient time to allow a defender to arrange his defence is a matter of fact. This is to be determined by the court of the state of enforcement by looking at all the circumstances concerning the service of the documents, including those occurring after service is made. In *Debaecker v Bowman*[2], the pursuer had used a mode of fictitious service on the defender. Later the defender, who was unaware that proceedings had started against him, wrote to the pursuers on a matter relating to the dispute between the parties. Although this correspondence disclosed the defender's actual address, the pursuer took no further steps to intimate to the defender that he had been served with documents instituting proceedings against him. Judgment in default of appearance by the defender was subsequently granted. The European Court held that this failure by the pursuer did not automatically render the judgment unenforceable in another contracting state but was a relevant factor for the court of the state where enforcement was sought to consider when deciding whether service had been sufficient to allow the defender to prepare a defence in the action.

The Court also noted that article 27(2) is to be determined in an 'independent' way and not by the criteria of national law (either of the contracting state of origin or of enforcement).

1 Case 166/80 *Klomps v Michel* [1981] ECR 1593, [1982] 2 CMLR 773.
2 Case 49/84 *Debaecker v Bowman* [1986] 2 CMLR 400.

11.60   Investigation by a court dealing with an application for enforcement of a judgment given in default of appearance by the defender is facilitated by the requirement of article 46(1) that such an application contains the original or certified true copy of the document which established that the party in default was served the document instituting the proceedings or with an equivalent document[1].

1 1968 Convention, art 46(1); cp RC 249E(2)(a)(iii); RC 249N(2).

11.61   Where a Scottish judgment is to be enforced in a contracting state other than the United Kingdom, the appropriate modes of service to be considered by the foreign court to which application for enforcement is made are those set out in RC 74A, 74B, 75, 192, OCR 12 and SCR 9. Since the bringing into force of the 1982 Act, the standard induciae in actions in the Court of Session and the sheriff court are twenty-one days where the defender is resident or has a place of business within Europe, which time should in most cases allow for the defender to prepare his defences and enter appearance[1].

1 RC 72, 192; OCR 7; SCR 4; SMCR 4.

11.62   One effect of the rule that a judgment cannot be enforced under the provisions of the Convention where due notice of the proceedings has not been made on the defender is that all ex parte orders and judgments cannot be enforced in another contracting state. This is the case even in regard to *ex parte* orders for provisional and protective measures, whose rationale usually presupposes that no notice is given to the opposite party[1]. Where one litigant wishes to use *ex parte* provisional and protective measures in another contracting state he must make separate application under article 24 for those measures in the courts of each contracting state in which he wishes to enforce them. However, where notice of proceedings has been made on the other party, a judgment in default of appearance by that party can still be enforced in another contracting state even where the judgment is provisional or interim in nature[1].

1 Case 125/79 *Denilauler v SNC Couchet Frères* [1980] ECR 1553, [1981] 1 CMLR 62.

Conflicting judgment in state of enforcement (article 27(3))

11.63   A judgment of a court of one contracting state cannot be enforced in another contracting state 'if the judgment is irreconcilable with a judgment given in a dispute between the same parties in the State in which recognition [and/or enforcement] is sought'. Articles 21–23 of the Convention lay down various rules which are designed to prevent simultaneous proceedings by courts of different contracting states with the same cause of action. However, the conflicting judgment in the state of enforcement must concern a dispute between the same parties but need not involve the same cause of action. What constitutes the 'giving' of a judgment in the state of enforcement is to be decided by the court dealing with the application for enforcement[1]. It is not clear that a judgment has been given in a state where it was first made in one state and then recognised or made subject to an order for enforcement in a second state and a later irreconcilable judgment is sought to be enforced in the second state. It has been suggested that in certain circumstances this wide definition of 'given' is necessary to give effect to the meaning of article 27(3)[2].

1 *Jenard* p 45.
2 G C Cheshire and P M North *Private International Law* (11th edn) p 422.

11.64   The conflicting judgment is one which has been given in the state, rather than the legal system, in which enforcement of the later judgment is sought. Thus, where application is made for enforcement in Scotland of a judgment of a court of another contracting state, the Court of Session must refuse enforcement if there is an irreconcilable judgment given in any part of the United Kingdom[1].

1 *Maxwell Report* p 121.

11.65   A particular problem arises in the cases of maintenance judgments. By virtue of articles 2 and 5(2) of the Convention, it is possible for courts in more than one contracting state to have jurisdiction to vary a maintenance judgment[1]. In most cases, variation of an existing maintenance judgment will take the form of a new judgment which is to supersede the original judgment. A difficulty arises therefore where a variation judgment is the subject of an application for enforcement in the contracting state where the original judgment was made. Jenard states that 'any judgment by a second court, in order to vary that of the first court, would have to be based on changed facts, and in those circumstances it could not be maintained that the judgments were in conflict'[2]. However, as the Maxwell Report notes, if the second judgment was made where there had been no change of circumstances, enforcement of the varying judgment could be refused on the basis of article 27(3)[3].

1 *Maxwell Report* pp 50–51; *Schlosser* paras 98–108.
2 *Jenard* p 25.
3 *Maxwell Report* p 157.

Conflicting judgment given in a non-contracting state (article 27(5))

11.66 A judgment of a court of a contracting state shall not be enforced in another contracting state where it is irreconcilable with an earlier judgment given in a non-contracting state involving the same cause of action and between the same parties. The judgment of the non-contracting state must be capable of recognition or enforcement in the state addressed. Thus, where there are two conflicting judgments on the same cause of action between the same parties, and one judgment is given in a contracting state and the other judgment given in a non-contracting state, the judgment in the non-contracting state will be enforced provided it is the earlier of the two judgments. Whether the judgment of the non-contracting state is entitled to recognition or enforcement in the contracting state of enforcement is to be determined by the law of that state. In the case of a judgment which is to be enforced in the United Kingdom, it appears that it is sufficient that the judgment of the non-contracting state must be entitled to recognition or enforcement in any of the legal systems of the United Kingdom[1].

1 For discussion of the problems of applying article 27(5) to judgments varying earlier maintenance judgments see the *Maxwell Report* pp 156–157.

Decisions on preliminary or incidental matters (article 27(4))

11.67 Article 27(4) provides that a judgment will not be enforced if the court of the contracting state in which the judgment was given has decided a preliminary question on certain matters in a way which conflicts with a rule of international private law of the contracting state in which the enforcement is sought. These matters are:
(i) the status or legal capacity of natural persons;
(ii) rights in property arising out of a matrimonial relationship;
(iii) wills or succession.
However, this ground for non-enforcement does not arise (a) where the decision on the preliminary matter was not necessary for the judgment, or (b) where the same outcome would have been arrived at if the correct rules of international private law had been applied. These issues are to be determined by the court dealing with the application for enforcement.

Where enforcement is sought in the United Kingdom, it would seem that a judgment must be refused registration for enforcement, where the judgment was given in an action which dealt with such a preliminary matter in a way conflicting with the rules of international private law of any of the legal systems of the United Kingdom and not only those of the legal system of the court to which application is made.

Anton notes that the effect of article 27(4) is to ensure that the enforcement and recognition provisions of the Convention are not used so as to allow indirect recognition and enforcement of judgments on matters outwith the scope of the Convention[1]. However, article 27(4) allows review of the application of choice of law rules only in respect of the matters listed above and does not apply in respect of all the matters excluded from the scope of the Convention (eg social security or bankruptcy).

1 A E Anton *Civil Jurisdiction in Scotland* p 137.

Conflicts with certain jurisdictional provisions (article 28)

11.68   Although the general rule is that the court to which application for enforcement is made cannot examine the basis of jurisdiction of the court which made the judgment, the court of enforcement must refuse to enforce a judgment if the judgment conflicts with certain jurisdictional provisions of the Convention. These provisions are those dealing with:
(i) insurance (articles 7–12A);
(ii) consumer contracts (articles 13–15);
(iii) exclusive jurisdiction dealt with in article 16.
The role of the court of enforcement is limited to considering whether the court of origin has correctly applied the rules of jurisdiction in the particular case, and in considering this matter it must accept the findings of fact which the court of origin has made in respect of the basis of its jurisdiction[1].

1 1968 Convention, art 28(2).

11.69   The general rules forbidding examination of jurisdiction of the court of origin by the court of enforcement continue to apply where jurisdiction is based on article 17 of the Convention, even where it appears to involve a breach of that provision. Article 17 gives exclusive jurisdiction to the court of a legal system where the parties have prorogated the jurisdiction of that court. Thus, where a court of one contracting state has assumed jurisdiction in ignorance of, or breach of, a prorogation agreement, a court in another contracting state to which application is made must still recognise and enforce the judgment of that court[1].

1 But see A E Anton *Civil Jurisdiction in Scotland* p 139 for doubts about this conclusion.

Case provided for by article 59 (article 28(1))

11.70   A judgment cannot be enforced in another contracting state where the judgment is covered by article 59 of the Convention. Article 59 is designed to avoid difficulties which may arise from the situation that a judgment may be covered by the provisions of the Convention on recognition and enforcement where the defender is not domiciled in any of the contracting states to the Convention and the basis of jurisdiction of the court of origin is not a ground permitted by the Convention (eg the nationality of the pursuer or the arrestment of the defender's moveable property)[1]. What article 59 does is to allow a contracting state to agree with a non-contracting state in a Convention on recognition and enforcement of judgments that it will *not* recognise and enforce a judgment given in any other contracting state against defenders domiciled or habitually resident in that non-contracting state.

1 For an explanation of some of the problems that may arise see A E Anton *Civil Jurisdiction in Scotland* pp 137–138.

11.71   However, such an agreement not to recognise or enforce a judgment given in another contracting state against defenders domiciled in non-contracting states is to apply only where the only possible ground of jurisdiction of the court of origin was a ground specified in article 3, paragraph 2, of the Convention, namely:

in Belgium	article 15 of the civil code (*Code civil – Burgerlijk Wetboek*) and article 638 of the Judicial Code (*Code judiciare – Gerectelijk Wetboek*);
in Denmark	article 248(2) of the law on civil procedure (*Lov om rettens pleje*) and chapter 3, article 3 of the Greenland law on civil procedure (*Lov for Gronland on rettens pleje*);
in the Federal Republic of Germany	article 23 of the code of civil procedure (*Zivilprozessordung*);
in France	articles 14 and 15 of the civil code (*Code civil*);
in Ireland	the rules which enable jurisdiction to be founded on the document instituting the proceedings having been served on the defendant during his temporary presence in Ireland;
in Italy	articles 2 and 4, nos 1 and 2 of the code of civil procedure (*Codice di procedura civile*);
in Luxembourg	articles 14 and 15 of the civil code (*Code civil*);
in the Netherlands	articles 126(3) and 127 of the code of civil procedure (*Wetboek van Bergerlijke Rechtsvordering*);
in the United Kingdom	the rules which enable jurisdiction to be founded on: (a) the document instituting the proceedings having been served on the defendant during his temporary presence in the United Kingdom; or (b) the presence within the United Kingdom of property belonging to the defendant; or (c) the seizure by the plaintiff of property situated in the United Kingdom.

Furthermore, article 59 does not allow for such a non-recognition and non-enforcement agreement with a non-contracting state where the jurisdiction is based on presence, or seizure by the plaintiff, of the defendant's property in the state of origin *and*
(1) the action is brought to assert or declare proprietary or possessory rights in that property or seeks to obtain authority to dispose of it, or arises from another issue relating to such property; or
(2) if the property constitutes the security for a debt which is the subject-matter of the action.

Accordingly, article 59 has application in Scotland in respect of judgments of Scottish courts where jurisdiction was based on the arrestment of moveable property of the defender *ad fundandam jurisdictionem* or the *situs* of heritable property in which the defender has a beneficial interest[1], unless the action was directly concerned with the property in question. It may be that where an action is raised for payment of a sum of money and the pursuer arrests moveable property both to found jurisdicton and on the dependence of the action, the arrested property is to be treated as a 'security for a debt which is the subject-matter of the action' and so any judgment in the action will not be within the scope of article 59.

Article 59 also applies in respect of actions in Scotland where jurisdiction is based on rule 2(1) of Schedule 8 to the 1982 Act (where the defender has no fixed residence and is personally cited) provided it can be shown that the defender was 'temporarily present' in the United Kingdom at the time of personal service.

1 Civil Jurisdiction and Judgments Act 1982, Sch 8, r 2(8).

11.72 It should be noted that the court of the contracting state of enforcement must satisfy itself that no possible basis exists for the jurisdiction of the court of origin other than one of the specified exorbitant jurisdictions. This is so whatever ground of jurisdiction may be specified by the court of origin. The court of enforcement is probably bound by findings of fact made by the court of origin concerning its basis of jurisdiction[1].

1 Cp C G Cheshire and P M North *Private International Law* (11th edn) p 425.

11.73 As far as concerns any such non-recognition and non-enforcement agreement made between the United Kingdom and a non-contracting state, section 9(2) of the 1982 Act allows for Orders in Council to declare that a convention on recognition and enforcement of judgments entered into by the United Kingdom is a provision whereby the United Kingdom has assumed an obligation of non-recognition and non-enforcement provided for by article 59 of the Convention.

To date the United Kingdom has made one such declaration, namely in respect of a Convention with Canada. The United Kingdom has agreed not to recognise or enforce under the 1968 Convention, judgments covered by article 59 of that Convention which have been made by courts of other contracting states against a person domiciled or habitually resident in Canada[1].

1 Recognition and Enforcement of Foreign Judgments (Canada) Order 1987, SI 1987/468. Article IX(2) of the relevant Convention with Canada contains definitions of domicile in Canada.

Judgment on civil liability in criminal action tried without appearance (Annexed Protocol, article II)

11.74 A judgment may be refused enforcement in another contracting state where the provisions of article II of the Annexed Protocol apply. These provisions relate to criminal proceedings for an offence not involving intent against a person who has a domicile in a contracting state and is prosecuted in a contracting state in which he is neither domiciled nor a national. The accused need not appear in person but may be defended by a legally qualified representative. However, if the criminal court orders appearance of the accused in person and the accused fails to appear, a judgment given in the 'civil action' where the accused has not had an opportunity to arrange his defence need not (but may) be recognised or enforced in another contracting state.

It is not clear what is meant by a judgment given in the civil action in this context. In the legal systems of some contracting states (but not in Scotland) criminal courts have jurisdiction to adjudicate on issues of civil liability arising out of the criminal conduct, and it is clear that civil judgments in these circumstances are covered by article II of the Annexed Protocol. However, in *Rinkau*[1], the European Court held that article II also applied to criminal proceedings on which the accused's civil liability might subsequently be based, and if the conditions set out in paragraph 2 of article II obtain in respect of criminal proceedings, then a judgment in later civil proceedings need not be enforced in other contracting states. In such a case, article II might apply in respect of a civil judgment given in Scottish courts where reliance is made on sections 10 and 12 of the Law Reform (Miscellaneous Provisions) (Scotland) Act 1968 to use as evidence a conviction of an accused where the accused was not present in court and the offence was not one involving criminal intent. It may be, however, that this wider interpretation of the idea of civil liability, adopted by the European court in *Rinkau*, applies only where the decision in the criminal proceedings is binding in subsequent civil proceedings[2]. In such a case, it might still have application in respect of Scottish civil judgments where section 12 of the 1968 Act has been used.

1 Case 157/80, [1981] ECR 1391, [1983] 1 CMLR 205.
2 See the opinion of the Advocate General in Case 157/80, [1981] ECR 1391 at 1408–1409.

Outline of procedure for enforcement

11.75   The general procedure for enforcing a Convention judgment in another contracting state is provided by articles 31–49 of the Convention. More detailed rules as applying to each contracting state are governed by the law of the contracting state in which enforcement is sought[1]. Where a judgment is given in a contracting state other than the United Kingdom and is to be enforced in Scotland, procedure is further regulated by RC 249D–RC 249L.

1 1968 Convention, art 33(1).

11.76   In outline the procedure for enforcement of a Convention judgment is that the party seeking enforcement in another contracting state lodges an application in a specified court of the contracting state concerned. The application is to be accompanied by various documents. The application is considered by the court in which the enforcement is sought. The court's decision on granting or refusing the application is subject to a set of appeals by the parties concerned. Where the application is granted, the judgment is registered by the enforcing court and made enforceable in that legal system.

Before a judgment can be subject to an application for enforcement in another contracting state, various conditions must be satisfied:
(1) The judgment must be within the scope of the 1968 Convention.
(2) The judgment must not be open to an objection against enforcement as specified in the Convention.
(3) The judgment must be enforceable in the contracting state of origin[1]. Documentary evidence from the contracting state of origin that the judgment is enforceable in that state must be produced when application for enforcemnt is made in another contracting state.
(4) The judgment must not have been satisfied in full. This condition is not expressly stated in the Convention but is a consequence of its having to be enforceable in the contracting state of origin. Furthermore this condition is implied by article 42(2) which permits the partial enforcement of a judgment.

(5) The judgment must have been 'served' on the party against whom enforcement is sought. Such service must have been made according to the law of the contracting state of origin of the judgment[2].

(6) Where the judgment orders periodic payment by way of penalty, the amount of the payment must have been finally determined by the court of origin[3]. This provision is aimed at provisions of some Contracting States that certain judgments attract penalty payments during the period in which the judgment is unsatisfied[4].

1 1968 Convention, arts 31, 47(1).
2 Ibid, art 47(1).
3 Ibid, art 43.
4 *Schlosser* p 132; A E Anton *Civil Jurisdiction in Scotland* p 143.

Title to apply for enforcement of a Convention judgment

11.77 Article 31 of the Convention lays down that a Convention judgment shall be enforceable in another contracting state if an order for its enforcement has been made in that contracting state following the application of 'any interested party'. No definition of interested party is provided in the Convention, but it appears that where a Convention judgment is to be enforced in Scotland, it is for Scots law to determine who has an interest in the enforcement of the judgment[1].

1 *Maxwell Report* p 97, citing Droz *Competence Judiciare et Effets des Jugements dans le Marche Commun* (1972) para 549.

Courts to which application for enforcement is made

11.78 Article 32 of the Convention specifies the following courts as the appropriate courts for submitting an application for enforcement of a judgment of a court of another contracting state:

Belgium:	to the *tribunal de première instance* or *rechtbank van eerste aanleg*;
Denmark:	to the *underret*;
Federal Republic of Germany:	to the presiding judge of a chamber of the *Landgericht*;
France:	to the presiding judge of the *tribunal de grande instance*;
Ireland:	to the High Court;
Italy:	to the *corte d'appello*;
Luxembourg:	to the presiding judge of the *tribunal d'arrondissement*;
The Netherlands:	to the presiding judge of the *arrondissementsrechtbank*

In the United Kingdom application is made to different courts depending on whether the judgment is or is not a maintenance judgment. Where the judgment is a non-maintenance one, application is to be made as follows:

in England and Wales:	to the High Court of Justice;
in Scotland:	to the Court of Session;
in Northern Ireland:	to the High Court of Justice.

Where application is made for the enforcement in the United Kingdom of a maintenance judgment of a court of another contracting state, the application is made to a local court by way of transmission from the Secretary of State[1]:

in England and Wales:	to the magistrates' court on transmission from the Secretary of State;
in Scotland:	to the sheriff court on transmission from the Secretary of State;
in Northern Ireland:	to the magistrates' court on transmission from the Lord Chancellor.

1 Civil Jurisdiction and Judgments Act 1982, s 5(1).

11.79   Except in the case of non-maintenance judgments which are to be enforced in the United Kingdom, the court which deals with an application for enforcement is a local court. The appropriate court in each contracting state is that of the place of the domicile of the party against whom enforcement is sought or if that party has no domicile in that state, the court of the place of enforcement[1].

1 1968 Convention, art 32(2).

11.80   It will be noted that where a judgment is to be enforced in the United Kingdom, separate application must be made to the appropriate courts in each of the constituent legal systems if enforcement is sought in more than one of the law districts of the United Kingdom.

Procedure for application

11.81   An application for enforcement must provide an address for service of process within the area of jurisdiction of the court applied to. In *Carron v West Germany*[1], the European Court held that the detailed procedure to be followed in respect of providing an address for service was to be regulated according to the law of the state where enforcement was sought. However, that law could not allow provision of such an address later than the time of service on the party liable under the judgment of the decision of the court authorising enforcement.

Where provision is made by the law of the state of enforcement for such an address being provided, any sanction for failure to provide it is also to be regulated by that law. However this law must conform to the aims of the Convention, and in particular any sanction cannot cast doubt on the validity of the order authorising enforcement or prejudice the rights of the other party.

If the law of that legal system does not have rules providing for such an address, the appellant must appoint a local representative *ad litem*[2]. Where a non-United Kingdom Convention judgment is to be enforced in Scotland, the application must be accompanied by an affidavit which states, inter alia, an address within the jurisdiction of the Court of Session for service on the application[3].

1 Case 198/85, [1987] 1 CMLR 838.
2 1968 Convention, art 33(2).
3 RC 249E(2)(b)(iv).

11.82 An application for enforcement must also provide various supporting documents. Articles 46 and 47 require that the party applying for enforcement of a judgment in another contracting state must produce:
(a) a copy of the judgment which satisfies the conditions necessary to establish its authenticity. Where a judgment of a court of another contracting state is to be enforced in the United Kingdom, the United Kingdom court dealing with the application shall treat a duly authenticated document which purports to be a copy of the judgment as a true copy unless the contrary is shown. A document purporting to be a copy of the judgment is duly authenticated for this purpose (i) if it purports to bear the seal of that court or (ii) if it purports to be certified by any person in his capacity as a judge or officer of that court to be a true copy of the judgment given by the court[1].
(b) in the case of a judgment given in default of appearance, the original or certified true copy of the document which establishes that the party in default was served with the document instituting the proceedings or with an equivalent document;
(c) documents establishing that the judgment is enforceable and has been served according to the law of the state in which it was given;
(d) where appropriate, a document showing that the applicant is in receipt of legal aid in the state in which the judgment was given.
Where application is made for enforcement in Scotland of a judgment of a court of another contracting state, the original or a copy of the documents specified in (b) to (d) above shall be sufficient evidence of any matter to which it relates[2].

If these documents are not produced with the application, the court dealing with the application has power to specify time-limits for their production. It may accept alternative documents, or if it considers that it has sufficient information before it, dispense with the production of the documents. The court may also require a translation of the documents[3].

1 Civil Jurisdiction and Judgments Act 1982, s 11(1)(a), (2).
2 Ibid, s 11(1)(b).
3 1968 Convention, art 48.

Application to the Court of Session: Convention judgments other than maintenance judgments

11.83 Where a non-United Kingdom Convention judgment (other than a maintenance judgment) is the subject of application for enforcement in Scotland, the application is made *ex parte* using Form 53 of the Rules of Court. The application is to be signed by the applicant, by an advocate, or by a solicitor entitled to practise before the Court of Session. With the application, there must be produced[1]:
(a) the following documents;
(i) a certified copy of the judgment to be registered;

(ii) a document which establishes that, according to the law of the country in which the judgment has been given, the judgment is enforceable and has been served;

(iii) where judgment has been given in default of appearance, the original or certified copy of the document which establishes that the party against whom the judgment was given was served with the document initiating the proceedings or with an equivalent document;

(iv) where appropriate, a document showing that the applicant is in receipt of legal aid in the country in which the judgment was given;

(v) where the judgment or any other document produced is in a language other than English, a translation into English certified by a person qualified as a translator;

(b) an affidavit stating:

(i) whether the judgment provides for the payment of a sum of money;

(ii) whether interest is recoverable on the judgment in accordance with the law of the country in which judgment was given, and if so, the rate of interest, the date from which interest is due and the date on which interest ceases to accrue;

(iii) where appropriate, the sterling equivalent at the relevant rate of exchange of the amount of money expressed in a foreign currency which is recoverable by the applicant. It is not clear when such a conversion into sterling is appropriate. Scots law recognises the issue of appropriate currency of a judgment to be a substantive matter to be determined by the appropriate proper law[2]. Conversion into sterling is required only if that is necessary for enforcement in Scotland but the date of conversion is to be as near as possible to the execution of diligence enforcing the decree[3]. For the court to examine whether the foreign currency of the judgment was the proper currency of the judgment would be inconsistent with the prohibition on review of substance of a judgment by a court dealing with an application for enforcement of the judgment in another contracting state[4].

Furthermore, the position that there need not be any conversion of the sum into sterling as at the date of application seems to be implicit in a Court of Session Practice Note of 8 December 1988[5] which allows for a certificate of conversion of the sum due under the judgment into sterling to be presented under RC 249(2), ie at time of seeking extract of an already-registered judgment.

(iv) an address within the jurisdiction of the court for service on the applicant[6];

(v) so far as known to the deponent, the usual or last known address or place of business of the person against whom the judgment was given;

(vi) to the knowledge and belief of the deponent the grounds on which the applicant is entitled to enforce the judgment;

(vii) whether at the date of the application the judgment has not been satisfied or the part or amount in respect of which it is unsatisfied.

1 RC 249E(2).
2 *Commerzbank AG v Large* 1977 SC 375. For discussion see ch 1 above at paras 1.44–1.49.
3 *Commerzbank AG v Large* 1977 SC 375 at 383.
4 1968 Convention art 34(3).
5 See 1989 SLT (News) 3.
6 Case 198/85 *Carron v West Germany* [1987] 1 CMLR 838.

11.84 Rule of Court 249E(3) reflects the provisions of article 48(1) of the Convention dealing with the situation where the documents mentioned in

paragraph (a) above are not produced. In these circumstances the court may
(i) fix a time within which the documents are to be lodged in process;
(ii) accept equivalent documents; or
(iii) dispense with the requirement to produce the documents.
However, these powers do not exist in connection with failure to produce the
appropriate affidavit in (b) above at paragraph 11.83. Failure to produce the
affidavit in full terms as required may lead the court to refuse the application
because of procedural irregularity, unless the terms of affidavit are not
appropriate to the application. However, given the decision of the European
Court in *Carron v West Germany*[1], any sanction for failure by the applicant to
provide an address for service cannot include refusing to deal with the
application or invalidating any order granting enforcement.

1 Case 198/85, [1987] 1 CMLR 838.

Application to the sheriff court: Convention maintenance judgments

11.85 Where a non–United Kingdom Convention maintenance judgment
is the subject of application for enforcement in Scotland, the application is
made *ex parte* in writing addressed to the Secretary of State. The application is
to be signed by the applicant, or by a solicitor or professional person,
qualified to act in such matters in the contracting state of origin, on his behalf.
  The application must specify[1]:
(a) an address within Scotland for service on the applicant. Where the sheriff
clerk is informed by a solicitor practising in Scotland that he is acting on
behalf of the applicant, the business address of the solicitor is to be treated as
the address for service on the applicant[2];
(b) the usual or last known address of the person against whom the judgment
was granted;
(c) the place where the applicant seeks to enforce the judgment;
(d) whether at the date of the application the judgment has been satisfied in
whole or in part;
(e) whether interest is recoverable on the judgment in accordance with the
law of the country in which it was granted, and if so, the rate of interest and
the date from which interest became due; and
(f) whether the time for bringing an appeal against the judgment has expired
without an appeal having been brought, or whether an appeal has been
brought against the judgment and is pending or has been finally disposed of.

1 AS (Enforcement of Judgments under the Civil Jurisdiction and Judgments Act 1982) 1986,
  SI 1986/1947, para 6(1).
2 Ibid, para 6(4).

11.86 In addition, an application shall be accompanied by[1]:
(a) a copy of the judgment authenticated by the court which made the order;
(b) documents which establish that, according to the law of the country in
which the judgment has been given, the judgment is enforceable and has been
served;
(c) where judgment has been given in default of appearance, documents
which establish that the party in default was served with the document
initiating the proceedings or with an equivalent document;

(d) where appropriate, a document showing that the applicant is in receipt of legal aid in the country in which the judgment was given; and
(e) a translation into English, certified as correct by a person qualified to make it, of the judgment or any documents in (a) to (d) above where they are in a language other than English.

1 SI 1986/1947, para 6(2).

11.87   Where any of the documents required under para 6(2) of the Sheriff Court Enforcement Act of Sederunt are not produced the sheriff clerk may
(a) fix a time within which the document is to be produced;
(b) accept an equivalent document; or
(c) dispense with the production of the document.
However, these powers do not exist in connection with failure to provide the information required by para 6(1) of the Act of Sederunt. As with applications to the Court of Session, failure to produce this information may lead the sheriff clerk to refuse the application because of procedural irregularity. However, given the decision of the European Court in *Carron v West Germany*[1], any sanction for failure by the applicant to provide an address for service cannot include refusing to deal with the application or invalidating any order granting enforcement.

1 Case 198/85, [1987] 1 CMLR 838.

11.88   Where a Convention maintenance judgment is to be enforced in the United Kingdom, sums payable under the order are to be paid in sterling. Where the judgment is expressed in a non-sterling currency, the amounts due under it are to be converted into sterling on the basis of the exchange rate prevailing at the date of registration of the order[1].

1 Civil Jurisdiction and Judgments Act 1982, ss(1), (2). By s 5(3) a written certificate purporting to be signed by an officer of any bank in the United Kingdom and stating the exchange rate prevailing on a specified date shall be sufficient evidence of the facts so stated.

Dealing with an application for enforcement

11.89   The procedure for dealing with an application for enforcement of a judgment of a court of a contracting state in another contracting state is intended to be expeditious. Procedure is *ex parte* and must allow for decisions on the application to be given without delay. Even if the party against whom enforcement is sought becomes aware of the application (which in Scotland might happen where a schedule of arrestment or inhibition is served prior to any decision on the application) that party probably cannot enter the proceedings until a decision on the enforcement of the judgment has been made. The court may refuse the application only if there has been a procedural irregularity invalidating the application or where the judgment is not entitled to enforcement under the provisions of the Convention[1]. It is not clear to what extent the court has power at this stage of the proceedings to undertake investigations of matters contained in the application or to require the submission of further evidence. Anton[2] argues that the court is not bound by the uncontested averments of the applicant but the Maxwell Report[3] states that the court shall act on the basis of the documents before it and not undertake any investigations.

Applications to the Court of Session are dealt with by a Lord Ordinary, Such applications do not require an appearance for the applicant unless the Lord Ordinary so requires, in which case the hearing is in chambers[4].

1 See above at paras 11.57–11.74. Most of the grounds for refusing enforcement under the Convention are mandatory. However in the case of a judgment covered by article II of the Annexed Protocol, the court of enforcement has a discretion to refuse enforcement.
2 A E Anton *Civil Jurisdiction in Scotland* p 146.
3 *Maxwell Report* p 133.
4 RC 249F.

11.90 In the case of maintenance judgments, applications are sent to the Secretary of State whose functions are exercised through the Scottish Courts Administration. Once the documents have been checked they are transmitted to the sheriff clerk of the appropriate sheriff court, who is the official responsible for registering the maintenance judgment in a register kept for that purpose in each sheriff court district[1].

1 *Maxwell Report* pp 148–151; SI 1986/1947, para 6(5).

Refusal of an application

11.91 Where the application is refused, the court must intimate its decision to the applicant without delay. The applicant then has the right to make an appeal against the refusal of the application. The appeal is heard by the appropriate court in the state or legal system concerned as specified by article 40:

Belgium:	by the *cour d'appel* or *hof van beroep*;
Denmark:	by the *landsret*;
Federal Republic of Germany:	by the *Oberlandesgericht*;
France:	by the *cour d'appel*;
Ireland:	by the High Court;
Italy:	by the *corte d'appello*;
Luxembourg:	by the *Cour superieure de Justice* sitting as a court of civil appeal;
The Netherlands:	by the *gerechtshof*;
The United Kingdom:	
(1) In England and Wales:	by the High Court of Justice, or in the case of a maintenance judgment, by the magistrates' court;
(2) In Scotland:	by the Court of Session, or in the case of a maintenance judgment, by the sheriff court;
(3) In Northern Ireland:	by the High Court of Justice, or in the case of a maintenance judgment, by the magistrates' court.

The party against whom enforcement is sought is to be summoned to appear before the court hearing the appeal. Where he does not appear, the provisions of article 20 of the Convention apply. These provisions require the sisting of proceedings until it can be shown that the other party has been able to receive the document instituting the proceedings or its equivalent in sufficient time to prepare his defence. This is the case even if the other party is domiciled in a non-contracting state[1].

1 1968 Convention, arts 20(2)(3), 40.

11.92   The decision given in the appeal against a refusal to accept an application for enforcement of a judgment is itself subject to only limited rights of further appeal, specified by article 41 as:

in Belgium, France, Italy, Luxembourg, and the Netherlands:	by an appeal in cassation;
in Denmark:	by an appeal to the *hojesteret*, with the leave of the Minister of Justice;
in the Federal Republic of Germany:	by a *Rechtsbeschwerde*;
in the Republic of Ireland:	by an appeal on a point of law to the Supreme Court;
in the United Kingdom:	by a single further appeal on a point of law. In Scotland the single further appeal is to the Inner House of the Court of Session. This applies as regards both maintenance and non-maintenance judgments[1].

Such further appeal may be made by either party.

1 Civil Jurisdiction and Judgments Act 1982, s 6(1), (3).

11.93   Where an application has been made to the Court of Session and has resulted in refusal to grant the application, the court must intimate this decision to the applicant by sending him a copy of the interlocutor in a registered or recorded delivery letter to his address for service in Scotland[1]. An appeal made by the applicant against refusal to grant the application is to be made to the Outer House in Form 42[2].

The appeal is governed by RC 290 except that it must be made within one month of the interlocutor refusing the application[3]. Furthermore, where the respondent is domiciled furth of the United Kingdom, whether or not he is domiciled in a contracting state, intimation to him, as required by RC 290(f), must be made in accordance with RC 74B or where appropriate RC 75[4].

A further appeal from the interlocutor dealing with the 'appeal' against the refusal to grant the application may be made on a point of law by motion for review by the Inner House in accordance with RC 262–264[5].

1 RC 249H.
2 RC 249K(2).
3 RC 249K(5)(b).
4 RC 249K(4)(b). Domicile here is to be determined in accordance with art 52 and 53 of the 1968 Convention and with ss 41–46 of the Civil Jurisdiction and Judgments Act 1982: RC 249D(1).
5 RC 249L(1).

11.94   Where an application for registration of a maintenance judgment has been refused, the sheriff clerk must at once serve a notice on the applicant *and* on the person against whom enforcement is sought[1]. This notice is in Form 6 of the Act of Sederunt. The application may appeal by way of summary application to the sheriff within one month. There is a single further appeal on a point of law to the Inner House of the Court of Session, but none to the sheriff principal. This further appeal proceeds in accordance with the rules of procedure for appeals to the Inner House in the Ordinary Cause Rules[2].

1 SI 1986/1947, para 6(8).
2 Ibid, para 6(11).

Granting of application: effect

11.95 Where the application for enforcement is granted, the judgment becomes enforceable in the legal system where application was granted. The Convention itself is silent on the issue of the effect to be given to the judgment in the legal system of enforcement[1]. As far as concerns non-United Kingdom Convention judgments which are subject to application for enforcement in one of the legal systems of the United Kingdom, the court granting the application registers the judgment in that court in the manner prescribed by the relevant rules of court. The effect of such registration is that for purposes of enforcement the judgment is to be treated as if it had been a judgment given by the registering court[2].

1 A E Anton *Civil Jurisdiction in Scotland* p 146.
2 Civil Jurisdiction and Judgments Act 1982, ss 4(3), 5(4).

11.96 Where application is made for enforcement in Scotland of a non-United Kingdom Convention judgment, the Lord Ordinary, on being satisfied that the requirements of the Convention and of the 1982 Act are satisfied, grants warrant for registration of the judgment. At the same time, he will also grant decree in terms of the judgment to be enforced, or, where the terms of the judgment require 'translation' into the concepts and language of Scots law (which is likely in cases of non-money judgments), will grant decree in accordance with Scots law[1]. In the case of enforcement of a maintenance judgment, the sheriff clerk registers the judgment in a register kept for that purpose in each sheriff court district. Where a maintenance judgment has been registered and is superseded by a subsequent judgment itself registered under the Convention provisions, the sheriff clerk is to make an appropriate entry in respect of the later order against the entry for the original judgment[2].

1 RC 264G(1).
2 SI 1986/1947, para 6(5), (6).

11.97 It will be noted that the scheme of the Convention is that applications for enforcement of a judgment proceed on an *ex parte* basis. For that reason caveats in respect of such applications would be disallowed as inconsistent with the aims of the Convention, which protects the position of the judgment debtor by other means. Nonetheless, it would be unfair for the party against whom enforcement is sought if the judgment became fully enforceable on the grant of the application without his having an opportunity to make any representations. On the other hand, the applicant for enforcement is entitled to a element of security to prevent the other party from defeating enforcement of the judgment by removing his assets from the jurisdiction of the court dealing with the application. To satisfy these conflicting interests, the Convention requires that the party against whom enforcement is sought is to be informed of the granting of any application for enforcement and is also given various rights of appeal against that decision. During the time in which any such appeal is available or is being heard the party making the application can take only limited steps to enforce the judgments, namely such steps as will provide him with protection of his interests.

These two aspects of the effect of granting an application for registration of a judgment require further consideration.

Rights of appeal against the granting of application

11.98 The court to which appeal is made by the party contesting registration is set out in article 37:

Belgium:	to the *tribunal de première instance* or *rechtbank van eerste aanleg*;
Denmark:	to the *landsret*;
Federal Republic of Germany:	to the *Oberlandesgericht*;
France:	to the *cour d'appel*;
Ireland:	to the High Court;
Italy:	to the *corte d'appello*;
Luxembourg:	to the *Cour superieure de Justice* sitting as a court of civil appeal;
The Netherlands:	to the *arrondissementsrechtbank*;
The United Kingdom:	
(1) In England and Wales:	to the High Court of Justice, or in the case of a maintenance judgment, to the magistrates' court;
(2) In Scotland:	to the Court of Session, or in the case of a maintenance judgment, to the sheriff court;
(3) In Northern Ireland:	to the High Court of Justice, or in the case of a maintenance judgment, to the magistrates' court.

The appeal is to be dealt with as a matter of contentious proceedings requiring the service on the original applicant to allow him to appear. At the hearing of such an appeal, the court is able to consider the whole issue of enforcement afresh in the light of information supplied by the appellant[1]. In many cases, the information which a court requires to consider whether a judgment should be enforced will be available only where such an appeal is made (eg whether payment of the debt due has been made).

1 *Jenard* p 51.

11.99 There is no express provision in the Convention requiring notification of the party against whom enforcement has been authorised, but this is implicit in the express right given to that party by article 36 to appeal against that decision[1].

Such an appeal must be made within one month of service on that party of the order authorising enforcement unless the party is domiciled in another contracting state in which case the period is two months[2].

Article 36 gives a right of appeal against a decision granting an application for enforcement, only to the party against whom the judgment is to be enforced, and does not extend an appeal to any other party. However, article 36 is concerned only with the procedure for the enforcement of a Convention judgment in another contracting state but not with the execution of the judgment once it becomes enforceable in that state. Matters of execution are governed by the national law of the legal system of enforcement, which may allow appeals by third parties on matters of execution[3].

1 In Scotland such notice to the other party is to be given by the successful applicant in the case of non-maintenance judgments, and by the sheriff clerk in the case of maintenance judgments. See below at paras 11.100–11.101.
2 Article 36; RC 249K(5)(a); SI 1986/1947, para 6(10).
3 Case 148/84 *Deutsche Genossenschaftsbank v Brasserie du Pecheur SA* [1986] 2 CMLR 496. Cp 1987 Act, s 40, for an example of a third party having a right to appeal on a matter of diligence. See further ch 7 above at para 7.33.

11.100 In Scotland, where an application to the Court of Session for enforcement of a non-maintenance judgment is granted, the court must intimate the decision to the applicant by sending to him a copy of the interlocutor in a registered or recorded delivery letter to his address for service in Scotland specified in the affidavit lodged with the application[1].

The decree granted on application and the warrant for registration of the judgment must be intimated by the applicant to the person against whom the judgment was given and against whom the decree and warrant was granted. This intimation is made by service of a notice in Form 54 with the appropriate service in terms of RC 74A, 74B, or 75[2]. There is no time-limit specified in the rule of court for making this intimation. However, any diligence in execution or other protective measures taken after the granting of the application will be of no avail unless such intimation is made within twenty-one days from the date of execution of the diligence or other protective measure[3].

The appeal against the granting of an application for enforcement is made to the Outer House in Form 42. The appeal is governed by RC 290 except that where the respondent is domiciled furth of the United Kingdom (whether or not in another contracting state) the intimation required by RC 290 should be made to the address for service of the respondent in Scotland[4]. RC 290 is further modified, to reflect article 36(2) of the Convention, that the appeal must be made within one month of intimation of decree and warrant for registration of the judgment or within two months of intimation of such decree and warrant where intimation was made on a person domiciled in another contracting state[5].

Where there is a successful appeal against the granting of an application for enforcement of a judgment, the court, on motion of the appellant, must pronounce an interlocutor recalling any protective measure[6].

1 RC 249H; 249E(2)(b)(iv).
2 RC 249J. Notice is to be given by service of Form 54, which is headed 'Intimation of decree and warrant for registration of a judgment under section 4 of the Civil Jurisdiction and Judgments Act 1982'. (It should be noted that the Rules of Court contain two different Forms 54.)
3 RC 249G(4). See below at paras 11.107–11.116.
4 RC 249K(4)(a).
5 RC 249K(5)(a).
6 RC 249K(6).

11.101 Where a maintenance judgment has been registered in the sheriff court, notice in Form 6 of the Act of Sederunt must be served on both parties by the sheriff clerk immediately after the registering of the judgment[1]. The party against whom enforcement of the judgment is sought may appeal by way of summary application to the sheriff within one month of service of the appropriate notice by the sheriff clerk. Where the person against whom enforcement is sought is domiciled in a contracting state other than the United Kingdom, such an appeal may be made within two months of service of the notice[2].

1 SI 1986/1947, para 6(8). The mode of service of the notice is governed by para 6(9) of the Act of Sederunt.
2 Ibid, para 6(10).

11.102 The decision given in the appeal against an order accepting an application for enforcement of a judgment is itself subject to only limited rights of further appeal, specified by article 37(2) as:
in Belgium, France, Italy, Luxembourg, and the Netherlands, by an appeal in cassation;
in Denmark, by an appeal to the *hojesteret*, with the leave of the Minister of Justice;
in the Federal Republic of Germany, by a *Rechtsbeschwerde*;
in Ireland, by an appeal on a point of law to the Supreme Court;
in the United Kingdom, by a single further appeal on a point of law.
In Scotland this further appeal is made to the Inner House of the Court of Session as regards both maintenance and non-maintenance judgments.
    Such further appeal may be made by either party.
    In Scotland a further appeal from the interlocutor of the Lord Ordinary may be made on a point of law by motion for review by the Inner House in accordance with RC 262–264. Where such a reclaiming motion against the registration of a judgment is successful, the court, on the motion of the appellant, must pronounce an interlocutor, recalling any protective measure[1].

1 RC 249L.

11.103 A single further appeal from the decision of a sheriff may be made on a point of law to the Inner House of the Court of Session, but not to the sheriff principal. Procedure for the appeal is in accordance with the rules on appeals in the Ordinary Cause Rules[1].

1 SI 1986/1947, para 6(10).

11.104 Article 38 of the Convention further provides for the situation where there has been an appeal against the granting of application to have a judgment registered. The appellant (ie the party against whom enforcement has been ordered) may request the court to sist proceedings where a so-called 'ordinary' appeal has been lodged against the judgment in the state of origin[1]. This language reflects distinctions in the legal systems of the orginal contracting states between ordinary and extra-ordinary appeals, which have different effects on whether a judgment is enforceable during the period of the appeal. The European Court of Justice has held that the ideas of ordinary and extra-ordinary appeals should be given 'independent' ie Convention-based, interpretations[2].

1 1968 Convention, art 38.
2 Case 43/77 *Industrial Diamonds v Riva* [1977] ECR 2175, [1978] 1 CMLR 349.

11.105 Where the time for the making of an appeal against an order allowing enforcement of a judgment has not expired, the court dealing with a request to sist that appeal may specify the time within which the 'ordinary' appeal in the contracting state of origin is to be made.

As far as concerns judgments given in the United Kingdom and Ireland, any form of appeal against a judgment is to be treated as an ordinary appeal for this purpose.

Where an ordinary appeal has been made in the contracting state of origin, the court considering an appeal against an order allowing enforcement may instead of sisting the appeal before it confirm the order authorising the enforcement of the judgment. However, to protect the party liable under the judgment in case he is successful in the 'ordinary' appeal in the state of origin, when the court upholds an order for enforcement it may make enforcement of the judgment conditional on the applicant providing security[1].

1 1968 Convention, art 38(3); Case 258/83 *Calzaturificio Brennero SAS v Wendel GmbH Schuhproduktion International* [1984] ECR 3971, [1986] 2 CMLR 59.

11.106 It appears that the court upholding an order for enforcement cannot make an order for provision of security by the applicant under article 38(3) during the hearing of any such further appeal (unless there is also an 'ordinary' appeal in the State of origin or the time for such an appeal is still running)[1]. Furthermore there is no right of appeal against any interim decision by the court which is dealing with the 'appeal' against an order granting an application for enforcement.

1 Case 258/83 *Calzaturificio Brennero SAS v Wendel GmbH Schuhproduktion International* [1984] ECR 3971, [1986] 2 CMLR 59.

Restrictions on enforcement and use of protective measures during the period of appeal

11.107 During the time allowed by article 36 for an appeal against the granting of an application for enforcement and until any such appeal has been disposed of, no measure may be taken by the applicant to enforce the judgment except for protective measures against the property of the person against whom enforcement has been sought[1]. Both of the aspects of this rule, namely the prohibition on enforcement and the permission to use protective measures, are expressly provided by the Convention and neither requires an order by the court which granted the application for enforcement or which is dealing with the appeal.

1 1968 Convention, art 39.

11.108 Article 39 has been the subject of interpretation by the European Court in *Capelloni and Aquilini v Pelkmans*[1], a decision which has been critically received. In *Capelloni* the court held that once the period of the article 36 appeal had started[2], there was no need for any specific authorisation for the applicant to use protective measures against the property of the other party nor for any specific order prohibiting enforcement during that period. What is not dealt with is the situation before the article 36 period begins. It may be that the European Court assumes that notification of a decision granting an application will be made at once by the court itself to the other party, but as has been noted this is not the situation in respect of non-maintenance judgments which are registered in Scotland.

The *Capelloni* decision also emphasised that during the article 36 period these protective measures and the prohibition on enforcement are 'automatic' and do not require any court order confirming their effect. Furthermore the only time-limits for these protective measures and the prohibition on enforcement are those specified in article 39 itself (ie the period in which an appeal against the granting of enforcement can be made or until any such appeal has been disposed of). What is not explicitly decided in *Capelloni* is the issue of what protective measures are available during the article 36 period. At least by implication the European Court appears to take the view that the nature of such measures is to be determined by the national law of the state of enforcement but that once article 36 comes into play article 39 introduces into the national law governing these measures the implications that no authority is required for taking protective measures other than the decision authorising enforcement, and that no steps can be taken to enforce or execute the judgment.

1 Case 119/84, [1986] 1 CMLR 388.
2 Ie with service of the decision authorising enforcement of the judgment on the party against whom enforcement is sought.

11.109   In Scotland, these provisions require some adaptation, chiefly because in Scots law there is no clear distinction between diligence in execution and protective measures designed to secure the position of a creditor. Indeed, protective measures in the form of arrestment (other than arrestment against earnings), and poinding are stages in diligences in execution, and inhibition is itself a diligence though it is a diligence which does not transfer property rights to the party using it.

For purposes of enforcing a Convention judgment in Scotland, the approach taken is to allow diligence in execution to be used as soon as an application has been granted and the appropriate decree and warrant registered, but to place restrictions on using some (but not all) of the diligences which have the effect of realising or transferring property or funds. Further, an applicant may use protective measures (as defined). To bring the article 39 provisions into effect (which as noted start to run only once service of the order granting application has been made on the party liable under the judgment), any diligence in execution or protective measure used or taken by the applicant will be of no effect unless such service is made within a specified period of time.

RC 249G states that the interlocutor of the Lord Ordinary which grants decree and warrant for registration of a Convention judgment will give notice that 'the applicant may extract the decree and proceed to do diligence in execution, save that –
(i) no action of furthcoming following upon an arrestment;
(ii) no sale following upon a poinding; and
(iii) no adjudication following upon an inhibition,
shall be competent until the expiry of the period of lodging an appeal and any appeal has been disposed of.'
RC 249G(3) provides that the applicant 'may apply to the court at any time in the process of the application under rule 249E(1) for protective measures until the expiry of the period for lodging an appeal and any appeal has been

disposed of.' Protective measures here include arrestment, inhibition, poinding, and interim interdict[1].

Any diligence in execution or other protective measure will be of no effect unless intimation of decree and warrant for registration is made to the judgment debtor 'within 21 days from the date or execution of the diligence or other protective measure[2].'

1 RC 249D(1).
2 RC 249G(4).

11.110 The effect of RC 249G is by no means clear and its provisions do not always sit easily with those of article 39 of the Convention. In particular the following points can be noted.

11.111 RC 249G(4) invalidates diligence in execution and other protective measures, unless service of the decree and warrant has been made on the judgment debtor 'within 21 days from the date or execution of the diligence or other protective measure'. The word 'execution' is ambiguous and may refer to the actual carrying out or performing of the diligence etc, or to the official report of the carrying out of the diligence which the officer of court makes to the court. An 'execution' in the latter sense may have a date later than that of the performing of the diligence itself. Accordingly the period set out in RC 249G(4) may be more than twenty-one days from the date on which the diligence was performed. The Rule of Court uses the expression 'date *or* execution of the diligence' etc, and this would seem to imply that the term execution is being used in the sense of official report[1].

Some diligences (eg poinding and sale and earnings arrestment) require a prior charge to be served on the debtor. It is probably more correct to say that a charge is not a step in these diligences but a precondition of doing them. Nor is it clear that a charge is itself a diligence or a protective measure. Accordingly the twenty-one-day limit for serving notice will not run from the date of serving a charge but from the date of 'execution' of the poinding, earnings arrestment etc.

1 It can be noted that even if the Rule had stated 'date of execution of the diligence' etc, the same ambiguity as to the meaning of execution would have remained.

11.112 RC 249G(3) states that 'The applicant may apply to the court at any time in the process of the application under rule 249E(1) for protective measures until the expiry of the period for lodging an appeal and any appeal has been disposed of.' It is not clear whether the phrase 'until the expiry of the period for lodging an appeal' etc qualifies the protective measures or the time in which the applicant may apply to the court. In any case, the clear effect of the *Capelloni* ruling is that once the period of appeal has begun by service under RC 249J(1), no application for a protective measure against the property of the other party is necessary, and RC 249G(3) must be read as applying only to applications for such protective measures prior to service under RC 249J.

However, by virtue of RC 249G(2)(b), from the date of registration of the judgment, the applicant can in any case use arrestment and poinding as inchoate steps of diligence in execution, and may also use inhibition (without a subsequent adjudication). Accordingly, specific authorisation for use of protective measures in respect of a registered judgment is necessary only

(a) in respect of measures sought during the process of an application for registration. However, the time-scale between presentation of an application and a decision upon it should be minimal; and

(b) in respect of protective measures other than those of arrestment, poinding and inhibition (eg interim interdict) after registration has been authorised but before service on the judgment debtor of the decision authorising the registration.

Again it is clear from the *Capelloni* decision that once the judgment debtor has been served with the decree and warrant for registration of the judgment, no authorisation is required for any protective measure against the debtor's property by virtue of article 39.

It may be, however, that application is always required for use of interim interdict as a protective measure. Article 39 restricts the automatic nature of protective measures to measures against the property of the party against whom enforcement is sought. If the view is taken that interdict is by its nature always a personal measure and is not a measure against property then article 39 would not apply in respect of it.

11.113   Before the article 36 appeal period begins by appropriate service on the judgment debtor, RC 249G contains no prohibition on the types of diligence in execution which may be used to enforce the registered judgment. However, limitations exist in that an arrestment cannot be completed by furthcoming, a poinding cannot be followed by sale, and an inhibition cannot be followed by an adjudication. Moreover, any diligence in execution will be of no effect unless service on the judgment debtor under RC 249J is made within twenty-one days of the 'execution' of the diligence. It must be noted that these provisions allow for the possibility of a diligence being completed prior to the twenty-one-day limitation. This could arise when the diligence of earnings arrestment is used. Such a diligence requires a prior charge to be served on the debtor[1]. But, as noted above, it may be that the twenty-one-day period for service under RC 249J does not run until the subsequent schedule of arrestment has been served on the debtor's employer, and the debt could be recovered in full by the time twenty-one days has elapsed.

It is also possible that various other forms of diligence could be completed in a period of twenty-one days from the registration of the judgment. In the first place it should be noted that in some circumstances arrestment is completed not by an action of furthcoming but by an action of sale[2]. RC 249G(2) does not prohibit sale as a way of completing an arrestment.

Furthermore where the judgment is one requiring some act to be done, it is likely that the Court of Session will repronounce the judgment in terms which reflect Scottish decrees *ad factum praestandum*. But this allows for the possibility of the applicant taking steps under section 1 of the Law Reform (Miscellaneous Provisions) (Scotland) Act 1940 to enforce the judgment before service of decree and warrant under RC 249J.

A similar result could arise where the judgment is one ordering the delivery of property to the applicant.

It is no doubt the case that in these circumstances the debtor could apply to the court to have the diligence sisted as he will have received indirect notice that a Convention judgment has been registered against him. But such indirect notice does not trigger the time for the article 36 appeal and it is not clear that the court will always sist diligence until the debtor's right of appeal under article 36 has arisen and article 39 comes into effect to prevent enforcement of the registered judgment. Where the applicant fails to serve notice under RC 249J by the twenty-one-day time-limit, any diligence, including any completed diligence, will be of no effect. But this might be of little protection for a debtor as funds or property will have been transferred into the possession of the creditor.

1 1987 Act, s 90(1). See further ch 6 above at para 6.06.
2 See ch 5 above at para 5.51.

11.114   RC 246G does not explicitly deal with the situation where warrant to arrest or to inhibit has been granted prior to the application for registration of a Convention judgment. Section 27 of the 1982 Act allows the Court of Session to grant warrant to arrest or inhibit on the dependence of an action commenced in another part of the United Kingdom or in another contracting state on a matter within the scope of the Convention. The situation may arise where eg arrestment on the dependence is used on the basis of a warrant granted under section 27 of the 1982 Act. The question then arises of the effect on the arrestment of RC 249G(4) which states that any 'diligence in execution or other protective measure shall be of no effect unless intimation of the decree and warrant for registration under rule 249J(1) is made within 21 days from the date or execution of the diligence or other protective measures.'

It should be noted that an action of furthcoming can be raised on the basis of an arrestment of the dependence which has not been followed by an arrestment in execution[1]. What is not clear is whether an arrestment of the dependence of a foreign action can be the basis of an action of furthcoming only if the judgment has been registered under the Convention for enforcement in Scotland. If the registration in Scotland is not necessary, then the protection for the judgment debtor provided by articles 36 and 39 of the Convention are in effect bypassed. In *De Wolf v Cox*[2], the European Court held that a judgment within the scope of the Convention can be enforced in another contracting state only under the provisions of the Convention. On the other hand, if registration of the judgment is required before an action of furthcoming can be raised on an arrestment granted under section 27 of the 1982 Act, then RC 249G(4) has the effect of nullifying the arrestment unless intimation of the registration is made on the judgment debtor within twenty-one days of the 'execution' of the arrestment. In most, if not indeed all, cases, an application for registration of a Convention judgment will take place more than twenty-one days after arresting on the dependence of the action. In effect, an application for registration of a Convention judgment will cause any arrestment on the dependence to fly off. A judgment creditor in this situation must, prior to the application for registration being granted, make application to the court for warrant to arrest funds or property which at that time are already subject to an arrestment previously made by him.

1 *Abercrombie v Edgar and Crerar* 1923 SLT 271; Graham Stewart *The Law of Diligence* p 231. See further ch 4 above at para 4.40.
2 Case 42/76, [1976] ECR 1759, [1977] 2 CMLR 43.

11.115   RC 249G fails to reflect fully the provisions of article 39 that once the period has started for the judgment debtor to lodge an appeal against the granting of an application, no steps in the enforcement of the judgment may be taken. Indeed the rule gives the impression that diligence in execution can be done up to twenty-one days prior to service under RC 249J and also that even after such service diligence in execution can still be done. What RC 249G does is to render incomplete the use of arrestment, poinding and inhibition as diligences in execution or steps towards such diligence, whereas article 39 is to the effect that no execution can be done within the period of the article 36 appeal once service is made on the debtor. It therefore falls to be implied that RC 249G, notwithstanding its express words, does nothing to authorise diligence in execution (eg arrestment and sale, earnings arrestment, application under section 1 of the 1940 Act) once this appeal period has started to run.

Where the judgment being registered is one prohibiting the other party from doing some act, it is likely to be repronounced to reflect a Scottish decree of interdict. Enforcement of interdict is by way of petition and complaint. Once the article 39 provisions are in effect, it is not clear whether petition and complaint procedure is struck at as being a mode of enforcing the judgment or is permitted as being a protective measure, which follows from the nature of interdict. It can be noted that the Maxwell Committee took the view that interdict can be taken as a protective measure and that enforcement by way of petition and complaint is available during the appeal period[1].

1 *Maxwell Report* p 139.

II.II6 The situation as regards protective measures in respect of maintenance judgments which are registered in sheriff courts, causes fewer problems. This is partly because only maintenance judgments can be registered in the sheriff court and accordingly specialities in executing non-money judgments do not arise. Furthermore, notice of registration of a maintenance judgment is given at once to the party against whom it is to be enforced and so the problems in the Court of Session rules about diligence in execution done before such notice are avoided.

Where a maintenance judgment has been registered in the sheriff court, the applicant may obtain an extract and proceed on that basis to arrest in execution, to inhibit and to charge and poind. However, until the time for the appeal by the other party against registration has elapsed or any such appeal has been disposed of, the applicant may not proceed to
(i) an action of furthcoming in respect of an arrestment;
(ii) an adjudication in respect of an inhibition; or,
(iii) a sale in respect of a poinding[1].
As with the Court of Session rule, this provision fails to reflect fully the extent of the prohibition on execution during the appeal period. It gives the impression that other diligences in execution, apart from those specified in the rule (eg arrestment and sale, current maintenance arrestment), may be done, though on one reading of the rule, *only* the three diligences stated there can be done on the basis of the extract of the registered order. Furthermore, the rules give no guidance on what other protective measures are available to the applicant during the appeal period (eg interim interdict) or how any such measures are to be given automatic effect.

1 SI 1986/1947, para 6(7).

Registration of decree and warrant

11.117   In the Court of Session, where the court grants an application for enforcement and to that effect issues decree and warrant for registration of the judgment, the Deputy Principal Clerk is under a duty to enter the decree in a register of judgments which require registration under the 1982 Act[1]. This is done immediately after the court order has been made[2]. The Keeper of the Registers, on receiving from the applicant a certified copy of the decree and warrant for registration and a certified copy of the judgment to be registered, must register these documents in the Books of Council and Session in a Register of Judgments. Where the judgment is in a language other than English, the Keeper must also be presented with a translation of the judgment into English by a person qualified as a translator. On making registration, the Keeper is under a duty to issue an extract of the registered judgment with warrant for execution.

In the sheriff court, the sheriff clerk registers a maintenance judgment, authorised to be enforced under the Convention provisions, in a register to be kept for the purpose in each sheriff court district[3].

1 RC 2491.
2 Cp *Maxwell Report* p 128.
3 SI 1986/1947, para 6(4), (5).

Execution of registered judgments

11.118   Once a judgment becomes fully enforceable in the contracting state of enforcement (ie the prohibition contained in article 39 no longer applies), the mode of execution is determined by the legal system of enforcement. A non-maintenance Convention judgment which is registered in Scotland has, as regards execution, the same force and effect as if the judgment has been originally given by the Court of Session, and similarly a Convention maintenance judgment registered in Scotland has the same effect as if it were a judgment of the sheriff court where it is registered[1]. Thus, once extract has been obtained and the period of appeal has expired, all appropriate diligence against the other party's property may proceed on the basis of the extract. A foreign judgment registered in Scotland for enforcement, apart from a registered maintenance judgment, is subject to the provisions of the Debtors (Scotland) Act 1987 on time to pay orders, which prevent a creditor from using certain diligences while the debtor is making payment under a scheme for payment approved by the court[2].

Time to pay orders are not available in respect of a debt due under an order of a court in criminal proceedings and the types of foreign decrees to which the time to pay provisions apply are expressly limited to civil judgments[2]. It is submitted, however, that this does not prevent a time to pay order being made where the original judgment was a Convention judgment of a criminal court of another contracting state. Section 4(3) of the 1982 Act states that a Convention judgment registered for enforcement has the same force and effect and proceedings for its enforcement may be taken 'as if the judgment has been originally given by the registering court' which in Scotland is the Court of Session.

1 Civil Jurisdiction and Judgments Act 1982, s 4(3).
2 1987 Act, s 15(3). For time to pay orders see ch 3 above.

Recovery of interest and expenses

11.119   The scheme of the Convention is that the judgment once registered in another contracting state is to be enforced there in the same manner as a judgment of courts of that contracting state. The steps in execution are left to the legal system of the contracting state of enforcement[1]. However, what is due under the judgment is to be treated as a matter of substance, and as such not reviewable by the court of enforcement. It would appear, accordingly, that questions of interest and expenses due are matters of substance.

1 Case 148/84 *Deutsche Genossenschaftsbank v Brasserie du Pecheur SA* [1986] 2 CMLR 496.

11.120   Where a maintenance or a non-maintenance judgment is registered for enforcement in a United Kingdom court, section 7(1) of the 1982 Act provides that where the applicant shows (a) that the judgment provides for the payment of a sum of money, and (b) that in accordance with the law of the contracting state of origin, interest on that sum is recoverable under the judgment from a particular date or time, the rate of interest and date or time from which it is recoverable are registered with the judgment and continue to have effect from the date of registration. In applications for enforcement of judgments in Scotland, the applicant must include in the affidavit which he is to lodge with his application, a statement whether interest is recoverable on the judgment in accordance with the law of the country in which the judgment was given and if so, the rate of interest, the date from which interest is due and the date on which interest ceases to accrue[1].

Expenses or costs due will be registered provided they are due under the judgment in the contracting state of origin.

1 RC 249E(b)(ii); cp SI 1986/1947, para 6(1)(e).

11.121   Once a non-maintenance judgment has been registered for enforcement in a legal system of the United Kingdom, the reasonable costs or expenses of and incidental to its registration are recoverable as if they were sums due under the judgment[1]. These expenses carry interest as if they were the subject of an order for payment of expenses made by the registering court on the date of registration[2].

1 Civil Jurisdiction and Judgments Act 1982, s 4(2).
2 Ibid, s 7(3).

Legal aid

11.122   Where an applicant for enforcement had received full or partial legal aid or exemption from costs in the contracting state of origin of the judgment, he is entitled to the most favourable legal aid or exemption from costs provided for in the contracting state of enforcement[1]. Thus, in Scotland an applicant who has received any form of legal aid or exemption from costs in the country of origin is entitled to full legal aid, without assessment of resources, where under Scots law legal aid is available in respect of the enforcement of judgments.

1 1968 Convention, art 44. See Civil Legal Aid (Scotland) Regulations 1987, SI 1987/381, reg 47.

11.123 However, such legal aid or exemption from costs is to be provided in the contracting state of enforcement only in respect of the procedures provided for in articles 32–35 of the Convention. These provisions deal with the initial procedures for applying for enforcement of a judgment. Thus legal aid need not be made available in the contracting state of enforcement in respect of appeals against the granting or the refusal of an application, or in respect of executing the judgment.

Security for costs

11.124 Article 45 of the Convention provides that no security, bond or deposit shall be required of a party who applies for the enforcement of a Convention judgment in another contracting state on the grounds that he is not a national of the contracting state of enforcement or that he is not domiciled or resident there.

The exact meaning of this provision is not clear. The article refers to the applicant 'in one Contracting State' who applies for the enforcement of a judgment in another contracting state. Thus, the article may apply only to domiciliaries or residents (and possibly also nationals) of the contracting state of origin of the judgment. The precise scope of the prohibition contained in the article is not certain. In a Scottish context it is not clear that the article strikes at the procedural step of requiring a party making an application for enforcement to sist a mandatary[1].

1 *Maxwell Report* pp 143–144; A E Anton *Civil Jurisdiction in Scotland* p 154.

11.125 It should be noted that article 44 applies only to the procedures for the enforcement of judgments under the Convention. It has no effect on the separate issue whether the procedures available for Scottish judgments being enforced in other contracting states prohibit Scottish courts from ordering caution for expenses or requiring a mandatary to be sisted, when an action is raised in Scotland by a national or domiciliary of another contracting state[1].

1 Cp *Zaeschmar v Shaw* 1988 SCLR 269; *Porzelack KG v Porzelack (United Kingdom) Ltd* [1987] 2 CMLR 33.

Enforcement of Scottish judgments in a contracting state (other than the United Kingdom)

11.126 Provision has been made by rules of court for the procedure to be used when a Convention judgment given in Scotland is to be made the subject of an application for enforcement in a contracting state outwith the United Kingdom[1].

1 Cp Civil Jurisdiction and Judgments Act 1982, s 12.

11.127 In the Court of Session, a party seeking to enforce a decree or interlocutor in another contracting state must first serve the decree or interlocutor on the person against whom it is to be enforced. Service is made in accordance with the appropriate mode set out in RC 74A, RC 74B or

RC 75. The next stage is that of applying in writing, along with an execution of the service of the decree, to the Deputy Principal Clerk for[1]
(a) a certificate in Form 55 (headed 'Certificate under section 12 of the Civil Jurisdiction and Judgments Act 1982');
(b) a certified copy interlocutor;
(c) if required, a certified copy of the opinion of the court.

1 RC 249N(1). (It should be noted that the Rules of Court currently contain two different Forms 55.)

11.128   In the sheriff court, the first step is also that of service of a copy of the judgment on all parties against whom the judgment was given. Service is made in accordance with the appropriate mode of service provided for by OCR 10 or 12, accompanied by a notice in Form 4 set out in the Act of Sederunt on Enforcement of Judgments under the 1982 Act. Execution of the service of the interlocutor or decree is in Form 5 unless a form of execution of service is provided by the person executing service in the other contracting state where service was effected[1]. The party seeking enforcement must then apply in writing, along with an execution of the service of the judgment, to the sheriff clerk for
(a) a certificate in Form 3 of the Act of Sederunt[2];
(b) a certified copy interlocutor;
(c) if required, a certified copy of the opinion of the sheriff.

1 SI 1986/1947, para 5(1).
2 Ibid, para 5(2), (3).

11.129   Once these certificates and various documents have been obtained the next stage is to make an application to the appropriate court[1] in the contracting state in which enforcement is sought[1] in accordance with articles 46–49 of the Convention.

1 As set out in art 32 of the 1968 Convention.

Enforcement of authentic instruments and court settlements

11.130   Special provision is made by articles 50 and 51 for the enforcement of authentic instruments and court settlements in other contracting states. Broadly speaking these documents are enforced in the same way as judgments.

The notion of authentic instrument is not defined by article 50. The Maxwell Report states[1] that 'the expression "authentic instrument" is intended to refer to those documents authenticated by a notary or other public officer or by registration in a special register which by virtue of such authentication are enforceable by diligence in certain legal systems in the same way as a judgment'. A document registered for execution in the Books of Council and Session or sheriff court books is an authentic instrument for the purposes of article 50[2].

1 *Maxwell Report* p 165.
2 *Schlosser* p 136.

11.131   Article 50 provides that the authentic instrument must be properly drawn up according to the law of the state of origin and must also be enforceable there. The mode of enforcing an authentic instrument in other contracting states is broadly similar to that used for enforcing judgments. However there are only limited grounds requiring the court dealing with an application for enforcement of an authentic instrument to refuse enforcement. These are that:

(a) the subject-matter of the instrument is not within the scope of the Convention;

(b) the authentic instrument is not properly drawn up according to the legal system of origin;

(c) the authentic instrument is not enforceable in the contracting state of origin;

(d) enforcement of the authentic instrument is contrary to public policy in the contracting state where enforcement is sought.

An application for enforcement must be accompanied by the documents specified in articles 45–49 as these are appropriate to authentic instruments. However, the provisions of article 46(2) on judgments in default have no equivalent as regards authentic instruments and do not apply, nor is it necessary to show that the authentic instrument has been served prior to making an application for its enforcement in another contracting state.

When an authentic instrument of another contracting state is to be enforced in Scotland, it appears that is for the Court of Session to require specific evidence in the application that the instrument is authentic[1].

1 Cp Civil Jurisdiction and Judgments Act 1982, s 13.

11.132 Where a document registered for execution in the Books of Council and Session is to be enforced in another contracting state, the applicant must apply in writing to the Keeper of the Registers for a certificate in Form 59 of the Rules of Court. With the application to the Keeper, there must be produced[1]:

(a) an extract of the writ in respect of which the certificate is sought; and

(b) an affidavit verifying that enforcement has not been suspended and that the time available for enforcement has not expired.

1 RC 249N(3). There appears to be no equivalent provisions in respect of enforcement in other contracting states of documents registered in sheriff court books.

11.133 Article 51 provides that a 'settlement' which has been approved by a court in the course of proceedings and is enforceable in the contracting state in which it was concluded is enforceable in other contracting states on the same conditions as an authentic instrument. This provision deals with the procedure in certain contracting states whereby settlements approved by a court in the course of proceedings are enforceable, in the same way as a judgment, without further formality[1].

1 See further A E Anton *Civil Jurisdiction in Scotland* pp 151–152.

11.134 Where such a settlement is to be enforced in Scotland, the Court of Session will require indication that the settlement has the authority of a court and is enforceable in the contracting state of origin but no specific provisions are made in the 1982 Act or rules of court.

It appears that there is little scope for the application of article 51 to Scottish settlements. In Scots law, a settlement is a contract between the parties but by itself cannot be enforced directly by diligence. The agreement of the parties is usually embodied in a joint minute to which the court interpones its authority and decree is granted in terms of the minute as far as relevant. In these circumstances it is the decree rather than the settlement which is open to enforcement in another contracting state. Alternatively, the parties might register their agreement for execution in the books of court but in this situation the provisions of article 50 on authentic instruments rather than those of article 51 would be appropriate where enforcement in another contracting state is being considered.

RECIPROCAL ENFORCEMENT OF UNITED KINGDOM CIVIL JUDGMENTS

Nature and extent of the United Kingdom enforcement scheme

11.135   The 1982 Act provides a scheme for the reciprocal enforcement of judgments in civil courts and tribunals in Scotland, Northern Ireland, and England and Wales[1]. The scheme applies to all civil judgments subject to a number of stated exceptions, and covers both money and non-money judgments, given by superior and inferior courts. Enforcement is made by application to the superior court of the legal system where enforcement of the judgment is sought and involves the presentation of a number of prescribed documents.

1 Civil Jurisdiction and Judgments Act 1982, s 18, Schs 6, 7.

11.136   The procedure for enforcement under the scheme is in general an expeditious one, and little exists by way of a power of the court of the country of enforcement to review the judgment given by a court of another United Kingdom legal system. In particular, a court dealing with the enforcement of a judgment given elsewhere in the United Kingdom cannot examine the jurisdictional basis of that other court. In some cases jurisdictional review is otiose because of the rules of jurisdiction of Schedule 1 and Schedule 4 to the 1982 Act. These rules lay down a common set of jurisdictional rules for contracting states to the 1968 Convention, and a set of broadly similar common rules for civil courts in the United Kingdom. Moreover, the prohibition on various 'exorbitant' grounds of jurisdiction in the 1968 Convention means that where the action falls within the scope of the Convention, no such exorbitant ground can found jurisdiction in any case where the defender is domiciled in any contracting state, including the United Kingdom.

However, such exorbitant grounds of jurisdiction could be at the basis of judgments covered by the scheme for reciprocal enforcement of United Kingdom judgments. This would occur where (1) the defender or defendant is domiciled (in the sense of the 1982 Act) outwith any contracting state, or (2) whatever the domicile of the defender, the action relates to a matter outwith the scope of the 1968 Convention but within the scope of the United Kingdom scheme for reciprocal enforcement. Even in these situations, however, a judgment subject to the United Kingdom scheme cannot be reviewed as to jurisdiction by the court in another part of the United Kingdom dealing with its enforcement.

Exclusion of other modes of reciprocal enforcement

11.137 Where a judgment falls within the scheme of the 1982 Act for the enforcement of a judgment given in one part of the United Kingdom in another part of the United Kingdom, it must be enforced in accordance with the procedures set out in Schedules 6 and 7 to the 1982 Act[1]. Thus an action for decree conform in relation to any such judgment given by a court in Northern Ireland, or in England and Wales is incompetent. This prohibition on other modes of enforcement of judgments in other parts of the United Kingdom does not apply to certain arbitration awards[2].

1 Civil Jurisdiction and Judgments Act 1982, s 18(8).
2 Ibid, s 18(2)(e), (8).

Scope of the scheme for reciprocal enforcement of United Kingdom judgments

11.138 The 1982 Act scheme for the reciprocal enforcement of United Kingdom judgments applies generally to civil judgments. The scope of the scheme is much wider than that of the 1968 Convention, and includes such matters as judgments relating to revenue and customs, matrimonial property rights, wills and succession, and arbitration, all of which are excluded from the 1968 Convention. Generally speaking, the 1982 Act scheme applies to all civil judgments of United Kingdom courts except those for which other and more appropriate statutory schemes exist for reciprocal enforcement.

The 1982 Act scheme for reciprocal enforcement applies to[1]:
(a) any judgment or order (by whatever name called) given or made by[2]
   (i) the House of Lords;
   (ii) the Court of Session and a sheriff court in Scotland;
   (iii) the Court of Appeal, the High Court, the Crown Court, and a county court in England and Wales, or Northern Ireland;
(b) any judgment or order not within (a) above which has been entered in England and Wales or Northern Ireland in the High Court or a county court;
(c) any document which in Scotland has been registered for execution in the Books of Council and Session or in the sheriff court books kept for any sheriffdom;
(d) any award or order made by a tribunal in any part of the United Kingdom which is enforceable in that part without an order of a court of law. The idea of 'court of law' is defined in section 50 of the 1982 Act, and in Scotland covers the House of Lords, the Court of Session, and the sheriff court. The effect of this category of included judgments is that the scheme applies to orders of courts such as employment appeal tribunals, and the Lands Tribunal for Scotland. However it is not clear whether it extends to orders of other 'courts' (as opposed to tribunals) which are not courts defined by section 50, such as the Restrictive Practices Court.

Awards of industrial tribunals in Scotland are enforceable as an order of a sheriff court[3] and clearly fall within this category of judgments included in the enforcement scheme.

(e) an arbitration award which has become enforceable in the part of the United Kingdom in which it was given in the same manner as a judgment given by a court of law in that part.

In particular the scheme applies, whatever the nature of the proceedings in which it was made, to[4]

(i) a decree issued under section 13 of the Court of Exchequer (Scotland) Act 1856 (which concerns the recovery of certain rent-charges and penalties by process of the Court of Session);

(ii) an order which is enforceable in the same manner as a judgment of the High Court in England and Wales by virtue of section 16 of the Contempt of Court Act 1981 or section 140 of the Supreme Court Act 1981 (which relates to fines for contempt of court and forfeiture of recognisances). These are orders which may have been made by criminal courts.

1 Civil Jurisdiction and Judgments Act 1982, s 18(2).
2 Ibid, ss 18(3), 50.
3 Employment Protection (Consolidation) Act 1978, Sch 11, para 21A.
4 Civil Jurisdiction and Judgments Act 1982, s 18(4).

11.139 However, the scheme does *not* extend to[1]:

(a) a judgment given in proceedings in a magistrates' court in England and Wales and Northern Ireland. Exceptions to this exclusion are orders covered by section 18(4)(b) of the 1982 Act (ie orders for fines for contempt of court and forfeiture of recognisances);

(b) a judgment given in proceedings other than civil proceedings. In this context 'civil proceedings' are contrasted with criminal proceedings, and so orders of courts in administrative law matters and appropriate orders of administrative tribunals are not excluded. Judgments excluded under this heading would include fines, compensation orders, and orders for costs made by criminal courts;

(c) a judgment given in the exercise of jurisdiction in relation to insolvency law within the meaning of section 426 of the Insolvency Act 1986;

(d) a judgment given in proceedings relating to the obtaining of title to administer the estate of a deceased person. It should be noted that judgments on all other matters concerning wills and succession, apart from title to administer an estate, are not covered by this exclusion and thus fall within the scheme of the 1982 Act for reciprocal enforcement of United Kingdom judgments;

(e) a confiscation order made under the Drug Trafficking Act 1986 or the Criminal Justice (Scotland) Act 1987 or the Criminal Justice Act 1988;

(f) a judgment or so much of any judgment as is an order to which section 16 of the Maintenance Orders Act 1950 applies. The enforcement of these orders in other parts of the United Kingdom is provided for by Part II of the 1950 Act;

(g) a judgment or so much of a judgment as concerns the status or legal capacity of an individual. Included within this category are decrees of judicial separation or of separation, and any provision relating to guardianship or custody, but the idea of status or legal capacity is not exhausted by these specific issues;

(h) a judgment or so much of a judgment as is a provisional (including protective) measure other than an order for the making of an interim payment.

The idea of a provisional and protective measure is not defined in the 1982

Act but it can be given a narrower and a wider construction. In the narrower sense of provisional measure, what are excluded from the enforcement scheme are court orders which regulate *ad interim* the course of a continuing litigation, and are concerned more with preserving the status quo than deciding the merits of the action[2]. Examples would be interim interdicts, and warrants for arrestment and inhibition on the dependence of an action. Excluding such interim orders from the enforcement scheme has a rationale given the terms of sections 24–28 of the 1982 Act. These sections allow such provisional and protective measures to be brought in a United Kingdom court in the absence of substantive proceedings before that court but in respect of proceedings in other contracting states to the 1968 Convention or before courts in other parts of the United Kingdom. The Maxwell Report suggested that provisional measures of this type tend to be cast in the language and concepts of the legal proceedings in each country and would not easily lend themselves to speedy enforcement in other United Kingdom legal systems[3].

An important category of such awards made *ad interim* until the merits of the case are finally disposed of, are awards of interim damages in cases of actions relating to personal injuries made under RC 89A and OCR 147–148[4]. However, the 1982 Act makes clear that awards for interim payment are not excluded from the scheme of enforcement.

However, if a wider sense of provisional measures is taken, interim decrees which deal with part of the merits of a case (eg where defences to an action show that the defender has a statable defence to only some of the conclusions of the action) are also excluded from the scope of the enforcement scheme. A wider definition of provisional measures might also exclude provisional damages awarded under section 12 of the Administration of Justice Act 1982. Such damages are awarded, not *ad interim* of a continuing action, but as the final determination of an action subject to the reservation of the right of the pursuer to return to the court where a risk of further damages, identified in the action, subsequently occurs. Awards of provisional damages are expressly made final decrees under rules of court[5].

It is submitted that the scheme of the reciprocal enforcement of United Kingdom judgments excludes only provisional measures in the narrower of the two senses of provisional measure. Provisional measures of this type can in effect be obtained in courts in each part of the United Kingdom. There is no reason why interim decrees in the wider sense or awards of provisional damages should be excluded from the scheme.

A judgment of a court outside the United Kingdom falls to be treated for purposes of its enforcement as a judgment of a court of law in the United Kingdom by virtue of any of the following enactments:

(1) Part II of the Administration of Justice Act 1920;
(2) Part I of the Foreign Judgment (Reciprocal Enforcement) Act 1933;
(3) Part I of the Maintenance Orders (Reciprocal Enforcement) Act 1972;
(4) Section 4 or 5 of the Civil Jurisdiction and Judgments Act 1982, which deals with enforcement within the United Kingdom of judgments covered by the 1968 Convention.

1 Civil Jurisdiction and Judgments Act 1982, s 18(3), as amended by the Insolvency Act 1985, Sch 8, para 36, the Insolvency Act 1986, Sch 10, Pt IV and Sch 14; Drug Trafficking Offences Act 1986, s 39; Criminal Justice (Scotland) Act 1987, s 45(3); Criminal Justice Act 1988, Sch 15, para 82.
2 See ch 1 above at paras 1.20–1.22.

3 *Maxwell Report* p 304.
4 In England similar interim damages are awarded under RSC Ord 29, r 11.
5 RC 134D.

Procedure for enforcement: obtaining a certificate or certified copy of the judgment

11.140   Detailed procedure for enforcing a judgment to which section 18 of the 1982 Act applies in another part of the United Kingdom is set out in Schedules 6 and 7 to the 1982 Act. Procedure under both Schedules is broadly similar, and variations reflect the differences appropriate for the enforcement of money provisions (regulated by Schedule 6) and non-money provisions (regulated by Schedule 7). A money provision is defined as one requiring payment of one or more sums of money; a non-money provision is defined negatively as a provision for any relief or remedy not requiring payment of a sum of money[1]. An example would be an interdict or decree *ad factum praestandum*.

1 Civil Jurisdiction and Judgments Act 1982, Sch 6, para 1; Sch 7, para 1.

11.141   Judgments may be severable both in respect of part of a judgment being within the scope of section 18 of the 1982 Act and part of it not so covered; and also in the sense that a judgment may contain both money and non-money provisions (eg a decree of interdict with payment of expenses). All such money provisions are regulated by Schedule 6 and only non-money elements of a judgment fall within Schedule 7.

11.142   The first step in enforcing a judgment in another part of the United Kingdom is for any interested party to make application to the court of origin of the judgment for an appropriate document which sets out the terms of the judgment or provision to be registered for enforcement elsewhere in the United Kingdom. In the case of a money provision this document is a certificate which sets out the details of the relevant part of the judgment. In the case of a non-money provision, application is made for a certified copy of the judgment itself. This step is necessary in the case of a non-money provision as the court where enforcement is sought may not be able to give full effect to non-money remedies unless it can refer to the terms of the entire judgment.

The expression 'interested party' who has title to apply for the certificate or certified copy of the judgment is not defined. Clearly a party other than one of the original litigants may have a title to make such an application but it is not clear whether the question of interest in the judgment is to be determined by the law of the court giving the judgment or the law of the court which registers it for enforcement.

The application is made to the proper officer of the court or tribunal which gave the original judgment. In the case of an arbitration award which has become enforceable in the same manner as a judgment, as covered by section 18(2)(e) of the 1982 Act, application for a certificate is made to the court which gave the order making the award enforceable as a judgment. Where a Scottish judgment is to be enforced in another part of the United Kingdom, application is made to the Deputy Principal Clerk of the Court of Session in the case of a Court of Session decree or interlocutor, and to the Keeper of the

Registers in the case of a document registered for execution in the Books of Council and Session. In respect of sheriff court judgments, application for certificates or certified copies of the judgment is made to the sheriff clerk of the appropriate sheriff court[1].

An application must be made in writing and is to be accompanied by an affidavit:

(1) verifying that the time for enrolling a reclaiming motion or appeal has expired without a reclaiming motion or appeal having been enrolled, or where a reclaiming motion or appeal has been enrolled, that such motion or appeal has been finally disposed of; and that enforcement of the judgment has not been suspended and the time available for its enforcement has not expired;

(2) stating the address of the party entitled to enforce the judgment, and the usual or last-known address of the party liable to execution on it. The basis of the title of the party to enforce the judgment should also be contained in the affidavit. In most cases this will be the extract decree, which should be forwarded to the court to which the application is made;

(3) only in the case of application to the Deputy Principal Clerk or sheriff clerk in respect of money judgments, stating the sum or aggregate of the sums, including expenses, payable and unsatisfied.

1 RC 249P(1); 249Q(1); SI 1986/1947, paras 2(1), 3(1).

11.143 The clerk or the Keeper issues the appropriate certificate or certified copy of the judgment (and where necessary, a certified copy of the court's opinion or note) on being satisfied that[1]:

(a) an appeal against the judgment can no longer be brought;

(b) any appeal which has been brought has been disposed of;

(c) the enforcement of the judgment is not for the time being stayed or sisted; and

(d) the time available for enforcing the judgment has not expired.

It is not clear to what extent the officer dealing with an application can insist on proof of each of these requirements in addition to what is set out in the applicant's supporting affidavit.

1 Civil Jurisdiction and Judgments Act 1982, Sch 6, paras 3, 4; Sch 7, paras 3, 4.

11.144 Where application is made for enforcement of a money provision of a Scottish judgment or registered document elsewhere in the United Kingdom, the appropriate certificates etc are in the forms set out in the rules of court[1].

In a case of non-money provision in judgments, the clerk issues both a copy of the decree or interlocutor (and if necessary a copy of the court's opinion or note) and also a certificate in the appropriate form[2]. The certified copy of the decree or interlocutor contains the whole judgment including any money provisions or matter not within the scope of the enforcement procedures of section 18 of the 1982 Act.

1 RC Form 56 concerning Court of Session decrees or interlocutors; RC Form 60 concerning documents registered in the Books of Council and Session; Form 1 of SI 1986/1947 for sheriff court judgments.

2 RC Forms 57 and 61 respectively for Court of Session decrees or interlocutors and documents registered in the Books of Council and Session; Form 2 of SI 1986/1947 for sheriff court judgments. No provision appears to have been made in respect of documents registered in sheriff court books.

11.145 It is possible to make an application for more than one certificate, certified copy judgment etc. This allows enforcement of the judgment in both of the other parts of the United Kingdom. Conversely provided all the preconditions obtain for making an application, more than one application may be made for a certificate or certified copy judgment in respect of the same judgment[1].

1 Civil Jurisdiction and Judgments Act 1982, Sch 6, para 4(2); Sch 7, para 4(3).

Registration of certificates and certified copies of judgments

11.146 Once the appropriate certificate and/or certified copy of the judgment have been obtained from the court of origin, the next stage is to make application for the registration of these documents in the other part or parts of the United Kingdom where enforcement of the judgment is sought. Application for registration is made in Scotland to the Court of Session, and to the High Court in England and Wales, and in Northern Ireland. Application must be made within six months of the issuing of the certificate or certified copy of the judgment. As these documents can be issued by the court of origin only where the judgment is still enforceable in that legal system, the six-month time limit for registration reduces, though it does not eliminate, the possibility of a judgment being enforceable in another part of the United Kingdom, though it is no longer enforceable in the legal system of its origin. Enforcement of a judgment in England is not automatic after six years from the date it was given. This means that a Scottish judgment registered in England must be executed there within six years of the date of registration. After this period has expired, execution of a judgment requires permission of the court. However, provided the decree is still enforceable in Scotland, a further application can be made to the court there and the certificate etc reregistered in England.

In the case of a money provision, the procedure for registration is essentially administrative. Where application is made for registration in the Court of Session of a certificate relating to a money provision of a judgment given in another part of the United Kingdom, application is made by producing to the Keeper of the Registers the appropriate certificate issued by the court of origin. On presentation of this certificate the Keeper registers the certificate in the Register of Judgments of the Books of Council and Session, and issues an extract of the certificate with warrant for execution. Once a certificate has been registered, it has effect as far as execution is concerned as if it had been a judgment originally given in the registering court[1].

1 Civil Jurisdiction and Judgments Act 1982, Sch 6, para 6; Sch 7, para 6.

11.147 In England and Wales procedure for registration of a certificate relating to a money provision of a Scottish or Northern Irish judgment is regulated by RSC Order 71, rule 37. Application is made by producing to the Central Office of the High Court the certificate together with a copy certified, by the applicant's solicitor, to be a true copy. The certificate is filed at the Central Office and the certified copy, sealed with the Central Office seal, is returned to the applicant's solicitor. Once registered, the certificate is equated with a judgment of the High Court which has been entered under RSC Ord 12 and may also be enforced in a county court under section 105 of the County Courts Act 1984. A judgment in England may be enforced after six years of its being given only with the leave of the court. This applies also to a United Kingdom judgment registered in England under the 1982 Act.

11.148 In the case of non-money provisions, potential problems concerning the effect to be given to such provisions in another legal system require a degree of judicial scrutiny when dealing with application for registration of such a provision for enforcement in another part of the United Kingdom. Application for registration in the Court of Session of a non-money provision of a judgment of another part of the United Kingdom is made in Form 58, accompanied with the certified copy of the judgment of the court of origin and the certificate issued by that court. The application is dealt with in the Outer House by a Lord Ordinary in chambers. An appearance for the applicant is not necessary unless the court so requires[1].

Where application is made for registration of a non-money provision in England and Wales, procedure is governed by RSC Order 71, rule 38. Procedure is by way of *ex parte* application.

Where a superior court is dealing with an application for registration of a non-money provision of a judgment from another part of the United Kingdom, it must refuse registration if compliance with the provision would involve a breach of the law of the part of the United Kingdom in which it sits. No guidance is given as to when this rule would be applicable, nor as to the procedure to be followed if the court is minded to refuse the application on this ground. In England and Wales, the High Court has power to direct the issue of a summons when application is made for registration of a non-money provision[2], but the Court of Session Rules are silent on whether the court can require the applicant to notify the party against whom enforcement is sought when dealing with an application for registration of a money or non-money provision. It would appear that the remedy of any party affected by such an application is to petition to have the registration set aside (see below).

Where the Lord Ordinary is satisfied that an application for registration meets the various requirements, he must grant warrant for registration of the judgment and where necessary pronounce decree in accordance with Scots law. The warrant (and decree) is then registered in the Register of Judgments[3]. Once a non-money provision has been registered it has the same effect as regards execution as if the provision had been contained in a judgment given by the registering court[4].

1 RC 249Q(4)–(6).
2 RSC Ord 71, r 38(1).
3 RC 249Q (7), (8).
4 Civil Jurisdiction and Judgments Act 1982, Sch 6, para 6; Sch 7, para 6.

11.149 Scots law does not require notice to be given of the registration on the party liable to enforcement of it. Such notice is required where registration of a non-money provision is made in England and Wales[1].

1 RSC Ord 71, r 38(3) which concerns registration under the Civil Jurisdiction and Judgments Act 1982, Sch 7.

Costs or expenses of registration

11.150 The reasonable costs or expenses of, and incidental to, obtaining a certificate and certified copy of a judgment, and registering the documents, are recoverable. In the case of a money provision, these expenses are recoverable as if they were stated to be payable as a money provision in the original judgment[1]. In the case of expenses concerning a non-money provision, they are recoverable as if on the date of registration there had also been registered in the registering court, a certificate under Schedule 6 treating the expenses as a money provision[2].

Interest is due in respect of such expenses or costs relating to both a money and a non-money provision, as if the expenses had been ordered by the registering court on the date of registration of the certificate or registration of the judgment[3]. The rate of interest accordingly is that of the court of registration, even in respect of expenses incurred in another part of the United Kingdom.

1 Civil Jurisdiction and Judgments Act 1982, Sch 6, para 7.
2 Ibid, Sch 7, para 7.
3 Ibid, Sch 6, para 8(3); Sch 7, para 7(2).

Interest

11.151 Where a money provision has been registered, interest is due only in respect of:
(1) sums due as costs or expenses relating to the registration and
(2) sums stated in the certificate as carrying interest. The rate of interest and time or date from which it runs is also as stated in the certificate[1].

1 Civil Jurisdiction and Judgments Act 1982, Sch 6, para 8(1); Sch 7, para 7(2). Provision may be made by rules of court as to the manner in which and the periods by reference to which any interest due in respect of sums stated in the judgment is to be calculated and paid, including provision for such interest to cease to accrue as from a prescribed date: Sch 6, para 8(2).

Sisting of execution

11.152 No provision is made in the Rules of Court for notification of the registration in Scotland of a money or non-money judgment to be given to the party against whom the judgment is to be enforced[1]. Accordingly, it would appear that the first intimation that a United Kingdom judgment has been registered in Scotland which any such person will have, occurs when the first stage of diligence is taken against that party's property to execute the registered judgment[2].

1 In England and Wales notice that a non-money provision has been registered must be given. There is no similar requirement as regards money judgments: RSC Ord 71, r 38(3).
2 It is not clear whether a caveat be lodged in respect of registration of a United Kingdom money or non-money judgment.

11.153 Schedules 6 and 7 to the 1982 Act both provide that the court has power to sist proceedings for enforcing the registered judgment or certificate where the person against whom it is sought to be enforced is entitled or intends to apply in the legal system of origin to have the judgment set aside or quashed[1]. Diligence may be sisted for such a period as is reasonable to allow the application for setting aside of the original judgment to be disposed of in the legal system of origin. Where it is sought to have diligence sisted on this basis, procedure is by way of petition to the Outer House and is governed by RC 191–198[2].

1 Civil Jurisdiction and Judgments Act 1982, Sch 6, para 9; Sch 7, para 8.
2 RC 249P(4)(a), 249Q(9)(a).

Setting aside of registration of certificate (or judgment)

11.154 A further remedy, available once a certificate or judgment has been registered, is for an interested party to seek to have the registration set aside. Procedure in the Court of Session for setting aside registration is by way of petition to the Outer House and is governed by RC 191–198[1].

1 RC 249P(4)(b), 249Q(9)(b).

11.155 There are two bases for the registering court setting aside the registration of a judgment or certificate[1]:
(1) The registering court must set aside registration where on application of an interested party it is satisfied that the registration was contrary to the provisions of Schedule 6 in the case of money judgments or of Schedule 7 in the case of non-money judgments. This would include cases where the judgment, or certificate relating to the judgment, was outwith the scope of section 18 of the 1982 Act provisions on reciprocal enforcement of United Kingdom judgments, or where an application for registration had been made after the six-month time-limit from date of issue of the appropriate certificate or certified copy of the judgment, or where the judgment was no longer enforceable in the legal system of origin.
(2) The registering court has a discretion to set aside registration where on such an application by an interested party, it is satisfied that the matter in dispute in the proceedings in which judgment was given, had previously been the subject of a judgment by another court or tribunal having jurisdiction in the matter. The scope of this discretion is not clear. The 'other' court or tribunal having jurisdiction is a court or tribunal other than that giving the judgment which is the subject of the registration. It may be a court in the same or any other legal system as the court of origin of the judgment being registered, including a court of the same legal system as that of the registering court. The discretion does not exist where the judgment of the other court was later than that of the judgment of the registration. Whether the registration should be set aside depends not so much on the existence of a previous judgment as on whether the two judgments are in conflict, in which case deference will normally be made to the earlier of the two judgments.

1 Civil Jurisdiction and Judgments Act 1982, Sch 6, para 10; Sch 7, para 9.

MAINTENANCE ORDERS

Common law

11.156 Where a judgment of a foreign court for payment of maintenance may be varied, it is not a final decree and does not call for recognition or enforcement in Scotland at common law[1]. However, where the foreign court does not have power to vary or modify the amount of arrears of maintenance, arrears may be recovered in Scotland by action of decree conform on the foreign judgment[2].

1 A E Anton *Private International Law* p 587; E M Clive *The Law of Husband and Wife in Scotland* (2nd edn) p 224.
2 *Beatty v Beatty* [1924] 1 KB 807.

Maintenance Orders Act 1950

EXTENT AND SCOPE OF PART II OF THE 1950 ACT

11.157 Part II of the Maintenance Orders Act 1950 contains provisions for the registration in Scotland, England and Wales, and Northern Ireland of certain types of maintenance order made in another part of the United Kingdom. The types of Scottish order which may be registered under the 1950 Act elsewhere in the United Kingdom are decrees for payment of aliment granted by a court in Scotland, including[1]:
(i) an order for the payment of an annual or periodical allowance or a capital sum under section 2 of the Divorce (Scotland) Act 1938, or an order for the payment of a periodical allowance under section 26 of the Succession (Scotland) Act 1964 or section 5 of the Divorce (Scotland) Act 1976 or section 29 of the Matrimonial and Family Proceedings Act 1984, or an order for financial provision in the form of monetary payment under section 8 of the Family Law (Scotland) Act 1985;
(ii) an order for the payment of weekly or periodical sums under subsection (2) of section 3 or subsection (4) of section 5 of the Guardianship of Infants Act 1925;
(iii) an order for payment of sums in respect of aliment under subsection (3) of section 1 of the Illegitimate Children (Scotland) Act 1930;
(iv) a decree for payment of aliment under section 44 of the National Assistance Act 1948, or under section 26 of the Children Act 1948;
(v) an order under section 43 of the National Assistance Act 1948;
(vi) a contribution order under section 80 of, or a decree or an order made under section 81 of, the Social Work (Scotland) Act 1968;
(vii) an order for payment of weekly or other periodical sums under subsection (3) of section 11 of the Guardianship Act 1973;
(viii) an order made on an application under section 18 or 19(8) of the Supplementary Benefits Act 1976;
(ix) an order made on an application under section 24 of the Social Security Act 1986.

1 Maintenance Orders Act 1950, s 16(2)(b). For the relevant types of English and Northern Irish orders which can be registered in Scotland, see 1950 Act, s 16(2)(a) and s 16(2)(c) respectively.

APPLICATION FOR REGISTRATION; TRANSMISSION OF APPLICATION

11.158 The first step in registering a maintenance order under the 1950 Act is for the person entitled to receive payment under it to apply to the appropriate court or judicial authority for registration. Application is made to the court which made the order, which in the case of maintenance orders made by the Court of Session is the Deputy Principal Clerk and the sheriff clerk in the case of sheriff court orders[1]. Application is made by lodging[2]:

(a) a letter of application for registration in the appropriate court in England and Wales or in Northern Ireland;

(b) an affidavit by the applicant which includes –

   (i) the name and address of the person liable to make payments under the decree;

   (ii) arrears due under the decree, if any, and the date to which they are calculated;

   (iii) the reason for the application; and

   (iv) a statement that the decree is not already registered under the 1950 Act;

(c) a copy of the affidavit;

(d) a certified copy of the decree.

1 Maintenance Orders Act 1950, s 17(1).
2 AS Maintenance Orders Acts Rules 1980 (Court of Session), SI 1980/1727, r 6; AS Maintenance Orders Acts Rules 1980 (Sheriff Court), SI 1980/1732, r 7.

11.159 The court to which application is made may (but does not have to) order transmission for registration if (1) it appears that the person liable to make payment under the order resides in another part of the United Kingdom and (2) it is convenient that the order should be enforceable there[1]. If transmission is to be made, a certified copy of the maintenance order is sent by the Deputy Principal Clerk or sheriff clerk to the appropriate officer of the court in which the order is to be registered. Where the maintenance order was made in a superior court[2], it is sent for registration in the superior court of the country of registration. Similarly, maintenance orders made in lower courts are transmitted for registration in the corresponding lower courts. On receiving the transmitted order, the officer of that court enters it in the books of the court[3].

1 Maintenance Orders Act 1950, s 17(2).
2 Ie, the Court of Session in Scotland, the Supreme Court of Judicature in England and Wales and the Supreme Court of Judicature of Northern Ireland.
3 Maintenance Orders Act 1950, s 17(3)–(5); AS Maintenance Orders Acts Rules 1980 (Court of Session) SI 1980/1727, rr 7, 8, 15; AS Maintenance Orders Acts Rules 1980 (Sheriff Court) SI 1980/1732, rr 8, 15.

ENFORCEMENT

11.160 Once a maintenance order has been registered under the 1950 Act, it may be enforced in the part of the United Kingdom where it has been registered as if it had been an order by the court of registration[1]. It should be noted that where an order is registered in another part of the United Kingdom, it cannot be registered under the Act in another court (this requires cancellation of the earlier registration) nor can it be enforced elsewhere, even in the legal system of origin of the order[2].

1 Maintenance Orders Act 1950, s 18(1). Special provision is made for recovery of interest (Maintenance Orders act 1950, s 18(1A), (1B)) and of arrears (Maintenance Orders Act 1950, s 20). Note should also be made of rules which allow for the reregistration of Court of Session maintenance orders in the magistrates' courts and re-registration of sheriff court maintenance orders in the High Court. These steps have implications for use of the system of collecting officers elsewhere in the United Kingdom: A S Maintenance Orders Acts Rules 1980 (Court of

Session) SI 1980/1727, rr 9–12; AS Maintenance Orders Acts Rules 1980 (Sheriff Court), SI 1980/1732, rr 10–11.
2 Maintenance Orders Act 1950, ss 17(7), 18(6).

DISCHARGE AND VARIATION

11.161 The power to discharge or vary a maintenance order made by the Court of Session or the High Court in England and Wales or in Northern Ireland which has been registered under the Maintenance Orders Act 1950 rests with the court which made the order[1]. However, the person liable to make payment under the order who is seeking discharge or variation may adduce evidence in support of his application before the court of registration. A transcript or summary of such evidence is sent by the court of registration to the court of origin of the maintenance order.

1 Maintenance Orders Act 1950, s 21; AS Maintenance Order Acts Rules 1980 (Court of Session), SI 1980/1727, r 5.

11.162 A similar rule applies in respect of a registered maintenance order made by a sheriff court or magistrates' court, except that a variation of such an order in respect of the rate of payment may be made only by the court of registration, following application by the person liable to make payment or the person entitled to payment under the order[1]. Furthermore the 'shuttlecock' procedure of adducing evidence to the court of registration which then transmits the evidence to the court of origin of the order is open in the case of sheriff court and magistrates' court orders to both the persons entitled to payment and the person liable to pay[2].

Where a maintenance order registered under the Act has been discharged or varied by any court, the appropriate officer of that court sends notice of the discharge or variation to the other court concerned[3].

1 Maintenance Orders Act 1950, s 2(1); AS Maintenance Orders Acts Rules 1980 (Sheriff Court), SI 1980/1732, r 15: *Thompson v Thompson* (1953) 69 Sh Ct Rep 193; *Akram v Akram* 1965 SLT (Sh Ct) 26. For this purpose the court of registration takes judicial notice of the law in force in any other part of the United Kingdom: Maintenance Orders Act 1950, s 22(2); *Cowan v Cowan* 1952 SLT (Sh Ct) 8; *Thompson v Thompson* (1953) 69 Sh Ct Rep 193.
2 Maintenance Orders Act 1950, s 22(4), (5).
3 Maintenance Orders Act 1950, s 23; AS Maintenance Orders Acts Rules 1980 (Court of Session), SI 1980/1727, rr 13, 16; AS Maintenance Orders Rules 1980 (Sheriff Court), SI 1980/1732, rr 12, 17.

CANCELLATION

11.163 Where a maintenance order has been registered in one part of the United Kingdom under the 1950 Act and it is later sought to enforce it in a different part of the United Kingdom (including the legal system of origin), the registration must first be cancelled[1]. Application is made by or on behalf of the person entitled to payment under the order, and generally speaking cancellation is granted as of right.

1 Maintenance Orders Act 1950, s 24; AS Maintenance Orders Acts Rules 1980 (Court of Session), SI 1980/1727, rr 14, 17; AS Maintenance Orders Acts Rules 1980 (Sheriff Court), SI 1980/1732, rr 13, 18.

Maintenance Orders (Reciprocal Enforcement) Act 1972

11.164 The Maintenance Orders (Reciprocal Enforcement) Act 1972 contains three sets of provisions on enforcement abroad of maintenance orders made in Scotland and elsewhere in the United Kingdom and the enforcement in the United Kingdom of foreign maintenance orders[1].

1 For full discussion, see E M Clive *The Law of Husband and Wife in Scotland* (2nd edn, 1982) pp 230–259.

MAINTENANCE ORDERS (RECIPROCAL ENFORCEMENT) ACT 1972,
PART I — RECIPROCATING COUNTRIES

*Scope and extent of Part I of the Maintenance Orders (Reciprocal Enforcement)
Act 1972*

11.165 A scheme for the reciprocal enforcement of maintenance orders contained in Part I of the 1972 Act applies in respect of an order (including interlocutor or decree) or variation of an order which is[1]:
(a) an order (including an affiliation order or order consequent upon an affiliation order) which provides for the periodical payment of sums of money towards the maintenance of any person, being a person whom the person liable to make payments under the order is, according to the law applied in the place where the order was made, liable to maintain;
(b) an order which has been made in Scotland, on or after the granting of decree of divorce, for the payment of a periodical allowance by one party to the marriage to the other party; and
(c) an affiliation order or order consequent upon an affiliation order, being an order which provides for the payment by a person adjudged, found or declared to be a child's father of expenses incidental to the child's birth, or, where the child has died, of his funeral expenses.

An order is a maintenance order only so far as it concerns periodical payment or payments of periodical allowance in (a) or (b) or payment of birth or funeral expenses by a child's father in (c)[2]. Awards of a lump sum are not maintenance for this purpose.

The scheme provided for in Part I of the 1972 Act has been applied by Order in Council to a large number of countries[3].

1 Maintenance Orders (Reciprocal Enforcement) Act 1972, s 21(1).
2 Ibid, s21(2).
3 Reciprocal Enforcement of Maintenance Orders (Designation of Reciprocating Countries) Orders: SI 1974/556, SI 1975/2187, SI 1979/115, SI 1983/1125. In most cases the scheme applies with exceptions. For a full list see E M Clive *The Law of Husband and Wife in Scotland* (2nd edn, 1982) p 231.

Enforcement of Scottish orders in reciprocating country

11.166 Where the payer under the order made by a United Kingdom court is resident or has assets in a reciprocating country, the payee under the order may apply for the order to be sent to that country for enforcement[1]. Application is made to the appropriate officer of the court which made the order, which in Scotland is the Deputy Principal Clerk in the Court of Session and the sheriff clerk in the sheriff court. If the application is in proper form, the officer sends various documents to the Secretary of State for transmission to the reciprocating country[2]. The documents will be transmitted only if the requisite statement relating to the whereabouts of the payer gives sufficient information to require this step being taken[3].

The transmission of an order to a reciprocating country does not prevent the order being varied or recalled in the United Kingdom country of origin[4].

1 Maintenance Orders (Reciprocal Enforcement) Act 1972, s 2(1).
2 Ibid, s 2(3), (4); AS (Maintenance Orders (Reciprocal Enforcement) Act 1972 Rules) 1974, SI 1974/939, rr 4, 10.
3 Maintenance Orders (Reciprocal Enforcement) Act 1972, s 2(4).
4 For procedure where an order is varied or revoked, see SI 1974/939, rr 5, 18(a).

Enforcement in Scotland of orders made in reciprocating country

11.167   Similarly an order made by a court in a reciprocating country may be sent to the Secretary of State for enforcement in the United Kingdom. A copy of the order is then sent to the appropriate officer of the court in whose area the payer under the order appears to reside, which in Scotland is the sheriff clerk of the relevant sheriff court[1]. The order is then registered in the sheriff court, and is enforced as if it had been made by that court[2].

1 Maintenance Orders (Reciprocal Enforcement) Act 1972, s 6.
2 Ibid, s 8. For discussion of the effect of variation and revocation of such orders, see E M Clive *The Law of Husband and Wife in Scotland* (2nd edn, 1982) pp 237–239.

Provisional order procedure

11.168   Part I of the 1972 Act also contains a procedure whereby the maintenance creditor applies in the country of his or her residence for a provisional maintenance order to be made. Such order and other relevant documents are then sent to the reciprocating country where the maintenance debtor is resident. The maintenance debtor is given the opportunity in that country to state a defence to the order available to him under the law of the country of origin of the order. Unless such a defence is established, the provisional order is confirmed in the country of residence of the maintenance debtor and may be enforced there[1].

1 Maintenance Orders (Reciprocal Enforcement) Act 1972, ss 4, 7, 8; AS (Maintenance Orders (Reciprocal Enforcement) Act 1972 Rules) 1974, SI 1974/939, rr 6–9, 12, 14, 17; *Killen v Killen* 1981 SLT (Sh Ct) 77; E M Clive *The Law of Husband and Wife in Scotland* pp 239–243.

1972 ACT, PART II – CONVENTION COUNTRIES

11.169   Part II of the 1972 Act sets out a scheme for the reciprocal enforcement of orders for maintenance[1] between countries which have ratified the 1956 United Nations Convention on the Recovery Abroad of Maintenance[2].

The procedure under Part II of the 1972 Act is for the person wishing to recover maintenance from a person subject to the jurisdiction of a Convention country to make an application in his or her own country. The application with various accompanying documents is then transmitted to the relevant Convention country, where proceedings are taken under the law of that country for recovery of the maintenance[3].

1 As regards Scotland, maintenance includes aliment and any sums payable following divorce by one spouse for the support of the other: Maintenance Orders (Reciprocal Enforcement) Act 1972, s 39.

2 For a list of these countries, see SI 1975/43, SI 1978/279.
3 See discussion in E M Clive *The Law of Husband and Wife in Scotland* pp 244–248.

1972 ACT, PART III – BILATERAL ARRANGEMENTS

11.170 Part III of the 1972 Act allows for bilateral arrangements to be made with countries for the reciprocal enforcement of maintenance orders. Orders in Council may apply, in respect of such countries, modified versions of the provisions of the 1972 Act[1]. To date, Orders in Council have been made in respect of
(i) the Republic of Ireland[2];
(ii) countries which have ratified the 1973 Hague Convention on the Recognition and Enforcement of Decisions Relating to Maintenance Obligations[3]; and
(iii) certain states of the United States of America[4].

1 Maintenance Orders (Reciprocal Enforcement) Act 1972, s 40.
2 SI 1974/2140, applying a version of Part I of the 1972 Act. See also AS (Reciprocal Enforcement of Maintenance Orders (Republic of Ireland) Order 1974 Rules) 1975, SI 1975/475.
3 SI 1979/1317, applying a version of Part I of the 1972 Act. See also AS (Reciprocal Enforcement of Maintenance Orders (Hague Convention Countries) 1980 Rules), SI 1980/291. The countries concerned are: Czechoslovakia, Finland, France, Italy, Luxembourg, The Netherlands, Norway, Portugal, Sweden, Switzerland, and Turkey.
4 SI 1979/1314, applying a modified version of Part II of the 1972 Act. The states concerned are: Arizona, Arkansas, California, Colorado, Connecticut, Florida, Idaho, Illinois, Indiana, Kansas, Kentucky, Louisiana, Maine, Michigan, Minnesota, Montana, Nebraska, Nevada, New Hampshire, New Mexico, New York, North Carolina, North Dakota, Ohio, Oklahoma, Oregon, Pennsylvania, Texas, Vermont, Virginia, Washington, Wisconsin, and Wyoming.

Civil Jurisdiction and Judgments Act 1982

SCOPE OF THE 1968 CONVENTION

11.171 Maintenance orders are judgments to which the provisions on recognition and enforcement of the 1968 Convention apply[1]. However, maintenance orders are excluded from the scope of the inter-United Kingdom scheme set out in sections 18 and 19 of the 1982 Act[2].

1 1968 Convention, art 1. For discussion see above at paras 11.41–11.42.
2 Civil Jurisdiction and Judgments Act 1982, ss 18(5), 19(2). See above at para 11.139.

OVERLAP OF 1968 CONVENTION AND OTHER SCHEMES

11.172 The 1968 Convention scheme for recognition and enforcement of maintenance judgments applies in addition to other such schemes, including the 1973 Hague Convention which was implemented into the legal systems of the United Kingdom by the 1972 Act[1]. The maintenance creditor has a choice as to which scheme he elects to use[2]. Similarly, the 1968 Convention scheme operates alongside the scheme of the 1972 Act as it applies to the Republic of Ireland, and again the decision as to which set of provisions to adopt is for the maintenance creditor[3].

1 The countries to which the 1968 Convention extends are set out at para 11.35 above and those which have ratified the 1973 Hague Convention at para 11.170 above.
2 *Maxwell Report* p 163.
3 A E Anton *Civil Jurisdiction in Scotland* p 149.

PROCEDURE FOR ENFORCEMENT OF MAINTENANCE JUDGMENTS

11.173 Procedure under the 1968 Convention for enforcement of maintenance judgments is generally speaking the same as that used in respect of other types of judgment within the scope of the 1968 Convention. However, where a non–United Kingdom Convention maintenance judgment is being enforced in the United Kingdom, application is made to the Secretary of State who is responsible for transmitting the application to the appropriate sheriff court or magistrates' court[1].

Another variation in respect of Convention maintenance judgments which are being enforced in the United Kingdom under the 1982 Act is that sums due under the judgment must be paid in sterling. Where the judgment is in another currency, conversion is to be made on the basis of the exchange rate at the date of the registration of the order[2].

In the context of maintenance orders, special note may also be made of article 27(4) of the 1968 Convention. This provides a ground for refusing enforcement of a judgment, namely that the court which made the judgment was required to consider a preliminary question relating to status in a way that leads to a different result from the application of the appropriate rule of international private law in the state where enforcement is sought[3].

1 1968 Convention, art 31, Civil Jurisdiction and Judgments Act 1982, s 5. See above at paras 11.85–11.88.
2 Civil Jurisdiction and Judgments Act 1982, s 8. A written certificate purporting to be signed by an officer of any bank in the United Kingdom which states the exchange rate prevailing on a specified date is sufficient evidence of the facts so stated.
3 1968 Convention, article 27(4). For discussion, see above at para 11.67.

CHAPTER 12

WRONGFUL DILIGENCE

INTRODUCTION

12.01 When considering wrongful diligence, a distinction has to be drawn between two situations in which diligence can be carried out. The first is where there is an existing warrant and so diligence may be done without further application to the court eg arrestment on the dependence and in execution, inhibition on the dependence and in execution and poinding. In such cases, there is no liability for a mere mistake. Liability will arise only if it can be shown that there was malice and lack of probable cause. The second situation is where a warrant is required from the court and the warrant is obtained on *ex parte* statements eg landlord's sequestration for rent, and arrestment and inhibition in security of a future or contingent debt. In these circumstances, the person applying for the warrant is responsible for the accuracy of the statements made to the court and he will be liable in damages if these statements are shown to be incorrect. The position is clearly set out by Lord Justice-Clerk Inglis in *Wolthekker v Northern Agricultural Co*[1]:

> 'A litigant using any legal right or remedy, to which he is absolutely entitled and which he requires to apply for no special warrant to enable him to use, can never be made liable for the consequences of its use, unless he is shown to have resorted to it maliciously and without probable cause. . . It would be most unreasonable and inconsistent to give the pursuer of an action the right to use inhibition and arrestment on the dependence, and, at the same time, to make him answerable in damages, merely because he fails in obtaining a judgment against the defender, though he used his legal remedy moderately and in good faith. I think it would be quite as reasonable [*sic*] to make him answerable for damages arising from his having raised an action in which he has succeeded. His right to raise the action and to state in his summons everything pertinent, though injurious to the defender, is not more unqualifiedly secured to him as a litigant than his right to use diligence on the dependence. But the rule does not hold in those cases where a party applies to a Court for some special diligence or remedy, and requires to make a statement or representation to the Court, to induce the Court to give him the requisite authority, as in the cases of interdict, landlord's sequestrations, and warrants against parties *in meditatione fugae*. In such cases the applicant must be answerable for the truth of the statement on the faith of which he obtains his warrant. Whether that statement was made in good faith or in bad faith, if it was inconsistent with fact, and unjustifiable, he must answer for the consequences.'

For the purposes of an action based on wrongful diligence, malice means spite or malevolence such as would be required to rebut a defence of qualified privilege in an action for defamation[2]. Absence of probable cause means absence of any just cause.[3].

If diligence is shown to have been wrongful, liability may be imposed on the creditor, his agent, the officer of court and the judge[4].

1 (1862) 1 M 211 at 212–3, per Lord Justice-Clerk Inglis.
2 *Young v Leven* (1822) 1 Sh App 210.
3 *Robertson v Keith* 1936 SC 29, SLT 9, per Lord Justice-Clerk Aitchison.
4 See paras 12. 21 et seq, below.

Diligence following upon a valid decree

12.02 If the creditor has a valid decree, he does not incur any liability for enforcing it, if the diligence itself is regular[1]. Diligence done on such a decree will not be invalidated merely because the decree is reduced, or recalled[2], but diligence done after the reduction or recall of the decree will be actionable without any need to establish malice and lack of probable cause. The creditor should know what has happened to his decree and that he no longer has authority to do diligence on it[3].

1 *MacGregor v McLaughlin* (1905) 8 F 70, 13 SLT 348, per Lord Dunedin.
2 *Keene v Aitken* (1875) 12 SLR 308.
3 *Clark v Beattie* 1909 SC 299, 1 SLT 28.

Diligence following upon an invalid decree

12.03 If the decree is defective, eg because it has been granted by an incompetent court, or the decree goes beyond, or is not in conformity with, the crave or conclusions, and the decree has been reduced, the mere doing of diligence involves liability[1]. Once again the reason is that the creditor should know that his decree is invalid. It would not, however, be necessary to reduce the decree where it had been agreed that diligence would not be done on it[2]. In each case, it is not necessary to aver malice and want of probable cause.

1 *MacRobbie v MacLellan's Trs* (1891) 18 R 470.
2 *Sturrock v Welsh & Forbes* (1890) 18 R 109.

Diligence following upon a document other than a decree

12.04 The document may be one which has been registered in the Books of Council and Session, or the sheriff court books, eg a personal bond, or a decision of a body which can be so registered such as a decision of the Lands Tribunal which can be registered in the Books of Council and Session, or one which by statute is deemed to be the equivalent of an extract decree arbitral bearing a warrant issued from the Books of Council and Session or those of a sheriff court[1]. In such a case, any irregularity may be founded upon without the need for reduction[2] and any diligence is actionable without the need to aver malice and want of probable cause.

1 For further details, see ch 2.
2 A T Glegg *The Law of Reparation in Scotland* (4th edn) pp 208–209. The case cited, *Buchan v Melville* (1902) 4 F 620, 9 SLT 459, does not however support that proposition.

Execution of diligence

12.05 No action will lie in respect of diligence carried out on a decree or its equivalent which is regular, even although the creditor might have been able to recover his debt by some other means. For example, in *Johnston v Commercial Bank*[1], the debtor had granted bills of exchange in favour of the bank. The bank did diligence on the bills of exchange, but they could have debited an account of the debtor's. It was held that their action was unobjectionable.

1 (1858) 20 D 790.

Irregularity in execution

12.06 Any material irregularity in execution of the diligence will give rise to an action without the need to establish want of probable cause and malice. An example would be a charge where the days of charge are wrong in that they give the debtor a shorter time to pay[1]. The debtor is entitled to the minimum period laid down and so if he were charged on a longer *induciae*, it is submitted that that should not invalidate the diligence. However, the 1987 Act has clarified the law in relation to days of charge and there is less excuse for making mistakes[2]. There is authority for the view that a defect which is merely a clerical error is not actionable, but where the date on which the charge was made was omitted, it was held that that was invalid as was the diligence which followed[3].

However, a distinction requires to be drawn between the record of the execution of the diligence which becomes part of the court process and the charge or other document which is given to the debtor at the time of execution. Information in the court process which is obviously wrong to the trained eye will not invalidate the diligence as where the date of the decree was incorrectly stated in the execution, but the execution made reference to the decree, the correct date of which would have been ascertainable from an examination of the process. Furthermore, the execution was on a separate piece of paper from the decree, but it was attached to it and that did not invalidate the execution[4].

However, wrong information given to the debtor may mislead him and so the diligence may be invalid[4], as where the debtor is charged in the wrong name eg 'Isabella' instead of 'Barbara'[5], but where the correct person is charged, the charge is not invalidated merely because there was a minor error in the name[6]. It is submitted, however, that the name of a company is unique and that any error in the name will invalidate diligence done, unless the 'error' is one which is specifically provided for in the Companies Act eg 'Ltd' instead of 'Limited'[7]. The person must, however be charged in his correct capacity eg as an individual, or trustee[8].

1 *Smith & Co v Taylor* (1882) 10 R 291.
2 1987 Act, s 90(3).
3 *Beattie v MacLellan* (1844) 6 D 1088.
4 *Henderson v Rollo* (1871) 10 M 104.
5 *Brown v Rodger* (1884) 12 R 340.
6 *Spalding v Vallentine* (1883) 10 R 465.
7 Companies Act 1985, s 26.
8 *Campbell v Gordon* (1844) 6 D 1030.

Diligence following tender of payment

12.07 The 1987 Act alters the law on tendering of payment in respect of the diligences of poinding and sale, an earnings arrestment and an arrestment and furthcoming (or sale). In these cases diligence must cease if the full amount is tendered[1]. That means the principal sum, interest on it and the expenses of the action, together with the expenses of doing the diligence[2]. If therefore, that sum is paid, but the creditor nevertheless continues, he will be liable in damages, without proof of malice and want of probable cause. Under the Act, payment may now be made to either a messenger-at-arms or a sheriff officer[3].

In relation to other diligences, the common law rules still apply and so diligence must cease if the debtor tenders the amount in the decree and the expenses of the extract[4].

1 1987 Act, s 95.
2 Ibid, s 94(2).
3 Ibid, s 75; AS (Messenger-at-Arms and Sheriff Officers) Rules 1988, SI 1988/2097, r 16.
4 *Inglis v Macintyre* (1862) 24 D 541.

The effect of a sist

12.08 If diligence is sisted, eg on the granting of a time to pay direction or order, and the creditor nevertheless proceeds with diligence, he will be liable in damages[1], but other creditors who are not affected by the sist may continue with diligence.

1 *Stewart v Stewart* (1751) Mor 10535.

12.09 It is appropriate to consider separately, diligence against the person, diligence against moveables and diligence against heritage.

DILIGENCE AGAINST THE PERSON

Civil imprisonment

12.10 The circumstances in which it is competent to imprison a debtor for non-payment of a debt are very restricted[1], and where the creditor is seeking to enforce a decree *ad factum praestandum*, he must now obtain a decree from the court[2]. However, in the limited circumstances in which the remedy is available, it is incumbent on the creditor to adhere strictly to the procedure as any departure from the procedure is regarded as wrongful and will render him liable in damages[3]. However, if the diligence is carried out properly, it is not open to the debtor to argue that the creditor has been acting oppressively[4]. The creditor is vicariously responsible for the actings of the officer in taking the debtor into custody[5].

1 See above at paras 8.32–8.43.
2 1987 Act, s 102.
3 *Strachan v Stoddart* (1828) 7 S 4. This action was raised against the magistrate.
4 *Cameron v Mortimer* (1872) 10 M 461.
5 *Ross v McBean* (1845) 8 D 250.

DILIGENCE AGAINST MOVEABLE PROPERTY

Arrestment

12.11 A party raising an action is entitled to use arrestment on the dependence and a person holding a decree is entitled to use arrestment in execution, provided it is competent to do so in the circumstances. So far as arrestment on the dependence or in security is concerned, the pursuer is not liable for their use merely because the action fails and as a consequence, the diligence falls[1]. Nor is the pursuer liable if he abandons the action[2]. In order to render the pursuer liable in damages, it must be shown that he acted maliciously and without probable cause[3], or that the proceedings upon which arrestment was used were irregular[4]. The best example of irregular proceedings is where the arrestment is used without proper warrant. For example, should a person be sued in his capacity as executor, that does not permit an arrestment of his private funds[5]. Again, diligence done on a decree which is subsequently reduced is wrongful and there is no need to aver malice[6]. In these circumstances, there is no need to prove actual damage[7]. Arrestment in execution may proceed on a decree or on an extract of a registered deed. There is no need to apply for a special warrant to arrest, but the creditor will be liable if the warrant is defective, or the diligence is otherwise irregular eg where the debt has been paid[8]. On the analogy of a poinding, where an earnings arrestment proceeds on a defective charge, or without a charge, the creditor will be liable.

1 *Duff v Bradberry* (1825) 4 S 23.
2 *Brodie v Young* (1851) 13 D 737.
3 *Wilson v Mackie* (1875) 3 R 18.
4 *Meikle v Sneddon* (1862) 24 D 720; *Grant v Magistrates of Airdrie* 1939 SC 738, SLT 559.
5 *Wilson v Mackie* (1875) 3 R 18.
6 *Clarke v Beattie* 1909 SC 299, 1 SLT 28.
7 *Meikle v Sneddon* (1862) 24 D 720.
8 *Graham Stewart* p 803; *Taylor v Rutherford* (1888) 15 R 608.

Furthcoming

12.12 As furthcoming is a court action, it will be necessary for the debtor to establish that there was malice and an absence of probable cause before the creditor will be liable[1].

1 *Kinnes v Adam* (1882) 9 R 698.

Poinding and sale

12.13 A creditor who holds a decree is entitled to use the diligence of poinding if the days of charge have expired and there is nothing otherwise to prevent him doing diligence, such as a time to pay order. A poinding is subject to the same rules as the charge and, of course, the charge upon which the poinding proceeds must be regular[1]. While a poinding need not be limited to the precise amount of the debt[2], the creditor will be liable in damages if he poinds goods far in excess of the amount due[3]. The officer of court must appraise the goods and if there is no appraisal, or where it has been done by guesswork, the creditor will be liable. In *Le Conte v Douglas*[4], articles of furniture and drawings were appraised without examination and the appraised value was fixed at a sum sufficient to meet the debt and expenses.

Because the sale will be conducted by an auctioneer, and under the 1987 Act it will usually be held in an auction room, it is unlikely that there will be irregularities. However, in one case[5] the creditor allowed goods to be sold at low prices and it was held that that was oppressive and rendered the creditor liable in damages.

1 *Struthers v Dykes* (1845) 7 D 436, where there was a mistake in the debtor's name.
2 *MacKinnon v Hamilton* (1868) 7 M (HL) 173.
3 *MacKnight v Green* (1866) 4 M 852.
4 (1880) 8 R 175.
5 *Robertson v Galbraith* (1857) 19 D 1016, a sale under a landlord's sequestration for rent.

Sequestration for rent

12.14   The landlord sequestrates for rent on the basis of statements made by him to the court that the lessee is due rent which he delays or refuses to pay, and accordingly is liable if these statements are inaccurate, eg where the amount due is overstated[1]. The landlord will also be liable if he sells goods which are not subject to the hypothec[2]. Where the decree awarding sequestration is irregularly or illegally executed, eg where the debtor has tendered payment, the landlord will be liable for wrongful sequestration[3].

1 *Pollock v Goodwin's Trs* (1898) 25 R 1051, 6 SLT 72.
2 For a statement of what is subject to the hypothec, see J Rankine *The Law of Leases in Scotland* (3rd edn) pp 373–383, and paras 8.44–8.55 above.
3 *Gilmour v Craig* (1908) 45 SLR 362.

Poinding of the ground and maills and duties

12.15   These are court actions, and malice and want of probable cause must be averred. The principles applicable to personal poindings apply equally to poindings of the ground[1].

1 *Graham Stewart* p 776.

DILIGENCE AGAINST HERITAGE

Inhibition

12.16   Although inhibition is a personal or prohibitory diligence, it prevents the voluntary disposal by the debtor of his heritable property[1]. The pursuer has the right to inhibit and in order to render him liable, the defender must show malice and lack of probable cause. If the inhibition is registered, it prevents the disposal of all the debtor's heritable property, but it may be restricted or recalled by the court, if it is nimious or oppressive[2]. Accordingly, if a debtor claims damages for the oppressive use of inhibition, he will not succeed if he could have had the inhibition recalled or restricted when it was first put on[3].

1 See ch 9 above.
2 G L Gretton *The Law of Inhibition and Adjudication* pp 35–36.
3 *MacLeod v MacLeod* (1836) 15 S 248.

Adjudication

12.17 Adjudication is a court action which can be raised following upon an inhibition, or it may be raised without a prior inhibition. In either case, it is necessary to aver malice and want of probable cause[1].

1 *Kinnes v Adam* (1882) 9 R 698 at 702, per Lord President Inglis.

Ejection

12.18 In order to justify a claim for damages, it will be necessary for the defender to establish that the landlord or other pursuer has acted maliciously and without probable cause, or that there was some irregularity in the procedure[1].

1 *Fairbairn v Cockburn's Trs* (1878) 15 SLR 705.

SUMMARY DILIGENCE

12.19 Summary diligence will be actionable if there has been some irregularity in the procedure eg failure to produce an extract registered protest with the execution of diligence[1], or the diligence was unjustifiable eg because the debt had been paid[2]. As an alternative, the debtor would have to establish malice and want of probable cause.

1 *Watts v Barbour* (1828) 6 S 1048.
2 *Gibb v Edinburgh Brewery* (1873) 11 M 705.

LIABILITY FOR WRONGFUL DILIGENCE

Liability of the creditor

12.20 The creditor is liable for his own fault and also for negligence on the part of his agent or of the officer of court[1]. Although the creditor is not obliged to employ a solicitor, diligence can be done only by an officer of the court. In both cases, however, the creditor will be liable for the actions of the solicitor and the officer[1]. Thus, in every case where the diligence is wrongful, an action will lie against the creditor.

1 *Anderson v Ormiston and Lorain* (1750) M 13949.

Liability of the solicitor

12.21 A claim for damages against the solicitor will lie if he has been personally at fault. Accordingly, the defect complained of must be one which the solicitor should have noticed[1]. Thus, a solicitor will be liable if he takes decree knowing that the debt has been paid[2].

1 *Henderson v Rollo* (1872) 10 M 104.
2 *Graham Stewart* pp 763–764.

Liability of the officer

12.22 The officer of court will be liable in damages if he knows or ought to know that there is an irregularity in the proceedings eg an obviously illegal or defective warrant[1], or if he poinds goods at unrealistically low figures[2]. He will also be liable if he knows or ought to know that the use of diligence is unjustifiable eg where he knows that the debt has been paid, or that the debtor has been discharged, or that the creditor and the debtor have made arrangements about payment, or that a sist of diligence is in operation[3]. In *Reid v Clark*[4], however, an action of removing was raised but was not properly served on the defender. After decree in absence, the officer executed the decree which was *ex facie* valid and regular. In a subsequent action against the officer, the court held that he was entitled and probably obliged to proceed on a decree which was in proper form and the action was dismissed.

The officer will be liable to the creditor if he fails to carry out diligence in accordance with the instructions, provided they are proper, or fails to do diligence with all due speed[5].

1 *Graham Stewart* p 806: the author says that the officer will not be liable if he does diligence on a warrant where essential parts have been typed on erasure.
2 *Le Conte v Douglas* (1880) 7 R 175; see also *Murray v Bonn* (1913) 29 Sh Ct Rep 62; *Broomberg v Reingold* (1944) 60 Sh Ct Rep 45.
3 *Graham Stewart* pp 806–808.
4 1913 2 SLT 330.
5 *Graham Stewart* p 822; *Troup v Hendry* (1906) 22 Sh Ct Rep 271; cp *Couper v Bain* (1868) 7 M 102; *Monteith v Hutton* (1900) 8 SLT 250.

Liability of judges

12.23   Judges of the Supreme Courts are exempt from civil liability[1], but other judges are not[2]. However, in order to establish liability on the part of a sheriff for wrongful diligence, it would have to be established either that his actions were 'the result of special malice under the cloak and pretext of judicial authority'[3] or that there was gross irregularity eg for imprisoning a person without any citation or notice[4].

1 *Taaffe v Downes* (1839) 3 Moo PC 36 (Note).
2 *McCreadie v Thomson* 1907 SC 1176; 15 SLT 216, per Lord Justice-Clerk Macdonald.
3 *Hamilton v Anderson* (1856) 18 D 1003 at 1019, per Lord Justice-Clerk Hope.
4 *Pitcairn v Deans* (1715) Mor 13948.

Liability of court staff

12.24   Court staff do not enjoy the same immunity as judges[1]. However, while the 1987 Act requires sheriff clerks to assist debtors, they are not liable for any error or omission[2]. That apart, however, they would be liable if, for example, they grant irregular warrants.

1 *Watt v Thomson* (1868) 6 M 1112.
2 1987 Act, s 96(2).

CHAPTER 13

EXPENSES AND LEGAL AID

EXPENSES

13.01 The general rule is that a creditor is entitled to recover the expenses of diligence from the debtor[1]. This is not changed by the 1987 Act. Prior to the Act, it was competent to use another diligence under the same decree, or to raise a separate action for recovery of the expenses of diligence. That rule now applies only to diligences not covered by the 1987 Act. The 1987 Act deals with the expenses of: arrestments and furthcoming (or sale); earnings arrestments; current maintenance arrestments; conjoined arrestment orders; and, poindings and sale.

It does this by introducing three basic rules. The first rule is that the expenses chargeable against a debtor should be recoverable from the debtor's property, funds or earnings. That applies to the expenses chargeable against the debtor which are incurred in: executing a charge and a poinding and sale; executing a charge and an earnings arrestment; an application for, or to be included in, a conjoined arrestment order; and, an arrestment and action of furthcoming[2]. The second rule is that the creditor should be entitled to continue with diligence until the expenses of that diligence are paid together with the principal sum, interest and expenses, if any[3]. The third rule is that the expenses of any diligence should be recoverable only by that diligence and the debtor therefore ceases to be liable for any expenses which have not been so recovered[4].

There is an exception to the last rule in the case of the diligence of arrestment and furthcoming. The expenses of an action of furthcoming could be considerable and a debtor might defend an action of furthcoming for no good reason if he knew that he would not be liable for the expenses. The Act therefore provides that when a court grants decree in an action of furthcoming, it should grant a decree in favour of the creditor for the expenses of the diligence, so far as they are not recovered out of the arrested funds[5].

So far as the expenses of executing a current maintenance arrestment are concerned, the 1987 Act provides that such an arrestment covers current maintenance only. The expenses of executing that arrestment are an ordinary debt and must be recovered by other diligence[6].

The second rule is that the creditor may continue with his diligence until the expenses of it are paid along with the principal sum, interest and expenses. That changes the common law which was that diligence had to stop if the debtor paid the sum due under the decree, the expenses of the action and interest due from the date of the decree. If the creditor wishes to recover his diligence expenses, formerly he had to raise another action. The position is now that the expenses of diligence are recoverable by the diligence used to enforce the debt, and only once all of these are paid must diligence stop[7].

Under the 1987 Act, payment may be made to the officer of court[8].

1 *Graham Stewart* p 133 (arrestment), p 347 (poinding).
2 1987 Act, s 93(1).
3 Ibid, ss 48, 60, 93–95.
4 Ibid, s 95.
5 Ibid, s 93(2).
6 Ibid, s 51(3).
7 Ibid, s 95.
8 Ibid, s 75; AS (Messengers-at-Arms and Sheriff Officers Rules) 1988, SI 1988/2097, r 16.

Ascription

13.02　Because of the rule that expenses of diligence which are not recovered cease to be chargeable against the debtor, it was thought necessary to have a specific provision dealing with the ascription of sums recovered by diligence.

The Act provides that any sums recovered by a poinding and sale, an earnings arrestment, an arrestment and action of furthcoming or sale and a conjoined arrestment order for an ordinary debt are to be ascribed in the following order: expenses, interest and the principal sum.

EXPENSES

13.03　These are the expenses of the current diligence and of any previous diligence where these are recoverable from the debtor. These are set out in the Act[1] and are discussed below. Expenses also include the expenses of executing a current maintenance arrestment[2].

1 1987 Act, s 93(5).
2 Ibid, s 94(2)(a).

INTEREST

13.04　This is interest, due under the decree or other extracts where the obligation is contained in a registered document, which has accrued at the time of executing a poinding, an arrestment or an earnings arrestment, or which has accrued at the date of an application for[1], or a variation of[2], a conjoined arrestment order in respect of an ordinary debt[3].

1 1987 Act, s 60(2).
2 Ibid, s 62(5).
3 Ibid, s 94(2)(b).

THE PRINCIPAL SUM

13.05　This is the principal sum and any interest or expenses due under the decree or other document[1], but not either interest or expenses mentioned above.

1 1987 Act, s 94(2)(c).

Diligence recalled or rendered ineffectual

13.06 If the above rules were applied rigorously, the creditor would be disadvantaged if his diligence was recalled on the granting of a time to pay order or otherwise recalled by the court. The creditor would be equally disadvantaged if the diligence was rendered ineffectual, eg on sequestration.

The Act, therefore, provides for situations in which the expenses shall be recovered by further diligence under the original warrant[1] ie where a diligence is recalled on the making of a time to pay order or a conjoined arrestment order, or is rendered ineffectual by sequestration or on the presentation of a petition for the appointment of administrator or by the crystallisation of a floating charge on the commencement of a winding-up, or is rendered unenforceable because the debtor has entered into a composition contract or acceded to a trust deed.

1 1987 Act, s 93(4)–(5).

Diligence expenses

13.07 The 1987 Act draws a distinction between the expenses of diligence which do not involve an application to the court, and those which do.

NO APPLICATION TO THE COURT

Earnings arrestment

13.08 The creditor will be entitled to recover from the debtor the judicial expenses of the court proceedings or action required to obtain the equivalent of a court decree and, in addition, the debtor is liable for interest on those sums which have accrued at the date of execution of the earnings arrestment and for the expenses of serving the charge to pay and the schedule of arrestment on the debtor's employer and of intimating the same to the debtor[1].

1 1987 Act, s 48(1), (3).

Current maintenance arrestment

13.09 The creditor will be able to recover the expenses of serving a schedule of arrestment on the debtor's employer[1] and of intimating the same to the debtor[2]. However, these expenses are recoverable from the debtor as an ordinary debt or by other diligence in pursuance of the warrant[3].

1 1987 Act, s 51(3).
2 Ibid, s 54(1).
3 Ibid, s 51(3).

Conjoined arrestment order

13.10 A creditor will have to apply to the sheriff for the making of such an order. If he succeeds, then he will be entitled to recover his expenses as an ordinary debt under the conjoined arrestment order[1].

So far as the sums due to the first creditor are concerned, they will be set out in the earnings arrestment schedule and will be repeated in the conjoined arrestment order[2]. So far as the second creditor is concerned (the one who is applying for the conjoined arrestment order), the sums due to him are recoverable only in so far as they are specified in his application[3].

1 1987 Act, s 61(4).
2 Ibid, s 48.
3 Ibid, s 61(4).

Poinding and sale

13.11 Schedule 1 to the 1987 Act details the expenses of poinding and sale which are recoverable from the debtor[1]. These are the expenses incurred:
(a) subject to section 90(7), in serving a charge;
(b) in serving a notice under section 18 before entering a dwellinghouse for the purpose of executing a poinding;
(c) in executing a poinding under section 20;
(d) in making a report under section 21(4) of the redemption by the debtor of any poinded article;
(e) in granting a receipt under section 21(5) for payment for redemption under subsection (4) of that section (ie redemption after poinding);
(f) in making a report under section 22 of the execution of a poinding, but not in applying for an extension of time for the making of such a report;
(g) in applying for a warrant of sale under section 30(1);
(h) in granting a receipt under section 33(3) for payment for the redemption of any poinded article (ie redemption after a warrant of sale);
(j) in making a report under section 33(5)(b) of the release or redemption of poinded articles;
(k) in making intimation, serving a copy of the warrant of sale and giving public notice under section 34;
(l) in removing any articles for sale in pursuance of a warrant of sale;
(m) in making arrangements for, conducting and supervising a warrant sale;
(n) where the arrangements for a sale have been cancelled under section 36(1) (ie on payment), in returning poinded articles to any premises from which they have been removed for sale;
(o) in making a report of an agreement under section 36(2);
(p) subject to section 39(3), in making a report of sale under that section;
(q) granting a receipt under section 41(4) for payment for the release from a poinding of any article which is owned in common;
(r) in making a report under section 41(5)(b) of the release of any such article;
(s) in opening shut and lockfast places in the execution of the diligence;
(t) by a solicitor in instructing an officer of court to take any of the steps specified above.
That list may be altered by the Lord Advocate[2].

1 1987 Act, s 44, Sch 1, para 1.
2 Ibid, Sch 1, para 2.

Removal, damage or destruction of poinded articles

13.12 Where the debtor has been given permission to move poinded goods to another location, an officer may repoind any of the articles so removed[1]. The general rule is that the expenses of the second poinding are chargeable against the debtor, but not the expenses of the original poinding[2]. That is subject to exceptions. One exception is where the creditor has agreed to the removal of poinded goods only if the debtor agrees to be liable for the expenses of the original poinding and where the sheriff has directed that the debtor will be liable for the original expenses[3]. A similar rule applies to the situation in which a new date is fixed for the holding of a warrant sale.

1 1987 Act, s 28(2).
2 Ibid, Sch 1, para 5.
3 Ibid, Sch 1, para 6.

Variations in arrangment for sale

13.13 Where a warrant of sale is varied, the debtor will be liable for the expenses incurred in the application for the variation and the execution of the warrant of sale as varied, but, as a general rule, he will not be liable for the expenses of the application for, and the execution of, the original warrant of sale[1]. Where the arrangements for sale are cancelled after a warrant for sale has been granted, because the debtor and the creditor have reached agreement about payment, the debtor is liable for the expenses of any new arrangements[2]. Where the sale cannot take place for some other reason for which neither the creditor nor the officer is responsible, or the removal of poinded articles cannot take place on the date arranged, again the debtor meets the expenses of any new arrangements but not those of the original[3]. Where a warrant of sale is varied and the sheriff awards additional expenses these are recoverable from the debtor[4].

1 1987 Act, Sch 1, para 2.
2 Ibid, Sch 1, para 3.
3 Ibid, Sch 1, para 7.
4 Ibid, Sch 1, para 4.

APPLICATION TO THE COURT

13.14 The general philosophy of the 1987 Act is not to discourage debtors from making applications to the court. Accordingly, the Act provides that an application by the debtor to the sheriff under the provisions of Part II of the Act dealing with poindings and warrant sales will not result in the debtor being liable for the expenses. He will not be liable for any objections to applications made by the creditor under that part of the Act either. The same applies to applications or objections by a creditor. Likewise, neither party is to be liable for the expenses of a hearing on the question of recalling a poinding or on the refusal to grant a warrant of sale or on the refusal to grant a variation of the arrangements for the sale, or a hearing regarding the balance due by or to the debtor following up an auditor's report on the warrant sale[1].

If, however, the application is frivolous or the opposition is frivolous or the grounds for seeking a hearing are frivolous then the sheriff may award a sum of expenses not exceeding £25 against the party acting frivolously. That figure may be altered by the Lord Advocate[2].

1 1987 Act, s 92(1), Sch 1, para 10.
2 Ibid, s 92(2), Sch 1, para 11.

EXCEPTIONS

13.15   The 'no expenses due or by' rule does not apply (i) where there is an appeal[1] (an appeal is competent only on a point of law and the parties will probably be legally represented and legal aid is available[2]), (ii) to the expenses of the parties where the debtor applies for a time to pay direction[3] and (iii) where a third party's goods have been poinded and he has to establish his rights in the goods[4]. In all of these cases, the normal rules about expenses apply.

The rule does not apply either to the expenses of poinding and sale in so far as they are set out in Schedule 1[5], or to the expenses of poinding and sale under a summary warrant in so far as these are set out in Schedule 5[6]. The expenses of enforcing summary warrants are broadly similar[7].

1 1987 Act, s 92(3)(b)(ii).
2 See para 13.29, below.
3 1987 Act, s 92(3)(b)(i).
4 Ibid, s 92(3)(b)(iii).
5 Ibid, s 93(3)(a), Sch 1, para 1.
6 Ibid, s 92(3)(a), Sch 5, paras 25–34.
7 Ibid, Sch 5, paras 25–34.

EXPENSES AT DISCRETION OF THE SHERIFF

13.16   The sheriff is given a discretion to award expenses where poinded goods are removed, damaged or destroyed in breach of a poinding requiring the creditor to obtain a further order from the court regarding the goods[1].

The sheriff also has a discretion in relation to expenses of an order made for the security of poinded goods[2]. The reason given for the discretion is the variety of circumstances which are not amenable to rules[3].

1 1987 Act, s 44, Sch 1, para 8(b)(i); for summary warrants 1987 Act, s 74, Sch 5, para 30(b).
2 Ibid, s 44, Sch 1, para 8(b)(ii); for summary warrants ibid, s 74, Sch 5, para 30(b).
3 Report on Diligence and Debtor Protection (Scot Law Com no 95 (1985)) para 9.35.

EXPENSES OF OTHER DILIGENCES

13.17   The 1987 Act does not deal with the expenses of inhibition, adjudication, sequestration for rent, poinding of the ground and maills and duties. The rules governing expenses for these diligences therefore remain unaltered[1].

1 For expenses of recall of arrestment, see para 4.55 above. For expenses of an action of furthcoming, see para 5.50 above.

Inhibition

13.18   As a general proposition, one can say that if the inhibiting creditor loses or abandons his action, or the use of the inhibition was unjustified, he is liable in expenses for the inhibition and must discharge it or recall it. In all other cases, the debtor is liable.[1]. This is dealt with under the heading of inhibition on the dependence and inhibition in execution.

1 For further details see G L Gretton *The Law of Inhibition and Adjudication* pp 399–41.

13.19   *Inhibition on the dependence: (i) creditor fails.* If the inhibition is recalled on the ground of nimiety or oppression[1] or because of a procedural irregularity[2], the inhibiting creditor must meet the expenses of the recall.

The same applies where the action raised by the inhibiting creditor is dismissed or decree of absolvitor is granted or the action is abandoned. Hence the creditor must grant a discharge at his expense and, if he fails, the debtor may have it recalled at the creditor's expense[3].

1 *Stair v Agnew* (1822) 2 S 106.
2 *Lickley, Petnr* (1871) 8 SLR 624.
3 *Milne v Birrell* (1902) 4 F 879, 10 SLT 104.

13.20 *(ii) Creditor succeeds.* Where the inhibiting creditor succeeds in the action, the debtor is entitled to have the inhibition discharged on payment, but at his expense[1]. However, if the creditor fails to grant the discharge when asked, the debtor is entitled to have the inhibition recalled, probably at the creditor's expense[2]. If the debtor, however, seeks recall without first asking for a discharge, he will be liable in expenses[3]. The position is the same when the action is sisted[4].

1 *Laing v Muirhead* (1868) 6 M 282.
2 *Robertson v Park Dobson & Co* (1896) 24 R 30, 4 SLT 114.
3 *Gordon v Duncan* (1827) 5 S 602.
4 *Robertson v Park Dobson & Co* (1896) 24 R 30, 4 SLT 114.

13.21 *(iii) Caution or consignation.* Where the inhibition is recalled on caution or consignation, there is some authority for the view that the debtor is liable in expenses[1]. However, there is a preferable view and that is that expenses should follow the success of the action[2].

1 *Blochairn Iron Co v Flower* (1865) 1 SLR 45; *Graham Stewart* p 573.
2 *Dobbie v Duncanson* (1872) 10 M 810 at 816, per Lord President Inglis.

13.22 *Inhibition in execution.* Where inhibition is used and the debt is paid, the creditor is under an obligation to grant a discharge, but the debtor is liable for the expenses[1].

1 *Laing v Muirhead* (1868) 6 M 282.

Adjudication

13.23 *Adjudication in security/execution.* Graham Stewart expresses the view that since adjudication is a diligence, it is incompetent to have a conclusion for expenses[1].

1 *Graham Stewart* p 589: A E J G Mackay *Manual of Practice in the Court of Session* p 520; *Riley v Cameron* 1940 SLT (Sh Ct) 40.

13.24 *Adjudication in implement.* If the debtor opposes[1] an adjudication in implement, the pursuer is entitled to ask for expenses.

1 *Graham Stewart* p 589.

13.25 *Declaratory adjudication.* Although actions of declaratory adjudication are rare, expenses will be granted only in the event of opposition.

Sequestration for rent

13.26 Where the landlord sequestrates for rent, the expenses of the process are chargeable against the tenant[1]. However, where the rent is tendered or consigned, the sequestration will be recalled and the landlord is not entitled to continue with the sequestration to recover his expenses[2].

Where the landlord sequestrates in security and the rent is paid, the tenant is not, as a general rule, liable in expenses[3]. The tenant might be liable if the landlord could show that the tenant was *vergens ad inopiam* or that there were other exceptional circumstances[4].

1 *Galloway v McPherson* (1830) 8 S 539.
2 *Graham Stewart* p 478.
3 *Shaw v Browne* (1885) 1 Sh Ct Rep 341.
4 *Oswald v Graeme* (1851) 13 D 1229.

Poinding of the ground

13.27 Where an action of poinding of the ground is raised against a debtor in possession, there will usually be a crave of conclusion for expenses[1], but where the subjects are tenanted, there will be a conclusion for expenses against the debtors only if they oppose the action[2].

1 Mackay *Manual of Practice in the Court of Session* p 113.
2 *Encyclopaedia of Scottish Legal Styles* vol 1, p 105.

Maills and duties

13.28 There should be a crave or conclusion for expenses against the proprietor, and against tenants but only if they oppose the action[1].

1 Stair IV, 22, 15.

LEGAL AID

13.29 Before doing diligence, a client who to legally-aided must obtain the consent of the Scottish Legal Aid Board (SLAB). The only exceptions are an arrestment in execution of a decree for aliment under the Family Law (Scotland) Act 1985, or an order for payment of a periodic allowance, or an order for periodic payments of maintenance and the preceding charge[1]. The Board will not give retrospective sanction for diligence which has been executed without its approval. The 1987 Act provides that legal aid will not be available to either creditor or debtor except for applications for time to pay directions, recall of directions, or appeals[2]. However, others are eligible for legal aid[3]. Thus a third party whose goods have been poinded by mistake is eligible for legal aid.

1 Civil Legal Aid (Scotland) Regulations 1987, SI 1987/381, regs 22, 32(a)(i)–(iii).
2 1987 Act, s 98(4).
3 Ibid, s 98(5).

CHAPTER 14

ADMINISTRATION OF OFFICERS OF COURT

INTRODUCTION

14.01 This chapter is concerned with the law regulating the offices of messenger-at-arms and sheriff officer, the officers of court[1] most directly concerned with the administration of diligence.

1 In the 1987 Act, as normally also in this book, 'officer of court' is used to refer to messengers-at-arms and sheriff officers: cp 1987 Act, s 106. This usage though common is not precise for in a broader sense advocates, solicitors, and others are also officers of court.

General nature of the offices

14.02 The offices of messenger-at-arms and sheriff officer are of considerable antiquity[1]. As the nature of each office developed, three broad characteristics emerged, which continue to apply to both. These are:

(a) First that messengers-at-arms and sheriff officers are officers of court. Officers are appointed by, and are responsible in the exercise of their duties to, high judicial authority. In the case of messengers-at-arms, this authority was primarily the Lord Lyon King of Arms but, since the 1987 Act, the main role in the appointment and supervision of messengers-at-arms lies with the Court of Session. Sheriff officers are appointed by and are responsible to sheriffs principal.

(b) A second, and partly contrasting, feature about the nature of the offices is that messengers-at-arms and sheriff officers function not as agents or employees of the courts but as independent contractors who act on the basis of instructions from litigants and creditors. Suggestions have been made from time to time that officers of court should be administered on a salaried basis and employed as a separate unit within the court service or by the executive branch of the government, but none of these proposals has attracted widespread support[2].

(c) A third feature of the offices of officers of court is that there are two different such offices, messenger-at-arms and sheriff officer. The two levels of office reflect the duality of the civil court system in Scotland between the Court of Session and the sheriff court. As a broad generalisation, messengers-at-arms are concerned with citation and diligence in connection with the Court of Session, and sheriff officers are concerned with these matters in respect of the sheriff court. Similarly, the appointment, supervision and discipline of officers reflect the duality of the court structure[3].

1 For discussion, see Malcolm Innes of Edingight (the Lord Lyon King of Arms), *The Laws of Scotland: Stair Memorial Encyclopaedia* vol 14, para 1501 et seq.

2 Report on Diligence and Debtor Protection (Scot Law Com no 95 (1985)) pp 34–46, 72–74, 452–454.
3 For further discussion of the range of duties of officers of court see below at paras 14.19–14.28. The strict duality of the two offices is breached in that: (i) no person may be admitted as a messenger-at-arms unless he is already a sheriff officer: 1987 Act, s 77(1)–(3); (ii) 'spot-checks' on the work of messengers-at-arms and sheriff officers are made only at the level of the sheriff court: 1987 Act, s 78(3); (iii) application by an officer for authorisation to engage in extra-official activities is made to a sheriff principal: 1987 Act, s 75(2).

Scope of duties

14.03 Historically the range of official duties of officers of court extended to (a) apprehension of criminals and the service of court writs in criminal cases, (b) service of court writs in civil cases, and (c) civil diligence. The rise of a professional police force in the nineteenth century greatly reduced the role of officers of court in criminal matters, though officers are still empowered to serve warrants, citations, indictments, complaints, lists of witnesses etc in criminal cases[1]. It is also now clear that the police and procurator fiscal service have no duties to enforce, or to assist officers of court in enforcing, warrants and decrees of the civil courts[2]. However, the police may accompany an officer of court executing a civil warrant for the purpose of preventing or dealing with any breach of the criminal law.

The service of summonses and citations in civil cases still forms a significant part of the work of officers of court. However, since the Citation Amendment (Scotland) Act 1882, most service of summonses and citations is effected by way of postal service by qualified solicitors. The extra expense of using service by officer of court is normally permitted only where postal service has proved unsuccessful but it may also be advisable in other circumstances, eg where an action is in danger of becoming time-barred[3].

In addition to executing citation and diligences of Court of Session actions, messengers-at-arms as officers of Arms also have functions in connection with the Court of the Lord Lyon and the High Court of Parliament[4].

There are also various prohibitions and restrictions on the extra-official functions which an officer of court may undertake[5].

1 Criminal Procedure (Scotland) Act 1975, ss 71, 326, 426(1).
2 *Caldwell v Caldwell* 1983 SLT 610.
3 For this purpose an action is raised when the service of the summons or initial writ is effected: *Alston v McDougall* (1887) 15 R 78; *Wall's Trs v Drynan* (1888) 15 R 359, 363.
4 See Malcolm Innes of Edingight (the Lord Lyon King of Arms) in *The Laws of Scotland: Stair Memorial Encyclopaedia* vol 14, para 1504; Malcolm Innes of Edingight and Sir Crispin Agnew 'The Court of the Lord Lyon' in *The Laws of Scotland: Stair Memorial Encyclopaedia* vol 6, para 1021.
5 1987 Act, s 75(e), (f); SI 1988/2097, r 17. See further at paras 14.29–14.36 below.

Administration of officers of court

14.04 The general principle is that officers of court are supervised and controlled by the judicial authority by which they are appointed, ie by the Court of Session in the case of messengers-at-arms, and by sheriffs principal in the case of sheriff officers. The appointment, supervision and discipline of officers of court is discussed in detail later. Note can be made here of other bodies and institutions which are concerned with the administration of officers of court.

COURT OF SESSION

14.05 By section 75(1) of the 1987 Act, the Court of Session is empowered to make regulations by Act of Sederunt on a wide variety of matters relating to officers of court, including their organisation, training, conduct, scope of duties, and procedure in disciplinary proceedings.

ADVISORY COUNCIL ON MESSENGERS–AT–ARMS AND SHERIFF OFFICERS

14.06 There is an Advisory Council on Messengers-at-Arms and Sheriff Officers, whose duties are to advise the Court of Session on its power to make regulations on officers of court by Act of Sederunt[1]. The Advisory Council is also under a duty to keep under review all matters relating to officers of court.

The members of the Advisory Council are[2]:
(i) a judge of the Court of Session, who acts as chairman;
(ii) two sheriffs principal;
(iii) two officers of court;
(iv) two solicitors;
(v) the Lord Lyon King of Arms;
(vi) one further member, appointed by the Lord Advocate.
The Advisory Council has a secretary who is appointed by the Secretary of State[3].

1 1987 Act, s 76(1).
2 Ibid, s 76(2). Categories (i)–(iv) are appointed by the Lord President of the Court of Session. The length of tenure of members of the Advisory Council is regulated by ibid, s 76(4)–(8).
3 Ibid, s 76(3).

REGISTERS OF OFFICERS OF COURT

14.07 Registers are kept by the clerk to the Lord Lyon in respect of messengers-at-arms, and by the regional sheriff clerk of each sheriffdom in respect of each sheriff officer who holds a commission in that sheriffdom[1]. In these registers there are recorded the following details in respect of every officer of court:
(i) the address of his principal, and any other, place of business or employment, his private address and any change of such address;
(ii) every commission held by him as an officer of court;
(iii) any extra-official activities carried on by him for remuneration, and any authorisation by a sheriff principal in respect of any such activity;
(iv) any interest disclosed by him under rule 18(2) or 18(3)[2];
(v) any suspension or deprivation of office;
(vi) the date on which he ceased to practise where notice to that effect has been given; and
(vii) the dates of his accounting year.

1 SI 1988/2097, r 19. For discussion of the office of regional sheriff clerk, see I D Macphail p 14.
2 SI 1988/2097.

THE SOCIETY OF MESSENGERS-AT-ARMS AND SHERIFF OFFICERS

14.08 The Society of Messengers-at-Arms and Sheriff Officers, which was established in 1922 following the amalgamation of two local associations of officers of court, acts as a general representative and pressure group for the interests of officers of court[1]. It acts as a channel of communication between officers and various authorities concerned with the law of citation and diligence, including the Advisory Council on Messengers-at-Arms and Sheriff Officers. The Society is a purely voluntary body, but although membership is not compulsory, it is thought that the vast majority of officers of court are members.

Furthermore, the Society does have a number of official roles in the administration of officers of court, especially in connection with the examining of candidates for entry to each office[2].

1 See further Scot Law Com Report no 95 (1985), pp 456–457, 499.
2 See further below at paras 14.12, 14.16. SI 1988/2097, r 6.

APPOINTMENT

General

14.09 A sheriff officer is appointed by the sheriff principal of the sheriffdom in which the officer has authority to act. A messenger-at-arms is appointed by the Lord Lyon King of Arms. However, the Lord Lyon's role in appointment is largely formal and the active part in the appointment of messengers-at-arms is carried out by the Court of Session.

The following categories of person are disqualified from being officers of court[1]:

(a) a person below the age of twenty years;
(b) a person over the age of seventy years;
(c) an auctioneer with his own auction room;
(d) an elected or appointed member of a public or local authority;
(e) a house factor;
(f) a member of the Faculty of Advocates;
(g) a member of the Law Society of Scotland;
(h) a member of the United Kingdom or European Parliaments;
(i) a money lender; or
(j) a police officer.

An officer of court, whether or not appointed before the 1987 Act came into force, must retire from practice as an officer on attaining the age of seventy years[2].

1 SI 1988/2097, rr 3(1)(a), (b), 17(3).
2 SI 1988/2097, r 3(2), (3).

Sheriff officer

14.10 The stages to be followed in being granted a commission as a sheriff officer are as follows:

SERVICE OF TRAINEESHIP

14.11 An intending intrant must serve a period of traineeship of three years with a person who is in practice as an officer of court[1]. On written application by the trainee, this period may be reduced to one year by the sheriff principal to whom application for a first commission is made in the light of previous experience of the trainee[2]. The rules do not give any guidance as to what previous experience is relevant in this context. When an officer takes on an employee for the purpose of that employee becoming an officer of court the officer is responsible for providing the requisite training of the trainee.

Where the period of training of a trainee has been completed satisfactorily, the intrant is issued with a certificate to that effect by the officer who provided the training.

1 SI 1988/2097, rr 3(1)(c), (d), 5(1).
2 Ibid, r 5(2).

EXAMINATIONS; EDUCATIONAL STANDARD

14.12 A committee of examiners is set up by the Society of Messengers-at-Arms and Sheriff Officers to examine any person who seeks to apply to become a sheriff officer[1]. The committee, in consultation with the Society, is responsible for the setting and assessing of the examinations and with the general educational standard or qualifications for candidates. An applicant must have passed all the examinations set by the committee of examiners within five years before applying for a commission as a sheriff officer. The applicant must also by that time have attained the educational standard fixed by the committee[2].

1 SI 1988/2097, r 6(1), (3). The membership of the committee is determined in accordance with ibid, r 6(7).
2 Ibid, r 3(1)(e), (f).

APPLICATION TO THE SHERIFF PRINCIPAL

14.13 Application for commission as a sheriff officer is made by initial writ as a summary application to the sheriff principal of the relevant sheriffdom[1]. The application is in Form 2 of the Officers of Court rules[2]. It must be signed by the applicant or his solicitor. The application may be for a commission as sheriff officer throughout the sheriffdom or for a particular sheriff court district or districts in the sheriffdom.

With the initial writ there is to be lodged:
(i) an inventory of productions;
(ii) a copy of the entry in the Register of Births relating to the applicant;
(iii) a certificate of satisfactory completion of traineeship;
(iv) a certificate from the committee of examiners to the effect that the applicant has passed the examinations set by the committee; and
(v) two references of good character.

An application is ordained to be intimated on the walls of every sheriff court in the sheriffdom or sheriff court district or districts of the sheriffdom for which appointment as sheriff officer is sought. The application must also be advertised in newspapers circulating in the sheriffdom[3].

Where an application is made for commissions as sheriff officer in more than one sheriffdom, a separate application must be made in each of the sheriffdoms concerned[4].

1 SI 1988/2097, r 8(1)–(3).
2 Ibid.
3 The advertisement is in ibid, Form 3.
4 Where an officer already holds a commission and subsequently obtains a further commission, he must make intimation of all subsequent commissions to the relevant sheriffs principal and, where appropriate, the Lord Lyon: ibid, r 8(10), (11).

OBJECTIONS TO APPLICATION; DETERMINING AN APPLICATION

14.14 Any person who wishes to object to an application for commission as sheriff officer must lodge answers to the application with the sheriff clerk within one month from the date of intimation and advertisement of the application[1]. The grounds on which objections may be raised are not set out in the 1987 Act nor in the Officers of Court Rules. Usually objections are raised by sheriff officers who already hold commissions in the sheriffdom on the ground that the sheriffdom or sheriff court district is adequately served by the existing numbers of officers and that further appointments would have a deleterious effect on the amount of business available[2].

Whether or not objections are made, the sheriff principal must satisfy himself that the applicant is suitably qualified and is a fit and proper person to be a sheriff officer. However, the sheriff principal retains a discretion whether to appoint a qualified person, and in exercising this discretion[3]

'the sheriff principal has regard to the interest of the applicant, to the interest of any objectors opposing the application and to the public interest, which is paramount. Important factors in determining the public interest are that there should be an adequate but not excessive number of sheriff officers for the relevant district; that a single officer or firm of officers should not have a monopoly of business so that a choice is available to creditors; that the officer should be of good character; and that the officer should preferably have knowledge of the local community.'

In *MacPherson, Petitioner*[4], the sheriff principal said:

'No sheriff principal wishes to act arbitrarily in deciding to grant or refuse a commission. Yet it is not easy to formulate criteria to serve as a guide in individual cases. On the assumption that a petitioner has all the necessary qualifications, I am inclined to ask two questions, viz (1) is there need for a new sheriff officer in the districts applied for, or at least will the introduction of a new sheriff officer or sheriff officers seriously prejudice existing sheriff officers who have served the districts well over the years? and (2) will the new sheriff officer be in a position to offer the level of service which a sheriff principal is entitled to expect when he grants a commission? Other questions will obviously arise in different cases, and the importance of the two I have ventured to formulate may well vary from case to case. For example, the first seems to me of less importance in large cities than in small country areas where a new commission or commissions could put an existing sheriff officer out of business.'

The sheriff principal's discretion is not subject to appeal[5] but may fall within the scope of the power of judicial review by the Court of Session.

1 SI 1988/2097, r 8(4).
2 See eg *Lewis, Petr* 1963 SLT (Sh Ct) 6; *Thornton, Applicant* 1967 SLT (Sh Ct) 71; *MacPherson Petr* 1989 SLT (Sh Ct) 53.

3 Scot Law Com Report no 95 (1985), p 467.
4 1989 SLT (Sh Ct) 53 at 55.
5 Cp *Stewart v Reid* 1934 SC 69, 76.

GRANTING OF COMMISSION

14.15 If the sheriff principal decides to grant a commission, he may limit its scope to a particular sheriff court district or to a number of particular sheriff court districts within the sheriffdom.

Before a sheriff principal can grant a commission as a sheriff officer to an applicant, the applicant must have lodged with the sheriff clerk the requisite bond of caution and a premium receipt from an insurance company for professional indemnity insurance[1].

On issuing the commission the sheriff principal (or a sheriff) administers to the applicant the oath or declaration *de fideli administratione officii*[2]. The applicant, on becoming an officer, is also issued with an official identity card by each sheriff principal (and the Lord Lyon) from whom he holds a commission as an officer of court[3].

1 SI 1988/2097, r 8(6), (7). Where the sheriff officer already holds a commission as a sheriff officer, he need only lodge a copy letter of receipt of the bond and premium issued by the regional sheriff clerk.
2 Ibid, r 8(8).
3 1987 Act, s 86(1). When performing his official functions, an officer of court must exhibit his identity card on being requested to do so. The identity card must be the appropriate one in connection with the diligence concerned (eg it would not be enough, if executing a warrant issued by a sheriff court in a sheriffdom to display the identity card issued by the Lord Lyon or by the sheriff principal in another sheriffdom).

Messengers-at-arms

PREREQUISITES TO APPLICATION

14.16 An application for a commission as a messenger-at-arms may be made only by a sheriff officer[1]. Furthermore, prior to application the applicant must have been in practice as a sheriff officer for a period of not less than two years, though an application may be made after a shorter period in practice as a sheriff officer upon cause shown[2].

Before making an application, the applicant must also have passed all examinations set for the purpose of becoming a messenger by a committee of examiners of the Society of Messengers-at-Arms and Sheriff Officers[3].

1 1987 Act, s 77(1).
2 SI 1988/2097, r 4(1), (2).
3 Ibid, rr 4(1)(b), 6. These examinations must have been passed by the applicant within five years before the date of application.

MODE OF APPLICATION

14.17 Application by a sheriff officer to be a messenger-at-arms involves a two-part procedure. Application is made in the first place to the Court of Session by way of petition presented to the Outer House[1]. With the petition there is lodged:

(i) an inventory of productions;

(ii) a copy of the entry in the Register of Births relating to the petitioner;

(iii) a certificate from the Society of Messengers-at-Arms and Sheriff Officers that the petitioner has passed the examinations set by the committee of examiners of the Society; and

(iv) a certificate from another officer of court specifying the period that the petitioner has been in practice as a sheriff officer.

The petition does not require a process and is not intimated on the walls of court, served or advertised. It appears that there is now no procedure for lodging objections to the petition[2].

The Lord Ordinary, if he finds that the petition is in order may recommend the applicant's appointment as a messenger-at-arms to the Lord Lyon[3]. The language of the statute suggests that the Lord Ordinary has a discretion whether or not to make the recommendation, though it is thought that refusal to make a recommendation will be rare.

1 SI 1988/2097, r 7(1)–(3). The petition is in Form 1 of SI 1988/2097 and is signed by the petitioner or his solicitor.

2 1987 Act, s 77(4), overruling *Lindsay v Drummond* (1744) Mor 8889.

3 1987 Act, s 77(1).

TRANSMISSION OF APPLICATION TO THE LORD LYON KING OF ARMS

14.18 The second stage in an application for a commission as a messenger-at-arms is the transmission of the application to the Lord Lyon, after the Lord Ordinary has granted the prayer of the applicant's petition. The clerk of the Petition Department sends a copy of the petition, with the interlocutor granting the prayer written on it, to the clerk of the Lord Lyon[1]. Thereafter the Lord Lyon may grant the applicant a commission as a messenger-at-arms. Again it is to be noted that the language of the statute suggests a discretion on the part of the Lord Lyon[2].

Before a commission as a messenger-at-arms can be issued, the applicant must lodge with the Lyon clerk a copy letter of receipt issued by a regional sheriff clerk in respect of the applicant's bond of caution and premium receipt for professional indemnity insurance[3].

When the Lord Lyon issues a commission as a messenger-at-arms, he administers to the applicant the oath or declaration of allegiance[4]. The applicant is issued with an official identity card, and a wand and blazon as the insignia of office[5].

A messenger-at-arms ceases to be entitled to hold a commission as a messenger-at-arms if he no longer holds any commission as a sheriff officer[6].

1 SI 1988/2097, r 7(4).

2 1987 Act, s 77(1). It can be noted that there is no longer a limitation on the number of persons who may wear and bear the Sovereign's arms in Scotland: 1987 Act, Sch 8, repealing Officers of Arms Act 1587 (c 30).

3 SI 1988/2097, r 7(5). See further below at para 14.38.

4 Ibid, r 7(6).

5 1987 Act, s 86. The blazon is an ebony rod tipped at each end with silver and the blazon is attached to it by a ring. In the event of deforcement, the messenger 'breaks' the wand by moving the ring from one end of the rod to the other. See further Malcolm Innes of Edingight in *The Laws of Scotland: Stair Memorial Encyclopaedia* vol 14, para 1503.

6 1987 Act, s 77(3).

POWERS AND DUTIES

General nature

14.19   The range of official powers and duties of officers of court extends over diligence, civil citations, and to a considerably lesser extent, citation in criminal cases[1]. This section sets out the various powers, duties and disabilities of officers as regards their official functions in diligence, and also examines the limitations imposed on the extra-official duties which officers of court may undertake.

1 Messengers-at-arms also have various official functions concerning the Court of the Lord Lyon King of Arms: see Malcolm Innes of Edingight in *The Laws of Scotland: Stair Memorial Encyclopaedia* vol 14, para 1504.

Duty to serve the lieges

14.20   Officers of court have a duty, reflected in their oath *de fideli*, to serve all who lawfully instruct them on payment or tender of reasonable expenses[1]. An officer may refuse to accept lawful instructions only where it is not reasonably practicable for him to carry out the instructions and this has been intimated without delay on receipt of the instructions to the person instructing him[2].

1 *Stewart v Reid* 1934 SC 69, esp at 72–74. In this case, it was held that as a consequence of this rule any commission which sought to restrict the officer to one (or more) employer was incompetent. See also SI 1988/2097, r 16(4)(c).
2 SI 1988/2097, r 16(4)(b).

Scope of official functions relating to diligence

MESSENGERS-AT-ARMS

14.21   A commission as a messenger-at-arms empowers the messenger to perform his official functions throughout Scotland. However, as concerns diligence, a messenger may execute only decrees and warrants of the Court of Session, the Court of Teinds, the High Court of Justiciary, and the Lyon Court. Decrees include 'deemed' decrees such as documents registered for execution in the Books of Council and Session[1] and foreign judgments registered in the Court of Session for execution in Scotland[2].

A messenger-at-arms is not authorised by his commission as a messenger-at-arms to execute a decree or warrant granted by a sheriff or sheriff clerk[3].

1 See further ch 2 above.
2 See further ch 11 above.
3 1987 Act, s 77(2). A messenger-at-arms may execute sheriff court diligence in his capacity as a sheriff officer if he holds an appropriate commission as sheriff officer: see further para 14.22 below.

SHERIFF OFFICERS

14.22   The general rule concerning the scope of powers of sheriff officers is that a sheriff officer's official functions relate to decrees and warrants of the sheriff court and he cannot execute diligence or citation concerning Court of Session decrees or citation[1], nor may he exercise his powers as sheriff officer beyond the territorial limits set out in his commission or commissions as sheriff officer.

However, the following sheriff court warrants and precepts may be executed anywhere in Scotland without the need for any warrant of concurrence[2]:

(i) a warrant for execution contained in an extract of a decree granted by a sheriff;

(ii) a warrant for execution inserted in an extract of a document registered in sheriff court books;

(iii) a warrant of a sheriff for arrestment on the dependence of an action or in security;

(iv) a precept (issued by a sheriff clerk) of arrestment in security of a liquid debt the term of payment of which has not yet arrived.

Any of these warrants or precepts may be executed by a sheriff officer who holds a commission extending to the court which granted it or to the sheriff court district in which it is to be executed[3].

A decree of the sheriff court includes 'deemed' or registered decrees. Furthermore, any reference in any statute or statutory instrument to an order being enforceable in like manner as a recorded decree arbitral is to be construed as a reference to such an order being enforceable in the same manner as an extract registered decree arbitral bearing a warrant for execution issued by the sheriff court of any sheriffdom in Scotland[4].

1 This is subject to the provisions of the Execution of Diligence (Scotland) Act 1926. See further below at para 14.23.
2 1987 Act, s 91(1).
3 Ibid, s 91(2).
4 Ibid, Sch 6, para 1. See also 1987 Act, Sch 6, para 15 (amending Town and Country Planning (Scotland) Act 1972, s 267(8)) and para 20 (amending Patents Act 1977, ss 93(b), 107(3)).

EXECUTION OF DILIGENCE (SCOTLAND) ACT 1926

14.23 The 1926 Act was an attempt to deal with some of the difficulties of executing diligence in the remote areas of Scotland by allowing for execution by persons other than messenger-at-arms and local sheriff officers.

(1) In any sheriff court district in which there is no resident messenger-at-arms or in any of the islands of Scotland, a sheriff officer duly authorised to practise in any part of the sheriffdom comprising the sheriff court district or island has all the powers of a messenger-at-arms in regard to any summons, writ, citation or other proceedings, or to the execution of or diligence on any decree, warrant or order[1].

(2) Execution by means of registered or recorded delivery letter may be made[2] of

(a) an arrestment (other than an arrestment to found jurisdiction), proceeding on any warrant or decree of the sheriff in a summary cause, including a small claims action[3]; and

(b) a charge upon a decree for payment of money, granted by a sheriff in a summary cause (including a small claims action) if the place of execution is

(i)   in any of the islands of Scotland; or

(ii) in any sheriff court district in which there is no resident sheriff officer; or

(iii) more than twelve miles distant from the seat of the court where decree was granted.

The registered or recorded delivery letter may be sent by a sheriff officer who would be entitled to execute the arrestment or charge according to the law and practice existing at the passing of the 1926 Act, or by a messenger-at-arms resident in the sheriffdom in which the place of execution is situated, or if there is no messenger-at-arms or sheriff officer resident in the sheriffdom, by a solicitor enrolled in that sheriffdom[4].

(3) The sheriff within whose jurisdiction a decree or warrant granted by any court in Scotland requires to be executed may, if satisfied that no messenger-at-arms or sheriff officer is reasonably available to execute the decree or warrant, authorise any suitable person to execute it. Such a person cannot be the solicitor of the person making the application for such authorisation. The person so authorised has all the powers of a messenger-at-arms or sheriff officer for the purposes concerned[5].

1 Execution of Diligence (Scotland) Act 1926, s 1. This provision supersedes in practice the power of the Court of Session in the exercise of its *nobile officium* to authorise a sheriff officer to act as a messenger-at-arms for specific occasions or to execute diligence following on Court of Session decrees: see eg *Kennedy* (1862) 24 D 1132; *Whyte, Ridsdale & Co* 1912 SC 1095.
2 The precise steps to be followed in making such execution are set out in the Execution of Diligence (Scotland) Act 1926, s 2(2).
3 Ibid, ss 2(1)(a), 5.
4 Ibid, s 2(1)(b), (2)(b).
5 Ibid, s 3. It appears that resort to section 3 of the 1926 Act is very rarely made: Report of the Committee on Diligence (Chairman Sheriff H McKechnie) Cmnd 456 (1958), para 227.

Power to collect debts

14.24 As part of their official functions officers of court may collect debts on behalf of creditors from debtors, provided the debt has been constituted by decree or is recoverable by summary warrant[1]. A messenger-at-arms may collect such a debt only in the case of a decree (including a 'deemed' decree) of the Court of Session and likewise a sheriff officer's power is restricted to decrees and summary warrants of the sheriff court[2]. As collection of post-decree debts is part of the official functions of a sheriff officer, he may exercise this power only in respect of decrees and summary warrants granted by a sheriff court within the scope of his commission as sheriff officer or where such decree or warrant is being enforced.

A further consequence of the collection of post-decree debts being part of the official functions of an officer of court is that the debtor and creditor are protected by the officer's bond of caution in the case of embezzlement of funds by the officer of payment made to him by the debtor[3]. Such debt collection is a power rather than a duty of an officer of court and may be exercised only if authorised by a creditor. However, the presumption is that instructions to an officer of court to carry out diligence in execution, implies a mandate to receive payment for (or on account of) any debt in respect of which the diligence is executed[4]. A creditor may, of course, give express instructions to the contrary, but unless the debtor is informed of such contrary instructions, he is entitled to rely on the presumption that the officer may receive payment on behalf of the creditor.

It should be noted that the collection of post-decree debts, although part of the officer's official functions, is not itself part of the diligence process.

Collection charges made by the officer to the creditor are not diligence expenses and are not recoverable by the creditor from the debtor[5].

1 1987 Act, s 75(1)(d); SI 1988/2097, r 16(1)(a).
2 SI 1988/2097, r 16(2).
3 For a useful discussion of the pre-1987 Act law see *Ayr County Council v Wyllie* 1935 SC 836.
4 SI 1988/2097, r 30.
5 For this reason such charges are not regulated by SI 1988/2097.

Duty to provide information

14.25 In order to provide complete and reliable statistics on diligence and other areas of concern to officers of court, the Lord Advocate may require any officer of court to provide information, in a form and at times to be specified by the Lord Advocate, on the official functions of the officer of court[1]. The Lord Advocate may publish all or some of the information provided by officers of court but the form of publication must not identify, or allow for the identification of, the officer of court, or the persons against whom the diligence has been executed[2].

It is not clear who bears the expense of making and returning the information required by the Lord Advocate under this section. The Scottish Law Commission recommended that this cost should be borne by the Exchequer[3].

1 1987 Act, s 84(1).
2 Ibid, s 84(2), (3).
3 Scot Law Com Report no 95 (1985), pp 498–499.

Disqualifying interest in exercise of official functions

14.26 As officers of court hold public office, the duties of which must be performed in an impartial and independent manner, they may not perform these official functions in respect of any matter in which they have a direct personal interest. It has for long been a recognised principle that an officer cannot execute diligence concerning a debt due to him as an individual[1], and the 1987 Act reinforces this principle and extends it to citation and all diligence, whether or not related to debt enforcement, in which the officer has an interest as an individual[2]. Any diligence, citation etc purported to be done in breach of these provisions is void[2].

1 *Dalgleish v Scott* (1822) 1 S 506.
2 1987 Act, s 83(1)(a). This extends to any charge for payment, execution of diligence or warrant in any proceedings in which the officer has an interest as an individual in the subject-matter of the charge, diligence or proceedings.

14.27 Where the citation, diligence, etc does not concern a debt, an officer is not disqualified because of an interest in the subject-matter if that interest is not a personal, individual one. Thus an officer is able to execute citation or diligence, eg in an action of interdict or declarator where a person with an interest in the action is a relative or a firm of which he is a partner or member.

However, where the subject-matter of the diligence, citation, etc consists of, or includes, a debt, the officer is disqualified from acting where[1]:

(1) the debt is due to a relative of the officer;

(2) the debt is due to an associate of the officer;

(3) the debt is due to a firm or company in which the officer is a partner or director or has a controlling interest;

(4) the debt is due to a firm or company in which the officer along with a relative has a controlling interest;

(5) the debt is due to a firm or company in which the officer along with an associate has a controlling interest;

(6) the debt is due to a firm or company in which a relative of the officer is a partner, director or has a controlling interest;

(7) the debt is due to a firm or company in which an associate of the officer is a partner, director or has a controlling interest;

(8) the debt is due to a firm or company whose principal business is debt-purchasing and the officer has a pecuniary interest in the firm or company;

(9) the debt is due to a firm or company whose principal business is debt-purchasing and a relative of the officer has a pecuniary interest in the firm or company;

(10) the debt is due to a firm or company whose principal business is debt-purchasing and an associate of the officer has a pecuniary interest in the firm or company.

Where any of the above circumstances apply, diligence or citation executed by the officer is void[2].

For the purposes of the above rules the term 'relative' refers to any of the following members of the officer's family[3]:

spouse
parent
child
grandparent
grandchild
brother
sister.

Any such relationship may be constituted, as the case may be, of the full-blood, half-blood or by affinity.

The term 'associate' in the above rules means[4]:

co-director
partner
employer
employee
agent
principal (but not a principal in a contract for the service of a charge or the execution of diligence or warrant in relation to the debt concerned)[5].

A 'controlling interest' in a company means control of a majority of votes in the company[6].

1 1987 Act, s 83(1)(b), (2).
2 Ibid, s 83(1)(b).
3 Ibid, s 83(3)(b).
4 Ibid, s 83(3)(a).
5 Ibid, s 83(4).
6 Ibid, s 83(3)(c); Finance Act 1975, Sch 4, para 13(7).

14.28   It should be noted that the various circumstances which give rise to a disqualifying interest on the part of an officer, where a matter of debt is concerned, arise when the debt 'is due' to the person or person specified above. These rules therefore apply when an officer serves warrants on the dependence of an action which later result in decree for payment of a principal sum of money to any person within one of the specified categories. In those circumstances, the effect of the decree is that the sum was always due, though not yet fully constituted. However, the rules do not apply in respect of diligence in security of a future debt which is not due at the time of the diligence.

Extra-official activities; debt collecting

14.29   There are restrictions on the activities, other than their official functions, which officers of court may undertake. Such extra-official activities are of three types.

PROHIBITED ACTIVITIES

14.30   The Court of Session has power to prohibit officers of court from undertaking extra-official duties which are incompatible with their official functions[1]. To date regulations have been made which prohibit officers of court from being[2]:
(1) an auctioneer with his own auction room;
(2) an elected or appointed member of a public or local authority;
(3) a house factor;
(4) a member of the Faculty of Advocates;
(5) a member of the Law Society of Scotland;
(6) a member of the United Kingdom or European Parliaments;
(7) a money lender; or
(8) a police officer.

1 1987 Act, s 75(1)(e).
2 SI 1988/2097, r 17(3).

PERMITTED ACTIVITIES

14.31   The Court of Session may also make provisions for permitting officers of court to undertake extra-official activities for remuneration[1]. To date provisions have been made which permit officers[2]:
(1) to collect debts not constituted by decree (this is discussed further below);
(2) to serve on a person any notice required to be served under any statute. This power may not be used where there is statutory provision to the contrary.
     In performing any of these permitted extra-official activities, the officer of court must not state or imply that he is acting in his capacity as officer of court.

1 1987 Act, s 75(1)(f).
2 SI 1988/2097, r 17(1), (2).

ACTIVITIES NEITHER PROHIBITED NOR PERMITTED

14.32　Any extra-official activity not within either of the above two categories may not be undertaken by an officer of court unless he has obtained the permission of the sheriff principal[1]. Application is made to the sheriff principal from whom the officer holds a commission, though presumably permission is required for extra-official activities only where they are to be carried out in the sheriffdom concerned. The sheriff principal in dealing with an application may not withhold permission unless it appears to him that the officer's undertaking such an activity would be incompatible with the officer's official functions. A sheriff principal may attach conditions to any permission granted to an officer.

1 1987 Act, s 75(2), (3).

DEBT–COLLECTING

14.33　Prior to the 1987 Act, the extra-official activity of officers of court which aroused most controversy was that of debt-collecting[1]. Under the 1987 Act and regulations implementing it, this activity is now subject to the following rules.

1 See *British Relay v Keay* 1976 SLT (Sh Ct) 23; Scot Law Com Report no 95 (1985), pp 489–493. An officer's interest in a debt-purchasing as opposed to a debt-collecting organisation is governed by 1987 Act, s 83. See above at para 14.27.

Collection, in official capacity, of debts not constituted by decree

14.34　It is not part of the official function of an officer of court to collect debts in his capacity as officer, where the debt has not been constituted by decree[1].

1 SI 1988/2097, r 17(2). It can also be noted that the Director General of Fair Trading has refused to issue the appropriate license as required under Part III of the Consumer Credit Act 1974 to allow officers of court to engage in debt-collecting using their official designations: see Scot Law Com Report no 95 (1985), p 489.

Collection, not in official capacity, of debts not constituted by decree

14.35　An officer of court may collect debts for remuneration where the debts have not been constituted by decree and he is not acting or purporting to act in his capacity as officer[1]. An officer may so act only on being granted authority to do so by a sheriff principal, following an application in writing by the officer which must disclose any material interest held by the officer, a member of his family or a business associate in any organisation on behalf of which he seeks authority to collect debts.

1 SI 1988/2097, r 18. A further application must be made to continue in debt-collecting where any subsequent interest in a debt-collecting organisation is acquired by the officer, a member of his family or business associate.

Collection of debts constituted by decree

14.36　The collection of debts constituted by decree or recoverable under summary warrant is now part of the official functions of an officer of court[1].

1 SI 1988/2097, r 16(1), (2). See further para 14.24 above.

ORGANISATION OF OFFICERS OF COURT

Nature of business organisation

14.37 Officers of court may operate as sole practitioners or as firms. It is not possible to grant a commission to an officer of court in such terms as to tie the officer to a particular employer[1], but an officer may be employed under a contract of service by another officer or by a firm of officers. However, an officer may not form a private or public company (within the meaning of the Companies Act 1985) for the purpose of exercising any of his official functions nor may he exercise any of his official functions as an employee of such a company[2].

The sharing of business premises between solicitors and officers of court is a breach of the solicitors' professional practice rules[3].

1 *Stewart v Reid* 1934 SC 69.
2 SI 1988/2097, r 16(5).
3 Scot Law Com Report no 95 (1985), p 495; cp *John Temple Ltd v Logan* 1973 SLT (Sh Ct) 41.

Caution and professional indemnity insurance

14.38 An officer of court must be covered by a bond of caution to the value of £50,000 from an approved guarantee company in respect of any commission held as a sheriff officer and a messenger-at-arms[1]. The language of the Officers of Court Rules refers to a bond of caution in respect of 'any commission' as a sheriff officer and messenger-at-arms, and this seems to suggest that a separate bond of guarantee must be taken in respect of each commission held. On the other hand, the bond of caution must be renewed each year within thirty days after the expiry of any current bond but it appears sufficient if there is only one renewal, a copy of which is intimated to other sheriff clerks. Failure to renew the bond timeously may result in the officer being suspended from office until a premium receipt for renewal of the bond has been properly lodged.

Similarly an officer of court and any partnership of officers of court must be covered by a policy for professional indemnity insurance from an insurance company to a minimum limit of £100,000[2]. The language of the rule suggests that cover is required in respect of each commission as officer of court in the case of an officer, and in the case of a partnership in respect of the firm and also in respect of the employees of the firm. Each year every officer of court must lodge a premium receipt from an insurance company stating that he is covered for professional indemnity insurance to a minimum of £100,000 within thirty days after the date of expiry of any current premium receipt. No explicit provision is made for the lodging of a renewed premium receipt by partnerships of officers. Failure by the officer (as opposed to failure by a firm of officers) to lodge a premium receipt renewing the professional indemnity insurance may lead to suspension of the officer from practice.

1 SI 1988/2097, rr 9–10.
2 Ibid, rr 11–12.

Accounts

14.39 Every officer of court must keep[1] (a) written books and accounts, separately in respect of each client account, to show all monies collected by him from the creditor's debtor, and (b) a separate bank account in respect of client creditors.

Furthermore, an officer of court must deliver annually to every sheriff principal from whom he holds a commission, a certificate by an accountant[2]. The certificate, which must be lodged within six months of the end of the officer's accounting year, must state that in the opinion of the accountant, the officer has kept satisfactory accounts[3]. If after examination of the officer's accounts the accountant is unable to sign such a certificate, he must prepare a report giving his reasons. A copy of the report is sent to each sheriff principal from whom the officer holds a commission as sheriff officer, and if the officer is also a messenger-at-arms to the clerk of the Lord Lyon. A copy is also sent to the officer concerned.

1 SI 1988/2097, rr 14, 15; cp *John Temple v Logan* 1973 SLT (Sh Ct) 41.
2 For the category of accountants who may prepare such a certificate, see SI 1988/2097, r 15(6).
3 To enable the accountant to grant such a certificate, the officer must make available to him all books and accounts which the accountant may reasonably require: ibid, r 15(3).

Duty to employ competent staff

14.40 As holders of public officers, officers of court must, if delegating any aspect of their work, employ competent staff[1]. Certain kinds of work should not be delegated.

1 *Lawrence Jack Collections v Hamilton* 1976 SLT (Sh Ct) 18.

Intimation of information for registers

14.41 Various items of information must be intimated by an officer of court to the person who maintains the relevant register, ie the Lyon clerk in the case of a messenger-at-arms, and the regional clerk of every sheriffdom in which a commission is held as sheriff officer in the case of a sheriff officer[1].
The information which must be intimated is:
(a) any change of the employment, business or private address of the officer of court. Intimation must be made within twenty-one days of such change;
(b) all extra-judicial activities, any authorisation to collect debts not constituted by decree, and any interests disclosed in an application for such authorisation[2];
(c) where the officer intends to give up practice as a sheriff officer or messenger-at-arms, prior notice of the date on which he will so cease to practise; and
(d) the dates of his accounting year.

1 SI 1988/2097, r 20.
2 See above at paras 14.32, 14.35.

Advertising

14.42 There are no restrictions on officers or firms of officers advertising or canvassing for business[1]. However the Court of Session has power to make regulations on these matters, if thought necessary[2].

1 Scot Law Com Report no 95 (1985) p 496.
2 1987 Act, s 75(1)(c).

SUPERVISION; DISCIPLINE OF OFFICERS OF COURT

Inspection of work

14.43   A system for the inspection of the work of officers of court is provided by section 78 of the 1987 Act. That section gives a sheriff principal power to appoint a suitable person to inspect the work, or any particular aspect of the work, of a sheriff officer who holds a commission from him. An inspection may follow a complaint being received by the sheriff principal from a member of the public, or it may be by way of a random or 'spot check'. The person appointed[1] has power to inspect the official functions, or specified official functions, of a sheriff officer but his powers as regards the officer's extra-official activities for remuneration are limited to making inquiries.

Where the activities (official and/or extra-official) of a messenger-at-arms are to be inspected or made the subject of inquiry, the Court of Session has power to order a sheriff principal to make the appropriate appointment[2].

The person appointed by a sheriff principal must make a report of his inspection or inquiry to the sheriff principal. Where an appointment has been made in connection with the activities of a messenger-at-arms, a copy of the report is also to be sent to the Deputy Principal Clerk of Session, who places the report before a judge nominated by the Lord President[3].

1   The Scottish Law Commission envisaged that the sort of person who might act as inspectors are senior officers of court, solicitors, and former sheriff clerks. Accountants would be suitable persons where investigation is to be made into the expenses and fees charged by officers: Scot Law Com Report no 95 (1985), p 472. The person appointed is entitled to a fee (unless he is already a full-time civil servant) and to payment of outlays: 1987 Act, s 78(4).
2   The appropriate sheriff principal is the one from whom the officer holds a commission as a sheriff officer.
3   1987 Act, s 78(3); SI 1988/2097, r 21(1).

Investigation of alleged misconduct

14.44   Where an allegation of misconduct[1] has been made against an officer of court, the officer must be given an opportunity to admit or deny the allegation[2]. Such an allegation may have been made where evidence of misconduct by the officer has been disclosed during the inspection of the officer's activities, or a complaint has been made to the Court of Session or a sheriff principal, or where a judge of the Court of Session or a sheriff principal has reason to believe that an officer may have been guilty of misconduct[3].

Where the allegation has been put to the officer and he does not admit the misconduct in writing or he fails to give a satisfactory explanation, a judge of the Court of Session appointed by the Lord President, or the sheriff principal, may appoint a solicitor to investigate the matter[4]. After making appropriate investigations, the solicitor must bring disciplinary proceedings at his instance against the officer if of the opinion that there is a probable case of misconduct and that there is sufficient evidence to justify proceedings. Where the solicitor considers that there is not a probable case of misconduct or that there is insufficient evidence for proceedings to be brought against the officer, he must report accordingly to the Court of Session judge or sheriff principal who appointed him[5].

1 For the meaning of misconduct see below at para 14.45.
2 1987 Act, s 79(2); SI 1988/2097, r 22.
3 1987 Act, s 79(1).
4 Ibid, s 79(2), (4), (7). If a person appointed to make a spot check investigation of the officer's work is a solicitor he may also be appointed to investigate the alleged misconduct. The solicitor appointed is entitled to a fee and payment of outlays incurred.
5 1987 Act, s 79(3), (8).

Nature of misconduct

14.45 The nature of misconduct justifying disciplinary proceedings against an officer of court is not defined in the 1987 Act. Section 79(9) states that misconduct includes conduct tending to bring the office of messenger-at-arms or sheriff officer into disrepute, but this must be read as a non-exclusive description rather than an exhaustive definition. The commission of a criminal offence is explicitly dealt with elsewhere in the 1987 Act and probably does not count as a separate heading of misconduct[1]. Examples of misconduct which have been suggested include[2]:

(i)   deliberate overcharging of fees or outlays[3];
(ii)   knowingly executing diligence in which the officer has a disqualifying interest;
(iii)   refusing to act when properly instructed;
(iv)   sharing business premises with a solicitor;
(v)   dealing with goods sold under warrant[4];
(vi)   engaging in prohibited or unauthorised activities, including collecting debts without authorisation;
(vii)   refusal or delay in submitting a report of sale of poinded goods[5];
(viii) financial improbity, including failure to keep proper accounts.

1 See below at para 14.48.
2 See Scot Law Com Report no 95 (1985), ch 8; D I Nichols *The Debtors (Scotland) Act 1987* p 18–97.
3 Cp 1987 Act, s 80(5)(d).
4 SI 1988/2097, r 31.
5 1987 Act, s 39(3).

Disciplinary hearings

14.46 Disciplinary hearings against an officer of court for misconduct are brought at the instance of the solicitor who conducted the investigation into the alleged misconduct[1]. Proceedings are brought in the Court of Session or before the sheriff principal, depending upon the origin of the appointment[2].

Proceedings against sheriff officers are brought by way of initial writ in a summary application, and the officer concerned is the respondent[3]. An application must include averments which specify the alleged misconduct, and the facts established by investigation which are alleged as the 'probable cause of the misconduct'. This is probably to be read, not as a matter of causation, but as the factual basis of the type of misconduct being charged against the officer. The application must also include a crave seeking the sheriff principal to order:
(i) service of the application on the respondent;
(ii) the respondent to lodge defences within fourteen days from the date of service;

(iii) intimation of the application to the Lord Advocate;

(iv) a date for a hearing for further procedure; and

(v) in the event of the respondent being found guilty of misconduct, such order under section 80(7) of the 1987 Act, if any, as the court shall think proper.

When making the first order for service and intimation, the sheriff principal fixes a date for the hearing for further procedure. The applicant must intimate that date to the respondent and to the Lord Advocate. The hearing will be held in public unless the officer requests otherwise or the sheriff principal considers that it would be prejudicial to the interests of justice if the hearing (or part of it) was not held in private[4].

Disciplinary proceedings against a messenger-at-arms follow the same broad procedure, but in this case the proceedings are brought by way of petition to the Outer House of the Court of Session, and the officer will normally be given twenty-one days to lodge answers[5].

1 1987 Act, s 79(3)(a). The solicitor has no right of audience before the Court of Session by virtue of raising such proceedings.

2 Ibid, s 79(8).

3 SI 1988/2097, r 25.

4 Procedure is as determined by the sheriff principal subject to the provisions of ibid, r 26. An appeal may be made to the Inner House of the Court of Session but there is no further appeal: 1987 Act, s 82; SI 1988/2097, r 29. Expenses may be awarded in disciplinary hearings in favour of or against either party: 1987 Act, s 79(5), (6).

5 SI 1988/2097, rr 23, 24.

Powers of court where officer guilty of misconduct

14.47 Where an officer admits in writing that he is guilty of misconduct or where the sheriff principal or Lord Ordinary is satisfied of the officer's guilt after disciplinary proceedings[1], the court may make

(a) an order that the officer be suspended from practice for a specified period or be deprived of office[2]. A sheriff principal's power extends only to his own sheriffdom. However, all such orders, whether made by the Court of Session or a sheriff principal must be intimated to the Court of Session, the Lord Lyon and other sheriffs principal if the officer holds a commission from these authorities. These authorities then give similar effect to the order of suspension and deprivation in respect of commissions granted by them[3];

(b) an order that the officer pay a fine not exceeding £2,500[4];

(c) an order censuring the officer[5];

(d) where the misconduct consists of, or includes, the charging of excessive fees or outlays, an order decerning for repayment by the officer of court to the person who paid them of the amount of the excess[6].

1 There is no authority on the standard of proof required but it is submitted that proof on the balance of probabilities does not suffice. The Discipline Tribunal of the Law Society of Scotland requires a 'high standard of evidence and proof': J G Mathiseon, 'Professional Ethics' (1985) 30 JLSS 278, 279. In *Lanford v General Medical Council* [1989] 2 All ER 921, the Privy Council held, in relation to a charge of serious professional misconduct before the General Medical Council, that the onus and standard of proof were those applicable to a criminal trial.

2 1987 Act, s 80(5)(a); 7(a).

3 Ibid, s 81.

4 Ibid, s 80(5)(b); (7)(b). Details of the fine are intimated to the Lord Advocate, who is responsible for recovery of the fine: 1987 Act, s 80(8), (9); SI 1988/2097, rr 24(10), (11), 26(9), (10).

5 1987 Act, s 80(5)(c), (7)(b).

6 Ibid, s 80(5)(d), (7)(b). The order is intimated by the clerk of court to the person to whom repayment is to be made: SI 1988/2097, rr 24(10)(b), 26(9)(b).

Criminal offences

14.48 An application for a commission as a sheriff officer or a messenger-at-arms must disclose any convictions of the applicant of a criminal offence other than a 'spent' offence in terms of the Rehabilitation of Offenders Act 1974[1]. Failure to disclose this information would no doubt be a form of misconduct on the part of the officer and could form the basis of disciplinary proceedings against him[2].

Where a sheriff principal becomes aware that a sheriff officer who holds a commission from him has been convicted of any offence, he may make an order suspending or depriving him of office[3]. The Court of Session has a similar power in respect of messengers-at-arms convicted of offences. 'Offence' includes any offence of which the officer has been convicted before or after the officer was granted a commission but does not extend to a 'spent' conviction nor to an offence disclosed in his application for commission[4].

Before making an order suspending the officer or depriving him of office, the sheriff principal or the Court of Session judge must give the officer an opportunity to make representations orally or in writing, and may also ordain him to appear[5].

Any order made is intimated to other authorities from whom the officer holds a commission. These authorities must give effect to the order in respect of the commissions granted by them[6].

1 SI 1988/2097, Forms 1, 2.
2 It is not clear whether the officer could be suspended or deprived of office where he has failed to disclose a conviction in his application for a commission, and the conviction has become spent by the time the failure is brought to light: Rehabilitation of Offenders Act 1974, s 4(3)(b).
3 1987 Act, s 80(1), (2).
4 Ibid, s 80(3).
5 SI 1988/2097, r 28.
6 1987 Act, s 81.

INDEX

Absence, decree in. *See* DECREE
Absolvitor, decree of, 1.26, 1.28,
   1.30*n*
competent and omitted, 1.28
mixed decree, 1.30
res judicata, 1.28
Acquirenda
inhibition, 9.24
Ad factum praestandum
action, 8.24, 8.25
decree, failure to obtemper—
   imprisonment for, 8.32, 8.40, 8.43
obligation, 2.28
Adjudger
sequestration for rent by, 8.50
Adjudication, 3.03
competition, 10.33
   equalisation as result of bankruptcy,
      10.43
debitum fundi, 3.38*n*
debt, for, time to pay provisions, 3.03,
   3.38, 3.63, 3.85, 3.94, 3.95, 9.37
declaratory, expenses, 13.25
disadvantage of, 9.30
expenses, 13.23–13.25
heritable property, 9.30
in execution, 9.37, 9.38–9.46
   basis, 9.40
   common property, 9.42
   competition, 9.45
   completion of title, 9.43
   decree, 9.43
   expenses, 13.23
   expiry of the legal, 9.44
   jointly owned property, 9.42
   meaning, 9.38
   notice of litigiosity, 9.41
   procedure, 9.39
   property affected, 9.42
   receivership, 9.46
in implement, 9.37, 9.49
   expenses, 13.24
in security, 9.37, 9.48
   expenses, 13.23

Adjudication – *contd.*
in security – *contd.*
   inhibition, superseded by, 3.46
   time to pay provisions, 3.46, 3.99
on the dependence, 9.47
ranking, 9.45
Register of Inhibitions and
   Adjudications, 9.43
Scottish Law Commission, reforms
   proposed by, 9.50
time to pay direction, effect, 3.38,
   3.38*n*
wrongful diligence, 12.17
**Administration of Justice Act
   (1920)**, 11.02–11.14
application—
   time-limit, 11.07
   title to make, 11.06
enforcement of Court of Session
   judgments, 11.03
geographical extent, 11.02
registration—
   effect of, 11.3
   procedure, 11.05–11.10
   refusal, 1.11, 11.12
   setting aside, 11.11, 11.12
scope, 11.03, 11.04
Affiliation order
Maintenance Orders (Reciprocal
   Enforcement) Act (1972), 11.165
Agricultural holdings
notice to quit, 9.71, 9.74, 9.79
Agricultural Marketing Act (1958)
disciplinary committee, registration of
   awards, 2.07
Aliment
Alimentary payments not arrestable,
   5.30
arrears, arrestment of, 5.30
contingent debt, as, 4.07
crave for, arrestment on the
   dependence, 4.03
decree for, arrestment in execution,
   legal aid, 13.29

Hypothec
competition, 10.07, 10.17, 10.26
　equalisation as a result of bankruptcy,
　　10.45
enforcement by sequestration for rent,
　8.44–8.55

Imprisonment. *See* CIVIL
　IMPRISONMENT
Income support
deductions for community charges
　arrears, 8.12
exemption from arrestment, 5.32
maintenance creditor in receipt of, 6.35
Income tax
current maintenance arrestment, 6.43
summary warrant, recovery by, 2.12,
　8.04
Indictments
service of, 14.03
Industrial tribunal
decisions as basis for inhibitions, 9.06
orders, arrestment, 5.14
Infeftment
heritable bonds, 5.12
Inhibition
adjudication by inhibitor, 9.30
adjudication in security superseded by,
　3.46
arrestment by inhibitor, 9.31
bases, 9.03
competence, 2.03
　documents of debt, 2.06
　competition—
　equalisation as result of bankruptcy,
　　10.37–10.39
　priority among inhibitions, 10.18
　with floating charge, 1.21
　with missives, 10.23
　with other creditors, 10.19, 10.20
　with receiver, 10.22
　with standard security, 10.24
　with voluntary trust deed, 10.25
debtor *in meditatione fugae*, 4.65
definition, 9.02
document of debt, 2.06, 9.03,
　9.10
　Bills and Letters, obtained by, 9.10
executors, 9.16
expenses, 13.18–13.22
in execution, 9.01–9.36
　acquirenda, 9.24
　adjudication, 9.28, 9.30
　arrestment, 9.28, 9.31
　bankruptcy and liquidation, 9.28,
　　9.32–9.35
　basis, 9.03

Inhibition – *contd.*
in execution – *contd.*
　Books of Council and Session,
　　documents registered in, 9.07
　books of the sheriff court, documents
　　registered in, 9.07
　creditor, acts to prejudice of, 9.18
　decree—
　　Court of Session, 9.04
　　foreign, 9.04
　　Scottish Land Court, 9.04
　　sheriff court, 9.04
　effect, 9.13–9.27
　　real rights not vested by, 9.14
　Employment Appeal Tribunal
　　decisions, 9.06
　enforcement, 9.28
　executries, 9.27
　expenses, 9.11, 13.22
　floating charges, 9.26
　future voluntary acts, 9.14, 9.15, 9.16
　heritable property, 9.19
　　corporeal, 9.20
　　incorporeal, 9.21–9.23
　　lease, 9.21–9.23
　industrial tribunals, decisions of, 9.06
　insolvency, 9.14
　Land Register, 9.11
　Land Tribunal orders as basis of, 9.05
　leases, 9.16, 9.21–9.23
　malice and lack of probably cause,
　　12.01
　mistake, 12.01
　moveable property, 9.19
　property affected, 9.19–9.27
　purchaser under missives, 9.19
　ranking process, 9.14, 9.17, 9.36
　reduction, 9.28, 9.29
　securities, inhibition against granting,
　　9.25
　sequestration, 9.14
　summary warrants not basis for,
　　9.08
　trusts, 9.27
in security, 4.01, 4.63–4.85, 4.65
　aliment actions, 4.65
　caution, consignation and nimiety,
　　4.78
　consistorial actions, 4.65
　debtor *vergens ad inopiam*, 4.65
　defender's heritage, action relating
　　to, 4.66
　divorce actions, 4.65
　expenses, 4.66
　extinction, 4.73–4.85
　　caution, consignation and nimiety,
　　　4.78

Interlocutor – *contd.*
decree distinguished, 1.01
decree in absence, recalling, 1.14
extract of, 1.59
reponing note, refusing, 1.14
Interlocutory decree, 1.18, 1.19
Invalidity benefit
exemption from arrestment, 5.32
IOU
whether document of debt, 9.10
Irritancy
extraordinary removings, 9.52, 9.53

Jointly liable
meaning, 7.34
Jointly owned property
adjudication, 9.42
arrestment not allowed, 5.26
inhibition, 9.20
meaning, 7.34
poinding and sale, 7.31, 7.34
Judge
wrongful diligence, liability for, 12.23
Judgment
acts, 1.01
as basis for diligence, 1.01, 2.01
decrees, 1.01
foreign. *See* FOREIGN JUDGMENT,
    ENFORCEMENT OF
interlocutors, 1.01
meaning, 1.01
money, requirement to pay 3.01
orders, 1.01
warrants, 1.01
Judicial factor
inhibition, 9.16
loco absentis, time to pay provisions,
    3.08, 3.61
loco tutoris, time to pay provisions, 3.08,
    3.61
Judgments Convention (1968), *see*
    CONVENTION ON JURISDICTION AND
    THE ENFORCEMENT OF JUDGMENTS IN
    CIVIL AND COMMERCIAL MATTERS
Judicial separation
reciprocal enforcement scheme, 11.139
status or legal capacity, 11.41

Land
corporeal heritable property, as, 9.20
jointly owned, inhibition, 9.20
poinding of the ground. *See* POINDING
    OF THE GROUND
Landlord
death of, 9.81
hypothec. *See* HYPOTHEC

Landlord – *contd.*
sequestration for rent. *See*
    SEQUESTRATION FOR RENT
Land Register
adjudication in execution, 9.38, 9.43
inhibition in execution, 9.11
reduction of deed or debt by inhibiting
    creditor, 9.29
Lands Tribunal for Scotland
awards registrable in Books of Council
    and Session, 2.07
orders as basis of inhibition in
    execution, 9.05
Lease
incorporeal heritable property,
    inhibition, 9.21–9.23
inhibition, 9.16
irritancy in, 9.52, 9.53
notice to quit, actions of removing,
    9.57–9.82
removings, 9.51. *See also* REMOVINGS
    AND EJECTIONS
summary diligence, 2.25
tacit relocation, 9.57, 9.58
Legal aid
appeals, 13.15
Judgments Convention, 11.122,
    11.123
Scottish Legal Aid Board consent,
    13.29
third party eligibility, 13.29
Legitim, right to
arrestment, 5.20
Lessee
inhibition, 9.23
Lessor
inhibition, 9.22
Liferent
poinding and sale, 7.41
Liquidation
common debtor, 5.44
company, arrestment on the
    dependence actions, 4.56
competition, equalisation as result of
    bankruptcy, 10.40
inhibitions in relation to, 9.16, 9.35
Liquidator
inhibition, 9.16
Local authority
recovery of rates and community
    charges. *See* COMMUNITY CHARGES;
    RATES
Lord Advocate
arrestment served on, 4.26
Lord Lyon King of Arms
Advisory Council on Messengers-at-
    arms and Sheriff Officers, 14.06